New Testament
Breakthrough KJV

Fifth Edition

Translated by Ray Geide

Greek Text: Textus Receptus Scrivener 1894
(Scrivener 1894 is the Textus Receptus that is closest to the KJV)

For our translation of the Nestle27/UBS4 (the Critical/Minority Text), please get the New Testament: Breakthrough Version

Breakthrough Version Publishing
Wichita, KS
breakthroughversion.com

BREAKTHROUGH KJV (BKJV)

The Breakthrough KJV (BKJV) text may be quoted in any form (written, visual, electronic or audio), up to and inclusive of one hundred (100) verses without express written permission of the publisher, providing the verses do not amount to a complete book of the Bible nor do the verses quoted account for twenty-five percent (25%) or more of the total text of the work in which they are quoted.

When the BKJV is quoted in works that exercise the above fair use clause, the following notice of copyright must appear on the title or copyright page or opening screen of the work (whichever is appropriate):

BREAKTHROUGH KJV™, BKJV™ Copyright © 2017-2020, 2026 by Ray Geide. Used by permission. All rights reserved worldwide. breakthroughversion.com

When quotations from the BKJV text are used in non-saleable media such as church bulletins, orders of service, posters, projections, or similar media, a complete copyright notice is not required, but the letters BKJV must appear at the end of each quotation, and the web address, breakthroughversion.com, must appear on the same page or presentation.

Permission requests for commercial use that exceed the above guidelines must be directed to, and approved in writing by, Breakthrough Version Publishing, 1725 Faulders Lane, Wichita, KS 67218.

Breakthrough Version Publishing
www.breakthroughversion.com

Legal Disclaimer - The publisher and the author make no representations or warranties with respect to the accuracy or completeness of the contents of this work and specifically disclaim all warranties, including without limitation warranties for a particular purpose. No warranty may be created or extended by sales or promotional materials. The advice and strategies contained herein may not be suitable for every situation.

ISBN-13: 978-0-9628012-6-7
Version 5.01 - 04/03/2026

© Copyright 2017-2020, 2026 by Ray Geide All rights reserved.
Published 2026

Table of Contents

Matthew 1
Mark 55
Luke 89
John 149
Acts 193
Romans 249
First Corinthians 273
Second Corinthians 295
Galatians 309
Ephesians 317
Philippians 325
Colossians 331
First Thessalonians 337
Second Thessalonians 343
First Timothy 347
Second Timothy 353
Titus 359
Philemon 363
Hebrews 365
James 383
First Peter 389
Second Peter 395
First John 399
Second John 405
Third John 407
Jude 409
Revelation 411

Translation Notes

Italics in the Bible text indicate words that have been added by the translator and are not in the Greek.

Matthew

1

1 A scroll of *the* birth of Jesus, *the* Anointed King, David's son, Abraham's son.
2 Abraham fathered Isaac. Isaac fathered Jacob. Jacob fathered Judah and his brothers.
3 Judah fathered Phares and Zerah, from Tamar. Phares fathered Hezron. Hezron fathered Aram.
4 Aram fathered Aminadab. Aminadab fathered Nahshon. Nahshon fathered Salmon.
5 Salmon fathered Boaz, from Rahab. Boaz fathered Obed, from Ruth. Obed fathered Jesse.
6 Jesse fathered David, the king. David, the king, fathered Solomon, from the *widow* of Uriah.
7 Solomon fathered Rehoboam. Rehoboam fathered Abijah. Abijah fathered Asa.
8 Asa fathered Jehoshaphat. Jehoshaphat fathered Joram. Joram fathered Uzziah.
9 Uzziah fathered Jotham. Jotham fathered Ahaz. Ahaz fathered Hezekiah.
10 Hezekiah fathered Manasseh. Manasseh fathered Amon. Amon fathered Josiah.
11 Josiah had *several sons*, Jeconiah and his brothers, at Babylon's resettlement *of Judeans*.
12 After Babylon's resettlement *of Judeans*, Jeconiah fathered Shealtiel. Shealtiel fathered Zerubbabel.
13 Zerubbabel fathered Abiud. Abiud fathered Eliakim. Eliakim fathered Azor.
14 Azor fathered Zadok. Zadok fathered Achim. Achim fathered Eliud.
15 Eliud fathered Eleazar. Eleazar fathered Matthan. Matthan fathered Jacob.
16 Jacob fathered Joseph, the husband of Mary, from whom was born, Jesus, the *One* who is called *the* Anointed King.
17 So all the generations from Abraham until David *are* fourteen generations. And from David until Babylon's resettlement *of Judeans are* fourteen generations. And from Babylon's resettlement *of Judeans* until the Anointed King *are* fourteen generations.
18 The birth of Jesus, *the* Anointed King, was like this: you see, when His mother Mary was promised to Joseph, before *the time* for them to even come together, she was found having *a baby* in *her* womb from *the* Sacred Spirit.
19 Joseph, her man, who did what is right and who did not want to make a public exhibit of her, intended to dismiss her in an unnoticed way.
20 When he contemplated these *things*, look, an angel of *the* Master appeared to him throughout a dream, saying, "Joseph, son of David, you should not be afraid to take along Mary, your woman. You see, what is born in her is from *the* Sacred Spirit.

21 She will deliver a son, and you will call His name Jesus. You see, He will rescue His ethnic group from their sins."
22 This whole *thing* had happened so that what was stated by the Master through the preacher *in Isaiah 7:14* might be accomplished that says,
23 "Look, the virgin will have *a baby* in *her* womb and deliver a son. And they will call His name Immanuel, that is translated *from Hebrew as* 'God with us'."
24 When Joseph was wide awake from the slumber, he did as the angel of *the* Master instructed him, and he took his woman along.
25 And he was not knowing her until *the time* that she delivered her son, the firstborn *one*. And he called His name Jesus.

2

1 When Jesus was born in Bethlehem, Judea in *the* days of Herod the king, look, Magian gurus from eastern regions showed up in Jerusalem
2 saying, "Where is the King of the Jewish *people* that was delivered *in birth*? You see, we saw His star in the east, and we came to bow down to Him."
3 When King Herod heard *this*, he was uneasy and all of Jerusalem with him.
4 And when he gathered together all of the head priests and *Old Testament* transcribers of the ethnic group, he was inquiring from the side of them where the Anointed King should be born.
5 The *transcribers* said to him, "In Bethlehem, Judea." You see, this is what has been written through the preacher *in Micah 5:2*,
6 "And you, Bethlehem, land of Judah, you are by no means *the* smallest among the leaders of Judah. You see, a *person* who is a leader will come out of you, someone who will shepherd My ethnic group Israel."
7 At that time, after Herod in an unnoticed way called for the Magian gurus, he verified from the side of them the time of the shining star.
8 And when he sent them to Bethlehem, he said, "After traveling *there*, question specifically about the young child. Whenever you find *him*, report to me in order that after going *there*, I also might bow down to him."
9 After the *Magian gurus* listened to the king, they traveled, and, look, the star that they saw in the east was going ahead of them until after going, it stood up on top of where the young child was.
10 When they saw the star, they were terribly happy with great happiness.
11 And when they went into the house, they saw the young child with Mary, His mother. And after they got down, they bowed to Him. And when they opened their stockpiles *of supplies*, they offered up contributions to Him: gold, high quality incense, and myrrh *(expensive perfume)*.
12 And when they were *divinely* notified throughout a dream not to double back to Herod, they took a back way using another road to their rural area.
13 After they took a back way, look, an angel of *the* Master appears throughout a dream to Joseph, saying, "After you get up, take along the young child and His mother, escape into Egypt, and be there until I tell you. You see, Herod is going to be looking for the young child for the *purpose* to ruin Him."
14 After *Joseph* got up, he took along the young child and his mother at night and took a back way into Egypt.

15 And he was there until the passing away of Herod so that what was stated by the Master through the preacher *in Hosea 11:1* might be accomplished that says, "Out of Egypt I called My Son."
16 At that time, when Herod saw that He was mocked by the Magian gurus, he was very angry. And after sending *soldiers* out, he executed all the boys in Bethlehem and in all its borders from two years *of age* and below according to the time that he verified from the side of the Magian gurus.
17 Then what was stated by Jeremiah, the preacher, *in Jeremiah 31:15* was accomplished that says,
18 "A sound was heard in Ramah, much wailing, crying, and mourning, Rachel crying for her children. And she was not wanting to be encouraged because they are not."
19 After Herod passed away, look, an angel of *the* Master appeared throughout a dream to Joseph in Egypt,
20 saying, "After you get up, take along the young child and His mother, and be traveling into *the* land of Israel. You see, the *people* looking for the soul of the young child have died."
21 After *Joseph* got up, he took along the young child and His mother, and went into *the* land of Israel.
22 After hearing that Archelaus is king over Judea in place of Herod his father, he was afraid to go off to there. After being *divinely* notified throughout a dream, he took a back way into the parts of Galilee.
23 And after going, he lived in a city called Nazareth in order that what was stated through the preachers might be accomplished, "He will be called a Nazarene."

1 In those days, John the Submerger shows up speaking publicly in the backcountry of Judea
2 and saying, "Change your ways. You see, the monarchy of the heavens has come near;
3 for this is what was stated by Isaiah, the preacher, *in Isaiah 40:3* that says, 'A voice shouting in the backcountry, Get the road of *the* Master ready. Make His paths straight.'"
4 The same John was having his attire out of camel's hair and a leather sash around his waist. His meal was grasshoppers and wild honey.
5 At that time, Jerusalem, all Judea, and all the surrounding rural area of Jordan were traveling out to him.
6 And they were being submerged in the Jordan by him, acknowledging their sins out loud.
7 When he saw many of the Separatists and Sadducees coming up to his submersion, he said to them, "Offspring of poisonous snakes, who put in front of your face to escape away from the punishment that is going *to come*?
8 So produce fruits deserving of the change of ways.
9 And it should not seem *good* to you to be saying among yourselves, 'We have a father, Abraham.' You see, I say to you that God is able from these stones to raise up children for Abraham.

10 The ax is also already lying facing the root of the trees. So every tree that does not produce nice fruit is chopped out and thrown into a fire.
11 I certainly submerge you in water for a change of ways, but the *One* coming behind me is stronger than me, whose sandals I am not adequate to haul. He will submerge you in *the* Sacred Spirit and fire,
12 whose shovel *is* in His hand. And He will completely clear off His processing floor and will gather His grain together into the grain bin, but the husks will be burned up with unextinguished fire."
13 At that time, Jesus shows up from Galilee to John on the Jordan for the "to be submerged by him" *part*.
14 John was flatly refusing Him, saying, "I have a need to be submerged by You, and You are coming to me?"
15 But when Jesus responded, He said to him, "Leave *it* just now. You see, this is how it is appropriate for us to accomplish every *bit of the* right way." Then he leaves it.
16 And after Jesus was submerged, right away he stepped up out of the water and, look, the heavens were opened to Him. And He saw the Spirit of God stepping down as if *It were* a dove and coming over Him.
17 And look, a voice from the heavens saying, "This is My Son, the loved *One*, in whom I am delighted."

4

1 At that time, Jesus was led up into the backcountry by the Spirit to experience trouble by the Accuser.
2 And after He went without food for forty days and forty nights, later He was hungry.
3 And when the *one* who tries to cause trouble came forward to Him, he said, "If you are a son of God, say that these stones will become *loaves of* bread."
4 When *Jesus* answered, He said, "It has been written *in Deuteronomy 8:3*, 'Not on bread alone will a person live, but on every statement traveling out through God's mouth.'"
5 Then the Accuser takes Him along into the sacred city, stands Him on the winglet of the temple grounds,
6 and says to Him, "If you are a son of God, throw Yourself down. You see, it has been written *in Psalm 91:11–12*, 'He will demand His angels concerning You, and they will pick You up on *their* hands so that You will not ever stub Your foot on a stone.'"
7 Jesus was declaring to him, "Again it has been written *in Deuteronomy 6:16*, 'You will not try to harass *the* Master, your God.'"
8 Again, the Accuser takes Him along to a very high mountain and shows Him all the monarchies of the world and their magnificence.
9 And he said to Him, "I will give you all these if, after you get down, you will bow to me."
10 At that time, Jesus says to him, "Make *your* way back, Opponent. You see, it has been written *in Deuteronomy 6:13*, 'You will bow down to *the* Master, your God, and minister to Him alone.'"

11 Then the Accuser leaves Him and, look, angels came forward and were serving Him.
12 When Jesus heard that John was turned in, He took a back way into Galilee.
13 And after leaving Nazareth down *there*, after going, He lived in Capernaum, the *city* beside the sea in *the* borders of Zebulon and Naphtali,
14 so that what was stated through Isaiah, the preacher, *in Isaiah 9:1–2* might be accomplished that says,
15 "*The* land of Zebulon and *the* land of Naphtali, *the* way of *the* sea, on *the* other side of the Jordan *River*, Galilee of the non-Jews,
16 the ethnic group, the *one* sitting in darkness, saw a great light. And to the *people* sitting in a rural area and in death's shadow, a light came up to them."
17 From then on, Jesus began to be speaking publicly and to be saying, "Change your ways. You see, the monarchy of the heavens has come near."
18 As Jesus walked around along the Sea of Galilee, He saw two brothers, Simon (the *one* who is called Peter) and Andrew (his brother) throwing a throw net into the sea. You see, they were fishermen.
19 And He says to them, "Come on behind Me, and I will make you fishermen of people."
20 Right away, after the *brothers* left the nets, they followed Him.
21 And when He walked on from there, He saw two other brothers, James (the *son* of Zebedee) and John (his brother) in the boat with Zebedee (their father) developing their nets. And He invited them.
22 Right away, after the *brothers* left the boat and their father, they followed Him.
23 And Jesus was leading *them* around all of Galilee teaching in their synagogues, speaking publicly about the good news of the monarchy, and healing every illness and every frailty among the group.
24 And the talk about Him went off into all of Syria. And they brought to Him all the *people* who had *it* bad, who were constrained by various illnesses and excruciating pains, who had lesser deities, who were struck by the moon *(that is, people who had seizures)*, and who were disabled. And He healed them.
25 And big crowds followed Him out of Galilee, Decapolis, Greater Jerusalem, Judea, and *the* other side of the Jordan *River*.

5

1 When He saw the crowds, He climbed up into the mountain. And after He was seated, His students came to Him.
2 And when He opened His mouth, He was teaching them, saying,
3 "The *people who are* poor in the spirit *are* blessed because the monarchy of the heavens is theirs.
4 The grieving *people are* blessed because they will be encouraged.
5 The submissive *people are* blessed because they will inherit the earth.
6 The *people* hungering and thirsting for the right way *are* blessed because they will be full.
7 The kind forgiving *people are* blessed because they will receive forgiving kindness.

8 The *people who are* clean in the heart *are* blessed because they will see God.
9 The peacemaking *people are* blessed because they will be called God's sons.
10 The *people* who have been persecuted on account of *the* right way *are* blessed because the monarchy of the heavens is theirs.
11 You are blessed when on account of Me they will criticize you, persecute *you*, and, lying, say every evil statement against you.
12 Be happy and excited because your pay in the heavens *is* much. You see, this is how they persecuted the preachers, the *ones* before you.
13 You are the salt of the earth. But if the salt lost its flavor, what will be salted with it? It no longer has *the* strength for anything except to be thrown outside and to be trampled on by the people.
14 You are the light of the world. A city is not able to be hidden lying up on top of a mountain.
15 Neither are they burning a lamp and placing it under the two gallon measuring bucket, but on the lampstand, and it is shining for everyone in the house.
16 This is how your light must shine in front of the people in order that they might see your nice actions and praise the magnificence of your Father, the *One* in the heavens.
17 You should not assume that I came to tear the Law or the Preachers down. I did not come to tear down, but to accomplish *what they say*.
18 You see, amen, I tell you, until the sky and the earth pass, one small letter or one hook of a letter will not in any way pass out of the Law until all *things* happen.
19 So whoever breaks one of the smallest of these demands and teaches the people that way, he will be called smallest in the monarchy of the heavens. But whoever will do and teach *them*, this *person* will be called great in the monarchy of the heavens.
20 You see, I tell you that unless your right way overflows *to be* more *right* than the *Old Testament* transcribers' and Separatists', you will not in any way go into the monarchy of the heavens.
21 You heard that it was stated to the original *people*, 'You will not murder. Whoever murders will be eligible for sentencing at the judgment.'
22 I tell you that everyone who is enraged at his brother for no reason will be eligible for sentencing at the judgment. Whoever says to his brother, 'Stupid!' will be eligible for sentencing at the council. Whoever says, 'Fool!' will be eligible for sentencing into the Hinnom Valley of the fire.
23 So if you are offering up your contribution on the altar and there you remember that your brother has something against you,
24 leave your contribution there in front of the altar, and make *your* way back. First, settle *the problem* with your brother, and then when you come, offer up your contribution.
25 You must quickly maintain good relations with your opponent in the court case up to the time that you are with him on the way *to court* so that the opponent in the court case will not turn you over to the judge, the judge turn you over to the underling, and you will be thrown into jail.

26 Amen, I tell you, you will not in any way come out from there until you give back the last penny.
27 You heard that it was stated to the original *people*, 'You will not cheat on *your* spouse.'
28 I tell you that everyone looking at a woman with the *intent* to desire *something* of her, he has already cheated on *his* spouse with her in his heart.
29 If your eye, the right *one*, causes you to stumble, take it out and throw it away from you. You see, it is advantageous to you that one of your body parts be ruined and your whole body not be thrown into Hinnom Valley.
30 And if your right hand causes you to stumble, chop it out and throw *it* away from you. You see, it is advantageous to you that one of your body parts be ruined and your whole body not be thrown into Hinnom Valley.
31 It was stated that whoever dismisses his wife must give her a divorce.
32 I tell you that whoever dismisses his wife, besides *and* outside of a matter of sexual sin, makes her to be cheated on, and whoever marries a *woman* who has been dismissed is cheating.
33 Again you heard that it was stated to the original *people*, 'You will not break an oath, but you will give back your oath to the Master.'
34 I tell you not to guarantee at all, not with the sky because it is a throne of God,
35 neither with the earth because it is a footrest for His feet, neither with Jerusalem because it is a city of the great King.
36 Neither should you guarantee with your head because you are not able to make one hair white or black.
37 Your answer must be yes, yes, no, no. *Whatever is* much more than this is from the evil *one*.
38 You heard that it was stated, 'An eye for an eye and a tooth for a tooth.'
39 I tell you to not stand in opposition to the evil, but anyone who will slap you on your right cheek, also turn the other to him.
40 And the *person* who wants you to be judged and to take your long undershirt, also leave *your* robe to him.
41 And anyone who will sequester help from you for one mile, lead the way with him for two.
42 Give to the *person* who asks you. And you will not turn away the *person* who wants to get an interest loan from you.
43 You heard that it was stated, 'You will love the *person* near you and hate your enemy.'
44 I tell you, love your enemies, confer blessings on the *people* putting a curse on you, do nicely to the *people* hating you, and pray over the *people* being spiteful to you and persecuting you
45 in order that you might become sons of your Father, the *One* in the heavens, because He brings His sun up on evil and good *people* and rains on *people* who do what is right and *people* who do what is wrong.
46 You see, if you love the people who love you, what pay do you have? Don't the tax collectors also do the same *thing*?
47 And if you say hello only to your brothers, what are you doing much more *than others*? Don't the tax collectors also do this?

48 So you will be complete *people* even as your Father, the *One* in the heavens, is complete."

6

1 "Pay attention to not be doing your charitable donation in front of the people with the *intent* to be viewed by them. But if not, you definitely are getting no pay beside your Father, the *One* in the heavens.
2 So when you make a charitable donation, do not blow a trumpet in front of you, even as the fakers do in the synagogues and in the streets in order that they might be elevated to a place of magnificence by the people. Amen, I tell you, they have all of their pay.
3 But as you make a charitable donation, your left *hand* must not know what your right *hand* is doing
4 in order that your charitable donation may be in the hidden *realm*. And your Father, the *One* who sees in the hidden *realm*, He will give back to you in the shown *realm*.
5 And when you pray, you will not even be as the fakers because they are fond of standing to pray in the synagogues and in the corners of the plazas in order that they might be shown to the people. Amen, I tell you that they have all of their pay.
6 But when you pray, go into your storage room. And after you close your door, pray to your Father, the *One* in the hidden *realm*, and your Father, the *One* who sees in the hidden *realm*, will give back to you in the shown *realm*.
7 As you *all* pray, you will not babble words, even as the non-Jewish *people do*. You see, it seems to them that they will be listened to in their many words.
8 So you should not be like them. You see, your Father realizes what *things* you have a need of before the *time* for you to ask Him.
9 So this is how you must pray: 'Our Father, the *One* in the heavens, Your name must be made sacred.
10 Your monarchy must come. What You want must happen, as in heaven, also on the earth.
11 Give us our bread (the next day *bread*) today.
12 And forgive us of the things we owe as we also are forgiving the people who owe us.
13 And you will not carry us into trouble, but save us from the evil because the monarchy, the ability, and the magnificence for the spans of time is Yours. Amen'
14 You see, if you will forgive the people *of* their infractions, your Father, the heavenly *One*, will also forgive you.
15 But if you will not forgive the people *of* their infractions, neither will your Father forgive your infractions.
16 When you go without food, do not even become as the sad-faced fakers. You see, they cause their *true* faces to disappear in order that it will appear to the people that they are going without food. Amen, I tell you that they have all of their pay.
17 But as you go without food, dab *perfume* on your head, and wash your face

18 in order that you will not appear to the people *as a person* going without food, only to your Father, the *One* in the hidden *realm*. And your Father, the *One* who sees in the hidden *realm*, will give back to you in the shown *realm*.
19 Do not stockpile stockpiles *of stuff* for yourselves on the earth where moth and dinner cause *them* to disappear and where thieves break in and steal.
20 But stockpile stockpiles *of stuff* for yourselves in heaven where neither moth nor dinner cause *them* to disappear and where thieves do not break in, nor steal.
21 You see, where your stockpile is, there your heart will also be.
22 The lamp of the body is the eye. So if your eye is dedicated, your whole body will be lit up.
23 But if your eye is evil, your whole body will be dark. So if the light, the *one* in you, is darkness, how great *is* the darkness.
24 No one is able to be a slave to two masters. You see, either he will hate the one and love the different *one*, or he will have one in front of *him* and ignore the different *one*. You are not able to be a slave to God and to wealthiness.
25 Because of this I tell you, do not worry about your soul, what you will eat and what you will drink, neither about your body, what you will put on. Isn't the soul more than the meal and the body *more than* the attire?
26 Look into the winged birds of the sky, because they do not seed, nor harvest, nor gather into grain bins, and your Father, the heavenly *One*, nurtures them. Aren't you much more substantial than they?
27 Who from among you by worrying is able to add on to his size one cubit (*an elbow to fingertip length*)?
28 And why must you worry about attire? Carefully study the wild flowers of the field, how it grows. It does not labor, nor spin yarn.
29 But I tell you that not even Solomon in all of his magnificence put *clothes* around himself as one of these.
30 If God decks out the grass of the field like this, that exists today and that tomorrow is thrown into a fire pit, *will He* not *do* much more for you, seldom trusting *people*?
31 So do not worry, saying, 'What will we eat?', or 'What will we drink?', or 'What *clothes* will we put around ourselves?'
32 You see, the non-Jews, he searches for all these *things*. You see, your Father, the heavenly *One*, realizes that you need absolutely all these *things*.
33 Look for the monarchy of God first and His right way, and all these *things* will be added to you.
34 So you will not worry for the *day* tomorrow. You see, the *day* tomorrow will worry about its own *things*. Its badness *is* enough for the day."

7

1 "Do not judge so that you will not be judged.
2 You see, with *the* judgment that you judge, you will be judged, and with *the* measurement that you measure out, it will be measured back to you.
3 Why do you see the wood chip, the *one* in the eye of your brother, but the log in your eye you do not take a closer look at?

4 Or how will you state to your brother, 'Leave *it*. I will take the wood chip out from your eye' and, look, the log *is* in your eye?
5 Faker, first take the log out of your eye, and then you will see clearly to take the wood chip out of the eye of your brother.
6 You should not give what is sacred to the dogs. Neither should you throw your pearls in front of the hogs so that they might not trample on them with their feet and, after turning around, rip you.
7 Ask and it will be given to you. Look and you will find. Knock and it will be opened to you.
8 You see, everyone who asks receives, the *person* who looks finds, and to the *person* who knocks, it will be opened.
9 Or what person is from among you, whom if his son asks for bread — he will not give a stone over to him, will he?
10 And if he asks for a fish — he will not give a snake over to him, will he?
11 So if you, who are evil, know to be giving good presents to your children, how much more will your Father, the *One* in the heavens, give good *things* to the *people* who ask Him?
12 So everything, however many *things* that you may want that the people do to you, this is what you also must be doing to them. You see, this is the Law and the Preachers.
13 Go in through the narrow gate because the wide gate and *its* spacious road *is* the *gate* leading off into the ruin, and the *people* going in through it are many
14 because the gate and the road that has gone through hard times *is* narrow (the *one* leading off into the life), and the *people* finding it are few.
15 Be cautious of the counterfeit preachers, some who come to you in sheep costumes, but on *the* inside they are vicious wolves.
16 From their fruits, you will correctly understand them. They do not gather up grape clusters from thorns, or figs from thistles, do they?
17 In this way, every good tree produces nice fruits, but the defective tree produces evil fruits.
18 A good tree is not able to be producing evil fruits. Neither *is* a defective tree *able* to be producing nice fruits.
19 Every tree that does not produce nice fruit is chopped out and thrown into a fire.
20 Clearly, from their fruits you will definitely correctly understand them.
21 Not everyone saying to Me, 'Master, Master,' will go into the monarchy of the heavens, only the *person* doing what My Father (the *One* in *the* heavens) wants.
22 Many will state to Me in that day, 'Master, Master, didn't we preach with Your name, with Your name throw lesser deities out, and with Your name show many abilities?'
23 And at that time, I will acknowledge to them, 'I never ever knew you. Distance yourself away from me, *you*, the *people* who work for the crime.'
24 So everyone, any who listen to these My messages and do them I will liken him to an attentive man, someone who built his house on the rock.

25 And the rain tumbled down, the rivers came, the winds blew, they fell toward that house, and it did not fall. You see, *the* foundation had been laid on the rock.
26 And everyone who listens to these My messages and does not do them, he will be like a foolish man, someone who built his house on the sand.
27 And the rain tumbled down, the rivers came, the winds blew, they beat against that house, and it fell. And its fall was great."
28 And it happened when Jesus completely finished these messages; the crowds were being impressed based on His teaching.
29 You see, He was teaching them as *a person* having authority and not as the *Old Testament* transcribers.

8

1 After He walked down out of the mountain, big crowds followed Him.
2 And look, when a skin-diseased *man* came, he was bowing down to Him, saying, "Master, if you want, you are able to clear me up."
3 And when Jesus put out the hand, He touched him, saying, "I want to. Be cleared up." And right away his skin disease was cleared up.
4 And Jesus says to him, "See, you should say nothing, but make *your* way back, show yourself to the priest, and offer the contribution that Moses instructed for a witness to them."
5 When Jesus went into Capernaum, a lieutenant came forward to Him encouraging Him
6 and saying, "Master, my servant boy has been confined *to bed* in the house, disabled, being tortured dreadfully."
7 And Jesus says to him, "When I come, I will heal him."
8 And when the lieutenant responded, he was declaring, "Master, I am not adequate that you come in under my roof, but just say a word, and my servant boy will be cured.
9 You see, I also am a person under authority having soldiers under me. And I say to this *one*, 'Travel,' and he travels; to another, 'Go,' and he goes; and to my slave, 'Do this,' and he does *it*."
10 When Jesus heard *this*, He was amazed and said to the *people* following *Him*, "Amen, I tell you, I did not find so much trust even in Israel.
11 I tell you that many will arrive from eastern regions and western regions and recline with Abraham, Isaac, and Jacob in the monarchy of the heavens,
12 but the sons of the monarchy will be thrown out into the darkness, the *darkness* further out. There will be the crying and the grinding of the teeth there."
13 And Jesus said to the lieutenant, "Make *your* way back, and as you trusted, it must happen to you." And his servant boy was cured in that hour.
14 And when Jesus came into the house of Peter, He saw his mother-in-law who had been confined *to bed* and had a fever.
15 And He touched her hand, the fever left her, and she got up and was serving them.

16 When it became evening, they brought many *people* to Him who had lesser deities. And He threw the spirits out with a word and healed all the *people* who had *it* bad

17 in order that what was stated through Isaiah, the preacher, *in Isaiah 53:4* might be accomplished that says, "He took our weaknesses and hauled the illnesses."

18 When Jesus saw big crowds around Him, He gave the order to go off to the other side.

19 And when one *Old Testament* transcriber came forward, he said to Him, "Teacher, I will follow You wherever You go off to."

20 And Jesus says to him, "The foxes have burrows, the winged birds of the sky *have* nests, but the Son of the Person does not have *a place* where He may rest *His* head."

21 A different *one* of His students said to Him, "Master, give me permission to first go off and bury my father."

22 But Jesus said to him, "Follow Me, and leave the dead to bury their *own* dead."

23 And when He climbed on board into the boat, His students followed Him.

24 And look, a large quake happened in the sea in such a way for the boat to be covered by the swells, but He was sleeping.

25 And when His students came forward, they got Him up, saying, "Master, rescue *us*. We are being ruined."

26 And He says to them, "Why are you cowardly, seldom trusting *people*?" Then after He got up, He told the winds and the sea to stop, and there became a great calm.

27 The people were amazed, saying, "What kind of *person* is this that even the winds and the sea obey Him?"

28 And after He came to the other side, to the rural area of the Gergesenes, two *people* who had lesser deities came to meet Him, coming out of the burial vaults, very fierce in such a way for no one to have strength to pass by through that way.

29 And, look, they yelled, saying, "What *is there between* us and you, Jesus, Son of God? Did you come here before *the* appointed time to torture us?"

30 A long way away from them, there was a herd of many hogs grazing.

31 The lesser deities were encouraging Him, saying, "If you throw us out, give us permission to go off into the herd of the hogs."

32 And He said to them, "Make *your* way out." When the *lesser deities* went out, they went off into the herd of the hogs. And, look, the entire herd of the hogs rushed down the steep slope into the sea and died in the water.

33 The *people* grazing *them* escaped. And when they went off into the city, they reported everything, even the *circumstances* of the *two* with lesser deities.

34 And, look, the entire city came out for a meeting together with Jesus. And when they saw Him, they encouraged *Him* in order that He might walk somewhere else away from their borders.

9

1 And after He climbed on board into the boat, He crossed all the way over and went to *His* own city.

2 And look, they were bringing to Him a disabled *man* on a cot who had been confined *to bed*. And when Jesus saw their trust, He said to the disabled *man*, "Be courageous, child. Your sins have been forgiven to you."
3 And look, some of the *Old Testament* transcribers said among themselves, "This *Person* is insulting *God*."
4 And after Jesus saw their contemplations, He said, "Why do you contemplate evil *things* in your hearts?
5 You see, which is easier to say, 'The sins have been forgiven to you,' or to say 'Get up and walk around?'
6 But so that you may realize that the Son of the Person has authority on the earth to be forgiving sins...." At that time, He says to the disabled *man*, "After getting up, pick up your cot, and make *your* way back to your house."
7 And after getting up, he went off to his house.
8 When the crowds saw *it*, they were amazed and praised the magnificence of God, the *One* who gave this type of authority to the people.
9 And as Jesus passed by from there, He saw a person called Matthew sitting at the tax booth. And He says to him, "Follow Me." And after he stood up, he followed Him.
10 And it happened that He was reclining in the house. And look, when many tax collectors and sinful *people* came, they were reclining together with Jesus and His students.
11 And when the Separatists saw *it*, they said to His students, "Why is your Teacher eating with the tax collectors and sinful *people*?"
12 When Jesus heard *it*, He said to them, "The *people* who have strength have no need of a doctor, but the *people* who have *it* bad *do*.
13 After you travel *off*, learn what *Hosea 6:6* is, 'I want forgiving kindness and not sacrifice.' You see, I did not come to invite *people* who do what is right, but sinful *people*, to a change of ways."
14 At that time, the students of John came to Him, saying, "Why do we and the Separatists go without food often, but Your students do not go without food?"
15 And Jesus said to them, "The sons of the bridal room are not able to be grieving as long as the groom is with them, are they? But days will come when the groom will be taken away from them, and then they will go without food.
16 No one puts a patch of unprocessed cloth on a worn out robe. You see, what fills it in takes away from the robe, and *the* tear becomes worse.
17 Neither do they put young wine into worn out leather bags. If *they do*, the leather bags definitely are ripped, the wine is spilled out, and the leather bags are ruined. But they put young wine into new leather bags, and both are preserved."
18 As He was speaking these *things* to them, look, when one head person came, he was bowing down to Him, saying, "My daughter passed away just now, but when You come, place Your hand on her, and she will live."
19 And when Jesus got up, He and His students followed him.
20 And look, when a woman who was bleeding for twelve years came up from behind, she touched the fringe of His robe.

21 You see, she was saying to herself, "If only I might touch His robe, I will be rescued."
22 When Jesus turned around and saw her, He said, "Daughter, be courageous, your trust has rescued you," and the woman was rescued from that hour.
23 And when Jesus came into the house of the head person and saw the flute players and the crowd causing a disturbance,
24 He says, "Get back. You see, the girl did not die, but she is sleeping." And they were laughing at Him.
25 After the crowd was thrown out, when He went in, He took hold of her hand, and the girl got up.
26 And the news about her went out into all of that land.
27 And as Jesus passed by from there, two blind *men* followed Him, yelling and saying, "Show forgiving kindness to us, son of David."
28 After He came into the house, the blind *men* came forward to Him, and Jesus says to them, "Do you trust that I am able to do this?" They say to Him, "Yes, Master."
29 Then He touched their eyes, saying, "It must happen to you according to your trust."
30 And their eyes were opened, and Jesus was stern with them, saying, "Look. No one must know."
31 After the *blind men* went out, they thoroughly spread *the news* about Him in all of that land.
32 As they were going out, look, they brought to Him a speech-impaired person who had a lesser deity.
33 And when the lesser deity was thrown out, the speech-impaired *person* spoke, and the crowds were amazed, saying, "*Something* like this never ever appeared in Israel."
34 But the Separatists were saying, "He throws the lesser deities out by the head of the lesser deities."
35 And Jesus led *them* around to all the cities and the villages teaching in their synagogues, speaking publicly about the good news of the monarchy, and healing every illness and every frailty among the ethnic group.
36 When He saw the crowds, He had sympathy concerning them because they were *people* who had given up and had been tossed as if *they were* sheep that don't have a shepherd.
37 At that time, He says to His students, "The harvest certainly *is* big, but the workers *are* few.
38 So plead with the master of the harvest in order that he might put workers out into his harvest."

10

1 And when He called for His twelve students, He gave them authority over spirits that are not clean in such a way to be throwing them out and to be healing every illness and every frailty.

2 These are the names of the twelve missionaries: first, Simon (the *one* called Peter) and Andrew (his brother); James (the *son* of Zebedee) and John (his brother);

3 Philip and Bartholomew; Thomas and Matthew (the tax collector); James (the *son* of Alpheus) and Lebbeus (who was also called Thaddeus);
4 Simon (the Kananite - *Aramaic for Zealot*) and Judas (the *one* from Kerioth who also turned Him in).
5 Jesus sent these twelve out *on a mission* after He passed the order on to them, saying, "You will not go off to a road of non-Jews, and you will not go into a city of Samaritans.
6 But instead travel to the sheep of Israel's house, the *ones* that have been lost.
7 As you travel, speak publicly, saying, 'The monarchy of the heavens has come near.'
8 Heal *people* who are weak. Clear up skin-diseased *people*. Get *the* dead up. Throw lesser deities out. You received for free, give for free.
9 You will not get gold, nor silver, nor copper for your sashes,
10 not a tote bag for *the* way, nor two long undershirts, nor sandals, nor staffs. You see, the worker is deserving of his meal.
11 Into whatever city or village you might go, question who in it is deserving, and stay there until you go out.
12 As you go into the house, say hello to it.
13 And if the house is certainly deserving, your peace must come on it. But if it is not deserving, your peace must be returned back to you.
14 And whoever does not accept you, nor hear your messages, as you go out of the house or that city, shake the dust of your feet off.
15 Amen, I tell you, it will be more tolerable for *the* land of Sodom and Gomorrah in a day of judgment than for that city.
16 Look, I am sending you out *on a mission* as sheep in *the* middle of wolves. So become focused as the snakes and unpolluted as the doves.
17 Be cautious of the people. You see, they will turn you into councils and in their synagogues whip you.
18 You will also be led before leaders and kings on account of Me for a witness to them and the non-Jews.
19 When they turn you in, do not worry how or what you should speak. You see, it will be given to you in that hour what you will speak;
20 for you are not the *ones* speaking, but the Spirit of your Father *is* the *One* speaking in you.
21 A brother will turn a brother in for death, and a father *will turn* a child *in*. And children will stand up on parents and will put them to death.
22 And you will be hated by all *kinds of people* because of My name, but the *person* who persists *to do what is right* to *the* conclusion, this *person* will be rescued.
23 When they pursue you in this city, escape to the other *city*. You see, amen, I tell you, you will not in any way finish the cities of Israel until the Son of the Person comes.
24 A student is not over the teacher. Neither *is* a slave over his master.
25 *It is* enough for the student that he might become as his teacher and the slave as his master. If they called the homeowner Beelzebub, how much more the people in His house?

26 So don't fear them. You see, there is nothing having been covered up that will not be uncovered, and hidden that will not be known.
27 What I tell you in the dark, say in the light, and what you hear in the ear speak publicly on the top of houses.
28 And do not be afraid from the *people* who kill the body, but the soul they are not able to kill. Instead fear the *One* who is able to ruin both soul and body in Hinnom Valley.
29 Are not two little sparrows sold for an assarius *($2)*? And one from them will not fall on the earth unaccompanied by your Father.
30 Even the hairs of your head are all *hairs* that have been numbered.
31 So do not be afraid, you are more substantial than many little sparrows.
32 So everyone, any who will acknowledge *being* in Me in front of the people, I will also acknowledge *being* in him in front of My Father, the *One* in *the* heavens.
33 But whoever denies Me in front of the people, I will also deny him in front of My Father, the *One* in *the* heavens.
34 Do not assume that I came to put peace on the earth. I did not come to put peace, but a dagger.
35 You see, I came to pit a person against his father, a daughter against her mother, and a bride against her mother-in-law.
36 And the person's enemies *are* the people in his house.
37 The *person* who is fond of a father or mother over Me is not deserving of Me, and the *person* who is fond of a son or daughter over Me is not deserving of Me.
38 And a *person* who does not take his cross and follow behind Me is not deserving of Me.
39 The *person* who finds his soul will lose it, and the *person* who loses his soul on account of Me will find it.
40 The *person* who accepts you accepts Me, and the *person* who accepts Me accepts the *One* who sent Me out *on a mission*.
41 The *person* who accepts a preacher for *the* name of a preacher will receive a preacher's pay. And the *person* who accepts a *person* who does what is right for *the* name of a *person* who does what is right will receive *the* pay of a *person* who does what is right.
42 And whoever gives one of these little *ones* a cup of cold *drink* to drink just for *the* name of a student, amen, I tell you, he will not in any way lose his pay."

11

1 And it happened when Jesus finished specifically assigning His twelve students; He walked somewhere else away from there for the "to be teaching and to be speaking publicly in their cities" *part*
2 In the prison, when John heard about the actions of the Anointed King, after sending two of his students,
3 he said to Him, "Are you the *One* coming or should we expect a different *One*?"
4 And when Jesus answered, He said to them, "After you travel *back*, report to John *things* that you hear and see.

5 Blind *people* see again, and crippled *people* walk around. Skin-diseased *people* are cleared up, and hearing-impaired *people* hear. Dead *people* are gotten up, and poor *people* are told good news.
6 And whoever does not stumble in Me is blessed."
7 As these *students* traveled *off*, Jesus began to be saying to the crowds about John, "What did you go out into the backcountry to view, a stick disturbed by wind?
8 But what did you go out to see, a person who had been decked out in elegant clothes? Look, the *people* wearing the elegant *clothes* are in the houses of the kings.
9 But what did you go out to see, a preacher? Yes, I tell you, and much more than a preacher.
10 You see, this is *the person* about whom it has been written *in Malachi 3:1*, 'Look, I am sending My announcer out *on a mission* before Your face who will construct Your road in front of You.'
11 Amen, I tell you, among *the people* born of women, there has not risen *a person* greater than John the Submerger. But the *person* who is littler in the monarchy of the heavens is greater than him.
12 From the days of John the Submerger until now, the monarchy of the heavens is forced, and forceful people snatch it.
13 You see, all the Preachers and the Law preached until John.
14 And if you want to accept *it*, he is Elijah, the *one* who is going to be coming.
15 The *person* who has ears to listen must listen.
16 What will I liken this generation to? It is like little boys sitting in marketplaces, hollering to their friends,
17 and saying, 'We played the flute for you, and you did not dance. We wailed for you, and you did not beat your chests in grief.'
18 You see, John came neither eating, nor drinking, and they say, 'He has a lesser deity.'
19 The Son of the Person came eating and drinking, and they say, 'Look, a person, an excessive eater and a wine drinker, a friend of tax collectors and sinful *people*.' And the insight was made right from its children."
20 At that time, He began to be criticizing the cities in which most of His abilities happened because they did not change their ways.
21 "What a tragedy *it is* to you, Chorazin! What a tragedy *it is* to you, Bethsaida! because if the abilities happened in Tyre and Sidon, the *ones* that happened in you, they would have changed their ways a long time ago in cloth made of hair and *in* ash.
22 More importantly, I tell you, it will be more tolerable for Tyre and Sidon in a day of judgment than for you.
23 And you, Capernaum, the *city* that was put up high until heaven. You will be made to walk down until Hades *(the underworld of the dead)* because if the abilities happened in Sodom, the *ones* that happened in you, it would have stayed up to the *day* today.
24 More importantly, I tell you, that it will be more tolerable for *the* land of Sodom in a day of judgment than for you."

25 In that time period, when Jesus responded, He said, "I acknowledge to you out loud, Father, Master of the heaven and the earth, that You hid these *things* away from insightful and understanding *people* and uncovered them to infants,
26 yes, Father, because in this way it became a good notion in front of You.
27 All *things* were turned over to Me by My Father. And no one correctly understands the Son except the Father. Neither does anyone correctly understand the Father except the Son and whomever the Son intends to uncover *Him* to.
28 Come on toward Me, all the *people* who are laboring and have been loaded down, and I will relax you.
29 Take My crossbeam upon you, learn from Me because I am humble and lowly in the heart, and you will find relief for your souls.
30 You see, My crossbeam *is* kind, and My load is light."

12

1 In that time period, Jesus traveled on the Sabbaths through the croplands. His students were hungry and began to be pulling off heads *of grain* and to be eating.
2 When the Separatists saw *it*, they said to Him, "Look, your students are doing what is not allowed to be doing during *the* Sabbath."
3 *Jesus* said to them, "Didn't you read what David did when he and the *people* with him were hungry?
4 How he went into the house of God and ate the *loaves of* bread of the display, *loaves* that were *something* not allowed for him to eat, nor the *people* with him, just the priests alone?
5 Or did you not read in the Law that on the Sabbaths the priests on the temple grounds profane the Sabbath and they are innocent?
6 I tell you that *someone* greater than the temple grounds is here.
7 But if you had known what *this* is, 'I want forgiving kindness and not sacrifice,' you would not have found the innocent *people* guilty.
8 You see, *the* Master even of the Sabbath is the Son of the Person."
9 And after He walked somewhere else away from there, He went into their synagogue.
10 And look, there was a person who had the dried-up hand. And they asked Him, saying, "*Tell us* if it is allowed to be healing on the Sabbaths," so that they might level a complaint against Him.
11 *Jesus* said to them, "What person will be from among you who will have one sheep, and if this *sheep* should fall into a hole on the Sabbaths, will he not take hold of it and get *it* up?
12 So how much more substantial is a person than a sheep? In such a way, it is allowed to be doing nicely on the Sabbaths."
13 Then He says to the person, "Put out your hand." And he put *it* out, and it was reestablished healthy as the other *hand*.
14 The Separatists received counsel against Him (after they went out) in order that they might ruin Him.

15 When Jesus knew *it*, He took a back way from there, and big crowds followed Him. And He healed them all
16 and shushed them so that they would not make Him known
17 in order that what was stated through Isaiah, the preacher, *in Isaiah 42:1–4* might be accomplished that says,
18 "Look, My Servant Boy whom I picked, My Loved *One*, in whom My soul is delighted. I will put My Spirit on Him, and He will report judgment to the non-Jews.
19 He will not fight, neither will He make a yell, neither will anyone hear His voice in the plazas.
20 He will not break a stick that has been crushed, and He will not extinguish a wick that is smoldering until He puts out the judgment for victory.
21 And non-Jews will anticipate good in His name."
22 Then a blind and speech-impaired *man* who had a lesser deity was brought to Him. And He healed him in such a way for the blind and speech-impaired *man* both to be speaking and to be seeing.
23 And all the crowds were being astounded and saying, "This isn't the son of David, is it?"
24 When the Separatists heard *it*, they said, "This *Person* does not throw out the lesser deities except with Beelzebub, *the* head of the lesser deities."
25 When Jesus realized their contemplations, He said to them, "Every monarchy divided against itself becomes uninhabited, and every city or house divided against itself will not be established.
26 And if the Opponent throws the Opponent out on himself, he is divided. So how will his monarchy stand?
27 And if I throw the lesser deities out with Beelzebub, your sons, with whom do they throw *them* out? Because of this, they will be your judges.
28 But if I throw the lesser deities out with God's Spirit, clearly the monarchy of God has already come on you.
29 Or how is anyone able to go into the house of the strong *person* and to ransack his containers if he will not first tie up the strong *person* and then ransack his house?
30 The *person* who is not with Me is against Me, and the *person* who does not gather with Me scatters.
31 Because of this, I tell you, every sin and insult will be forgiven to the people, but the insult against the Spirit will not be forgiven to the people.
32 And whoever says a word against the Son of the Person, it will be forgiven to him, but whoever says *a word* against the Spirit, the Sacred *Spirit*, it will not be forgiven to him, not in this span of time, nor in the *span of time* that is going *to come*.
33 Either make the tree nice and its fruit nice, or make the tree defective and its fruit defective. You see, the tree is known from the fruit.
34 Offspring of poisonous snakes, how are you who are evil able to be speaking good *things*? You see, from the excess of the heart, the mouth speaks.
35 The good person throws the good *things* out from the good stockpile of the heart, and the evil person throws evil *things* out from the evil stockpile.

36 I tell you that every idle statement that the people might speak, they will give back an answer concerning it in a day of judgment.
37 You see, from your words, you will be made right, and from your words, you will be found guilty."
38 At that time, some of the *Old Testament* transcribers and Separatists responded, saying, "Teacher, we want to see an indicator from You."
39 But when He answered, He said to them, "An evil and cheating generation searches for an indicator, and an indicator will not be given to it except the indicator of Jonah, the preacher.
40 You see, even as Jonah was in the belly of the large fish three days and three nights, so will the Son of the Person be in the heart of the earth three days and three nights.
41 Ninevite men will stand up in the judgment with this generation and find it guilty because they changed their ways into the public speaking of Jonah and, look, a greater *thing* than Jonah *is* here.
42 A queen of *the* south will be gotten up in the judgment with this generation and will find it guilty because she came from the ends of the earth to hear the insight of Solomon and, look, a greater *thing* than Solomon *is* here.
43 When the spirit that is not clean comes out from the person, it passes through places without water looking for relief and does not find *it*.
44 At that time, it says, 'I will return back to my house from where I went out.' And when it comes, it finds a hangout that has been swept and decorated.
45 Then it travels and takes along with itself seven different spirits more evil than itself. And when it goes in, it lives there, and the last of that person becomes worse than the first. This is how it will also be for this generation, the evil *generation*."
46 As He was still speaking to the crowds, look, His mother and brothers had stood outside looking to speak to Him.
47 Someone said to Him, "Look, Your mother and Your brothers have stood outside looking to speak to You."
48 But when *Jesus* answered, He said to the *person* who told Him, "Who is My mother? And who are My brothers?"
49 And when He put out His hand over His students, He said, "Look, My mother and My brothers.
50 You see, whoever does what My Father (the *One* in *the* heavens) wants, he is My brother, sister, and mother."

13

1 During that day after Jesus came out away from the house, He was sitting along the sea.
2 And big crowds were gathered together to Him in such a way that for Him to be sitting down He climbed on board into the boat, and all the crowd had stood on the beach.
3 And He spoke many *things* to them in illustrations, saying, "Look, the *one* who seeds went out for the "to be seeding" *part*.
4 And during the *time* for him to be seeding, some fell along the road. And the winged birds came and ate them up.

5 Others fell on the rocky *places* where they did not have much soil, and right away they came up because of the *fact for them* to not be having *the* depth of *the* soil.
6 When *the* sun came up, they were scorched and, because of the *fact for them* to not be having root, they shriveled up.
7 Others fell on the thorns, and the thorns climbed up and choked them out.
8 Others fell on the soil, the nice *soil*, and they were giving fruit: *one* that *gave* a hundred, *another* that *gave* sixty, *another* that *gave* thirty.
9 The *person* who has ears to listen must listen."
10 And when the students came forward, they said to Him, "Why do you speak to them in illustrations?"
11 When *Jesus* answered, He said to them, "Because it has been given to you to know the secrets of the monarchy of the heavens, but to those *people* it has not been given.
12 You see, anyone who has, it will be given to him, and it will overflow, but anyone who does not have, even what he has will be taken away from him.
13 Because of this, I speak to them in illustrations because as they see, they don't see, and as they hear, they don't hear, nor understand.
14 And the preaching of Isaiah *in Isaiah 6:9–10* is being fully accomplished on them, the *preaching* that says, 'With the sense of hearing, you will hear and not in any way understand, and as you look, you will look and not in any way see.
15 You see, the heart of this ethnic group became fat, they hardly heard with the ears, and they shut their eyes so that they would never see with the eyes, hear with the ears, understand with the heart, return back, and I would cure them.'
16 But your eyes *are* blessed because they see, and your ears because they hear.
17 You see, amen, I tell you that many preachers and *people* who did what is right desired to see *things* that you are looking at, and they did not see, and to hear *things* that you hear, and they did not hear.
18 So you must listen to the illustration of the *one* who seeds.
19 Everyone who hears the message of the monarchy and does not understand, the evil one comes and snatches up what has been seeded in his heart. This is the *one* who was seeded along the road.
20 The *one* seeded on the rocky *places*, this is the *person* who hears the message and right away takes it with happiness.
21 It does not have root in him, but it is for the time being. When hard times or persecution because of the message happens, right away he stumbles.
22 The *one* seeded into the thorns, this is the *person* who hears the message, and the worry of this span of time and the fraud of the wealth come together and choke off the message, and he becomes fruitless.
23 The *one* seeded on the soil, the nice *soil*, this is the *person* hearing and understanding the message, who for sure produces fruit and makes: *one* that *makes* a hundred, *another* that *makes* sixty, *another* that *makes* thirty."
24 He placed another illustration beside them, saying, "The monarchy of the heavens is like a person who seeded nice seed in his field.

25 During the *time* for the people to be sleeping, his enemy came, seeded ryegrass up in *the* middle of the wheat, and went away.
26 When the stem budded and produced fruit, then the ryegrass also appeared.
27 When the slaves of the property owner came forward, they said to him, 'Master, didn't you seed nice seed in your field? So where does it have the ryegrass from?'
28 The *property owner* was declaring to them, 'A person *who is* an enemy did this.' The slaves said to him, 'So do you want *that* after going off, we will gather them up?'
29 The *property owner* was declaring, 'No, don't, so that as you gather up the ryegrass you will not uproot the *good* wheat with them at the same time.
30 Leave both *of them* to be grown together up to the harvest. And at the harvest time, I will state to the harvesters, "Gather up the ryegrass first, and tie it up into bundles with the *intent* to burn it. But bring the *good* wheat together into my grain bin."'"
31 He placed another illustration beside them, saying, "The monarchy of the heavens is like a kernel of mustard that, when a person took, he seeded in his field,
32 that not only is littler than all of the seeds, but when it is grown, it is greater than the vegetables, and it becomes a tree in such a way for the winged birds of the sky to come and to be nesting in its branches."
33 He spoke another illustration to them, "The monarchy of the heavens is like yeast that when a woman took, she hid in three loads of dough until *the time* that all of it was raised."
34 Jesus spoke all these *things* to the crowds in illustrations, and without an illustration, He was not speaking to them
35 in order that what was stated through the preacher *in Psalm 78:2* might be accomplished that says, "I will open my mouth in illustrations. I will utter *things* that have been hidden since *the* founding of *the* world."
36 At that time, after leaving the crowds, Jesus went into the house, and His students came to Him saying, "Explain to us the illustration of the ryegrass of the field."
37 When *Jesus* answered, He said to them, "The *person* seeding the nice seed is the Son of the Person.
38 The field is the world. The nice seed, they are these *people*, the sons of the monarchy. The ryegrass is the sons of the evil *one*.
39 The enemy, the *one* who seeded them is the Accuser. The harvest is *the* very conclusion of the span of time. The harvesters are angels.
40 So even as the ryegrass is gathered up and burned with fire, so will it be at the very conclusion of this span of time.
41 The Son of the Person will send His angels out *on a mission*, and they will gather up from His monarchy all the obstacles and the *people* doing the crime.
42 And they will throw them into the furnace of the fire. There will be the crying and the grinding of the teeth there.

43 At that time, the *people* who did what is right will shine brightly as the sun in the monarchy of their Father. The *person* who has ears to listen must listen.
44 Again the monarchy of the heavens is like a stockpile of treasure that has been hidden in the field, that when a *person* found, he hid, and out of his happiness he makes *his* way back, sells everything, as much as he has, and buys that field.
45 Again the monarchy of the heavens is like a person, a wholesaler, looking for nice pearls,
46 who, when he found one very valuable pearl, after he went away, he has put everything up for sale, as much as he had, and bought it.
47 Again the monarchy of the heavens is like a seine net that was thrown into the sea and gathered *some* of every kind together,
48 that when it was filled, after they hauled *it* up on the beach and were seated, they gathered up the nice *ones* into buckets, but threw the defective *ones* out.
49 This is how it will be at the very conclusion of the span of time. The angels will go out and isolate the evil *people* from *the* middle of the *people* who did what is right.
50 And they will throw them into the furnace of the fire. There will be the crying and the grinding of the teeth there."
51 Jesus says to them, "Do you understand all these *things*?" They say to Him, "Yes, Master."
52 *Jesus* said to them, "Because of this, every *Old Testament* transcriber who becomes a student in the monarchy of the heavens is like a person, a homeowner, someone who takes out from his stockpile new *things* and former *things*."
53 And it happened when Jesus finished these illustrations; He took off from there.
54 And when He went into His hometown, He was teaching them in their synagogue in such a way for them to be impressed and to be saying, "Where *does* this *Person get* this insight and the abilities from?
55 Isn't this the son of the builder? Isn't His mother called Mary and His brothers, James, Joses, Simon, and Jude?
56 And aren't His sisters all with us? So where *does* this *Person get* all these *things* from?"
57 And they were stumbling in Him. But Jesus said to them, "A preacher is not worthless except in his hometown and in his house."
58 And He did not show many abilities there because of their lack of trust.

14

1 In that time period, Herod, the head of one of *Palestine's* four regions, heard the talk about Jesus.
2 And he said to his servant boys, "This is John the Submerger. He was gotten up from the dead, and because of this, the abilities are active in him."
3 You see, when Herod took John into custody, he tied him up and put *him* in jail because of Herodias (the wife of Philip, his brother);
4 for John was saying to him, "It is not allowed for you to be having her."

5 And wanting to kill him, he feared the crowd because they had him as a preacher.
6 As Herod's birthday celebrations were conducted, Herodias' daughter danced in the middle of *them*, and Herod liked it.
7 From this, with an oath, he acknowledged to give her whatever she asked for.
8 The *daughter*, who was forced forward by her mother, declares, "Give me here on a plate, the head of John the Submerger."
9 And the king was sad. But because of the oaths and the *people* reclining together with *him*, he gave the order *for it* to be given.
10 And after sending *someone*, he beheaded John in the jail.
11 And his head was carried on a plate and given to the girl. And she carried *it* to her mother.
12 And when his students came forward, they took the body away and buried it. And when they came, they reported *it* to Jesus.
13 And when Jesus heard *it*, He took a back way from there in a boat to an uninhabited place by Himself. And when the crowds heard, they followed Him on foot out of the cities.
14 And when Jesus came out *of the boat*, He saw a big crowd, had sympathy on them, and healed their sick.
15 When it became evening, His students came to Him, saying, "The place is uninhabited, and the hour already passed by. Dismiss the crowds so that after going away into the villages, they might buy food for themselves."
16 But Jesus said to them, "They have no need to go away. You give them *something* to eat."
17 The *students* say to Him, "We don't have *anything* here except five *loaves of* bread and two fish."
18 *Jesus* said, "Bring them to Me here."
19 And after He gave the order for the crowds to recline on the grasses and took the five *loaves of* bread and the two fish, when He looked up into the sky, He conferred a blessing *on them*. And after He split *them*, He gave the *pieces of* bread to the students, the students to the crowds.
20 And everyone ate and was full. And they picked up what was left over of the pieces, twelve full baskets.
21 The *people* eating were as if *they were* five thousand men, besides women and young children.
22 And right away Jesus urged His students to climb on board into the boat and to be going ahead of Him to the other side until *the time* that He will dismiss the crowds.
23 And after dismissing the crowds, He climbed up into the mountain by Himself to pray. When it became evening, He was there alone.
24 The boat already in *the* middle of the sea was being tortured by the swells. You see, the wind was opposing *them*.
25 In *the* fourth guard shift of the night (*3:00 to 6:00 a.m.*), Jesus went off toward them walking around on the sea.
26 When the students saw Him walking around on the sea, they were uneasy, saying, "It is a ghost," and they yelled from the fear.

27 Right away Jesus spoke to them, saying, "Be courageous. *It* is Me. Don't be afraid."
28 When Peter responded to Him, he said, "Master, if *it* is You, give the order for me to come toward You on the water."
29 *Jesus* said, "Come." And after Peter climbed down out of the boat, he walked around on the water to go toward Jesus.
30 But seeing the strong wind, he was afraid, and after he began to be dropped down, he yelled, saying, "Master, rescue me."
31 Right away when Jesus put out *His* hand, He latched on to him and says to him, "Seldom trusting *Peter*, why did you doubt?"
32 And when they climbed on board into the boat, the wind stopped blowing.
33 When the *people* in the boat came, they bowed down to Him, saying, "You truly are a son of God."
34 And when they crossed all the way over, they came into the land of Gennesaret.
35 And when the men of that place recognized Him, they sent out into all of that surrounding rural area, and they brought to Him all the *people* who had *it* bad.
36 And they were encouraging Him so that they might just touch the fringe of His robe. And as many as touched were completely rescued.

15

1 At that time, the *Old Testament* transcribers and Separatists from Greater Jerusalem came forward to Jesus, saying,
2 "Why do your students walk in violation of the tradition of the older *men*? You see, they are not washing their hands when they eat bread."
3 When *Jesus* answered, He said to them, "Why do you also walk in violation of the demand of God because of your tradition?
4 You see, God demanded, saying *in Deuteronomy 5:16*, 'Value your father and mother,' and *in Exodus 21:17*, 'The *person* who says bad things about a father or mother must pass away with death.'
5 But you say, 'Whoever says to the father or the mother, "Whatever you should have been benefited with from me *is* a contribution *now*,"
6 will not in any way even value his father or his mother.' And you nullified the demand of God because of your tradition.
7 Fakers, Isaiah nicely preached about you *in Isaiah 29:13*, saying,
8 'This ethnic group comes near to Me with their mouth and values Me with the lips, but their heart has *itself* far away from Me.
9 They worship Me in a futile way, teaching instructions *that are* people's regulations.'"
10 And after calling for the crowd, He said to them, "Hear and understand.
11 What goes into the mouth does not make the person shared, but what travels out of the mouth, this makes the person shared."
12 Then, after His students came forward, they said to Him, "Do you realize that when the Separatists heard the message, they were offended?"

13 When *Jesus* answered, He said, "Every plant that My Father, the heavenly *One*, did not plant will be uprooted.
14 Leave them. They are blind guides of blind *people*. If a blind *person* guides a blind *person*, both will fall into a hole."
15 When Peter responded, he said to Him, "Explain this illustration to us."
16 Jesus said, "Are you also still clueless?
17 Are you not yet aware that everything traveling into the mouth, takes up room in the belly, and is thrown out into *the* sewer?
18 But the *things* traveling out of the mouth come out of the heart, and those *things* make the person shared.
19 You see, out of the heart comes evil ponderings, murders, cheatings on a spouse, sexual sins, thefts, lies from witnesses, insults.
20 These are the *things* that make the person shared, but the "to eat with unwashed hands" *thing* does not make the person shared."
21 And when Jesus went out from there, He took a back way into the parts of Tyre and Sidon.
22 And, look, when a Canaannite woman came out from those borders, she made a yell at Him, saying, "Show forgiving kindness to me, Master, Son of David. My daughter has a lesser deity in a bad way."
23 But *Jesus* did not answer her a word, and when His students came forward, they were asking Him, saying, "Dismiss her because she is yelling behind us."
24 When *Jesus* answered, He said, "I was not sent out except to the sheep of Israel's house, the *ones* that have been lost."
25 When the *woman* came, she was bowing down to Him, saying, "Master, help me."
26 When *Jesus* answered, He said, "It is not nice to take the bread of the children and throw it to the puppies."
27 But the *woman* said, "Yes, Master. You see, even the puppies eat out of the crumbs, the *ones* falling off of their masters' table."
28 Then when Jesus responded, He said to her, "O ma'am, your trust *is* great. It must happen to you as you want." And her daughter was cured from that hour.
29 And when Jesus walked somewhere else away from there, He went along the Sea of Galilee. And after He climbed up into the mountain, He was sitting there,
30 and big crowds came forward to Him having with them crippled *people*, blind *people*, physically wounded *people*, speech-impaired *people*, also many different *people*. And they tossed them beside Jesus' feet, and He healed them
31 in such a way for the crowds to be amazed seeing speech-impaired *people* speaking, physically wounded *people* well, crippled *people* walking around, and blind *people* seeing. And they praised the magnificence of the God of Israel.
32 After Jesus called for His students, He said, "I have sympathy on the crowd because already for three days they are still staying with Me and they do not have what they will eat. And I do not want to dismiss them with nothing to eat so that they will not be exhausted on the road."

33 And His students say to Him, "Where *do* we *get* so many *loaves of* bread from in an uninhabited place in such a way to make so big a crowd full?"
34 And Jesus says to them, "How many *loaves of* bread do you have?" The *students* said, "Seven and a few small fish."
35 And He gave the order to the crowds to settle down on the ground,
36 and when He took the seven *loaves of* bread and the fish, after He was thankful, He split *them* and gave *them* to His students, the students to the crowds.
37 And they all ate and were full. And they picked up what was left over of the pieces: seven full big baskets.
38 The *people* eating were four thousand men, besides women and young children.
39 And after He dismissed the crowds, He climbed on board into the boat and went to the borders of Magdala.

16

1 And when the Separatists and Sadducees came forward, trying to cause trouble, they asked Him to show them an indicator from the sky.
2 When He answered, He said to them, "When it becomes evening, you say, 'Nice weather, you see, the sky is fiery.'
3 And in *the* morning, 'Today, a storm, you see, the disappointing sky is fiery.' Fakers, you certainly know to be considering the appearance of the sky to be different, but the indicators of the appointed times, you are not able to.
4 An evil and cheating generation searches for an indicator, and an indicator will not be given to it except the indicator of Jonah, the preacher." And after leaving them down *there*, He went away.
5 And when His students went to the other side, they forgot to take *loaves of* bread.
6 Jesus said to them, "Look, and be cautious of the yeast of the Separatists and Sadducees."
7 The *students* were pondering *it* among themselves, saying, "*It is* because we did not take *loaves of* bread."
8 When Jesus knew, He said to them, "Why are you pondering among yourselves, seldom trusting *people*, that you did not take *loaves of* bread?"
9 Are you not yet aware of, nor remember, the five *loaves of* bread of the five thousand and how many baskets you took?
10 Nor the seven *loaves of* bread of the four thousand and how many big baskets you took?
11 How are you not aware that I did not talk to you about bread? *You are* to be cautious of the yeast of the Separatists and Sadducees."
12 Then they understood that He did not say to be cautious of the yeast of the bread, but of the teaching of the Separatists and Sadducees.
13 When Jesus came into the parts of Caesarea of Philip, He was asking His students, saying, "Who do the people say for Me, the Son of the Person, to be?"
14 The *students* said, "Some, John the Submerger; others, Elijah; but different *ones*, Jeremiah or one of the preachers."

15 He says to them, "You, who do you say for Me to be?"
16 When Simon Peter answered, he said, "You are the Anointed King, the Son of God, the living *God*."
17 When Jesus responded, He said to him, "Simon, Bar (*'son of' in Hebrew*) Jonah, you are blessed because a physical body and blood did not uncover *this* to you, but My Father, the *One* in the heavens.
18 I also say to you that you are Peter, on this rock I will build My assembly, and gates of Hades *(the underworld of the dead)* will not be strong against it.
19 And I will give you the keys of the monarchy of the heavens. And whatever you lock up on the earth will be *a thing* that has been locked up in the heavens, and whatever you release on the earth will be *a thing* that has been released in the heavens."
20 At that time, He warned His students that they should tell no one that He is Jesus, the Anointed King.
21 From then on, Jesus began to be showing His students that it is necessary for Him to go off to Jerusalem, to suffer many *things* from the older *men*, head priests, and *Old Testament* transcribers, to be killed, and to be gotten up on the third day.
22 And after Peter took Him aside, he began to be telling Him to stop, saying, "*God has it* remedied for You, Master. This will not in any way be for You."
23 But when He turned, He said to Peter, "Make *your* way back behind Me, opponent. You are an obstacle to Me because you do not focus on the *things* of God, but on the *things* of the people.
24 Then Jesus said to His students, "If anyone wants to come behind Me, he must flatly deny himself, pick up his cross, and follow Me.
25 You see, whoever wants to rescue his soul will lose it, but whoever loses his soul on account of Me will find it;
26 for how is a person benefited if he gains the whole world, but his soul he sustains loss to? Or what will a person give in exchange for his soul?
27 You see, the Son of the Person is going to be coming in the magnificence of His Father with His angels. And at that time, He will give back to each *person* aligned with what he repeatedly did.
28 Amen, I tell you, some of the *people* who have stood here are some who will not in any way taste death until they see the Son of the Person coming in His monarchy."

17

1 And after six days, Jesus takes along Peter, James, and John (his brother) and brings them up into a high mountain by themselves.
2 And He was transformed in front of them, and His face shined as the sun. His clothes became white as the light.
3 And, look, Moses and Elijah were seen by them speaking together with Him.
4 When Peter responded, he said to Jesus, "Master, it is nice for us to be here. If you want, I will make three tents here, one for You, one for Moses, and one for Elijah."

5 As he was still speaking, look, the shadow of a lit up cloud fell on them, and look, a voice from the cloud, saying, "This is My Son, the loved *One*, in whom I am delighted. Listen to Him."
6 And when the students heard *it*, they fell down on their face and were terribly afraid.
7 And when Jesus came forward, He touched them and said, "Get up. And don't be afraid."
8 When they raised their eyes, they saw no one except Jesus alone.
9 And as they walked down out of the mountain, Jesus demanded them, saying, "You will tell no one of the sighting until *the time* that the Son of the Person will come back to life from *the* dead."
10 And His students asked Him, saying, "So why are the *Old Testament* transcribers saying that it is necessary for Elijah to come first?"
11 When Jesus answered, He said to them, "Elijah not only comes and will reestablish all *things*,
12 but I tell you that Elijah already came, and they did not recognize him. But they did with him as much as they wanted. This is also how the Son of the Person is going to be suffering under them."
13 At that time, the students understood that He talked to them about John the Submerger.
14 And when they came to the crowd, a person came to Him, kneeling before Him and saying,
15 "Master, show forgiving kindness to my son because he is struck by the moon *(that is, he has seizures)* and suffers badly. You see, many times he falls into the fire and many times into the water.
16 And I brought him to your students, and they were not able to heal him.
17 When Jesus responded, He said, "O generation, untrusting and that has been twisted, until when will I be with you? Until when will I tolerate you? Bring him here to Me."
18 And Jesus told it to stop, the lesser deity came out of him, and the boy was healed from that hour.
19 Then when the students came to Jesus by themselves, they said, "Why weren't we able to throw it out?"
20 Jesus said to them, "Because of your lack of trust. You see, amen, I tell you, if you have trust as a kernel of mustard, you will state to this mountain, 'Walk from here to there,' it will walk, and nothing will be impossible to you.
21 But this kind does not travel out except in prayer and a time of going without food.
22 As they were busy in Galilee, Jesus said to them, "The Son of the Person is going to be turned over to people's hands,
23 they will kill Him, and He will be gotten up on the third day." And they were terribly sad.
24 After they came into Capernaum, the *people* who take *up* the double drachmas *(the temple tax)* came to Peter and said, "Isn't your teacher paying the double drachmas?"
25 He says, "Yes." And when he went into the house, Jesus already came to him first, saying, "How does it seem to you, Simon? The kings of the earth, from

whom do they take taxes or enrollment? From their sons, or from the *ones* belonging to others?"
26 Peter said to Him, "From the *ones* belonging to others." Jesus was declaring to him, "Clearly the sons are definitely free.
27 But so that we won't cause them to stumble, after you travel to the sea, throw a hook *in*, and pick up the fish that tumbles up first. And when you open its mouth, you will find a stater *(a silver coin)*. After taking that, give *it* to them for Me and you."

18

1 In that hour, the students came to Jesus, saying, "So who is greater in the monarchy of the heavens?"
2 And when Jesus called for a young child, He stood him in *the* middle of them.
3 And He said, "Amen, I tell you, if you will not turn and become as the young children, you will not in any way go into the monarchy of the heavens.
4 So anyone who will put himself down low as this young child, this is the greater *one* in the monarchy of the heavens.
5 And whoever accepts one young child of this type based on My name accepts Me.
6 But whoever causes one of these little *ones* to stumble, the *ones* who trust in Me, it is advantageous to him that a millstone *(the kind turned by* a donkey) be hung on his neck and he be dropped down in the deep part of the sea.
7 What a tragedy *it is* to the world from the obstacles! You see, there is an obligation for the obstacles to come. More importantly, what a tragedy it is to that person through whom the obstacle comes!
8 But if your hand or your foot causes you to stumble, chop them out, and throw *them* away from you. Is it nice for you to go into the life crippled or physically wounded, or having two hands or two feet to be thrown into the fire, the *one* that spans *all* time?
9 And if your eye causes you to stumble, take it out, and throw *it* away from you. Is it nice for you to go into the life one-eyed, or having two eyes to be thrown into the Hinnom Valley of the fire?
10 Look. No one should ignore one of these little *ones*. You see, I tell you that their angels in *the* heavens look through everything at the face of My Father, the *One* in *the* heavens.
11 You see, the Son of the Person came to rescue the lost *sheep*.
12 What does it seem to you? If it happens *that* a certain person *has* a hundred sheep and one from them wanders off, will he not leave the ninety-nine on the mountains and, after traveling *away*, search for the *one* that wandered off?
13 And if he happens to find it, amen, I tell you that he is happy based on it rather than based on the ninety-nine, the *ones* that have not wandered off.
14 In this way, it is not *something* wanted in front of your Father, the *One* in *the* heavens, that one of these little *ones* would be ruined.
15 If your brother does something sinful to you, make *your* way back and reprimand him between you and him alone. If he listens to you, you gained your brother.

16 But if he does not listen, take along with you one or two more so that based on *the* mouth of two or three witnesses every statement might be established.
17 If he disregards them, talk to the assembly. If he also disregards the assembly, he must be to you even as the non-Jewish *person* and the tax collector.
18 Amen, I tell you, whatever you lock up on the earth will be *things* that have been locked up in the heaven, and whatever you release on the earth will be *things* that have been released in the heaven.
19 Again, I tell you that if two of you on the earth harmoniously agree about every item, whatever they ask for, it will happen to them from the side of My Father, the *One* in *the* heavens.
20 You see, where there are two or three that have been gathered together into My name, I am there in *the* middle of them."
21 At that time, when Peter came forward to Him, he said, "Master, how many times will my brother do something sinful to me and I will forgive him, until seven times?"
22 Jesus says to him, "I do not say to you, until seven times, but until seventy times *multiplied by* seven.
23 Because of this, the monarchy of the heavens is like a person, a king, who wanted to settle an account with his slaves.
24 After he began to be settling, one was brought to him, a person who owed ten thousand talents (*ten million dollars*).
25 Since he did not have *a way* to give *it* back, his master gave the order for him, his wife, *his* children, and everything (as much as he has) to be put up for sale and *for it* to be given back.
26 So after the slave got down *on the ground*, he was bowing to him, saying, 'Master, be patient over me, and I will give everything back to you.'
27 After the master of that slave had sympathy, he dismissed him and forgave him of the debt.
28 But after that slave went out, he found one of his fellow slaves who owed him one hundred denarii *($5000)*, and when he took hold of him, he was choking *him*, saying, 'Give me back anything that you owe.'
29 So when his fellow slave got down at his feet, he was encouraging him, saying, 'Be patient over me, and I will give everything back to you.'
30 The *slave* was not wanting to. But when he went away, he threw him into jail until *the time* that he would give back what was owed.
31 When his fellow slaves saw the *things* that happened, they were terribly sad. And after they went, they explained all the *things* that happened to their master.
32 At that time, after his master called for him, he says to him, 'Evil slave, I forgave you every *bit of* that amount owed *by you* since you encouraged me *to*.
33 Wasn't it necessary for you to also show forgiving kindness to your fellow slave as I also showed forgiving kindness to you?'
34 And after being enraged, his master turned him over to the torturers until *the time* that he will give back every *bit of* what was owed to him.
35 My Father, the heavenly *One*, will also do like this to you if each *of you* do not forgive his brother from your hearts of their infractions."

19

1 And it happened when Jesus finished these messages; He took off out of Galilee and went to the borders of Judea on *the* other side of the Jordan *River*.
2 And big crowds followed Him, and He healed them there.
3 And the Separatists came to Him trying to cause Him trouble and saying to Him, "*Tell us* if a person is allowed to dismiss his wife regarding every accusation."
4 When *Jesus* answered, He said to them, "Didn't you read that the *One* who made *them*, from *the* beginning made them male and female
5 and said *in Genesis 2:24*, 'On account of this, a person will leave the father and the mother down *there*, be stuck like glue to his wife, and the two will be in one physical body'?
6 In such a way, they are no longer two, but one physical body. So *a thing* that God strapped together, a person must not separate.
7 They say to Him, "So why did Moses demand to give a scroll of divorce and to dismiss her?"
8 He says to them, "Moses for your hardheartedness gave you permission to dismiss your wives, but from *the* beginning it has not happened like that.
9 But I tell you that whoever dismisses his wife, except *it is* based on sexual sin, and marries another is cheating on *his* wife. And the *one* who marries *a wife* who has been dismissed is cheating."
10 His students say to Him, "If this is how the accusation of the person with the wife is, it is not advantageous to marry."
11 *Jesus* said to them, "Not everyone makes room for this message, but *it is for the people* to whom it has been given.
12 You see, there are castrated men, some who were born like this from *their* mother's belly, there are castrated men, some who were castrated by the people, and there are castrated men, some who castrated themselves because of the monarchy of the heavens. The *person* who is able to be making room must make room.
13 At that time, young children were brought to Him so that He might place *His* hands on them and pray. But the students stopped them.
14 But Jesus said, "Leave the young children, and don't hinder them to come to Me. You see, the monarchy of the heavens is *made up* of these types of *children*."
15 And after He placed *His* hands on them, He traveled from there.
16 And look, when one *person* came to Him, he said, "Good Teacher, what good thing should I do so that I may have life that spans *all* time?"
17 *Jesus* said to him, "Why do you call Me good? No one *is* good except one, God. But if you want to go into the life, keep the demands."
18 He says to Him, "Which ones?" Jesus said, "The 'you will not murder, you will not cheat on *your* spouse, you will not steal, you will not lie when you are a witness,
19 value your father and *your* mother, also you will love the *person* near you as yourself' *thing*."
20 The young lad says to Him, "I observed all these from my youth. What do I still lack?"

21 Jesus was declaring to him, "If you want to be complete, make *your* way back; sell the *things* that are yours, give to poor *people,* you will have a stockpile of treasure in heavens, and come here; follow Me."
22 When the young lad heard the message, He went away sad. You see, he was *a person* who had many properties.
23 Jesus said to His students, "Amen, I tell you that *it* will *be* hard *for* a wealthy *person as he* goes into the monarchy of the heavens.
24 Again I tell you, it is easier for a camel to go through an eye of a needle than for a wealthy *person* to go into the monarchy of God.
25 After His students heard *this,* they were being terribly stunned, saying, "So who is able to be rescued?"
26 When Jesus looked at *them,* He said to them, "Beside people this is impossible, but beside God everything is possible."
27 At that time, when Peter responded, he said to Him, "Look, we left everything and followed You. So what will we have?"
28 Jesus said to them, "Amen, I tell you that you, the *people* who followed Me, in the rebirth when the Son of the Person will be seated on a throne of His magnificence, you will also sit on twelve thrones judging the twelve family lines of Israel.
29 And everyone who left houses, or brothers, or sisters, or a father, or a mother, of a wife, or children, or fields on account of My Name will receive a hundred times *that* and inherit life that spans *all* time.
30 Many first *people* will be last, and last *people* first."

20

1 "You see, the monarchy of the heavens is like a person, a property owner, someone who went out at the same time as morning to hire workers for his vineyard.
2 After he harmoniously agreed with the workers for a denarius *(a fifty-dollar coin) for* the day, he sent them out into his vineyard.
3 And when he went out around *the* third hour *(9:00 a.m.),* he saw others that had stood idle in the marketplace.
4 And to those *people* he said, 'You also must make *your* way back into the vineyard, and whatever is right I will give you.' But the *people* went away.
5 Again when he went out around *the* sixth *(noon)* and *the* ninth hour *(3:00 p.m.),* he did similarly.
6 Around the eleventh hour *(5:00 p.m.)* when he went out, he found others who had stood idle, and he says to them, 'Why have you stood here idle the whole day?'
7 They say to him, 'Because no one hired us.' He says to them, 'You also must make *your* way back into the vineyard, and whatever is right, you will receive.'
8 When it becomes evening, the master of the vineyard says to his administrator, 'Call the workers, and give out the pay to them, beginning from the last until the first.'
9 And when the 'around the eleventh hour *(5:00 p.m.)*' *workers* came, they received a denarius *(a fifty-dollar coin)* apiece.

10 And when the first *workers* came, they assumed that they will receive more, and they also received a denarius *(a fifty-dollar coin)* apiece.
11 After they received *it*, they were grumbling against the property owner,
12 saying, 'These last *workers* made one hour, and you made them equal to us, the *ones* who hauled the heavy weight of the day and the hot wind.'
13 When the *property owner* responded, he said to one of them, 'Comrade, I did not *do anything* wrong *to* you. Didn't you harmoniously agree with me for a denarius *(a fifty-dollar coin)*?
14 Take what *is* yours, and make *your* way back *home*. I want to give to this last *worker* as *I* also *gave* to you.
15 Or am I not allowed to do what I want with my *things*? *Tell me* if your eye is evil because I am good.'
16 This is how the last will be first and the first last. You see, many are invited, but few *are people* who choose *to come*."
17 And as Jesus was walking up into Jerusalem, He took the twelve students along by themselves on the way and said to them,
18 "Look, I am walking up into Jerusalem. And the Son of the Person will be turned over to the head priests and *Old Testament* transcribers, and they will find Him guilty with death.
19 And they will turn Him over to the non-Jews for the 'to mock, to whip, and to nail to a cross' *part*. And on the third day, He will stand up."
20 At that time, the mother of the sons of Zebedee came to Him with her sons, bowing down and asking for something from the side of Him.
21 He said to her, "What do you want?" She says to Him, "Say that these two sons of mine will be seated, one at *places to the* right of You and one at *places to the* left of You, in Your monarchy."
22 When Jesus answered, He said, "You do not realize what you are asking for. Are you able to drink the cup that I am going to be drinking and be submerged in the submersion that I am being submerged in?" They say to Him, "We are able."
23 And He says to them, "You will certainly drink My cup and be submerged in the submersion that I am submerged in, but the *permission* to be seated at *places to the* right of Me and at *places to the* left of Me is not Mine to give. But *it is* for whom it has been readied by My Father."
24 And when the ten heard, they were frustrated about the two brothers.
25 When Jesus called for them, He said, "You realize that the head people of the non-Jews act like masters over them and the great *people* put themselves in authority over them.
26 It will not be like this among you, but whoever wants to become great among you, he must be a servant of you.
27 And whoever wants to be first among you, he must be a slave of you,
28 even as the Son of the Person did not come to be served, but to serve and to give His soul as a payment for the release of many."
29 And as they traveled out from Jericho, a big crowd followed Him.
30 And look, when two blind *people* sitting along the road heard that Jesus is passing by, they yelled, saying, "Show us forgiving kindness, Master, Son of David."

31 The crowd shushed them so that they would be silent. But the *two* were yelling louder, saying, "Show us forgiving kindness, Master, Son of David."
32 And when Jesus stood *still*, He hollered for them and said, "What do you want *that* I would do for you?"
33 They say to Him, "Master, that our eyes would be opened."
34 After Jesus had sympathy, He touched their eyes. And right away their eyes saw again, and they followed Him.

21

1 And when they were near to Jerusalem and came to Bethphage toward the Mountain of the Olives, at that time, Jesus sent two students out *on a mission*,
2 saying to them, "Travel into the village, the *one* up in front of you. And right away you will find a donkey that has been tied up and a foal with her. After you release *them*, lead *them* to Me.
3 And if anyone says something to you, you will state, 'The Master has need of them.' He will send them out right away."
4 This whole *thing* has happened so that what was stated through the preacher *in Zechariah 9:9* might be accomplished that says,
5 "Tell the daughter of Zion, look, your king comes to you submissive and having climbed up on a donkey and a foal, a son of a workhorse."
6 When the students traveled and did just as Jesus instructed them,
7 they led the donkey and the foal and placed their robes up on top of them, and they sat *Him* up on top of them.
8 The biggest crowd spread out their *own* robes in the road. Others were chopping branches off the trees and spreading *them* out in the road.
9 The crowds, the *ones* going ahead and the *ones* following, were yelling, saying, "Hosanna *(Hebrew for 'O, rescue us')* to the Son of David, the *One* coming in *the* Master's Name that has been conferred with blessings. Hosanna in the highest *things*."
10 And when He came into Jerusalem, the entire city was shook, saying, "Who is this?"
11 The crowds were saying, "This is the preacher Jesus, the *One* from Nazareth, Galilee."
12 And Jesus went onto God's temple grounds and threw out all the *people* buying and selling on the temple grounds. And He turned over the tables of the currency exchangers and the benches of the *people* selling the doves.
13 And He says to them, "It has been written *in Isaiah 56:7*, 'My house will be called a house of prayer,' but you made it a cave of bandits."
14 And blind and crippled *people* came to Him on the temple grounds, and He healed them.
15 But when the head priests and the *Old Testament* transcribers saw the amazing *things* that He did and the boys yelling on the temple grounds and saying, "Hosanna to the Son of David," they were frustrated.
16 And they said to Him, "Do you hear what these are saying?" But Jesus says to them, "Yes, did you never even once read *in Psalm 8:2*, 'From *the* mouth of infants, even nursing *infants*, You developed praise?'"

17 And after He left them down *there*, He went outside of the city to Bethany, and spent the night there outside.
18 In *the* morning, as He was taking *them* up into the city, He was hungry.
19 And when He saw one fig tree up the road, He went up to it and found nothing in it except leaves only. And He says to it, "No fruit will ever come into existence from you for the span of time," and the fig tree shriveled up at once.
20 And when the students saw *it*, they were amazed, saying, "How did the fig tree shrivel up at once?"
21 When Jesus answered, He said to them, "Amen, I tell you, if you have trust and do not consider *it* to be wrong, not only will you do the *thing* of the fig tree, but even if you say to this mountain, 'Be picked up, and be thrown into the sea,' it will happen.
22 And everything, however many *things* that you will ask for in the prayer, trusting, you will receive."
23 And after He came onto the temple grounds, the head priests and the older *men* of the ethnic group came to Him as He was teaching, saying, "In what kind of authority do you do these *things*, and who gave you this authority?"
24 When Jesus answered, He said to them, "I will also ask you one saying that, if you tell me, I will also state to you in what kind of authority I do these *things*.
25 The submersion of John, where was it from, from heaven or from people?" The *men* were pondering *it* beside themselves, saying, "If we say from heaven, He will state to us, 'So why didn't you trust him?'
26 But if we say from people, we fear the crowd. You see, all hold John as a preacher."
27 And when they answered Jesus, they said, "We do not know." He also was declaring to them, "Neither do I tell you in what kind of authority I do these *things*.
28 What does it seem to you? A person had two children. And when he came to the first, he said, 'Child, make *your* way back today. Work in my vineyard.'
29 When the *child* answered, he said, 'I don't want to.' But later after he regretted *his response*, he went off.
30 And when he came to the second *child*, he said similarly. When the *child* answered, he said, 'I *am going*, master,' and he did not go off.
31 Which *one* from the two did what the father wanted?" They say, "The first." Jesus says to them, "Amen, I tell you that the tax collectors and the prostitutes are going ahead of you into the monarchy of God.
32 You see, to you came John on a road of *the* right way, and you did not trust him. But the tax collectors and the prostitutes trusted him. When you saw *it*, you did not later regret *your response* for the *purpose* to trust him.
33 Listen to another illustration. There was a certain person, a property owner, someone who planted a vineyard, put a barrier wall around it, dug a grape smashing pit in it, built a tower, gave it out to farmers, and left the area.
34 When the right time for the fruits was near, he sent his slaves out to the farmers to take its fruits.

35 And after the farmers took his slaves, *there was one* that they beat, *another* that they killed, *another* that they threw stones at.
36 Again he sent out other slaves, more than the first, and they did similarly to them.
37 Later he sent out his son to them, saying, 'They will be embarrassed around my son.'
38 But when the farmers saw the son, they said among themselves, 'This is the inheritor. Come on, we should kill him, and we will hold down his inheritance.'
39 And after they took him, they threw *him* outside of the vineyard and killed *him*.
40 So when the master of the vineyard comes, what will he do to those farmers?"
41 They say to Him, "Bad *farmers*, in a bad way he will ruin them and give the vineyard out to other farmers, some who will give him back the fruits at their right times."
42 Jesus says to them, "Did you never even once read in the *Old Testament* writings *in Psalm 118:22, 23*, 'A stone that the *people* who are building rejected, this became for a corner's head; this happened from the side of *the* Master, and it is amazing in our eyes'?
43 Because of this, I tell you that the monarchy of God will be taken away from you and given to a nation producing its fruits."
44 And the *person* who falls on this stone will be smashed, and whoever it falls on, it will grind him up.
45 And when the head priests and the Separatists heard His illustrations, they knew that He was talking about them.
46 And as they looked to take Him into custody, they feared the crowds since, for sure, they held Him as a preacher.

22

1 And when Jesus responded, again He talked to them in illustrations, saying,
2 "The monarchy of the heavens is like a person, a king, someone who did wedding *events* for his son.
3 And he sent his slaves out *on a mission* to invite the *people* who had been invited to the wedding *events*, and they were not wanting to come.
4 Again he sent other slaves out, saying, 'Say to the *people* who have been invited, look, I got my breakfast ready. My bulls, the grain-fed steers (that have been killed), and everything *are* ready. Come on to the wedding *events*.'
5 But the *people* who did not care went off, the *one* to *his* own field, the *other* to his business.
6 The rest, after taking hold of his slaves, injured and killed *them*.
7 When the king heard, he was enraged. And after he sent his military forces, he ruined those murderers and incinerated their cities.
8 Then he says to his slaves, 'Not only is the wedding ready, but the *people* who had been invited were not deserving.
9 So travel on the intersections of the roads, and invite however many that you find into the wedding *events*.'

10 And when those slaves went out to the roads, they gathered everyone together, as many as they found, both evil and good, and the wedding was full of reclining *people*.
11 But when the king came in to view the reclining *people*, he saw a person there who had not put on *the* attire of a wedding.
12 And he says to him, 'Comrade, how did you come in here not having *the* attire of a wedding?' But the *person* was quiet.
13 Then the king said to the servants, 'After you tie him up, feet and hands, pick him up, and throw him out into the darkness, the *darkness* further out. There will be the crying and the grinding of the teeth there.'
14 You see, many are invited, but few *are people* who choose *to come*."
15 At that time, after the Separatists traveled *away*, they received counsel on how they might trap Him in an answer.
16 And they are sending their students out to Him with the Herod supporters, saying, "Teacher, we realize that You are valid, You teach the way of God in truth, and there is no concern in You about anyone. You see, You do not look at people's appearance.
17 So tell us, what does it seem to you? Is it allowed to give an enrollment *tax* to Caesar or not?"
18 But when Jesus knew their evilness, He said, "Why are you trying to cause trouble with Me, fakers?
19 Show Me the legal tender of the enrollment." The *people* brought Him a denarius *(a fifty-dollar coin)*.
20 And He says to them, "Whose image and inscription *is* it?"
21 They say to Him, "Caesar's." Then He says to them, "So give the *things* of Caesar back to Caesar, and the *things* of God *back* to God."
22 And when they heard *this*, they were amazed. And after they left Him, they went away.
23 During that day, Sadducees (who say *there is* to be no return back to life) came to Him and asked Him,
24 saying, "Teacher, Moses said, 'If anyone dies not having children, his brother will also marry his wife and stand up a seed for his brother.'
25 There were seven brothers beside us, and after the first married, he passed away. And not having a seed, he left his wife to his brother,
26 likewise also the second and the third until the seven *brothers passed away*.
27 Later the wife of *them* all also died.
28 So in the return back to life, whose wife will she be of the seven? You see, *they* all had her."
29 When Jesus answered, He said to them, "You are misled, not knowing the *Old Testament* writings nor the ability of God.
30 You see, in the return back to life, neither do they marry, nor are they given out in marriage, but they are as God's angels in heaven.
31 But about the return back to life of the dead, didn't you read what was stated to you by God *in Exodus 3:6 and 15* that says,
32 'I am the God of Abraham, the God of Isaac, and the God of Jacob?' God is not the God of dead *people*, but of living."

33 And when the crowds heard *this*, they were being impressed based on His teaching.
34 When the Separatists heard that He quieted the Sadducees, they were gathered together based on the same *thing*.
35 And one from among them, a law *expert*, asked, trying to cause Him trouble and saying,
36 "Teacher, which demand *is the* great *demand* in the law?"
37 Jesus said to him, "'You will love *the* Master, your God, with your whole heart, with your whole soul, and with your whole mind.'
38 This is *the* first and great demand.
39 *The* second is like it, 'You will love the *person* near you as yourself.'
40 In these two demands are hung the whole Law and the Preachers."
41 Since the Separatists had been gathered together, Jesus asked them,
42 saying, "What does it seem to you concerning the Anointed King? Whose son is he?" They say to him, "David's."
43 He says to them, "So how does David in *the* Spirit call him Master, saying *in Psalm 110:1*,
44 'The Master said to my Master: sit down at *places to the* right of Me until I put Your enemies *as* a footrest of Your feet?'
45 So if David calls Him Master, how is He his son?"
46 And no one was able to answer Him a word, neither did anyone dare to ask Him anymore after that day.

23

1 Then Jesus spoke to the crowds and to His students,
2 saying, "On Moses' bench are seated the *Old Testament* transcribers and the Separatists.
3 So everything, however many *things* that they tell you to keep, do and keep, but do not do aligned with their actions. You see, they say and do not do.
4 They detain heavy and hard-to-haul loads and place *them* on the shoulders of the people. But they with their finger don't want to move them.
5 They do all their actions with the *intent* to be viewed by the people. They widen their scripture boxes and make the fringes of their robes large.
6 They are fond of the front reclining places in the feasts, the front benches in the synagogues,
7 the greetings in the marketplaces, and to be called Rabbi Rabbi by the people.
8 But you will not be called Rabbi. You see, there is One *who is* your Mentor, the Anointed King. You all are brothers.
9 And you should not call *any* of you on the earth, Father. You see, one *Person* is your Father, the *One* in the heavens.
10 Neither should you be called mentors. You see, one of you is the mentor, the Anointed King.
11 Your greater *person* will be your servant.
12 Anyone who will put himself up high will be put down low, and anyone who will put himself down low will be put up high.

13 What a tragedy *it is* to you, *Old Testament* transcribers and Separatists, fakers, because you close up the monarchy of the heavens in front of the people. You see, you do not go in, neither do you leave the *people* going in to go in.
14 What a tragedy *it is* to you, *Old Testament* transcribers and Separatists, fakers, because you eat up the widows' houses even as you pray for a long time for a sham. Because of this, you will receive much more judgment.
15 What a tragedy *it is* to you, *Old Testament* transcribers and Separatists, fakers, because you go around the sea and the dry land to make one convert, and when it happens, you make him two times more a son of Hinnom Valley than you.
16 What a tragedy *it is* to you, blind guides, the *ones* who say, 'Whoever guarantees with the temple, it is nothing, but whoever guarantees with the gold of the temple is obligated.'
17 Foolish and blind *people*, you see, which is greater, the gold or the temple, the *thing* that makes the gold sacred?
18 And, 'Whoever guarantees with the altar, it is nothing, but whoever guarantees with the contribution, the *thing* up on top of it, is obligated.'
19 Foolish and blind *people*, you see, which is greater, the contribution or the altar, the *thing* that makes the contribution sacred?
20 So the *person* who guarantees with the altar, guarantees with it and with everything up on top of it.
21 And the *person* who guarantees with the temple, guarantees with it and with the *One* living in it.
22 And the *person* who guarantees with heaven, guarantees with the throne of God and with the *One* sitting up on top of it.
23 What a tragedy *it is* to you, *Old Testament* transcribers and Separatists, fakers, because you take ten percent out of the sweet smelling mint, the dill plant, and the fennel plant and leave the heavier *things* of the law: the judgment, the forgiving kindness, and the trust. These *things* it was necessary to do and not to be leaving those,
24 blind guides, the *ones* who strain out the gnat, but swallow up the camel.
25 What a tragedy *it is* to you, *Old Testament* transcribers and Separatists, fakers, because you clean the outside of the cup and the dish, but on *the* inside they are packed full from looting and a lack of restraint.
26 Blind Separatist, first clean the inside of the cup and the dish so that its outside might also become clean.
27 What a tragedy *it is* to you, *Old Testament* transcribers and Separatists, fakers, because you resemble gravesites that have been whitened with chalk, some that on the outside certainly appear beautiful, but on *the* inside are packed full of dead *people's* bones and all of what is not clean.
28 This is how you also on the outside certainly appear to the people *as people* who do what is right, but on *the* inside you are full of faked behavior and crime.
29 What a tragedy *it is* to you, *Old Testament* transcribers and Separatists, fakers, because you build the gravesites of the preachers, decorate the burial vaults of the *people* who did what is right,

30 and say, 'If we were in the days of our fathers, we would not have been their partners in the blood of the preachers.'
31 In such a way, you are witnesses to yourselves that you are sons of the murderers of the preachers.
32 You also must fill in your fathers' amount.
33 Snakes, offspring of poisonous snakes, how will you escape away from the judgment of the Hinnom Valley?
34 Because of this, look, I am sending out preachers, insightful *people*, and transcribers to you. And *people* from among them, you will kill and nail to crosses. And *people* from among them, you will whip in your synagogues and pursue from city to city
35 in order that every *drop of* blood that did what is right being spilled out on the earth will come on you, from the blood of Abel (who did what is right) until the blood of Zacharias (a son of Barachias, whom you murdered between the temple and the altar).
36 Amen, I tell you, all these *things* will arrive on this generation.
37 Jerusalem, Jerusalem, the *city* that kills the preachers and throws stones at the *people* who have been sent out to it, how many times did I want to bring your children together in one place, *the* way that a hen brings her own chicks together under *her* wings, and you did not want *it*.
38 Look, your house is left to you uninhabited.
39 You see, I tell you, you will not in any way see Me from now *on* until you say, 'The *One* coming in *the* Master's name has been conferred with blessings.'"

1 And after Jesus went out, He was traveling away from the temple grounds. And His students came forward to show Him the buildings of the temple grounds.
2 Jesus said to them, "Don't you see all these *things*? Amen, I tell you, a stone will not in any way be left on a stone here that will not be torn down."
3 As He was sitting on the Mountain of the Olives, the students came to Him by themselves, saying, "Tell us, when will these *things* be, and what *is* the indicator of Your arrival and the very conclusion of the span of time?
4 And when Jesus answered, He said to them, "See *that* no one misleads you.
5 You see, many will come based on My name, saying, 'I am the Anointed King,' and they will mislead many.
6 You will be about to be hearing wars and much talk about wars. Look. Do not be alarmed. You see, it is necessary for all *of these things* to happen, but it is not the conclusion yet;
7 for a nation will rise up on a nation and a monarchy on a monarchy. And there will be famines, diseases, and earthquakes throughout places.
8 All these *things* are *the* beginning of pains.
9 At that time, they will turn you in for hard times, they will kill you, and you will be hated by all the nations because of My name.
10 And then many will stumble, will turn each other in, and will hate each other.

11 And many counterfeit preachers will rise up and mislead many.
12 And because of the *fact* for the crime to be increased, the love of many will be cooled.
13 The *person* who persisted *to do what is right* to *the* conclusion, this *person* will be rescued.
14 And this good news of the monarchy will be spoken publicly in the whole civilized world for a witness to all the non-Jews, and then the conclusion will arrive.
15 So when you see the disgusting thing of the uninhabitedness (the *thing* that was stated through Daniel, the preacher) having stood in *the* sacred place (the *person* who reads *this* must be aware),
16 at that time, the *people* in Judea must escape up to the mountains.
17 The *person* on the top of a house must not climb down to take the *things* from his house,
18 and the *person* in the field must not return back behind to take his robes.
19 What a tragedy to the *women* having *a baby* in *their* womb and the *women* nursing in those days!
20 Pray that your escape might not happen during a storm, nor on a Sabbath.
21 You see, at that time, there will be great hard times, such as has not happened from *the* beginning of *the* world until the present, no, nor ever will happen.
22 And if those days were not halted, every physical body would not be rescued, but because of the *people* who choose *God's way*, those days will be halted.
23 At that time, if someone tells you, "Look, here *is* the Anointed King, or here," you should not trust *it*.
24 You see, counterfeit anointed kings and counterfeit preachers will rise and will do great indicators and incredible things in such a way to mislead, if possible, even the *people* who choose *God's way*.
25 Look, I have stated *it* to you beforehand.
26 So if they tell you, "Look, He is in the backcountry," you should not go out *there*. "Look, *He is* in the storage rooms," you should not trust *it*.
27 You see, even as the lightning goes out from eastern regions and shines to western regions, this is also how the arrival of the Son of the Person will be.
28 You see, wherever the corpse is, there the raptors will be gathered together.
29 After the hard times of those days, right away the sun will be made dark, the moon will not give her glow, the stars will fall out of the sky, and the abilities of the heavens will be disturbed.
30 And then the indicator of the Son of the Person will appear in the sky. And then all the family lines of the earth will beat their chests in grief, and they will see the Son of the Person coming on the clouds of the sky with ability and much magnificence.
31 And He will send His angels out *on a mission* with a great trumpet sound, and they will bring the *people* who chose Him together in one place from the four winds *(compass directions)*, out of edges of heavens to *other* edges of them.

32 From the fig tree, learn the illustration: when its branch already becomes tender and it may sprout out the leaves, you know that the summer is near.
33 In the same way, when you also see all these *things*, you know that it is near, at the door.
34 Amen, I tell you *that* this generation will not in any way pass until all these *things* happen.
35 The sky and the earth will pass, but My messages will not in any way pass.
36 But about that day and the hour, no one knows, not even the angels of the heavens, except My Father alone.
37 Even as the days of Noah *were*, so also will the arrival of the Son of the Person be.
38 You see, even as they were in the days, the *ones* before the flood (chewing and drinking, marrying and giving out in marriage) till *the* day that Noah went into the box,
39 and did not know until the flood came and took every single one *of them*, so also will the arrival of the Son of the Person be.
40 At that time, two will be in the field; the one is taken along, and the one is left;
41 two grinding *flour* in the mill; one is taken along, and one is left.
42 So stay awake because you do not realize which hour your Master is coming.
43 But that *thing* you know, that if the homeowner had realized in which guard shift the thief comes, he would have stayed awake and not allowed his house to be broken into.
44 Because of this, you also must become ready, because the Son of the Person comes at an hour that it doesn't seem to you *he will*.
45 So who is the reliable and attentive slave whom his master put in charge over his attendants for the *purpose* to give them the meal at *the* right time?
46 That slave *is* blessed whom his master will find doing this when he comes.
47 Amen, I tell you that he will put him in charge over all the *things* that are his.
48 But if that bad slave says in his heart, 'My master is taking a long time to come,'
49 he might also begin to be hitting *his* fellow slaves, to be eating and to be drinking with the *people* who are drunk.
50 The master of that slave will arrive during a day that he is not expecting and at an hour that he does not know.
51 And he will cut him in two and place his part with the fakers. There will be the crying and the grinding of the teeth there."

25

1 "At that time, the monarchy of the heavens will be like ten virgins, some who, after taking their torches, went out for a face-to-face meeting of the groom.
2 Five from among them were attentive, and five *were* foolish.
3 When some who *were* foolish took their own torches, they did not take olive oil with them.

4 But the attentive *women* took olive oil in their buckets with their torches.
5 As the groom was taking a long time, they all nodded off and were sleeping.
6 In *the* middle of *the* night, a yell has happened, 'Look, the groom is coming, come out for his face-to-face meeting.'
7 At that time, all those virgins got up and assembled their torches.
8 The foolish *virgins* said to the attentive *virgins*, 'Give us *some* from your olive oil because our torches are extinguished.'
9 But the attentive *virgins* answered, saying, 'No, there will never be enough for us and you. Instead travel to the sellers, and buy *some* for yourselves.'
10 As they went off to buy *olive oil*, the groom came, the *virgins* who were ready went in with him into the wedding *events*, and the door was closed.
11 Later the rest *of the* virgins also come, saying, 'Master, master, open *the door* to us.'
12 When he answered, he said, 'Amen, I tell you, I do not know you.'
13 So stay awake because you do not know the day nor the hour in which the Son of the Person comes,
14 you see, even as a person leaving the area called *his* own slaves and turned over to them the *things* that are his:
15 even *one* to whom he gave five talents ($5000); *another* to whom *he gave* two; *another* to whom *he gave* one; to each according to *his* own ability. And he left the area. Right away,
16 after the *slave* who received the five talents ($5000) traveled, he worked with them and made another five talents ($5000).
17 Similarly also, the *slave who received* the two also himself gained another two.
18 But after the *slave* who received the one *talent* went off, he dug in the ground and hid the silver of his master away.
19 After much time, the master of those slaves comes and settles *his* account with them.
20 And when the *slave* who received the five talents ($5000) came forward, he brought another five talents ($5000), saying, 'Master, you turned five talents ($5000) over to me. Look, I gained another five talents ($5000) on them.'
21 His master was declaring to him, 'Well *done*, good and reliable slave. On a few *things* you were reliable. On many *things* I will put you in charge. Come into the happiness of your master.'
22 When the *slave* who received the two talents ($2000) also came forward, he said, 'Master, you turned two talents ($2000) over to me. Look, I gained another two talents ($2000) on them.'
23 His master was declaring to him, 'Well *done*, good and reliable slave. On a few *things* you were reliable. On many *things* I will put you in charge. Come into the happiness of your master.'
24 But when the *slave* who had received the one talent ($1000) also came forward, he said, 'Master, I knew you that you are a harsh person, harvesting where you did not seed and gathering from where you did not disperse.
25 And because I was afraid, after I went off, I hid your talent ($1000) in the ground. Look, you have what *is* yours.'

26 When his master responded, he said to him, 'Evil and lazy slave, you realized that I harvest where I did not seed and gather from where I did not disperse.
27 So it was necessary for you to throw my silver coins to the bankers' tables, and when I came I would retrieve what *is* mine together with interest.
28 So take the talent (*$1000*) away from him, and give *it* to the *slave* who has the ten talents (*$10,000*).
29 You see, to everyone who has, it will be given, and it will overflow, but from the *person* who does not have, even what he has will be taken away from him.
30 And throw the mediocre slave out into the darkness, the *darkness* further out. There will be the crying and the grinding of the teeth there.'
31 When the Son of the Person comes in His magnificence and all the sacred angels with Him, at that time, He will be seated on a throne of His magnificence.
32 And all the nations will be gathered together in front of Him, and He will isolate them away from each other, even as the shepherd isolates the sheep away from the goats.
33 And He will certainly stand the sheep at *places to the* right of Him, but the goatlings at *places to the* left.
34 Then the King will state to the *sheep* at *places to the* right of Him, 'Come on, the *people* who have been conferred with blessings from My Father, inherit the monarchy that has been readied for you since *the* founding of *the* world.
35 You see, I was hungry, and you gave Me *something* to eat. I was thirsty, and you gave Me a drink. I was a stranger, and you gathered Me together *with you*.
36 *I was* naked, and you put *a robe* around Me. I was weak, and you kept an eye on Me. I was in jail, and you came to Me.
37 Then the *people* who did what is right will respond to Him, saying, 'Master, when did we see You being hungry and we nurtured *You*, or being thirsty and we gave *You* a drink?
38 When did we see You a stranger and gathered *You* together *with us*, or naked and we put *a robe* around *You*?
39 When did we see You weak or in jail, and we came to You?'
40 And when the King answers, He will state to them, 'Amen, I tell you, based on as much as you did to one of these brothers of Mine, the smallest *ones*, you did *it* to Me.'
41 Then He will also state to the *goats* at *places to the* left, 'Travel away from Me, the *people* who have been cursed to the fire, the *fire* that spans *all* time, the *fire* that has been readied for the Accuser and his angels.
42 You see, I was hungry, and you did not give Me *anything* to eat. I was thirsty, and you did not give Me a drink.
43 I was a stranger, and you did not gather Me together *with you*; naked, and you did not put *a robe* around Me; weak and in jail, and you did not keep an eye on Me.'

44 Then they will also respond to Him, saying, 'Master, when did we see You being hungry, or being thirsty, or a stranger, or naked, or weak, or in jail, and we did not serve You?'
45 Then He will answer them, saying, 'Amen, I tell you, based on as much as you did not do to one of these, the smallest *ones*, neither did you do *it* to Me.'
46 And these *people* will go off into confinement that spans *all* time, but the *people* who did what is right into life that spans *all* time."

26

1 And it happened when Jesus finished all these messages; He said to His students,
2 "You realize that after two days the Passover is happening and the Son of the Person is turned in for the 'to be nailed to a cross' *execution*."
3 At that time, the head priests, the *Old Testament* transcribers, and the older *men* of the ethnic group were gathered together into the courtyard of the head priest, the *one* called Caiaphas.
4 And together they advised that they might take Jesus into custody with deception and they may kill *Him*.
5 But they were saying, "Not at the festival so that a riot won't happen among the group."
6 When Jesus became in Bethany in Simon's house, the skin-diseased *man*,
7 a woman who had an alabaster jar of high-priced perfume came to Him and spilled *it* down on His head as He reclined.
8 But when His students saw *it*, they were frustrated, saying, "What *is* this ruin for?
9 You see, this perfume was able to be put up for sale for much and given to poor *people*."
10 When Jesus knew *it*, He said to them, "Why are you bothering the woman? You see, she worked nice work for Me;
11 for the poor you always have with you, but Me you don't always have.
12 You see, when she put this perfume on My body, she did it with the *intent* to prepare Me for burial.
13 Amen, I tell you, wherever this good news is spoken publicly in the whole world, what she did will also be spoken for a reminder of her."
14 At that time, when one of the Twelve, the *one* called Judas from Kerioth, traveled to the head priests,
15 he said, "What do you want to give me, and I will turn Him over to you?" The *head priests* stacked up thirty silver coins for him.
16 And from then on, he was looking for a good time that he might turn Him over.
17 On the first of the Yeast-free *Loaves Festival*, the students went to Jesus, saying to Him, "Where do You want *that* we should get *things* ready for You to eat the Passover *meal*?"
18 *Jesus* said, "Make *your* way back into the city to [NAME REDACTED] and say to him, 'The Teacher says, My time is near. I am doing the Passover toward you with My students.'"

19 And the students did as Jesus dictated to them, and they got the Passover *meal* ready.
20 When it became evening, He was reclining with the Twelve.
21 And as they ate, He said, "Amen, I tell you that one from among you will turn Me in."
22 And they being terribly sad began to be saying to Him, each of them, "*It* isn't me, is it, Master?"
23 When *Jesus* answered, He said, "The *one* who dips *his* hand with Me in the bowl, this *one* will turn Me in.
24 The Son of the Person certainly makes *His* way back, just as it has been written about Him, but what a tragedy *it is* to that person through whom the Son of the Person is turned in. It was nice for him if that person was not born.
25 When Judas responded (the *one* turning Him in), he said, "*It* isn't me, is it, Rabbi?" He says to him, "You said *it*."
26 As they were eating, after Jesus took the bread and conferred a blessing on *it*, He split *it* and was giving *it* to the students. And He said, "Take *it*. Eat *it*. This is My body."
27 And when He took the cup and was thankful, He gave *it* to them, saying, "Drink from it, everyone.
28 You see, this is My blood, the *blood* of the new deal, the *blood* that is spilled out concerning many *people* for forgiveness of sins.
29 I tell you that I will not in any way drink from this produce of the vine from now *on* until that day when I drink it new with you in the monarchy of My Father."
30 And after they sang praise songs, they went out to the Mountain of the Olives.
31 At that time, Jesus says to them, "You all will stumble in Me in this night. You see, it has been written *in Zechariah 13:7*, 'I will forcibly strike the shepherd, and the sheep of the flock will be dispersed.'
32 After the *time* for Me to be gotten up, I will go ahead of you into Galilee."
33 When Peter responded, he said to Him, "Even if everyone will stumble in You, I will never ever stumble."
34 Jesus was declaring to him, 'Amen, I tell you that in this night before *the time* for a rooster to crow, three times you will flatly deny Me."
35 Peter says to Him, "Even if it may be necessary for me to die together with You, I will not in any way flatly deny You." All the students also talked likewise.
36 At that time, Jesus comes with them into a parcel of land called Gethsemane and says to the students, "Be seated here until *the time* that, after going off, I will pray there."
37 And after He took along Peter and the two sons of Zebedee, He began to be sad and heavyhearted.
38 At that time, He says to them, "My soul is overcome with sadness up to death. Stay here, and stay awake with Me."
39 And after He went on ahead a little, He got down on His face, praying and saying, "My Father, if it is possible, this cup must pass away from Me. More importantly, not as I want, but as You *want*."

40 And He comes to the students, finds them sleeping, and says to Peter, "Is this how *it is*? Didn't you have strength to stay awake with Me for one hour?
41 Stay awake, and pray that you will not get into trouble. The spirit certainly *is* eager, but the physical body *is* weak."
42 Again after He went off from a second *time*, He prayed, saying, "My Father, if this cup is not able to pass away from Me unless I drink it, what You want must happen."
43 And when He came, He found them sleeping again. You see, it was their eyes that had been weighted down.
44 And after He left them, when He went off again, He prayed at a third *time*, after saying the same words.
45 Then He comes to His students and says to them, "Are you sleeping for the rest *of the time* and relaxing? Look, the hour has come near, and the Son of the Person is turned over into hands of sinful *people*."
46 "Get up. We may lead. Look, the *person* who is turning Me in has come near."
47 And as He was still speaking, look, Judas, one of the Twelve, came, and with him a big crowd (with daggers and wooden clubs) out from the head priests and older *men* of the ethnic group.
48 The *one* turning Him in gave them an indicator, saying, "Whoever I will be friendly with is Him. Take Him into custody."
49 And right away when he came to Jesus, he said, "Happy to meet You, Rabbi," and was very friendly to Him.
50 Jesus said to him, "Comrade, on to what you are beside *Me* for." At that time, when they came forward, they put *their* hands on Jesus and took Him into custody.
51 And look, when one of the *men* with Jesus put out *his* hand, he pulled away his dagger, and when he forcibly struck the slave of the head priest, he took off his ear lobe.
52 Then Jesus says to him, "Return your dagger back into its place. You see, all who take a dagger will be ruined by a dagger.
53 Or does it seem to you that I am not able now to call My Father here, and He will stand up next to Me more than twelve legions *(the Latin word for regiments)* of angels?
54 So how will the *Old Testament* writings be accomplished that *say* it is necessary *for it* to happen like this?"
55 In that hour, Jesus said to the crowds, "As on a bandit, you came out with daggers and wooden clubs to apprehend Me. Daily I was seated facing you teaching on the temple grounds, and you did not take Me into custody.
56 But this whole *thing* has happened so that the preachers' writings might be accomplished." Then after all the students left Him, they escaped.
57 After the *underlings* took Jesus into custody, they led Him away to Caiaphas, the head priest, where the *Old Testament* transcribers and the older *men* were gathered together.
58 Peter was following Him off at a distance until the courtyard of the head priest. And when he went inside, he was sitting with the underlings to see the conclusion.

59 The head priests, the older *men*, and the whole council were looking for a lie against Jesus from a witness in order that they might put Him to death.
60 And they did not find *any*. Even after many lying witnesses came forward, they did not find *any*. Later, when two lying witnesses came forward,
61 they said, "This *Person* was declaring, 'I am able to tear the temple of God down and to build it through three days.'"
62 And when the head priest stood up, he said to Him, "You are answering nothing. What are these *people* witnessing against you?"
63 But Jesus was keeping silent. And when the head priest responded, he said to Him, "I am forcing you into an oath under God, the living *God*, so that You might tell us if you are the Anointed King, the Son of God."
64 Jesus says to him, "You said *it*. More importantly, I tell you, from now *on* you will see the Son of the Person sitting at *places to the* right of the Ability and coming on the clouds of the sky."
65 At that time, the head priest ripped apart his clothes, saying, "He insulted *God*. What? Do we still have a need for witnesses? Look. Now you heard His insult.
66 What does it seem to you?" When the *men* answered, they said, "He is eligible to be sentenced to death."
67 Then they spit in His face and slugged Him. The *people* slapped *Him*,
68 saying, "Prophesy to us, Anointed King. Who is the *person* who struck You?"
69 But Peter was sitting outside in the courtyard, and one servant girl came to him, saying, "You also were with Jesus, the Galilean."
70 *Peter* denied *it* in front of everyone, saying, "I do not know what you are saying."
71 When he went out into the gateway, another *girl* saw him and says to the *people*, "This *person* was also there with Jesus, the Nazarene."
72 And again he denied *it* with an oath, "I do not know the person."
73 After a little while, when the *people* who had stood *there* came forward, they said to Peter, "You also are truly from among them. You see, your speech also makes you obvious."
74 At that time, he began to be vowing under the penalty of being adversely doomed and to be guaranteeing, "I do not know the person," and right away a rooster crowed.
75 And Peter remembered Jesus' statement that He had stated to him, "Before *the time* for a rooster to crow, three times you will flatly deny Me." And after going outside, he cried bitterly.

27

1 When it became morning, all the head priests and the older *men* of the ethnic group received counsel against Jesus in such a way to put Him to death.
2 And after they tied Him up, they led *Him* away and turned Him over to Pontius Pilate, the leader.
3 At that time, when Judas (the *one* who turned Him in) saw that He was found guilty, after regretting *what he had done*, he returned the thirty silver coins back to the head priests and the older *men*,

4 saying, "I sinned when I turned in blood *that is* not guilty," but the *head priests* said, "What *is that* to us? You will see."
5 And after he tossed the silver coins in the temple, he took a back way, and after going off, he hung himself.
6 When the head priests took the silver coins, they said, "It is not allowed to throw these into the Corban *(the name of the offering boxes in the temple)* since it is a price of blood."
7 After receiving counsel, they bought the field of the clay worker from them for burial of the strangers.
8 For this reason, that field was called "Field of Blood" until the *day* today.
9 At that time, what was stated through Jeremiah, the preacher, *in Zechariah 11:12–13* was accomplished that says, "And they took the thirty silver coins, the price of the *One* who had been priced, whom they priced apart from Israel's sons.
10 And they gave these for the field of the clay worker aligned with what *the* Master dictated to me."
11 Jesus stood in front of the leader, and the leader asked Him, saying, "Are You the king of the Jewish *people*?" Jesus was declaring to him, "You say *so*."
12 And during the *time* for complaints to be leveled against Him by the head priests and the older *men*, He answered nothing.
13 At that time, Pilate says to Him, "Don't You hear how many *things* they are witnessing against You?"
14 And He did not respond to him toward even one statement in such a way for the leader to be very amazed.
15 At each festival the leader had been accustomed to dismiss one prisoner to the crowd, whom they were wanting.
16 At that time, they had a well-known prisoner called Barabbas.
17 So since they had been gathered together, Pilate said to them, "Who do you want *that* I should dismiss to you, Barabbas or Jesus, the *One* called *the* Anointed King?"
18 You see, he realized that they turned Him in because of envy.
19 As he sat down on the judicial bench, his wife sent *someone* out to him, saying, "*There must be* nothing *between* you and that *Person* who does what is right. You see, I suffered many *things* today throughout a dream because of Him."
20 But the head priests and the older *men* persuaded the crowds so that they would ask for Barabbas, but ruin Jesus.
21 When the leader responded, he said to them, "Which out of the two do you want *that* I should dismiss to you." The *crowds* said, "Barabbas."
22 Pilate says to them, "So what should I do with Jesus, the *One* who is called *the* Anointed King?" Everyone says to him, "He must be nailed to a cross."
23 The leader was declaring, "You see, what bad *thing* did He do?" But the *crowds* were yelling much more, saying, "He must be nailed to a cross."
24 Pilate, after seeing that he is not benefiting in any way, but instead a riot is happening, when he took water, he washed off *his* hands up in front of the crowd, saying, "I am not guilty for the blood of this *Person* who does what is right. You will see."

25 And when the entire group responded, it said, "His blood *is* on us and on our children."
26 At that time, he dismissed Barabbas to them. But after thrashing Jesus with a whip, he turned *Him* over so that He might be nailed to a cross.
27 Then when the soldiers of the leader took Jesus along into the Roman palace, they gathered the whole regiment together over Him.
28 And after they stripped Him, they placed a red military cape around Him.
29 And after they wove an award wreath from thorns, they put *it* on His head and a stick on His right *hand*. And after kneeling in front of Him, they were mocking Him, saying, "Happy to meet You, the King of the Jewish *people*."
30 And after they spit onto Him, they took the stick and were hitting onto His head.
31 And after they mocked Him, they stripped the military cape off Him, put His clothes on Him, and led Him away for the "to be nailed to a cross" *part*.
32 As they came out, they found a person, a Cyrenian with *the* name, Simon. They sequestered help from this *person* so that he might pick up His cross.
33 And when they came to a place called Golgotha, that is called Place of a Skull,
34 they gave Him sour wine that had been mixed with bile to drink. And when He tasted *it*, He was not wanting to drink *it*.
35 After they nailed Him to a cross, they divided up His clothing, throwing dice, so that what was stated by the preacher *in Psalm 22:18* might be accomplished, "They divided up my clothes for themselves, and on my clothing they threw dice."
36 And sitting down, they were keeping guard of Him there.
37 And they placed His accusation up on top of His head that had been written, "This is Jesus, the King of the Jewish *people*."
38 At that time, two bandits were nailed to crosses together with Him, one at *places to the* right and one at *places to the* left.
39 As the *people* were traveling by, they were insulting Him, shaking their heads
40 and saying, "The *One* who tears the temple down and builds *it* in three days, rescue Yourself. If You are a son of God, climb down off the cross."
41 Likewise, as the head priests with the *Old Testament* transcribers and older *men* also mocked, they were saying,
42 "Others, He rescued. Himself, He is not able to rescue. If He is *the* King of Israel, He must climb down off the cross now, and we will trust Him.
43 He has been confident based on God. He must save Him now if He wants Him. You see, He said, 'I am a son of God.'"
44 Also the bandits, the *ones* that were nailed to crosses together with Him, were criticizing Him the same *way*.
45 From *the* sixth hour (*noon*), darkness happened on all the earth until *the* ninth hour (*3:00 p.m.*).
46 Around the ninth hour (*3:00 p.m.*) Jesus shouted out with a loud voice, saying, "Eli, Eli, lama sabachthani?" That is *Aramaic for* "My God, My God, why did You leave Me down in *here*?"

47 Some of the *people* who had stood there, when they heard *it*, were saying, "This *Person* is hollering for Elijah."
48 And right away, when one from among them ran and took a sponge, after he both filled *it* with sour wine and put *it* around a stick, he was giving Him a drink.
49 But the rest were saying, "Leave *Him alone*. We should see if Elijah comes so that he will rescue Him."
50 When Jesus yelled again with a loud voice, He left the spirit *to God*.
51 And, look, the curtain of the temple was torn in two from top to bottom, the earth was shook, the rocks were torn *apart*,
52 the burial vaults were opened, and many bodies of the sacred *people* who had been asleep were gotten up
53 (and after coming out of the burial vaults with His getting up, they went into the sacred city and were made apparent to many).
54 When the lieutenant and the *soldiers* with him (who were keeping guard of Jesus) saw the earthquake and the *things* that happened, they were terribly afraid, saying, "This truly was a son of a god."
55 Many women were there watching off at a distance, some who followed Jesus from Galilee serving Him,
56 among whom were Mary (the Magdalene), Mary (the mother of James and Joses), and the mother of the sons of Zebedee.
57 When it became evening, a wealthy person from Arimathaea came named Joseph, who himself also made students for Jesus.
58 When this *person* came to Pilate, he asked for Jesus' body. At that time, Pilate gave the order for the body to be given back.
59 And after Joseph took the body, he wound a clean linen cloth around it
60 and put it in his new burial vault that he chiseled out in the rock. And after he rolled a large stone over the doorway of the burial vault, he went away.
61 Mary (the Magdalene) and the other Mary were there sitting up in front of the gravesite.
62 On the next day, a certain *day* that is after the preparation *day*, the head priests and the Separatists were gathered together to Pilate,
63 saying, "Master, we remembered that that misleader said as He was still living, 'After three days I am being gotten up.'
64 So give the order for the gravesite to be made secure until the third day so that when His students come at night, they won't steal Him and tell the group, 'He was gotten up from the dead,' and the last misleading lie will be worse than the first."
65 Pilate was declaring to them, "You have a Roman guard unit. Lead the way back, secure *it* as you have seen."
66 After the *head priests* traveled *off*, they secured the gravesite when they put a seal on the stone with the Roman guard unit *present*.

28

1 In *the* evening of *the* Sabbaths, the *day* emerging into *Day* 1 after *the* Sabbaths, Mary (the Magdalene) and the other Mary went to watch the gravesite.

2 And look, a large earthquake happened. You see, after an angel of *the* Master stepped down from heaven, when he came forward, he rolled the stone away from the door and was sitting up on top of it.

3 The sight of him was as lightning, and his attire white as if *it were* snow.

4 The *soldiers* who were keeping guard were shook from the fear of him and became as if *they were* dead *people*.

5 When the angel responded, he said to the women, "You must not be afraid. You see, I realize that you are looking for Jesus, the *One* who has been nailed to a cross.

6 He is not here. You see, He was gotten up, just as He said. Come on. Look at the place where the Master was lying.

7 And after traveling quickly, tell His students that He was gotten up from the dead, and look, He is going ahead of you into Galilee. There you will see Him. Look, I told you."

8 And when they quickly went out of the burial vault with fear and great happiness, they ran to report *it* to His students.

9 As *the angel instructed*, they were traveling to report to His students, and look, Jesus came to meet them, saying, "Happy to meet you." When the *women* came forward, they took hold of His feet and bowed down to Him.

10 At that time, Jesus says to them, "Don't be afraid. Make *your* way back, report to My brothers that I will go off into Galilee and they will see Me there."

11 As they were traveling, look, after some of the Roman guard unit went into the city, they reported to the head priests absolutely all of the *things* that happened.

12 And after they were gathered together with the older *men* and received counsel, they gave an adequate amount of silver coins to the soldiers,

13 saying, "Say that when His students came at night, they stole Him as you were sleeping.

14 And if this is heard up to the leader, we will persuade him and make you without worries."

15 After the *soldiers* took the silver coins, they did as they were taught, and this saying is thoroughly spread beside Jewish *people* up to the *day* today.

16 The eleven students traveled into Galilee into the mountain where Jesus arranged with them.

17 And when they saw Him, they bowed down to Him, but the *people* doubted.

18 And when Jesus came forward, He spoke to them, saying, "Every authority in heaven and on earth was given to Me.

19 So after traveling, make students of all the nations, submerging them into the name of the Father, the Son, and the Sacred Spirit,

20 teaching them to be keeping all *things*, as many as I demanded you. And look, I am with you all the days until the very conclusion of the span of time. Amen.

Mark

1

1 *The* beginning of the good news of Jesus, *the* Anointed King, God's Son,
2 as it has been written in the Preachers, *in Isaiah 40:3*, "Look, I am sending My announcer out *on a mission* before Your face, who will construct Your road in front of You.
3 A voice shouting in the backcountry, 'Get the road of *the* Master ready. Make His paths straight.'"
4 John became *a person* submerging *people* in the backcountry and speaking publicly about a change of ways submersion for forgiveness of sins.
5 And all the rural area (Judea) and the Jerusalemites were traveling out to him, and everyone was being submerged in the Jordan River by him acknowledging their sins out loud.
6 John was *a person* who had put on camel hair and a leather sash around his waist and was eating grasshoppers and wild honey.
7 And he was speaking publicly, saying, "The *One* stronger than me is coming behind me of whom I am not adequate, after stooping, to release the strap of His sandals.
8 I certainly submerged you in water, but He will submerge you in *the* Sacred Spirit."
9 And it happened in those days; Jesus came out of Nazareth, Galilee and was submerged by John in the Jordan *River*.
10 And right away as He stepped up out of the water, He saw the skies being torn and the Spirit as if *It were* a dove stepping down on Him.
11 And a voice happened from the heavens, "You are My Son, the loved *Son*, in whom I am delighted."
12 And right away the Spirit threw Him out into the backcountry.
13 And He was there in the backcountry forty days experiencing trouble under the Opponent. And He was with the wild animals, and the angels were serving Him.
14 After the *time* for John to be turned in, Jesus went into Galilee speaking publicly about the good news of the monarchy of God
15 and saying, "The appointed time has been accomplished, and the monarchy of God has come near. Change your ways, and trust in the good news."
16 As He was walking around along the Sea of Galilee, He saw Simon and Andrew (his brother), throwing a throw net in the sea. You see, they were fishermen.
17 And Jesus said to them, "Come on behind Me, and I will make you to become fishermen of people."
18 And right away after leaving their nets, they followed Him.
19 After He walked on from there for a little while, He saw James (the *son* of Zebedee) and John (his brother), as they were also developing the nets in the boat.

20 And right away He invited them. And after they left their father Zebedee in the boat with the hired workers, they went off behind Him.
21 And they travel into Capernaum, and right away on the Sabbaths, when He went into the synagogue, He was teaching.
22 And they were being impressed based on His teaching. You see, He was teaching them as *a person* having authority and not as the *Old Testament* transcribers.
23 And in their synagogue there was a person with a spirit that was not clean, and he yelled out,
24 saying, "Ahhhh! What *is there between* us and You, Jesus, Nazarene? Did You come to ruin us? I realize who You are, the Sacred *One* of God."
25 And Jesus stopped it, saying, "Be quiet, and come out of him."
26 And after the spirit that was not clean sent him into convulsions and yelled with a loud voice, He came out of him.
27 And everyone was perplexed in such a way to together be posing questions to themselves, saying, "What is this *thing*? What *is* this new teaching? Because He even gives directives aligned with authority to the spirits, the *ones* that are not clean, and they obey Him."
28 The talk about Him went out right away into the whole surrounding rural area of Galilee.
29 And right away after they went out of the synagogue, they went into the house of Simon and Andrew with James and John.
30 The mother-in-law of Simon was lying down having a fever. And right away they tell Him about her.
31 And when He came forward, He got her up after taking hold of her hand. And the fever left her right away, and she was serving them.
32 When it became evening after the sun set, they were bringing to Him all the *people* who had *it* bad, and the *people* who had lesser deities.
33 And the whole city had come together in one place to the door.
34 And He healed many *people* who had *it* bad with various illnesses and threw out many lesser deities. And He was not leaving the lesser deities to be speaking because they knew Him.
35 And in *the* morning (very *much* in *the* night), after getting up, He went out, went off to an uninhabited place, and was praying there.
36 And Simon and the *people* with him hunted Him down,
37 and when they find Him, they say to Him, "Everyone is looking for You."
38 And He says to them, "We should lead into the next towns so that I might speak publicly there also. You see, for this I have come out.
39 And He was in their synagogues in all of Galilee speaking publicly and throwing out the lesser deities.
40 And a skin-diseased *man* came to Him encouraging Him, kneeling to Him, and saying to Him, "If You want to, You are able to clear me up."
41 When Jesus had sympathy, after He put out the hand, He touched him and says to him, "I want to. Be cleared up."
42 And when He spoke, right away the skin disease went away from him, and he was cleared up.
43 And after being stern with him, He put him out right away.

44 And He says to him, "See, you shouldn't say anything to anyone. But Make *your* way back. Show yourself to the priest, and offer up what Moses instructed concerning your cleansing for a witness to them."
45 But when the *man* went out, he began to be speaking publicly a lot and to be thoroughly spreading the message *of what happened to him* in such a way for Him to no longer be able to go into a city in a shown way. But He was outside in uninhabited places, and they were coming to Him from all directions.

2

1 And He went into Capernaum again after some days, and it was heard that He is in a house.
2 And right away, many *people* were gathered together in such a way *for there* to no longer be *any* room, not even the *areas* toward the door. And He was speaking the message to them.
3 And they come bringing a disabled *man* to Him picked up by four.
4 And not being able to come close to Him because of the crowd, they unroofed the roof where He was. And after digging *it* out, they lower the mattress on which the disabled *man* was lying.
5 When Jesus sees their trust, He says to the disabled *man*, "Child, your sins have been forgiven you."
6 Some of the *Old Testament* transcribers were sitting there and pondering in their hearts,
7 "Why is this *Person* speaking insults like this? Who is able to be forgiving sins except One, God?"
8 And right away when Jesus correctly understood with His spirit that this is what they are pondering among themselves, He said to them, "Why are you pondering these *things* in your hearts?
9 Which is easier to say to the disabled *man*, 'The sins have been forgiven you,' or to say, 'Get up, pick up your mattress, and walk around?'
10 But so that you may realize that the Son of the Person has authority to be forgiving sins on the earth...." He says to the disabled *man*,
11 "I tell you, get up, pick up your mattress, and make *your* way back into your house."
12 And He got up right away, and after picking up the mattress, he went out directly in front of everyone in such a way for everyone to be astounded and to be praising the magnificence of God, saying, "We have never ever seen anything like this."
13 And He went out again along the sea, the entire crowd was coming to Him, and He was teaching them.
14 And as He passed by, He saw Levi (the *son* of Alphaeus) sitting at the tax booth. And He says to him, "Follow Me," and after he got up, he followed Him.
15 And it happened during the *time* for Him to be lounging in his house; many tax collectors and sinful *people* were also reclining together with Jesus and His students. You see, there were many, and they were following Him.
16 And when the *Old Testament* transcribers and the Separatists saw Him eating with the tax collectors and sinful *people*, they were saying to His

students, "How *is it* that He is eating and drinking with the tax collectors and sinful *people*?"

17 And when Jesus hears, He says to them, "The *people* who have strength have no need of a doctor, but the *people* who have *it* bad *do*. I did not come to invite *people* who do what is right to a change of ways, but sinful *people*."

18 And the students of John and the *students* of the Separatists were going without food. And they come and say to Him, "Why do the students of John and the *students* of the Separatists go without food, but Your students do not go without food?"

19 And Jesus said to them, "The sons of the bridal room are not able to be going without food during *the time* that the groom is with them, are they? For as much time as they have the groom with themselves, they are not able to be going without food.

20 But days will come when the groom will be taken away from them, and then in those days, they will go without food.

21 And no one sews a patch of unprocessed cloth on a worn out robe, but if *they do*, what fills in *the hole* takes away from it, the new from the old, and a tear becomes worse.

22 And no one puts young wine into worn out leather bags, but if *they do*, the wine, the young *wine*, rips the leather bags, the wine is spilled out, and the leather bags will be ruined. But young wine *is a thing that* must be put into new leather bags."

23 And it happened for Him to be traveling along on the Sabbaths through the croplands, and His students began to be making a way pulling off the heads *of grain*.

24 And the Separatists were saying to Him, "Look, why are they doing what is not allowed on the Sabbaths?"

25 And He was saying to them, "Have you never even once read what David did when he had a need and he was hungry, he and the *people* with him?

26 How he went into the house of God before head priest Abiathar, ate the *loaves of* bread of the display (that no *one* is allowed to eat except the priests), and also gave *it* to the *people* who were together with him?"

27 And He was saying to them, "The Sabbath happened because of the person, not the person because of the Sabbath.

28 In such a way, the Son of the Person is even Master of the Sabbath."

3

1 And He went into the synagogue again, and a person was there who had the hand that had been shriveled up.

2 And they were watching Him closely whether He would heal him on the Sabbaths so that they might level a complaint against Him.

3 And He says to the person, the *one* who has the hand that had been shriveled up, "Get up in the middle."

4 And He says to them, "Is it allowed on the Sabbaths to do good or to do bad? To rescue a soul or to kill?" But the *people* were silent.

5 And after He looked around at them with rage, being saddened over the stone hardness of their hearts, He says to the person, "Put out your hand." And he put *it* out, and his hand was reestablished healthy, as the other.
6 And when the Separatists went out right away with the Herod supporters, they were taking counsel against Him on how they might ruin Him.
7 And Jesus took a back way to the sea with His students, and a very large number from Galilee followed Him, also from Judea,
8 from Greater Jerusalem, and from Idumaea, *the* other side of the Jordan River, and the *people* around Tyre and Sidon. As a very large number heard as many *things* as He was doing, they came to Him.
9 And He told His students that a small boat should stay close to Him because of the crowd so that they may not give Him a hard time.
10 You see, He healed many in such a way *for them* to be falling on Him so that as many as had ailments might touch Him.
11 And whenever the spirits, the *ones* that were not clean, were seeing Him, they were falling toward Him and yelling, saying, "You are the Son of God."
12 And He was shushing many *spirits* in them so that they would not make Him known.
13 And He climbs up into the mountain and calls for whom He was wanting. And they went off to Him.
14 And He made twelve so that they may be with Him and so that He may send them out *on missions* to be speaking publicly
15 and to be having authority to be healing the illnesses and to be throwing out the lesser deities.
16 *Simon* (He added to Simon a name, Peter),
17 James (the *son* of Zebedee), John (the brother of James; He also added names to them, Boanerges, that is *Hebrew for* Sons of Thunder),
18 Andrew, Philip, Bartholomew, Matthew, Thomas, James (the *son* of Alphaeus), Thaddeus, Simon (the Kananite - *Aramaic for Zealot*),
19 and Judas from Kerioth (who also turned Him in). And He went into a house,
20 and the crowd again came together in such a way for them not to be able to even eat bread.
21 And when the *people* from the side of Him heard, they went out to take Him into custody. You see, they were saying that He was deranged.
22 And the *Old Testament* transcribers, the *ones* who walked down out of Greater Jerusalem, were saying that He has Beelzebub and that with the head of the lesser deities He is throwing out the lesser deities.
23 And after calling for them, He was talking to them in illustrations, "How is *the* Opponent able to be throwing *the* Opponent out?
24 And if a monarchy is divided on itself, that monarchy is not able to be established.
25 And if a house is divided on itself, that house is not able to be established.
26 And if the Opponent stands up on himself and has been divided, he is not able to be established, but has a conclusion.

27 No one is able to ransack the containers of the strong *person* after going into his house unless he first ties up the strong *person*, and then he will ransack his house.
28 Amen, I tell you that all sins will be forgiven to the sons of the people and insults, however many things they might insult.
29 But whoever insults into the Spirit, the Sacred *Spirit*, does not have forgiveness for the span of time, but he is eligible for sentencing for judgment that spans *all* time."
30 *He said this* because they were saying, "He has a spirit that is not clean."
31 So His brothers and mother come. And having stood outside, they sent out *someone* to Him, hollering at Him.
32 And a crowd was sitting around Him. They said to Him, "Look, Your mother and Your brothers outside are looking for You."
33 And He responded to them, saying, "Who is My mother or My brothers?"
34 And after looking around in a circle at the *people* sitting around Him, He says, "Look, My mother and My brothers.
35 You see, whoever does what God wants, this *person* is My brother, My sister, and mother."

4

1 And again He began to be teaching along the sea. And a great crowd was gathered together facing Him in such a way that for Him to be sitting in the sea He climbed on board into the boat. And the entire crowd was on the land facing the sea.
2 And He was teaching them many *things* in illustrations. And He was saying to them in His teaching,
3 "Listen. Look. The *person* who seeds went out to seed.
4 And it happened during the *time* to be seeding; *one* that fell along the road, and the winged birds of the sky came and ate it.
5 Another fell on the rocky *place* where it did not have much soil, and right away it came up because of the *fact for it* not to be having depth of soil.
6 When *the* sun came up, it was scorched, and because of the *fact for it* not to be having root, it shriveled up.
7 And another fell into the thorns. And the thorns climbed up, came together, and choked it off. And it did not give fruit.
8 And another fell into the soil, the nice *soil*, and was giving fruit as it was climbing up and growing. And one was carrying thirty, one sixty, and one a hundred."
9 And He was saying to them, "The *person* who has ears to be listening must listen."
10 And when He became in *places where they were* alone, the *people* around Him together with the Twelve asked Him about the illustration.
11 And He was saying to them, "It has been given to you to know the secret of the monarchy of God, but to those *people* outside all *things* are happening in illustrations
12 so that as they look, they may look and not see, and as they hear, they may hear and not understand. They will never return back, and it (the sins) be forgiven them."

13 And He says to them, "Don't you realize this illustration? And how will you know all the illustrations?
14 The *person* who seeds, seeds the message.
15 These are the *people* along the road where the message is seeded. And when they hear, right away the Opponent comes and takes away the message, the *one* that has been seeded in their hearts.
16 And these likewise are the *people* seeded on the rocky *places*, who, when they hear the message, right away with happiness they take it.
17 And they don't have root in themselves, but they are for the time being. After that, when hard times or persecution happens because of the message, right away they stumble.
18 And these are the *people* seeded into the thorns, the *people* who heard the message,
19 and the worries of this span of time, the fraud of the wealth, and the desires concerning the rest *of the things*, as they travel into *them*, come together and choke off the message. And they become fruitless.
20 And these are the *people* seeded on the soil, the nice *soil*, any who hear the message and accept *it* with a warm welcome. And they produce fruit, one thirty, one sixty, and one a hundred."
21 And He was saying to them, "The lamp doesn't come *into a room* so that it might be placed under the two gallon measuring bucket or under the cot, does it? No, *it comes into a room* so that it might be placed on the lampstand.
22 You see, something is not hidden if *it is* not *a thing* that might be shown, neither did it become hidden away, but so that it might come into a shown *place*.
23 If anyone has ears to be listening, he must listen."
24 And He was saying to them, "Look out what you listen to. With *the* measurement that you measure, it will be measured to you, and it will be added to you, the *people* who listen.
25 You see, whoever has, it will be given to him. And *a person* who does not have, even what he has will be taken away from him."
26 And He was saying, "The monarchy of God is like this, as if a person would throw the batch of seeds on the ground.
27 And he may sleep and get up night and day, and the batch of seeds may bud and get longer. How? He does not know.
28 You see, the earth automatically produces fruit, first a stem, after that a head *of grain*, after that full grain in the head.
29 But when the fruit turns up, right away he sends out the sickle because the harvest has offered *itself*."
30 And He was saying, "What will we liken the monarchy of God to? Or in what kind of illustration will we illustrate it?
31 *It is* as a kernel of mustard, that, when it is seeded on the earth, it is *a seed* littler than all the seeds, the *seeds* on the earth.
32 And when it is seeded, it climbs up and becomes greater than all the vegetables. And it makes large branches in such a way for the winged birds of the sky to be able to be nesting under its shadow."

33 And with many of these types of illustrations, He was speaking the message to them, just what they were able to be hearing.
34 Without an illustration, He was not speaking to them. But by themselves to His students, He was explaining everything.
35 And He says to them during that day when it becomes evening, "We will go across to the other side."
36 And after leaving the crowd, they take Him along as He was in the boat. There were also other small boats with Him.
37 And a large blast of wind happens. It was throwing the swells up into the boat in such a way for it to already be full.
38 And He was on the back of the boat on the cushion sleeping. And they wake Him up and say to Him, "Teacher, isn't it a concern to You that we are being ruined?"
39 And when He was wide awake, He shushed the wind and said to the sea, "Silence. Be quiet." And the wind stopped blowing, and there became a great calm.
40 And He said to them, "Why are you cowardly like this? How *is it that* you do not have trust?"
41 And they were afraid with great fear and were saying to each other, "So who is this *Person*, because even the wind and the sea obey Him?"

5

1 And they went to the other side of the sea to the rural area of the Gadarenes.
2 And when He came out of the boat, right away a person met Him from the burial vaults with a spirit that was not clean,
3 who was having *his* residence in the burial vaults. And not even with a chain was anyone able to lock him up,
4 because of the *fact* for him to have been locked up many times with foot shackles and chains, and for the chains to have been pulled apart by him, and for the foot shackles to have been crushed. And no one had *the* strength to tame him.
5 And through everything, night and day, in the mountains and in the graves, he was yelling and cutting himself up with stones.
6 When he saw Jesus off at a distance, he ran and bowed down to Him.
7 And after he yelled with a loud voice, he said, "What *is there between* me and You, Jesus, son of God, the highest? I place you under an oath to God that you not torture me."
8 You see, He was saying to him, "Come out of the person, the spirit, the *one* that is not clean."
9 And He was asking him, "What is a name for you?" And he answered, saying, "Legion *(the Latin word for regiment) is* a name for me, because we are many."
10 And he was encouraging Him a lot so that He would not send them outside of the rural area.
11 A large herd of hogs were there toward the mountains, grazing.
12 And all the lesser deities encouraged Him, saying, "Send us into the hogs so that we might go into them."

13 And Jesus gave them permission right away. And when the spirits, the *ones* that were not clean, came out, they went into the hogs, and the herd (they were as two thousand) rushed down the steep slope into the sea and were drowning in the sea.
14 The *people* grazing the hogs escaped and announced to the city and to the fields. And they went out to see what is the *thing* that has happened.
15 And they are coming to Jesus and watching the *man* who had lesser deities, sitting, having been clothed, and properly focused, the *one* who has had the legion. And they were afraid.
16 And the *people* who saw *it* described to them how it happened to the *man* who had lesser deities and about the hogs.
17 And they began to be encouraging Him to go away from their borders.
18 And when He climbed on board into the boat, the *man* who had lesser deities was encouraging Him so that he may be with Him.
19 Jesus did not leave him *alone*, but He says to him, "Make *your* way back into your house to your *people* and announce to them how much the Master has done for you and showed you forgiving kindness."
20 And He went off and began to be speaking publicly in Decapolis about how much Jesus did for him, and all were being amazed.
21 And after Jesus crossed all the way over in the boat again to the other side, a big crowd was gathered together up to Him, and He was beside the sea.
22 And look, one of the synagogue's head rulers with *the* name Jairus comes, and when he sees Him, he gets down facing His feet
23 and was encouraging Him much, saying, "My little daughter has *her* last *days*. O that after coming, You would place *Your* hands on her in order that she would be rescued and will live."
24 And He went off with him. And a big crowd was following Him and squeezing in on Him.
25 And a certain woman being in a discharge of blood twelve years
26 and who suffered many *things* under many doctors, who spent everything from the side of herself, and who was not benefited in any way, but instead was coming into the worse *part*,
27 after hearing about Jesus, when she came in the crowd from behind, she touched His robe.
28 You see, she was saying, "If I just touch His clothes, I will be rescued."
29 And right away the spring of her blood dried up, and she knew in *her* body that she had been cured from the ailment.
30 And right away after Jesus recognized in Himself the ability from Him that went out, when He turned around in the crowd, He was saying, "Who touched My clothes?"
31 And His students were saying to Him, "You see the crowd squeezing in on You, and You are saying, 'Who touched Me?'"
32 And He was looking around to see the *woman* who did this.
33 But the woman, who was afraid and trembling, realizing what had happened over her, came, got down facing Him, and told Him all the truth.
34 *Jesus* said to her, "Daughter, your trust has rescued you. Make *your* way back into peace and be well from your ailment."

35 As He is still speaking, they come from the synagogue's head ruler's *house*, saying, "Your daughter died. Why are you still irritating the teacher?"
36 Right away when Jesus hears the message being spoken, He says to the synagogue's head ruler, "Don't be afraid. Just trust."
37 And He did not leave anyone to follow along with Him except Peter, James, and John (the brother of James).
38 And He goes into the house of the synagogue's head ruler and watches *the* disturbance as *people* are both crying and clanging many *things*.
39 And after going in, He says to them, "Why are you causing a disturbance and crying? The young child did not die, but is sleeping."
40 And they were laughing at Him. But after throwing everyone out, He takes along the father of the young child, the mother, and the *three* with Him and travels into where the young child was reclining.
41 And after taking hold of the hand of the young child, He says to her, "Talitha Cumi," that is translated *from Aramaic as* "The girl, I tell you, get up."
42 And right away the girl got up and was walking around. You see, she was twelve years *old*. And they were astounded with great astonishment.
43 And He warned them many *times* that no one should know this, and He said to give her *something* to eat.

6

1 And He went out from there and went into His hometown. And His students follow Him.
2 And when a Sabbath happened, He began to be teaching in the synagogue, and many listening were being impressed, saying, "Where *are* these *things* from *that* this *Person has*?" and "What is the insight, the *insight* given to Him, that even these types of abilities happen through His hands?
3 Isn't this the builder, the son of Mary, a brother of James, Joses, Judah, and Simon? And aren't His sisters here with us?" And they were stumbling in Him.
4 Jesus was saying to them, "A preacher is not worthless except in his hometown, among *his* relatives, and in his house."
5 And He was not able to show even one ability there, except after placing *His* hands on a few sick *people*, He healed *them*.
6 And He was being amazed because of their lack of trust. And He was leading *His students* around the circling villages, teaching.
7 And He calls for the Twelve and began to be sending them out *on missions* two *by* two. And He was giving them authority over the spirits, the *ones* that are not clean.
8 And He passed the order on to them that they should take nothing for *the* road except a staff only: no tote bag, no bread, no copper in the waist sash;
9 but having tied sole pads on under *their feet*, not to also put two long undershirts on.
10 And He was saying to them, "Whatever house you go into, stay there until you go out from there.
11 And however many that do not accept you, nor listen to you, as you travel out from there, shake off the dirt, the *dirt* beneath your feet, for a witness to

them. Amen, I tell you, it will be more tolerable for Sodom and Gomorrah in *the* judgment day than for that city.

12 And after they went out, they were speaking publicly that they should change their ways.

13 And they were throwing many lesser deities out, dabbing olive oil on many sick *people*, and healing *them*.

14 And King Herod heard (you see, His name became shown), and he was saying, "John, the *one* who submerges, was gotten up from *the* dead, and because of this, the abilities are active in Him."

15 Others were saying, "He is Elijah." Others were saying, "He is a preacher or as one of the preachers."

16 When Herod heard, he said, "John, whom I beheaded, this is him. He was gotten up from *the* dead."

17 You see, when Herod himself sent *someone* out, he took John into custody and locked him up in the jail because of Herodias, the wife of his brother Philip, because he married her;

18 for John was saying to Herod, "It is not allowed for you to be having the wife of your brother."

19 Herodias was holding a grudge against him. And she was wanting to kill him and was not able to.

20 You see, Herod feared John, realizing him *to be* a man who does what is right and *is* sacred. And he was preserving him. And when he listened to him, he was doing many *things* and was gladly listening to him.

21 And a well-timed day happened when Herod at his birthday celebrations was making a feast for his greatest people, the commanding officers, and the most important *people* of Galilee.

22 And when the daughter of Herodias herself came in, danced, and Herod and the *people* reclining together with *him* liked it, the king said to the girl, "Ask me for whatever you want, and I will give *it* to you."

23 And he guaranteed *it* to her, "Whatever you ask me for, I will give to you, up to half of my monarchy."

24 After going out, the *girl* said to her mother, "What will I ask for?" The *mother* said, "The head of John the Submerger."

25 And when she went in right away in a hurry to the king, she asked, saying, "I want that you might immediately give me on a plate the head of John the Submerger."

26 And though the king became overcome with sadness, because of the oaths and the *people* reclining together with *him*, he did not want to invalidate her.

27 And right away when the king sent a bodyguard out, he gave the directive for his head to be brought. After the *bodyguard* went off, he beheaded him in the jail.

28 And he brought his head on a plate and gave it to the girl, and the girl gave it to her mother.

29 And when his students heard, they went, took his corpse away, and put it in a burial vault.

30 And the missionaries are gathered together to Jesus. And they reported to Him everything, both as much as they did and as much as they taught.

31 And He said to them, "Come on, you yourselves by yourselves, into an uninhabited place and relax for a little while." You see, the *people* coming and the *people* making *their* way back were many, and they were not even having a good time to eat.

32 And they went off to an uninhabited place in the boat by themselves.

33 And the crowds saw them making *their* way back. And many correctly understood Him and ran there together on foot from all of the cities. And they went on ahead of them and came together to Him.

34 And when Jesus came out, He saw a big crowd, and He had sympathy on them because they were as sheep not having a shepherd. And He began to be teaching them many *things*.

35 And after a late hour already happened, when His students came to Him, they are saying, "The place is uninhabited, and *it is* already a late hour.

36 Dismiss them so that when they go off into the circling fields and villages, they might buy bread for themselves. You see, they don't have what they will eat."

37 When *Jesus* answered, He said to them, "You must give them *something* to eat." And they say to Him, "After we go off, we might buy two hundred denarii *($10,000) worth* of *loaves of* bread and give *it* to them to eat."

38 *Jesus* says to them, "How many *loaves of* bread do you have? Make *your* way back and look." And when they know, they say, "Five *loaves* and two fish."

39 And He gave the directive to them for everyone to recline, social groups *by* social groups, on the green grass.

40 And they settled down, plots *by* plots, of a hundred apiece and of fifty apiece.

41 And after He took the five *loaves of* bread and the two fish, when He looked up into the sky, He conferred a blessing *on them*. And He split the *loaves of* bread up and was giving *them* to His students so that they may place them beside them. And He divided the two fish to everyone.

42 And everyone ate and was full.

43 And they picked up twelve baskets full of pieces and from the fish.

44 And the *men* eating the *loaves of* bread were as if *they were* five thousand men.

45 And right away He urged his students to climb on board into the boat and to be going ahead to the other side to Bethsaida until He would dismiss the crowd.

46 And after He said good-bye to them, He went off into the mountain to pray.

47 And when it became evening, the boat was in *the* middle of the sea, and He *was* alone on the land.

48 And He saw them being tortured during the *time* to be driving *the boat* forward (you see, the wind was opposing them), and around *the* fourth guard shift of the night *(3:00 to 6:00 a.m.)* He comes to them walking around on the sea. And He was wanting to pass by them.

49 But when the *students* saw Him walking around on the sea, it seemed to them to be a ghost, and they yelled out.

50 You see, everyone saw Him, and they were uneasy. And right away He spoke with them. And He says to them, "Be courageous. *It* is Me. Don't be afraid."
51 And He climbed up to them into the boat, and the wind stopped blowing. And they were being much more *than* very astounded among themselves and amazed.
52 You see, they did not understand based on the *loaves of* bread; for their heart had become hard as stone.
53 And when they crossed all the way over, they came up to the land of Gennesaret and were anchored *there*.
54 And when they came out of the boat, right away when *people* recognized Him,
55 after they ran around that whole surrounding rural area, they began to be carrying around on the mattresses the people who had *it* bad to where they were hearing that He is there.
56 And wherever He was traveling into villages, or cities, or fields, they were placing the *people* who were weak in the marketplaces and encouraging Him so that they might just touch the fringe of His robe. And however many that touched Him, they were being rescued.

7

1 And the Separatists and some of the *Old Testament* transcribers who came out of Greater Jerusalem were gathered together to Him.
2 And when they saw some of His students eating *loaves of* bread with shared hands, that is with unwashed *hands*, they found fault.
3 You see, the Separatists and all the Jewish *people* do not eat unless they wash the hands with a fist, holding on to the tradition of the older *men*.
4 And *after coming* from *the* marketplace, they do not eat unless they submerge themselves, and there are many other *regulations* that they took in to be holding on to: submersions of cups, pots, copper items, and cots.
5 Following that, the Separatists and the *Old Testament* transcribers ask Him, "Why do Your students not walk around aligned with the tradition of the older *men*, but eat the bread with unwashed hands?"
6 When *Jesus* answered, He said to them, "Isaiah nicely preached about you, the fakers, as it has been written *in Isaiah 29:13*, 'This ethnic group values Me with the lips, but their heart has *itself* far away from Me.
7 They worship Me in a futile way, teaching instructions *that are* people's regulations.'
8 You see, after leaving the demand of God, you hold on to the tradition of the people, submersion of pots and cups. And you are doing many other *things* resembling these types of *things*."
9 And He was saying to them, "You nicely invalidate the demand of God so that you might keep your tradition.
10 You see, Moses said *in Exodus 20:12*, 'Value your father and your mother,' and *in Exodus 21:17*, 'The *person* who says bad things about a father or mother must pass away with death.'

11 But you say if a person says to the father or the mother, '*It is* a Corban (that is *Hebrew for* a contribution), whatever should have benefited you from me,'
12 you even leave him to no longer do anything for his father or his mother,
13 nullifying the message of God with your tradition that you gave out. And you are doing many *things* resembling these types of *things*."
14 And after He called for all the crowd, He was saying to them, "Listen to Me everyone, and understand.
15 There is nothing outside of the person, traveling into him, that is able to make him shared, but the *things* traveling out from him, these are the *things* that make the person shared.
16 If someone has ears to be listening, he must listen."
17 And when He went into a house away from the crowd, his students were asking Him about the illustration.
18 And He says to them, "Are you also clueless like this? Aren't you aware that everything on the outside traveling into the person is not able to make him shared
19 because it is not traveling into his heart, but into the belly? And it travels out into the sewer, cleaning all the food."
20 He was saying, "The *thing* traveling out of the person, that *thing* makes the person shared.
21 You see, the ponderings, the bad *ones*, travel out from *the* inside, from the heart of the people. Cheatings on a spouse, sexual sins, murders,
22 thefts, desires for more, evils, deception, indulgent activity, an evil eye, an insult, pride, distraction:
23 all these evil *things* travel out from *the* inside and make the person shared."
24 And when He got up from there, He went off into the adjoining borders of Tyre and Sidon. And when He went into the house, He was not wanting anyone to know. And He was not able to be unnoticed.
25 You see, after a woman heard about Him (whose little daughter of hers had a spirit that was not clean), when she came, she got down facing His feet.
26 The woman was Greek, a Syrian-Phoenician by birth. And she was asking Him that He would throw the lesser deity out of her daughter.
27 But Jesus said to her, "First, leave the children to be full. You see, it is not nice to take the bread of the children and throw *it* to the puppies."
28 But the *woman* answered and says to Him, "Yes, Master, you see, even the puppies beneath the table eat from the crumbs of the young children."
29 And He said to her, "Because of this answer, make *your* way back; the lesser deity has come out of your daughter."
30 And when she went off to her house, she found that the lesser deity had come out and that the daughter had been thrown on the cot.
31 And again when He came out from the borders of Tyre and Sidon, He went to the Sea of Galilee up in *the* middle of the borders of Decapolis.
32 And they bring to Him a hearing-impaired tongue-tied *man* and encourage Him that He might place *His* hand on him.
33 And after He took him off away from the crowd by Himself, He put his fingers into his ears, and after He spit, He touched his tongue.

34 And when He looked up into the sky, He groaned and says to him, "Ephphatha," that is *Aramaic for*, "Open completely."
35 And right away the hearing of his ears was completely opened, the restraint of his tongue was released, and he was speaking correctly.
36 And He warned them that they should tell *it* to no one, but as much as He was warning them, instead they were speaking publicly much more.
37 And they were being impressed even much more, saying, "He has done everything nicely. He makes both the hearing-impaired *people* to be hearing, and the nonspeaking to be speaking."

8

1 In those days, as *the* crowd is very big and *people* do not have what they will eat, after calling for His students, Jesus says to them,
2 "I have sympathy on the crowd because already for three days they are still staying with Me and they do not have what they will eat.
3 And if I dismiss them with nothing to eat to their house, they will be exhausted on the road. You see, some of them have arrived from a distance."
4 And His students responded to Him, "Where will anyone be able *to get loaves of* bread from to make these *people* full here on an uninhabited place?"
5 And He was asking them, "How many *loaves of* bread do you have?" The *students* said, "Seven."
6 And He passed the order on to the crowd to settle down on the ground. And when He took the seven *loaves of* bread, after He was thankful, He split *them* and was giving *them* to His students so that they might place *them* beside *them*. And they placed *them* beside the crowd.
7 And they had a few small fish. And after He conferred a blessing, He said to also place them beside *them*.
8 They ate and were full. And they picked up leftovers of pieces, seven big baskets.
9 The *people* eating were as *if it were* four thousand. And He dismissed them.
10 And right away after climbing on board into the boat with His students, He went to the parts of Dalmanutha.
11 And the Separatists came out and began to together be posing questions to Him, looking for an indicator from the side of Him out from the sky, trying to cause trouble with Him.
12 And after groaning deeply to His spirit, He says, "Why is this generation searching for an indicator? Amen, I tell you, if an indicator will be given to this generation, *may I be punished*."
13 And after leaving them, when He again climbed on board into the boat, He went off to the other side.
14 And the students forgot to take *loaves of* bread, and except for one *loaf of* bread they did not have *any* with them in the boat.
15 And He was warning them, saying, "See. Look out for the yeast of the Separatists and the yeast of Herod."
16 And they were pondering to each other saying that they did not have *loaves of* bread.

17 And when Jesus knows *it*, He says to them, "Why are you pondering that you do not have *loaves of* bread? Are you not yet aware, nor understand? Do you still have your heart that has become hard as stone?
18 Having eyes, do you not see? And having ears, do you not hear? And do you not remember?
19 When I split the five *loaves of* bread for the five thousand, how many full baskets of pieces did you pick up?" They say to Him, "Twelve."
20 "When *I split* the seven for the four thousand, how many full big baskets of pieces did you pick up?" The *students* say, "Seven."
21 And He was saying to them, "How do you not understand?"
22 And He is coming into Bethsaida. And they bring a blind *man* to Him and encourage Him so that He might touch him.
23 And when He latched on to the hand of the blind *man*, He led him outside of the village. And after He spit into his eyes, when He placed the hands on him, He was asking him if he sees anything.
24 And when he looked up, he was saying, "I see the people as trees walking around."
25 After that, again He placed the hands on his eyes and made him look up. And he was reestablished and was seeing absolutely all far away *things* clearly.
26 And He sent him out to his house, saying, "Don't go into the village, nor tell *it* to anyone in the village."
27 And Jesus and His students went out to the villages of Caesarea of Philip, and on the road He was asking His students, saying to them, "Who do the people say for Me to be?"
28 The *students* answered, "John the Submerger; and others, Elijah; but others, one of the preachers."
29 And He says to them, "But you, who do you say for Me to be?" When Peter answers, he says to Him, "You are the Anointed King."
30 And He shushed them so that they may tell no one about Him.
31 And He began to be teaching them that it is necessary for the Son of the Person to suffer many *things*, to be rejected from the older *men*, head priests, and *Old Testament* transcribers, to be killed, and to get up after three days.
32 And He was speaking the message with a clear public statement. And after Peter took Him aside, he began to be telling Him to stop.
33 But when *Jesus* turned around and saw His students, He told Peter to stop, saying, "Make *your* way back behind Me, opponent, because you do not focus on the *things* of God, but on the *things* of the people."
34 And when He called for the crowd together with His students, He said to them, "Anyone who wants to come behind Me, he must flatly deny himself, pick up his cross, and follow Me.
35 You see, whoever wants to rescue his soul will lose it, but whoever loses his soul on account of Me and the good news, this *person* will rescue it.
36 You see, what will it benefit a person if he will gain the whole world and sustain loss to his soul?
37 You see, what will a person give in exchange for his soul?
38 You see, whoever is ashamed of Me and My messages in this generation, the cheating and sinful *one*, the Son of the Person will also be ashamed of him

when He comes in the magnificence of His Father with the angels, the sacred *ones*."

1 And He was saying to them, "Amen, I tell you that some of the *people* who have stood here are some who will not in any way taste death until they see the monarchy of God that has come in ability."
2 And after six days Jesus takes along Peter, James, and John and brings them up into a high mountain alone by themselves. And He was transformed in front of them.
3 And His clothes became very sparkling white as snow, such as a laundry on the earth is not able to whiten.
4 And Elijah was seen together with Moses by them, and they were *there* speaking together with Jesus.
5 And when Peter responds, he says to Jesus, "Rabbi, it is nice for us to be here. And we should make three tents: one for You, one for Moses, and one for Elijah."
6 You see, he did not know how he should speak; for they were frightened.
7 And there became a cloud, its shadow falling on them, and a voice happened from the cloud, saying, "This is My Son, the loved *One*. Listen to Him."
8 And all of a sudden when they looked around, they did not see anyone anymore but only Jesus with them.
9 As they walked down out of the mountain, He warned them that they should not describe what they saw to anyone except after the Son of the Person gets up from *the* dead.
10 And they took hold of the message together posing questions to themselves, what is the "to get up from *the* dead" *thing*?
11 And they were asking Him, saying, "*Why* do the *Old Testament* transcribers say that it is necessary for Elijah to come first."
12 When *Jesus* answered, He said to them, "When Elijah certainly comes first, he reestablishes everything. And how has it been written on the Son of the Person that He will suffer many *things* and be treated as a nobody?
13 But I tell you that even Elijah has come, and they did to him as much as they wanted, just as it has been written on him."
14 And when He came to the students, He saw a big crowd around them, and *Old Testament* transcribers together posing questions to them.
15 And right away when the entire crowd saw Him, it was puzzled, and, running up, they were greeting Him.
16 And He asked the *Old Testament* transcribers, "What questions are you together posing to them?"
17 And when one *man* from the crowd answered, He said, "Teacher, I brought my son to You, who has a nonspeaking spirit.
18 And whenever it takes him down, it rips him, he foams at the mouth, he grits his teeth, and he is shriveled up. And I said to Your students that they should throw it out, and they didn't have *the* strength."
19 When *Jesus* responds to them, He says, "O untrusting generation, until when will I be facing you? Until when will I tolerate you? Bring him to Me."

20 And they brought him to Him, and when he saw Him, right away the spirit sent him into convulsions. And after he fell on the ground, he was rolling around, foaming at the mouth.
21 And He asked his father, "How much time is it *that* it has happened to him as this?" The father said, "Since childhood.
22 And many times it also threw him into fire and into water so that it might ruin him. But if you are able *to do* something, help us after having sympathy on us."
23 Jesus said to him, "The *thing is* whether you are able to trust. All things *are* possible to the *person* who trusts."
24 And right away, after the father of the young child yelled, he was saying with tears, "I trust, Master. Help my lack of trust."
25 When Jesus saw that a crowd is running together up to *them*, He stopped the spirit, the *one* that was not clean, saying to him, "The spirit, the nonspeaking and hearing-impaired *one*, I give the directive to you, come out of him, and don't go into him anymore."
26 And after it yelled and sent him into many convulsions, it came out, and he became as if *he were* a dead *man* in such a way for many to be saying that he died.
27 But when Jesus took hold of him by the hand, He got him up, and he stood up.
28 And when He went into a house, His students were asking Him by themselves, "*Why* weren't we able to throw it out?"
29 And He said to them, "This kind is not able to go out in any way except in prayer and a time of going without food."
30 And when they went out from there, they were traveling along through Galilee, and He was not wanting that anyone should know.
31 You see, He was teaching His students and telling them, "The Son of the Person is turned over to people's hands. And they will kill him, and when He is dead, on the third day, He will be gotten up."
32 The *students* were unaware of the statement and were afraid to ask Him.
33 And He went into Capernaum. And when He became in the house, He was asking them, "What were you pondering to each other on the road?"
34 But the *students* were keeping silent. You see, they had a discussion toward each other on the road *about* who *is* greater.
35 And when He was seated, He hollered for the Twelve. And He says to them, "If anyone wants to be first, he will be last of all and servant of all."
36 And when He took a young child, He set him in *the* middle of them. And after He took him in His arms, He said to them,
37 "Whoever accepts one of these types of young children based on My name accepts Me, and whoever accepts Me does not accept Me but the *One* who sent Me out *on a mission*."
38 John answered Him, saying, "Teacher, we saw someone throwing lesser deities out in Your name who is not following us, and we hindered him because he is not following us."

39 But Jesus said, "Don't hinder him. You see, there is no one who will do an ability based on My name and will be able to quickly say bad things about Me;
40 for *a person* who is not against us is over with us.
41 You see, whoever gives you a cup of water to drink in My name because you are *the* Anointed King's, amen, I tell you that he will not in any way lose his pay.
42 And whoever causes one of these little *ones* to stumble, the *ones* trusting in Me, it is nice for him instead if a stone belonging to a mill is laid around his neck and he has been thrown into the sea.
43 And if your hand causes you to stumble, chop it off. Is it nice for you to go into the life physically wounded, or having the two hands to go off into the Hinnom Valley into the fire, the unextinguished *fire*?
44 Where their maggot does not pass away and the fire is not extinguished.
45 And if your foot causes you to stumble, chop it off. Is it nice for you to go into the life crippled, or having the two feet to be thrown into the Hinnom Valley into the fire, the unextinguished *fire*?
46 Where their maggot does not pass away and the fire is not extinguished.
47 And if your eye causes you to stumble, throw it out. Is it nice for you to go into the monarchy of God one-eyed, or having two eyes to be thrown into the Hinnom Valley of the fire?
48 Where their maggot does not pass away and the fire is not extinguished.
49 You see, everyone will be salted with fire, and every sacrifice will be salted with salt.
50 The salt *is* nice, but if the salt became not salty, what will you season it with? Have salt among yourselves, and be peaceful among each other.

10

1 And when He got up from there, He went to the borders of Judea across to the other side of the Jordan *River*. And crowds again traveled together to Him, and as He had been accustomed to, He was teaching them again.
2 And when the Separatists came forward, they asked Him if it is allowed for a husband to dismiss a wife, trying to cause trouble with Him.
3 When *Jesus* answered, He said to them, "What did Moses demand to you?"
4 The *Separatists* said, "Moses gave permission to write a scroll of divorce and to dismiss."
5 And when Jesus responded, He said to them, "Toward your hardheartedness He wrote you this demand.
6 But from *the* beginning of creation, God made them male and female.
7 On account of this, a person will leave his father and mother down *there* and be stuck like glue to his wife.
8 And the two will be in one physical body. In such a way, they are no longer two, but one physical body.
9 So what God strapped together, a person must not separate."
10 And in the house again, His students asked Him about the same *thing*.
11 And He says to them, "Whoever dismisses his wife and marries another is cheating on her.

12 And if a wife dismisses her husband and is married to another, she is cheating on *her* husband."
13 And they were bringing young children to Him so that He might touch them, but the students were stopping the *ones* bringing *them*.
14 When Jesus saw *it*, He was frustrated and said to them, "Leave the young children to be coming to Me, and don't hinder them. You see, the monarchy of God is *made up* of these types of *children*.
15 Amen, I tell you, whoever does not accept the monarchy of God as a young child will not in any way go into it."
16 And after He took them in His arms, placing *His* hands on them, He was conferring a blessing *on them*.
17 And as He was traveling out to a road, after one *person* ran up and kneeled to Him, he was asking Him, "Good Teacher, what will I do so that I might inherit life that spans *all* time?"
18 Jesus said to him, "Why are you calling Me good? No one *is* good except One, God.
19 You know the demands: you will not cheat on *your* spouse, you will not murder, you will not steal, you will not lie when you are a witness, you will not rob, you must value your father and mother."
20 When the *person* answered, He said to Him, "Teacher, all these *things* I observed from my youth."
21 When Jesus looked at him, He loved him and said to him, "One *thing* is lacking for you. Make *your* way back. Sell as much as you have, give to the poor (and you will have a stockpile of treasure in heaven), and come here; follow Me after you pick up the cross."
22 After being disappointed over the answer, the *person* went away sad. You see, he was *a person* who had many properties.
23 And after Jesus looks around, He says to His students, "How hard *it* will *be for* the *people* who have the stacks of money *as they* go into the monarchy of God."
24 The students were perplexed over His messages. When Jesus responds again, He says to them, "Children, how hard it is for the people who have been confident based on the stacks of money to go into the monarchy of God!
25 It is easier for a camel to go through the eye of the needle than for a wealthy *man* to go into the monarchy of God."
26 The *students* were being stunned much more, saying to themselves, "And who is able to be rescued?"
27 When Jesus looks at them, He says, "Beside people *it is* impossible, but not beside God. You see, all *things* are possible beside God."
28 And Peter began to be saying to Him, "Look, we left everything and followed You."
29 When Jesus answered, He said, "Amen, I tell you, there is no one who left a house, or brothers, or sisters, or a father, or a mother, or a wife, or children, or fields on account of Me and the good news,
30 except he will receive a hundred times *as much* now in this time (houses, brothers, sisters, mothers, children, and fields) with persecutions and in the span of time, the coming *one*, life that spans *all* time.

31 Many *who are* first will be last, and the last first."
32 They were on the road walking up to Jerusalem, Jesus was going ahead of them, they were perplexed, and as they followed, they were afraid. And when He took the Twelve alongside of *Him* again, He began to be telling them the *things* that were going to be transpiring with Him.
33 "Look, I am walking up to Jerusalem, and the Son of the Person will be turned over to the head priests and the *Old Testament* transcribers. And they will find Him guilty with death and turn Him over to the non-Jews.
34 And they will mock Him, whip Him, spit at Him, kill Him, and on the third day, He will be gotten up."
35 And James and John (the sons of Zebedee) are traveling to Him, saying, "Teacher, we want that whatever we will ask, You will do for us."
36 But *Jesus* said to them, "What do you want Me to do for you?"
37 The *brothers* said to Him, "Give us so that we might be seated, one at *places to the* right of You and one at *places to the* left of You in Your magnificence."
38 Jesus said to them, "You do not realize what you are asking for. Are you able to drink the cup that I am drinking and to be submerged in the submersion that I am submerged in?"
39 The *brothers* said to Him, "We are able." But Jesus said to them, "The cup that I drink, you will certainly drink, and the submersion that I am submerged in, you will be submerged in,
40 but the *right* to be seated at *places to the* right of Me and at *places to the* left of Me is not Mine to give. But *it is* for the *people* it has been readied for."
41 And when the ten heard, they began to be getting frustrated about James and John.
42 When Jesus calls for them, He says to them, "You realize that the *people* who seem to be heading the non-Jews act like masters over them and their great *people* put themselves in authority over them.
43 This is not how it will be among you. But whoever wants to become great among you will be your servant.
44 And whoever of you wants to become first will be everyone's slave.
45 You see, the Son of the Person also did not come to be served, but to serve and to give His soul *as* a payment for the release of many."
46 And they are coming into Jericho. And as He, His students, and an adequate crowd traveled out from Jericho, a son of Timaeus, blind Bartimaeus, was sitting along the road begging.
47 And when he hears that it is Jesus, the Nazarene, he began to be yelling and to be saying, "The Son of David, Jesus, show me forgiving kindness."
48 And many were shushing him so that he would be silent, but the *beggar* was yelling much more, "Son of David, show me forgiving kindness."
49 And when Jesus stood *still*, He said to holler for him. And they are hollering for the blind *man*, saying to him, "Be courageous. Get up. He is hollering for you."
50 After throwing off his robe, when the *man* stood up, he went to Jesus.
51 And when Jesus responded, He says to him, "What do you want *that* I would do for you?" The blind *man* said to Him, "Rabboni *(Great Rabbi)*, that I might see again."

52 Jesus said to him, "Make *your* way back. Your trust has rescued you." And right away he saw again and was following Jesus on the road.

11

1 And when they are near to Jerusalem, to Bethphage and Bethany, toward the Mountain of the Olives, He sends two of His students out *on a mission*.
2 And He says to them, "Make *your* way back into the village, the *one* directly facing you, and right away as you travel into it, you will find a foal that has been tied up on which not one person has been seated. After releasing it, lead *it here*.
3 And if anyone says to you, 'Why are you doing this?' say, 'The Master has a need for it, and right away He will send it back here.'"
4 They went off and found the foal that had been tied to the door outside on the road around *the village*. And they are releasing it.
5 And some of the *people* that had stood there were saying to them, "What are you doing releasing the foal?"
6 The *students* said to them just as Jesus demanded, and they left them.
7 And they led the foal to Jesus, they threw their robes on it, and He sat on it.
8 Many spread out their robes in the road. Others were chopping vegetation from the trees and spreading *it* in the road.
9 And the *people* going ahead and the *people* following were yelling, saying, "Hosanna *(Hebrew for 'O, rescue us')*. The *One* coming in *the* Master's name that has been conferred with blessings,
10 the coming monarchy in *the* name of *the* Master of our father David that has been conferred with blessings, hosanna in the highest."
11 And Jesus went into Jerusalem and onto the temple grounds. And after He looked around at everything, since it was already the evening hour, He went out to Bethany with the Twelve.
12 And the next day when they went out from Bethany, He was hungry.
13 And when He saw a fig tree at a distance that had leaves, He went, if maybe He will find something in it. And when He came up to it, He found nothing except leaves. You see, it was not *the* right time for figs.
14 And when Jesus responded, He said to it, "No one will eat fruit from you anymore for the span of time." And His students were listening.
15 And they are going into Jerusalem. And when Jesus went onto the temple grounds, He began to be throwing out the *people* selling and buying on the temple grounds. And He turned over the tables of the currency exchangers and the benches of the *people* selling the doves.
16 And He was not leaving so that no one would carry a container through the temple grounds.
17 And He was teaching, saying to them, "Has it not been written *in Isaiah 56:7*, 'My house will be called a house of prayer for all the nations?' But you have made it a cave of bandits."
18 And the *Old Testament* transcribers and the head priests heard and were looking for how they might ruin Him. You see, they feared Him because the entire crowd was being impressed based on His teaching.
19 And when it became evening, He was traveling outside of the city.

20 And as they were traveling along in *the* morning, they saw the fig tree that had shriveled up from *its* roots.
21 And when Peter was reminded again, he says to Him, "Rabbi, look, the fig tree that you put a curse on has shriveled up."
22 And when Jesus responds, He says to them, "Have a trust of God.
23 You see, amen, I tell you that whoever might say to this mountain, 'Be picked up and thrown into the sea,' and in his heart does not consider *it* to be wrong, but trusts that what he says is happening, it will *belong* to him, whatever he said.
24 Because of this, I tell you, everything, however many *things* that you ask for as you pray, trust that you are receiving *them*, and it will *belong* to you.
25 And whenever you stand praying, forgive (if you have anything against anyone) so that your Father, the *One* in the heavens, also might forgive you of your infractions.
26 But if you do not forgive, neither will your Father, the *One* in the heavens, forgive your infractions."
27 And they come again into Jerusalem. And as He is walking around on the temple grounds, the head priests, the *Old Testament* transcribers, and the older *men* come to Him.
28 And they say to Him, "In what kind of authority do You do these *things*, and who gave You this authority so that You may do these *things*?"
29 When Jesus answered, He said to them, "I will also ask you one saying. Also answer Me, and I will state to you in what kind of authority I do these *things*.
30 The submersion of John, was it from heaven or from people? Answer Me."
31 And they were considering *it* to themselves, saying, "If we say 'from heaven', He will state, 'So why didn't you trust him?'
32 But if we say 'from people'" — they feared the ethnic group (you see, absolutely everyone was holding that John really was a preacher).
33 And when they answer Jesus, they say, "We do not know." And when Jesus answers, He says to them, "Neither am I telling you in what kind of authority I do these *things*."

12

1 And He began to be talking to them in illustrations. "A person planted a vineyard, put a barrier wall around it, dug a trough beneath *the grape smashing area*, built a tower, gave it out to farmers, and left the area.
2 And he sent a slave out *on a mission* to the farmers at the right time so that he might receive out of the fruit of the vineyard from the side of the farmers.
3 After the *farmers* took him, they beat *him* and sent *him* out empty.
4 And again he sent another slave out *on a mission* to them. And after throwing stones, they hit that *slave* in the head and sent *him* off having been abused.
5 And again he sent another out, and they killed that *one*. And *there were* many others, *some* the *ones* that they beat, *others* the *ones* that they killed.
6 So still having one son, his loved *son*, he also sent him out to them last, saying, 'They will be embarrassed around my son.'

7 But those farmers said to themselves, 'This is the inheritor. Come on. We should kill him, and the inheritance will be ours.'
8 And after taking him, they killed *him* and threw *him* outside of the vineyard.
9 So what will the master of the vineyard do? He will come, ruin the farmers, and give the vineyard to others.
10 Didn't you even read this *Old Testament* writing, *Psalm 118:22–23*? 'A stone that the *people* who are building rejected, this became for a corner's head.
11 This happened from the side of *the* Master, and it is amazing in our eyes.'"
12 And they were looking to take Him into custody. And they feared the crowd. You see, they knew that He said the illustration to them. And after leaving Him, they went away.
13 And they are sending some of the Separatists and the Herod Supporters out to Him so that they might catch Him in an answer.
14 When they come, they say to Him, "Teacher, we realize that You are valid, and there is no concern in You about anyone. You see, You do not look into people's appearance, but based on truth You teach the way of God. Is it allowed to give an enrollment *tax* to Caesar or not?
15 Should we give or not give?" But *Jesus*, realizing their faked behavior, said to them, "Why are you trying to cause trouble with Me? Bring Me a denarius *(a fifty-dollar coin)* so that I might see *it*."
16 The *people* brought *it*, and He says to them, "Whose *is* this image and inscription?" The *people* said to Him, "Caesar's."
17 And when Jesus responded, He said to them, "Give the *things* of Caesar back to Caesar and the *things* of God to God." And they were amazed over Him.
18 And Sadducees are coming to Him (some who say *there is* not to be a return back to life). And they asked Him, saying,
19 "Teacher, Moses wrote to us that if someone's brother dies and leaves a wife down *here*, and he does not leave a child, that his brother should take his wife and bring up from *her* a seed of his brother.
20 So there were seven brothers. And the first took a wife, and as he died, he did not leave a seed.
21 And the second took her, died, and he didn't leave a seed either, and the third similarly.
22 And the seven *brothers* took her and did not leave a seed. Last of all, the wife also died.
23 So in the return back to life, whenever they come back to life, whose wife will she be of them? You see, the seven had her *as* a wife."
24 And when Jesus answered, He said to them, "Aren't you misled because of this: not realizing the *Old Testament* writings, nor the ability of God?
25 You see, whenever they come back to life from *the* dead, they are neither marrying nor being given away in marriage, but they are as the angels in the heavens.
26 But about the dead that they are gotten up, didn't you read in Moses' scroll *in Exodus 3:6 and 18* on the bush, how God said to him, saying, 'I *am* the God of Abraham, the God of Isaac, and the God of Jacob?'

27 He is not a God of dead *people*, but a God of living. So you are misled in many *things*."
28 And when one of the *Old Testament* transcribers came forward after he listened to them as they were together posing questions, when he realized that He answered them nicely, he asked Him, "Which is *the* first demand of all?"
29 Jesus answered him, "First of all of the demands, 'Listen, Israel, *the* Master, our God, is One Master.
30 And you will love *the* Master, your God, from your whole heart, from your whole soul, from your whole mind, and from your whole strength.' This *is the* first demand.
31 And *the* second *is* like this, 'You will love the *person* near you as yourself.' There is no other demand greater than these."
32 And the *Old Testament* transcriber said to Him, "Teacher, You said nicely based on truth because God is one, and there is not another, other than Him.
33 And the "to be loving Him from the whole heart, from the whole understanding, from the whole soul, and from the whole strength" *thing*, and the "to be loving the *person* nearby as oneself" *thing* is more than all the entirely burned offerings and the sacrifices."
34 And when Jesus saw him, that he answered thoughtfully, He said to him, "You are not a long way away from the monarchy of God." And no one was daring to ask Him *anything* anymore.
35 And when Jesus responded, He was saying as He taught on the temple grounds, "How do the *Old Testament* transcribers say that the Anointed King is a son of David?
36 You see, David himself said in the Spirit, the Sacred *Spirit, in Psalm 110:1*, 'The Master said to my Master: sit down at *places to the* right of Me until I put Your enemies *as* a footrest of Your feet.'
37 So David himself calls Him Master. And where is He a son of him from?" And the big crowd was gladly listening to Him.
38 And He was saying to them in His teaching, "Look out for the *Old Testament* transcribers, the *ones* who want to be walking around in long robes, *who want* greetings in the marketplaces,
39 front benches in the synagogues, and front reclining places in the feasts,
40 the *ones* eating up the houses of the widows and praying long *prayers* for a sham. These *people* will receive much more judgment."
41 And when Jesus was seated directly facing the treasury vault, He was watching how the crowd throws copper *coins* into the treasury vault. And many wealthy *people* were throwing *in* much.
42 And when one poor widow came, she threw *in* two tiny coins that are a quadrans (*fifty cents*).
43 And after He calls for His students, He says to them, "Amen, I tell you that this widow, the poor *one*, has thrown *in* more than all the *people* who threw into the treasury vault.
44 You see, everyone threw *in* from what they had left over, but she, from her deficit, threw *in* everything, as much as she had, her whole livelihood."

13

1 And as He is traveling out of the temple grounds, one of His students says to Him, "Teacher, look! What stones! And what buildings!"

2 And when Jesus answered, He said to him, "Do you see these large buildings? A stone will not in any way be left on a stone that will not in any way be torn down."

3 And as He sat in the Mountain of the Olives directly facing the temple grounds, Peter, James, John, and Andrew were asking Him by themselves,

4 "Tell us when these *things* will be, and what the indicator *is* whenever all these *things* are going to be completely finished."

5 When Jesus answered them, He began to be saying, "See *that* no one misleads you.

6 You see, many will come based on My name, saying, 'I am *Him*,' and they will mislead many.

7 Whenever you hear wars and much talk about wars, do not be alarmed. You see, it is necessary *for them* to happen, but *it is* not the conclusion yet.

8 You see, a nation will rise up on a nation and a monarchy on a monarchy. And there will be earthquakes throughout places, and there will be famines and agitations. These *are the* beginnings of pains.

9 You must look out for yourselves. You see, they will turn you in to councils. And in synagogues you will be beaten. And you will be led before leaders and kings on account of Me for a witness to them.

10 And first, it is necessary for the good news to be spoken publicly to all the nations.

11 And whenever they lead you, turning *you* in, do not worry beforehand what you will speak or even be concerned about *it*, but whatever is given to you in that hour, this speak. You see, you are not the *ones* speaking, but the Spirit, the Sacred *Spirit, is speaking*.

12 A brother will turn a brother in for death; and a father, a child. And children will stand up on parents and put them to death.

13 And you will be *people* that are hated by everyone because of My name, but the *person* who persists *to do what is right* to *the* conclusion, this *person* will be rescued.

14 Whenever you see the disgusting thing of the uninhabitedness, the *thing* stated by Daniel, the preacher, *in Daniel 11:31 and 12:11*, that he has stood where it is not necessary (the *person* reading *this* must be aware), at that time the *people* in Judea must escape into the mountains.

15 The *person* on the top of a house must not climb down into the house, nor go in to take anything from his house.

16 And the *person* that is in the field must not return back to the *things left* behind to take his robe.

17 What a tragedy *it will be* to the *women* having *a baby* in *their* womb and the *women* nursing in those days.

18 Be praying so that your escape will not happen during a storm.

19 You see, those days will be this type of hard times, such as has not happened from *the* beginning of *the* creation (that God created) until the present and will not in any way happen.

20 And if *the* Master did not halt the days, every physical body would not be rescued, but because of the *people* who chose *Him, the people* whom He chose, He halted the days.
21 And at that time, if someone says to you, 'Look, the Anointed King *is* here, or look there,' do not trust *it*.
22 You see, counterfeit anointed kings and counterfeit preachers will get up and give indicators and incredible things, with the *intent* to be misleading away *from God*, if possible, even the *people* who chose *God*.
23 You must look out. See, I have stated all *things* to you beforehand.
24 But in those days after those hard times, the sun will be made dark, the moon will not give its glow,
25 there will be the stars of the sky that fall out, and the abilities, the *ones* in the heavens, will be disturbed.
26 And then they will see the Son of the Person coming in clouds with much ability and magnificence.
27 And then He will send out His angels, and He will bring the *people* who chose Him together in one place from the four winds *(compass directions)*, out of *one* edge of *the* earth to *the other* edge of heaven.
28 Learn the illustration from the fig tree. Whenever its branch already becomes tender and it sprouts the leaves out, you know that the summer is near.
29 In this way also, whenever you see these *things* happening, know that it is near, at *the* door.
30 Amen, I tell you that this generation will not in any way pass up to *the point* that all these *things* happen.
31 The sky and the earth will pass, but My messages will not in any way pass.
32 About that day and hour, no one knows except the Father, not the angels, the *ones* in heaven, nor the Son.
33 Look out! Don't go to sleep! And pray! You see, you do not realize when the appointed time is.
34 As a person out of town, who left his house and gave the authority to his slaves and to each his *own* work, and to the doorkeeper he demanded that he should stay awake,
35 so stay awake. You see, you do not realize when the master of the house is coming: evening, or middle of the night, or at rooster-crowing time *(3:00-6:00 a.m.)*, or in *the* morning.
36 When he comes unexpectedly, he will not find you sleeping, will he?
37 What I say to you, I say to everyone, stay awake."

14

1 After two days, it was the Passover and the Yeast-free *Loaves Festival*. And the head priests and the *Old Testament* transcribers were looking for how, when they take Him into custody using deception, they may kill *Him*.
2 But they were saying, "Not in the festival so that there will not be a riot of the group."
3 And as He was in Bethany in the house of Simon (the skin-diseased *man*), as He was lounging, a woman came having an alabaster jar of very expensive

authentic Spikenard perfume. And after she crushed the alabaster jar, she spilled *it* down on His head.
4 There were some who were frustrated to themselves and saying, "Why has this ruining of the perfume happened?
5 You see, this was able to be put up for sale for over three hundred denarii ($15,000) and to be given to the poor." And they were being stern with her.
6 But Jesus said, "Leave her *alone*. Why are you bothering her? She worked nice work for Me.
7 You see, you always have the poor with you. And whenever you want you are able to make them well, but Me you do not always have.
8 She did what she had. She took *it* beforehand to perfume My body for the embalming.
9 Amen, I tell you, whenever this good news is spoken publicly in the whole world, what she did also will be spoken for a reminder of her."
10 And Judas, the *one* from Kerioth, one of the Twelve, went off to the head priests so that he might turn Him in to them.
11 When the *head priests* heard *it*, they were happy and promised to give him silver. And he was looking for how he might turn Him in at easy times.
12 And for the first day of the Yeast-free *Loaves Festival* (when they were sacrificing the Passover *lamb*), His students say to Him, "Where do You want *that* after going off we might get *things* ready so that you might eat the Passover *meal*?"
13 And He sends two of His students out and says to them, "Make *your* way back into the city, and a person will meet you hauling a clay pitcher of water. Follow him.
14 And wherever he goes in, tell the homeowner, 'The teacher says, "Where is the guest room where I might eat the Passover *meal* with My students?"'
15 And he will show you a large room above the ground floor that has been set up, *that is* ready. Get ready for us there."
16 And His students went out, went into the city, and found *it* just as He told them. And they got the Passover *meal* ready.
17 And when it became evening, He came with the Twelve.
18 And as they reclined and ate, Jesus said, "Amen, I tell you that one from among you will turn Me in, the *one* eating with Me."
19 The *students* began to be sad and to be saying to Him, one by one, "It isn't me, *is it*?" And another, "It isn't me, *is it*?"
20 When *Jesus* answered, He said to them, "*It is* one from the Twelve, the *one* dipping with Me into the bowl.
21 The Son of the Person certainly makes *His* way back just as it has been written about Him, but what a tragedy *it is* to that person by whom the Son of the Person is turned in. It was nice for him if that person was not born."
22 And as they were eating, when Jesus took bread, after conferring a blessing *on it*, He split *it*, gave *it* to them, and said, "Take *it*. Eat *it*. This is My body."
23 And when He took the cup, after being thankful, He gave *it* to them, and everyone drank from it.

24 And He said to them, "This is My blood, the *blood* of the new deal, the *blood* that is spilled out concerning many.
25 Amen, I tell you that I will not in any way drink anymore from the produce of the vine until that day, whenever I drink it new in the monarchy of God."
26 And after they sang praise songs, they went out to the Mountain of the Olives.
27 And Jesus says to them, "You will all stumble in Me in this night because it has been written *in Zechariah 13:7*, 'I will forcibly strike the shepherd, and the sheep will be dispersed.'
28 But after the *time* for Me to be gotten up, I will go ahead of you into Galilee."
29 Peter was declaring to Him, "Even if everyone will stumble, still I *will* not."
30 And Jesus says to him, "Amen, I tell you that today, in this night, before *the time* for a rooster to even crow twice, three times you will flatly deny Me."
31 But *Peter* was saying much more instead, "If it is necessary for me to die together with You, I will not in any way flatly deny You." They all were also saying similarly.
32 And they come into a parcel of land, the name of which *is* Gethsemane, and He says to His students, "Be seated here while I will pray."
33 And He takes Peter, James, and John along with Himself. And He began to be puzzled and heavyhearted.
34 And He says to them, "My soul is overcome with sadness to death. Stay here and stay awake."
35 And when He went on ahead a little, He got down on the ground and was praying that, if it is possible, the hour might pass away from Him.
36 And He was saying, "Daddy, the Father, all *things are* possible for You. Carry this cup off away from Me. But not what I want. But what You *want*."
37 And He comes and finds them sleeping. And He says to Peter, "Simon, are you sleeping? Didn't you have strength to stay awake one hour?
38 Stay awake and pray that you will not get into trouble. The spirit certainly *is* eager, but the physical body *is* weak."
39 And when He went off again, He prayed when He said the same words.
40 And when He returned, He found them sleeping again. You see, their eyes had been weighted down, and they did not know how to respond to Him.
41 And He comes the third *time* and says to them, "Sleep the rest *of the time*, and relax. He has *it* all. The hour came. Look, the Son of the Person is turned over into the hands of the sinful *people*.
42 Get up. We should lead. Look, the *person* turning Me in has come near."
43 And right away as He is still speaking, Judas, who is one of the Twelve, shows up, and with him a big crowd with daggers and wooden clubs from the side of the head priests, the *Old Testament* transcribers, and the older *men*.
44 The *one* turning Him in had given them a signal, saying, "Whoever I am friendly with is Him. Take Him into custody and lead *Him* away securely."
45 And after he came, right away when he came forward to Him, he says, "Rabbi, Rabbi," and was very friendly to Him.
46 The *men* put their hands on Him and took Him into custody.

47 A certain one of the *students* that had stood nearby, after pulling out the dagger, forcibly struck the slave of the head priest and took off his ear lobe.
48 And when Jesus responded, He said to them, "As on a bandit, you came out with daggers and wooden clubs to apprehend Me.
49 Daily I was facing you on the temple grounds teaching, and you did not take Me into custody. But *this is happening* so that the *Old Testament* writings might be accomplished."
50 And after leaving Him, everyone escaped.
51 And one certain young lad was following Him, having put a linen cloth around himself over *his* naked *body*, and the young men take hold of him.
52 But the *young man*, after leaving the linen cloth down *there*, escaped away from them naked.
53 And they led Jesus away to the head priest. And all the head priests, the older *men*, and the *Old Testament* transcribers are coming together to Him.
54 And Peter followed Him off at a distance until inside, in the courtyard of the head priest. And he was sitting together with the underlings and warming himself facing the light.
55 The head priests and the whole council were looking for a witness account against Jesus for the "to put Him to death" *part*, and they were not finding *one*.
56 You see, many were lying when they were witnessing against Him, and the witness accounts were not equal.
57 And when some stood up, they were lying when they were witnessing against Him, saying,
58 "We listened to Him saying, 'I will tear down this temple, the handmade *one*, and through three days I will build another made without hands.'"
59 And like this neither was their witness account equal.
60 And after the head priest stood up in the middle, he asked Jesus, saying, "Are You not answering anything? What are these *people* witnessing against You?"
61 But *Jesus* was being silent and answered nothing. Again the head priest was asking Him. And he says to Him, "Are You the Anointed King, the Son of the *One* conferred with blessings?"
62 Jesus said, "I am, and you will see the Son of the Person sitting at *places to the* right of the Ability and coming with the clouds of the sky."
63 After the head priest rips apart his long undershirt, he says, "What? Do we still have a need for witnesses?
64 You listened to the insult. How does it appear to you?" The *men* all found Him guilty to be eligible to be sentenced to death.
65 And some began to be spitting at Him, to be blindfolding His face, to be slugging Him, and to be saying to Him, "Prophesy." And the underlings were taking Him with slaps.
66 And as Peter is in the courtyard below, one of the servant girls of the head priest comes.
67 And when she sees Peter warming himself, after looking at him, she says, "You also were with the Nazarene, Jesus."
68 But *Peter* denied *it*, saying, "I do not know nor am even aware of what you are saying." And he went outside into the front yard, and a rooster crowed.

69 And when the servant girl saw him again, she began to be saying to the *people* who had stood nearby, "This *person* is from them."
70 But *Peter* again was denying *it*. And again after a little while, the *people* who had stood nearby were saying to Peter, "You are truly from them. You see, you are even a Galilean, and your speech is similar."
71 But *Peter* began to be vowing under the penalty of being doomed and to be guaranteeing, "I do not know this person whom you are saying."
72 And from a second *time* a rooster crowed, and Peter was reminded again of the statement that Jesus said to him, "Before *the time* for a rooster to crow twice, three times you will flatly deny Me." And when he threw up *Jesus' statement in his mind*, he was crying.

15

1 And right away, after the head priests took up the counsel in *the* morning with the older *men*, *Old Testament* transcribers, and the whole council, after tying Jesus up, they carried *Him* off and turned *Him* over to Pilate.
2 And Pilate asked Him, "Are you the king of the Jewish *people*?" When *Jesus* answered, He said to him, "You are saying *it*."
3 And the head priests were leveling many complaints against Him. But He answered nothing.
4 Pilate asked Him again, saying, "Are you answering nothing? Look at how many complaints they are witnessing against you."
5 But Jesus did not answer anything anymore in such a way for Pilate to be amazed.
6 At each festival he dismissed one prisoner to them, even whom they were requesting.
7 There was the *prisoner* called Barabbas who had been locked up with the disruptors, some who had committed murder in the disruption.
8 And after the crowd shouted out, it began to be asking *him to do* just as he was always doing for them.
9 Pilate answered them, saying, "Do you want *that* I dismiss the King of the Jewish *people* to you?"
10 You see, he knew that because of envy the head priests had turned Him in.
11 But the head priests shook up the crowd so that he might dismiss Barabbas to them instead.
12 When Pilate responded again, he said to them, "So what do you want *that* I should do *to Him* whom you say *to be* King of the Jewish *people*?"
13 The *people* again yelled, "Nail Him to a cross."
14 But Pilate was saying to them, "You see, what bad *thing* did He do?" But the *people* yelled much more, "Nail Him to a cross."
15 Pilate, intending to do the adequate *thing* for the crowd, dismissed Barabbas to them and turned Jesus over, after he thrashed *Him* with a whip, so that He might be nailed to a cross.
16 The soldiers led Him away inside the courtyard that is a Roman palace. And they call the whole regiment together,
17 put purple on Him, and place a thorny award wreath around Him that they wove together.

18 And they began to be greeting Him, "Happy to meet You, King of the Jewish *people*."
19 And they were hitting His head with a stick, spitting at Him, and, as they placed *their* knees *on the ground*, bowing down to Him.
20 And when they mocked Him, they stripped the purple off Him and put the clothes, *His* own *clothes*, on Him. And they lead Him out so that they might nail Him to a cross.
21 And they sequester help from someone passing by, Simon, a Cyrenian, coming from a field, the father of Alexander and Rufus, so that he might pick up His cross.
22 And they carry Him on to *the* place, Golgotha, that is translated *from Aramaic as* "Place of a Skull."
23 And they were giving Him wine that had been mixed with myrrh to drink, but *Jesus* did not take *it*.
24 And after they nailed Him to a cross, they were dividing up His clothes throwing dice on them *to determine* who would take what.
25 It was *the* third hour *(9:00 a.m.)*, and they nailed Him to a cross.
26 And the inscription of His accusation that had been inscribed was, "The King of the Jewish *people*."
27 And together with Him, they nail two bandits on crosses, one at *places to the* right and one at *places to the* left of Him.
28 And the *Old Testament* writing was accomplished, the *one* that says *in Isaiah 53:12*, "And he was considered with criminals."
29 And the *people* traveling by were insulting Him, shaking their heads and saying, "Ah, the *One* who tears the temple down and in three days builds *it*.
30 Rescue yourself and climb down off the cross."
31 Likewise, the head priests mocking to each other with the *Old Testament* transcribers were also saying, "Others He rescued, Himself He is not able to rescue.
32 The Anointed King, the king of Israel, must climb down now off the cross so that we might see and trust." Also the *bandits* that had been nailed on crosses together with Him were criticizing Him.
33 When *the* sixth hour *(noon)* happened, darkness happened on the whole earth until *the* ninth hour *(3:00 p.m.)*.
34 And at the hour, the ninth *one (3:00 p.m.)*, Jesus shouted with a loud voice, saying, "Eloi, Eloi, lamma sabachthani," that is translated *from Aramaic as* "My God, My God, why did You leave Me down in *here*?"
35 And when some of the *people* that had stood nearby heard *it*, they were saying, "Look, He is hollering for Elijah."
36 When one *person* ran, filled a sponge full of sour wine, and put *it* around a stick, he was giving Him a drink, saying, "Leave *Him alone*, we will see if Elijah comes to take Him down."
37 But when Jesus left, He breathed out a loud sound.
38 And the curtain of the temple was torn in two from top to bottom.
39 When the centurion *(Latin for lieutenant)*, the *one* who had stood nearby facing Him, saw that after yelling He breathed out *His last breath* like this, he said, "This person truly was a son of a god."

40 There were also women watching off at a distance, among whom were also Mary (the Magdalene), Mary (the mother of little James and Joses), Salome,
41 (who also, when He was in Galilee, were following Him and serving Him), and many other *women* who walked up together with Him to Jerusalem.
42 And when it already became evening, since it was a preparation *day* (that is, *the* pre-Sabbath day),
43 Joseph (the *one* from Arimathaea, a reputable advisor who himself also was awaiting the monarchy of God) came, who was daring. He went in to Pilate and asked for the body of Jesus.
44 Pilate was amazed if He had already died. And after he called for the centurion, he asked him if He died a long time ago.
45 And when he knew *it* from the centurion, he gave the body to Joseph for free.
46 And after purchasing linen cloth and taking Him down, he wrapped *Him* in the linen cloth and laid Him down in a burial vault that was *one* that had been chiseled from rock. And he rolled a stone over the door of the burial vault.
47 Mary (the Magdalene) and Mary (*mother* of Joses) were watching where He is placed.

16

1 And after the Sabbath had elapsed, Mary (the Magdalene), Mary (the *mother* of James), and Salome bought fragrant resins so that when they go, they might dab *them* on Him.
2 And very much in *the* morning on the *Day* 1 after the Sabbaths, they come up to the burial vault when the sun comes up.
3 And they were saying to themselves, "Who will roll the stone away for us from the door of the burial vault?"
4 And when they look up, they see that the stone has been rolled away. You see, it was terribly large.
5 And when they went into the burial vault, they saw a young lad sitting in the *parts to the* right, around whom a long white robe had been put, and they were puzzled.
6 The *young lad* says to them, "Don't be puzzled. You are looking for Jesus, the Nazarene, the *One* who has been nailed to a cross. He was gotten up. He is not here. Look, the place where they put Him.
7 But make *your* way back. Tell His students and Peter, 'He is going ahead of you into Galilee. There you will see Him, just as He told you.'"
8 And after they went out quickly, they escaped away from the burial vault. Trembling and astonishment had *a hold on* them, and they did not say anything to anyone; for they were afraid.
9 After He came back to life in *the* morning on *the* first *day* after *the* Sabbath, He appeared first to Mary (the Magdalene), out of whom He had thrown out seven lesser deities.
10 After that *woman* traveled *off*, she reported *it* to the grieving and crying *people* who became with Him.
11 And when those *people* hear that He is alive and was seen by her, they did not trust.

12 After these *things*, as two from among them were walking around, He was shown in a different form as they traveled to a field.
13 And after those *two* went away, they reported *it* to the rest. Neither did they trust those *two*.
14 Later as they reclined, He was shown to the eleven. And He criticized their lack of trust and hardheartedness because they did not trust with the *ones* who viewed Him who had been gotten up.
15 And He said to them, "When you travel into absolutely all of the world, speak publicly about the good news to every created being.
16 The *person* who trusts and is submerged will be rescued, but the *person* who does not trust will be found guilty.
17 These indicators will follow alongside the *people* who trust in My name: they will throw lesser deities out, they will speak with new languages,
18 they will pick up snakes, and if they drink something deadly, it will not in any way hurt them. They will place hands on sick *people*, and they will have *it* nicely."
19 So certainly the Master, after the *time for Him* to speak to them, was taken up into the sky and was seated at *places to the* right of God.
20 When those *people* went out, they spoke publicly everywhere as the Master worked together *with them* and authenticated the message through the indicators following closely behind. Amen.

Luke

1

1 Since for sure it is true that many attempted to again arrange a description about the items that have been well-established among us,

2 just as the eyewitnesses from *the* beginning turned *it* over to us after they also became underlings of the message,

3 it also seemed *good* to me, who has followed alongside everything from the top, to accurately write to you in order, most powerful Theophilus,

4 so that you might correctly understand about the certainty of the messages that echoed down to you.

5 It happened in the days of Herod, the king of Judea; a certain priest with *the* name Zacharias from *the* Abijah priest rotation and his wife from the daughters of Aaron (and her name *was* Elisabeth),

6 both were doing what was right in the sight of God, traveling in all the demands and right paths of the Master, faultless *people*.

7 And there was no child with them due to the fact that Elisabeth was infertile and both were *people* who *were advanced in years* (*literally*, had walked on in their days).

8 It happened during the *time* for him to be performing the priest duties in the arrangement of his priest rotation directly in front of God

9 aligned with the custom of the office of the priesthood; he took his turn of the "to burn incense after going into the temple of the Master" *kind*.

10 And there was the entire large number of the group praying outside at the hour of the incense.

11 An angel of *the* Master was seen by him that had stood at *places to the* right of the incense altar.

12 And Zacharias was uneasy when he saw *him* and fear fell on him.

13 The angel said to him, "Don't be afraid, Zacharias, because your plea was listened to, your wife Elisabeth will give birth to a son for you, and you will call his name John.

14 And happiness and excitement will be with you. And many will be happy based on his birth.

15 You see, he will be great in the sight of the Master. And he should not in any way drink wine and alcoholic beverages, he will be filled with *the* Sacred Spirit (still from his mother's belly),

16 he will turn many of the sons of Israel back to *the* Master, their God,

17 and he will go on ahead in His sight in Elijah's spirit and ability to turn back hearts of fathers to children, and *to turn back* unbelieving *people* in *the* focus of *people* who do what is right, to get an ethnic group ready that has been constructed for *the* Master."

18 And Zacharias said to the angel, "How will I know this *is true*? You see, I am an old man, and my wife *is a woman* that *is advanced in years* (*literally*, has walked on in her days)."

19 And when the angel answered, he said to him, "I am Gabriel, the *one* who has stood by in the sight of God. And I was sent out *on a mission* to speak to you and to share the good news of these *things* with you.
20 And look, you will be silent and not able to speak till *the* day that these *things* happen for *the times* that you did not trust my words, some that will be accomplished in their appointed time."
21 And the group was expecting Zacharias and were amazed during the *time* for him to be taking a long time in the temple.
22 When he came out, he was not able to speak to them. And they correctly understood that he has seen a sighting in the temple. And he was gesturing during the whole time to them and through *it all* staying speech-impaired.
23 And it happened as *soon as* the days of his public service culminated; he went off to his house.
24 After these days, Elisabeth, his wife, conceived and hid herself from everyone for five months, saying,
25 "Because this is what the Master has done to me in days that He looked on *me* to take away the disdain of me among people."
26 During the month, the sixth, the angel Gabriel was sent out from God *on a mission* to a city of Galilee to which *belongs the* name Nazareth
27 to a virgin that had been promised to a man to whom *belongs the* name Joseph from David's house. And the name of the virgin *was* Mary.
28 And when the angel went into *a house* to her, he said, "Be happy, *you* who have been shown generosity. The Master *is* with you, you who have been conferred with blessing among women."
29 When the *virgin* saw *him*, she was very upset over his message and was pondering what kind of greeting this might be.
30 And the angel said to her, "Don't be afraid, Mary. You see, you found generosity beside God.
31 And look, you will conceive in *your* womb and will deliver a son. And you will call His name Jesus.
32 This *son* will be great and will be called Son of *the* Highest. And *the* Master, God, will give Him the throne of David, His father.
33 And He will be king over the house of Jacob for the spans of time, and of His monarchy there will not be a conclusion."
34 Mary said to the angel, "How will this be since I do not know a man?"
35 And when the angel answered, he said to her, "*The* Sacred Spirit will come on you, and the shadow of *the* ability of *the* Highest will fall on you. For this reason, the sacred *Child* being born from you also will be called Son of God.
36 And look, Elisabeth, your relative, she has also conceived a son in her old age. And this is *the* sixth month for her, the *one* who is called infertile,
37 because every statement beside God will not be impossible."
38 Mary said, "Look, the slave of *the* Master. May it happen to me aligned with your statement." And the angel went away from her.
39 When Mary got up in those days, she traveled to the mountainous *area* in a hurry, into a city of Judah.
40 And she went into Zacharias' house and greeted Elisabeth.

41 And it happened as Elisabeth heard the greeting of Mary; the baby skipped in her belly, and Elisabeth was filled with *the* Sacred Spirit.
42 And she hollered loudly with a loud voice and said, "You (who have been conferred with blessing among women) and the fruit of your belly (that has been conferred with blessing),
43 and where *does* this *come* to me from, that the mother of my Master would come to me?
44 You see, look, as the voice of your greeting became in my ears, the baby skipped with excitement in my belly.
45 And the *woman* who trusted *is* blessed because there will be a completion to the *things* that have been spoken to her from the side of *the* Master."
46 And Mary said, "My soul makes the Master great.
47 And my spirit is excited based on God, my Rescuer,
48 because He took a look at the lowliness of His slave. You see, look, from the present *on* all the generations will consider me to be blessed
49 because the Competent *One* did great *things* for me and His name is sacred.
50 And His forgiving kindness *is* for generations of generations to the *people* who fear Him.
51 He made power with His arm. He dispersed proud *people* with a mind of their heart.
52 He took competent rulers down from thrones and put lowly *people* up high.
53 He filled up *people* who were hungry with good and sent *people* who were wealthy off empty.
54 He assisted His servant boy Israel to be remembered for forgiving kindness,
55 just as He spoke to our fathers (to Abraham and his seed) for the span of time."
56 Mary stayed together with her as if *it were* three months and returned to her house.
57 For Elisabeth, the time of the "for her to deliver" *part* culminated, and she gave birth to a son.
58 And the houses around *there* and her relatives heard that *the* Master was making His forgiving kindness great with her, and they were happy together with her.
59 And it happened during the eighth day; they came to circumcise the young child, and they were calling him based on the name of his father Zacharias.
60 And when his mother responded, she said, "Definitely not, but he will be called John."
61 And they said to her, "There is no one among your relatives who is called by this name."
62 They were gesturing at his father the "what he would want him to be called" *thing*.
63 And after he asked for a writing pad, he wrote, saying, "John is his name." And everyone was amazed.

64 At once his mouth and his tongue were opened, and he was speaking, conferring blessings on God.
65 And fear became on everyone housed around them. And in the whole mountainous *area* of Judea all these statements were spoken in detail.
66 And everyone who heard placed *it* in their heart, saying, "So what kind of young child will this be?" And *the* Master's hand was with him.
67 And Zacharias, his father, was filled with *the* Sacred Spirit and preached, saying,
68 "*The* Master, the God of Israel, *is* conferred with blessings because He kept an eye on and made *the* release payment for His ethnic group.
69 And He raised up a horn of rescue for us in the house of David, His servant boy,
70 just as He spoke through *the* mouth of His preachers, the sacred *ones*, since *the* span of time *began*,
71 a rescue from our enemies and from *the* hand of all the *people* who hate us,
72 to show forgiving kindness with our fathers and to remember His sacred deal,
73 an oath that He guaranteed to Abraham, our father,
74 for the *purpose* to give to us, after we were saved from *the* hand of our enemies, to be ministering to Him fearlessly
75 in holiness and *the* right way in His sight all the days of our life.
76 And you, young child, will be called a preacher of *the* Highest. You see, you will travel ahead before *the* face of *the* Master to get His way ready,
77 for the *purpose* to give information about rescue to His ethnic group in forgiveness of their sins,
78 because of our God's sympathy of forgiving kindness in which a rising from a high position will keep an eye on us
79 to shine on the *people* sitting in darkness and a shadow of death for the *purpose* to direct our feet to a road of peace."
80 The young child was growing and gaining power in *the* spirit. And he was in the backcountry until *the* day of his public showing to Israel.

2

1 It happened in those days; a rule went out from the side of Caesar Augustus to be registering all the civilized world.
2 This registration first happened as Cyrenius was the leader of Syria.
3 And all were traveling to be registered, each to *his* own city.
4 Joseph also walked up out of Galilee from *the* city of Nazareth into Judea into a city of David, a certain *city* that is called Bethlehem, because of the *fact* for him to be from a house and family tree of David,
5 to be registered together with Mary, the woman who had been promised to him, being in the later stages of pregnancy.
6 It happened during the *time* for them to be there; the days of the "for her to deliver" *part* culminated.
7 And she delivered her son, the firstborn, wrapped Him in a strip of cloth, and reclined Him in the feed trough because there was no place for them in the guest room.

8 And shepherds were in the rural area, the same *rural area,* playing the flute in the field and standing guard over their flock *during the* guard shifts of the night.
9 And look, an angel of *the* Master stood over them, and *the* magnificence of *the* Master shined around them. And they feared great fear.
10 And the angel said to them, "Don't be afraid. You see, look, I am sharing the good news with you of great happiness, something that will be for all the ethnic group
11 because there was delivered to you *in birth* today, a rescuer, who is *the* Anointed King, *the* Master, in a city of David.
12 And this *is* the indicator for you. You will find a baby that has been wrapped in a strip of cloth, lying in the feed trough.
13 And unexpectedly there became together with the angel a large number of a heavenly army praising God and saying,
14 "Magnificence in *the* highest *belongs* to God, and on earth peace among people, a good notion."
15 And it happened as *soon as* the angels went away from them into the sky, and the people, the shepherds, said to each other, "We will for sure go through until Bethlehem and see this statement, the *one* that has happened, that the Master made known to us."
16 And they went hurrying. And they looked for and found both Mary and Joseph, and the baby lying in the feed trough.
17 After seeing *them,* they made the statement known throughout *there,* the *one* that was spoken to them about this young child.
18 And all the *people* who heard were amazed about the *things* that were spoken by the shepherds to them.
19 But Mary was preserving all these statements as she deliberated in her heart.
20 And the shepherds returned back elevating *God* to a place of magnificence and praising God based on everything that they heard and saw, just as it was spoken to them.
21 And when eight days culminated of the *requirement* to circumcise the young child, His name was also called Jesus, what *He* was called by the angel before the *time* for Him to be conceived in the belly.
22 And when the days of her cleansing culminated according to the law of Moses, they led Him up into Jerusalem to offer *Him* to the Master
23 (just as it has been written in *the* law of *the* Master *in Exodus 13:2,* "Every male completely opening *the* womb will be called sacred to the Master")
24 and for the *purpose* to give a sacrifice according to what has been stated in *the* law of *the* Master *in Leviticus 12:8,* "a pair of cooing doves or two young chicks of doves."
25 And look, a person was in Jerusalem whose name *was* Simeon. And this person did what is right and *was* devout, awaiting Israel's encouragement. And *the* Sacred Spirit was on him.
26 And it was for him (having been *divinely* notified by the Spirit, the Sacred *Spirit*) to not even see death before he would see the Anointed King of *the* Master.

27 And he went in the Spirit onto the temple grounds even during the *time* for the parents to lead the young child Jesus in for the *purpose* of them to do according to what had been made the custom of the law concerning Him."
28 And he accepted Him into his cradling arms, conferred blessings on God, and said,
29 "Now You are dismissing Your slave, *my* Owner, aligned with Your statement in peace
30 because my eyes saw Your rescue *process*
31 that You got ready right in front of *the* face of all the ethnic groups,
32 a light for uncovering non-Jews and *for the* magnificence of Your ethnic group, Israel."
33 And there was Joseph and His mother being amazed based on the *things* spoken about Him.
34 And Simeon conferred a blessing on them and said to Mary, His mother, "Look, this *child* lies *here* for a fall and return back to life of many *people* in Israel and for an indicator to which opposition is expressed
35 (a sword will also go through your very soul) in order that ponderings from many hearts will be uncovered."
36 And Anna was a female preacher, Phanuel's daughter from Asher's family line. She *was a woman far advanced in years* (*literally*, having walked on in many days) who lived with a husband *for* seven years out from her puberty.
37 And she *was* a widow as *if it were* eighty-four years who was not standing off away from the temple grounds ministering with times of going without food and with pleas, night and day.
38 And when she in the same hour stood over *them*, she was responding and acknowledging the Master and speaking about Him to all of the *people* awaiting *the* release payment in Jerusalem.
39 And as *soon as* they finished absolutely all the *things* according to the law of *the* Master, they returned into Galilee into their city, Nazareth.
40 The young child was growing and gaining power in *the* spirit being filled with insight. And God's generosity was on Him.
41 And His parents were traveling each year to Jerusalem to the Festival of the Passover.
42 And when He became twelve years *old*, after they walked up to Jerusalem aligned with the custom of the festival
43 and completed the days, during the *time* for them to be returning, Jesus, the boy, persisted *to do what is right* in Jerusalem, and Joseph and His mother did not know *it*.
44 When they assumed Him to be among the group *traveling* together on the road, they went a day's trip and were looking up *and down* for Him among the relatives and among the *people they* knew.
45 And when they did not find Him, they returned to Jerusalem looking for Him.
46 And it happened after three days; they found Him on the temple grounds seated in *the* middle of the teachers, listening to them, and asking them *questions*.

47 All the *people* listening to Him were being astounded based on His understanding and responses.
48 And when they saw Him, they were impressed, and His mother said to Him, "Child, why did You do like this to us? Look, Your father and I, being in agony, were looking for You."
49 And He said to them, "Why *is it* that you were looking for Me? Didn't you realize that it is necessary for Me to be among the *things* of My Father?"
50 And they did not understand the statement that He spoke to them.
51 And He walked down with them, went into Nazareth, and was placing Himself under them. And His mother was carefully keeping all these statements in her heart.
52 And Jesus was progressing in insight, in age, and in generosity beside God and people.

3

1 In *the* fifteenth year of the leadership of Tiberius Caesar, as Pontius Pilate was the leader of Judea and Herod was the head of one of *Palestine's* four regions (Galilee), as Philip (his brother) was the head of one of *Palestine's* four regions (the Ituraea and Trachonitis rural area), and Lysanias was the head of one of *Palestine's* four regions (Abilene),
2 on head priests Annas and Caiaphas, a statement of God came on John (Zacharias' son) in the backcountry.
3 And he went into all the rural area surrounding the Jordan *River* speaking publicly about a submersion of a change of ways for forgiveness of sins,
4 as it has been written in a scroll of messages of the preacher Isaiah *in Isaiah 40:3–5*, that says, "A voice shouting in the backcountry, 'Get *the* Master's road ready. Make His paths straight.'
5 Every valley will be filled in, every mountain and hill will be put down low, and it will be the crooked *things* into a straight *road* and the rugged *roads* into smooth roads.
6 And every physical body will see the rescue *process* of God."
7 So he was saying to the crowds traveling out to be submerged by him, "Offspring of poisonous snakes, who put in front of your face to escape away from the punishment that is going *to come*?
8 So produce fruits deserving of the change of ways, and you should not begin to be saying among yourselves, we have a father — Abraham. You see, I tell you that God is able from these stones to raise up children for Abraham.
9 Already even the ax is lying facing the root of the trees. So every tree not producing nice fruit is chopped out and thrown into a fire."
10 And the crowds were asking him, saying, "So what will we do?"
11 When he answers, he says to them, "The *person* who has two long undershirts must give *one* out to the *person* who does not have *one*, and the *person* who has food must do likewise."
12 Tax collectors also went to be submerged, and they said to him, "Teacher, what will we do?"
13 *John* said to them, "You must collect nothing more beyond what has been specifically assigned to you."

14 *Men* serving in the military also were asking him, saying, "And we, what will we do?" And he said to them, "You should shake no one violently, nor make false accusations. And be content with your wages."

15 As the ethnic group was expecting and everyone was pondering in their hearts about John that perhaps he is the Anointed King,

16 John responded to absolutely everyone, saying, "I certainly submerge you in water, but the *One* stronger than I is coming whose strap of His sandals I am not adequate to release. He will submerge you in *the* Sacred Spirit and fire,

17 whose shovel *is* in His hand. And He will completely clear off His processing floor and gather the grain together into His grain bin, but the husks will be burned up with unextinguished fire."

18 So as he was encouraging in many and different *ways*, he certainly was sharing good news with the ethnic group.

19 But Herod, the head of one of *Palestine's* four regions, being reprimanded by him about Herodias (the wife of his brother Philip) and about all the evil *things* that Herod did,

20 added even this on everything, he also shut John up in the jail.

21 It happened during the *time* for absolutely all the group to be submerged, after Jesus also was submerged (and as He was praying), for the sky to be opened

22 and the Spirit, the Sacred *Spirit*, to step down on Him in a bodily, visual image as if *It were* a dove, and a voice to happen from heaven, saying, "You are My Son, the loved *One*. I am delighted with You."

23 And Jesus Himself was as if *He were* thirty years *old* as He began, being (as it was assumed) a son of Joseph, the *son* of Eli,

24 the *son* of Matthat, the *son* of Levi, the *son* of Melchi, the *son* of Janna, the *son* of Joseph,

25 the *son* of Mattathias, the *son* of Amos, the *son* of Nahum, the *son* of Esli, the *son* of Naggai,

26 the *son* of Maath, the *son* of Mattathias, the *son* of Shimei, the *son* of Joseph, the *son* of Judah,

27 the *son* of Joanna, the *son* of Rhesa, the *son* of Zerubbabel, the *son* of Shealtiel, the *son* of Neri,

28 the *son* of Melchi, the *son* of Addi, the *son* of Kosam, the *son* of Elmodam, the *son* of Er,

29 the *son* of Joses, the *son* of Eliezer, the *son* of Jorim, the *son* of Matthat, the *son* of Levi,

30 the *son* of Simeon, the *son* of Judah, the *son* of Joseph, the *son* of Jonan, the *son* of Eliakim,

31 the *son* of Melea, the *son* of Menan, the *son* of Mattatha, the *son* of Nathan, the *son* of David,

32 the *son* of Jesse, the *son* of Obed, the *son* of Boaz, the *son* of Salmon, the *son* of Nahshon,

33 the *son* of Aminadab, the *son* of Aram, the *son* of Hezron, the *son* of Phares, the *son* of Judah,

34 the *son* of Jacob, the *son* of Isaac, the *son* of Abraham, the *son* of Terah, the *son* of Nahor,
35 the *son* of Serug, the *son* of Reu, the *son* of Peleg, the *son* of Eber, the *son* of Shelah,
36 the *son* of Cainan, the *son* of Arphaxad, the *son* of Shem, the *son* of Noah, the *son* of Lamech,
37 the *son* of Methushelah, the *son* of Enoch, the *son* of Jared, the *son* of Mahalaleel, the *son* of Cainan,
38 the *son* of Enos, the *son* of Seth, the *son* of Adam, the *son* of God.

4

1 Jesus, full of *the* Sacred Spirit, returned from the Jordan *River* and was being led in the Spirit into the backcountry
2 forty days as He experienced trouble under the Accuser. And He ate nothing in those days. And later, when they were completely finished, He was hungry.
3 The Accuser said to Him, "If You are a son of God, say to this stone that it should become bread."
4 And Jesus responded to him, saying, "It has been written *in Deuteronomy 8:3*, 'The person will not live on bread alone, but on every statement of God.'"
5 And after the Accuser led Him up into a high mountain, he showed Him all the monarchies of the civilized world in an instant of time.
6 And the Accuser said to Him, "I will give You absolutely all this authority and their magnificence because it has been turned over to me and to whomever I want to give it.
7 So if You bow down in my sight, all *things* will be Yours."
8 And when He responded to him, Jesus said, "Make *your* way back behind Me, Opponent. You see, it has been written *in Deuteronomy 6:13*, 'You will bow down to *the* Master, your God, and minister to Him only.'"
9 And he led Him into Jerusalem, stood Him on the winglet of the temple grounds, and said to Him, "If You are the Son of God, throw Yourself down from here.
10 You see, it has been written *in Psalm 91:11–12*, 'He will demand His angels concerning you for the *purpose* to guard you closely."
11 And they will pick you up on hands so that you will never stub your foot to a stone.'"
12 And when He answered, Jesus said to him, "It has been stated *in Deuteronomy 6:16*, 'You will not try to harass *the* Master, your God.'"
13 And after the Accuser completely finished every trouble, he stood off away from Him till *another* time.
14 And Jesus returned in the ability of the Spirit into Galilee, and news went throughout the whole surrounding rural area about Him.
15 And He was teaching in their synagogues, being elevated to a place of magnificence by everyone.
16 And He went into Nazareth where it was that He had been nurtured, and He went (according to what had been a custom for Him during the day of the Sabbaths) into the synagogue and stood up to read.

17 And a scroll of the preacher Isaiah was given over to Him. And when He unrolled the scroll, He found the place *in Isaiah 61:1-2* where it was that it had been written,
18 "*The* Master's Spirit *is* on Me, on account of which He anointed Me to share good news with poor *people*. He has sent Me out *on a mission* to cure the *people* whose heart has been crushed, to speak publicly to incarcerated people about forgiveness and about sight restoration to blind *people*, to send *people* out in forgiveness who have been shattered,
19 to speak publicly about *the* accepted year of *the* Master."
20 And when He rolled up the scroll, after He gave *it* back to the underling, He was seated. And the eyes of everyone in the synagogue were staring at Him.
21 He began to be saying to them, "Today, this writing has been accomplished in your ears."
22 And all were telling what they witnessed of Him and being amazed based on the messages of the generosity, the *messages* traveling out of His mouth. And they were saying, "Isn't this the son of Joseph?"
23 And He said to them, "By all means, you will state this illustration to Me, 'Doctor, heal yourself. As many *things* as we heard happened in Capernaum, do also here in your hometown.'"
24 He said, "Amen, I tell you that not even one preacher is accepted in his hometown.
25 But based on truth, I tell you, there were many widows in the days of Elijah in Israel when he closed the sky over three years and six months as a large famine happened on the entire earth.
26 And to not even one of them was Elijah sent except to Sarepta of Sidon, toward a woman, a widow.
27 And there were many skin-diseased *people* over *the time* of Elisha, the preacher, in Israel and not even one of them was cleared up except Naaman, the Syrian.
28 And everyone was filled with anger in the synagogue hearing these *things*.
29 And when they stood up, they threw Him outside of the city and led Him up to the overhang of the mountain on which their city had been built for the "to throw Him down the steep slope" *part*.
30 But He, after going through *the* middle of them, was traveling *off*.
31 And He went down to Capernaum, a city of Galilee, and was teaching them on the Sabbaths.
32 And they were being impressed based on His teaching because His message was with authority.
33 And in the synagogue, there was a person who had *the* spirit of a lesser deity that was not clean, and he yelled out with a loud voice,
34 saying, "Ahhhh! What *is there between* us and You, Jesus, Nazarene? Did you come to ruin us? I know who You are, the Sacred *One* of God."
35 And Jesus stopped him, saying, "Be quiet and come out of him." And after the lesser deity tossed him into the middle, he came out from him after not hurting him.

36 And bewilderment happened on everyone, and they were speaking together to each other, saying, "What is this saying? Because with authority and ability He gives directives to the spirits that are not clean, and they come out."
37 And an echo about Him was traveling out into every place of the surrounding rural area.
38 When He got up from the synagogue, He went into the house of Simon. Simon's mother-in-law was being constrained by a large fever, and they asked Him about her.
39 And when He stood over her, He told the fever to stop, and it left her. At once, after standing up, she was serving them.
40 As the sun was setting, everyone, as many as had *people* who were weak with various illnesses led them to Him. *Jesus*, after placing *His* hands on each one of them, healed them.
41 Lesser deities were also coming out of many, yelling and saying, "You are the Anointed King, the Son of God." And shushing *them*, He was not allowing them to be speaking because they knew Him to be the Anointed King.
42 When it became day, after going out, He traveled into an uninhabited place. And the crowds were looking for Him and went until *they found* Him. And they were holding Him up for the *purpose* to not be traveling off from them.
43 *Jesus* said to them, "It is necessary for Me to share the good news of the monarchy of God also with different cities, because I have been sent out *on a mission* for this."
44 And He was speaking publicly in the synagogues of Galilee.

5

1 It happened during the *time* for the crowd to be leaning on Him for the *purpose* to be hearing the message of God; He also had stood along Gennesaret Lake.
2 And He saw two boats that have stood along the lake. The fishermen, after stepping out of them, rinsed off the nets.
3 When He climbed on board into one of the boats that was Simon's, He asked him to take *Him* out a little bit away from the land. And after He was seated, He was teaching the crowds out of the boat.
4 As He stopped speaking, He said to Simon, "Take *us* out into the depth and lower your nets for a catch."
5 And when Simon answered, he said to Him, "Boss, after laboring through the whole night, we took nothing, but based on Your statement, I will lower the net."
6 And when they did this, they closed up a very large number of fish. Their net was being ripped apart.
7 And they motioned to the teammates, the *ones* in the different boat for the *purpose*, after coming, to take *them* in together with them. And they came and filled both of the boats in such a way for them to be sinking.
8 When Simon Peter saw *it*, he got down toward the knees of Jesus, saying, "Go out away from me because I am a sinful man, Master."
9 You see, bewilderment had itself around him and all the *people* together with him over the catch of the fish that they took in together,

10 likewise also, James and John (Zebedee's sons, who were partners with Simon). And Jesus said to Simon, "Don't be afraid. From the present *on*, you will be catching people alive."
11 And after they towed the boats down on the land, after leaving absolutely everything, they followed Him.
12 And it happened during the *time* for Him to be in one of the cities; and look, a man full of a skin disease. And when he saw Jesus, after he got down on *his* face, he pleaded with Him, saying, "Master, if you want to, you are able to clear me up."
13 And when He put out *His* hand, He touched him, saying, "I want *to*. Be cleared up." And right away the skin disease went away from him.
14 And He passed the order on to him to tell no one, but, "When you go away, show yourself to the priest, and offer concerning your cleansing just as Moses instructed for a witness to them."
15 But instead, the message about Him was going through *there*, and big crowds were coming together to be listening and to be healed by Him from their weaknesses.
16 He was slipping away secretly in the uninhabited *places* and praying.
17 And it happened during one of the days; He also was teaching, and Separatists and law teachers were sitting *there* who had come from every village of Galilee and Judea, and Jerusalem. And *the* Master's ability was *there* for the "to cure them" *thing*.
18 And, look, men carrying a person on a cot who had been disabled. And they were looking to carry him in and place *him* in His sight.
19 And when they did not find through which *way* they might carry him in because of the crowd, after climbing up on the top of the house, through the clay tiles they let him down together with the bedding into the middle, in front of Jesus.
20 And when He saw their trust, He said to him, "Sir, your sins have been forgiven you."
21 And the *Old Testament* transcribers and the Separatists began to ponder *it*, saying, "Who is this who is speaking insults? Who is able to forgive sins except God alone?"
22 After Jesus correctly understood their ponderings, when He responded, He said to them, "What are you pondering in your hearts?
23 Which is easier to say, 'Your sins have been forgiven you,' or to say, 'Get up and walk around?'
24 But so that you may realize that the Son of the Person has authority on the earth to be forgiving sins...." He said to the *man* who had been disabled, "I tell you, Get up and pick up your bedding. Travel to your house."
25 And at once, after he got up in their sight, when he picked up what he was laying down on, he went off to his house praising God's magnificence.
26 And astonishment took *hold of* absolutely everyone. And they were praising God's magnificence and were filled with fear, saying, "We saw unusual *things* today."
27 And after these *things*, He went out and viewed a tax collector with *the* name Levi sitting at the tax booth. And He said to him, "Follow Me."

28 And after leaving absolutely everything down *there*, when he got up, he followed Him.
29 And Levi made a large reception for Him in his house. And there was a big crowd of tax collectors and others who were lounging with them.
30 And their *Old Testament* transcribers and the Separatists were grumbling to His students, saying, "Why are you eating and drinking with tax collectors and sinful *people*?"
31 And when Jesus responded, He said to them, "The *people* who are healthy have no need of a doctor, but the *people* who have *it* bad *do*.
32 I have not come to invite *people* who do what is right, but sinful *people*, to a change of ways.
33 The *people* said to Him, "Why do the students of John go without food for frequent *things* and make pleas, likewise also the *students* of the Separatists, but Yours eat and drink?"
34 *Jesus* said to them, "You are not able to make the sons of the bridal room go without food during *the time* that the groom is with them, are you?
35 Days will also come when the groom is taken away from them, then they will go without food in those days."
36 He also was telling an illustration to them, "No one puts a patch of a new robe on a worn out robe, but if *they do*, definitely both the new *robe* will tear, and the patch from the new *robe* will not harmoniously agree with the worn out *robe*.
37 And no one puts young wine into worn out leather bags, but if *they do*, definitely the young wine will rip the leather bags, it will be spilled out, and the leather bags will be ruined.
38 But young wine *is a thing that* must be put into new leather bags, and both are preserved.
39 And no one after drinking worn out wants young right away. You see, he says the worn out is more useful."

1 It happened on *the* second-first Sabbath *after the Passover* for Him to be traveling through the croplands. And His students were pulling off the heads *of grain* and eating, rubbing *them* with the hands.
2 Some of the Separatists said to them, "Why are you doing what is not allowed to do in the Sabbaths?"
3 And when He answered, Jesus said to them, "Didn't you even read this, what David did back when he and the *people* who were with him were hungry?
4 How he went into the house of God, took the *loaves of* bread of the display, ate, and also gave to the *people* with him, *loaves* that no one is allowed to eat except the priests alone?"
5 And He was saying to them, "The Son of the Person is also Master of the Sabbath."
6 It happened on a different Sabbath for Him also to go into the synagogue and to be teaching. And a person was there, and his hand, the right *one*, was dried-up.

7 The *Old Testament* transcribers and the Separatists were watching Him closely *to see* if He will heal on the Sabbath so that they might find a criminal complaint against Him.

8 He realized their ponderings, and He said to the person, the *one* who had the dried-up hand, "Get up and stand in the middle." After he got up, he stood.

9 So Jesus said to them, "I will ask you, What is allowed with the Sabbath? To good or to do bad, to rescue a soul or to ruin *it*?"

10 And after He looked around at them all, He said to the person, "Put out your hand." The *person* did so, and his hand was reestablished healthy as the other.

11 They were filled with insanity and were speaking in detail with each other *about* what they should do to Jesus.

12 It happened in these days; He went out into the mountain to pray. And He was continuing through the night in the prayer of God.

13 And when it became day, He hollered out for His students. And after selecting twelve out of them, whom He also named missionaries,

14 Simon (whom He also named Peter) and Andrew (his brother), James and John, Philip and Bartholomew,

15 Matthew and Thomas, James (the *son* of Alphaeus) and Simon (the *one* who was called Zealot),

16 Judas (James's *brother*) and Judas from Kerioth (who also became a traitor),

17 and after walking down with them, He stood on a level place, also a crowd of His students and a very large number of the ethnic group out of all of Judea, Jerusalem, and the sea coast of Tyre and Sidon, who came to listen to Him and to be cured out of their illnesses.

18 And the *people* crowded by spirits that were not clean were also being healed.

19 And the entire crowd was looking to be touching Him because ability was going out from the side of Him and curing everyone.

20 And when He raised His eyes to His students, He was saying, "*You*, the poor *people, are* blessed because the monarchy of God is yours.

21 *You*, the *people* who are hungry now, *are* blessed because you will be full. *You*, the *people* who are crying now, *are* blessed because you will laugh.

22 You are blessed when the people hate you and when they isolate you, criticize *you*, and throw out your name as evil on account of the Son of the Person.

23 Be happy in that day and skip *for joy*. You see, look, your pay *is* much in heaven; for their fathers were doing to the preachers aligned with these *things*.

24 More importantly, what a tragedy *it is* to you, the wealthy *people*, because you have all of your encouragement.

25 What a tragedy *it is* to you, the *people* who have been filled up, because you will be hungry. What a tragedy *it is* to you, the *people* who are laughing now, because you will grieve and cry.

26 What a tragedy *it is* for you when all of the people talk nicely of you. You see, their fathers were doing to the counterfeit preachers aligned with these *things*.

27 But I tell you, the *ones* who are listening, love your enemies; do nicely to the *people* hating you;
28 confer a blessing on the *people* putting a curse on you, and pray over the *people* being spiteful to you.
29 To the *person* hitting you on the cheek, also provide the other *cheek*. And from the *person* taking your robe, you should also not hinder the long undershirt.
30 To everyone asking you, give, and from the *person* taking, do not ask for your *things* back.
31 And just as you want that the people should do to you, you also must do likewise to them.
32 And if you love the *people* loving you, what kind of generosity is with you? You see, even the sinful *people* love the *people* loving them.
33 And if you do good to the *people* doing good to you, what kind of generosity is with you? You see, even the sinful *people* do the same *thing*.
34 And if you give an interest loan *to the people* from the side of whom you anticipate to receive back, what kind of generosity is with you? You see, even the sinful *people* give an interest loan to sinful *people* so that they might receive the equal *things* back.
35 More importantly, love your enemies, do good, and give an interest loan anticipating nothing back. And your pay will be much, and you will be sons of the Highest because He is kind over the ungenerous and evil *people*.
36 So become compassionate just as your Father also is compassionate.
37 Do not judge, and you will not in any way be judged. Do not find *people* guilty, and you will not in any way be found guilty. Dismiss *people*, and you will be dismissed.
38 Give, and it will be given to you. A nice measurement that has been packed down, that has been shaken together, and that spills out over into your lap will they give. You see, the same measurement that you measure out will be measured back to you."
39 He told them an illustration, "A blind *person* isn't able to be guiding a blind *person*, is he? Won't both fall into a hole?
40 A student is not above his teacher, but everyone who has been trained will be as his teacher.
41 Why do you see the wood chip, the *one* in the eye of your brother, but the log, the *one* in *your* own eye, you do not take a closer look at?
42 Or how are you able to be saying to your brother, 'Brother, leave *it*. I will take out the wood chip, the *one* in your eye,' *you* yourself not seeing the log in your eye? Faker, first take the log out of your eye, and then you will see clearly to take out the wood chip, the *one* in the eye of your brother.
43 You see, a nice tree is not *one* that produces defective fruit, nor a defective tree, *one* that produces nice fruit;
44 for each tree is known from *its* own fruit; for they do not gather up figs from thorns, neither do they pick a cluster of grapes from a bush.
45 The good person from the good stockpile of his heart brings forward the good *thing*, and the evil person from the evil stockpile of his heart brings

forward the evil *thing*. You see, from the excess of the heart, his mouth speaks.
46 Why do you call Me, Master, Master, and do not do *things* that I say?
47 Everyone who comes to Me, who listens to My messages, and who does them, I will put in front of your face whom he is like:
48 he is like a person building a house, who excavated, went deep, and set a foundation on the rock. When a torrential rain happened, the river crashed toward that house and did not have *the* strength to disturb it. You see, *the* foundation had been laid on the rock.
49 But the *person* who listens and does not do, is like a person who built a house on the ground without a foundation, toward which the river crashed, and right away it fell. And the crash of that house became great.

7

1 Since He filled all His statements into the hearing of the group, He went into Capernaum.
2 A certain lieutenant's slave, who had *it* bad, was going to be passing away, who was valued by him.
3 When he heard about Jesus, he sent older *men* of the Jewish *people* out *on a mission* to Him, asking Him *a favor* in order that after coming He would completely rescue his slave.
4 When the *older men* showed up to *where* Jesus *was*, they were encouraging Him aggressively, saying that he is deserving, to whom He will provide this.
5 "You see, he loves our nation, and he built the synagogue himself for us."
6 Jesus was traveling together with them. As He already had *himself* not a long way away from the house, the lieutenant sent friends to Him saying to Him, "Master, don't be irritated. You see, I am not adequate that you would come in under my roof.
7 For this reason, neither did I think that *I* myself deserved to come to You, but say a word, and my servant boy will be cured.
8 You see, I also am a person assigned under an authority having soldiers under me, and I say to this *one*, 'Travel,' and he travels; to another, 'Go,' and he goes; and to my slave, 'Do this,' and he does *it*."
9 When Jesus heard these *things*, it amazed Him. And after turning to the crowd following Him, He said, "I tell you, not even in Israel did I find so much trust."
10 And when the *people* who were sent returned into the house, they found the slave who was weak healthy.
11 And it happened on the *day* afterward; He was traveling into a city called Nain, and an adequate amount of His students and a big crowd were traveling together with Him.
12 As He came near to the gate of the city, and look, *a body* that had died was being carried out to be buried, *the* only biological son to his mother, and she was a widow. And an adequate crowd from the city was together with her.
13 And when the Master saw her, He had sympathy on her and said to her, "Don't cry."
14 And when He came forward, He touched the coffin. The *people* hauling *it* stood *still*, and He said, "Young lad, I tell you, be gotten up."

15 And the dead *son* sat up on his own and began to be speaking. And He gave him to his mother.

16 Fear took *hold of* absolutely everyone, and they were praising God's magnificence, saying, "A great preacher has risen among us," and, "God kept an eye on His ethnic group."

17 And this message went out in all Judea about Him and in all the surrounding rural area.

18 And his students reported about all these *things* to John.

19 And after John called for any two of his students, he sent *them* to Jesus, saying, "Are You the *One* coming, or should we expect another?"

20 When the men showed up to *where* He *was*, they said, "John the Submerger has sent us out *on a mission* to You, saying, 'Are You the *One* coming, or should we expect another?'"

21 In the same hour, He healed many out of illnesses, ailments, and evil spirits. And as an act of generosity, He gave many blind *people* the *ability* to be seeing.

22 And when Jesus answered, He said to them, "After you travel, report to John *things* that you saw and heard, that blind *people* see again, crippled *people* walk around, skin-diseased *people* are cleared up, hearing-impaired *people* hear, dead *people* are gotten up, good news is shared with poor *people*.

23 And whoever does not stumble in Me is blessed."

24 When the announcers from John went away, He began to be saying to the crowds about John, "What have you gone out into the backcountry to view? A stick disturbed by wind?

25 But what have you gone out to see? A person who has been decked out in elegant clothes? Look, the *people* being in magnificent clothing and with lavish things are in the kingly *places*.

26 But what have you gone out to see? A preacher? Yes, I tell you, and much more than a preacher.

27 It is this *person* about whom it has been written *in Malachi 3:1*, 'Look, I am sending My announcer out *on a mission* before Your face who will construct Your road in front of You.'

28 You see, I tell you, among *people* born of women there is not even one preacher greater than John the Submerger. But the littler *person* in the monarchy of God is greater than him.

29 And all the ethnic group and the tax collectors who heard, made God right when they were submerged with the submersion of John.

30 But the Separatists and the law *experts* invalidated the intention of God for them when they were not submerged by him."

31 The Master said, "So what will I liken the people of this generation to? And what are they like?

32 They are like the young children sitting in a marketplace. And they holler to each other and say, 'We played the flute for you, and you did not dance. We wailed to you, and you did not cry.'

33 You see, John the Submerger has come, neither eating bread, nor drinking wine, and you say, 'He has a lesser deity.'

34 The Son of the Person has come eating and drinking, and you say, 'Look, a person, an excessive eater and a wine drinker, a friend of tax collectors and sinful *people*.'
35 And the insight was made right from all her children.
36 A certain *one* of the Separatists was asking Him that He might eat with him. And when He went into the house of the Separatist, He was reclined.
37 And, look, a woman in the city, someone who was sinful. When she correctly understood that He was reclining in the house of the Separatist, after she retrieved an alabaster jar of perfume
38 and stood behind beside His feet crying, she began to be dampening His feet with the tears, with the hairs of her head she was wiping *them* dry, she was being very friendly to His feet, and she was dabbing the perfume *on them*.
39 When the Separatist, the *one* who invited Him, saw *it*, he talked in himself, saying "This *Person*, if He was a preacher, should know who and what kind the woman *is*, someone who is touching Him, because she is sinful."
40 And when Jesus responded, He said to him, "Simon, I have something to say to you." *Simon* declares, "Teacher, say *it*."
41 "There were two owers of debt to a certain lender. The one was owing five hundred denarii *($25,000)*, the different *one* fifty *($2,500)*.
42 Since they did not have *a way* to give *it* back, in an act of generosity, he forgave both *of them*. So tell *Me* which of them will love him more?"
43 When Simon answered, he said, "I presume that *it would be the one* to whom he forgave more." *Jesus* said to him, "You judged correctly."
44 And after He turned toward the woman, He was declaring to Simon, "Do you see this woman? I came into your house. You did not give water on My feet, but she with the tears dampened My feet and with the hairs of her head wiped *them* dry.
45 A friendly gesture you did not give Me, but she, from *the moment* that I came in, did not take a break *from* being very friendly to My feet.
46 Olive oil you did not dab on My head, but she dabbed perfume on My feet.
47 Thanks to which, I tell you, her sins, the many *sins*, have been forgiven; that *is why* she loved much. But a *person* to whom little is forgiven loves little."
48 He said to her, "Your sins have been forgiven."
49 And the *people* reclining together with *Him* began to be saying among themselves, "Who is this that even forgives sins?"
50 He said to the woman, "Your trust has rescued you, travel into peace."

8

1 And it happened in the *time*; He also was making His way through each city and village in order speaking publicly and sharing the good news of the monarchy of God, and the Twelve *were* together with Him
2 and some women who had been healed from evil spirits and weaknesses: Mary (the *one* called "Magdalene" from whom seven lesser deities had come out),

3 Joanna (a wife of Chuza, Herod's administrator), Susanna, and many different *ones*, some who were serving Him out of the *things* that are with them.

4 As a big crowd was coming together and the *people* were also traveling to Him from each city, He said through an illustration:

5 "The *one* who seeds went out for the *purpose* to seed his batch of seeds. And during the *time* for him to be seeding, certainly *there was a seed* that fell along the road and was trampled on. And the winged birds of the sky ate it.

6 And a different *seed* fell on the rock. And after sprouting up, it shriveled up because of the *fact for it* to not be having moisture.

7 And a different *seed* fell in *the* middle of the thorns. And after sprouting up together with *it*, the thorns choked it out.

8 And a different *seed* fell on the soil, the good *soil*. And after sprouting up, it produced a hundred times *the* fruit." As He said these *things*, He was hollering, "The *person* who has ears to be listening must listen."

9 His students were asking Him, saying, "What is this illustration?"

10 *Jesus* said, "To you it has been given to know the secrets of the monarchy of God, but to the rest *I speak* in illustrations so that as they see, they may not see, and as they hear, they may not understand.

11 This is the illustration. The batch of seeds is the message of God.

12 The *people* along the road are the *people* who hear. After that, the Accuser comes and takes the message away from their heart so that they might not trust *and* be rescued.

13 The *people* on the rock *are people* who when they hear, with happiness they accept the message. And these do not have root, who trust for a time, and in a time of trouble, they stand off away.

14 The *seed* that fell into the thorns, these are the *people* who heard, and traveling under worries, wealth, and pleasures of the life, they come together, are choked off, and do not bring *it* to the conclusion.

15 The *seed* in the nice soil, these *people* are any who heard the message with a nice and good heart. They hold steady and produce fruit with persistence.

16 No one, after lighting a lamp, covers it up with a container or puts *it* beneath a cot, but he puts *it* on a lampstand so that the *people* traveling in may see the light.

17 You see, *a thing* is not hidden that will not become shown, nor hidden away that will not be known and come into a shown *place*.

18 So look out how you hear. You see, whoever has, it will be given to him, and whoever does not have, even what he seems to be having will be taken away from him."

19 His mother and brothers showed up to *where* He *was*, and they were not able to meet up with Him because of the crowd.

20 And it was reported to Him *by people* who said, "Your mother and Your brothers have been standing outside wanting to see You."

21 When *Jesus* responded, He said to them, "My mother and My brothers are these *people*, the *ones* listening to the message of God and doing it."

22 And it happened during one of the days; He and His students also climbed on board into a boat, He said to them, "We will go across to the other side of the lake," and they took off.
23 As they sailed, He fell asleep. And a blast of wind stepped down onto the lake, and they were being filled totally up and were in danger.
24 After coming forward, they woke Him up, saying, "Boss, boss, we are being ruined." When *Jesus* got up, He shushed the wind and the wave of water, they stopped, and there became a calm.
25 He said to them, "Where is your trust?" After being afraid, they were amazed, saying to each other, "So who is this *Person*? Because even to the winds and the water He gives the directive and they obey Him."
26 And they sailed down to the rural area of the Gadarenes, a certain *area* that is on the opposite side of Galilee.
27 When He came out on the land, a certain man came to meet Him from the city who had lesser deities for an adequate amount of time. And he was not dressing himself in clothes and not staying in a house, but among the graves.
28 When he saw Jesus and after yelling out, he fell toward Him and said with a loud voice, "What *is there between* me and You, Jesus, Son of God, the Highest *God*? I plead with You, You should not torture me."
29 You see, He passed the order on to the spirit, the *spirit* that was not clean, to come out from the person; for many times it had seized him, and he was being detained with a chain and foot shackles as he was guarded. And ripping the restraints apart, he was being driven by the lesser deity into the backcountry.
30 Jesus asked him, saying, "What is a name for you?" He said, "Legion" *(the Latin word for regiment)*, because many lesser deities went into him.
31 And they were encouraging Him so that He would not give the directive to them to go off into the bottomless area.
32 A herd of an adequate amount of hogs was there grazing on the mountain. And they were encouraging Him that He would give them permission to go into those *hogs*, and He gave them permission.
33 When the lesser deities came out from the person, they went into the hogs, the herd rushed down the steep slope into the lake, and they were choked out.
34 When the *people* grazing *them* saw what had happened, they escaped. And after going away, they reported *it* in the city and in the fields.
35 They came out to see what had happened. And they came to Jesus and found the person (from whom the lesser deities had come out) sitting (having been clothed) and properly focused beside the feet of Jesus, and they were afraid.
36 The *people* who also saw *it* reported to them how the *man* who had lesser deities was rescued.
37 And absolutely all the large number from the surrounding rural area of the Gadarenes asked Him to go away from them because they were being constrained by great fear. After He climbed on board into the boat, He returned.
38 The man from whom the lesser deities had come out was pleading with Him to be together with Him, but Jesus dismissed him, saying,

39 "Return to your house, and describe as many *things* as God did for you." And he went off speaking publicly throughout the whole city about as many *things* as Jesus did for him.

40 It happened in the *time* for Jesus to return; the crowd gladly accepted Him. You see, everyone was expecting Him.

41 And look, a man (to whom *belonged the* name Jairus) came, and he was a head of the synagogue. And after he got down beside Jesus' feet, he was encouraging Him to come into his house

42 because *the* only biological daughter to him was as *if she were* twelve years *old* and she was dying. But during the *time* for Him to be making *His* way back, the crowds were coming together and choking Him.

43 And a woman who was in a discharge of blood for twelve years (someone who consumed almost all of *her* livelihood on doctors) did not have *the* strength to be healed by any *of them*.

44 When she came up from behind, she touched the fringe of His robe, and at once the discharge of her blood stood *still*.

45 And Jesus said, "Who *is* the *one* who touched Me?" As everyone was denying *it*, Peter and the *people* with him said, "Boss, the crowds are constraining and shoving You, and You are saying, 'Who *is* the *one* that touched Me?'"

46 Jesus said, "Someone touched Me. You see, I knew *the* ability that went out from Me."

47 When the woman saw that she was not unnoticed, she came trembling and got down close to Him. She reported to Him in the sight of the entire group *the* reason why she touched Him and how she was cured at once.

48 *Jesus* said to her, "Daughter, be courageous. Your trust has rescued you. Travel into peace."

49 As He is still speaking, someone comes from the side of the synagogue's head ruler, saying, "Your daughter has died. Do not irritate the teacher."

50 When Jesus heard *it*, He responded to him, saying, "Don't be afraid. Just trust, and she will be rescued."

51 When He came into the house, He did not leave anyone to come in together with Him except Peter, John, James, the father of the girl, and the mother.

52 Everyone was crying and beating their chests in grief for her. *Jesus* said, "Don't cry. She did not die, but she is sleeping."

53 And they were laughing at Him, having seen that she died.

54 After He sent everyone outside and took hold of her hand, He hollered, saying, "The girl, get up."

55 And her spirit turned around, she got up at once, and He specifically arranged for her to be given *something* to eat.

56 And her parents were astounded. *Jesus* passed the order on to them to tell no one what had happened.

1 After calling His twelve students together, He gave them ability and authority over all the lesser deities and to be healing illnesses.

2 And He sent them out *on a mission* to be speaking publicly about the monarchy of God and to be curing the *people* who are weak.
3 And He said to them, "Take nothing for the road: not staffs, nor a tote bag, nor bread, nor silver, nor to be having two long undershirts apiece.
4 And whichever house you go into, stay there, and go out from there.
5 And however many that do not accept you, as you go out from that city, also knock off the dust from your feet for a witness over them."
6 As they went out, they were going throughout the villages sharing good news and healing everywhere.
7 Herod, the head of one of *Palestine's* four regions, heard all the *things* that were happening under Him, and he was dumbfounded because of the *fact for it* to be said by some that John had been gotten up from *the* dead,
8 by some that Elijah appeared, *by* others that one preacher of the original *ones* came back to life.
9 And Herod said, "I beheaded John, but who is this *Person* about whom I am hearing these types of *things*?" And he was looking for *an opportunity* to see Him.
10 And when the missionaries returned, they described to Him as many *things* as they did. And after taking them along, He slipped away secretly by Himself to an uninhabited place of a city called Bethsaida.
11 When the crowds knew *it*, they followed Him. And after accepting them, He was speaking about the monarchy of God to them. And the *people* who had a need of healing, He was curing.
12 The day began to be declining. When the Twelve came forward, they said to Him, "Dismiss the crowd so that after going off into the circling villages and the fields, they might settle down *for the night* and find groceries because here we are in an uninhabited place."
13 He said to them, "You must give them *something* to eat." The *students* said, "Not more than five *loaves of* bread and two fish are with us, unless after traveling, we buy food for this entire group."
14 You see, there were as if *it were* five thousand men. He said to His students, "Have them recline in reclining groups of fifty apiece."
15 And this is what they did. And absolutely everyone reclined.
16 After taking the five *loaves of* bread and the two fish, when He looked up into the sky, He conferred a blessing on them, split *them* up, and was giving *them* to the students to be placed beside the crowd.
17 And they ate, and everyone was full. And what was left over with them of *the* pieces was picked up, twelve baskets.
18 And it happened during the *time* for Him to be praying in *places where they were* alone (the students were together with Him); He also asked them, saying, "Who do the crowds say for Me to be?"
19 When the *students* answered, they said, "John the Submerger, others Elijah, others that a certain preacher of the original *ones* came back to life."
20 He said to them, "You, who do you say for Me to be?" When Peter answered, he said, "The Anointed King of God."
21 After *Jesus* shushed *him*, He passed the order on to them to tell this to no one,

22 after saying, "It is necessary for the Son of the Person to suffer many *things*, to be rejected out from the older *men*, head priests, and *Old Testament* transcribers, to be killed, and to be gotten up the third day."
23 He was saying to everyone, "If anyone wants to come behind Me, he must flatly deny himself, pick up his cross daily, and follow Me.
24 You see, whoever wants to rescue his soul will lose it, but whoever loses his soul on account of Me, this *person* will rescue it;
25 for how is a person benefited when he gains the whole world, but loses himself or sustains loss?
26 You see, whoever is ashamed of Me and My messages, this *person* the Son of the Person will be ashamed of when He comes in the magnificence of Him, the Father, and the sacred angels.
27 I tell you, there are truly some of the *people* who have been standing here who will not in any way taste death until they see the monarchy of God."
28 It happened as if *it were* eight days after these words; after taking Peter, James, and John along, He also climbed up into the mountain to pray.
29 And during the *time* for Him to be praying, the visual image of His face became different, and His clothing, dazzling white.
30 And, look, two men were speaking together with Him, certain *men* who were Moses and Elijah,
31 who, after being seen in magnificence, they were talking about His exit that was going to be accomplished in Jerusalem.
32 Peter and the *two* together with him had been weighted down with slumber. When they completely woke up, they saw His magnificence and the two men, the *men* that had been standing together with Him.
33 And it happened during the *time* for them to be completely separated away from Him; Peter said to Jesus, "Boss, it is nice for us to be here. And we should make three tents, one to You, one to Moses, and one to Elijah," not realizing what he is saying.
34 As he said these *things*, there became a cloud, and its shadow fell on them. They were afraid during the *time* for those *students* to go into the cloud.
35 And there became a voice from the cloud, saying, "This is My Son, the loved *Son*. Listen to Him."
36 And during the *time* for the voice to happen, Jesus was found alone. And they kept quiet and did not report anything to anyone in those days of what they had seen.
37 It happened on the day afterward; after they came down out of the mountain, a big crowd met together with Him.
38 And, look, a man out of the crowd shouted out, saying, "Teacher, I am pleading with You, take a look at my son because he is *the* only biological *son* to me.
39 And look, a spirit takes him, he unexpectedly yells, it sends him into convulsions with foam, and it distances itself from him with a lot of effort crushing him.
40 And I pleaded with Your students that they may throw it out, and they were not able to."

41 When Jesus answered, He said, "O generation, untrusting and that has been twisted, until when will I be facing you and tolerate you? Bring your son to *Me* here."
42 As he was still coming forward, the lesser deity ripped him and sent *him* into violent convulsions. Jesus stopped the spirit, the *one* that was not clean, cured the boy, and gave him back to his father.
43 All were being impressed based on the greatness of God. Since all were amazed based on all *the things* that He did, Jesus said to His students,
44 "You must put these words into your ears. You see, the Son of the Person is going to be turned over to people's hands."
45 The *students* were unaware of this statement, it was *a thing* that had been concealed from them so that they would not comprehend it, and they were afraid to ask Him about this statement.
46 A pondering went in among them: the "which of them would be *the* greatest" *thing*.
47 When Jesus saw the pondering of their heart, after He latched on to a young child, He stood him beside Him.
48 And He said to them, "Whoever accepts this young child based on My name accepts Me, and whoever accepts Me accepts the *One* who sent Me out. You see, the *person* who is littler among you all, this *person* will be great."
49 When John responded, he said, "Boss, we saw someone throwing out the lesser deities based on Your name, and we hindered him because he is not following with us."
50 And Jesus said to him, "Don't hinder *him*. You see, a *person* who is not against us is over with us."
51 It happened during the *time* for the days of His being taken up *to heaven* to be totally filled up; He also established His face of the "to be traveling to Jerusalem" *kind*
52 and sent out announcers before His face. And after traveling, they went into a village of Samaritans in such a way to get *things* ready for Him.
53 And they did not accept Him because His face was traveling to Jerusalem.
54 When His students, James and John, saw *it*, they said, "Master, do you want *that* we will tell fire to step down out of the sky and consume them, as Elijah also did?"
55 But after He turned, He shushed them and said, "You do not realize of what spirit you are.
56 You see, the Son of the Person did not come to ruin people's souls but to rescue *them*." And they traveled to a different village.
57 It happened as they traveled on the road; someone said to Him, "I will follow You wherever You go off to, Master."
58 And Jesus said to him, "The foxes have burrows, and the winged birds of the sky *have* nests, but the Son of the Person does not have *a place* where He may rest *His* head."
59 He said to a different *person*, "Follow Me." But the *person* said, "Master, first give me permission, after going off, to bury my father."
60 But Jesus said to him, "Leave the dead to bury their *own* dead, but, after going off, you must announce the monarchy of God everywhere."

61 A different *person* also said, "I will follow you, Master, but first give me permission to say good-bye to the *people* in my house."
62 But Jesus said to him, "No one who put his hand on a plow and is looking to the *things left* behind is suitable for the monarchy of God."

10

1 After these *things* the Master also publicly showed seventy different *ones* and sent them out *on a mission* (two apiece) before His face into every city and place where He was going to be going.
2 So He was saying to them, "The harvest certainly *is* big, but the workers *are* few. So plead with the master of the harvest in order that he may put workers out into his harvest.
3 Make *your* way back. Look, I am sending you out as lambs in *the* middle of wolves.
4 Do not haul a money bag, no tote bag, nor sandals. And you should say hello to no one along the way.
5 Into whatever house you go, first say, "Peace to this house."
6 And if the son of peace is certainly there, your peace will relax on it. But if definitely not, it will double back on you.
7 Stay in the same house eating and drinking the *things* from the side of them. You see, the worker is deserving of his pay. Do not walk from house to house.
8 Also into whatever city you go and they accept you, eat the *things* being placed beside you,
9 heal the weak *people* in it, and say to them, "The monarchy of God has come near over you."
10 But into whatever city you go and they do not accept you, after going out into its plaza, say,
11 'Even the dust, the *dust* that is stuck like glue to us from your city, we are wiping off against you. More importantly, know this that the monarchy of God has come near over you.'
12 I tell you that for Sodom in that day it will be more tolerable than for that city.
13 What a tragedy *it is* to you, Chorazin! What a tragedy *it is* to you, Bethsaida! because if the abilities that happened among you happened in Tyre and Sidon, they would have changed their ways a long time ago sitting in cloth made of hair and *in* ash.
14 More importantly, for Tyre and Sidon it will be more tolerable in the judgment than for you.
15 And you, the Capernaum that was put up high until the heaven. You will be made to walk down until Hades *(the underworld of the dead)*.
16 The *person* listening to you listens to Me, and the *person* invalidating you invalidates Me. The *person* invalidating Me invalidates the *One* who sent Me out *on a mission*."
17 The seventy returned with happiness, saying, "Master, even the lesser deities place themselves under us in Your name."

18 He said to them, "I was watching the Opponent who fell from the sky as lightning.
19 Look, I give you the authority of the 'to be trampling up on top of snakes and scorpions and on all the ability of the enemy' *kind*. And nothing will in any way harm you.
20 More importantly, don't be happy in this, that the spirits place themselves under you, but instead, be happy that your names were written in the heavens."
21 In the same hour, Jesus was excited in the Spirit and said, "I acknowledge out loud to You, Father, Master of the heaven and the earth, that You hid these *things* away from insightful and understanding *people* and uncovered them to infants, yes, the Father, because this is how it became a good notion in front of You.
22 Everything was turned over to Me by My father. And no one knows who the Son is except the Father and who the Father is except the Son and to whomever the Son intends to uncover *Him*.
23 And after turning to the students by themselves, He said, "The eyes, the *ones* seeing what you see, are blessed.
24 You see, I tell you that many preachers and kings wanted to see *things* that you are looking at and they did not see *them*, and to hear *things* that you hear and they did not hear *them*."
25 And look, a certain law *expert* stood up, trying to harass Him and saying, "Teacher, what *is a thing that* after doing *it*, I will inherit life that spans *all* time?"
26 *Jesus* said to him, "What has been written in the law? How do you read *it*?"
27 When the *law expert* answered, he said, "You will love *the* Master, your God, from your whole heart, from your whole soul, from your whole strength, and from your whole mind, and the *person* near you as yourself."
28 He said to him, "You answered correctly. Do this and you will live."
29 But the *law expert*, wanting to make himself right, said to Jesus, "And who is near me?"
30 When Jesus took *it* up, He said, "A certain person was walking down out of Jerusalem to Jericho and fell into being surrounded by bandits who, after both stripping him and putting wounds on *him*, went away after leaving *him* half dead (which he was obtaining).
31 By coincidence a certain priest was walking down on that road, and when he saw him, he passed by on the other side.
32 Likewise, when a Levite also became by the place, after he went and saw *him*, he passed by on the other side.
33 But as a certain Samaritan was on a trip, he went by him, and when he saw him, he had sympathy.
34 And when he came forward, he bandaged up his wounds pouring olive oil and wine on *them*. After loading him on *his* own animal, he led him into an inn and took care of him.
35 And on the next day, when he left, after he took out two denarii *(fifty-dollar coins)*, he gave *them* to the innkeeper and said to him, 'Take care of him, and anything more that you might spend, I, during the *time* for me to be coming back, will give *it* back to you.'

36 So which of these three does it seem to you to have become near the *man* who fell into the bandits?"
37 The *law expert* said, "The *one* who showed the forgiving kindness with him." So Jesus said to him, "Travel, and you must do likewise."
38 It happened during the *time* for them to be traveling; He also went into a certain village. A certain woman with *the* name Martha accepted Him under *her roof* into her house.
39 And here with *Martha* was a sister called Mary, who also (when she was seated beside the feet of Jesus) was hearing His message.
40 But Martha was being pulled around about much serving. When she stood over *Him*, she said, "Master, isn't it a concern to You that my sister left me down *there* to be serving alone? So tell her that she should assist together with me."
41 When He answered, Jesus said to her, "Martha, Martha, you are worried and flustered about many *things,*
42 but one *thing* is a need; Mary selected the good part, something that will not be taken away from her."

11

1 And it happened during the *time* for Him to be in a certain place praying; as He stopped, a certain one of His students said to Him, "Master, teach us to be praying, just as John also taught his students."
2 He said to them, "When you pray, say, Father, the *One* in the heavens, Your name must be made sacred. Your monarchy must come. What You want must happen, as in heaven, *so* also on the earth.
3 Give us the "daily" *thing,* our bread (the next day *bread).*
4 And forgive us our sins. You see, we ourselves also forgive everyone who owes us. And You will not carry us into trouble, but save us from the evil *one*."
5 And He said to them, "Who from among you will have a friend, will travel to him in *the* middle of the night, and might say to him, 'Friend, loan me three *loaves of* bread
6 since, for sure, my friend showed up to me from a trip and I don't have *anything* that I will place beside him'?
7 And when that *person* from inside answers, he might say, 'Don't bother me. The door has already been closed, and my young children are with me in the bed. I am not able after standing up to give *it* to you.'
8 I tell you, even if he will not give to him after standing up because of the *fact for him* to be his friend, because of his shameless audacity, he definitely, after being gotten up, will give him as much as he needs.
9 And I tell you, ask and it will be given to you. Look and you will find. Knock and it will be opened to you.
10 You see, everyone who asks receives, the *person* who looks finds, and to the *person* who knocks, it will be opened.
11 Whom of you (the father) will the son ask for bread? He will not give a stone over to him, will he? And if *he will ask* for a fish, he will not in place of a fish give a snake over to him, will he?

12 Or if he will also ask for an egg, he will not give a scorpion over to him, will he?
13 So if you *all* who are evil know to be giving good presents to your children, how much more will the Father, the *One* from heaven, give *the* Sacred Spirit to the *people* who ask Him?"
14 And He was throwing a lesser deity out, and it was speech-impaired. It happened when the lesser deity came out; the speech-impaired *man* spoke, and the crowds were amazed.
15 Some from among them said, "He throws the lesser deities out with Beelzebub, *the* head of the lesser deities."
16 Different *ones*, trying to cause trouble, were looking for an indicator from the side of Him from heaven.
17 He, realizing their thoughts, said to them, "Every monarchy that is divided *and* against itself becomes uninhabited, and a house against a house falls.
18 If the Opponent also was divided *and* against himself, how will his monarchy be established? Because you say for Me with Beelzebub to be throwing the lesser deities out.
19 If I throw the lesser deities out with Beelzebub, your sons, with whom do they throw *them* out? Because of this, they will be judges of you.
20 But if I with a finger of God throw the lesser deities out, clearly the monarchy of God already came on you.
21 When the strong *person* (having been fully armored) guards his *own* courtyard, the *things* that are his are in peace.
22 But whenever the *person* who is stronger than him comes on *him*, he conquers him. He takes his full body armor on which he had been confident and passes out his spoils.
23 The *person* who is not with Me is against Me, and the *person* who does not gather with Me scatters.
24 When the spirit that is not clean comes out from the person, it passes through places without water looking for relief. And not finding *it*, it says, 'I will return back into my house from where I went out.'
25 And when it comes, it finds that it has been swept and decorated.
26 Then it travels and takes along seven different spirits more evil than itself. And when they go in, it lives there, and the last of that person becomes worse than the first."
27 It happened during the *time* for Him to be saying these *things*; when a certain woman from the crowd raised up *her* voice, she said to him, "The belly, the *one* that hauled You, and *the* breasts that nursed *You are* blessed."
28 He said, "Yes, so of course the *people* hearing the message of God and observing it *are* blessed."
29 As the crowds gathered more, He began to be saying, "This generation is evil. An indicator it is looking for, and an indicator will not be given to it except the indicator of Jonah, the preacher.
30 You see, just as Jonah became an indicator to the Ninevites, so will the Son of the Person also be to this generation.
31 A queen of *the* south will be gotten up during the judgment with the men of this generation and find them guilty because she came from the ends of the

earth to hear the insight of Solomon and, look, *something* better than Solomon is here.

32 Men of Nineveh will stand up during the judgment with this generation and find it guilty because they changed their ways into the public speaking of Jonah and, look, *something* better than Jonah *is* here.

33 No one, after lighting a lamp, places *it* into a hidden *place* or under the two gallon measuring bucket, but on the lampstand so that the *people* traveling in may see the glow.

34 The lamp of the body is the eye. So when your eye is dedicated, your whole body also is lit up, but whenever it is evil, your body *is* also dark.

35 So keep an eye out for *this, that* the light, the *light* in you, is not darkness.

36 So if your whole body *is* lit up, not having any dark part, *the* whole will be lit up as when the lamp for the lightning lights *things* up for you."

37 During the *time* to speak, a certain Separatist was asking Him *a favor* in order that He might have breakfast beside him. When He went in, He settled down.

38 When the Separatist saw *it*, he was amazed because He was not first submerged *in water* before the breakfast.

39 The Master said to him, "You, the Separatists, now clean the outside of the cup and the plate, but your inside is packed full of looting and evilness.

40 Distracted *people*, didn't the *One* who made the outside also make the inside?

41 More importantly, give the *things* that are inside *as* a charitable donation and, look, all *things* are clean to you.

42 But what a tragedy *it is* to you, the Separatists, because you take ten percent out of the sweet smelling mint, the rue leaves, and every vegetable and pass by the judgment and the love of God. It was necessary to do these *things* and not to leave those.

43 What a tragedy *it is* to you, the Separatists, because you love the front bench in the synagogue and the greetings in the marketplaces.

44 What a tragedy *it is* to you, *Old Testament* transcribers and Separatists, fakers, because you are as the burial vaults, the obscure *ones*; and the people, the *ones* walking around up on top, do not realize *it*."

45 When one of the law *experts* responds, he says to Him, "Teacher, these *things* that you are saying also injure us."

46 Jesus said, "And to you, the law *experts*, what a tragedy *it is* because you load the people down with heavy hard-to-haul loads and you yourselves with one of your fingers do not *even* lightly touch the heavy loads.

47 What a tragedy *it is* to you because you build the burial vaults of the preachers, but your fathers killed them.

48 Clearly you are witnesses and agree that *you think* the actions of your fathers are good, because they not only killed them, but you build their burial vaults.

49 Because of this, the insight of God also said, 'I will send preachers and missionaries out to them, and *some* from among them they will kill, and *some* they will chase out,'

50 so that the blood of all the preachers, that is spilled out since *the* world's founding, will be intensively searched for from this generation,
51 from the blood of Abel to the blood of the Zacharias that was ruined between the altar and the house. Yes, I tell you, it will be intensively searched for from this generation.
52 What a tragedy *it is* to you, the law *experts*, because you take away the key to the information yourselves. You did not go in, and you hindered the *people* going in."
53 As He said these *things* to them, the *Old Testament* transcribers and Separatists began to dreadfully be holding a grudge and to be making Him speak impromptu about more *things*,
54 lying in wait for Him and looking to snag something from His mouth so that they might level a complaint against Him.

12

1 Meanwhile, when the tens of thousands of the crowd came together in one place in such a way to be trampling on each other, He first began to be saying to His students, "Be cautious yourselves of the yeast of the Separatists, something that is faked behavior.
2 There is nothing that has been covered up well that will not be uncovered, and hidden that will not be known,
3 for *the times* that as much as you said in the dark will be heard in the light and what you spoke to the ear in the storage rooms will be spoken publicly on the top of houses.
4 But I tell you, my friends, do not be afraid from the *people* who kill the body and after these *things* have nothing much more to do.
5 But I will put in front of your face who you should fear. Fear the *One* who, after the *time for Him* to kill, has authority to throw into the Hinnom Valley. Yes, I tell you, fear this *One*.
6 Are not five little sparrows sold for two assarii *($4)*? And there is not one of them that has been forgotten in the sight of God.
7 But even all the hairs of your head have been numbered. So do not be afraid, you are more substantial than many little sparrows.
8 I tell you, everyone, whoever acknowledged *being* in Me in front of the people, the Son of the Person will also acknowledge *being* in him in front of the angels of God.
9 But the *person* who denied Me in the sight of the people will be flatly denied in the sight of the angels of God.
10 And everyone who will state a word in reference to the Son of the Person, it will be forgiven to him, but to the *person* who insults into the Sacred Spirit, it will not be forgiven.
11 When they bring you forward before the synagogues, the head rulers, and the authorities, do not worry how or what you will defend or what you will say.
12 You see, the Sacred Spirit will teach you in the same hour *things* that it is necessary to say."

13 Someone from the crowd said to Him, "Teacher, tell my brother to divide the inheritance with me."
14 But *Jesus* said to him, "Sir, who put Me in charge *as* a referee or distributor over you?"
15 He said to them, "Look, and guard yourselves from the desire for more, because during the *time for things* to be overflowing to someone, his life is not from the *things* that are his."
16 He told an illustration to them, saying, "The rural area of a certain wealthy person was productive.
17 And He was pondering in himself, saying, 'What will I do because I do not have *a place* where I will gather my fruits?'
18 And he said, 'I will do this, I will take down my grain bins and build bigger. And I will gather everything there, my produce and my goods.
19 And I will state to my soul, "Soul, you have many goods lying *here* for many years. Relax. Eat. Drink. Celebrate."'
20 But God said to him, 'Distracted *person*, this night they are asking for your soul back from you. With whom will *the things* be that you got ready?'
21 This is how *it is with* the *person* stockpiling *stuff* for himself and not being wealthy to God."
22 He said to His students, "Because of this, I tell you, don't worry about your soul (what you might eat), nor about the body (what you might put on).
23 The soul is more than the meal, and the body *more* than the attire.
24 Take a closer look at the crows because they do not seed, nor harvest (with whom there is no storage room, nor grain bin), and God nurtures them. How much more substantial you are than the winged birds.
25 Who from among you by worrying is able to add on to his size one cubit (*an elbow to fingertip length*)?
26 So if you are not even capable of *the* smallest *thing*, why do you worry about the rest?
27 Take a closer look at the wild flowers, how *a wild flower* grows. It does not labor, nor spin yarn. But, I tell you, not even Solomon in all his magnificence put *clothes* around himself as one of these.
28 If God decks out the grass this way, that is in the field today and tomorrow is thrown into a fire pit, how much more *will He do for* you, seldom trusting *people*?
29 And you must not search for what you might eat or what you might drink. And don't be anxious.
30 You see, the nations of the world search for all these, but your Father realizes that you need these.
31 More importantly, look for the monarchy of God, and all these *things* will be added to you.
32 Do not be afraid, the little flock, because it seemed like a good idea to your Father to give you the monarchy.
33 Sell the *things* that are yours and give a charitable donation. Make money bags for yourself that do not wear out, permanent stockpile in the heavens, where a thief doesn't come near, neither does a moth devour.
34 You see, where your stockpile is, there your heart will also be.

35 Your waists must be *waists* around which a waist sash has been put, the lamps burning,
36 and you, like people awaiting their master when he will be released from the wedding *events*, so that when he comes and knocks, right away they might open *the door* to him.
37 Those slaves whom the master will find staying awake when he comes are blessed. Amen, I tell you that he will put a waist sash around himself, recline them, and, after coming alongside, will serve them.
38 And if he comes in the second guard shift *(9:00 p.m. – midnight)* and in the third guard shift *of the night (midnight – 3:00 a.m.)*, he comes and finds *them* like this, those slaves are blessed.
39 Know this, that if the homeowner realized at which hour the thief comes, he would have stayed awake and not left his house to be broken into.
40 So you also must become ready, because the Son of the Person comes at an hour that it doesn't seem to you *He will*."
41 Peter said to Him, "Master, are you telling this illustration to us or also to everyone?"
42 The Master said, "So who is the reliable and attentive manager? *One* whom the master will put in charge over his attendants for the *purpose* to be giving the grain portion at *the* right time.
43 That slave *is* blessed whom, when his master comes, he will find doing so.
44 I truly tell you that he will put him in charge over all the *things* that are his.
45 But if that slave says in his heart, 'My master is taking a long time to come,' and begins to be hitting the servant boys and the servant girls, to be eating and to be drinking, and to be getting drunk,
46 the master of that slave will arrive during a day that he is not expecting and in an hour that he does not know. And he will cut him in two, and place his part with the *people* who cannot be trusted.
47 That slave, the *one* who knew what his *own* master wanted and did not get *it* ready (or do *anything* pointed toward what he wanted), will be beaten many *times*.
48 But the *one* who did not know but did *things* deserving of wounds will be beaten a few *times*. To everyone whom much was given, much will be looked for from the side of him. And beside whom they placed much, they will ask him for much more.
49 I came to throw fire into the earth, and what do I want? If *only* it was already started.
50 I have a submersion to be submerged in, and how I am constrained *by it* until *the time* that it will be finished.
51 Does it seem to you that I showed up to give peace in the earth? Definitely not, I tell you, but instead bitter division.
52 You see, from the present *on*, there will be five that have been divided up in one house, three on two and two on three.
53 A father will be divided *and* against a son and a son against a father, a mother against a daughter and a daughter against a mother, a mother-in-law

against her daughter-in-law and a daughter-in-law against her mother-in-law."

54 He also was saying to the crowds, "When you see the cloud coming up out of western regions, right away you say, 'Severe weather is coming,' and that is what happens.

55 And when a south *wind* is blowing, you say, 'It will be a hot wind,' and it happens.

56 Fakers, you know to be checking the appearance of the earth and the sky, but how are you not checking this appointed time?

57 Why don't you also out from yourselves judge the right *thing*?

58 You see, as you make *your* way back with your opponent in the court case before a head person, on the way, give work to have been relieved from him so that he might not drag you down to the judge, the judge might turn you over to the bailiff, and the bailiff may throw you into jail.

59 I tell you, you will not in any way come out from there until *the time* that you will give even the last tiny coin back."

13

1 Some were beside *Him* at the same time, who reported to Him about the Galileans whose blood Pilate mixed with their sacrifices.

2 And when Jesus responded, He said to them, "Does it seem to you that these Galileans became sinful beyond all the Galileans because they have suffered these types of *things*?

3 Definitely not, I tell you, but if you do not change your ways, you all will similarly be ruined.

4 Or those ten and eight on whom the tower in Siloam fell and killed them. Does it seem to you that these became people who owed beyond all the people living in Jerusalem?

5 Definitely not, I tell you, but if you do not change your ways, you all will likewise be ruined."

6 He was telling this illustration, "A certain *person* had a fig tree that had been planted in his vineyard. And he went looking for fruit in it and found none.

7 He said to the vineyard worker, 'Look, for three years I am coming looking for fruit in this fig tree, and I am finding none. Chop it out. Why does it also make the ground useless?'

8 When the *vineyard worker* responds, he says to him, 'Master, leave it also this year until I will excavate around it and put *down* manure.

9 And certainly if it produces fruit, *good*. But if not, for the *time* that is going *to come*, you definitely will chop it out.'"

10 He was teaching in one of the synagogues on the Sabbaths.

11 And look, there was a woman who had a spirit of weakness for ten and eight years. And she was stooping over and not able to stand up straight to the maximum.

12 When Jesus saw her, He hollered out and said to her, "Ma'am, you have been dismissed from your weakness."

13 And He placed His hands on her, and at once she was straightened up and was praising God's magnificence.
14 When the synagogue's head ruler responded, frustrated because Jesus healed on the Sabbath, he was saying to the crowd, "There are six days during which it is necessary to be working. So as you come during these, be healed, and not on the day of the Sabbath."
15 So the Master responded to him and said, "Faker, doesn't each of you on the Sabbath release his cow or donkey from the feed trough and, after leading *it* off, give *it* a drink?
16 But this *woman*, who is a daughter of Abraham, whom the Opponent tied up, look, ten and eight years, isn't it necessary to release *her* from this restraint on the day of the Sabbath?"
17 And as He said these *things*, all the *people* lying in opposition to Him were ashamed, and the entire crowd was happy based on all the magnificent *things* happening under Him.
18 He was saying, "What is the monarchy of God like, and what will I liken it to?
19 It is like a kernel of mustard, that, after a person took, he threw into his garden. And it grew, became into a large tree, and the winged birds of the sky nested in its branches."
20 And again He said, "What will I liken the monarchy of God to?
21 It is like yeast that, after a woman took, she hid in three loads of dough until *the time* that *the* whole *thing* was raised."
22 And He was traveling throughout cities and villages teaching and making a journey to Jerusalem.
23 Someone said to Him, "Master, *tell us* if the *people* being rescued *are* few." *Jesus* said to them,
24 "Struggle to go in through the narrow gate, because many, I tell you, will look to go in and will not have *the* strength.
25 From *the time* that the homeowner got up and closed up the door, you also began to have been standing outside and to be knocking on the door, saying, 'Master, master, open to us.' And when he responds, he will state to you, 'I don't know you, where you are from.'
26 At that time, you will begin to be saying, 'We ate in your sight and drank, and you taught in our plazas.'
27 And He will state, 'I tell you, I don't know you, where you are from. Stand off away from Me, all the workers of the wrong.'
28 There will be the crying and the grinding of the teeth there when you see Abraham, Isaac, Jacob, and all the preachers in the monarchy of God, but you being thrown outside.
29 And they will arrive from eastern regions and western regions, and from *the* north and south, and will recline in the monarchy of God.
30 And look, *the* last *ones* are who will be first, and *the* first *ones* are who will be last."
31 In the same day, some Separatists came forward, saying to Him, "Go out and travel *away* from here because Herod wants to kill You."

32 And He said to them, "When you travel *back*, tell that fox, 'Look, I am throwing lesser deities out and finishing up cures today and tomorrow. And on the third *day*, I am finished.
33 More importantly, it is necessary for Me today, tomorrow, and the following *day* to be traveling because it is not acceptable for a preacher to be ruined outside of Jerusalem.'
34 Jerusalem, Jerusalem, the *city* killing the preachers and throwing stones at the *people* who have been sent out to her. How many times I wanted to bring your children together in one place, *the* way that a hen *gathers* her *own* young under the wings, and you did not want *it*.
35 Look, your house is left to you uninhabited. Amen, I tell you that you will not in any way see Me until *the time* will arrive when you will say, 'The *One* coming in *the* Master's name who has been conferred with blessings.'"

14

1 And it happened during the *time* for Him to go into a house of a certain *one* of the head people of the Separatists on *the* Sabbath to eat bread; they also were closely watching Him.
2 And look, a certain swollen person was in front of Him.
3 And when Jesus responded, He talked to the law *experts* and Separatists, saying, "*Tell me* if it is allowed to heal on the Sabbath."
4 The *people* remained calm. And after latching on to *him*, He cured him and dismissed *him*.
5 And when He responded to them, He said, "Whose donkey or cow of you *all* will fall into a well? And will he not right away pull it up during the day of the Sabbath?"
6 And they didn't have *the* strength to respond to Him in opposition to these *things*.
7 He was telling an illustration to the *people* who had been invited as He was fixing *His* attention on how they were selecting the front reclining places, saying to them,
8 "When you are invited by someone to wedding *events*, do not be reclined in the front reclining place; perhaps there is a more valued *person* than you who has been invited by him.
9 And when the *one* who invited you and him comes, he will state to you, 'Give *your* place to this *person*,' and then you will begin with shame to be holding down the last place.
10 But when you are invited, when you travel *there*, settle down in the last place so that when the *person* who has invited you comes, he will say to you, 'Friend, move further up.' Then there will be magnificence for you in the sight of the *people* reclining together with you
11 because everyone who puts himself up high will be put down low and the *person* who puts himself down low will be put up high."
12 He also was saying to the *person* who had invited Him, "When you make a breakfast or feast, do not holler for your friends, nor your brothers, nor your relatives, nor wealthy neighbors, so that they won't also invite you in return, and it might become a repayment to you.

13 But when you make a reception, invite poor *people*, badly wounded *people*, crippled *people*, blind *people*.
14 And you will be blessed because they don't have *a way* to repay you. You see, it will be repaid to you in the return back to life of the *people* who do what is right."
15 When a certain *person* of the *ones* reclining together with *Him* heard these *things*, he said to Him, "A *person* who will eat bread in the monarchy of God *is* blessed."
16 *Jesus* said to him, "A certain person made a large feast and invited many.
17 And he sent his slave out at the hour of the feast to tell the *people* who had been invited, 'Come because everything is already ready.'
18 And they all from one *consent* began to be giving excuses. The first said to him, 'I bought a field, and I have an obligation to go out and see it. I ask you, have me *as a person* who has been excused.'
19 And a different *person* said, 'I bought five pairs of cows, and I am traveling to check them. I ask you, have me *as a person* who has been excused.'
20 And a different *person* said, 'I married a wife, and because of this I am not able to come.'
21 And when that slave showed up, he reported these *things* to his master. At that time, after the property owner was enraged, he said to his slave, 'Go out quickly into the plazas and streets of the city, and lead the poor, badly wounded, crippled, and blind in here.'
22 And the slave said, 'Master, it has happened as the directive you gave, and still a place is *empty*.'
23 And the master said to the slave, 'Go out to the roads and barrier walls, and urge *people* to come in so that my house might be full.
24 You see, I tell you that none of those men who have been invited will taste my feast.'"
25 Big crowds were traveling together with Him. And after turning, He said to them,
26 "If someone comes to Me and does not hate his *own* father, mother, wife, children, brothers, and sisters, but still even his own soul, he is not able to be My student.
27 And anyone who does not haul his cross and come behind Me is not able to be My student.
28 You see, who from among you who wants to build a tower, does he not, after first being seated, count the expense if he has the *things* toward a complete development?
29 So that *it will* not ever *be that* after he has laid a foundation and as he does not have *the* strength to finish off *the tower*, all the *people* watching might begin to be mocking him,
30 saying, 'This person began to be building and didn't have *the* strength to finish *it* off.'
31 Or what king traveling to meet up with a different king for war, does he not, after first being seated, advise if it is possible with ten thousand to meet the *one* coming on him with twenty thousand?

32 If not, definitely, as he is still far away, after sending out a delegation of older men, he asks the *conditions* toward peace.
33 So in this way, everyone from among you who does not say good-bye to all the *things* that are his *own* is not able to be My student.
34 The salt *is* nice, but if the salt lost its flavor, with what will *food* be seasoned?
35 It is neither suitable for *the* ground, nor for manure. They throw it outside. The *person* who has ears to be listening must listen."

15

1 All the tax collectors and the sinful *people* were near Him to be listening to Him.
2 And the Separatists and the *Old Testament* transcribers were speaking in hushed tones among themselves, saying, "This *Person* accepts sinful *people* in and eats together with them."
3 He told this illustration to them, saying,
4 "What person from among you who has a hundred sheep, and when he loses one from them, does not leave the ninety-nine down in the backcountry and travel based on the *one* that has been lost until he finds it?
5 And when he finds *it*, he places *it* on his *own* shoulders being happy.
6 And when he comes into the house, he calls the friends and the neighbors together, saying to them, 'Be happy together with me because I found my sheep, the *one* that has been lost.'
7 I tell you that this is how there will be happiness in heaven over one sinful *person* changing his ways than over ninety-nine that do what is right, some that have no need of a change of ways.
8 Or what woman having ten drachmas (*silver coins*), if she loses one drachma, does she not light a lamp, sweep the house, and look carefully until a *certain* time that she will find *it*?
9 And after finding *it*, she calls the friends and the neighbors together, saying, 'Be happy together with me because I found the drachma that I lost.'
10 This is how, I tell you, happiness happens in the sight of the angels of God over one sinful *person* changing his ways."
11 He said, "A certain person had two sons.
12 And the younger of them said to *his* father, 'Father, give the part of the assets throwing *the inheritance* up to me.' And he divvied out the livelihood to them.
13 And after not many days, when the younger son gathered absolutely everything, he left the area *to go* to a distant rural area. And there he squandered his assets, living recklessly.
14 After he spent everything, a strong famine happened throughout that rural area, and he began to be lacking.
15 And after he traveled, he was stuck like glue to one of the citizens of that rural area. And he sent him into his fields to be feeding hogs.
16 And he was desiring to fill his belly from the raw carob pods that the hogs were eating. And no one was giving to him.
17 When he came to himself, he said, 'How many paid *workers* of my father have *loaves of* bread left over, but I am being ruined by a famine.

18 After getting up, I will travel to my father and state to him, "Father, I sinned to heaven and in your sight.
19 I am no longer even deserving to be called your son. Make me as one of your paid *workers*.'"
20 And after getting up, he went to his *own* father. But as he had *himself* still a long way away, his father saw him and had sympathy. And after running *to him*, he fell on his neck and was very friendly to him.
21 The son said to him, 'Father, I sinned to heaven and in your sight. I no longer am even deserving to be called your son.'
22 But the father said to his slaves, 'Bring out the long robe, the most important *one*, and put it on him. And give *him* a ring for his hand and sandals for *his* feet.
23 And after bringing the calf, the grain-fed *one*, kill *it*, and after eating, we will celebrate
24 because this *one*, my son, was dead, and he came back to life; and he had been lost and was found.' And they began to celebrate.
25 His son, the older *one*, was in a field. And going *home*, as he was near the house, he heard *musical* harmony and circle dancing.
26 And after calling for one of the servant boys, he was inquiring what these *things* might be.
27 The *boy* said to him, 'Your brother has arrived, and your father killed the calf, the grain-fed *one*, because he received him back healthy.'
28 He was enraged and did not want to go in. So after his father came out, he was encouraging him.
29 When the *son* responded, he said to *his* father, 'Look, for so many years, I am a slave to you, and I never even once passed by your demand. And you never even once gave me a goat so that I might celebrate with my friends.
30 When your son, this *one* who ate up your livelihood with prostitutes, came, you killed the calf for him, the grain-fed *calf*.'
31 But the *father* said to him, 'Child, you are always with me, and all my *things* are yours.
32 It was necessary to celebrate and to be happy because your brother, this *one*, was dead and came back to life, and had been lost and was found."'

16

1 He also was saying to His students, "There was a certain wealthy person who had a manager. And this *manager* was accused to him as *someone* squandering the *things* that are his.
2 And after he hollered for him, he said to him, 'What *is* this I hear about you? Give back the account of your management. You see, you will not be able to be managing anymore.'
3 The manager said in himself, 'What will I do because my master is taking the management away from me. I do not have *the* strength to plow *and* plant. I am ashamed to be asking for *money*.
4 I know what I will do so that when I am dislodged from the management, they will accept me into their houses.'
5 And after he called for each one of the owers of debt to his master, he was saying to the first, 'How much do you owe my master?'

6 The *person* said, 'A hundred baths *(800 gallons)* of olive oil.' And he said to him, 'Accept your documents, and after being seated quickly, write fifty.'
7 Following that, he said to a different *one*, 'You, how much do you owe?' The *person* said, 'A hundred cors *(1000 bushels)* of grain.' He says to him, 'Accept your documents and write eighty.'
8 And the master applauded the manager of the wrong, because he did *it* with a focus, because the sons of this span of time are more attentive (above the sons of the light) to their *own* generation.
9 And I tell you, make friends for yourselves from the wealthiness of the wrong way, so that when it ceases, they will accept you into the tents that span *all* time.
10 The *person who is* reliable in *the* smallest *thing* is also reliable in much, and the *person who is* wrong in *the* smallest *thing* is also wrong in much.
11 So if you did not become reliable in the wrong wealthiness, who will trust the true *wealthiness* to you?
12 And if you did not become reliable in the *thing* belonging to others, who will give you your *own things*?
13 Not even one domestic servant is able to be a slave to two masters. You see, either he will hate the one and love the different *one*, or he will have one in front of *him* and ignore the different *one*. You are not able to be a slave to God and wealthiness."
14 The Separatists, who are fond of money, were also listening to all these *things* and making a fool of Him out loud.
15 And He said to them, "You are the *ones* who make yourselves right in the sight of the people, but God knows your hearts because the high *thing* among people *is* a disgusting thing in the presence of God.
16 The Law and the Preachers *are* until John, from then on, the good news of the monarchy of God is shared, and everyone forces their way into it.
17 It is easier for the sky and the earth to pass than for one hook of a letter of the law to fall.
18 Everyone who dismisses his wife and marries a different *woman* is cheating on *his* wife and everyone who marries a *woman* who has been dismissed from a husband is cheating.
19 A certain person was wealthy and dressing himself in purple and elegant linen as he celebrated dazzlingly daily.
20 There was a certain poor *man* with *the* name Lazarus who had been put facing his gateway, having become full of sores
21 and desiring to be full from the crumbs, the *ones* falling from the table of the wealthy man, but even the dogs that came were licking off his sores.
22 It happened for the poor *man* to die and for him to be carried off by the angels into the arms of Abraham. The wealthy *man* also died and was buried.
23 And in the Hades *(the underworld of the dead)*, after raising his eyes, being in excruciating pains, he sees Abraham off at a distance and Lazarus in his arms.
24 And when he hollered, he said, 'Father Abraham, show me forgiving kindness and send Lazarus so that he might dip the edge of his finger in water and cool down my tongue because I am in agony in this blaze.

25 But Abraham said, 'Child, remember that you fully received your good *things* in your life, and Lazarus likewise, the bad *things*. Now the *man* here is encouraged, but you are in agony.
26 And on all these *things*, between us and you a large gap has been established in order that the *people* wanting to walk across from here to you are not able to. Neither may the *people* cross all the way over from there to us.'
27 He said, 'So I am asking you, father, that you might send him into the house of my father
28 (you see, I have five brothers) in order that he may be a strong witness to them so that they also might not come into this place of the excruciating pain.'
29 Abraham says to him, 'They have Moses and the Preachers. They must listen to them.'
30 The *wealthy man* said, 'Definitely not, father Abraham, but if someone out of *the* dead should travel to them, they will change their ways.'
31 But he said to him, 'If they do not listen to Moses and the Preachers, neither will they be persuaded if someone stands up from *the* dead.'"

17

1 He said to the students, "It is unacceptable, the 'for the obstacles not to come' *part*, but what a tragedy *it is* to *the person* through whom it comes.
2 It compensates for him if a millstone (*the kind turned by* a donkey) is laid around his neck, and he has been tossed into the sea, than that he might cause one of these little *ones* to stumble.
3 Pay attention to yourselves. If your brother does something sinful to you, tell him to stop, and if he changes his ways, forgive him.
4 And if seven times in the day he does something sinful to you and seven times in the day turns back to you, saying, 'I am changing my ways,' you will forgive him."
5 And the missionaries said to the Master, "Add trust to us."
6 The Master said, "If you were having trust as a kernel of mustard, you would be saying to this black mulberry tree, 'Be uprooted and be planted in the sea,' and it would obey you.
7 Who from among you, who has a slave plowing or shepherding, who comes in from the field, will state *to him* right away, 'When you pass by, settle down'?
8 But will he not state to him, 'Get something ready, I will eat dinner,' and, 'After putting a sash around your waist, serve me until I eat and drink, and after these, you will eat and drink'?
9 He doesn't have generosity for that slave because he did the *things* that were specifically assigned to him, does he? I don't think *so*.
10 In this way, you also, when you do all the *things* that were specifically assigned to you, say, 'We are mediocre slaves. We have done what we were obligated to do.'"
11 And it happened during the *time* for Him to be traveling to Jerusalem; He also was going through *the* middle of Samaria and Galilee.

12 And as He went into a certain village, ten skin-diseased men met Him, who stood far away.
13 And they raised *their* voice, saying, "Jesus, Boss, show us forgiving kindness."
14 And when He saw *them*, He said to them, "After you travel *back*, show yourselves to the priests." And it happened during the *time* for them to be making *their* way back; they were cleared up.
15 When one from among them saw that he was cured, he returned praising the magnificence of God with a loud voice.
16 And he got down on *his* face beside His feet thanking Him. And he was a Samaritan.
17 When Jesus responded, He said, "Weren't the ten cleared up? But the nine, where *are they*?
18 Were no *other men* found who returned to give magnificence to God except this *one* from another ethnicity?"
19 And He said to him, "When you stand up, travel *home*. Your trust has rescued you."
20 After being asked by the Separatists when the monarchy of God is coming, He answered them and said, "The monarchy of God is not coming with visual observation.
21 Neither will they state, 'Look, *it is* here,' or 'Look, *it is* there.' You see, look, the monarchy of God is inside of you."
22 He said to the students, "Days will come when you will desire to see one of the days of the Son of the Person, and you will not see *it*.
23 And they will state to you, 'Look, *He is* there,' or 'Look, *He is* here.' You should not go off, nor should you pursue *it*.
24 You see, even as the lightning, the *lightning* that is bright, shines from the *one place* under *the* sky to the *other* under *the* sky, so also will the Son of the Person be in His day.
25 But first, it is necessary for Him to suffer many *things* and to be rejected out from this generation.
26 And just as it happened in the days of Noah, so will it also be in the days of the Son of the Person.
27 They were eating; they were drinking; they were marrying; they were being given out in marriage till *the* day that Noah went into the box; and the flood came and ruined absolutely everyone.
28 Likewise, as it also happened in the days of Lot: they were eating; they were drinking; they were buying; they were selling; they were planting; they were building;
29 but on *the* day that Lot went out away from Sodom, it rained fire and sulfur out of heaven and ruined absolutely everyone.
30 It will be aligned with these *things* on *the* day that the Son of the Person is uncovered.
31 In that day, a *person* who will be on the top of a house (and his containers in the house) must not climb down to take them, and the *person* in the field likewise must not return back to the *things left* behind.
32 Remember the wife of Lot.

33 Whoever looks to rescue his soul will lose it, but whoever loses it will help it survive.
34 I tell you on that night, two will be on one cot; the one will be taken along, and the different *one* will be left.
35 There will be two *women* grinding *flour* on the same *mill*; the one will be taken along, and the different *one* will be left.
36 Two will be in the field; the one will be taken along, and the different *one* will be left."
37 And when they respond, they say to Him, "Where, Master?" *Jesus* said to them, "Where the body is, there the raptors will be gathered together."

18

1 He was also telling them an illustration with the *lesson for it* to be necessary to always be praying and not to be getting discouraged,
2 saying, "A certain judge was in a certain city who didn't fear God and wasn't embarrassed around a person.
3 A widow was in that city, and she was coming to him, saying, 'Retaliate for me from my opponent in the court case.'
4 And he did not want to over time, but after these *things* he said in himself, 'Even if I don't fear God and am not embarrassed around a person,
5 because of the *fact* for this widow to definitely be bothering me, I will retaliate for her so that for a conclusion as she comes she does not give me a black eye.'"
6 The Master said, "Hear what the judge of the wrong way says.
7 Will God not in any way make the retaliation for His *people* who choose *Him*, the *ones* who are shouting to Him day and night? He is even patient over them.
8 I tell you that He will make the retaliation for them quickly. More importantly, when the Son of the Person comes, will He find trust on the earth?"
9 He also told this illustration to some, the *ones* who have been confident based on themselves that they are right and treating the rest as nobodies.
10 "Two people walked up to the temple grounds to pray: the one a Separatist and the different *one* a tax collector.
11 After the Separatist was stood up, he was praying these *things* to himself, 'God, I thank You that I am not even like the rest of the people: vicious, wrong, cheating spouses, or even as this tax collector.
12 I go without food twice after the Sabbath. I take ten percent out of everything, as much as I get.'
13 And the tax collector who had stood at a distance was not wanting to even raise *his* eyes to the sky, but was hitting on his chest, saying, 'God, provide a remedy to me, the sinful *person*.'
14 I tell you, this *person* walked down to his house having been made right rather than that *person* because everyone putting himself up high will be put down low but the *person* putting himself down low will be put up high."
15 They were also bringing the babies to Him so that He may touch them. But when the students saw *it*, they stopped them.

16 After Jesus called for them *(the babies)*, He said, "Leave the young children to be coming to Me, and don't hinder them. You see, the monarchy of God is *made up* of these types of *young children*.
17 Amen, I tell you, whoever does not accept the monarchy of God as a young child will not in any way go into it."
18 And a certain head person asked Him, saying, "Good teacher, what *is it that* after I do *it*, I will inherit life that spans *all* time?"
19 Jesus said to him, "Why are you calling Me good? No one *is* good except One, God.
20 You know the demands. You will not cheat on *your* spouse. You will not murder. You will not steal. You will not lie when you are a witness. Value your father and your mother."
21 But the *head person* said, "I observed all these *things* from my youth."
22 When Jesus heard these *things*, He said to him, "One *thing* is still missing for you. Sell everything, as much as you have, pass *it* out to poor *people* (and you will have a stockpile of treasure in heaven), and come here, follow Me."
23 When the *head person* heard these *things*, he became overcome with sadness. You see, he was terribly wealthy.
24 When Jesus saw him, that he became overcome with sadness, He said, "How hard *it* will *be for* the *people* who have the stacks of money *as* they go into the monarchy of God.
25 You see, it is easier for a camel to go in through *the* eye of a needle than for a wealthy *person* to go into the monarchy of God."
26 The *people* listening said, "And who is able to be rescued?"
27 *Jesus* said, "The impossible *things* beside people are possible beside God."
28 Peter said, "Look, we left everything and followed You."
29 *Jesus* said to them, "Amen, I tell you that there is not even one *person* who left a house, or parents, or brothers, or a wife, or children on account of the monarchy of God,
30 who will not in any way receive back many times more in this time and in the span of time, the coming *one*, life that spans *all* time."
31 After He took the Twelve alongside, He said to them, "Look, we are walking up into Jerusalem and all the *things* that have been written through the preachers about the Son of the Person will be finished.
32 You see, He will be turned over to the non-Jews. And He will be mocked, injured, and spit at.
33 And after whipping *Him*, they will kill Him, and on the day, the third *one*, He will stand up."
34 And they understood none of these *things*, this statement was *one* that had been hidden from them, and they were not knowing the *things* being said.
35 It happened during the *time* for Him to be coming near to Jericho; a certain blind *man* was sitting along the road begging.
36 When he listened to a crowd traveling through, he was inquiring what this was.
37 They reported to him that Jesus the Nazarene is passing by.
38 And he shouted, saying, "Jesus, Son of David, show forgiving kindness to me."

39 And the *people* who were going ahead of *Him* were shushing him so that he would be silent. But he was yelling much more, "Son of David, show forgiving kindness to me."
40 When Jesus was stopped, He gave the order for him to be led to Him. When he was near, He asked him,
41 saying, "What do you want *that* I should do for you?" The *blind man* said, "Master, that I might see again."
42 And Jesus said to him, "See again. Your trust has rescued you."
43 And at once he saw again, and he was following Him praising God's magnificence. And when the entire group saw *it*, it gave praise to God.

19

1 And after He went in, He was going through Jericho.
2 And look, a man called by *the* name Zacchaeus. And he was a head tax collector, and he was wealthy.
3 And he was looking to see Jesus, who He is. And he was not able *to see Him* out of the crowd because he was little in size.
4 And after he ran ahead in front, he climbed up on a white mulberry tree so that he might see Him because He was going to be going through that *way*.
5 And as Jesus came up to the place, when He looked up, He saw him and said to him, "Zacchaeus, after hurrying up, climb down. You see, today it is necessary for Me to stay in your house."
6 And after hurrying up, he climbed down and, being happy, accepted Him under *his roof*.
7 And when absolutely everyone saw *it*, they were speaking in hushed tones among themselves, saying, "He went in beside a sinful man to settle down *for the night*."
8 But when Zacchaeus was stood up, he said to the Master, "Look, the halves of the *things* that are mine, Master, I am giving to the poor, and if I made false accusations of anything against anyone, I am giving *it* back quadruple."
9 Jesus said to him, "Today a rescue happened in this house due to the fact that he is also a son of Abraham.
10 You see, the Son of the Person came to look for and to rescue the *sheep* that has been lost."
11 As they listened, when He added to these *things*, He told an illustration because of the *fact* for Him to be near Jerusalem and for it to be seeming to them that the monarchy of God was going to be spotted at once.
12 So He said, "A certain person from a high-ranking family line traveled to a distant rural area to receive a monarchy for himself and to return.
13 After calling ten slaves of his, he gave them ten minas (*$17 coins*) and said to them, 'Invest until I come.'
14 His citizens were hating him. And they sent a delegation of older men out *on a mission* behind him, saying, 'We do not want this *person* to be king over us.'
15 And it happened during the *time* for him to come back after receiving the monarchy; he also said to holler for him to these slaves (to whom he gave the silver) so that he might know who earned what through investing.

16 The first *one* showed up, saying, 'Master, your mina *(a $17 coin)* earned ten minas *($170).*'
17 And he said to him, 'Well *done*, good slave. Because you became reliable in *the* smallest *thing*, have authority over ten cities.'
18 And the second *slave* came, saying, 'Master, your mina *(a $17 coin)* made five minas *($85).*'
19 He also said to this *slave*, 'And you, become over five cities.'
20 And a different *slave* came, saying, 'Master, look, your mina *(a $17 coin)* that I was keeping set-aside in a towel.
21 You see, I feared you because you are a rough person. You pick up what you did not set *down* and harvest what you did not seed.'
22 He says to him, 'From your mouth, I will judge you, evil slave. You realized that I am a rough person taking what I did not set *down* and harvesting what I did not seed.
23 And why didn't you give my silver on the *bank* table, and when I came, I would collect it together with interest?'
24 And to the *people* who had stood nearby, he said, 'Take the mina *(a $17 coin)* away from him, and give it to the *person* who has ten minas *($170).*'
25 And they said to him, 'Master, he has ten minas *($170).*'
26 'You see, I tell you that to everyone who has it will be given, but from the *person* who does not have, even what he has will be taken away from him.
27 More importantly, lead those enemies of mine here, the *ones* who did not want me to be king over them, and slaughter *them* down in front of me.'"
28 And after He said these *things*, He was traveling in front, as He walked up to Jerusalem.
29 And it happened as He came near to Bethphage and Bethany, toward the mountain, the *one* that is called, "of Olives;" He sent two of His students out *on a mission*,
30 after saying, "Make *your* way back into the village directly facing *you*, in which, as you travel into *it*, you will find a foal that has been tied up, on which no one (of people) has been seated at any time. After you release *it*, lead it *here*.
31 And if someone asks you why you are releasing *it*, this is what you will state to him, 'The Master has need of it.'"
32 After going off, the *two* who had been sent out found just what He said to them.
33 As they were releasing the foal, its masters said to them, "Why are you releasing the foal?"
34 The *two* said, "The Master has need of it."
35 And they led it to Jesus, and after tossing their *own* robes on the foal, they loaded Jesus on *it*.
36 As He traveled, they were spreading their robes out underneath in the road.
37 As He came near, already facing the descent of the Mountain of the Olives, absolutely all the large number of the students (as *the people* were happy) began to be praising God with a loud voice about all *the* abilities that they saw,

38 saying, "The *One* coming (the King) in *the* Master's name who has been conferred with blessings. Peace in heaven and magnificence in *the* highest *places*."
39 And some of the Separatists out of the crowd said to Him, "Teacher, stop Your students."
40 And when He responded, He said to them, "I tell you that if these *people* will be silent, the stones will yell."
41 And as He came near, when He saw the city, He cried over it,
42 saying, "If you knew, even you, and definitely in this your day, the *things* toward your peace. But now it was hidden away from your eyes
43 because days will arrive on you and your enemies will put a blockade around you, completely surround you, and hold you in on all sides.
44 And they will level you and your children in you down to terra firma, and they will not leave in you a stone on a stone for *the times* that you did not know the appointed time of your supervision."
45 And when He went onto the temple grounds, He began to be throwing out the *people* who were selling in it and buying,
46 saying to them, "It has been written *in Isaiah 56:7*, 'My house is a house of prayer,' but you made it a cave of bandits."
47 And He was teaching the "daily" *thing* on the temple grounds, but the head priests, the *Old Testament* transcribers, and the most important *men* of the ethnic group were looking to ruin Him,
48 and they were not finding the "what they would do" *thing*. You see, absolutely all of the group were hanging on to His *every word* as they listened.

20

1 And it happened during one of those days; as He was teaching the group on the temple grounds and sharing good news, the head priests and the *Old Testament* transcribers stood over *Him* together with the older *men*.
2 And they said to Him, saying, "Tell us, in what kind of authority are You doing these *things* or who is the *one* who gave You this authority?"
3 When He answered, He said to them, "I also will ask you one saying, and you must tell *it* to Me.
4 The submersion of John, was it from heaven or from people?"
5 Together the *men* considered to themselves, saying, "If we say from heaven, He will state, 'So why didn't you trust him?'
6 But if we say from people, the entire group will take us down by throwing stones *at us*. You see, it is *a group* that has been confident for John to be a preacher."
7 And they responded not to know where *it is* from.
8 And Jesus said to them, "Neither am I telling you in what kind of authority I do these *things*."
9 He began to be telling this illustration to the group, "A certain person planted a vineyard, gave it out to farmers, and left the area for an adequate amount of time.

10 And during *the* right time, he sent a slave out *on a mission* to the farmers so that they would give to him out of the fruit of the vineyard, but after the farmers beat *him*, they sent him off empty.

11 And he added a different slave to send. The *farmers* also, after beating and belittling that *one*, sent *him* off empty.

12 And he added a third to send. The *farmers* also, after wounding this *one*, threw *him* out.

13 The master of the vineyard said, 'What should I do? I will send my son, the loved *one*. They will likely be embarrassed when they see this *one*.'

14 But when the farmers saw him, they were pondering to themselves, saying, 'This is the inheritor. Come on. We should kill him so that the inheritance might become ours.'

15 And after they threw him outside of the vineyard, they killed *him*. So what will the master of the vineyard do to them?

16 He will come and ruin these farmers and give the vineyard to others." When they heard *this*, they said, "It could not happen."

17 After looking at them, *Jesus* said, "So, what is this *thing* that has been written *in Psalm 118:22*, 'A stone that the *people* who are building rejected, this became for a corner's head?'

18 Everyone who falls on that stone will be smashed. On whomever it falls, it will grind him up."

19 And the head priests and the *Old Testament* transcribers looked for *an opportunity* to put *their* hands on Him in the same hour. And they feared the group. You see, they knew that He told this illustration to them.

20 And after they watched *Him* closely, they sent undercover *people* (that were themselves faking to be *people* who do what is right) out *on a mission* so that they might attack His answer for the "to turn Him over to the head ruler and the authority of the leader" *part*.

21 And they asked Him, saying, "Teacher, we realize that you are talking and teaching correctly and You don't receive an appearance, but You teach the way of God based on truth.

22 Is it allowed to us to give a protection fee to Caesar or not?"

23 After taking a closer look at their slyness, He said to them, "Why are you trying to cause trouble with Me?

24 Show me a denarius *(a fifty-dollar coin)*. Whose image and inscription does it have?" When they answered, they said, "Caesar's."

25 *Jesus* said to them, "Now then, give the *things* of Caesar back to Caesar and the *things* of God *back* to God."

26 And they didn't have *the* strength to attack His statement directly in front of the group, and, amazed based on His response, they kept quiet.

27 When some of the Sadducees came forward (the *ones* expressing opposition to a return back to life, *for it* not to exist), they asked Him,

28 saying, "Teacher, Moses wrote to us, 'If someone's brother dies who has a wife and this *one* dies childless, that his brother should take the wife and bring up from *him* a seed for his brother.'

29 So there were seven brothers, and after the first took a wife, he died childless.

30 And the second *brother* took the wife, and this *one* died childless.
31 And the third took her. Similarly, even the seven also did not leave children down *here* and died.
32 Last of all, the wife also died.
33 So in the return back to life, whose wife of them does she become? You see, the seven had her *as* a wife."
34 And when Jesus answered, He said to them, "The sons of this span of time marry and are given out in marriage.
35 But the *people* who are considered deserving to obtain that span of time and the return back to life, the *return back to life* from *the* dead, neither marry, nor are given out in marriage.
36 You see, neither are they able to die anymore; for they are equal to angels, and they are sons of God, being sons of the return back to life.
37 That the dead are gotten up — even Moses disclosed *this* on the bush as he says, '*The* Master *is* the God of Abraham, the God of Isaac, and the God of Jacob.'
38 He is not a God of dead *people*, but of *people* living. You see, all are living to Him."
39 When some of the *Old Testament* transcribers responded, they said, "Teacher, nicely said."
40 No longer were they daring to be asking Him anything.
41 But He said to them, "How do they say the Anointed King *is* to be a son of David?
42 Even David himself says in a scroll of Psalms *in Psalm 110:1*, 'The Master said to my Master, Sit down at *places to the* right of Me
43 until I put Your enemies *as* a footrest of Your feet.'
44 So David calls Him a master. And how is He his son?"
45 As the entire group was listening, He said to His students,
46 "Be cautious of the *Old Testament* transcribers, the *ones* who want to be walking around in long robes and who are fond of greetings in the marketplaces, front benches in the synagogues, and front reclining places in the feasts,
47 who eat up the houses of the widows and for a sham, pray long *prayers*. These will receive much more judgment."

21

1 When He looked up, He saw the wealthy *people* throwing their contributions into the treasury vault.
2 He also saw a certain needy widow throwing two tiny coins there.
3 And He said, "I truly tell you that the widow, this poor *one*, threw *in* more than everyone.
4 You see, for the contributions of God, absolutely all these *people* threw *in* from what they had left over, but this *widow* from her deficiency threw in absolutely all the livelihood that she had."
5 And as some were telling about the temple grounds, that it had been decorated with nice stones and donations, He said,

6 "For these *things* that you see, days will come in which a stone will not be left on a stone that will not be torn down."
7 They asked Him, saying, "Teacher, so when will these *things* be, and what *is* the indicator when these *things* are going to be happening?"
8 *Jesus* said, "Look out. You should not be misled. You see, many will come based on My name, saying, 'I am *Him*,' and, 'The appointed time has come near.' So do not travel off behind them.
9 When you hear wars and conflicts, don't panic. You see, it is necessary for these *things* to happen first, but the conclusion *is* not right away."
10 At that time, He was saying to them, "A nation will rise up on a nation and a monarchy on a monarchy.
11 There will be both large earthquakes and throughout places, famines and diseases. There will be both fearful things and great indicators out of heaven.
12 Before all these *things*, they will put their hands on you and persecute *you*, turning *you* in to synagogues and jails being led before kings and leaders on account of My name.
13 It will step out to you for a witness.
14 So place into your hearts not to be concerned beforehand to defend yourself.
15 You see, I will give you a mouth and insight that all the *people* lying in opposition to you will not be able to talk in opposition, nor stand in opposition to.
16 You will even be turned in by parents, brothers, relatives, and friends. And they will put *some* from among you to death.
17 And you will be hated by everyone because of My name.
18 And a hair from your head will not in any way be ruined.
19 Get your souls in your persistence *to do what is right*.
20 When you see Jerusalem being surrounded by army camps, at that time know that her uninhabitedness has come near.
21 At that time, the *people* in Judea must escape into the mountains, the *people* in *the* middle of her must get a long way away, and the *people* in the rural areas must not go into her
22 because these are days of retaliation, of the 'to accomplish all the *things* that have been written' *kind*.
23 What a tragedy *it will be* to the *women* having *a baby* in *their* womb and the *women* nursing in those days. You see, there will be a large shortage on the earth and punishment in this ethnic group.
24 And they will fall by *the* mouth of a dagger and will be forcibly incarcerated into all the nations. And Jerusalem will be trampled by non-Jews till *the* appointed times of *the* non-Jews will be accomplished.
25 And indicators will be in *the* sun, moon, and constellations. And on the earth, *there will be* a distress of nations with perplexity of *the* sea and surge echoing
26 as people stop breathing out of fear and expectation of the *events* coming on the civilized world. You see, the abilities of the heavens will be disturbed.
27 And at that time, they will see the Son of the Person coming in a cloud with much ability and magnificence.

28 As these *events* begin to be happening, stand up straight and raise your heads up because your paid release is near."
29 And He told an illustration to them, "Look at the fig tree and all the trees.
30 When they already thrust *sprouts* forward, as you see out from yourselves, you know that the summer is already near.
31 In this way also, when you see these *things* happening, know that the monarchy of God is near.
32 Amen, I tell you that this generation will not in any way pass until all *these things* happen.
33 The sky and the earth will pass, but My messages will not in any way pass.
34 Pay attention to yourselves so that your hearts might not be heavy with a hangover, drunkenness, and worry about this life's things, and that day might stand over you unexpected.
35 You see, it will come as a trap on all the *people* sitting on the face of all the earth.
36 So don't go to sleep, pleading in every right time so that you might be considered deserving to escape from all these *things* that are going to be happening and to be established in front of the Son of the Person."
37 *During* the days, He was on the temple grounds teaching. *During* the nights, going out, He was spending the nights outside in the mountain, the *one* that is called "of Olives."
38 And the entire group was coming to Him at daybreak on the temple grounds to be listening to Him.

22

1 The Festival of the Yeast-free *Loaves*, the *festival* that is called *the* Passover, was near.
2 And the head priests and the *Old Testament* transcribers were looking for the "how they might execute Him" *thing*. You see, they were fearing the group.
3 The Opponent went into the Judas also called "from Kerioth", who was from the number of the Twelve.
4 And when he went off, he spoke together with the head priests and the captains *about* the "how he might turn Him over to them" *thing*.
5 And they were happy and agreed to give him silver.
6 And he acknowledged *it* out loud and was looking for a good time of the "to turn Him over to them void of a crowd" *part*.
7 The day of the Yeast-free *Loaves Festival* came, in which it was necessary for the Passover *lamb* to be sacrificed.
8 And He sent Peter and John out *on a mission* after saying, "After traveling *out*, get the Passover *meal* ready for us so that we might eat."
9 The *two* said to Him, "Where do you want *that* we might get *things* ready?"
10 *Jesus* said to them, "Look, when you go into the city, a person will meet together with you hauling a clay pitcher of water. Follow him into the house where he travels into *it*.

11 And you will state to the homeowner of the house, 'The Teacher says to you, "Where is the guest room where I might eat the Passover *meal* with My students?"'
12 And that *person* will show you a large room above the ground floor that has been set up. Get ready there."
13 After they went off, they found *it* just as He has stated to them. And they got the Passover *meal* ready.
14 And when the hour happened, He settled down and the twelve missionaries together with Him.
15 And He said to them, "With desire I have desired to eat this Passover *meal* with you before the *time* for Me to suffer.
16 You see, I tell you that I will no longer in any way eat from it until it will be accomplished in the monarchy of God."
17 And when He accepted a cup, after He was thankful, He said, "Take this, and divide *it* up to yourselves.
18 You see, I tell you that I will not in any way drink from the produce of the vine until the monarchy of God will come."
19 And when He took bread, after He was thankful, He split *it* and gave *it* to them, saying, "This is My body, the *body* given on your behalf. Do this for the reminder again of Me."
20 Similarly, *He* also *did* the cup after the *time for them* to eat dinner, saying, "This cup *is* the new deal in My blood, the *cup* spilled out on your behalf.
21 More importantly, look, the hand of the *person* turning Me in *is* with Me on the table.
22 And the Son of the Person certainly travels aligned with what has been designated. More importantly, what a tragedy *it is* to that person through whom He is turned in."
23 And they began to together be posing questions to themselves, the "so who would it be from among them, the *one* who is going to be repeatedly doing this *thing*" kind.
24 Also an argument that they liked to have among them happened, the "who of them seems to be greater" *argument*.
25 *Jesus* said to them, "The kings of the non-Jews are masters over them, and the *people* who have authority over them are called humanitarians.
26 You *will* not *be* like that, but the greater *person* among you must become as the younger *person* and the *person* being a leader as the *person* serving.
27 You see, who is greater, the *person* reclining or the *person* serving? Is it not the *person* reclining? But I *am* in *the* middle of you as the *person* serving *is*.
28 You are the *ones* who through it *all* have stayed with Me in My troubles.
29 And I am making a deal with you for a monarchy (just as My father made with Me)
30 so that you may eat and drink on My table in My monarchy and you will be seated on thrones judging the twelve family lines of Israel."
31 The Master said, "Simon, Simon, look, the Opponent made a request *concerning* you, of the 'to sift *you* as the grain' *kind*,
32 but I pleaded concerning you that your trust may not cease. And you, whenever you return back, establish your brothers."

33 *Peter* said to Him, "Master, I am ready to be traveling with You, even into jail and into death."
34 *Jesus* said, "I tell you, Peter, a rooster will not in any way crow today before you will flatly deny *Me*, even three times, to not know Me."
35 And He said to them, "When I sent you out *on missions* void of a money bag, a tote bag, and sandals, did you lack anything?" The *students* said, "Nothing."
36 So He said to them, "But now the *person* who has a money bag must take it, likewise also a tote bag. And the *person* who does not have *them* must sell his robe and buy a dagger.
37 You see, I tell you that still it is necessary for this *thing* that has been written *in Isaiah 53:12* to be finished in Me, the 'and He will be considered with criminals' *thing*; for *this thing* about Me also has a conclusion."
38 The *students* said, "Master, look, here *are* two daggers." *Jesus* said to them, "It is adequate."
39 And after going out, He traveled (aligned with the custom) to the Mountain of the Olives. His students also followed Him.
40 After they became on the place, He said to them, "Pray not to get into trouble."
41 And He was pulled away from them as if *it were* a stone's throw, and after placing *His* knees *on the ground*, He was praying,
42 saying, "Father, if You intend *to*, carry this cup off away from Me. More importantly, not what I want, but what You *want* must happen.
43 An angel out of heaven was seen with Him, invigorating Him.
44 And when He became in a struggle, He was praying more intensely. His perspiration became as if *it were* clots of blood tumbling down on the ground.
45 And after He got up from the prayer, when He went to the students, He found them asleep from the sadness.
46 And He said to them, "Why are you sleeping? After getting up, pray that you might not get into trouble."
47 As He was still speaking, look, a crowd, and the *one* called Judas (one of the Twelve) was going on ahead of them. And He came near to Jesus to be friendly with Him.
48 Jesus said to him, "Judas, are you turning the Son of the Person in with a friendly gesture?"
49 When the *people* around Him saw what will be, they said to Him, "Master, *tell us* if we will forcibly strike *them* with a dagger."
50 And a certain one from among them forcibly struck the slave of the head priest and took off his ear, the right *one*.
51 But when Jesus answered, He said, "Allow this for now." And when He touched his ear lobe, He cured him.
52 Jesus said to the *people* who showed up on Him (head priests, captains of the temple grounds, and older *men*), "Have you come out with daggers and wooden clubs as on a bandit?
53 Daily as I was with you on the temple grounds, you did not put out *your* hands on Me, but this is your hour and the authority of the darkness.

54 When they apprehended Him, they took and led Him into the house of the head priest. Peter was following at a distance.
55 When they lit a fire in *the* middle of the courtyard and were seated together, Peter was sitting in *the* middle of them.
56 When a certain servant girl saw him sitting toward the light and stared at him, she said, "This *person* also was together with Him."
57 But *Peter* denied Him, saying, "Ma'am, I do not know Him."
58 And after a bit, when a different *person* saw him, he was declaring, "You also are from among them." But Peter said, "Sir, I am not."
59 And after as if one hour went by, someone else was strongly insisting, saying, "Based on truth, this *person* also was with Him. You see, he also is a Galilean."
60 But Peter said, "Sir, I do not know what you are saying." And at once, as he was still speaking, the rooster crowed.
61 And after the Master turned, He looked at Peter, and Peter quietly remembered the message of the Master, how He said to him, "Before *the time* for a rooster to crow, you will flatly deny Me three times."
62 And after Peter went outside, he cried bitterly.
63 And the men, the *ones* holding Jesus, were mocking Him as they beat *Him*.
64 And after they blindfolded Him, they were hitting His face and asking Him, saying, "Prophesy. Who is the *one* who struck You?"
65 And many different *things* were they saying to Him, insulting *Him*.
66 And as it became day, the board of older men of the ethnic group, head priests, and *Old Testament* transcribers were gathered together. And they led Him up to their *own* council, saying,
67 "If You are the Anointed King, tell us." He told them, "If I tell you, you will not in any way trust.
68 If I also ask *you a question*, you will not in any way answer Me or dismiss *Me*.
69 From the present *on*, the Son of the Person will be sitting at *places to the* right of the ability of God."
70 Everyone said, "So are You the Son of God?" *Jesus* was declaring to them, "You are saying that I am."
71 The *men* said, "What? Do we still have a need of a witness? You see, we ourselves heard it out of His mouth."

23

1 And after absolutely all the large number of them got up, they led Him before Pilate.
2 They began to be leveling complaints against Him, saying, "We found this *Person* twisting the nation and hindering *people* to be giving protection fees to Caesar saying for He Himself to be a king, *the* Anointed King."
3 Pilate asked Him, saying, "Are You the king of the Jewish *people*?" When *Jesus* answered him, He was declaring, "You say *it*."
4 Pilate said to the head priests and the crowds, "I find no *legal* case in this person."

5 The *people* were getting stronger, saying, "He shakes up the ethnic group teaching throughout all of Judea after beginning from Galilee to here."
6 When Pilate heard Galilee, he asked if the person is a Galilean.
7 And when he correctly understood that He is from the jurisdiction of Herod, he sent Him up to Herod, since he was also in Greater Jerusalem during these days.
8 When Herod saw Jesus, he was very happy. You see, he was wanting to see Him from an adequate amount *of time* because of the *fact for him* to be hearing much about Him, and he was anticipating to see some indicator happening under Him.
9 He was asking Him in an adequate amount of words, but He answered him nothing.
10 The head priests and the *Old Testament* transcribers had stood methodically leveling complaints against Him.
11 After Herod together with his military forces treated Him as a nobody and mocked *Him*, after putting a dazzling outfit around Him, he sent Him up to Pilate.
12 They became friends (both Herod and Pilate) in the same day with each other. You see, they previously were in a hostile relationship as they were facing each other.
13 When Pilate called the head priests, the head people, and the group together,
14 he said to them, "You brought this person to me as a *person* who turns the ethnic group away, and look, when I investigated Him in your sight, I found in this person no *legal* case of *things* that you level against Him.
15 But neither *did* Herod. You see, I sent you up to him, and look, there is nothing deserving of death that has been repeatedly done by Him.
16 So after I discipline Him, I will dismiss *Him*."
17 He was having an obligation to be dismissing one *person* to them at each festival.
18 But they yelled out simultaneously, saying, "Take this *Person*. Dismiss Barabbas to us"
19 (someone who, because of a certain disruption that happened in the city and *because of* murder, had been thrown into jail).
20 So again Pilate hollered, wanting to dismiss Jesus.
21 But the *people* were hollering out, saying, "Nail *Him* to a cross. Nail Him to a cross."
22 A third *time Pilate* said to them, "You see, what bad *thing* did this *Person* do? I found no *legal* case of death in Him. So after I discipline Him, I will dismiss *Him*."
23 But the *people* were laying into *him* with loud voices asking for Him to be nailed to a cross, and the voices of them and the head priests were strong against *him*.
24 Pilate gave the sentence for their request to happen.
25 He dismissed to them the *one* who, because of disruption and murder, had been thrown into the jail, whom they were asking for, but turned Jesus over to what they wanted.

26 And as they led Him away, after latching on to a certain Simon, a Cyrenian, coming out of a field, they placed the cross on him to be carrying *it* behind Jesus.
27 A very large number of the group and of women (who were also beating their chests in grief and wailing for Him) were following Him.
28 When Jesus turned back toward them, He said, "Daughters of Jerusalem, don't cry over Me. More importantly, cry over yourselves and over your children
29 because, look, days are coming in which they will state, 'The infertile women, bellies that did not give birth, and breasts that did not nurse are blessed.'
30 At that time, they will begin to be saying to the mountains, 'Fall on us,' and to the hills, 'Cover us up,'
31 because if they are doing these *things* in the wet wood, what will happen in the dry?"
32 Two different outlaws were also being led together with Him to be executed.
33 And when they went off onto the place, the *place* called Skull, there they nailed Him and the outlaws (*one* that *was* at *places to the* right, *another* that *was* at *places to the* left) to crosses.
34 But Jesus was saying, "Father, forgive them. You see, they don't realize what they are doing." As they divided up His clothes, they threw dice.
35 And the group had stood *there* watching. The head people were even making a fool *of Him* out loud together with them, saying, "Others He rescued. He must rescue Himself if this is the Anointed King, the select *One* of God."
36 The soldiers also were mocking Him, coming forward, offering sour wine to Him,
37 and saying, "If You are the king of the Jewish *people*, rescue Yourself."
38 An inscription also had been written over Him with Greek, Latin, and Hebrew alphabetic characters, "This is the King of the Jewish *people*."
39 One of the outlaws hanging *there* was insulting Him, saying, "If You are the Anointed King, rescue Yourself and us."
40 When the different *outlaw* responded, he was shushing him, saying, "Don't you even fear God? Because you are in the same sentence,
41 and we, certainly rightly *so*. You see, we are receiving back deserving *things* of which we constantly did. But this *person* constantly did nothing out of place."
42 And he was saying to Jesus, "Remember me, Master, when You come in Your monarchy."
43 And Jesus said to him, "Amen, I tell you, today you will be with Me in the paradise."
44 It was as if *it were the* sixth hour *(noon)*, and darkness happened on the whole earth until *the* ninth hour *(3:00 p.m.)*.
45 And the sun was made dark, and the curtain of the temple was torn *down the* middle.

46 And when Jesus hollered with a loud voice, He said, "Father, into Your hands will I place My spirit beside *You*." And when He said these *things*, He breathed out *His last breath*.
47 When the lieutenant saw what happened, he praised God's magnificence, saying, "This person was really right."
48 And all the crowds that came out together on this spectator event, after watching what happened, were returning hitting their *own* chests.
49 All the *people* known of Him and the women who followed along with Him out of Galilee had stood at a distance looking at these *things*.
50 And look, a man with *the* name Joseph, an advisor, who was a good man and did what is right.
51 This *man*, who had not voted in agreement with their intention and what they repeatedly did, was from Arimathaea, a city of the Jewish *people*, who also even himself was awaiting the monarchy of God.
52 This *man*, after going forward to Pilate, asked for the body of Jesus.
53 And when he took it down, he wound a linen cloth around it and placed Him in a grave cut out of rock that no one was lying in yet.
54 And *the* day was a preparation *day*, and a Sabbath was emerging.
55 After women also (some who had come together from Galilee) followed behind him, they viewed the burial vault and how His body was placed.
56 When they returned, they got fragrant resins and perfumes ready. And they certainly calmed down on the Sabbath according to the demand.

24

1 On the *Day* 1 after the Sabbaths at deep daybreak, they and some *women* together with them came on the grave carrying fragrant resins that they got ready.
2 But they found the stone that had been rolled away from the burial vault.
3 And when they went in, they did not find the body of the Master, Jesus.
4 And it happened during the *time* for them to be dumbfounded about this; and look, two men stood over them in outfits that were bright.
5 When they became afraid, even putting *their* face down to the ground, *the men* said to them, "Why are you looking for the living with the dead?
6 He is not here, but He was gotten up. Remember how He spoke to you as He was still in Galilee,
7 saying, 'It is necessary for the Son of the Person to be turned over into sinful people's hands, to be nailed to a cross, and to stand up on the third day'?"
8 They remembered His statements.
9 And when they returned from the burial vault, they reported all these *things* to the eleven and all the rest.
10 They were the Magdalene Mary, Joanna, Mary (*the mother* of James), and the rest *of the women* together with them, who were telling these *things* to the missionaries.
11 And their statements appeared in their sight as if *it were* nonsense, and they were not trusting them.

12 But when Peter got up, he ran up to the burial vault. And when he stooped and peered in, he saw the linen strips lying alone. And he went off to himself, amazed at what happened.
13 And look, two from among them were traveling in the same day to a village having *itself* sixty track laps *(7 1/2 miles)* away from Jerusalem to which *belongs the* name Emmaus.
14 And they were chatting to each other about all these *things* that had transpired.
15 And it happened during the *time* for them to be chatting and to together be posing questions; after Jesus Himself came near, He also was traveling together with them.
16 Their eyes were being held on to, of the "not to recognize Him" *kind*.
17 He said to them, "What *are* these words that you are throwing back and forth to each other as you walk around and are sad-faced?"
18 When the one with whom *is the* name Cleopas answered, he said to Him, "Are you just a tourist in Jerusalem? And didn't you know the *things* that happened in it in these days?"
19 And He said to them, "What kind of *things*?" The *two* said to Him, "The *things* about Jesus, the Nazarene, a man who became a preacher, competent in action and message directly in front of God and all the ethnic group,
20 and how the head priests and our head people turned Him over to a sentence of death and nailed Him to a cross.
21 We were anticipating that He is the *One* who is going to be paying the price to release Israel. But, definitely, together with all these *things*, it leads this third day, today, from *the time* that these *things* happened.
22 But also some women from among us astounded us who became daybreaking *women* on the burial vault.
23 And when they did not find His body, they came, saying to have also seen a sighting of angels that say for Him to be alive.
24 And some of the *people* together with us went off up to the burial vault and this is how they found *it*, just as also the women said, but they did not see Him."
25 And He said to them, "O unobservant *people* and slow with the heart of the 'to be trusting based on all *the things* that the preachers spoke' *thing*.
26 Was it not necessary for the Anointed King to suffer these *things* and to go into His magnificence?"
27 And beginning from Moses and from all the Preachers, He thoroughly interpreted to them the *things* about Himself in all the *Old Testament* writings.
28 And they were near to the village where they were traveling to, and He was pretending to be traveling farther.
29 And they compelled Him, saying, "Stay with us because it is toward late afternoon and the day has declined down." And He went in for the *purpose* to stay together with them.
30 And it happened during the *time* for Him to be reclined with them; after taking the bread, He conferred a blessing on *it*, and after splitting *it*, He was giving *it* over to them.

31 Their eyes were completely opened, they recognized Him, and He became disappeared away from them.
32 And they said to each other, "Was our heart not burning in us as He was speaking to us on the road, as He was completely opening the *Old Testament* writings to us?"
33 And after standing up the same hour, they returned to Jerusalem, and they found the eleven and the *people* who had accumulated together with them,
34 who said that the Master really was gotten up and was seen by Simon.
35 And they were recounting the *things* on the road and how He was known to them in the splitting of the bread.
36 As they were speaking these *things*, Jesus stood in *the* middle of them. And He says to them, "Peace to you."
37 After panicking and becoming afraid, they were seeming to be seeing a spirit.
38 And He said to them, "Why have you been uneasy? And why do questions step up in your hearts?
39 Look at My hands and My feet because I am Me, Myself. Feel Me and look because a spirit does not have a physical body and bones just as you see Me having."
40 And after He said this, He showed them *His* hands and feet.
41 While they still did not trust out of the happiness and being amazed, He said to them, "What edible *thing* do you have here?"
42 The *students* gave a part of cooked fish over to Him and *a piece* out of a honeycomb.
43 And after taking *it*, He ate *it* in their sight.
44 He said to them, "These *are* the words that I spoke to you as I was still together with you, 'It is necessary for all the *things* that have been written in the Law of Moses, *the* Preachers, and Psalms about Me to be accomplished.'"
45 At that time, He completely opened their way of thinking for the "to be understanding the *Old Testament* writings" part.
46 And He said to them, "This is how it has been written, and this is how it is necessary for the Anointed King to suffer, to come back to life from *the* dead the third day,
47 and to speak publicly based on His name about a change of ways and forgiveness of sins for all the nations beginning out from Jerusalem.
48 You are witnesses of these *things*.
49 And look, I am sending the promise of My Father out on you. You must be seated in the city of Jerusalem until *the time* that you will put on ability from a high position."
50 He led them outside until *they came* to Bethany, and when He raised up His hands, He conferred a blessing on them.
51 And it happened during the *time* for Him to be conferring a blessing on them; He stood further away from them and was being carried up into the sky.
52 And they, after bowing down to Him, returned to Jerusalem with great happiness.

53 And through everything they were on the temple grounds praising and conferring blessings on God. Amen.

John

1

1 In *the* beginning, there was the Message, the Message was pointed toward God, and the Message was God.
2 This *Message* was pointed toward God in *the* beginning.
3 All *things* came into existence through Him, and separate from Him not even one *thing* came into existence that has come into existence.
4 In Him, there was life, and the life was the light of the people.
5 And the light shines in the dark, and the dark did not take it down.
6 There became a person who had been sent out *on a mission* from the side of God. *The* name *belonging* to him *is* John.
7 This *person* came for a witness account, so that he might tell what he witnessed about the Light, so that all might trust through him.
8 That *person* was not the Light, but *he came* so that he might tell what he witnessed about the Light.
9 The Light (the true *One* that lights *things* up for every person) was coming into the world.
10 He was in the world, the world came into existence through Him, and the world did not know Him.
11 He went to *His* own *places*, and *His* own *people* did not receive Him in.
12 But as many as received Him, to them He gave authority to become God's children, to the *people* trusting in His name
13 who were born, not from bloodlines, nor from what a physical body wants, nor from what a man wants, but from God.
14 And the Message became a physical body and camped among us. And we viewed His magnificence, magnificence as of *the* only biological *child* from the side of *the* Father, full of generosity and truth.
15 John tells what he witnessed about Him, and he has yelled, saying, "This was whom I said, 'The *One* coming behind me has become in front of me because He was first *over* me.'"
16 And we all received from His fullness, even generosity for generosity.
17 Because the law was given through Moses, the generosity and the truth happened through Jesus, the Anointed King.
18 No one has seen God at any time. The only biological Son, the *One* being in the arms of the Father, that *One* recounted *Him*.
19 And this is the witness account of John when the Jewish *people* from Greater Jerusalem sent out priests and Levites so that they might ask him, "Who are you?"
20 And he acknowledged. And he did not deny. And he acknowledged, "I am not the Anointed King."
21 And they asked him, "So who *are you*? Are you Elijah?" And he says, "I am not." "Are you the Preacher?" And he answered, "No."

22 So they said to him, "Who are you? So that we might give a response to the *people* who sent us. What do you say about yourself?"
23 He was declaring, "I *am* a voice shouting in the backcountry, 'Make the road of *the* Master straight,' just as Isaiah, the preacher, said *in Isaiah 40:3*."
24 And the *people* who had been sent out were from the Separatists.
25 And they asked him and said to him, "So why do you submerge if you are not the Anointed King, nor Elijah, nor the Preacher?"
26 John answered them, saying, "I submerge in water. But *in the* middle of you, He has stood, whom you have not seen.
27 He is the *One* coming behind me, who has become in front of me, of whom I am not deserving that I might release the strap of His sandal."
28 These *things* happened in Bethabara on *the* other side of the Jordan *River* where John was submerging.
29 The next day, John sees Jesus coming to him and says, "Look, the Lamb of God, the *One* taking away the sin of the world.
30 It is this *One* about whom I said, 'Behind me, a Man is coming who has become in front of me because He was first *over* me.'
31 And I had not seen Him, but *I had seen* that He would be shown to Israel. Because of this, I came submerging in the water."
32 And John told what he witnessed, saying, "I have viewed the Spirit stepping down as if *He were* a dove from heaven, and He stayed on Him.
33 And I had not seen Him, but the *One* who sent me to be submerging in water, that *One* said to me, 'On whomever you see the Spirit stepping down and staying on Him, this *One* is the *One* who submerges in *the* Sacred Spirit.'
34 And I have seen and told what I witnessed, that this is the Son of God."
35 The next day, again, John and two from his students had been standing.
36 And when he looks at Jesus walking around, he says, "Look, the Lamb of God!"
37 And the two students listened to him speaking, and they followed Jesus.
38 When Jesus turns around and sees them following, He says to them, "What are you looking for?" The *two* said to Him, "Rabbi," (that is said *in place of* Teacher, being interpreted *from Hebrew*), "where are You staying?"
39 He says to them, "Come and see." They went and saw where He stays and stayed beside Him that day. *The* hour was as *if it were the* tenth *(4:00 p.m.)*.
40 Andrew (the brother of Simon Peter) was one from the two, the *two* who heard from the side of John and followed Him.
41 This first *man* finds the brother, *his* own, Simon, and says to him, "We have found the Messiah," (that is translated *from Hebrew as* the Anointed King).
42 And he led him to Jesus. When Jesus looked at him, He said, "You are Simon, the son of Jonah. You will be called Cephas" (*Aramaic for Peter*, that is interpreted rock).
43 The next day Jesus wanted to go out into Galilee. And He finds Philip and says to him, "Follow Me."
44 Philip was out of Bethsaida, from the city of Andrew and Peter.
45 Philip finds Nathanael and says to him, "Whom Moses in the Law and the Preachers wrote about, we have found, Jesus, the son of Joseph, the *one* out of Nazareth."

46 And Nathanael said to him, "What good *thing* is able to be from Nazareth?" Philip says to him, "Come and see."
47 Jesus saw Nathanael coming to Him and says concerning him, "Look, an Israeli in whom is truly no deception."
48 Nathanael says to Him, "Where do You know me from?" Jesus answered and said to him, "Before the *time* for Philip to holler to you, being under the fig tree, I saw you."
49 Nathanael responded and says to Him, "Rabbi, You are the Son of God. You are the King of Israel."
50 Jesus responded and said to him, "Because I said to you, 'I saw you beneath the fig tree,' do you trust? You will see greater *things* than these."
51 And He says to him, "Amen, amen, I tell you, from now *on* you will see the heaven having opened and the angels of God stepping up and stepping down on the Son of the Person."

2

1 And on the day, the third *one*, a wedding happened in Cana, Galilee, and the mother of Jesus was there.
2 Jesus and His students were also invited to the wedding.
3 And when wine was lacking, the mother of Jesus says to Him, "They do not have wine."
4 Jesus says to her, "What *is there between* Me and you, ma'am? My hour has not arrived yet."
5 His mother says to the servants, "Whatever He says to you, do."
6 There were six stone water jars lying there according to the cleansing of the Jewish *people* having a capacity of two or three measurers *(18 or 27 gallons)* apiece.
7 Jesus says to them, "Fill the water jars full of water." And they filled them full up to the top.
8 And He says to them, "Draw *it* out now, and carry *it* to the head waiter." And they carried *it to him*.
9 As the head waiter tasted the water that had become wine and did not realize where it is from (but the servants who had drawn out the water realized *where it was from*), the head waiter hollers for the groom.
10 And he says to him, "Every person puts the nice wine *out* first, and when they are drunk, then the lesser *wine*. You have kept the nice wine until now."
11 This beginning of the indicators Jesus did in Cana, Galilee. And He showed His magnificence, and His students trusted in Him.
12 After this, He, His mother, His brothers, and His students walked down to Capernaum. And they did not stay there many days.
13 And the Passover of the Jewish *people* was near, and Jesus walked up to Jerusalem.
14 And He found on the temple grounds the *people* selling cattle, sheep, and doves, and the traders of small change sitting.
15 And after making a whip from ropes, He threw all *of them* out of the temple grounds (even the sheep and the cattle), spilled out the small change of the currency exchangers, and turned over the tables.

16 And He said to the *people* selling the doves, "Take these *things* out of here. Do not make the house of My Father a house of merchandise."
17 His students remembered that it is *a thing* that has been written *in Psalm 69:9*, "The passion of Your house ate me up."
18 So the Jewish *people* responded and said to Him, "What indicator do You show us because You are doing these *things*?"
19 Jesus answered and said to them, "Break down this temple and in three days I will raise it up."
20 So the Jewish *people* said, "In forty and six years, this temple was built, and you in three days will raise it up?"
21 But that *Jesus* was talking about the temple of His body.
22 So when He got up from *the* dead, His students remembered that He was saying this to them, and they trusted in the *Old Testament* writing and in the message that Jesus told.
23 As He was in Greater Jerusalem during the Passover, many in the festival trusted in His name as they watched His indicators that He was doing.
24 But Jesus Himself was not trusting Himself to them because of the *fact* for Him to be knowing everyone
25 and because He did not have a need that someone might tell what he witnessed about the person. You see, He knew what was in the person.

3

1 There was a person from the Separatists — Nicodemus *is the* name *belonging* to him — a head *person* of the Jewish *people*.
2 This *person* came to Jesus at night and said to Him, "Rabbi, we realize that You have come out from God *as* a teacher. You see, no one is able to be doing these indicators that You do unless God is with him."
3 Jesus responded and said to him, "Amen, amen, I tell you, unless someone is born all over *again*, he is not able to see the monarchy of God."
4 Nicodemus says to Him, "How is a person able to be born being an old man? He is not able to go into the belly of his mother a second time and to be born, is he?"
5 Jesus answered, "Amen, amen, I tell you, unless someone is born from water and spirit, he is not able to go into the monarchy of God.
6 The *thing* that has been born from the physical body is a physical body, and the *thing* that has been born from the Spirit is a spirit.
7 You should not be amazed that I said to you, 'It is necessary for you to be born all over *again*.'
8 The *breeze* (Spirit) blows where it wants, and you hear its voice, but you don't know where it comes from and where it makes *its* way back to. This is how everyone is who has been born from the Spirit."
9 Nicodemus responded and said to Him, "How are these *things* able to happen?"
10 Jesus answered and said to him, "You are the teacher of Israel, and you do not know these *things*?

11 Amen, amen, I tell you that what we know, we speak, and what we have seen, we tell that we witnessed *it*, and you do not receive our witness account.
12 If I told the earthly *things* to you and you do not trust, how will you trust if I tell you the heavenly *things*?
13 And no one has stepped up into the heaven, except the *One* who stepped down from the heaven, the Son of the Person, the *One* who is in the heaven.
14 And just as Moses put the snake up high in the backcountry, so it is necessary for the Son of the Person to be put up high
15 so that everyone who trusts in Him might not be ruined, but may have life that spans *all* time.
16 You see, this is how God loved the world in such a way that He gave His Son, the only biological *Son*, so that everyone trusting in Him would not be ruined, but may have life that spans *all* time;
17 for God did not send His Son out *on a mission* into the world so that He may judge the world, but so that the world might be rescued through Him.
18 The *person* trusting in Him is not judged, but the *person* not trusting has already been judged because he has not trusted in the name of the only biological Son of God.
19 This judgment is because the light has come into the world and the people loved the darkness rather than the light. You see, their actions were evil;
20 for everyone who repeatedly does useless *things* hates the light and does not come to the light so that his actions might not be reprimanded.
21 But the *person* doing the truth comes to the light so that it might be shown that it is in God that his actions have been worked."
22 After these *things*, Jesus and his students went into the Jewish land. And He was spending time there with them and submerging.
23 John also was in Aenon near Salim submerging because there was a lot of water there and *people* were showing up and being submerged.
24 You see, John had not yet been thrown into the jail.
25 So a questioning happened from the students of John with Jewish *people* about cleansing.
26 And they came to John and said to him, "Rabbi, *the Person* who was with you on *the* other side of the Jordan *River*, of whom you have told what you witnessed, look, this *Person* is submerging and all are going to Him."
27 John responded and said, "A person is not able to be receiving anything unless it has been given to him from the heaven.
28 You yourselves are witnesses of me that I said *that* I am not the Anointed King, but that I am *a person* who has been sent out *on a mission* in front of that *Person*.
29 The *person* who has the bride is a groom. But the friend of the groom, the *person* who has stood and is listening to him is happy with happiness because of the voice of the groom. So this, the happiness, my *happiness*, has been filled up.
30 It is necessary for that *Person* to be growing, but for me to be made less.

31 The *Person* coming from above is over all *things*. The *person* who is from the earth is from the earth and speaks from the earth. The *Person* coming from the heaven is over all *things*.
32 And the *thing* that He has seen and heard, He tells that He witnessed this, and no one receives His witness account.
33 The *person* who received His witness account put a seal on *it* that God is valid;
34 for He whom God sent out *on a mission* speaks the statements of God. You see, God doesn't give the Spirit from a measurement.
35 The Father loves the Son and has given all *things* in His hand.
36 The *person* trusting in the Son has life that spans *all* time, but the *person* not believing the Son will not see life, but the punishment of God stays on him."

4

1 So as *soon as* the Master knew that the Separatists heard that Jesus makes and submerges more students than John
2 (and yet Jesus definitely Himself was not submerging, but His students *were*),
3 He left Judea and went off again into Galilee.
4 But it was necessary for Him to be going through Samaria.
5 So He goes to a city of Samaria called Sychar, near the parcel of land that Jacob gave to Joseph, his son.
6 A spring of Jacob was there. So Jesus, who was fatigued from the road travel, was seated like this on the spring. *The* hour was as if *it were the* sixth *(noon)*.
7 A woman from Samaria comes to draw out water. Jesus says to her, "Give Me *some water* to drink."
8 You see, His students had gone off into the city so that they might buy meals.
9 So the woman, the Samaritess, says to Him, "How *is it that* you, who are a Jewish *man*, is asking to drink from the side of me, who is a woman, a Samaritess?" You see, Jewish *people* do not associate with Samaritans.
10 Jesus answered and said to her, "If you realized the free handout of God and who is the *One* saying to you, 'Give Me *some water* to drink', you would ask Him, and He would give you living water."
11 The woman says to Him, "Master, You don't even have anything to get water with, and the well is deep. So where do You have the water, the living *water*, from?
12 You are not greater than our father Jacob who gave us the well, are You? And he, his sons, and his livestock drank from it."
13 Jesus answered and said to her, "Everyone who drinks from this water will be thirsty again,
14 but whoever drinks from the water that I will give him will not in any way be thirsty for the span of time. But the water that I will give him will become in him a spring of water gushing out into life that spans *all* time."
15 The woman says to Him, "Master, give me this water so that I may not be thirsty, nor come here to be drawing out *water*."
16 Jesus says to her, "Make *your* way back. Holler for your husband, and come here."

17 The woman responded and said, "I don't have a husband." Jesus says to her, "Nicely, you said, 'I don't have a husband.'
18 You see, you had five husbands, and now who you have is not your husband. This *that* you have stated *is* valid."
19 The woman says to Him, "Master, I see that You are a preacher.
20 Our fathers bowed down in this mountain, and you *all* say that in Greater Jerusalem is the place where it is necessary to be bowing down."
21 Jesus says to her, "Ma'am, trust Me, because an hour is coming when neither in this mountain, nor in Greater Jerusalem, will you bow down to the Father.
22 You *all* bow down to what you have not seen. We bow down to what we have seen because the rescue is from the Jewish *people*.
23 But an hour is coming, and it is now, when the true bowers will bow down to the Father in spirit and truth. You see, the Father is even looking for these types of *people*, the *ones* who are bowing down to Him.
24 God *is* a spirit, and it is necessary for the *people* bowing down to Him to be bowing down in spirit and truth."
25 The woman says to Him, "I realize that a messiah is coming, the *One* who is called, 'Anointed King'. When that *One* comes, He will announce everything to us."
26 Jesus says to her, "I, the *One* speaking to you, am *Him*."
27 And on this, His students came and were amazed that He was speaking with a woman; however, no one said, "What are You looking for?" or "Why are You speaking with her?"
28 So the woman left her water jar and went off into the city. And she says to the people,
29 "Come on. Look, a person who told me everything, as much as I did. This isn't the Anointed King, is it?"
30 So they came out of the city and were coming to Him.
31 In the meantime, the students were asking Him, saying, "Rabbi, eat."
32 But *Jesus* said to them, "I have a dinner to eat that you do not realize."
33 So the students were saying to each other, "Someone didn't bring Him *something* to eat, did they?"
34 Jesus says to them, "My food is that I may do what the *One* who sent Me wants and I might complete His work.
35 Do you not say that there is yet a four-month *wait* and the harvest comes? Look, I tell you, raise your eyes and view the rural areas because they are white already toward a harvest.
36 And the *person* harvesting receives pay and gathers fruit for life that spans *all* time so that both the *person* seeding and the *person* harvesting may be happy at the same time.
37 You see, in this, the saying is true, 'Another *person* is the *one* seeding, and another, the *one* harvesting.'
38 I sent you out *on a mission* to be harvesting what you have not labored for. Others have labored, and you have come into their labor."
39 From that city, many of the Samaritans trusted in Him because of the message of the woman telling what she witnessed, "He told me all *kinds of things*, as much as I did."

40 So as the Samaritans came to Him, they were asking Him to stay beside them, and He stayed there two days.
41 And many more trusted because of His message.
42 And they were saying to the woman, "We no longer trust because of your speech. You see, we ourselves have heard, and we realize that this is truly the Rescuer of the world, the Anointed King."
43 After the two days, He went out from there and went off into Galilee.
44 You see, Jesus Himself told what He witnessed, that a preacher in His own hometown does not have value.
45 So when He went into Galilee, the Galileans accepted Him having seen all *the things* that He did in Greater Jerusalem during the festival. You see, they also went to the festival.
46 So Jesus went again to Cana, Galilee, where He made the water wine. And there was a certain royal *person* whose son was weak in Capernaum.
47 When this *man* heard that Jesus has arrived from Judea into Galilee, he went off to Him and was asking Him that He would walk down and cure his son. You see, he was going to be dying.
48 So Jesus said to him, "If you *all* don't see indicators and incredible things, you will not in any way trust."
49 The royal *person* says to Him, "Master, walk down before *the time* for my young child to die."
50 Jesus says to him, "Travel *back*. Your son is alive." The person trusted the answer that Jesus said to him, and he was traveling *back*.
51 As he was already walking down, his slaves met him and reported, saying, "Your boy is alive."
52 So he inquired the hour from the side of them in which he got better. And they said to him, "Yesterday, *the* seventh hour *(1:00 p.m.)*, the fever left him."
53 So the father knew that *it was* in that hour in which Jesus said to him, "Your son is alive." And he and his whole house trusted.
54 This second indicator again Jesus did when He went from Judea into Galilee.

5

1 After these *things*, there was a festival of the Jewish *people*, and Jesus walked up to Jerusalem.
2 In Greater Jerusalem at the sheep *gate* is a swimming pool, the *one* also called Bethesda in Hebrew, that has five columned shelters.
3 In these, a very large number was laying down, of the *people* who were weak, blind, crippled, dried-up, waiting for the shaking of the water.
4 You see, an angel was stepping down according to a certain time in the swimming pool and agitating the water. So the first *person* who climbed in after the agitation of the water became well of whatever ill he was steadily having.
5 A certain person was there having thirty and eight years in *his* weakness.
6 When Jesus sees this *person* lying down and knows that he already has a lot of time *there*, He says to him, "Do you want to become well?"

7 The *person* who was weak answered him, "Master, I don't have a person so that when the water is agitated he may throw me into the swimming pool. But in *the time* that I am going, another *person* steps down before me."
8 Jesus says to him, "Get up. Pick up your mattress, and walk around."
9 And right away the person became well, picked up his mattress, and was walking around. But a Sabbath was on that day.
10 So the Jewish *people* were saying to the *person* who had been healed, "It is a Sabbath, and you are not allowed to pick up the mattress."
11 He responded to them, "That *Person* who made me well said to me, 'Pick up your mattress, and walk around.'"
12 So they asked him, "Who is the person, the *one* that said to you, 'Pick up your mattress, and walk around'?"
13 The *person* who was healed did not realize who it is. You see, Jesus slipped off since a crowd was in the place.
14 After these *things*, Jesus finds him on the temple grounds. And He said to him, "Look, you have become well. Don't sin anymore so that something worse won't happen to you."
15 The person went off and announced to the Jewish *people* that Jesus is the One who made him well.
16 And because of this, the Jewish *people* were pursuing Jesus and looking to kill Him because He was doing these *things* on a Sabbath.
17 But Jesus responded to them, "My Father until now is working, and I am working."
18 So because of this, the Jewish *people* were looking to kill Him more because not only was He breaking the Sabbath, but He was also calling God *His* own Father, making Himself equal to God.
19 So Jesus responded and was saying to them, "Amen, amen, I tell you, the Son is not able to be doing anything out from Himself if *it is* not something He sees the Father doing. You see, whatever that *One* does, these *things* the Son also does likewise;
20 for the Father is fond of the Son and shows Him all *kinds of things* that He does. And He will show Him greater actions than these so that you may be amazed.
21 You see, even as the Father gets the dead *people* up and gives *them* life, so also the Son gives life to whom He wants;
22 for the Father does not judge anyone either, but He has given every judgment to the Son
23 so that everyone may value the Son, just as they value the Father. The *person* who does not value the Son does not value the Father, the *One* who sent Him.
24 Amen, amen, I tell you that the *person* hearing My message and trusting the *One* who sent Me has life that spans *all* time and does not go into judgment, but has stepped from the death to the life.
25 Amen, amen, I tell you that an hour is coming, and it is now, when the dead will listen to the voice of the Son of God, and the *ones* who listen will live.
26 You see, even as the Father has life in Himself, so also did He give to the Son to be having life in Himself.

27 And He gave Him authority to also be making judgment because He is a son of a person.
28 Don't be amazed at this because an hour is coming in which all the *people* in the burial vaults will listen to His voice
29 and will travel out: the *ones* who did the good *things* to a return back to life of life, but the *ones* who constantly did the useless *things* to a return back to life of judgment.
30 I am not able to be doing anything on My own. Just as I hear, I judge. And the judgment, My *judgment*, is right because I don't look for what is wanted, what I *want*, but *for* what the Father who sent Me wants.
31 If I should tell what I witnessed about Myself, My witness account is not valid.
32 There is another, the *One* who tells what He witnessed about Me, and I have seen that the witness account that He tells about Me is valid.
33 You have sent *people* out *on a mission* to John, and he has told what he witnessed of the truth.
34 I do not receive the witness account from the side of a person, but these *things* I say so that you might be rescued.
35 That *man* was the lamp, the burning and shining *lamp*. You wanted to be excited toward an hour in his light.
36 But I have the witness account greater than John's. You see, the actions that the Father gave to Me so that I might complete them, the very actions that I do, they tell what they witness about Me, that the Father has sent Me out *on a mission*.
37 And the Father who Himself sent Me has told what He witnessed about Me. Neither His voice have you heard at any time, nor His visual image have you seen.
38 And you do not have His message staying in you because you do not trust this *One* whom that *One* sent out *on a mission*.
39 Examine the *Old Testament* writings because in them it seems to you *for you* to be having life that spans *all* time. And those *writings* are the *ones* that tell what they witnessed about Me,
40 and you don't want to come to Me so that you may have life.
41 I don't receive magnificence from the side of people.
42 But I have known you that you don't have the love of God in yourselves.
43 I have come in the name of My Father, and you don't receive Me. If another comes in the name, *his* own, you will receive that *one*.
44 How are you able to trust magnificence that you receive from the side of each other, and the magnificence, the *magnificence* from the side of the only God, you don't look for?
45 Don't think that I will level a complaint against you to the Father. The *one* leveling a complaint against you is Moses, in whom you have anticipated good.
46 You see, if you were trusting Moses, you would be trusting Me; for that *man* wrote about Me.
47 But if you don't trust the alphabetic characters of that *man*, how will you trust My statements?

1 After these *things*, Jesus went off to *the* other side of the Sea of Galilee (of Tiberias).
2 And a big crowd was following Him because they were watching His indicators that He was doing on the *people* who were weak.
3 Jesus went up into the mountain and was sitting there with His students.
4 The Passover, the festival of the Jewish *people*, was near.
5 So when Jesus raises *His* eyes and sees that a big crowd is coming to Him, He says to Philip, "Where will we buy *loaves of* bread from so that these *people* might eat?"
6 But He was saying this, trying to trouble him. You see, He realized what He was going to be doing.
7 Philip answered Him, "Two hundred denarii *($10,000) worth* of *loaves of* bread is not enough for them that each of them might take some bit."
8 One from among His students, Andrew (the brother of Simon Peter), says to Him,
9 "There is one little boy here who has five *loaves of* barley bread and two Opsarius *(a certain species of fish)*, but what are these for so many *people*?"
10 Jesus said, "Make the people settle down *on the ground*." There was a lot of grass in the place. So the men (the number as if *it were* five thousand) settled down *on the ground*.
11 Jesus took the *loaves of* bread, and after being thankful, He passed *them* out to the students, but the students to the reclining *people* (likewise also from the Opsarius), as much as they were wanting.
12 As they were filled up, He says to His students, "Gather up the leftover pieces so that nothing will be ruined."
13 So they gathered and filled twelve baskets full of pieces from the five *loaves* of bread, the barley *bread*, that were left over with the *people* who had dined.
14 So when the people saw that He did an indicator, they were saying, "This truly is the Preacher, the *one* that is coming into the world."
15 So when Jesus knows that they are going to be coming and to be snatching Him so that they might make Him king, He took a back way again into the mountain Himself alone.
16 As it became evening, His students walked down on the sea,
17 and after they climbed on board into the boat, they were going to *the* other side of the sea to Capernaum. And it had already become dark, and Jesus had not come to them.
18 And the sea was wide awake, a large wind blowing.
19 So having driven *the boat* forward as *if it were* twenty-five or thirty track laps *(3 or 4 miles)*, they see Jesus walking around on the sea and becoming near the boat. And they were afraid.
20 But *Jesus* says to them, "*It* is Me. Don't be afraid."
21 So they were wanting to take Him into the boat. And right away the boat became up to the land to which they were making *their* way back.
22 The next day the crowd, the *one* that had stood on *the* other side of the sea, saw that no other small boat was there except that one into which His students

climbed on board, and that Jesus did not go into the small boat together with His students, but only His students went away.

23 (But other small boats came from Tiberias near the place where they ate the bread after the Master was thankful.)

24 So when the crowd saw that Jesus isn't there, nor His students, they also climbed on board into the boats and went to Capernaum looking for Jesus.

25 And when they found Him on the other side of the sea, they said to Him, "Rabbi, when have You become here?"

26 Jesus answered them and said, "Amen, amen, I tell you, you are looking for Me, not because you saw indicators, but because you ate from the *loaves of* bread and were full.

27 Work, not for the dinner, the *dinner* that gets ruined, but for the dinner, the *dinner* that stays for life that spans *all* time, that the Son of the Person will give to you. You see, God, the Father, put a seal on this *One*."

28 So they said to Him, "What should we do so that we may work God's actions *of work*?"

29 Jesus answered and said to them, "This is the work of God, that you should trust in whom that *One* sent out."

30 So they said to Him, "So what indicator are you doing so that we might see *it* and trust You? What are You working?

31 Our fathers ate the manna in the backcountry, just as it has been written *in Psalm 78:24*, 'He gave them bread from the heaven to eat.'"

32 So Jesus said to them, "Amen, amen, I tell you, Moses has not given you the bread from the heaven, but My Father gives you the bread from the heaven, the true *bread*.

33 You see, the bread of God is the *One* stepping down from the heaven and giving life to the world."

34 So they said to Him, "Master, always give us this bread."

35 Jesus said to them, "I am the Bread of the life. The *one* coming to Me will not in any way be hungry, and the *one* trusting in Me will not in any way be thirsty at any time.

36 But I said to you, 'You have even seen Me, and you do not trust.'

37 Everything that the Father gives Me will arrive to Me. And the *person* coming to Me, I will not in any way throw outside

38 because I have stepped down from the heaven, not so that I may do what is wanted, what I *want*, but what the *One* who sent Me wants.

39 This is what the Father who sent Me wants, that everything that He has given to Me, I would not lose *anything* from it, but I will get it up during the last day.

40 This is what the *One* who sent Me wants, that everyone watching the Son and trusting in Him may have life that spans *all* time, and I will get him up at the last day."

41 So the Jewish *people* were grumbling about Him because He said, "I am the Bread, the *Bread* that stepped down from the heaven."

42 And they were saying, "Isn't this Jesus, the son of Joseph, whose father and mother we know? How does He now say, 'I have stepped down from the heaven?'"

43 So Jesus answered and said to them, "Don't grumble with each other.
44 No one is able to come to Me unless the Father, the *One* who sent Me, draws on him. And I will get him up at the last day.
45 It has been written in the Preachers *in Isaiah 54:13*, 'And all will be *people* taught of God.' So everyone who heard from the side of the Father and who learned comes to Me
46 because no one has seen the Father except the *One* who is from the side of God. This *One* has seen the Father.
47 Amen, amen, I tell you, the *person* trusting in Me has life that spans *all* time.
48 I am the Bread of the life.
49 Your fathers ate the manna in the backcountry and died.
50 This is the Bread, the *One* stepping down from the heaven so that anyone might eat from Him and not die.
51 I am the Bread, the Living *Bread*, that stepped down from the heaven. If anyone eats from this Bread, he will live for the span of time. Also the bread that I will give is My physical body that I will give on behalf of the life of the world."
52 So the Jewish *people* were arguing to each other, saying, "How is this *Person* able to give us *His* physical body to eat?"
53 So Jesus said to them, "Amen, amen, I tell you, if you do not eat the physical body of the Son of the Person and drink His blood, you do not have life in yourselves.
54 The *person* chewing My physical body and drinking My blood has life that spans *all* time, and I will get him up at the last day.
55 You see, My physical body truly is a dinner, and My blood truly is a drink.
56 The *person* chewing My physical body and drinking My blood stays in Me and I in him.
57 Just as the living Father sent Me out *on a mission* and I live because of the Father, also the *person* chewing Me, that *person* will also live because of Me.
58 This is the Bread, the *One* that stepped down from heaven. Unlike how your fathers ate the manna and died, the *person* chewing this Bread will live for the span of time."
59 These *things* He said in a synagogue teaching in Capernaum.
60 So when many from among His students heard *it*, they said, "This message is harsh. Who is able to be listening to it?"
61 But Jesus, who realized in Himself that His students are grumbling about this, said to them, "Does this cause you to stumble?
62 So *what* if you watch the Son of the Person stepping up to where He was the prior *time*?
63 The spirit is what gives life. The physical body is not a benefit in any way. The statements that I speak to you; it is spirit and it is life.
64 But there are some from among you who do not trust." You see, Jesus realized from *the* beginning which *people* are the *ones* not trusting and which *person* is the *one* who will turn Him in.
65 And He was saying, "Because of this I have stated to you, 'No one is able to come to Me unless it is *a thing* that has been given to him from My Father.'"

66 From this, many of His students went off to the *things left* behind and no longer walked around with Him.
67 So Jesus said to the Twelve, "You don't also want to be making *your* way back, do you?"
68 So Simon Peter answered Him, "Master, who will we go off to? You have statements of life that spans *all* time.
69 And we have trusted and have known that You are the Anointed King, the Son of God, the living *God*."
70 Jesus responded to them, "Didn't I select you, the Twelve, and one from among you is an accuser?"
71 He was talking *about* Judas (*a son* of Simon) from Kerioth. You see, this *man* was going to be turning Him in, one who was from among the Twelve.

7

1 And after these *things*, Jesus walked around in Galilee. You see, He was not wanting to be walking around in Judea because the Jewish *people* were looking to kill Him.
2 The festival of the Jewish *people*, the Tent-Setting-Up *Festival*, was near.
3 So His brothers said to Him, "Walk somewhere else away from here, and make *your* way back into Judea so that Your students will also see Your actions that You do.
4 You see, no one does something in a hidden *way* and looks for it to be in a clear public statement. If You do these *things*, show Yourself to the world."
5 You see, neither were His brothers trusting in Him.
6 So Jesus says to them, "The right time, the *right time* for Me, is not beside *Me* yet, but the right time, the *right time* for you, is always ready.
7 The world is not able to be hating you, but it hates Me because I tell what I witness about it, that its actions are evil.
8 You *all* walk up to this festival. I am not walking up to this festival yet because the right time, the *right time* for Me, has not yet been accomplished."
9 After He said these *things* to them, He stayed in Galilee.
10 As His brothers walked up, at that time He also walked up to the festival, not in a shown way, but as *if it were* in a hidden *way*.
11 So the Jewish *people* were looking for Him during the festival and were saying, "Where is that *Man*?"
12 And there was much grumbling about Him in the crowds. The *people* certainly were saying, "He is a good *man*." But others were saying, "No, but He is misleading the crowd."
13 However, no one was speaking with a clear public statement about Him because of the fear of the Jewish *leaders*.
14 The festival already being halfway through, Jesus walked up onto the temple grounds and was teaching.
15 And the Jewish *people* were amazed, saying, "How does this *Man* know documents, not having learned?"
16 Jesus answered them and said, "My teaching is not Mine, but *His*, the *One* who sent Me.

17 If anyone wants to be doing what He wants, he will know about the teaching, whether it is from God or I am speaking on My own.
18 The *person* speaking out from himself looks for the magnificence, *his* own, but the *person* looking for the magnificence of the *one* who sent him, this *person* is valid, and there is no wrong in him.
19 Hasn't Moses given you the law? And not even one from among you does the law. Why are you looking to kill Me?"
20 The crowd answered and said, "You have a lesser deity. Who is looking to kill You?"
21 Jesus answered and said to them, "I did one action, and everyone is amazed
22 because of this. Moses has given you the circumcision (not that it is from Moses, but from the fathers), and during a Sabbath you circumcise a person.
23 If a person receives circumcision during a Sabbath so that the law of Moses might not be broken, are you nasty to Me because I made an entire person well during a Sabbath?
24 Do not judge according to *the* eyes, but judge the right judgment."
25 So some from the Jerusalemites were saying, "Isn't this who they are looking for to kill?
26 And look, He is speaking with a clear public statement, and they are saying nothing to Him. Perhaps the head *people* truly know that this is truly the Anointed King.
27 But we have seen where this *Man* is from. Whenever the Anointed King comes, no one knows where He is from."
28 So Jesus yelled on the temple grounds teaching and saying, "You have both seen Me and seen where I am from. And I have not come on My own, but it is the True *One* who sent Me whom you have not seen.
29 I have seen Him because I am from the side of Him, and that *One* sent Me out *on a mission*."
30 So they were looking to arrest Him. And no one put *their* hand on Him because His hour had not yet come.
31 Many from the crowd trusted in Him and were saying, "When the Anointed King comes, He won't do more indicators than these that this *Man* did, will He?"
32 The Separatists listened to the crowd grumbling these *things* about Him, and the Separatists and the head priests sent underlings out so that they might arrest Him.
33 So Jesus said to them, "I am still with you for a short time. And I am making *My* way back to the *One* who sent Me.
34 You will look for Me and will not find *Me*. And where I am, you are not able to go."
35 So the Jewish *people* said to themselves, "Where is this *Man* going to be traveling to, that we will not find Him? He is not going to be traveling to the scattering of the Greeks and to be teaching the Greeks, is He?
36 What is this saying that He said? 'You will look for Me and will not find *Me*. And where I am, you are not able to go.'"

37 During the last day (the great *one*) of the festival, Jesus had stood, and He yelled, saying, "If anyone is thirsty, come to Me and drink.
38 The *person* trusting in Me, just as the *Old Testament* writing said, 'Rivers of living water will flow from his belly.'"
39 (He said this about the Spirit that they were going to be receiving, the people who trust in Him. You see, *the* Sacred Spirit was not yet *given* because Jesus was not yet elevated to a place of magnificence.)
40 So many from the crowd who heard the message were saying, "Truly this is the Preacher."
41 Others were saying, "This is the Anointed King." But others were saying, "You see, the Anointed King does not come from Galilee, does He?
42 Didn't the *Old Testament* writing say that from the seed of David and out of Bethlehem (the village where David was) comes the Anointed King?"
43 So there became a rift in the crowd because of Him.
44 Some from among them were wanting to arrest Him, but no one put *their* hands on Him.
45 So the underlings went to the head priests and Separatists, and those *leaders* said to them, "Why didn't you lead Him *here*?"
46 The underlings answered, "A person never ever spoke like this, as this Person *does*."
47 So the Separatists responded to them, "You have not also been misled, have you?
48 Someone from the head people or from the Separatists didn't trust in Him, did they?
49 But this crowd, the *crowd* that does not know the law, is cursed."
50 Nicodemus (the one who came to Him at night, who is from among them) said to them,
51 "Our law does not judge the person unless it might previously hear from the side of him and know what he does, does it?"
52 They answered and said to him, "You aren't also from Galilee, are you? Examine and see that a preacher does not raise up from Galilee."
53 And each traveled to his house.

8

1 Jesus traveled to the Mountain of the Olives.
2 At daybreak again, He showed up on the temple grounds, and the entire group was coming to Him. And after He was seated, He was teaching them.
3 The *Old Testament* transcribers and the Separatists lead a woman to Him who has been taken down while cheating on *her* spouse. And after they stand her in *the* middle,
4 they say to Him, "Teacher, this woman was taken down over *the* very act, cheating on *her* spouse.
5 In the law, Moses demanded us to be having stones thrown at these types of *women*. So what do You say?"
6 They were saying this, trying to cause trouble with Him, so that they may have a complaint to be leveling against Him. But after Jesus stooped down, He was writing in the soil with *His* finger pretending to not *hear them*.

7 As they were staying at *it*, asking Him, when He stood up straight, He said to them, "Your first sinless *person* must throw the stone on her."
8 And again after stooping down, He was writing in the soil.
9 The *people* who heard *it* and were reprimanded by *their* conscience were going out one by one, beginning from the older *men* until the last. And Jesus was left down *there* alone and the woman who had stood in *the* middle.
10 When Jesus stood up straight and saw no one other than the woman, He said to her, "The woman — where are those complainants against you? Did no one find you guilty?"
11 The *woman* said, "No one, Master." Jesus said to her, "Neither do I find you guilty. Travel *home*, and do not sin anymore."
12 So again Jesus spoke to them, saying, "I am the Light of the world. The *person* following Me will not in any way walk around in the dark, but will have the light of the life."
13 So the Separatists said to Him, "You are telling what You witness about Yourself. Your witness account is not valid."
14 Jesus answered and said to them, "Even if I should tell what I witness about Myself, My witness account is valid because I realize where I came from and where I am making *My* way back to. But you do not realize where I come from and where I am making *My* way back to.
15 You judge aligned with the physical body. I do not judge anyone.
16 Even if I judge, the judgment, My *judgment*, is valid because I am not alone, but *it is* I and the Father who sent Me,
17 and in the law, your *law*, it has been written *in Deuteronomy 17:6 and 19:15*, 'The witness account of two people is valid.'
18 I am the *One* who tells what I witness about Myself, and He tells what He witnesses about Me, the Father who sent Me."
19 So they were saying to Him, "Where is Your Father?" Jesus answered, "You know neither Me, nor My Father. If you knew Me, you would also know My Father."
20 Jesus spoke these statements at the treasury vault as He taught on the temple grounds. And no one arrested Him because His hour had not come yet.
21 So Jesus said to them again, "I am making *My* way back, and you will look for Me and die in your sin. Where I am making *My* way back to, you are not able to go to."
22 So the Jewish *people* were saying, "He won't kill Himself, will He? Because He says, 'Where I am making *My* way back to, you are not able to go to'?"
23 He also said to them, "You are from the *ones* below. I am from the *ones* above. You are from this world. I am not from this world.
24 So I said to you, 'You will die in your sins.' You see, if you do not trust that 'I am', you will die in your sins."
25 So they were saying to Him, "You, who are you?" Jesus said to them, "Primarily, something that I am also speaking to you.
26 I have many *things* to be speaking and to be judging about you, but the *One* who sent Me is valid, and I say these *things* to the world that I heard from the side of Him."

27 They did not know that He was telling them of the Father.
28 So Jesus said to them, "When you put the Son of the Person up high, at that time, you will know that 'I am', and I do nothing on My own, but just as My Father taught Me, I am speaking these *things*.
29 And the *One* who sent Me is with Me. The Father did not leave Me alone because I always do the *things* that He likes."
30 As He was speaking these *things*, many trusted in Him.
31 So Jesus was saying to the Jewish *people* who had trusted Him, "If you stay in the message, My *message*, you truly are My students.
32 And you will know the truth, and the truth will set you free."
33 They responded to Him, "We are Abraham's seed and have not been slaves at any time to anyone. How are you saying, 'You will become free?'"
34 Jesus answered them, "Amen, amen, I tell you that everyone committing the sin is a slave of the sin.
35 The slave does not stay in the house for the span of time. The Son stays for the span of time.
36 So if the Son set you free, you will really be free.
37 I realize that you are Abraham's seed, but you are looking to kill Me because there is no room in you for the message, My *message*.
38 I am speaking what I have seen beside My Father, so you also are doing what you have seen beside your father."
39 They responded and said to Him, "Our father is Abraham." Jesus says to them, "If you were Abraham's children, you would do the actions of Abraham.
40 But now you are looking to kill Me (a person who — I have spoken the truth to you that I heard from the side of God). This, Abraham did not do.
41 You are doing the actions of your father." So they said to Him, "We haven't been born from sexual sin. We have one Father, God."
42 Jesus said to them, "If God were your Father, you would be loving Me. You see, I came out from God, and I have arrived; for neither have I come on My own, but that *One* sent me out *on a mission*.
43 Why don't you know the speech, My *speech*? Because you are not able to be hearing the message, My *message*.
44 You are from a father, the Accuser, and you want to be doing the desires of your father. That *Accuser* was a people-killer from *the* beginning and has not stood in the truth because truth is not in him. Whenever he speaks the lie, he speaks on his own because he is a liar and its father.
45 But because I tell the truth, you do not trust Me.
46 Who from among you reprimands Me about a sin? If I tell *the* truth, why don't you trust Me?
47 The *person* who is from God hears the statements of God. Because of this, you don't hear, because you are not from God."
48 So the Jewish *people* responded and said to Him, "Don't we nicely say that you are a Samaritan and have a lesser deity?"
49 Jesus responded, "I do not have a lesser deity, but I value My Father, and you belittle Me.

50 I am not looking for My magnificence. He is the *One* looking for *it* and judging.
51 Amen, amen, I tell you, if anyone keeps the message, My *message*, he will not in any way see death for the span of time."
52 So the Jewish *people* said to Him, "Now we have known that you have a lesser deity. Abraham and the preachers died, and You are saying, 'If anyone keeps My message, he will not in any way taste death for the span of time.'
53 You are not greater than our father Abraham, someone who is dead, are You? And the preachers died. Who are You making Yourself *out to be*?"
54 Jesus answered, "If I elevate Myself to a place of magnificence, My magnificence is nothing. My Father is the *One* who elevates Me to a place of magnificence, whom you say that He is your God,
55 and you have not known Him, but I have seen Him. If I even say that I have not seen Him, I will be like you, a liar, but I have seen Him, and I keep His message.
56 Your father Abraham was excited that he might see the day, My *day*. And he saw *it* and was happy."
57 So the Jewish *people* said to Him, "You don't yet have fifty years, and You have seen Abraham?"
58 Jesus said to them, "Amen, amen, I tell you, before *the time* for Abraham to come into existence, I am."
59 So they picked up stones so that they might throw *them* on Him, but Jesus hid and went out of the temple grounds, going through *the* middle of them and in this way was passing on by.

9

1 And as He passed on by, He saw a person, blind from birth.
2 And His students asked Him, saying, "Rabbi, who sinned, this *person* or his parents, that he would be born blind?"
3 Jesus answered, "Neither this *person* sinned, nor his parents, but *it happened* so that the actions of God might be shown in him.
4 It is necessary for Me to be working the actions *of work* of the *One* who sent Me while it is day. Night is coming when no one is able to be working.
5 Whenever I am in the world, I am a light of the world."
6 After He said these *things*, He spat on the ground, made mud from the spit, smeared the mud on the eyes of the blind *person*,
7 and said to him, "Make *your* way back, wash in the swimming pool of Siloam" (that is interpreted *from Hebrew* as "Having been sent out"). So he went off, washed, and came seeing.
8 So the neighbors and the *people* who saw him the prior *time*, that he was blind, were saying, "Isn't this the *one* sitting and begging?"
9 Others were saying, "This is *him*." But others, "He is like him." That *person* was saying, "I am *him*."
10 So they were saying to him, "How were your eyes opened?"
11 That *person* answered and said, "A person called Jesus made mud, smeared *it* on my eyes, and said to me, 'Make *your* way back into the swimming pool of the Siloam and wash.' When I went off and washed, I saw again."
12 They said to him, "Where is that *Person*?" He says, "I don't know."

13 They lead him (the *person* blind in the past) to the Separatists.
14 It was a Sabbath when Jesus made the mud and opened his eyes.
15 So again the Separatists also were asking him how he saw again. The *person* said to them, "He put mud on my eyes, I washed, and I see."
16 So some from the Separatists were saying, "This Person is not from the side of God because He does not keep the Sabbath." Others were saying, "How is a sinful person able to be doing these types of indicators?" And there was a rift among them.
17 They say to the blind *person* again, "What do you say about Him, that He opened your eyes?" The *person* said, "He is a preacher."
18 So the Jewish *leaders* didn't trust *this* about him, that he was blind and saw again, until they hollered for his parents, *the parents* of the *person* who saw again.
19 And they asked them, saying, "Is this your son whom you say that he was born blind? So how does he see now?"
20 His parents answered them and said, "We know that this is our son and that he was born blind.
21 But how does he now see? We do not know. Or who opened his eyes? We do not know. He has *the* age. Ask him. He will speak concerning himself."
22 His parents said these *things* because they feared the Jewish *leaders*. You see, the Jewish *leaders* were already agreeing that if anyone acknowledged Him *as the* Anointed King, he would become excommunicated from the synagogue.
23 Because of this, his parents said, "He has *the* age. Ask him."
24 So from a second *time* they hollered for the person who was blind and said to him, "Give magnificence to God. We know that this Person is sinful."
25 So that *person* responded and said, "If He is sinful, I do not know. One *thing* I know, that I, being a blind *person*, now see."
26 They said to him again, "What did He do to you? How did He open your eyes?"
27 He answered them, "I already told you, and you did not listen. Why do you want to be listening *to it* again? You don't also want to become His students, do you?"
28 So they put him down and said, "You are a student of that *Person*, but we are students of Moses.
29 We know that God has spoken to Moses, but this *Person*, we don't know where He is from."
30 The person responded and said to them, "You see, in this is an amazing *thing*, that you don't know where He is from, and He opened my eyes.
31 We know that God doesn't listen to sinful *people*, but if anyone is God-worshipping and does what He wants, He listens to this *person*.
32 From the span of time, it has not been heard that anyone opened *the* eyes of a *person* who has been born blind.
33 If this *Person* wasn't from the side of God, He wasn't able to be doing anything."
34 They responded and said to him, "In sins you were born, *the* whole *you*, and you are teaching us?" And they threw him outside.

35 Jesus heard that they threw him outside. And when He found him, He said to him, "Do you trust in the Son of God?"
36 That *person* answered and said, "Who is He, Master, so that I might trust in Him?"
37 Jesus said to him, "You have both seen Him and the *One* speaking with you is that *Son*."
38 The *person* was declaring, "I trust, Master," and he bowed down to Him.
39 And Jesus said, "For judgment I came into this world so that the *people* not seeing may see and the *people* seeing might become blind."
40 And *some* from the Separatists heard these *things* (the *ones* who were with Him) and said to Him, "We are not also blind, are we?"
41 Jesus said to them, "If you were blind, you would not have sin. But now you say, 'We see.' So your sin stays."

10

1 "Amen, amen, I tell you, the *person* not going in through the door into the yard of the sheep, but climbing up some other way, that *person* is a thief and a bandit.
2 The *one* going in through the door is a shepherd of the sheep.
3 To this *one*, the doorkeeper opens up, and the sheep listen to his voice. And he hollers for *his* own sheep by name and leads them out.
4 And whenever he takes *his* own sheep out, he travels in front of them, and the sheep follow him because they know his voice.
5 *A shepherd* belonging to others they won't in any way follow, but they will escape away from him because they don't know the voice of the *shepherds* belonging to others."
6 Jesus told this analogy to them, but those *people* didn't know what *things* it was that He was speaking to them.
7 So Jesus said to them again, "Amen, amen, I tell you, I am the door of the sheep.
8 Everyone, as many as came before Me are thieves and bandits, but the sheep didn't listen to them.
9 I am the door. Through Me, if anyone goes in, he will be rescued. And he will go in and go out, and will find pasture.
10 The thief doesn't come except so that he might steal, kill, and ruin. I came so that they may have life and have much more.
11 I am the Shepherd, the Nice *One*. The Shepherd, the Nice *One*, puts His soul *out there* on behalf of the sheep.
12 The hired worker (not also being a shepherd, whose sheep are not *his* own) sees the wolf coming, leaves the sheep, and escapes. And the wolf snatches them and scatters the sheep.
13 The hired worker escapes because he is a hired worker and there is no concern in him about the sheep.
14 I am the Shepherd, the Nice *One*, I know My *sheep*, and I am known by My *sheep*,
15 just as the Father knows Me and I know the Father. And I put My soul *out there* on behalf of the sheep.

16 And I have other sheep that are not from this yard. And it is necessary for Me to lead those *sheep*. And they will listen to My voice, and it will become one flock, one Shepherd.

17 Because of this, the Father loves Me, because I put my soul *out there* so that I might receive it again.

18 No one takes it away from Me, but I put it *out there* on My own. I have authority to put it *out there*, and I have authority to receive it again. I received this demand from the side of My Father."

19 So there became a rift again among the Jewish *people* because of these messages.

20 Many from among them were saying, "He has a lesser deity and is crazy. Why are you listening to Him?"

21 Others were saying, "These are not the statements of a *person* who has a lesser deity. A lesser deity is not able to be opening eyes of blind *people*, is it?"

22 It became *Hanukkah* (the initiations) in Greater Jerusalem, and there was a storm.

23 And Jesus was walking around on the temple grounds in the Columned Shelter of Solomon.

24 So the Jewish *people* surrounded Him and were saying to Him, "Until when are You raising our souls? If You are the Anointed King, tell us with a clear public statement."

25 Jesus answered them, "I told you, and you do not trust. The actions that I do in the name of My Father, these *things* are witnesses concerning Me.

26 But you do not trust. You see, you are not from the sheep, My *sheep*, just as I told you.

27 The sheep, My *sheep*, listen to My voice, I know them, and they follow Me.

28 And I give them life that spans *all* time, they will not in any way be ruined for the span of time, and someone will not snatch them from My hand.

29 My Father, who has given *them* to Me, is greater than everyone, and no one is able to be snatching *them* from the hand of My Father.

30 I and the Father are one."

31 So again the Jewish *people* hauled stones so that they might attack Him with stones.

32 Jesus responded to them, "I showed you many nice actions from My Father. Because of which action of these are you attacking Me with stones?"

33 The Jewish *people* answered Him, saying, "We are not attacking You with stones concerning a nice action, but concerning an insult and because You, being a person, make Yourself a god."

34 Jesus responded to them, "Is it not *a thing* that has been written in your law *in Psalm 82:6*, 'I said, You are gods'?

35 If He called those *people* gods to whom the message of God happened, and the *Old Testament* writing is not able to be undone,

36 are you saying *concerning* whom the Father made sacred and sent out into the world, 'You are insulting *God*,' because I said, 'I am a son of God'?

37 If I am not doing the actions of My Father, don't trust Me.

38 But if I am doing *them*, even if you don't trust Me, trust the actions so that you might know and trust that the Father *is* in Me and I in Him."

39 So they were looking again to arrest Him, and He went out of their hand.
40 And He went off again to *the* other side of the Jordan *River* to the place where John was submerging the first *time*, and He stayed there.
41 And many went to Him and were saying, "John certainly didn't do even one indicator, but everything as much as John said about this *Man* was valid."
42 And many trusted in Him there.

11

1 There was a certain man who was weak, Lazarus, out of Bethany, from the village of Mary and her sister Martha.
2 Mary was the *woman* who dabbed perfume on the Master and wiped His feet dry with her hair, whose brother Lazarus was weak.
3 So the sisters sent *someone* out to Him, saying, "Master, look, *a person* whom You are fond of is weak."
4 When Jesus heard, He said, "This weakness is not to death, but on behalf of the magnificence of God, so that the Son of God might be elevated to a place of magnificence through it."
5 Jesus was loving Martha, her sister, and Lazarus.
6 So as He heard that he is weak, at that time, He certainly stayed in a place where He was two days.
7 Following after this, He says to the students, "We may lead into Judea again."
8 The students say to Him, "Rabbi, the Jewish *people* now were looking to attack You with stones, and You are making *Your* way back there again?"
9 Jesus answered, "Are there not twelve hours of the day? If anyone walks around during the day, he doesn't trip because he sees the light of this world.
10 But if anyone walks around in the night, he trips because the light is not in him."
11 He said these *things*, and after this He says to them, "Our friend Lazarus has fallen asleep, but I am traveling *there* so that I might wake him up."
12 So His students said, "Master, if he has fallen asleep, he will be rescued."
13 Jesus had stated about his death, but to those *students* it seemed that He is talking about the sleep of the slumber.
14 So at that time, Jesus said to them with a clear public statement, "Lazarus died,
15 and I am happy because of you (so that you might trust) that I wasn't there, but we may lead toward him."
16 So Thomas (the *one* called Twin) said to *his* fellow students, "We may also lead so that we might die with him."
17 So when Jesus came, He found him already having four days in the burial vault.
18 Bethany was near Greater Jerusalem, as *if it were* fifteen track laps *(almost 2 miles)* away.
19 Many from the Jewish *people* had come to the *women* around Martha and Mary so that they might comfort them concerning their brother.
20 So Martha, as she heard that Jesus is coming, went to meet with Him. But Mary was seated in the house.

21 So Martha said to Jesus, "Master, if You were here, my brother wouldn't have died.
22 But I realize even now that however many *things* that You ask God for, God will give to You."
23 Jesus says to her, "Your brother will come back to life again."
24 Martha says to Him, "I realize that he will come back to life again in the return back to life in the last day."
25 Jesus said to her, "I am the Return Back to Life and the Life. The *person* trusting in Me, even if he were dead, he will live.
26 And everyone living and trusting in Me will not in any way die for the span of time. Do you trust this?"
27 She says to Him, "Yes, Master. I have trusted that You are the Anointed King, the Son of God, the *One* coming into the world."
28 And after she said these *things*, she went away and hollered in an unnoticed way for Mary, her sister, when she said, "The Teacher is beside *us* and is hollering for you."
29 That *sister*, as she heard, gets up quickly and goes to Him.
30 Jesus hadn't yet come into the village, but was in the place where Martha went to meet Him.
31 So the Jewish *people*, the *ones* who were with her in the house and were comforting her, when they saw that Mary quickly got up and went out, followed her, saying that she is making *her* way back to the burial vault so that she might cry there.
32 So Mary, as she came to where Jesus was, when she saw Him, fell to His feet, saying to Him, "Master, if You were here, my brother would not have died."
33 So Jesus, as He saw her crying and the Jewish *people* who came together with her crying, was stern in the spirit and agitated Himself.
34 And He said, "Where have you put him?" They say to Him, "Master, come and see."
35 Jesus teared up.
36 So the Jewish *people* were saying, "Look, how fond He was of him!"
37 But some from among them said, "Wasn't this *Man*, the *One* who opened the eyes of the blind, able to make *it* so that this *man* also would not die?"
38 So Jesus again being stern in Himself comes to the burial vault. It was a cave and a stone was lying on it.
39 Jesus says, "Take the stone away." The sister of the *one* who had died, Martha, says to Him, "Master, he already stinks. You see, he is a four-day-old *corpse*."
40 Jesus says to her, "Didn't I tell you that if you trust, you will see the magnificence of God?"
41 So they took the stone away from where the *one* that had died was lying. Jesus raised up *His* eyes and said, "Father, I thank You that You listened to Me.
42 I knew that You always listen to Me, but because of the crowd, the *one* that has stood around, I said *it* so that they might trust that You sent Me out *on a mission*."

43 And after saying these *things*, He made a yell with a loud voice, "Lazarus, come here outside."
44 The *one* who had died came out having been tied up (the feet and the hands) with strips of cloth, and his eyes had a towel tied around them. Jesus says to them, "Release him, and leave *him* to be making *his* way back *home*."
45 So many from the Jewish *people*, the *ones* who came to Mary and saw what Jesus did, trusted in Him.
46 But some from among them went off to the Separatists and told them *things* that Jesus did.
47 So the head priests and the Separatists gathered a council together and were saying, "What do we do? Because this Person is doing many indicators.
48 If we leave Him like this, everyone will trust in Him, and the Romans will come and take away both our place and nation."
49 A certain one from among them, Caiaphas, who was *the* head priest that year, said to them, "You don't know anything.
50 Neither are you pondering that it is advantageous to us that one person die on behalf of the ethnic group and the whole nation not be ruined."
51 This he didn't say out from himself, but being a head priest that year, he prophesied that Jesus was going to be dying on behalf of the nation,
52 and not just on behalf of the nation, but so that He might also gather the children of God (the *ones* that had been dispersed) together into one.
53 So from that day they together advised that they should kill Him.
54 So Jesus was no longer walking around among the Jewish *people* with a clear public statement, but He went away from there into the rural area near the backcountry into a city called Ephraim. And He was spending time there with His students.
55 The Passover of the Jewish *people* was near, and many walked up to Jerusalem from the rural area before the Passover so that they might consecrate themselves.
56 So they were looking for Jesus and were talking with each other (who had stood on the temple grounds), "What? Does it seem to you that He won't in any way come to the festival?"
57 Both the head priests and the Separatists had given a demand that if anyone knew where He is, he should disclose *it* in order that they might arrest Him.

12

1 So Jesus, six days before the Passover, went into Bethany where Lazarus was, the *one* that had died, whom He got up from *the* dead.
2 So they made a feast there for Him, and Martha was serving. Lazarus was one of the *people* reclining together with Him.
3 So after Mary took twelve ounces of very valuable authentic Spikenard perfume, she dabbed it on the feet of Jesus, and wiped His feet dry with her hair. The house was filled from the aroma of the perfume.
4 So one from His students, Judas (a son of Simon from Kerioth, the *one* who is going to be turning Him in), says,
5 "Why wasn't this perfume put up for sale for three hundred denarii ($15,000) and given to *the* poor?"

6 He said this, not because it was a concern to him about the poor, but because he was a thief and had the money box. And he was hauling out the *money* being put in *it*.
7 So Jesus said, "Leave her *alone*. She has kept it for the day of My embalming.
8 You see, the poor you always have with you, but Me you don't always have."
9 So a big crowd from the Jewish *people* knew that He is there, and they came not only because of Jesus, but so that they also might see Lazarus, whom He got up from *the* dead.
10 But the head priests advised that they should also kill Lazarus
11 because many of the Jewish *people* were making *their* way back and trusting in Jesus because of him.
12 On the next day when a big crowd that came to the festival heard that Jesus is coming to Jerusalem,
13 they took the limbs of the palm trees and went out for an encounter with Him. And they were yelling, "Hosanna *(Hebrew for 'O, rescue us')*, the *One* coming in *the* Master's name and the king of Israel that has been conferred with blessings."
14 When Jesus found a little donkey, He was seated on it, just as it has been written *in Zechariah 9:9,*
15 "Don't be afraid, daughter of Zion. Look, your king is coming sitting on a foal of a donkey."
16 His students didn't know these *things* the first *time*, but when Jesus was elevated to a place of magnificence, at that time they remembered that these *things* had been written on Him and they did these *things* to Him.
17 So the crowd was telling what they witnessed (the *crowd* that was with Him when He hollered for Lazarus *to come* out of the burial vault and got him up from *the* dead).
18 Because of this, the crowd also went to meet Him, because they heard this: for Him to have done the indicator.
19 So the Separatists said to themselves, "Do you see that you are not benefiting in any way? Look, the world went off behind Him."
20 Greeks were some from among the *people* walking up so that they might bow down in the festival.
21 So these *Greeks* came forward to Philip (the *one* out of Bethsaida, Galilee) and were asking him, saying, "Master, we want to see Jesus."
22 Philip goes and tells *it* to Andrew. And Andrew and Philip tell *it* again to Jesus.
23 But Jesus answered them, saying, "The hour has come that the Son of the Person will be elevated to a place of magnificence.
24 Amen, amen, I tell you, unless the kernel of the grain, after falling into the ground, dies, it stays alone. But if it dies, it carries much fruit.
25 The *person* who is fond of his soul will lose it, and the *person* who hates his soul in this world will guard it for a life that spans *all* time.
26 If anyone serves Me, he must follow Me, and where I am, there the servant, My *servant*, will also be. If anyone serves Me, the Father will value him.

27 Now My soul has been uneasy. And what should I say? Father, rescue Me from this hour? But because of this, I came to this hour.
28 Father, elevate Your name to a place of magnificence." So a voice came from the sky, "I both elevated *it* and again will elevate *it*."
29 So the crowd (the *crowd* that had stood *there* and heard *it*) were saying for thunder to have happened. Others were saying an angel has spoken to Him.
30 Jesus responded and said, "This voice hasn't happened because of Me, but because of you.
31 Now is a judgment of this world. Now the head of this world will be thrown out.
32 And I, if I be put up high from the earth, I will draw everyone to Myself."
33 This He was saying indicating what kind of death He was going to be dying.
34 The crowd responded to Him, "We heard from the law that the Anointed King stays for the span of time. And how are You saying that it is necessary for the Son of the Person to be put up high? Who is this Son of the Person?"
35 So Jesus said to them, "The light is with you for a short time yet. Walk around while you have the light so that darkness might not take you down. The *person* walking around in the dark doesn't even realize where he is making *his* way back to.
36 While you have the light, trust in the light so that you might become sons of light." Jesus spoke these *things*, and when He went away, He was hidden away from them.
37 Although He had done so many indicators in front of them, they were not trusting in Him,
38 so that the message of Isaiah, the preacher, might be accomplished that He said *in Isaiah 53:1*, "Master, who trusted what was heard from us, and the arm of *the* Master, to whom was it uncovered?"
39 Because of this, they were not able to be trusting, because Isaiah again said *in Isaiah 6:9-10*,
40 "He has blinded their eyes and has made their heart hard as stone so that they might not see with the eyes, be aware with the heart, return back, and I might cure them."
41 Isaiah said these *things* when he saw His magnificence and spoke about Him.
42 In the same manner, however, even many from the head people trusted in Him, but because of the Separatists they weren't acknowledging *it* so that they wouldn't become excommunicated from the synagogue.
43 You see, they loved the magnificence of the people rather than even the magnificence of God.
44 Jesus yelled and said, "The *person* trusting in Me does not trust in Me, but in the *One* who sent Me.
45 And the *person* watching Me watches the *One* who sent Me.
46 I have come — a light into the world — so that everyone trusting in Me might not stay in the dark.

47 And if anyone listens to My statements and doesn't trust, I don't judge Him. You see, I didn't come so that I may judge the world, but so that I might rescue the world.
48 The *person* invalidating Me and not receiving My statements has the *message* judging him, the message that I spoke. That will judge him in the last day
49 because I didn't speak from Myself, but the Father who sent Me, He gave Me a demand, what I might say and what I might speak.
50 And I realize that His demand is life that spans *all* time; so *things* that I am speaking, just as the Father has stated to Me, so I am speaking."

13

1 Before the Festival of the Passover, after Jesus realized that His hour had come so that He might step from this world to the Father, He, who loved *His* own *people* (the *people* in the world), loved them to *the* conclusion.
2 And after *the* feast happened, when the Accuser had already put in the heart of Judas, *a son* of Simon from Kerioth, that he would turn Him in,
3 Jesus realizing that the Father has given everything to Him, into *His* hands, and that He came out from God and is making *His* way back to God,
4 He gets up from the feast, puts *His* clothes *down*, and after taking a linen towel, tied *it* around Himself.
5 After that He puts water into the large bowl and began to be washing the feet of the students and to be wiping *them* dry with the linen towel that had been tied around.
6 So He comes to Simon Peter. And that *Peter* says to Him, "Master, are You washing my feet?"
7 Jesus answered and said to him, "What I am doing, you don't realize now. You will know after these *things*."
8 Peter says to Him, "You will not in any way wash my feet for the span of time." Jesus answered him, "If I will not wash you, you have no part with Me."
9 Simon Peter says to Him, "Master, not just my feet, but also the hands and the head."
10 Jesus says to him, "The *person* who has been given a bath has no need than to wash the feet, but *the* whole *body* is clean. And you are clean, but definitely not all."
11 You see, He knew the *person* turning Him in. Because of this, He said, "You are definitely not all clean."
12 So when He washed their feet and took His clothes, after settling down again, He said to them, "Do you know what I have done to you?
13 You holler at Me, 'the Teacher' and 'the Master', and nicely you say *it*. You see, *that is what* I am.
14 So if I, the Master and the Teacher, washed your feet, you are obligated to also be washing the feet of each other.
15 You see, I gave you a demonstration so that, just as I did to you, you also may do.

16 Amen, amen, I tell you, a slave is not greater than his master, neither a missionary greater than the *one* who sent him.
17 If you realize these *things*, you are blessed if you do them.
18 I am not talking about all of you. I realize whom I selected, but *I selected him* so that the *Old Testament* writing *in Psalm 41:9* might be accomplished, 'The *one* chewing the bread with me raised up his heel on Me.'
19 From now *on* I am telling you before the *time for it* to happen so that you might trust (when it happens) that I am *Him*.
20 Amen, amen, I tell you, the *person* receiving whomever I sent receives Me. The *person* receiving Me receives the *One* who sent Me."
21 After Jesus said these *things*, He was uneasy in the spirit. And He told what He witnessed and said, "Amen, amen, I tell you that one from among you will turn Me in."
22 So the students were looking at each other, not sure what to think about what He says.
23 One of His students was reclining in the front of Jesus (whom Jesus *kept* loving).
24 So Simon Peter gestures to this *person* to inquire who it might be that He is talking about.
25 When that *person* got down on the chest of Jesus, he says to Him, "Master, who is it?"
26 Jesus answers, "It is that *person* to whom, after dipping the piece *of bread*, I will give *it* over to." And after dipping the piece, He gives *it* to Judas, *the son* of Simon, from Kerioth.
27 And after the piece *of bread*, at that time, the Opponent went into that *man*. So Jesus says to him, "Do what you are doing faster."
28 None of the *people* reclining knew why He said this to him.
29 You see, it seemed to some, since Judas had the money box, that Jesus says to him, "Buy what *things* we have a need of for the festival" or that he should give something to the poor.
30 So after that *man* took the piece, he went out right away. It was night.
31 So when he went out, Jesus says, "Now the Son of the Person was elevated to a place of magnificence, and God was elevated to a place of magnificence in Him.
32 If God was elevated to a place of magnificence in Him, God will also elevate Him to a place of magnificence in Himself, and right away He will elevate Him to a place of magnificence.
33 Little children, for yet a little *while* I am with you. You will look for Me, and just as I said to the Jewish *people* ('Where I am making *My* way back to, you are not able to come'), I also tell you now.
34 I am giving you a new demand so that you may love each other just as I loved you, that you also may love each other.
35 In this, all will know that you are students to Me, if you have love among each other."
36 Simon Peter says to Him, "Master, where are you making *Your* way back to?" Jesus answered him, "Where I am making *My* way back to, you are not able to follow with Me now. You will follow with Me later."

37 Peter says to Him, "Master, why am I not able to follow with You now? I will put my soul *out there* on Your behalf."
38 Jesus answered him, "Will you put your soul *out there* on My behalf? Amen, amen, I tell you, a rooster will not in any way crow until *the time* that you will flatly deny Me three times."

14

1 "Your heart must not be uneasy. You trust in God. Also trust in Me.
2 In the house of My Father are many places to stay, but if not, I would tell you. I am traveling to get a place ready for you.
3 And if I travel and get a place ready for you, I am coming again, and I will receive you in to Myself, so that where I am, you also may be.
4 And where I am making *My* way back to, you know, and the way you know."
5 Thomas says to Him, "Master, we don't know where You are making *Your* way back to. How are we even able to know the way?"
6 Jesus says to him, "I am the Way, the Truth, and the Life. No one goes to the Father if *it is* not through Me.
7 If you had known Me, you also would have known My Father. And from now *on*, you know Him and have seen Him."
8 Philip says to Him, "Master, show us the Father, and it is enough."
9 Jesus says to him, "Am I with you for so much time, and you have not known Me, Philip? The *person* who has seen Me has seen the Father. How are you saying, 'Show us the Father'?
10 Don't you trust that I *am* in the Father, and the Father is in Me? The statements that I speak to you I don't speak on My own, but the Father who stays in Me is doing His actions.
11 Trust Me because I *am* in the Father and the Father *is* in Me, but if not, trust Me because of the very actions.
12 Amen, amen, I tell you, the *person* trusting in Me, the actions that I do, that *person* will also do, and he will do greater *things* than these because I am traveling to My Father.
13 And whatever you ask for in My name, this I will do so that the Father might be elevated to a place of magnificence in the Son.
14 If you ask for anything in My name, I will do *it*.
15 If you love Me, keep the demands, My *demands*.
16 And I will ask the Father, and He will give another Encourager to you so that He may stay with you for the span of time,
17 the Spirit of the Truth (that the world is not able to receive because it does not see Him, nor know Him). You know Him because He stays beside you and will be in you.
18 I will not leave you orphans. I am coming to you.
19 Yet a little *while* and the world no longer sees Me, but you see Me because I am living and you will live.
20 In that day you will know that I *am* in My Father, you in Me, and I in you.

Breakthrough KJV   **John 15**

21 The *person* having My demands and keeping them, that *person* is the *one* loving Me. The *one* loving Me will be loved by My Father, I will love him, and I will make Myself apparent to him."

22 Judas (not the *one* from Kerioth) says to Him, "Master, what has happened that to us You are going to be making Yourself apparent and definitely not to the world?"

23 Jesus answered and said to him, "If anyone loves Me, he will keep My message, My Father will love him, We will come to him, and We will make a place to stay beside him.

24 The *person* not loving Me, doesn't keep My messages. And the message that you hear isn't Mine, but the Father's who sent Me.

25 I have spoken these *things* to you as I stay beside you.

26 But that Encourager (the Spirit, the Sacred *Spirit*, that the Father will send in My name) will teach you all *things* and will quietly remind you of all that I said to you.

27 I am leaving peace with you. My peace I am giving to you (unlike how the world gives, I am giving to you). Your heart must not be uneasy, neither must it be cowardly.

28 You heard that I said to you, 'I am making *My* way back and coming to you.' If you were loving Me, you would be happy that I said, 'I am traveling to the Father,' because My Father is greater than Me.

29 And now I have stated *it* to you before *it is* to happen so that when it happens you might trust.

30 I no longer will speak much with you. You see, the head of this world is coming, and he has nothing in Me.

31 But *it will happen* so that the world might know that I love the Father, and just as the Father demanded Me, so I am doing. Get up. We should lead from here."

15

1 "I am the Vine, the True *Vine*, and My Father is the Farmer.

2 Every vine branch in Me not carrying fruit, He takes it off. And every *vine branch* carrying fruit, He prunes it so that it may carry more fruit.

3 You are already clean because of the message that I have spoken to you.

4 Stay in Me and I in you. Just as the vine branch isn't able to be carrying fruit out from itself if it doesn't stay in the vine, so neither *can* you if you don't stay in Me.

5 I am the Vine. You *are* the vine branches. The *person* staying in Me and I in him, this *person* carries much fruit because separate from Me you are not able to be doing anything.

6 If anyone didn't stay in Me, he was thrown outside as the vine branch, he was shriveled up, they gather them together, they throw *them* into a fire, and he is burned.

7 If you stay in Me and My statements stay in you, whatever you want you will ask for *it*, and it will happen to you.

8 In this My Father was elevated to a place of magnificence, so that you may carry much fruit and you will become students to Me.
9 Just as the Father loved Me, I also loved you. Stay in the love, My *love*.
10 If you keep My demands, you will stay in My love, just as I have kept the demands of My Father, and I stay in His love.
11 I have spoken these *things* to you so that the happiness, My *happiness*, might stay in you and your happiness might be filled up.
12 This is the demand, My *demand*, that you should love each other, just as I loved you.
13 No one has a greater love than this, that someone would put his soul *out there* on behalf of his friends.
14 You are My friends if you do as many *things* as I demand you.
15 I no longer call you slaves because the slave does not realize what his master is doing, but I have stated *that* you *are* friends because everything that I heard from the side of My Father I made known to you.
16 You did not select Me, but I selected you and placed you so that you may make *your* way back, carry fruit, and your fruit stay, so that whatever you ask the Father for in My name, He might give you.
17 These *things* I demand you so that you may love each other.
18 If the world hates you, you know that it has hated Me first *over* you.
19 If you were from the world, the world would be fond of *its* own. Because you are not from the world, but I selected you from the world, because of this the world hates you.
20 Remember the message that I said to you, 'A slave is not greater than his master.' If they pursued Me, they also will pursue you. If they kept My message, they also will keep yours.
21 But they will do all these *things* to you because of My name, because they do not know the *One* who sent Me.
22 If I did not come and speak to them, they were not having sin, but now they do not have a sham about their sin.
23 The *person* hating Me also hates My Father.
24 If I didn't do the actions among them that no one else has done, they were not having sin. Now, they have both seen and hated both Me and My Father.
25 But *it happened* so that the message (the *one* that has been written in their law *in Psalm 35:19 and 69:4*) might be accomplished, 'They hated Me for nothing.'
26 When that Encourager comes whom I will send to you from the side of the Father (the Spirit of the Truth that travels out from the side of the Father), He will tell what He witnesses about Me.
27 And you are telling what you witnessed because from *the* beginning you are with Me."

16

1 "I have spoken these *things* to you so that you might not stumble.
2 They will make you excommunicated from the synagogue. But an hour is coming that everyone who kills you will seem to be bringing a sacrifice ritual to God.

3 And they will do these *things* to you because they didn't know the Father, nor Me.
4 But I have spoken these *things* to you so that when the hour comes you may remember them, that I told *them* to you. I didn't tell you these *things* from *the* beginning because I was with you.
5 Now I am making *My* way back to the *One* who sent Me, and no one from among you is asking Me, 'Where are You making *Your* way back to?'
6 But because I have spoken these *things* to you, the sadness has filled your heart.
7 But I am telling you the truth. It is advantageous to you that I go away. You see, if I don't go away, the Encourager will not come to you. If I travel *away*, I will send Him to you.
8 And when that *Encourager* comes, He will reprimand the world concerning sin, concerning *the* right way, and concerning judgment
9 (certainly concerning sin because they don't trust in Me,
10 but concerning *the* right way because I am making *My* way back to My Father and you no longer see Me,
11 but concerning judgment because the head of this world has been judged).
12 I still have many *things* to be saying to you, but you are not able to be hauling *them* now.
13 When that *Encourager* comes, the Spirit of the Truth, He will guide you into all the truth. You see, He won't speak out from Himself, but however many *things* that He might hear He will speak, and He will announce to you the *things* coming.
14 That *Encourager* will elevate Me to a place of magnificence because He will receive from My *Person* and announce *it* to you.
15 All *things*, as many as the Father has, are Mine. Because of this, I said that He will receive from My *Person* and announce *it* to you.
16 A little *while* and you do not see Me, and again, a little *while* and you will look at Me because I am making *My* way back to the Father."
17 So *some* from among His students said to each other, "What is this that He is saying to us, 'A little *while* and you do not see Me, and again a little *while* and you will look at Me,' and 'Because I am making *My* way back to the Father'?"
18 So they were saying, "What is this that He is saying, the 'little *while*'? We don't know what He is speaking."
19 So Jesus knew that they were wanting to be asking Him. And He said to them, "Are you looking with each other for *what I meant* about this that I said, 'A little *while* and you don't see Me, and again, a little *while* and you will look at Me'?
20 Amen, amen, I tell you that you will cry and wail. The world will be happy. You will be sad, but your sadness will become for happiness.
21 When the woman is delivering, she has sadness because her hour came, but when the young child is born, she does not remember the hard times anymore, because of the happiness, that a person was born into the world.
22 So you also now certainly have sadness, but I will see you again, your heart will be happy, and your happiness no one takes away from you.

23 And in that day, you won't ask Me anything. Amen, amen, I tell you, that however many *things* that you ask the Father for in My name, He will give to you.
24 Until now you did not ask for anything in My name. Ask and you will receive so that your happiness may be *happiness* that has been filled up.
25 I have spoken these *things* to you in analogies. An hour is coming when I will no longer speak to you in analogies, but I will announce to you with a clear public statement about the Father.
26 In that day, you will ask for *things* in My name, and I am not telling you that I will ask the Father about you.
27 You see, the Father Himself is fond of you because you have been fond of Me and have trusted that I came out from the side of God.
28 I came out from the side of the Father, and I have come into the world. Again I am leaving the world and traveling to the Father."
29 His students say to Him, "Look, now you are speaking with a clear public statement and not telling any analogy.
30 Now we know that You know everything and have no need that anyone should ask You *questions*. We trust in this, that You came out from God."
31 Jesus responded to them, "Do you trust now?
32 Look, an hour is coming and has now come that you will be scattered each to *your* own *places* and will leave Me alone. And I am not alone because the Father is with Me.
33 I have spoken these *things* to you so that you may have peace in Me. In the world, you will have hard times, but be courageous, I have conquered the world."

17

1 Jesus spoke these *things* and raised His eyes to the sky. And He said, "Father, the hour has come. Elevate Your Son to a place of magnificence so that the Son might also elevate You to a place of magnificence,

2 just as You gave Him authority over every physical body so that for everything that You have given Him, He might give them life that spans *all* time.
3 This is the life that spans *all* time: that they may know You (the only true God) and whom You sent out *on a mission* (Jesus, *the* Anointed King).
4 I elevated You to a place of magnificence on the earth. I completed the work that You have given Me that I might do.
5 And now, You, Father, elevate Me to a place of magnificence beside Yourself with the magnificence that I was having beside You before the *time* for the world to exist.
6 I showed Your name to the people whom You have given to Me from the world. They were Yours, You have given them to Me, and they have kept Your message.
7 Now they have known that all *things,* as many as You have given to Me, they are from the side of You

8 because the statements that You have given to Me I have given to them and they received *them*, they truly knew that I came out from the side of You, and they trusted that You sent Me out *on a mission*.
9 I ask concerning them. I don't ask concerning the world, but concerning whom You have given Me because they are with You.
10 And all My *things* are Yours, Your *things are* Mine, and I have been elevated to a place of magnificence in them.
11 And I am no longer in the world, these are in the world, and I am coming to You, Sacred Father. Keep them in Your name (whom You have given to Me) so that they may be one, just as We *are*.
12 When I was with them in the world, I was keeping them (whom You have given to Me) in Your name. I guarded *them*, and no one from among them was ruined except the son of the ruin, so that the *Old Testament* writing might be accomplished.
13 Now I am coming to You, and I am speaking these *things* in the world so that they may have the happiness, My *happiness*, that has been filled up in them.
14 I have given them Your message, and the world hated them because they are not from the world, just as I am not from the world.
15 I don't ask that You might take them from the world, but that You might keep them from the evil *one*.
16 They are not from the world, just as I am not from the world.
17 Make them sacred in Your truth. The message, Your *message*, is truth.
18 Just as You sent Me out *on a mission* into the world, I also sent them out *on a mission* into the world.
19 And on their behalf I make Myself sacred so that they themselves may also be *people* who have been made sacred in truth.
20 I am not only asking concerning these *people*, but also concerning the *people* who will trust in Me through their message,
21 so that all may be one, just as You, Father, *are* in Me and I in You, so that they also may be one in Us, so that the world may trust that You sent Me out *on a mission*.
22 And I have given them the magnificence that You have given Me so that they may be one, just as We are one.
23 I in them and You in Me, so that they may be *people* who have been completed into one and so that the world may know that You sent Me out *on a mission* and You loved them, just as You loved Me.
24 Father, I want whom You have given Me so that where I am those *people* also may be with Me, so that they may see the magnificence, My *magnificence*, that You gave to Me because You loved Me before *the* founding of *the* world.
25 Father, who does what is right, even the world didn't know You. I knew You, and these *people* knew that You sent Me out *on a mission*.
26 And I made Your name known to them, and I will make *it* known so that the love that You loved Me with may be in them and I in them.

18

1 After Jesus said these *things*, He went out together with His students to *the* other side of the stormwater basin of the Kidron where there was a garden into which He and His students went.
2 Judas (the *one* turning Him in) also knew the place because Jesus gathered there many times with His students.
3 So after Judas takes the regiment and underlings from the head priests and Separatists, he comes there with lanterns, torches, and weapons.
4 So Jesus, who knew all the *things* coming on Him, when He went out, said to them, "Who are you looking for?"
5 They answered Him, "Jesus, the Nazarene." Jesus says to them, "I am *Him*." Judas (the *one* turning Him in) had also stood with them.
6 So as He said to them, "I am *Him*," they went off into the *things left* behind and fell on the ground.
7 So again He asked them, "Who are you looking for?" The *people* said, "Jesus, the Nazarene."
8 Jesus answered, "I told you that I am *Him*. So if you are looking for Me, leave these *people* to be making *their* way back *home*."
9 *He said this* so that the message that He said might be accomplished, 'I ruined no one from them whom You have given Me.'
10 So Simon Peter, having a dagger, pulled it, struck the slave of the head priest, and chopped off his ear lobe, the right *one*. *The* name *belonging* to the slave was Malchus.
11 So Jesus said to Peter, "Put your dagger into the sheath. The cup that the Father has given Me, should I not in any way drink it?"
12 So the regiment, the commanding officer, and the underlings of the Jewish *leaders* apprehended Jesus and tied Him up.
13 And they led Him off to Annas first. You see, he was *the* father-in-law of Caiaphas who was that year's head priest.
14 Caiaphas was the *one* who strongly advised to the Jewish *people* that it is advantageous for one person to be ruined on behalf of the ethnic group.
15 Simon Peter and another student were following Jesus. That student was known to the head priest, and he went into the courtyard of the head priest together with Jesus.
16 Peter had stood outside toward the door. So the student (the other *one* who was known by the head priest) went out, talked to the doorkeeper, and led Peter in.
17 So the servant girl (the doorkeeper) says to Peter, "You aren't also from the students of this Person, are you?" That *Peter* says, "I am not."
18 The slaves and the underlings had been standing *there*, who had made a bed of hot coals because it was cold, and they were warming *themselves*. Peter was with them, having stood *there* and warming himself.
19 So the head priest asked Jesus about His students and about His teaching.
20 Jesus answered him, "I spoke with a clear public statement to the world. I always taught in the synagogue and on the temple grounds where the Jewish *people* always come together, and in a hidden way I spoke nothing.
21 Why are you asking Me? Ask the *people* who have heard what I spoke to them. Look, these *people* know what I said."

22 When He said these *things*, one of the underlings who had stood nearby gave Jesus a slap, after saying, "Are you answering the head priest like this?"
23 Jesus answered him, "If I spoke in a bad way, tell what you witnessed about the bad *thing*. If *I spoke* nicely, why do you beat Me?"
24 So Annas sent Him out, who had been tied up, to Caiaphas, the head priest.
25 Simon Peter had been standing and warming himself. So they said to him, "You aren't also from His students, are you?" That *Peter* denied and said, "I am not."
26 One from among the slaves of the head priest (who is a relative of *the man* whose ear lobe Peter chopped off) says, "Didn't I see you in the garden with Him?"
27 So again Peter denied, and right away a rooster crowed.
28 So they lead Jesus out from Caiaphas into the Roman palace. It was morning, and they didn't go into the Roman palace so that they might not be desecrated, but so that they might eat the Passover.
29 So Pilate came out to them and said, "What criminal complaint are you bringing against this person?"
30 They answered and said to him, "If this *man* wasn't a *person* who does bad things, we wouldn't have turned Him over to you."
31 So Pilate said to them, "You must take Him and judge Him according to your law." So the Jewish *leaders* said to him, "It is not allowed for us to kill anyone."
32 (*This happened* so that the message of Jesus might be accomplished that He said indicating what kind of death He was going to be dying.)
33 So Pilate went into the Roman palace again, hollered for Jesus, and said to Him, "Are You the king of the Jewish *people*?"
34 Jesus answered him, "Are you saying this out from yourself, or did others tell you about Me?"
35 Pilate answered, "I'm not Jewish, am I? The nation, Your *nation*, and the head priests turned You over to me. What did You do?"
36 Jesus answered, "The monarchy, My *monarchy*, isn't from this world. If the monarchy, My *monarchy*, was from this world, the underlings, My *underlings*, would be struggling so that I wouldn't be turned over to the Jewish *people*. But now, the monarchy, My *monarchy*, isn't from here."
37 So Pilate said to Him, "So aren't You a king?" Jesus answered, "You are saying that I am a king. I have been born for this, and for this I have come into the world, so that I might tell what I witnessed of the truth. Everyone who is from the truth hears My voice."
38 Pilate says to Him, "What is truth?" And after saying this, again he went out to the Jewish *leaders* and says to them, "I don't find even one accusation in Him.
39 But it is a policy with you that I should dismiss one *person* to you during the Passover. So do you intend *that* I should dismiss the King of the Jewish *people* to you?"
40 So all *of them* made a yell again, saying, "Not this *Man*, but Barabbas." Barabbas was a bandit.

19

1 So at that time Pilate took Jesus and whipped *Him*.
2 And the soldiers who wove an award wreath from thorns placed *it* on His head and put a purple robe around Him.
3 And they were saying, "Happy to meet You, the King of the Jewish *people*," and they were giving Him slaps.
4 So Pilate came outside again and says to them, "Look, I lead Him outside to you so that you might know that in Him I don't find even one accusation."
5 So Jesus came outside wearing the thorny award wreath and the purple robe. And he says to them, "Look, the Person."
6 So when the head priests and the underlings saw Him, they made a yell, saying, "Nail *Him* to a cross. Nail *Him* to a cross." Pilate says to them, "You must take Him and nail *Him* to a cross. You see, I don't find in Him an accusation."
7 The Jewish *people* responded to him, "We have a law, and according to our law He ought to die because He made Himself a son of God."
8 So when Pilate heard this saying, he was more afraid.
9 And he went into the Roman palace again. And he says to Jesus, "Where are You from?" But Jesus did not give him a response.
10 So Pilate says to Him, "Are You not speaking to me? Don't You realize that I have authority to nail You to a cross and I have authority to dismiss You?"
11 Jesus answered, "You don't have even one *bit* of authority against Me unless it has been given to you from above. Because of this, the *one* who turned Me over to you has a bigger sin."
12 From this *time on*, Pilate was looking to dismiss Him, but the Jewish *people* were yelling, saying, "If you dismiss this *Man*, you are not a friend of Caesar. Everyone making himself a king is expressing opposition to Caesar."
13 So when Pilate heard this saying, he led Jesus outside and was seated on the judicial bench in a place called "Paved with Stone" ("Gabbatha" in Hebrew).
14 It was a preparation *day* of the Passover, but an hour as if *it were the* sixth *(noon)*. And he says to the Jewish *people*, "Look, your King."
15 But the *people* made a yell, "Take *Him* away. Take *Him* away. Nail Him to a cross." Pilate said to them, "Will I nail your King to a cross?" The head priests answered, "We do not have a king except Caesar."
16 So at that time, he turned Him over to them so that He might be nailed to a cross. They took Jesus along and led *Him* away.
17 And hauling His cross, He went out to the *place* called Place of a Skull, that in Hebrew is called Golgotha,
18 where they nailed Him to a cross and two others with Him, on this side and on this side, but Jesus in *the* middle.
19 Pilate also wrote a placard and placed it on the cross. It had been written, "Jesus, the Nazarene, the King of the Jewish *people*."
20 So this placard many of the Jewish *people* read because the place where Jesus was nailed to a cross was near the city and it had been written in Hebrew, in Latin, in Greek.
21 So the head priests of the Jewish *people* were saying to Pilate, "Don't write, 'The King of the Jewish *people*,' but 'That *Man* said I am a king of the Jewish *people*'."

22 Pilate answered, "What I have written, I have written."
23 So the soldiers, when they nailed Jesus to a cross, took His clothes and made four parts, a part for each soldier, and the long undershirt. But the long seamless undershirt was woven from the top through all of *it*.
24 So they said to each other, "We should not tear it up, but we should throw dice concerning it, whose it will be." *This happened* so that the *Old Testament* writing *in Psalm 22:18* might be accomplished that says, "They divided up my clothes for themselves and threw dice on my clothing." So the soldiers certainly did these *things*.
25 His mother, the sister of His mother, Mary (the *wife* of Clopas), and Mary (the Magdalene) had stood beside the cross of Jesus.
26 So when Jesus saw *His* mother and the student whom He *kept* loving standing nearby, He says to His mother, "Ma'am, look, your son."
27 After that He says to the student, "Look, your mother." And from that hour, the student took her to *his* own *places*.
28 After this, Jesus realizing that He had already finished everything, so that the *Old Testament* writing *in Psalm 69:21* might be completed, He says, "I am thirsty."
29 So a container was lying *there* full of sour wine. After they filled a sponge with sour wine and put *it* around a hyssop *stick*, they offered *it* to His mouth.
30 So when Jesus took the sour wine, He said, "It has been finished." And when He put *His* head down, He gave up the spirit.
31 So the Jewish *people*, since it was a preparation *day*, so that the bodies wouldn't stay on the cross during the Sabbath (you see, the day of that Sabbath was great), they asked Pilate that their legs would be broken and they would be taken away
32 So the soldiers went and certainly broke the legs of the first *man* and of the other *man*, the *man* who was nailed to a cross together with Him.
33 But when they came up to Jesus, as they saw that He had already died, they didn't break His legs.
34 But one of the soldiers stabbed His side with a spear, and right away blood and water came out.
35 And the *person* who has seen *it* has told what he witnessed, and his witness account is true. And that *person* realizes that he is saying valid *things*, so that you might trust.
36 You see, these *things* happened so that the *Old Testament* writing *in Exodus 12:46, Numbers 9:12, and Psalm 34:20* might be accomplished. "A bone of His will not be crushed."
37 And again a different *Old Testament* writing says *in Zechariah 12:10*, "They will look to whom they impaled."
38 After these *things*, Joseph (the *one* out of Arimathaea, who was a student of Jesus, but had been hid because of *his* fear of the Jewish *people*) asked Pilate that he might take the body of Jesus, and Pilate gave permission. So he went and took the body of Jesus.
39 Nicodemus (the *one* who came to Jesus at night the first *time*) also came, bringing a mixture of myrrh *(expensive perfume)* and aloe, as if *it were* seventy-five pounds.

40 So they took the body of Jesus and tied it up in linen strips with the fragrant resins, just as *the* custom is for the Jewish *people* to be preparing *a corpse* for burial.

41 In the place where He was nailed to a cross, there was a garden, and in the garden a new burial vault in which no one was placed yet.

42 So they put Jesus there because of the preparation *day* of the Jewish *people,* because the burial vault was near.

20

1 On the *Day* 1 after the Sabbaths, Mary (the Magdalene) comes to the burial vault in *the* morning, it still being dark, and sees the stone that has been taken away from the burial vault.

2 So she runs and comes to Simon Peter and to the other student whom Jesus *kept* being fond of. And she says to them, "They took the Master from the burial vault, and we don't know where they put Him."

3 So Peter and the other student went out and were going to the burial vault.

4 The two were running at the same time. And the other student ran ahead faster than Peter and came first to the burial vault.

5 And when he stooped and peered in, he sees the linen strips lying there; however, he did not go in.

6 So Simon Peter comes following him. And he went into the burial vault and sees the linen strips lying there

7 and the towel that was on His head, not lying with the linen strips, but separate from *them,* having been wound up into one place.

8 So at that time, the other student, the *one* who came first, also went into the burial vault, looked, and trusted.

9 You see, they didn't yet realize the *Old Testament* writing that *says* it is necessary for Him to come back to life from *the* dead.

10 So the students went off again to their *own places.*

11 But Mary had stood facing the burial vault crying outside. So as she was crying, she stooped and peered into the burial vault,

12 and she sees two angels in white seated, one near the head and one near the feet, where the body of Jesus was lying.

13 And those *angels* say to her, "Ma'am, why are you crying?" She says to them, "Because they took my Master away and I don't know where they put Him."

14 And after she said these *things,* she turned to the *things left* behind, sees Jesus who has stood *there,* and didn't realize that it is Jesus.

15 Jesus says to her, "Ma'am, why are you crying? Who are you looking for?" That *Mary* thinking that He is the gardener says to Him, "Master, if you hauled Him off, tell me where you put Him, and I will take Him away."

16 Jesus says to her, "Mary." When that *Mary* turned, she says to Him, "Rabboni" *(Great Rabbi),* that is said *in place of* Teacher.

17 Jesus says to her, "Don't touch Me. You see, I have not yet stepped up to My Father. Travel *off* to My brothers, and tell them I am stepping up to My Father, your Father, My God, and your God."

18 Mary (the Magdalene) comes, reporting to the students that she had seen the Master and He said these *things* to her.

19 So being evening on that day, the *Day* 1 after the Sabbaths, and the doors having been closed where the students were gathered together because of the fear of the Jewish *people*, Jesus went, stood in the middle, and says to them, "Peace to you."
20 And when He said this, He showed them *His* hands and His side. So the students were happy when they saw the Master.
21 So Jesus said to them again, "Peace to you. Just as the Father has sent Me out *on a mission*, I am also sending you."
22 And when He said this, He puffed on *them* and says to them, "Receive *the* Sacred Spirit.
23 If you forgive the sins of any, they are forgiven to them. If you hold on to *the sins* of any, they have been held on to."
24 But Thomas, one from among the Twelve, the *one* being called Twin, was not with them when Jesus came.
25 So the other students were saying to him, "We have seen the Master." But *Thomas* said to them, "Unless I see the impression of the spikes in His hands, put my finger into the impression of the spikes, and put my hand into His side, I won't in any way trust."
26 And after eight days, again His students were inside, and Thomas *was* with them. Jesus comes, the doors having been closed, stood in the middle, and said, "Peace to you."
27 After that He says to Thomas, "Bring your finger here, and see My hands. And bring your hand and put *it* into My side. And don't become untrusting, but *become* trusting."
28 And Thomas answered and said to Him, "My Master and My God."
29 Jesus says to Him, "Because you have seen Me, Thomas, you have trusted. The *people* who do not see and *yet* trust *are* blessed."
30 So Jesus also certainly did many other indicators in the sight of His students, that have not been written in this scroll.
31 These *things* have been written so that you might trust that Jesus is the Anointed King, the Son of God, and so that as you trust, you may have life in His name.

21

1 After these *things*, Jesus showed Himself again to the students on the Sea of Tiberias. He showed *Himself* like this.
2 They were at the same place: Simon Peter, Thomas (the *one* called Twin), Nathanael (the *one* out of Cana, Galilee), the *sons* of Zebedee, and two others from His students.
3 Simon Peter says to them, "I am making *my* way back to be fishing." They say to him, "We are also going together with you." They went out, climbed up into the boat right away, and in that night captured nothing.
4 After it already became morning, Jesus stood on the beach; however, the students did not realize that it is Jesus.
5 So Jesus says to them, "Young children, you don't have anything to eat with bread, do you?" They answered Him, "No."

6 *Jesus* said to them, "Throw the net into the parts *on the* right of the boat, and you will find *them*." So they threw *it*, and they weren't having *the* strength anymore to pull it out of the large number of the fish.

7 So that student whom Jesus *kept* loving says to Peter, "It is the Master." So when Simon Peter heard that it is the Master, he tied the jacket around himself (you see, he was naked), and threw himself into the sea.

8 The other students came in the small boat (you see, they weren't a long way away from the land, but as *if it were* two hundred cubits (*300 feet*) away) dragging the net of the fish.

9 So as they stepped out onto the land, they see a bed of hot coals laid out, Opsarius *(a certain species of fish)* lying on *it*, and bread.

10 Jesus says to them, "Bring out the Opsarius that you now captured."

11 Simon Peter climbed up and pulled the net onto the land full of large fish, one hundred fifty-three. Even though there were so many, the net did not tear.

12 Jesus says to them, "Come on. Have breakfast." None of the students were daring to question Him, "Who are You?" realizing that it is the Master.

13 So Jesus comes, takes the bread, and gives *it* to them (and the Opsarius likewise).

14 This *is* already *the* third *time* Jesus was shown to His students after He got up from *the* dead.

15 So when they had breakfast, Jesus says to Simon Peter, "Simon, *son* of Jonah, do you love Me more than these?" He says to Him, "Yes, Master. You realize that I am fond of You." He says to him, "Feed My lambs."

16 He says to him again a second time, "Simon, *son* of Jonah, do you love Me?" He says to Him, "Yes, Master. You realize that I am fond of You." He says to him, "Shepherd My sheep."

17 The third *time* He says to him, "Simon, *son* of Jonah, are you fond of Me?" Peter was sad because He said to him the third *time*, "Are you fond of Me?" And he said to Him, "Master, You realize everything. You know that I am fond of You." Jesus says to him, "Feed My sheep.

18 Amen, amen, I tell you, when you were younger, you were putting your waist sash on by yourself and walking around where you were wanting to. But when you age, you will put your hands out, and another *person* will put your waist sash on for you and carry *you* where you don't want *to go*."

19 He said this indicating what kind of death he will elevate God to a place of magnificence with. And after saying this, He says to him, "Follow Me."

20 When Peter turns around, he sees the student whom Jesus *kept* loving following (who also settled down in the feast on His chest and said, "Master, who is the *one* turning You in?").

21 When Peter sees this *student*, he says to Jesus, "Master, what *about* this *one*?"

22 Jesus says to him, "If I want him to be staying until I come, what *is that* to you? You must follow Me."

23 So this message went out to the brothers that that student doesn't die. Jesus didn't even tell him that he doesn't die, but "if I want him to be staying until I come, what *is that* to you?"

24 This is the student, the *one* who is telling what he witnessed about these *things* and who wrote these *things*. And we realize that his witness account is valid.
25 There are also many other *things*, as many as Jesus did, some that if each one is written, I suppose the world itself to not have enough room for the written scrolls. Amen.

Acts

1

1 I certainly made the first message, O Theophilus, about all that Jesus began both to be doing and to be teaching
2 till *the* day that He was taken up after He gave a demand to the missionaries whom He selected through *the* Sacred Spirit,
3 to whom He also presented Himself alive (after the *time* for Him to suffer) in many evidences, being seen by them through forty days and telling the *things* about the monarchy of God.
4 And convening with them, He passed the order on to them out of Greater Jerusalem, "*You are* not to be separating, but to be staying around for the promise of the Father that you heard from Me,
5 because John certainly submerged with water, but you will be submerged in *the* Sacred Spirit after not many of these days."
6 So certainly when the *people* came together, they were asking Him, saying, "Master, *tell us* if during this time You are reestablishing the monarchy to Israel."
7 He said to them, "It is not yours to know amounts of time or appointed times that the Father placed in *His* own authority.
8 But you will receive ability after the Sacred Spirit comes on you, and you will be witnesses for Me both in Jerusalem and in all Judea and Samaria, even until *the* last *person* of the earth."
9 And after saying these *things*, as they watched Him, He raised up, and a cloud took Him up away from their eyes.
10 And as they were staring into the sky as He traveled *away*, also look, two men had been standing by them in a white outfit,
11 who also said, "Men, Galileans, why have you been standing looking into the sky? This Jesus, the *One* who was taken up away from you into the sky, will come like this: *the* way that you watched Him traveling into the sky."
12 At that time, they returned into Jerusalem out of the mountain called "Of An Olive Orchard," that is near Jerusalem, having a Sabbath's trip.
13 And when they went in, they climbed up into the upstairs room where they were staying permanently: Peter, James, John and Andrew; Philip and Thomas; Bartholomew and Matthew; James of Alpheus, Simon the Zealot, and Judas of James.
14 These all were unanimously staying close to the prayer and the plea, together with women, Mary (the mother of Jesus), and His brothers.
15 And in these days, after Peter stood up in *the* middle of the students, he said (a crowd of names were at the same *place*, as *if it were* one hundred twenty),
16 "Men, brothers, it was necessary for this *Old Testament* writing to be accomplished that the Spirit, the Sacred *Spirit*, already said through David's mouth about Judas, the *one* who became a guide to the *people* who apprehended Jesus,

17 because he had been numbered down together with us and took his turn in the portion of this *task of* serving.
18 (So this *man* certainly got a parcel of land from the pay of the wrong way, and when he became front first, he broke open in *the* middle and all his guts spilled out.
19 And it became known to all the *people* living in Jerusalem in such a way for that parcel of land to be called in *their* own dialect, Aceldama, that is, "Land Parcel of Blood.")
20 You see, it has been written in a scroll of psalms *in Psalm 69:25 and 109:8*, 'His hut must become uninhabited, the *person* must not be living in it, and his supervision, a different *person* should take.'
21 So it is necessary of the men who went together with us in all *the* time in which the Master Jesus went in and went out on us,
22 beginning off at John's submersion until the day that He was taken up away from us, for one of these to become a witness of His return back to life together with us."
23 And they stood up two: Joseph (the *one* called Barsabas, who was also called Justus) and Matthias.
24 And when they prayed, they said, "You, Master, *the* Heart-Knower of all, publicly show from these two, *the* one whom You selected
25 to take the portion in this *task of* serving and mission that Judas walked in violation from, to travel into the place, *his* own."
26 And they gave their dice, the die fell on Matthias, and he was counted as an additional *member* of the eleven missionaries.

2

1 And during the *time* for the Day of the Fiftieth to be totally filled up, absolutely all of them were unanimous at the same *place*.
2 And an echo suddenly happened from the sky (even like a forceful breath being driven) and filled the whole house where they were sitting.
3 And tongues being divided up as if *they were* fire were seen by them, and it was seated on each one of them.
4 And absolutely all of them were filled with *the* Sacred Spirit and began to be speaking with different languages just as the Spirit was giving them *the ability* to be verbalizing clearly.
5 Jewish *people* were living in Jerusalem, devout men out of every nation, the *nations* under the sky.
6 After this sound happened, the large number came together and were stirred up because they (each one) were listening to them speaking in *their* own dialect.
7 They all were being astounded and amazed, saying to each other, "Look, aren't all these, the *ones* speaking, Galileans?
8 And how do we each hear in our own dialect in which we were born?
9 Parthians, Medes, Elamites, and the *people* living in Mesopotamia; both Judea and Cappadocia; Pontus and Western Turkey;

10 both Phrygia and Pamphylia; Egypt, the parts of Libya (the *one* along Cyrene), and the Romans making *this their* home (both Jewish *people* and converts);

11 Cretans and Arabians, we are listening to them speaking the great *things* of God with our languages."

12 All were being astounded and dumbfounded, saying another to another, "What is this wanting to be?"

13 Different *people* joking were saying that they are *people* who have been full of sweet wine.

14 But when Peter was stood up together with the eleven, he raised up his voice and verbalized clearly to them, "Jewish men and absolutely all the *people* living in Jerusalem, this must be known to you, and you must open your ears to my statements.

15 You see, these *people* are not drunk as you presume; for it is *the* third hour of the day *(9:00 a.m.)*.

16 But this is what has been stated through the preacher Joel *in Joel 2:28–32,*

17 'And it will be in the last days, says God, *that* I will spill out from My Spirit on every physical body. And your sons and your daughters will preach. And your young lads will see sightings, and your older *men* will be inspired while they sleep with sleep inspirations.

18 And definitely on My *male* slaves and on My *female* slaves in those days, I will spill out from My Spirit, and they will preach.

19 And I will give incredible things in the sky above and indicators on the earth below: blood, fire, and fog from smoke.

20 The sun will turn into darkness and the moon into blood before *the time* for the great and conspicuous day of *the* Master to even come.

21 And it will be *that* everyone, whoever calls on the name of *the* Master will be rescued.'

22 Men, Israelis, hear these words: Jesus the Nazarene, a man who has been substantiated from God to you with abilities, incredible things, and indicators that God did through Him in *the* middle of you, just as you yourselves also have seen,

23 this *Man* (resigned to the intention that had been designated and to what God knew beforehand), after you took, when you fastened *to a cross* through hands of criminals, you executed,

24 whom God brought back to life after He released the pains of the death due to the fact that it was not possible for Him to be held on to by it.

25 You see, David *in Psalm 16:8–11* says for Him, 'I was seeing the Master before *me* in my sight through everything, because He is at *places to the* right of me so that I will not be disturbed.

26 Because of this, my heart celebrated, and my tongue was excited. Even my physical body will still sleep in *my* tent based on anticipation,

27 because you will not leave My soul down in Hades *(the underworld of the dead)*, nor give Your Holy *One* to see decay.

28 You made roads of life known to me. You will make me full of celebration with Your face.'

29 Men, brothers, *a thing* that is allowed *is* to talk with a clear public statement facing you about the head father, David, that he both passed away and was buried. And his grave is among us till this day.

30 So being a preacher and realizing that God guaranteed to him with an oath *a person* from *the* fruit of his groin (the 'aligned with *the* physical body *in the future* to bring the Anointed King back to life' *thing*) to be seated on his throne,

31 after seeing *it* beforehand, he spoke about the return back to life of the Anointed King, that His soul was not left down in Hades *(the underworld of the dead)*, nor did His physical body see decay.

32 God brought this Jesus back to life, of which we all are witnesses.

33 So when He was put up high to the right *side* of God and received the promise of the Sacred Spirit from the side of the Father, He spilled this out that you now see and hear.

34 You see, David did not step up into the heavens. He himself says, 'The Master said to my Master, sit down at *places to the* right of Me

35 until I will place Your enemies *as* a footrest of Your feet.'

36 So all *the* house of Israel must securely know that God made Him both Master and Anointed King, this Jesus whom you nailed to a cross."

37 When they heard *this*, they were stabbed in the heart. And they said to Peter and the rest *of the* missionaries, "Men, brothers, what will we do?"

38 Peter was declaring to them, "Change your ways. And each of you must be submerged based on the name of Jesus, *the* Anointed King, for forgiveness of your sins, and you will receive the free handout of the Sacred Spirit.

39 You see, the promise is for you, your children, and all the *people* a long way away, however many that *the* Master, our God, will call forward."

40 With more, different words, he was being a strong witness and was encouraging *them*, saying, "Be rescued out of the generation, this crooked *generation*."

41 So certainly the *people* who with pleasure gladly accepted his message were submerged, and souls were added that day, as if *they were* three thousand.

42 They were staying close to the teaching of the missionaries, to the sharing, to the splitting of the bread, and to the prayers.

43 Fear happened to every soul. And many incredible things and indicators were happening through the missionaries.

44 All the *people* trusting were at the same *place* and were having absolutely everything shared.

45 And they were putting *their* properties and possessions up for sale and dividing them up out to each and every one according to whoever was having a need.

46 And daily unanimously staying close by on the temple grounds and splitting bread in each house, they were receiving a meal with *others* in excitement and plainness of heart,

47 praising God and having generosity toward the whole group. The Master was adding the *people* being rescued daily to the assembly.

1 At the same *time*, Peter and John were walking up to the temple grounds at the hour of the prayer, the ninth *hour (3:00 p.m.)*.
2 And a certain man who was crippled from his mother's belly was being hauled, whom they were putting daily facing the door of the temple grounds (the *one* called Beautiful) for the *purpose* to be asking for a charitable donation from the side of the *people* traveling onto the temple grounds,
3 who, when he saw Peter and John who were going to be entering onto the temple grounds, was asking for a charitable donation.
4 When Peter stared at him together with John, he said, "Look at us."
5 The *man* was fixing *his* attention on them, expecting to receive something from the side of them.
6 Peter said, "Silver and gold is not with me, but what I have, this I give to you. In the name of Jesus, *the* Anointed King, the Nazarene, get up and walk around."
7 And when he grabbed him by the right hand, he got up. His insteps and ankles at once became solid.
8 And leaping up, he stood, was walking around, and went together with them onto the temple grounds, walking around, jumping, and praising God.
9 And the entire group saw him walking around and praising God.
10 And they were recognizing him, that this was the *man* who sat toward the charitable donation at the Beautiful Gate of the temple grounds, and they were filled with bewilderment and astonishment based on what had transpired with him.
11 As the crippled *man* who was cured held on to Peter and John, the entire group ran together to them at the columned shelter (the *one* called Solomon's) puzzled.
12 When Peter saw *it*, he responded to the group, "Men, Israelis, why are you amazed based on this? Or why do you stare at us as if *it is* with *our* own ability or godliness that we have done the 'for him to be walking around' *thing*?
13 The God of Abraham, Isaac, and Jacob, the God of our fathers, elevated His Servant Boy Jesus to a place of magnificence, whom you turned in and denied right in front of *the* face of Pilate when that *man* decided to be dismissing *Him*,
14 but you denied the Sacred and Right *One* and asked for a man, a murderer, to be given to you as an act of generosity.
15 You killed the Head Leader of the Life, whom God got up from *the* dead, of which we are witnesses.
16 And based on the trust of His name, His name made this *man* solid (whom you see and know). And the trust, the *trust* through Him, gave him this wholeness up in front of you all.
17 And now, brothers, I realize that aligned with a lack of awareness you repeatedly did *what you did*, even as your head people also *did*.
18 This is how God accomplished *things* that He previously proclaimed through *the* mouth of all His preachers — for the Anointed King to suffer.

19 So change your ways, and return back for the 'for your sins to be erased' *part* in order that times of refreshment would come out of the face of the Master

20 and He would send out the *One* who has been publicly spoken about to you beforehand, Jesus, *the* Anointed King,

21 whom it is necessary for heaven to certainly accept till *the* times of *the* reestablishment of everything that God spoke of through *the* mouth of all His sacred preachers since *the* span of time *began.*

22 You see, Moses certainly said to the fathers *in Deuteronomy 18:15,* 'The Master, your God, will stand a preacher up for you from your brothers. You will listen to Him as me *(Moses)* regarding everything, however many *things* that He might speak to you.

23 It will be *that* every soul, any that do not listen to that preacher, will be eradicated from the ethnic group.'

24 Even all the preachers from Samuel and the *preachers* in order, as many as spoke, also previously proclaimed these days.

25 You are sons of the preachers and of the deal that God made facing your fathers, saying facing Abraham, 'And in your seed, all the family trees of the earth will be conferred with blessings.'

26 To you first, after God brought His Servant Boy Jesus back to life, He sent Him out *on a mission,* conferring blessings on you during the *time* for each *of you* to be turning away from your evils."

4

1 As they spoke to the group, the priests, the captain of the temple grounds, and the Sadducees stood over them

2 being thoroughly anguished because of the *fact* for them to be teaching the group and to be proclaiming in Jesus the return back to life, the *return* from *the* dead.

3 And they put *their* hands on them and put *them* in a holding cell for the next day. You see, it was already late afternoon.

4 Many of the *people* who heard the message trusted, and the number of the men became as if *it were* five thousand.

5 It happened on the next day for their head people, older *men,* and *Old Testament* transcribers to be gathered together

6 into Jerusalem, also Annas (the head priest), Caiaphas, John, Alexander, and as many as were from *the* head priest's family.

7 And when they stood them in the middle, they were inquiring, "In which ability or in which name did you do this?"

8 Then Peter, filled with the Sacred Spirit, said to them, "Head people of the ethnic group and older *men* of Israel,

9 if we today are being investigated on a humane thing to a weak person, in which this *person* has been rescued,

10 be it known to you all and to all the ethnic group of Israel that in the name of Jesus, *the* Anointed King, the Nazarene, whom you nailed to a cross, whom God got up from *the* dead, in this, this *man* has stood here in your sight well.

11 This is the stone, the *one* that was treated as a nobody by you, the *people* who are building, the *one* that became for a corner's head.

12 And the rescue is in no one else. You see, neither is there a different name under the sky that has been given among people in which it is necessary for us to be rescued."
13 As they watched the clear public statement of Peter and John, and when they took down that they are unlearned and uneducated people, they were being amazed and recognizing them that they were together with Jesus.
14 Seeing the person who had stood together with them, the *one* who had been healed, they had nothing to say in opposition to *it*.
15 After giving them the order to go off outside of the council, they deliberated to each other,
16 saying, "What will we do to these people, you see, because a known indicator has certainly happened through them. *It is* shown to all the *people* living in Jerusalem, and we are not able to deny *it*.
17 But so that it might not be circulated any further into the group, we should threaten them with a threat to no longer be speaking based on this name to any people."
18 And after calling them *back in*, they passed the order on to them, the "not to ever be verbalizing, nor to be teaching, based on the name of Jesus" *order*.
19 But when Peter and John responded to them, they said, "Whether it is right in the sight of God to be listening to you rather than God, you must judge.
20 You see, we are not able to not be speaking *things* that we saw and heard."
21 The *leaders*, after threatening more, dismissed them (finding nothing of the "how they might curtail them" *sort*) because of the group, because everyone was praising God's magnificence based on what had happened.
22 You see, the person on whom this indicator of the cure happened was more than forty years *old*.
23 After being dismissed, they went to *their* own *people* and reported as many *things* to them as the head priests and the older *men* said.
24 The *people* who heard *it* raised a voice unanimously to God and said, "*Our* Owner, You *are* God, the *One* who made the sky, the earth, the sea, and all the *things* in them,
25 the *One* who through *the* mouth of David, Your servant boy, said *in Psalm 2:1–2*, 'Why were non-Jews riled up and ethnic groups concerned about empty *things*?
26 The kings of the earth stood by, and the head people were gathered together over the same *thing*: against the Master and against His Anointed King.'
27 You see, based on truth, over Your Sacred Servant Boy Jesus, whom You anointed, both Herod and Pontius Pilate together with non-Jews and ethnic groups of Israel were gathered together,
28 to do as much as Your hand and Your intention designated beforehand to happen.
29 And the things now, Master, look on their threats, and give to Your slaves to be speaking Your message with every clear public statement
30 during the *time* for You to be putting out Your hand for a cure, and indicators and incredible things to be happening through the name of Your Sacred Servant Boy Jesus."

31 And when they pleaded, the place in which they had been gathered together was disturbed, every single one of them were filled with *the* Sacred Spirit, and they were speaking the message of God with a clear public statement.
32 Of the large number of the *people* who trusted, there was one heart and soul. And neither was one *person* saying for any of the *things* that were with him to be *his* own, but absolutely everything with them was shared.
33 And the missionaries with great ability were giving out what they witnessed of the return back to life of the Master Jesus. And great generosity was on them all.
34 You see, neither was anyone destitute among them; for as many as were recipients of parcels of land or houses, as they sold *them*, were bringing the prices of the *things* that were put up for sale
35 and were placing *them* beside the feet of the missionaries. It was being passed out to each and every one according to whoever was having a need.
36 Joses (the *one* who was also called Barnabas by the missionaries, that is translated *from Hebrew as* son of encouragement, a Levite, a Cyprian by birth),
37 after selling a field that was with him, brought the stack of money and placed *it* beside the feet of the missionaries.

5

1 A certain man with *the* name Ananias together with Sapphira (his wife) sold property
2 and secretly kept *some* out of the price for himself, his wife also having been aware of *it*. And after bringing a certain part *of it*, he placed *it* beside the feet of the missionaries.
3 But Peter said, "Ananias, why did the Opponent fill your heart for you to lie to the Spirit, the Sacred *Spirit*, and to secretly keep *some* out of the price of the parcel of land for yourself?
4 As it stayed, was it not staying to you? And when it was put up for sale, was it *not* in your authority? What is this item that you placed in your heart? You did not lie to people, but to God."
5 As Ananias heard these words, after falling, he exhaled *his last breath*. And there became a great fear on all the *people* who heard these *things*.
6 When the younger men got up, they wrapped him up, and after carrying *him* out, they buried *him*.
7 An interval of as *if it were* three hours happened, and his wife, not realizing what had happened, came in.
8 Peter responded to her, "Tell me if you gave the parcel of land away for so much." She said, "Yes, for so much."
9 Peter *said* to her, "How *is it* that it was harmoniously agreed with you to try to cause trouble with the Spirit of *the* Master? Look, the feet of the *people* who buried your husband *are* at the door. And they will carry you out."
10 At once, she fell beside his feet and exhaled *her last breath*. When the young lads came in, they found her dead, and, after carrying *her* out, they buried *her* facing her husband.
11 And there became a great fear on the whole assembly and on all the *people* hearing these *things*.

12 Through the hands of the missionaries, many indicators and incredible things were happening among the group, and absolutely everyone was unanimous in the Columned Shelter of Solomon.
13 None of the rest were daring to be stuck like glue to them, but the group was magnifying them.
14 Trusting *people* were being added to the Master more, large numbers of both men and women,
15 in such a way *for them* to be carrying the weak out to each of the plazas and to be placing *them* on cots and mattresses so that as Peter went *by*, *his* shadow might just fall on some of them.
16 Even the large number of the cities around *there* were coming together to Jerusalem carrying weak *people* and *people* crowded by spirits that are not clean, some *people* who were being healed, every single one.
17 After the head priest and all the *people* together with him (the existing sect of the Sadducees) stood up, they were full of hostile passion,
18 they put their hands on the missionaries, and they put them in a public holding cell.
19 An angel of *the* Master through the night opened the doors of the jail, and after he led them out, he said,
20 "Travel *back*, and when you are stood up, speak on the temple grounds to the group all the statements of this life."
21 After listening, they went under the daybreak onto the temple grounds and were teaching. When the head priest and the *people* together with him showed up, they called together the council and all the senate of the sons of Israel and sent *underlings* out to the prison for them to be led *there*.
22 When the underlings showed up, they did not find them in the jail. After returning, they reported,
23 saying, "We certainly found the prison that had been closed in all certainty, and the jailors that had stood outside in front of the doors. But when we opened *it*, we found no one inside."
24 As they heard these words, both the priest, the captain of the temple grounds, and the head priests were dumbfounded about them, what this might become.
25 But when someone showed up, he reported to them, saying, "Look, the men that you put in the jail are on the temple grounds, who have been standing and are teaching the group."
26 Then after the captain went off together with the underlings, he led them without force. You see, they were fearing the group so that they might not be attacked with stones.
27 When they led them *in*, they stood in the council and the head priest asked them,
28 saying, "Didn't we pass an order on to you not to be teaching based on this name? And look, you have filled Jerusalem with your teaching, and you intend to bring the blood of this Person onto us."
29 When Peter and the missionaries answered, they said, "It is necessary to be loyal to God rather than people.

30 The God of our fathers got Jesus up whom you killed with your hands when you hung *Him* on a wooden cross.
31 This Head Leader and Rescuer, God put up high to His right *side* to give Israel a change of ways and forgiveness of sins.
32 And we are His witnesses of these statements but also *so is* the Spirit, the Sacred *Spirit*, that God gave to the *people* being loyal to Him."
33 The *people* who listened were being sawed in two and were advising to execute them.
34 But when someone in the council stood up (a Separatist with *the* name Gamaliel, a law teacher, valuable to all the ethnic group), he gave the order to make the missionaries *go* outside for some bit.
35 And he said to them, "Men, Israelis, pay attention to yourselves, what you are going to repeatedly be doing based on these people.
36 You see, before these days Theudas stood up saying for himself to be somebody, to whom a number of men were stuck like glue (as if *it were* four hundred), who was executed, and everyone, as many as were being persuaded by him dissipated and became for nothing.
37 After this, Judas, the Galilean, stood up in the days of the registration and stood an adequate group off behind him. And that *one* ruined himself, and all who were being persuaded by him were dispersed.
38 And the *things* now, I say to you, stand off away from these people and allow them because if this intention or this work is from people, it will be torn down.
39 But if it is from God, you aren't able to ever tear it down, and you will be found *to be people* who argue with God."
40 They were persuaded by him. And when they called for the missionaries, after beating *them*, they passed on the order not to be speaking based on the name of Jesus and dismissed them.
41 So the *missionaries* certainly traveled out of *the* face of the council, being happy, because they were considered deserving to be belittled on behalf of His name.
42 And every day, on the temple grounds and in each house, they did not stop teaching and sharing the good news of Jesus, the Anointed King.

6

1 In these days, as the students were increasing, grumbling from the Greek-speaking Jews happened to the Hebrew-speaking *Jews* because their widows were being overlooked in the serving, the daily *one*.
2 After the Twelve called for the large number of the students, they said, "It is not a *thing* that we like *to do*, leaving the message of God down *there* to be serving tables.
3 So, brothers, keep an eye on seven men from among you who are witnessed *by you to be* full of *the* Sacred Spirit and insight, whom we will put in charge over this need.
4 But we will stay close to the prayer and the serving of the message."

5 And the message was liked in the sight of all the large number, and they selected Stephen (a man full of trust and *the* Sacred Spirit), Philip, Prochorus, Nicanor, Timon, Parmenas, and Nicolas (an Antiochian convert),
6 whom they stood in the sight of the missionaries, and when they prayed, they placed *their* hands on them.
7 And the message of God was growing, and the number of the students in Jerusalem was increasing terribly. Even a big crowd of the priests were obeying the trust.
8 Stephen, full of trust and ability, was doing incredible things and great indicators among the group.
9 Some of the *people* from the synagogue, the *one* called "of Libertines *(Latin for free people)*, Cyrenians, Alexadrians, and the *people* out of Cilicia and Western Turkey," stood up, together posing questions to Stephen.
10 And they didn't have *the* strength to stand in opposition to the insight and the Spirit with which he was speaking.
11 Then they secretly threw in men who said, "We have listened to him speaking statements insulting into Moses and God."
12 And together they shook up the group, the older *men*, and the *Old Testament* transcribers. And when they stood over *him*, they seized him and led *him* into the council.
13 And they stood up lying witnesses that said, "This person doesn't stop speaking insulting statements against the place, this sacred *place*, and the law.
14 You see, we have listened to him saying that this Jesus, the Nazarene, will tear this place down and change the customs that Moses turned over to us."
15 And when absolutely all of the *people* seated on the council stared at him, they saw his face as if *it were the* face of an angel.

7

1 The head priest said, "So if this is how he has these *things*..."
2 But *Stephen* was declaring, "Men, brothers and fathers, listen. The God of the magnificence was seen by our father Abraham as he was in Mesopotamia before *the time* for him to even live in Haran.
3 And He said to him, 'Come out from your land and from your relatives, and come here into *the* land that I will show you.'
4 Then after he went out from *the* land of *the* Chaldeans, he lived in Haran. And from there, after the *time* for his father to die, He relocated him to this land in which you now live.
5 And He did not give him an inheritance in it, not even a step of a foot. And He promised to give it to him for a permanent possession and to his seed after him (a child not being with him).
6 God spoke like this: that his seed will be a foreign resident in land belonging to others, and they will enslave and do bad to it for four hundred years.
7 'And the nation in which they will be slaves, I will judge,' said God. 'And after these *things*, they will come out and minister to Me in this place.'

8 And He gave him a deal of circumcision. And this is how he fathered Isaac, and circumcised him on the day, the eighth *day*, Isaac *did the same to* Jacob, and Jacob *did the same to* the twelve head fathers.
9 And when the head fathers got mad at Joseph, they gave *him* away to Egypt, and God was with him.
10 And He took him out of all his hard times and gave him generosity and insight directly in front of Pharaoh, a king of Egypt. And He put him in charge, being a leader over Egypt and his whole house.
11 But a famine came over all of the land of Egypt and Canaan and very hard times. And our fathers were not finding feed *for their cattle*.
12 When Jacob heard that there was grain in Egypt, he sent our fathers off first.
13 And during the second *time*, Joseph revealed himself to his brothers, and the family of Joseph became shown to Pharaoh.
14 When Joseph sent *people* out, he summoned Jacob (his father) and all of his relatives (in souls, seventy-five).
15 Jacob walked down to Egypt. And he and our fathers passed away,
16 and they were transferred to Shechem and placed in the grave that Abraham purchased with a price of silver from the side of the sons of Emmor of Shechem.
17 Just as the time of the promise was coming near that God guaranteed to Abraham, the ethnic group grew and increased in Egypt
18 till *a time* that a different king stood up over Egypt who did not know Joseph.
19 After this *king* swindled our family, he did bad to our fathers, of the 'to be making their babies *to be* put out' *kind* for the 'to not survive' *part*,
20 in which time, Moses was born and to God he was well behaved, who was raised three months in the house of his father.
21 When he was placed outside, the daughter of Pharaoh took him up and raised him herself for a son.
22 And Moses was disciplined in every insight of Egyptians. He was competent in messages and in actions.
23 As a forty-year time was being accomplished with him, it stepped up on his heart to keep an eye on his brothers, the sons of Israel.
24 And when he saw someone being wronged, he fended *for him* and made a retaliation against the *Egyptian* oppressing *him* when he forcibly struck the Egyptian.
25 He was assuming for his brothers to be understanding that God through his hand is giving a rescue to them, but the *men* did not understand.
26 On the following day, he was seen by them as they were arguing, and he urged them together for peace, saying, 'Men, you are brothers. Why are you doing wrong to each other?'
27 The *man* doing wrong to the *man* nearby pushed him away, saying, 'Who put you in charge as a head person and referee over us?
28 You don't want to execute me *the* way that you executed the Egyptian yesterday, do you?'

29 Moses escaped during this saying and became a foreign resident in *the* land of Midian where he had two sons.
30 And when forty years were accomplished, there was seen by him in the backcountry of Mount Sinai, an angel of *the* Master in a blaze of fire of a bush.
31 When Moses saw *it*, he was amazed at the sighting. As he went forward to take a closer look, there became *the* Master's voice toward him.
32 'I *am* the God of your fathers, the God of Abraham, the God of Isaac, and the God of Jacob.' After there became trembling inside, Moses was not daring to take a closer look.
33 The Master said to him, 'Release the sandals of your feet. You see, the place in which you have stood is sacred ground.
34 When I looked, I saw the bad treatment of my ethnic group, the *one* in Egypt. And I listened to their groan and stepped down to take them out *of Egypt*. And now, come here. I will send you out *on a mission* to Egypt.'
35 This Moses, whom they denied when they said, 'Who put you in charge *as* a head person and referee?' this *man*, God sent out *on a mission to be* a head person and provider of *their* release in *the* hand of *the* angel who was seen by him in the bush.
36 This *man* led them out after he did incredible things and indicators in *the* land of Egypt, in *the* Red Sea, and in the backcountry for forty years.
37 This *man* is Moses, the *one* who said to the sons of Israel, '*The* Master, your God, will stand up a preacher to you from your brothers, as me. You will listen to him.'
38 This is the *one* who became in the assembly in the backcountry with the angel (the *one* speaking to him in Mount Sinai) and *with* our fathers, who accepted living utterances to give to us,
39 to whom our fathers didn't want to become obedient, but pushed away and turned back in their hearts to Egypt
40 when they said to Aaron, 'Make gods for us that will travel ahead of us. You see, this Moses who led us out from Egypt land, we don't know what happened to him.'
41 And they made a calf in those days, led a sacrifice up to the idol, and were celebrating in the works of their hands.
42 God turned and gave them up to be ministering to the army of the sky, just as it has been written in a scroll of the preachers *in Amos 5:25–27*, 'You didn't offer slaughtered animals and sacrifices up to Me forty years in the backcountry, house of Israel, did you?
43 You even took up the tent of Molech and the constellation of your god, Remphan, the examples that you made to be bowing down to them. And I will relocate you on that *side* of Babylon.'
44 The tent of the witness was with our fathers in the backcountry, just as the *One* speaking to Moses specifically arranged for it to be made aligned with the example that he had seen,
45 that our fathers also led in (after passing *it* down in succession) with Joshua in the permanent possession of the nations that God pushed out away from *the* face of our fathers until the days of David,

46 who found generosity in the sight of God and asked to find a shelter for the God of Jacob.
47 Solomon built Him a house.
48 But the Highest *One* does not live in handmade temples, just as the preacher says *in Isaiah 66:1,*
49 'The sky *is* a throne to Me. The earth *is* a footrest of My feet. What kind of house will you build Me, says *the* Master? Or what place *is* My resting place?
50 Didn't My hand make all these?'
51 Stiffnecked and uncircumcised in the heart and the ears, you always fall opposing the Spirit, the Sacred *Spirit.* As your fathers *did,* you also *do.*
52 Which of the preachers did your fathers not persecute? They even killed the *people* who previously proclaimed about the coming of the *Man* who did what is right, of whom now you have become traitors and murderers,
53 some who received the law for arrangements of announcers and didn't observe *it.*"
54 Hearing these *things,* they were being sawed in two by their hearts and were grinding *their* teeth at him.
55 Being full of *the* Sacred Spirit, when he stared into the sky, he saw God's magnificence and Jesus who had stood at *places to the* right of God.
56 And he said, "Look, I see the heavens that have been opened and the Son of the Person who has been standing at *places to the* right of God."
57 When they yelled with a loud voice, they held their ears and unanimously rushed on him.
58 And after throwing *him* outside of the city, they were throwing stones *at him.* And the witnesses put away their robes beside the feet of a young man called Saul.
59 And they were throwing stones at Stephen as he called over and said, "Master, Jesus, accept my spirit."
60 After placing his knees *on the ground,* he yelled with a loud voice, "Master, you shouldn't stack up this sin to them." And when he said this, he fell asleep.

8 1 Saul was agreeing that his execution was good. In that day a large persecution happened on the assembly, the *one* in Greater Jerusalem. Everyone was scattered throughout the rural areas of Judea and Samaria, other than the missionaries.
2 Together devout men retrieved Stephen, and they did a great beating of chests in grief over him.
3 Saul was wreaking havoc on the assembly. Traveling into each house and dragging out men and women, he was turning *them* in for jail.
4 So when the *people* were certainly scattered out, they went through *there* sharing the good news of the message.
5 When Philip went down to a city of Samaria, he was speaking publicly to them about the Anointed King.
6 The crowds were unanimously paying attention to the *things* being said by Philip, during the *time* for them to be hearing and to be seeing the indicators that he did.

7 You see, of the many *people* who had spirits that were not clean, as they were shouting with a loud voice, they were coming out. Many who had been disabled and crippled *people* were being healed.
8 And there became great happiness in that city.
9 A certain man with *the* name Simon previously was in the city using magic tricks and astounding the nation of Samaria, saying himself to be some great *person*,
10 to whom they all, from little to great, were paying attention, saying, "This *man* is the ability of God, the great *ability*."
11 They were paying attention to him because of the *fact for him* to have astounded them an adequate amount of time with the magic tricks.
12 When they trusted Philip (who was sharing the good news of the *things* about the monarchy of God and the name of Jesus, *the* Anointed King), they were being submerged, both men and women.
13 Even Simon himself trusted. And after he was submerged, staying close to Philip and watching abilities and indicators happening, he was being astounded.
14 When the missionaries in Greater Jerusalem heard that Samaria had accepted the message of God, they sent Peter and John out *on a mission* to them,
15 certain *men* who, after walking down, prayed about them in order that they might receive *the* Sacred Spirit.
16 (You see, He had not fallen on any of them yet. They had only been submerged in the name of the Master Jesus.)
17 Then they were placing *their* hands on them, and they were receiving *the* Sacred Spirit.
18 When Simon viewed that through the laying on of the hands of the missionaries the Sacred Spirit is given, he offered them stacks of money,
19 saying, "Give me this authority also, so that on whomever I place *my* hands, he may receive *the* Sacred Spirit."
20 Peter said to him, "May your silver be together with you for ruin because you assumed to be getting the free handout of God through stacks of money.
21 Not a part nor a portion in this message is with you. You see, your heart is not straight in the sight of God.
22 So change your ways away from this badness of yours and plead with God, if then the viewpoint of your heart will be forgiven to you.
23 You see, I see you being into bile of bitterness and bondage of *the* wrong way."
24 When Simon responded, he said, "You must plead on my behalf to the Master in order that none of what you have stated will come on me."
25 So after the *missionaries* certainly were strong witnesses and spoke the message of the Master, they returned to Jerusalem and shared good news with many villages of the Samaritans.
26 An angel of *the* Master spoke to Philip, saying, "Get up and travel throughout *the* middle of the day on the road, the *one* that steps down out of Jerusalem to Gaza" (it is backcountry).

27 And when he got up, he traveled and look, a man (an Ethiopian, a castrated man, a competent ruler *under* Candace, the Queen of Ethiopians, who was over all of her royal treasury), who had gone to Jerusalem so that he will bow down.
28 And he was returning and sitting on his chariot. He was reading the preacher Isaiah.
29 The Spirit said to Philip, "Go forward, and be stuck like glue to this chariot."
30 When Philip ran up, he listened to him reading Isaiah, the preacher, and said, "So do you definitely know what you are reading?"
31 The *Ethiopian* said, "You see, how would I be able to, if someone won't guide me?" And he encouraged Philip, after climbing up, to be seated together with him.
32 The passage of the *Old Testament* writing that he was reading was this *(Isaiah 53:7–8)*, "As a sheep at a slaughter was led, and as a lamb directly in front of the one shearing him *is* voiceless, this is how He doesn't open His mouth.
33 In His lowliness, His judgment was taken away. Who will describe His generation because His life is taken away from the earth?"
34 When the castrated man responded to Philip, he said, "I plead with you, who is the preacher talking about? *Is* this about himself or about someone different?"
35 When Philip opened his mouth and began out of this *Old Testament* writing, he shared the good news with him of Jesus.
36 As they were traveling along the road, they came upon some water, and the castrated man declares, "Look. Water. What is hindering me to be submerged?"
37 Philip said, "If you trust from *your* whole heart, it is allowed." When he answered, he said, "I trust the son of God to be Jesus, *the* Anointed King."
38 And he gave the order for the chariot to stand *still*. And they both climbed down into the water (both Philip and the castrated man), and he submerged him.
39 When they climbed up from the water, *the* Master's Spirit snatched Philip, and the castrated man did not see him anymore. You see, he was traveling *on* his way, being happy.
40 But Philip was found in Azotus. And as he went through *there*, he was sharing good news with all the cities until the *time* for him to come to Caesarea.

9

1 Saul still inhaling *the smell* of threat and murder for the students of the Master, after going forward to the head priest,
2 asked from the side of him letters to Damascus to the synagogues in order that if he found any *people* of the Way (being both men and women), he would lead *them* (having been tied up) to Jerusalem.

3 During the *time* to be traveling, it happened for him to be coming near Damascus. And unexpectedly, a light from the sky beamed down all around him.
4 And after he fell on the ground, he heard a voice saying to him, "Saul, Saul, why are you persecuting Me?"
5 He said, "Who are You, Master?" The Master said, "I am Jesus, whom you persecute. *Is it* harsh to you to be kicking toward cattle prods?"
6 Both trembling and perplexed, he said, "Master, what do you want me to do?" And the Master *said* to him, "Get up, go into the city, and it will be spoken to you what it is necessary for you to be doing."
7 The men, the *ones* who were on the trip together with him, had stood speechless, certainly listening to the voice, but seeing no one.
8 Saul got up off the ground, but when he had opened his eyes, he was seeing nothing. Leading *him* by the hand, they led him into Damascus.
9 And he was not seeing for three days. He also did not eat, nor drink.
10 There was a certain student in Damascus with *the* name Ananias. And the Master said to him in a sighting, "Ananias." *Ananias* said, "Look, *it is* me, Master."
11 The Master *said* to him, "When you get up, travel on the street, the *one* called Straight, and look in Jude's house for Saul by name, a Tarsean. You see, look, he is praying,
12 and he saw in a sighting a man with *the* name Ananias, who went in and placed a hand on him in order that he might see again."
13 Ananias responded, "Master, I have heard from many about this man, how many bad *things* he did to Your sacred *people* in Jerusalem.
14 And here he has authority from the side of the head priests to lock up all the *people* calling on Your Name."
15 But the Master said to him, "Travel *there* because he is a container of selection by Me. This *man is* of the 'to haul My name in the sight of non-Jews, kings, and sons of Israel' *kind*.
16 You see, I will put in front of his face how many *things* it is necessary for him to suffer on behalf of My name."
17 Ananias went off and went into the house. And when he placed *his* hands on him, he said, "Saul, brother, the Master has sent me out, Jesus, the *One* who saw you in the road that you were coming *on*, in order that you might see again and be filled with *the* Sacred Spirit."
18 And right away, as if *they were* flakes they fell off his eyes, and at once he saw again. And when he got up, he was submerged.
19 And after he received a meal, he was invigorated. Saul became with the students in Damascus for some days.
20 And right away he was speaking publicly about *the* Anointed King in the synagogues, that this is the Son of God.
21 All the *people* listening were being astounded and saying, "Isn't this the *one* who damaged the *people* calling on this name in Jerusalem and here he had come for this, so that he might lead them (having been tied up) before the head priests?"

22 Saul was becoming more competent, and he was stirring up the Jewish *people*, the *ones* living in Damascus, inferring that this is the Anointed King.
23 As an adequate amount of days were being accomplished, the Jewish *people* together advised to execute him.
24 Their conspiracy was known to Saul. They were even closely watching the gates both day and night in order that they might execute him.
25 After the students took him at night, they let *him* down through the wall after lowering *him* in a big basket.
26 When Saul showed up in Jerusalem, he was trying to be stuck like glue to the students. And all feared him, not trusting that he is a student.
27 But after Barnabas latched on to him, he led *him* to the missionaries and described to them how in the road he saw the Master, that He spoke to him, and how in Damascus he made clear public statements in the name of Jesus.
28 And he was with them traveling in and traveling out in Jerusalem.
29 And making clear public statements in the name of the Master Jesus, he was both speaking and together posing questions to the Greek-speaking Jews, but the *Greek-speaking Jews* were attempting to execute him.
30 When the brothers correctly understood *it*, they led him down to Caesarea and sent him off to Tarsus.
31 So the assemblies certainly were having peace throughout all of Judea, Galilee, and Samaria. Being built and traveling in the fear of the Master and the encouragement of the Sacred Spirit, they were increasing.
32 It happened for Peter, going through everywhere, to also go down to the sacred *people*, the *ones* living in Lydda.
33 There he found a certain person with *the* name Aeneas, laying down on a mattress for eight years, who had been disabled.
34 And Peter said to him, "Aeneas, Jesus, the Anointed King, is curing you. Stand up and spread *your mattress* out for yourself." And right away he stood up.
35 And all the people living in Lydda and *the plain of* Sharon saw him, some who turned back to the Master.
36 In Joppa there was a certain student with *the* name Tabitha, that being thoroughly interpreted *from Aramaic* she is called Gazelle. She was full of good actions and charitable donations that she was making.
37 She happened (in those days when she was weak) to die. After they gave *her* a bath, they placed her in an upstairs room.
38 Since Lydda is near Joppa, when the students heard that Peter is in it, they sent two men out to him encouraging *him* not to hesitate to come on through to them.
39 After Peter got up, he went together with them, whom, when he showed up, they led up to the upstairs room, and all the widows stood by him crying and showing as many long undershirts and clothes as the Gazelle was making as she was with them.
40 After Peter put everyone outside, when he placed *his* knees *on the floor*, he prayed. And when he turned around toward the body, he said, "Tabitha, get up." The *woman* opened her eyes, and when she saw Peter, she sat up on her own.

41 After giving her a hand, he got her up. When he hollered for the sacred *people* and the widows, he presented her alive.
42 It became known throughout all of Joppa, and many *people* trusted based on the Master.
43 It happened for him to stay an adequate amount of days in Joppa beside a certain Simon, a leatherworker.

10

1 There was a certain man in Caesarea with *the* name Cornelius, a lieutenant from the regiment called Italian.
2 *He was* a godly *man* and fearing God together with everyone in his house both making many charitable donations to the ethnic group and pleading with God through everything.
3 He saw in a sighting in a shown way as if *it were the* ninth hour of the day *(3:00 p.m.)* God's angel that came in toward him and said to him, "Cornelius."
4 When the *lieutenant* stared at him and became afraid, he said, "What is it, Master?" He said to him, "Your prayers and your charitable donations stepped up for a reminder in the sight of God.
5 And now send men to Joppa, and send for Simon, who is also called Peter.
6 This *man* is a guest by the side of a certain Simon, a leatherworker, with whom is a house along *the* sea. This *man* will speak to you what it is necessary for you to do."
7 As the angel (the *one* speaking to Cornelius) went away, after hollering for two of his domestic servants and a godly soldier of the *ones* who stayed close to him
8 and recounting to them absolutely everything, he sent them out *on a mission* to Joppa.
9 The next day as those *people* were traveling on the road and came near to the city, Peter climbed up on the top of the house to pray around *the* sixth hour *(noon)*.
10 He became very hungry, and he was wanting to taste *some food*, but as those *people* were preparing *it*, a trance fell on him.
11 And he watches the sky (that has been opened) and a certain container stepping down on him as a large sheet with four corners having been tied and being let down on the earth,
12 in which were all the four-legged animals of the earth, the wild animals, the reptiles, and the winged birds of the sky.
13 And there became a voice to him, "Get up, Peter. Kill and eat."
14 But Peter said, "No way, Master, because I never even once ate anything shared or not clean."
15 And a voice *came* again from a second *time* to him, "*Things* that God cleaned you must not make shared."
16 This happened at three times, and the container again was taken up into the sky.
17 As Peter was dumbfounded in himself *about* whatever the sighting that he saw might be, and look, the men, the *ones* that had been sent out by Cornelius, after asking around for the house of Simon, stood at the gateway.

18 And when they hollered, they were inquiring if Simon, the *one* who is also called Peter, was a guest there.
19 As Peter was contemplating about the sighting, the Spirit said to him, "Look, three men are looking for you.
20 But when you get up, climb down, and travel together with them, considering nothing to be wrong because I have sent them out."
21 After Peter climbed down to the men, the *ones* sent out from Cornelius to him, he said, "Look, I am who you are looking for. What *is* the reason why you are beside *us*?"
22 The *men* said, "Cornelius, a lieutenant, a man who does what is right and who fears God, also being witnessed by the whole nation of the Jewish *people*, was *divinely* notified by a sacred angel to send for you to his house and to hear statements from the side of you."
23 So after he invited them in, he provided a place *for them* to stay. On the next day, Peter went out together with them. And some of the brothers, the *ones* out of Joppa, went together with him.
24 And on the next day he went into Caesarea. Cornelius was expecting them after calling his relatives and essential friends together.
25 As it happened for Peter to go in, when Cornelius met together with him, after getting down at *his* feet, he bowed down.
26 But Peter got him up, saying, "Stand up. I myself also am a person."
27 And as he was chatting together with him, he went in and finds many who had come together.
28 And he was declaring to them, "You are well aware of how it is forbidden for a Jewish man to be stuck like glue to or to be coming forward to a *person* of another family line, and God showed me not to be calling any person shared or not clean.
29 For this reason, I also came without objecting when I was sent for. So I am inquiring, for what matter did you send for me?"
30 And Cornelius was declaring, "Out of *the* fourth day, up to this hour I was going without food and praying the ninth hour *(3:00 p.m.) prayer* in my house. And look, a man stood in my sight in a dazzling outfit.
31 And he declares, 'Cornelius, your prayer was listened to and your charitable donations were remembered in the sight of God.
32 So send to Joppa and summon Simon who is also called Peter. This *man* is a guest in *the* house of Simon, a leatherworker along *the* sea, who, when he shows up, will speak to you.'
33 So I immediately sent to you, and you did nicely showing up. So now we all are beside *you* in the sight of God to hear all the *things* that have been instructed to you by God."
34 When Peter opened *his* mouth, he said, "Based on truth I completely take *it* that God is not someone who is swayed by appearances.
35 But in every nation, the *person* who fears Him and works for *the* right way is accepted by Him.
36 The message that He sent out to the sons of Israel, sharing the good news of peace through Jesus, *the* Anointed King (this *Jesus* is Master of all) —

37 you realize the statement that became throughout all of Judea, after it started out of Galilee with the submersion that John spoke publicly about:
38 Jesus, the *One* out of Nazareth (as God anointed Him with *the* Sacred Spirit and ability), who went through *there* doing humane things and curing all the *people* suppressed by the Accuser because God was with Him.
39 And we are witnesses of all that He did, both in the rural area of the Jewish *people* and in Jerusalem, whom they executed when they hung *Him* on a wooden cross.
40 This *Man*, God got up the third day and gave Him to become explicitly shown,
41 not to all the ethnic group, but to witnesses, to the *people* who had been handpicked beforehand by God, to us, some who ate together and drank together with Him after the *time* for Him to come back to life from *the* dead.
42 And He passed the order on to us to speak publicly to the ethnic group and to be strong witnesses *to the fact* that He is the *One* who has been designated by God *to be the* Judge of living and dead *people*.
43 To this, all the Preachers are witnesses: for everyone who trusts in Him to receive forgiveness of sins through His name."
44 As Peter was still speaking these statements, the Spirit, the Sacred *Spirit*, fell on all the *people* hearing the message.
45 And the trusting *people* from *the* circumcision were astounded, as many as came together with Peter, because the free handout of the Sacred Spirit also had been spilled out on the non-Jews.
46 You see, they were listening to them speaking with languages and magnifying God. Then Peter responded,
47 "Someone is not able to hinder the water for the *purpose* of these *people* (some who received the Spirit, the Sacred *Spirit*, just as we also *did*) not to be submerged, is he?"
48 And He instructed them to be submerged in the name of the Master. Then they asked him to stay over for some days.

11

1 The missionaries and the brothers, the *ones* who were throughout Judea, heard that the non-Jews also accepted the message of God.
2 And when Peter walked up to Jerusalem, the *people* from *the* circumcision were considering *it* to be wrong for him,
3 saying, "You went in toward men having uncircumcision and ate together with them."
4 But when Peter began, he laid *it* out to them in order, saying,
5 "I was in *the* city *of* Joppa praying and I saw a sighting in a trance, a certain container stepping down as a large sheet being let down by four corners from the sky. And it came till me.
6 Into which, after staring, I was taking a closer look, and I saw the four-legged animals of the earth, the wild animals, the reptiles, and the winged birds of the sky.
7 I listened to a voice saying to me, 'Get up, Peter. Kill and eat.'

8 But I said, 'No way, Master, because never even once did anything shared or not clean come into my mouth.'
9 A voice responded to me from a second *time* from the sky, '*Things* that God cleaned you must not make shared.'
10 This happened at three times, and absolutely everything was pulled up again into the sky.
11 And look, immediately three men stood at the house that I was in, who had been sent out from Caesarea to me.
12 The Spirit said to me to go together with them considering nothing to be wrong. They went together with me and these six brothers. And we went into the house of the man.
13 He reported to us how he saw the angel in his house when it was stood up and said to him, 'Send men out to Joppa, and send for Simon, the *one* who is also called Peter,
14 who will speak statements to you in which you and all your house will be rescued.'
15 During the *time* for me to begin to be speaking, the Spirit, the Sacred *Spirit*, fell on them, even as *it* also *fell* on us in *the* beginning.
16 I remembered the statement of *the* Master, how He was saying, 'John certainly submerged with water, but you will be submerged in *the* Sacred Spirit.'
17 So if God gave them the free handout equal as also to us who trusted based on the Master Jesus, *the* Anointed King, who was I? *Was I* able to hinder God?"
18 After hearing these *things*, they calmed down and were praising God's magnificence, saying, "Clearly, definitely, even to the non-Jews, God gave the change of ways into life."
19 So not only did the *people* who were scattered out from the hard times, the hard times that happened over Stephen, go across as far as Phoenicia, Cyprus, and Antioch speaking the message to no one except to Jewish *people* only,
20 but some from among them were men, Cyprians and Cyrenians, certain *men* who, when they went into Antioch, were speaking to the Greek-speaking people, sharing the good news of the Master Jesus.
21 And *the* hand of *the* Master was with them. And a big number who trusted turned back to the Master.
22 The message about them was heard in the ears of the assembly, the *one* in Jerusalem, and they sent Barnabas off to go through as far as Antioch,
23 who, after showing up and seeing the generosity of God, was happy and was encouraging everyone in the purpose of *their* heart to still be staying in the Master,
24 because he was a good man and full of *the* Sacred Spirit and trust. And an adequate crowd was added to the Master.
25 Barnabas went out to Tarsus to look up *and down* for Saul.
26 And when he found him, he led him to Antioch. It happened a whole year for them to gather together in the assembly, to teach an adequate crowd, and for the students to first notify *people* in Antioch *that they are* Christians.
27 In these days, preachers went down out of Jerusalem into Antioch.

28 When one from among them with *the* name Agabus stood up, he indicated through the Spirit *for there in the future* to be going to be a large famine over the whole civilized world, even something that happened over Caesar Claudius.
29 Of the students, just as some had means, they (each of them) designated *money* for *the task of* serving to send to the brothers living in Judea,
30 that they also did when they sent *it* out to the older *men* through *the* hand of Barnabas and Saul.

12

1 Throughout that time, Herod, the king, put *his* hands on some of the *people* out of the assembly to do bad to *them*.
2 He executed James, the brother of John, with a dagger.
3 And after seeing that it is a *thing* that the Jewish *people* liked, he added to *it* to also apprehend Peter (but it was *the* days of the Yeast-free *Loaves Festival*),
4 whom also, after arresting, he put in jail after he turned him over to four squads of four soldiers to be guarding him, intending after the Passover to lead him up to the ethnic group.
5 So Peter certainly was being kept in the jail, but there was intensive prayer happening under the assembly to God over him.
6 When Herod was going to be bringing him out, that night Peter was asleep between two soldiers having been locked up with two chains. And jailors in front of the door were keeping guard of the jail.
7 And look, an angel of *the* Master stood over *him*, and a light shined in the cell. After forcibly striking the side of Peter, he got him up, saying, "Stand up quickly." And his chains fell from *his* hands.
8 And the angel said to him, "Tie your sash around your waist, and tie your sole pads on under *your feet*." He did so. And he says to him, "Put your robe around yourself, and follow me."
9 And when he went out, he was following him and did not realize that the *thing* happening through the angel is valid. He seemed to be seeing a sighting.
10 After going through *the* first and second jail, they came upon the gate, the iron *one*, the *one* leading to the city, something that automatically opened to them. And when they went out, they went on ahead down one street, and right away the angel stood off away from him.
11 And when Peter became in himself, he said, "Now I truly realize that *the* Master sent off His angel and took me out of Herod's hand and every expectation of the ethnic group of the Jewish *people*."
12 And when he became aware of *it*, he went up to the house of Mary, the mother of John (the *one* who is also called Mark), where an adequate amount of *people* were who had accumulated together and were praying.
13 When Peter knocked at the door of the gateway, a servant girl with *the* name Rhoda came forward to quietly listen.
14 And when she recognized the voice of Peter, out of the happiness, she didn't open the gateway, but after running inside, she reported for Peter to have stood in front of the gateway.

15 The *people* said to her, "You are crazy." The *girl* was strongly insisting to be having *it* like this. The *people* were saying, "It is his angel."
16 Peter was staying at *it*, knocking. When they opened, they saw him and were astounded.
17 After motioning to them with *his* hand to keep quiet, he described to them how the Master led him out of the jail. He said, "Report these *things* to James and the brothers." And when he went out, he traveled to a different place.
18 When it became day, there was not *just* a little agitation among the soldiers. "So what happened to Peter?"
19 When Herod searched for him and did not find *him*, after investigating the jailors, he gave the order for *them* to be led away. And after he went down out of Judea into Caesarea, he was spending time *there*.
20 Herod was in a heated argument with Tyrians and Sidonians. Unanimously they were beside *him* facing him, and after they persuaded Blastus (the person over the bedroom of the king), they were asking for peace because of the *fact* for their rural area to be nurtured out of the royal *treasury*.
21 On an appointed day, when Herod put on a royal outfit and was seated on the judicial bench, he was delivering a mob-inspiring speech facing them.
22 The mob was hollering out, "A voice of a god and not of a person."
23 At once, an angel of *the* Master forcibly struck him for *the times* that he did not give the magnificence to God. And after becoming infested with maggots, he exhaled *his last breath*.
24 The message of God was growing and increasing.
25 Barnabas and Saul returned from Jerusalem after they accomplished the serving, who also took John (the *one* who was also called Mark) along together with *them*.

13

1 Some preachers and teachers were throughout the existing assembly in Antioch: Barnabas, Simon (the *one* called Niger), Lucius (the Cyrenian), Manaen (a childhood companion of the head of one of *Palestine's* four regions, Herod), and Saul.
2 As they served the public for the Master and went without food, the Spirit, the Sacred *Spirit*, said, "Isolate to Me, for sure, both Barnabas and Saul for the work that I have called them to."
3 Then after they went without food, prayed, and placed *their* hands on *them*, they dismissed *them*.
4 So after these certainly were sent off by the Sacred Spirit, they went down to Seleucia, and from there they sailed off to Cyprus.
5 And when they became in Salamis, they were proclaiming the message of God in the synagogues of the Jewish *people*. They were also having John *as* an underling.
6 After they went through the island till Paphos, they found a certain Jewish *man*, a Magian guru, a counterfeit preacher with whom *was the* name Barjesus,
7 who was together with the Roman deputy Sergius Paul, an understanding man. When this *man* called for Barnabas and Saul, he searched to hear the message of God.

8 But Elymas, the Magian guru (you see, this is how his name is translated), was standing in opposition to them, looking to twist the Roman deputy away from the trust.
9 Saul, the *one who is* also Paul, who was filled with *the* Sacred Spirit and staring at him,
10 said, "O, full of every deception and every mischievousness, son of *the* Accuser, enemy of every right way, will you not stop twisting the ways of *the* Master (the straight *ways*)?
11 And now, look, *the* hand of the Master *is* on you, and you will be blind, not seeing the sun till a certain time." At once, blurriness and darkness fell on him, and going around he was looking for people to lead *him* by the hand.
12 Then when the Roman deputy saw what had happened, he trusted being impressed based on the Master's teaching.
13 When the *people* around Paul took off from Paphos, they went to Perga of Pamphylia. After John distanced himself away from them, he returned to Jerusalem.
14 After they went through *there* away from Perga, they showed up in Antioch of Pisidia. And when they went into the synagogue on the day of the Sabbaths, they were seated.
15 After the reading of the Law and the Preachers, the synagogue's head rulers sent out to them, saying, "Men, brothers, if there is a message among you of encouragement to the group, tell *it*."
16 When Paul stood up and motioned with *his* hand, he said, "Men, Israelis, and the *people* who fear God, listen.
17 The God of this ethnic group, Israel, selected our fathers and put the ethnic group up high in the foreign residency in a land, Egypt. And with a high arm, He led them out of it.
18 And for as *if it were* a forty-year time, He put up with them in the backcountry.
19 And after He took down seven nations in *the* land of Canaan, He portioned out their land to them for an inheritance.
20 And after these *things*, as *if it were* four hundred and fifty years, He also gave judges until Samuel, the preacher.
21 And from there, they asked for a king and God gave them Saul (a son of Kish, a man from Benjamin's family line) for forty years.
22 And after He dislodged him, He raised up David into a king for them, to whom He also said when He told what He witnessed, 'I found David, the *son* of Jesse, a man aligned with My heart, who will do all the *things* that I want.'
23 Out of the seed of this *man*, God, aligned with a promise, raised a rescuer for Israel, Jesus.
24 After John spoke publicly before *the* appearance of His entrance about a submersion of a change of ways to all the ethnic group of Israel,
25 as John was accomplishing the race, he was saying, 'Who do you suspect me to be? I am not *Him*. But look, He is coming after me, the sandal of whose feet I am not deserving to release.'
26 Men, brothers, sons of Abraham's family, and the *people* among you who fear God, to you was the message of this rescue sent out.

27 You see, when the *people* living in Jerusalem and their head people were unaware of this *Man* and the voices of the Preachers being read each *and* every Sabbath, after judging *Him*, they accomplished *what the voices said.*
28 And when they did not find even one accusation of death, they asked Pilate to execute Him.
29 As they finished absolutely all the *things* that had been written about Him, after taking *Him* down off the wooden cross, they placed *Him* into a burial vault.
30 God got Him up from *the* dead,
31 who was seen over several days by the *people* who walked up together with Him out of Galilee into Jerusalem, some who are witnesses of Him to the ethnic group.
32 And we are sharing the good news with you of the promise that happened to the fathers
33 that this *promise* God has completely fulfilled for their children, us, when He brought Jesus back to life, as it has also been written in the Psalm, the second *one (2:7),* 'You are My Son. I today have given birth to You.'
34 Because He brought Him back to life from *the* dead, who is no longer going to be returning to decay, this is what He has stated *in Isaiah 55:3,* 'I will give you the holy *things* of David, the *things* that can be trusted.'
35 For this reason, also in a different *place,* He says *in Psalm 16:10,* 'You will not give Your Holy *One* to see decay.'
36 You see, David, after working as an underling for *his* own generation in the intention of God, certainly fell asleep, was placed facing his fathers, and saw decay.
37 But *the One* whom God got up did not see decay.
38 So be it known to you, men, brothers, that through this *Man* forgiveness of sins is proclaimed to you.
39 And everything that you were not able in the law of Moses to be made right from, in this *Man,* everyone trusting is made right.
40 So look out *that* what has been stated in the Preachers *in Habakkuk 1:5* might not come on you:
41 'The people who ignore, look, be amazed, and disappear, because I am working a work in your days, a work that you will not in any way trust, *even* if someone describes *it* in detail to you.'"
42 When the Jewish *people* were out of the synagogue, the non-Jews were encouraging on the in-between Sabbath for these statements to be spoken to them.
43 When the synagogue was released, many of the Jewish *people* and the worshipping converts followed Paul and Barnabas, certain *men* who, as they spoke to them, were persuading them to be staying over in the generosity of God.
44 On the coming Sabbath, nearly all the city was gathered together to hear the message of God.
45 When the Jewish *people* saw the crowds, they were filled with hostile passion and were expressing opposition to the *things* being said by Paul, speaking against *them* and insulting *them.*

46 When Paul and Barnabas made a clear public statement, they said, "It was essential for the message of God to be spoken to you first. But since, for sure, you are pushing it away and judging yourselves not deserving of the life that spans *all* time, look, we are turned to the non-Jews.

47 You see, this is how the Master has demanded us *in Isaiah 49:6*, 'I have placed you for a light of *the* non-Jews, of the "for you to be for rescue out to *the* last *place* of the earth" *kind*.'"

48 As the non-Jews heard *this*, they were happy and praising the magnificence of the message of the Master. And they trusted, as many as had assigned themselves to life that spans *all* time.

49 The message of the Master was being carried through the whole rural area.

50 But the Jewish *people* incited the worshipping women, the reputable *women*, and the most important *people* of the city. And they roused up persecution on Paul and Barnabas and threw them out away from their borders.

51 After the *two* shook off the dust of their feet on them, they went to Iconium.

52 The students were being filled with happiness and *the* Sacred Spirit.

14

1 It happened in Iconium aligned with the same *process*, for them to go into the synagogue of the Jewish *people* and to speak this way, in such a way for a very large number of both Jewish *people* and Greeks to trust.

2 The Jewish *people* who did not believe roused up and did bad to the souls of the non-Jews against the brothers.

3 So they certainly spent an adequate amount of time making clear public statements on the Master, who was a witness of the message of His generosity and who gave indicators and incredible things to be happening through their hands.

4 The large number of the city were torn. And *some* were the *people* together with the Jewish *people*, but *the others*, the *people* together with the missionaries.

5 As there became a sudden impulse of both the non-Jews and *the* Jewish *people* together with their head people to injure and to throw stones at them,

6 when they became aware of *it*, they escaped down to the cities of Lycaonia: Lystra, Derbe, and the surrounding rural area.

7 And there they were sharing good news.

8 And a certain man in Lystra (unable with the feet) was sitting, being crippled from his mother's belly, who never even once walked around.

9 This *man* was listening to Paul speaking, who, when he stared at him and saw that he has trust of the "to be rescued" *kind*,

10 said with a loud voice, "Stand up straight on your feet." And he was jumping up and walking around.

11 When the crowds saw what Paul did, they raised up their voice in Lycaonian, saying, "The gods, after becoming like people, stepped down to us."

12 And they were calling Barnabas Zeus, but Paul Hermes, since, for sure, he was the *one* being a leader of the message.
13 The priest of Zeus, the *Zeus* that was in front of their city, after bringing bulls and wreaths up to the gateway, was wanting to be sacrificing together with the crowds.
14 But when the missionaries, Barnabas and Paul, heard it, after ripping apart their robes, they leaped into the crowd, yelling
15 and saying, "Men, why are you doing these *things*? We also are people suffering like you, sharing good news with you to be turning back away from these futile *gods* to God, the living *God*, who made the sky, the earth, the sea, and all the *things* in them,
16 who, in the generations that have gone by, allowed all the nations to be traveling their ways.
17 And yet He definitely did not leave *you* with no witness of Himself, working on good *things*, giving you showers from the sky and fruit-producing times, filling our hearts up with a meal and celebration."
18 And saying these *things*, with a lot of effort they quieted down the crowds for the *purpose* to not be sacrificing to them.
19 But Jewish *people* came on *them* out of Antioch and Iconium. And when they persuaded the crowds and attacked Paul with stones, they were dragging *him* outside of the city after assuming him to have died.
20 When the students surrounded him, after getting up, he went into the city. And on the next day, he went out together with Barnabas to Derbe.
21 After they both shared good news with that city and made an adequate amount of students, they returned to Lystra, Iconium, and Antioch
22 further establishing the souls of the students, encouraging *them* to be staying in the trust and that "through many hard times it is necessary for us to go into the monarchy of God."
23 After handpicking older *men* for them in each assembly, when they prayed with times of going without food, they placed them beside the Master in whom they had trusted.
24 And after going through Pisidia, they went to Pamphylia.
25 And after they spoke the message in Perga, they walked down to Attalia.
26 And from there, they sailed off to Antioch, from where they had been given over to the generosity of God for the work that they accomplished.
27 When they showed up and gathered the assembly together, they were announcing as many *of the things* as God did with them and that He opened a door of trust to the non-Jews.
28 They were spending not *just* a little time there together with the students.

15

1 And some who came down out of Judea were teaching the brothers, "If you are not circumcised with the custom of Moses, you are not able to be rescued."
2 So after a disruption and not *just* a little back and forth questioning happened with Paul and Barnabas toward them, they arranged for Paul, Barnabas, and some others from among them to be walking up to the missionaries and older *men* into Jerusalem about this question.

3 So the *men*, after being brought on their way by the assembly, certainly were going through Phoenicia and Samaria describing in detail the turnaround of the non-Jews and making great happiness for all the brothers.

4 When they showed up in Jerusalem, they were gladly accepted by the assembly, the missionaries, and the older *men*. And they announced as many *of the things* as God did with them.

5 Some of the *people* out of the sect of the Separatists who had trusted stood up from *them*, saying, "It is necessary to be circumcising them and to be passing the order on *to them* to be keeping the law of Moses."

6 The missionaries and the older *men* were gathered together to see about this matter.

7 After much back and forth questioning happened, when Peter stood up, he said to them, "Men, brothers, you are well aware that out of *the* beginning days among you, God selected through my mouth for the non-Jews to hear the message of the good news and to trust.

8 And the Heart-Knower, God, told what He witnessed of them when He gave them the Spirit, the Sacred *Spirit*, just as *He* also *gave* to us.

9 And He considered nothing to be different between both us and them with the trust when He cleaned out their hearts.

10 So why are you now trying to cause trouble with God, to put a crossbeam on the neck of the students that neither our fathers, nor we had *the* strength to haul?

11 But through the generosity of *the* Master Jesus, we trust to be rescued aligned with *the* way that those *people* also *do*."

12 All the large number *of people* kept quiet and were listening to Barnabas and Paul recounting how many indicators and incredible things God did among the non-Jews through them.

13 After the *time* for them to keep quiet, James responded, saying, "Men, brothers, listen to me.

14 Simon recounted just how God first kept an eye on *this*, to take an ethnic group from non-Jews based on His name.

15 And the messages of the Preachers harmoniously agree with this, just as it has been written *in Amos 9:11–12,*

16 "'After these *things,* I will return, I will rebuild the tent of David, the *tent* that has fallen, I will rebuild its *parts* that have been dug up and removed, and I will straighten it up

17 in order that the residual *ones* of the people and all the non-Jews on whom My name has been called on them will intensively search for the Master," says the Master doing all these *things*.

18 All His actions out of *the* span of time are known to God.'

19 For this reason, I judge to not be disturbing anymore the *people* out of the non-Jews turning back to God,

20 but to write a letter to them of the 'to be keeping themselves away from the contaminations of the idols, the sexual sin, the choked *animal*, and the blood' kind.

21 You see, from *the* beginning generations Moses has in each city the *people* speaking publicly about Him in the synagogues, he being read each *and* every Sabbath."

22 At that time, it seemed *good* to the missionaries and the older *men* together with the whole assembly, after selecting men from among them, to send to Antioch together with Paul and Barnabas, Judah (the *one* also called Barsabas) and Silas, men being leaders among the brothers,

23 after writing the *things* here through their hand, "*From*: The missionaries, the older *men*, and the brothers. To: The brothers throughout Antioch, Syria, and Cilicia, the *brothers* from non-Jews. Happy to meet you.

24 Since, for sure, we heard that some from us agitated you with messages plundering your souls, saying to become circumcised and to keep the law, with which we did not warn,

25 it seemed *good* to us, who became unanimous, to send selected men to you together with our loved *brothers*, Barnabas and Paul,

26 people who have given up their souls on behalf of the name of our Master Jesus, *the* Anointed King.

27 So we have sent Judah and Silas out *on a mission* (who themselves also through words are reporting the same *things*).

28 You see, it seemed *good* to the Sacred Spirit and to us not to be putting any more weight on you other than these crucial *things*:

29 to be keeping yourselves away from idol sacrifices, blood, choked *animals*, and sexual sin, from which *things, if you are* carefully keeping yourselves, you will constantly do well. Farewell."

30 So the *men*, after being dismissed, certainly went into Antioch. And when they gathered the large number together, they gave the letter over *to them*.

31 After reading, they were happy based on the encouragement.

32 Judah and Silas, themselves also being preachers, through many words encouraged and further established the brothers.

33 After they did time *there*, they were dismissed with peace out from the brothers *to go back* to the missionaries.

34 It seemed *good* to Silas to stay over there.

35 Paul and Barnabas were spending time in Antioch, teaching and sharing the good news of the message of the Master with many different *people* also.

36 After some days, Paul said to Barnabas, "After returning back, for sure we should keep an eye on our brothers in each *and* every city in which we proclaimed the message of the Master, how they have *it*."

37 Barnabas advised to take along John (the *one* who is called Mark) together with *them*.

38 Paul was thinking that the *one* who stood off away from them out of Pamphylia and did not go together with them into the work, deserved *for them* to not take this *one* along together with *them*.

39 So it became an annoyance in such a way for them to be separated apart from each other, and for Barnabas, who took Mark along, to sail out to Cyprus.

40 After Paul said *that* Silas *would* also *go with him*, he went out after being given over to the generosity of God by the brothers.

41 He was going through Syria and Cilicia further establishing the assemblies.

1 He made it to Derbe and Lystra and, look, a certain student was there with the name Timothy, a son of a certain trusting Jewish woman, but of a father *who was* Greek,
2 who was witnessed by the brothers in Lystra and Iconium.
3 Paul wanted this *student* to go out together with him. And after he took *him*, he circumcised him because of the Jewish *people*, the *ones* who were in those places. You see, absolutely everyone realized that his father was Greek.
4 As they were traveling through the cities, they were turning the rules over to them to be observing (the *ones* that had been decided by the missionaries and the *older men*, the *older men* in Jerusalem).
5 So the assemblies certainly were becoming solid in the trust and overflowing in the number daily.
6 When they went through Phrygia and the Galatian rural area, after they were hindered by the Sacred Spirit to speak the message in Western Turkey,
7 after going along Mysia, they were trying to travel down to Bithynia, and the Spirit did not allow them.
8 After they passed by Mysia, they walked down into Troas.
9 And a sighting was seen by Paul through the night. There was a certain man, a Macedonian, who had been standing, encouraging him and saying, "After walking across into Macedonia, help us."
10 As *soon as* he saw the sighting, right away we looked to go out into Macedonia, inferring that the Master has called us forward to share good news with them.
11 After taking off out of Troas, we sailed straight to Samothracia, the following *day* to Neapolis,
12 and from there to Philippi, a certain *city* that is a most important city of *that* part of Macedonia, a *Roman* colony. We were spending some days in that city.
13 And on the day of the Sabbaths, we went outside of the city along a river where we were assuming *there* to be prayer. And after we were seated, we were speaking to the women who came together.
14 And a certain woman with *the* name Lydia (a seller of purple cloth of a city of Thyatira, who worshipped God) was listening, whose heart the Master completely opened to be paying attention to the *things* being spoken by Paul.
15 As she and *the people from* her house were submerged, she encouraged *us*, saying, "If you have judged me to be *someone* the Master can trust, when you come into my house, you must stay." And she compelled us.
16 It happened as we were traveling to prayer, for a certain servant girl having a spirit, a Python *(a clairvoyant spirit)*, to come to meet us, someone who was providing much work for her masters using *her* psychic abilities.
17 When she followed behind Paul and us, she was yelling, saying, "These people are slaves of God, the highest *God*, some who are proclaiming a way of rescue to you."

18 This she was doing over many days. When Paul was thoroughly anguished and after turning around, he said to the spirit, "I pass the order on to you in the name of Jesus, *the* Anointed King, to come out away from her." And it came out the same hour.
19 When her masters saw that the good anticipation of their work came out, after latching on to Paul and Silas, they pulled *them* into the marketplace before the head people.
20 And when they brought them to the captains, they said, "These people, being Jewish, are greatly agitating our city.
21 And they proclaim customs that it is not allowed for us to be accepting with a warm welcome, nor to be doing, being Romans."
22 And the crowd stood up together against them. And when the captains ripped around their robes, they were giving orders to be beating *them* with sticks.
23 After putting many wounds on them, they threw *them* into jail after passing the order on to the prison guard to be keeping them securely,
24 who, when he received this type of an order, he threw them into the inner jail and secured their feet in the wooden restraint.
25 Throughout the middle of the night, as Paul and Silas prayed, they were singing praise songs to God. The prisoners were listening to them intently.
26 Suddenly, a large earthquake happened in such a way for the foundations of the prison to be disturbed. At once, all the doors were opened, and the restraints of everyone eased up.
27 When the prison guard became awakened and saw that the doors of the jail had been opened, after pulling out a dagger, he was going to be executing himself, assuming the prisoners to have escaped from *there*.
28 Paul hollered with a loud voice, saying, "You should repeatedly do nothing bad to yourself. You see, we are in here, every single one."
29 After he asked for lights, he leaped in. And after there became trembling inside, he fell toward Paul and Silas.
30 And after he brought them outside, he was declaring, "Masters, what is it necessary for me to be doing so that I might be rescued?"
31 The *two* said, "Trust based on the Master Jesus, *the* Anointed King, and you will be rescued, you and your house."
32 And they spoke the message of the Master to him and all the *people* in his house.
33 And after taking them along *with him* in that hour of the night, he gave *them* a bath *to wash* off the wounds. And he was submerged, he and all his *people* at once.
34 And when he led them up into his house, he placed a table *of food* beside them. And he was excited, having trusted God with everyone in *his* house.
35 When it became day, the captains sent out the sergeants, saying, "Dismiss those people."
36 The prison guard reported the words to Paul, "The captains have sent out *the sergeants* so that you might be dismissed. So now, when you go out, travel in peace."

37 Paul was declaring to them, "After beating us publicly, being Roman people not found guilty, they threw *us* into jail, and now, in an unnoticed way, are they throwing us out? You see, no, but when they come, they must lead us out."
38 The sergeants announced these statements to the captains. And they were afraid when they heard that they are Romans.
39 And when they came, they encouraged them. And after they led *them* out, they were asking *them* to go out of the city.
40 After going out of the jail, they went into *the house of* Lydia. And after they saw the brothers, they encouraged them and went out.

17

1 After making their way through Amphipolis and Apollonia, they went into Thessalonica where there was the synagogue of the Jewish *people*.
2 According to what had been a custom for Paul, he went in to them and over three Sabbaths was having discussions with them out of the *Old Testament* writings,
3 completely opening and placing beside *them* that it was necessary for the Anointed King to suffer and to come back to life from *the* dead. And, "This is the Anointed King Jesus whom I proclaim to you."
4 And some from them were persuaded and joined Paul and Silas (both a very large number of the worshipping Greeks and not *just* a few of the most important women).
5 But when the unbelieving Jewish *people* got mad, took in some evil men of the marketplace *bums*, and drew a crowd, they were disturbing the city. And when they stood over the house of Jason, they were looking to lead them into the mob.
6 When they did not find them, they were dragging Jason and some brothers before the city leaders, shouting, "These *people* who upset the civilized world are also here beside *us*,
7 whom Jason has accepted under *his roof*. And all these *people* are constantly doing *things* up against the rules of Caesar, saying *for there* to be a different king, Jesus."
8 They agitated the crowd and the city leaders hearing these *things*.
9 And after taking the adequate amount of *money* from the side of Jason and the rest, they dismissed them.
10 The brothers right away sent both Paul and Silas off through the night to Berea, certain *men* who, when they showed up, were off into the synagogue of the Jewish *people*.
11 These were a higher-ranking family line than the *people* in Thessalonica, some who accepted the message with every *bit of* eagerness for the "daily investigating the *Old Testament* writings whether this is how it has these *things*" *part*.
12 So certainly many from them trusted, both the Greek women (the reputable *ones*) and not *just* a few men.
13 As the Jewish *people* out of Thessalonica knew that also in Berea the message of God was proclaimed by Paul, they also went there, disturbing the crowds.

14 Then right away the brothers sent Paul off to be traveling as *if it were* on the sea. Both Silas and Timothy were persisting *to do what is right* there.
15 The *people* put in charge of Paul led him until Athens. And when they received a demand to Silas and Timothy that they should come to him as quickly as possible, they were out *of there*.
16 In Athens, as Paul was waiting for them, his spirit was being annoyed in him, watching the city being entirely idolatrous.
17 So he certainly was having discussions in the synagogue with the Jewish *people* and the worshipping *people* and in the marketplace each *and* every day toward the *people* who happened by.
18 Some of the Epicureans and the Stoics (people fond of insight) were deliberating about him. And some were saying, "Whatever might this scrap-collecting *person* want to be saying?" But the *people were saying*, "He seems to be a proclaimer of strange lesser deities," because he was sharing the good news with them of Jesus and the return back to life.
19 And after latching on to him, they led *him* onto Areopagus *(Mar's Hill)*, saying, "Are we able to know what this new *thing is*, the teaching being spoken by you?
20 You see, you are carrying some *ideas* that are strange into the hearing of our ears. So we intend to know what these *things* are wanting to be."
21 All Athenians and the strangers making *this their* home were having a good time in nothing different than to be saying and to be hearing something newer.
22 When Paul was stood up in *the* middle of Areopagus *(Mar's Hill)*, he was declaring, "Men, Athenians, in each *and* everything, I watch how you *are* more zealous of lesser deities.
23 You see, going through and observing your worshipped objects, I even found a platform on which it had been inscribed, 'To an unknown god.' So what, though unaware of, you reverence, this I am proclaiming to you.
24 God, who made the world and all the *things* in it, this *God* who is Master of heaven and earth, does not live in handmade temples.
25 Neither is He healed by people's hands as He Himself is pleading for something, since He gives life, breath, and all *things* to everything.
26 And from one blood, He made every nation of people to be living on every face of the earth, who designated times that have been prearranged and the limits of their residence
27 to be looking for the Master, if they might definitely feel Him and find *Him*, who yet also is definitely not a long way away from each one of us.
28 You see, in Him, we live, move, and exist even as some of the poets aligned with you have stated, 'You see, we are also a family of the *One*.'
29 So being a family of God, we are obligated not to be assuming gold, or silver, or stone (a statue from a person's skill and contemplation) to be like the divine *thing*.
30 So after God certainly looked past the times of the lack of awareness, for the *things* now He passes the order on to all the people everywhere to be changing their ways,

31 because He established a day in which He is going to be judging the civilized world in *the* right way, in a Man whom He designated after providing trust to all *people* when He brought Him back to life from *the* dead."
32 When they heard *of* a return back to life of dead *people*, the *people* certainly were joking, but the *others* said, "We will listen to you again about this."
33 And this is how Paul went out from *the* middle of them.
34 Some men who were stuck like glue to him trusted, among whom *were* also Dionysius (the Areopagite), a woman with *the* name Damaris, and different *ones* together with them.

18

1 After these *things*, after Paul separated from Athens, he went to Corinth.
2 And when he found a certain Jewish *man* with *the* name Aquila (a Pontican by birth, who recently had come from Italy because of the *fact* for Claudius to have specifically arranged to be separating all the Jewish *people* from Rome) and his wife Priscilla, he went to them.
3 And because of the *fact for him* to be of the same trade, he was staying beside them and working. You see, they were tentmakers by trade.
4 He was having discussions in the synagogue each *and* every Sabbath and was persuading Jewish *people* and Greeks.
5 As they came down from Macedonia, both Silas and Timothy, Paul was being constrained by the Spirit, being a strong witness to the Jewish *people* of the Anointed King Jesus.
6 As they were placing themselves in opposition *to it* and insulting *it*, after shaking off *his* clothes, he said to them, "Your blood *is* on your head. I *am* clean. From the present *on*, I will travel to the non-Jews."
7 And after walking somewhere else away from there, he went into a house of someone with *the* name Justus, who worshipped God, whose house was *one* that was up against the synagogue.
8 Crispus, the synagogue's head ruler, trusted the Master together with his whole house. And many of the Corinthians listening were trusting and being submerged.
9 The Master said to Paul through a sighting at night, "Don't be afraid, but speak, and you should not be silent
10 because I am with you and no one will put *his hand* on you (of the 'to do bad to you' *kind*) because a big group is with Me in this city."
11 And he was seated a year and six months teaching among them the message of God.
12 As Gallio was a Roman deputy of Achaia, the Jewish *people* unanimously stood up against Paul and led him before the judicial bench,
13 saying, "This *man* motivates the people to be worshipping God contrary to the law."
14 As Paul was going to be opening *his* mouth, Gallio said to the Jewish *people*, "So certainly if it were some wrong *thing* or evil mischief, O Jewish *people*, I should tolerate you regarding an answer,

15 but if it is a question about an answer, names, and the law according to you, you will see *to it* yourselves. You see, I do not intend to be a judge of these *things*."
16 And he drove them away from the judicial bench.
17 When all the Greeks latched on to Sosthenese, the synagogue's head ruler, they were hitting *him* in front of the judicial bench. And none of these *things* were a concern to Gallio.
18 When Paul still stayed yet an adequate amount of days, after saying good-bye to the brothers, he was sailing out into Syria (and together with him, Priscilla and Aquila) after cutting *the hair on his* head in Cenchrea. You see, he was having a vow.
19 They made it to Ephesus, and he left those *two* down there, but when he went into the synagogue, he had a discussion with the Jewish *people*.
20 As they were asking *him* to stay over a longer time beside them, he did not nod.
21 But he said good-bye to them, after saying, "It is necessary for me by all means to do the festival, the coming *one*, in Jerusalem. But I will double back to you again, as God wants." And he took off from Ephesus.
22 And when he went down to Caesarea, after walking up and saying hello to the assembly, he walked down to Antioch.
23 And after he did some time *there*, he went out, going in order through the Galatian rural area and Phrygia, further establishing all the students.
24 A certain Jewish *man* with *the* name Apollos, an Alexandrian by birth, a message man, made it to Ephesus being competent in the *Old Testament* writings.
25 This was *a man* that the way of the Master had been echoed down to, and being passionate in the Spirit, he was speaking and teaching accurately the *things* about the Master, being well acquainted only with the submersion of John.
26 And this *man* began to make clear public statements in the synagogue. After Aquila and Priscilla listened to him, they took him in and more accurately laid out to him the way of God.
27 Since he intended to go through into Achaia, the brothers wrote to the students beforehand urging *them* to gladly accept him, who, when he showed up, pitched in much with the *people* who had trusted through the generosity.
28 You see, he was methodically thoroughly disproving the Jewish *people*, publicly showing through the *Old Testament* writings Jesus to be the Anointed King.

19

1 It happened during the *time* for Apollos to be in Corinth; for Paul, after going through the upper parts, to go into Ephesus and to find some students.
2 He said to them, "*Tell me* if you received *the* Sacred Spirit after you trusted." The *students* said to him, "No, we did not even hear if *the* Sacred Spirit exists."
3 And he said to them, "So what were you submerged into?" The *students* said, "Into the submersion of John."

4 Paul said, "John certainly submerged *with* a submersion of a change of ways saying to the ethnic group that they should trust in the *One* coming after him, that is, in the Anointed King, Jesus."
5 When they heard *this*, they were submerged in the name of the Master Jesus.
6 And when Paul placed *his* hands on them, the Spirit, the Sacred *Spirit*, came on them. They were both speaking with languages and preaching.
7 All the men were as if *they were* twelve.
8 After going into the synagogue, he was making clear public statements over three months, having discussions and persuading *them in* the *things* about the monarchy of God.
9 As some were being hardened and were not believing, saying bad things about the Way in the sight of the large number *of people*, after standing off away from them, he isolated the students, having discussions daily in the public hall of a certain Tyrannus.
10 This happened over two years in such a way for all the *people* living in Western Turkey to hear the message of the Master Jesus, both Jewish *people* and Greeks.
11 And God was showing abilities (the *abilities* not *usually* obtained) through the hands of Paul
12 in such a way even on the *people* who were weak, for towels or aprons to be brought up off his skin and for the illnesses to be relieved from them and the spirits, the evil *ones*, to be coming out from them.
13 Some out of the Jewish exorcists going around attempted to be naming over the *people* having the spirits, the evil *spirits*, the name of the Master Jesus, saying, "We place you under an oath to the Jesus whom Paul speaks publicly about..."
14 Some were seven sons of a Jewish head priest, Sceva, doing this.
15 When the spirit, the evil *spirit*, responded, it said, "I know Jesus, and I am well aware of Paul, but who are you?"
16 And when the person that the spirit, the evil *spirit*, was in jumped on them, after he took control of them, he had strength against them in such a way for *them* to escape from that house naked and having been wounded.
17 This became known to everyone (both Jewish *people* and Greeks), the *people* living in Ephesus, and fear fell on them all. And the name of the Master Jesus was being made great.
18 And many of the *people* who had trusted were coming, acknowledging out loud and announcing the things they repeatedly did.
19 After an adequate amount of the *people* who repeatedly did the *things* that work *their way* around *work* (*magic*) brought the scrolls together, they were burning *them* up in the sight of everyone. And they added up the prices of them and found *it to be* fifty thousand *coins* of silver.
20 Regarding power, this is how the message of the Master was growing and having strength.
21 As these *things* were accomplished, Paul placed in *his* spirit after going through Macedonia and Achaia to be traveling to Jerusalem, saying, "After the *time* for me to become there, it is necessary for me to also see Rome."

22 After he sent out two of the *people* serving him (Timothy and Erastus) to Macedonia, he was fixing *his* attention on Western Turkey for a while.
23 Throughout that time, not *just* a little agitation happened about the Way.
24 You see, someone with *the* name Demetrius, a silversmith making silver temples of Artemis, was providing not *just* a little work to the skilled workers,
25 whom after he accumulated together (also the workers concerning these types of *things*), he said, "Men, you are well aware that our fortune is from this work.
26 And you see and hear that not only from Ephesus, but from nearly all of Western Turkey, when this Paul persuades, he dislodges an adequate crowd, saying, 'There are no gods coming into existence through hands.'
27 Not only is this in danger to us for *our* part to come into a reprimand, but also for the temple grounds of the great goddess Artemis to be considered for nothing, and for her greatness (that all of Western Turkey and the civilized world worship) to be going to also be taken down."
28 After listening and becoming full of anger, they were yelling, saying, "The Artemis of *the* Ephesian *people is* great."
29 And the whole city was filled with a commotion. And they unanimously rushed into the amphitheater after seizing Gaius and Aristarchus, Macedonian traveling companions of Paul.
30 (As Paul was intending to go into the mob, the students were not allowing him.
31 Even some of the Western Turkey head rulers, who were friends to him, after sending to him, were encouraging *him* not to give himself into the amphitheater.)
32 So others were certainly yelling some other *thing*. You see, the assembly had been stirred up, and the majority did not realize why they had come together.
33 They forced Alexander forward from the crowd as the Jewish *people* thrust him forward. When Alexander motioned with *his* hand, he was wanting to be giving a defense to the mob.
34 When they correctly understood that he is Jewish, there became one voice from everyone over as *if it were* two hours, yelling, "The Artemis of *the* Ephesian *people is* great."
35 After the *town* transcriber subdues the crowd, he declares, "Men, Ephesian *people*, you see, where is a person who does not know the city of *the* Ephesian *people* that is a temple servant of the great goddess Artemis and the *statue* that fell from Zeus.
36 So these being unobjected *things*, it is necessary for you to be *people* having been subdued and to repeatedly be doing nothing obnoxious.
37 You see, you led these men *here who are* neither people who pilfer temples, nor *people* insulting our goddess.
38 So certainly if Demetrius and the skilled workers together with him have a matter toward someone, the marketplace *courts* are being conducted, and there are Roman deputies. They must charge each other.

39 If you are searching for anything about different *matters*, it will be resolved in the lawful assembly.
40 You see, we are even in danger to be charged with disruption concerning the *day* today, since there is no *legal* case concerning which we will be able to give an answer back for this illegal plot."
41 And after saying these *things*, he dismissed the assembly.

20

1 After the *time* for the disturbance to stop, after Paul called for the students and said good-bye, he went out to travel to Macedonia.
2 After he went through those parts and encouraged them with many messages, he came to Greece.
3 And after he did three months *there*, when there became a conspiracy by the Jewish *people* against him as he was going to be taking off for Syria, there became an opinion of the "to be returning through Macedonia" *kind*.
4 Sopater (a Berean) was being accompanied by him till Western Turkey; of Thessalonians: Aristarchus and Secundus; and Gaius (a Derbaean) and Timothy; Western Turks: Tychicus and Trophimus.
5 After these *people* went on ahead, they were staying in Troas for us.
6 We sailed out away from Philippi after the days of the Yeast-free *Loaves Festival*, and till five days we came to them in Troas, where we spent seven days.
7 In the *Day* 1 after the Sabbaths, the students having been gathered together to split bread, Paul was having discussions with them. And since he was going to be out *of there* the next day, he was prolonging the message up to *the* middle of the night.
8 There were an adequate amount of torches in the upstairs room where they were, having been gathered together.
9 A certain young man with *the* name Eutychus *was* sitting on the window being overcome by deep slumber. As Paul was having discussions on more, when he was overcome from the slumber, he fell down from the third floor and was picked up dead.
10 After Paul climbed down, he got down on him, and when he hugged *him*, he said, "Don't cause a disturbance. You see, his soul is in him."
11 After climbing up, splitting bread, tasting, and chatting over an adequate amount *of time* till first light of day, this is how he went out.
12 They led the boy *off* alive and were encouraged immeasurably.
13 When we went on ahead on the boat, we took off to Assos since we were going to be taking up Paul from there. You see, this is what it was that he had specifically arranged since he was going to be going on foot.
14 As he met up with us in Assos, after taking him up, we went to Mitylene.
15 And from there, after we sailed off, the following day we made it to outside of Chios. We pulled in alongside Samos on the different *day* and stayed in Trogyllium. The *day* being held *after that*, we went to Miletus.
16 You see, Paul decided to sail past Ephesus in order that it might not happen to him to use up time in Western Turkey; for he was hurrying (if it was possible for him) to become in Jerusalem for the Day of the Fiftieth.

17 Out of Miletus, when he sent to Ephesus, he summoned the older *men* of the assembly.
18 As *soon as* they showed up to him, he said to them, "You are well aware out of *the* first day out of which I walked up to Western Turkey, how I became all the time with you,
19 being a slave to the Master with every *bit of* lowly focus, many tears, and troubles, the *ones* that transpired with me in the conspiracies of the Jewish *people*,
20 how I backed off from none of the *things* that were advantageous for the *purpose* to announce to you and to teach you publicly and in each house,
21 being a strong witness to both Jewish *people* and Greeks of the change of ways to God and the trust to our Master Jesus, *the* Anointed King.
22 And now, look, having been tied up by the spirit, I am traveling to Jerusalem, not realizing the *things* in it that will meet together with me,
23 more importantly, that the Spirit, the Sacred *Spirit*, in each city is a strong witness, saying that restraints and hard times remain for me.
24 But I make an account of nothing, neither do I hold my soul valuable to myself, as to complete with happiness my race and the *task of* serving that I received from the side of the Master Jesus, to be a strong witness of the good news of the generosity of God.
25 And now, look, I realize that you will no longer see my face, you all, among whom I went through *here* speaking publicly about the monarchy of God.
26 For this reason, I am a witness to you in the day today that I *am* clean from the blood of everyone.
27 You see, I did not back off in any way from the 'to announce every intention of God to you' *part*.
28 So pay attention to yourselves and to all the flock, among which the Spirit, the Sacred *Spirit*, placed you *as* supervisors to be shepherding the assembly of God that was acquired through *His* own blood.
29 You see, I realize this, that after my departure heavy wolves will come in among you not going easy on the flock.
30 And from among you yourselves, men will stand up speaking *things* that have been twisted, of the "to be pulling the students away behind them" *kind*.
31 For this reason, stay awake, remembering that for a three year period, night and day, I did not stop cautioning each one *of you* with tears.
32 And the *things* now, I place you, brothers, beside God and the message of His generosity, the *message* that is able to build *you* and give you an inheritance among all the *people* who have been made sacred.
33 I desired no one's silver, or gold, or clothing.
34 You yourselves know that for my needs and for the *people* who were with me, these hands worked as an underling.
35 I put everything in front of your face because laboring like this, it is necessary to be assisting the *people* who are weak and to be remembering the words of the Master Jesus that He Himself said, 'It is more blessed to be giving than to be receiving.'"
36 And after he said these *things*, after placing his knees *on the ground*, he prayed together with them all.

37 There became an adequate amount of crying from everyone. And after falling on the neck of Paul, they were being very friendly to him.
38 Being in agony especially based on the message that he had stated, that they no longer are going to be seeing his face, they were bringing him on his way to the boat.

21

1 As it happened for us to take off, after we pulled away from them, when we sailed straight, we went to Cos, but on the *day* afterward to Rhodes, and from there to Patara.
2 And when we found a boat crossing all the way over to Phoenicia, after climbing up on board, we took off.
3 When we spotted Cyprus and left it down to the left, we were sailing to Syria and landed at Tyre. You see, the boat was unloading the cargo there.
4 And when we looked for and found the students, we stayed over there for seven days, some who were saying to Paul through the Spirit not to be walking up to Jerusalem.
5 When it happened for us to fully develop the days, after coming out, we were traveling, everyone together with wives and children, bringing us on our way until outside of the city. And after placing *our* knees on the beach, we prayed.
6 And after we said good-bye to each other, we climbed up on board the boat. Those *people* returned to *their* own *places*.
7 We, after concluding the voyage out of Tyre, made it into Ptolemais, and after greeting the brothers, we stayed for one day beside them.
8 On the next day, after the *people* around Paul went out, we went to Caesarea, and when we went into the house of Philip (the sharer of good news who was from the seven), we stayed beside him.
9 With this *Philip* there were four daughters (virgins) who preach.
10 As we stayed over more days, a certain preacher came down out of Judea with *the* name Agabus.
11 And when he came to us and took the sash of Paul off, after tying his hands and feet, he said, "The Spirit, the Sacred *Spirit*, says the *things* here, 'The man whose sash this is, like this the Jewish *people* in Jerusalem will tie up and will turn over to *the* hands of *the* non-Jews.'"
12 As we heard these *things*, both we and the *people* in that place were encouraging of the "for him not to be walking up to Jerusalem" kind.
13 Paul responded, "What are you doing, crying and pulverizing my heart? You see, I have *myself* ready, not only to be tied up, but also to die in Jerusalem on behalf of the name of the Master Jesus."
14 Since he was not persuaded, we calmed down after saying, "What the Master wants must happen."
15 After these days, after packing *everything* away, we were walking up into Jerusalem.
16 *Some* of the students out of Caesarea also went together with us, leading *us* to the side of whom we would be guests, a certain Mnason, a Cyprian, an original student.
17 When we became in Jerusalem, the brothers accepted us with pleasure.

18 On the following *day*, Paul had entered together with us to James, and all the older *men* showed up.
19 And after he said hello to them, he was recounting regarding each one of *the things* that God did among the non-Jews through his serving.
20 The *people* listening were praising the Master's magnificence. And they said to him, "You are seeing, brother, how many tens of thousands there are of Jewish *people*, the *ones* who have trusted, and they are all people with passion for the law.
21 It was echoed down to them about you that you teach a divorce from Moses to all the Jewish *people* throughout the nations, saying for them not to be circumcising the children, nor to be walking around in the customs.
22 So what is *to be done*? By all means, it is necessary for a large number to come together. You see, they will hear that you have come.
23 So do this *thing* that we say to you. With us there are four men having a vow on themselves.
24 After taking these *men* along, be consecrated together with them, and spend *money* on them so that they might shave *their* head and everyone might know that what has been echoed down to them about you is nothing, but you yourself even march in step, observing the law.
25 About the non-Jews that have trusted, we wrote a letter after we judged for them to be keeping nothing of this type except to be guarding themselves from the idol sacrifice, the blood and choked *animal*, and sexual sin."
26 Then when Paul took the men along, after he was consecrated together with them on the day being held *after that*, he had entered onto the temple grounds announcing to everyone the complete accomplishment of the days of the consecration until *the time* that the offering was offered on behalf of each one of them.
27 As the seven days were going to be completely finished, when the Jewish *people* out of Western Turkey viewed him on the temple grounds, they were stirring up all the crowd and put *their* hands on him,
28 yelling, "Men, Israelis, help. This is the person, the *one* teaching everyone everywhere against the ethnic group, the law, and this place. And still he even led Greeks onto the temple grounds and has made this sacred place shared."
29 You see, there were *people* who had seen Trophimus the Ephesian *man* in the city together with him before, whom they were assuming that Paul led onto the temple grounds.
30 And the whole city was moved, and there became a rushing together of the group. And when they latched on to Paul, they were pulling him outside of the temple grounds, and right away the doors were closed.
31 As they were looking to kill him, news stepped up to the commanding officer of the regiment that all of Jerusalem had been stirred up,
32 who immediately, after taking along soldiers and lieutenants, ran down on them. When the *people* saw the commanding officer and the soldiers, they stopped hitting Paul.
33 At that time, when the commanding officer came near, he latched on to him and gave the order *for him* to be locked up with two chains. And he was inquiring who he may be and what it is that he had done.

34 Others in the crowd were shouting some other *thing*. Since he was not able to know the *thing* for certain because of the disturbance, he gave the order for him to be led into the barracks.
35 When he became on the stairs, it transpired for him to be hauled by the soldiers because of the force of the crowd.
36 You see, the large number of the group was following, yelling, "Take him away."
37 And as he is going to be led into the barracks, Paul says to the commanding officer, "*Tell me* if it is allowed for me to say something to you." The *commanding officer* was declaring, "Do you know Greek?
38 So aren't you the Egyptian, the *one* before these days who upset and led the four thousand men of the Assassins out into the backcountry?"
39 Paul said, "I certainly am a Jewish person, a Tarsean of Cilicia, a citizen of a city *that is* not insignificant. I plead of you, give me permission to speak to the group."
40 When he gave permission, Paul, having stood on the stairs, motioned with *his* hand to the group. When there became a big hush, he hollered out in the Hebrew dialect, saying,

22

1 "Men, brothers and fathers, listen now to my defense to you."
2 When they heard that he was hollering to them in the Hebrew dialect, they provided more calmness. And he declares,
3 "I certainly am a Jewish man who has been born in Tarsus of Cilicia, but who has been raised in this city beside the feet of Gamaliel, who has been disciplined aligned with *the* strictness of the paternal law, being a person with passion for God, just as you all are today,
4 who persecuted this Way till death, detaining and turning in to jails both men and women.
5 As both the head priest and all of the board of older men are a witness of me, from the side of whom, after accepting letters to the brothers, I was even traveling to Damascus so that I will also lead the *people* who are there to Jerusalem having been tied up, so that they might be kept from ruining a valuable thing.
6 It happened as I was traveling and coming near to Damascus around *the* middle of the day for an adequate amount of light from the sky to unexpectedly beam down all around me.
7 And I fell to the terra firma and listened to a voice saying to me, 'Saul, Saul, why are you persecuting Me?'
8 I answered, 'Who are you, Master?' And He said to me, 'I am Jesus, the Nazarene, whom you are persecuting.'
9 The *people* who were together with me certainly viewed the light and became afraid, but they did not hear the voice of the *One* speaking to me.
10 I said, 'What should I do, Master?' The Master said to me, 'When you get up, travel into Damascus and there it will be spoken to you about everything that has been arranged for you to do.'
11 As I was not seeing from the magnificence of that light, being led by the hand by the *people* who were together with me, I went into Damascus.

12 When Ananias (a certain godly man according to the law, being witnessed by all the living Jewish *people*)
13 came to me and stood over *me*, he said to me, 'Saul, brother, see again.' And the same hour, I saw again *and looked* at him.
14 *Ananias* said, 'The God of our fathers handed you *this* beforehand: to know what He wants, to see the *One* who does what is right, and to hear a voice from His mouth;
15 because you will be a witness of Him to all people of *things* that you have seen and heard.
16 And now, what are you going *to do*? When you get up, be submerged and douse off your sins when you call on the name of the Master.'
17 It happened to me after returning to Jerusalem, even as I was praying on the temple grounds, for me to become in a trance
18 and to see Him saying to me, 'Hurry up, and go out of Jerusalem quickly because they will not accept with a warm welcome what you say you witnessed about Me.'
19 And I said, 'Master, they are well aware that I was throwing in jail and beating the *people* throughout the synagogues who trusted based on You.
20 And when the blood of Stephen, Your witness, was being spilled out, I myself was even *a person* who had stood over him, both agreeing that his execution was good and guarding the robes of the *people* executing him.'
21 And He said to me, 'Travel *away*, because I will send you off a long way away to non-Jews.'"
22 They were listening to him till these words. And they raised up their voice, saying, "Take this type of *person* away from the earth. You see, *he is* not meeting even the lowest standard for him to be living."
23 As they were making a yell, tossing off *their* robes, and throwing dust into the air,
24 the commanding officer gave the order for him to be led into the barracks after saying for him to be interrogated with whips so that he might correctly understand *the* reason why they were hollering out at him like that.
25 As they stretched him out beforehand with the straps, Paul said to the lieutenant who had stood *there*, "If a person *is* a Roman and not found guilty, is it allowed for you to be having *him* whipped?"
26 After the lieutenant heard *this*, when he went forward to the commanding officer, he reported, saying, "Look! What are you going to be doing? You see, this person is a Roman."
27 When the commanding officer came forward, he said to him, "Tell me if you are a Roman." *Paul* was declaring, "Yes."
28 And the commanding officer responded, "I got this citizenship with much capital." Paul was declaring, "But I have actually been born *a Roman*."
29 So right away the *soldiers* who were going to be interrogating him stood off away from him. And the commanding officer was afraid when he correctly understood that he is a Roman and that he had locked him up.
30 On the next day, intending to know the *thing* for certain, the "what was the complaint leveled against *him* from the side of the Jewish *people*" *thing*, he released him from the restraints and gave the order for the head priests and

the whole council to come. And when he led Paul down, he stood among them.

23

1 When Paul stared at the council, he said, "Men, brothers, I have been a law-abiding citizen with every *bit of* a good conscience with God till this day."
2 The head priest, Ananias, gave the directive to the *people* who had been standing by him to be hitting his mouth.
3 At that time, Paul said to him, "God is going to be hitting you, chalk-whitened wall. You actually sit judging me aligned with the law, and going contrary to the law you give an order for me to be hit."
4 The *people* who had been standing by him said, "Are you putting the head priest of God down?"
5 And Paul was declaring, "I did not realize, brothers, that he is *the* head priest. You see, it has been written, 'You will not state *something* in a bad way about *the* head person of your ethnic group.'"
6 When Paul knew that the one part is Sadducees, but the different *part is* Separatists, he yelled in the council, "Men, brothers, I am a Separatist, a son of a Separatist, about anticipation and a return back to life of dead *people* I am being judged."
7 After he spoke this, there became a disruption *between* the Separatists and the Sadducees, and the large number *of people* were torn.
8 You see, Sadducees certainly say *for there* not to be a return back to life, nor angel, nor spirit, but Separatists acknowledge the both.
9 Great yelling happened. And when the *Old Testament* transcribers of the part of the Separatists stood up, they were arguing furiously, saying, "We find nothing bad in this person. If a spirit or angel spoke to him, we should not argue with God."
10 After *the* disruption became big, when the commanding officer took *it* seriously that Paul might be pulled apart by them, he gave the order for the military unit, after stepping down, to snatch him from *the* middle of them and to be leading *him* into the barracks.
11 In the following night when the Master stood over him, He said, "Be courageous, Paul. You see, as you were a strong witness of the *things* about Me in Jerusalem, so it is necessary for you to also tell in Rome what you witnessed."
12 When it became day, after some of the Jewish *people* made an illegal plot, they vowed under the penalty of dooming themselves, saying neither to eat nor drink until *the time* that they may kill Paul.
13 There were more than forty, the *ones* who had made this mutual guarantee,
14 some who, after coming forward to the head priests and the older *men*, said, "We vowed under the penalty of dooming ourselves with doom to not taste anything until *the time* that we may kill Paul."
15 So now you together with the council must make apparent to the commanding officer how that he should lead him down to you tomorrow as you are going to be knowing more accurately what *things* about him are

wrong. But we, before the *time* for him to come near, are ready for the *purpose* to execute him.
16 When the son of Paul's sister heard *about* the ambush, after showing up and going into the barracks, he reported *it* to Paul.
17 When Paul called for one of the lieutenants, he was declaring, "Lead this young man off to the commanding officer. You see, he has something to report to him."
18 So certainly when the *lieutenant* took him along, he led *him* to the commanding officer and declares, "When the prisoner, Paul, called for me, he asked *me* to bring this young man to you since he has something to speak to you."
19 After the commanding officer latched on to his hand and went in the back privately, he was inquiring, "What is *it* that you have to report to me?"
20 He said, "The Jewish *people* agreed for the *purpose* to ask you in order that tomorrow you might lead Paul down to the council as *if it is* going to be inquiring something more accurately about him.
21 So you should not be persuaded by them. You see, more than forty men from them are lying in wait for him, some who vowed under the penalty of dooming themselves neither to eat nor drink until *the time* that they will execute him. And now they are ready, awaiting the promise from you.
22 So the commanding officer certainly dismissed the young man, after passing the order on to *him*, "*You are* to speak out to no one that you made these *things* apparent to me."
23 And after he called for any two of the lieutenants, he said, "Get two hundred soldiers ready in order that they might travel until Caesarea (and seventy horsemen and two hundred lightly armed guards) out of *the* third hour of the night *(9:00 p.m.)*,
24 and for animals to stand by so that after loading Paul on *them*, they might keep *him* safe to Felix, the leader,"
25 who wrote a letter having itself around this format:
26 "*From*: Claudius Lysias. To: The most powerful leader, Felix. Happy to meet you.
27 After this man was apprehended by the Jewish *people* and as he was going to be executed by them, when I stood over *them* together with the military unit, I took him out when I learned that he is a Roman.
28 Intending to know the reason why they were charging him, I led him down into their council,
29 whom I found being charged concerning questions of their law, but not having a charge of anything deserving of death or restraints.
30 When *it* was disclosed to me *for there* to be going to be *in the future* a conspiracy by the Jewish *people* in reference to the man, I sent *him* immediately to you after I also passed the order on to the complainants to be talking to him before you. Farewell."
31 So certainly the soldiers, according to what had been specifically arranged with them, after taking up Paul, led *him* through the night to Antipatris.
32 On the next day after allowing the horsemen to be traveling together with him, they returned to the barracks,

33 some *horsemen* who, when they went into Caesarea and handed over the letter to the leader, also presented Paul to him.
34 After the leader read *the letter*, asked what kind of province he is from *(senatorial or imperial)*, and determined that *he is* out of Cilicia,
35 "I will hear you out," he was declaring, "whenever your complainants also show up." And he gave the order for him to be guarded in Herod's Roman palace.

24

1 After five days, the head priest, Ananias, walked down with the older *men* and a certain speaker, Tertullus, some who made *their* case against Paul apparent to the leader.
2 When he was called, Tertullus began to be leveling a complaint against *him*, saying, "Since we obtain much peace through you and improvements happen to this nation through your plan,
3 both every way and everywhere, we gladly accept *it*, most powerful Felix, with every *bit of* thankfulness.
4 But so that I may not interrupt you over more, I encourage you to listen to us briefly with your politeness.
5 You see, after finding this man a disease (even arousing disruptions with all the Jewish *people*, the *ones* throughout the civilized world) and *the* most prominent leader of the sect of the Nazarenes,
6 who was even trying to profane the temple grounds, whom we also took into custody and wanted to judge according to our law,
7 but when Lysias, the commanding officer, came alongside with much force, he led *him* away out of our hands
8 when he ordered his complainants to come before you, from the side of whom, you will be able, after investigating yourself, to correctly understand about all these *complaints* that we level against him."
9 The Jewish *people* also agreed, claiming to be holding these *things* like this.
10 Paul responded after the leader gestured to him to speak, "Being well aware that you are a judge of this nation for many years, I more cheerfully defend the *things* about myself,
11 you being able to correctly know that there are not more than twelve days with me from *the day* that I walked up so that I will bow down in Jerusalem.
12 And neither on the temple grounds did they find me having a discussion toward anyone or making tension in a crowd, nor in the synagogues, nor throughout the city.
13 Nor are they able to present *proof* concerning *the complaints* that they now level against me.
14 I acknowledge this to you, that aligned with the Way (that they call a sect), this is how I minister to the paternal God, trusting all *things*, the *things* aligned with the Law and the *things* that have been written by the preachers,
15 having an anticipation in God (that these *people* themselves also are awaiting) *for there* to be going to be *in the future* a return back to life of dead *people*, both *people* who do what is right and *people* who do what is wrong.
16 In this I exert myself: to be having a conscience not offensive toward God and the people through everything.

17 Through more years, I showed up so that I will make charitable donations to my nation and offerings,
18 in which, they found me, having been consecrated on the temple grounds, not with a crowd, nor with a disturbance. *There are* some Jewish *people* out of Western Turkey,
19 whom it was necessary to be beside *us* before you and to be leveling a complaint against *me* if they have anything toward me.
20 Or these *people* themselves must say if they found something wrong in me when I stood before the council.
21 Or *it is* about this one voice that I yelled having stood among them, 'About *the* return back to life of dead *people*, I am being judged today by you.'"
22 When Felix (who more accurately knows the *things* about the Way) heard these *things*, he put them off, after saying, "When Lysias, the commanding officer, walks down, I will know what *things* are wrong regarding you *all*"
23 (who specifically arranged with the lieutenant for Paul to be kept both to be having relief and to be hindering none of his own *people* to be working as an underling or to be coming to him).
24 After some days, when Felix together with Drusilla (his wife who is Jewish) showed up, he sent for Paul and listened to him about the trust in *the* Anointed King.
25 Having discussions about *the* right way, restraint, and the judgment (the *one* that is going to be *in the future*), when Felix became afraid, he responded, "For the *thing* having *our attention* now, travel *out*. After taking time with *others*, I will summon you,"
26 but at the same time, also anticipating that stacks of money will be given to him by Paul in order that he might release him. For this reason, sending for him more frequently, he was actually chatting with him.
27 After a two year period was accomplished, Felix took a successor, Porcius Festus. And wanting to lay down generosities for the Jewish *people*, Felix left Paul down *there* having been locked up.

25

1 So when Festus walked up on the province, after three days he walked up to Jerusalem out of Caesarea.
2 The head priest and the most important *people* of the Jewish *people* made *their case* against Paul apparent to him, and they were encouraging him,
3 asking for generosity against him in order that he might send him to Jerusalem as they made an ambush to execute him along the way.
4 So Festus certainly responded for Paul to be kept in Caesarea, but for he himself to be going to be traveling out quickly.
5 "So when the capable *people* among you walk down together," he declares, "if there is anything out of place in this man, they must level a complaint against him."
6 After spending more than ten days among them, when he walked down into Caesarea, after being seated on the judicial bench the next day, he gave the order for Paul to be led *in*.

7 When he showed up, the Jewish *people* who had walked down out of Greater Jerusalem stood around bringing many and heavy accusations against Paul that they did not have *the* strength to substantiate
8 as he defended himself, "Not to the law of the Jewish *people*, nor to the temple grounds, nor to Caesar did I do anything sinful *in* any way."
9 When Festus, who wanted to lay down generosity for the Jewish *people*, responded to Paul, he said, "Do you want, after walking up into Jerusalem, to be judged there before me concerning these *things*?"
10 Paul said, "Having stood before the judicial bench of Caesar, I am where it is necessary for me to be judged. I did nothing wrong to Jewish *people* as you also correctly understand more nicely *now*.
11 You see, if I certainly do wrong and I have repeatedly done something deserving of death, I do not refuse the "to die" *part*, but if nothing exists of *things* that these *people* level against me, no one is able to give me as an act of generosity to them. I call on Caesar."
12 Then after Festus spoke together with the counsel, he responded, "Caesar you have called on. Up to Caesar you will travel."
13 After some days had elapsed, Agrippa the king and Bernice made it to Caesarea, who will greet Festus.
14 As they were spending more days there, Festus laid out to the king the *things* regarding Paul, saying, "There is a certain man who has been left down *here* by Felix, a prisoner,
15 concerning whom, when I became in Jerusalem, the head priests and the older *men* of the Jewish *people* made *their case* apparent as they asked for justice against him,
16 to whom I answered that it is not a custom with Roman *people* to be giving any person for ruin as an act of generosity before even the *person* that a complaint is leveled against may have the complainants right in front of *his* face and he may receive a place of defense concerning the charge.
17 So after they came together here, after not making even one delay, the *day* afterward when I was seated on the judicial bench, I gave the order for the man to be led *in*,
18 concerning whom, when the complainants were stood up, they were not even bringing up one accusation of *things* that I suspected.
19 They were having some questions toward him about *their* own zeal for God and about a certain Jesus who had died, whom Paul was claiming to be living.
20 Since I wasn't sure what to think about in the questioning concerning this, I was saying *to him to tell me* if he intends to be traveling to Jerusalem and there to be judged concerning these *things*.
21 But when Paul called on for him to be kept for the scrutiny of the Worshipped *One*, I gave the order for him to be kept until *the time* that I will send him to Caesar."
22 Agrippa was declaring to Festus, "I was intending to also listen to the person myself." "Tomorrow," *Festus* declares, "you will listen to him."
23 So on the next day, after Agrippa and Bernice came with much fanfare and went into the hearing room together with both the commanding officers and

the men of the city aligned with prominence, and when Festus gave the order, Paul was led *in*.
24 And Festus declares, "King Agrippa and all the *people* who are together beside us, men, you see this *man* about whom all the large number of the Jewish *people* intervened with me both in Greater Jerusalem and here, shouting that it is not necessary for him to be living anymore.
25 After I took down for him to have repeatedly done nothing deserving of death, but when this *man* himself actually called on the Worshipped *One*, I decided to be sending him,
26 concerning whom, I don't have anything certain to write to the master. For this reason, I brought him out before you *all*, and especially before you, King Agrippa, in order that I might have something to write of the investigation that happened.
27 You see, it seems irrational to me, sending a prisoner and not to indicate the accusations against him."

26

1 Agrippa was declaring to Paul, "Permission is given to you to be talking on behalf of yourself." Then when Paul put out *his* hand, he was defending *himself*.
2 "Concerning everything that I am charged with by Jewish *people*, King Agrippa, I have regarded myself blessed that I am going to be defending myself before you today,
3 especially realizing that you are a knowledgeable person of all the *things* regarding Jewish *people*, both customs and questions. For this reason, I plead for you to listen to me patiently.
4 So certainly my way of life from *my* youth (the *way of life* that happened from *the* beginning in my nation in Greater Jerusalem) all the Jewish *people* realize,
5 since they know me from before, from the top, if they want to be telling what they witnessed, that I lived aligned with the strictest sect of our religion, a Separatist.
6 And now, based on an anticipation of the promise toward the fathers that happened under God, I have been standing being judged,
7 to which, as our twelve family lines minister in intensity night and day, they anticipate to make it — an anticipation, concerning which, I am charged by the Jewish *people*, King Agrippa.
8 Why is it judged *as something that* cannot be trusted beside you if God gets dead *people* up?
9 So it certainly seemed to me, to myself, toward the name of Jesus, the Nazarene, to be necessary to repeatedly do many *things* opposing *it*,
10 that I even did in Greater Jerusalem. And I also shut many of the sacred *people* up in jails after receiving the authority from the side of the head priests. And as they were being executed, I voted with a pebble.
11 And throughout all the synagogues, many times, as I was keeping a valuable thing from being ruined, I was urging them to be insulting *Jesus*. And becoming much more crazed by them, I was persecuting *them* until even into the outside cities,

12 among which, as I was even traveling to Damascus with the authority and permission from the side of the head priests,

13 in *the* middle of *the* day along the way, King, I saw a light from the sky over the brightness of the sun that shined around me and the *people* traveling together with me.

14 After we all fell down to the ground, I heard a voice speaking to me and saying in the Hebrew dialect, 'Saul, Saul, why are you persecuting Me? *Is it* harsh to you to be kicking at cattle prods?'

15 I said, 'Who are you, Master?' The *Master* said, 'I am Jesus, whom you persecute.

16 But get up and stand on your feet. You see, for this *reason* I was seen by you, to hand you beforehand *the job of* an underling and a witness both of *times* that you saw and of *times* that I will be seen by you,

17 taking you out of the ethnic group and the non-Jews, to whom I am now sending you out *on a mission*

18 to open their eyes and to turn *them* back out of darkness to light and *out* of the authority of the Opponent up to God of the "for them to receive forgiveness of sins and a portion among the *people* who have been made sacred by the trust in Me" *kind*.'

19 From this, King Agrippa, I did not become *a person* unbelieving to the heavenly sighting.

20 But I was reporting to the *people* in Damascus first, to Greater Jerusalem, into every rural area of Judea, and to the non-Jews to be changing their ways and to be turning back to God, repeatedly doing actions deserving of the change of ways.

21 On account of these *things*, when the Jewish *people* apprehended me on the temple grounds, they were trying to kill *me* with their hands.

22 So after obtaining assistance, the *kind* from the side of God, till this day, I have stood telling what I witnessed to both little and great, saying nothing outside of what both the preachers and Moses spoke was going to be happening.

23 Whether the Anointed King *is* capable of suffering, whether He *is* first from *the* return back to life of dead *people*, He is going to be proclaiming light to the ethnic group and to the non-Jews."

24 As he was defending *himself* with these *things*, Festus was declaring with a loud voice, "You are crazy, Paul. The many documents are turning you around into craziness."

25 *Paul* declares, "I am not crazy, most powerful Festus. But I am clearly verbalizing statements of truth and proper focus.

26 You see, the king is well aware concerning these *things*, to whom I also am speaking making clear public statements; for I am persuaded none of these *things* to be unnoticed by him. You see, this is not *a thing* that has repeatedly been done in a corner.

27 King Agrippa, do you trust the Preachers? I realize that you trust."

28 Agrippa was declaring to Paul, "In a little *while*, you persuade me to become a Christian."

29 Paul said, "I wish to God both in a little *while* and in a long *while*, not only you but also all the *people* listening to me today, for these types of *people* to become whatever kind of *thing* I also am, besides *and* outside of these restraints."
30 And after he said these *things*, the king, the leader, Bernice, and the *people* sitting together with them got up.
31 And when they went in the back, they were speaking to each other, saying, "This person is repeatedly doing nothing deserving of death or restraints."
32 Agrippa was declaring to Festus, "To have been dismissed, this person was able if he had not called on Caesar."

27

1 As *soon as* it was decided of the "to be sailing us off to Italy" *question*, they were turning both Paul and some different inmates over to a lieutenant with *the* name Julius of *the* Worshipped *One's* regiment.
2 After he climbed up on board an Adramyttium boat, as we were going to be sailing to the places along Western Turkey, we took off, Aristarchus (a Macedonian, a Thessalonian) being together with us.
3 And on the different *day*, we landed at Sidon. And when Julius behaved benevolently to Paul, he gave *him* permission to obtain care after traveling to *his* friends.
4 And from there, after taking off, we sailed under Cyprus, because of the *fact* for the winds to be opposing *us*.
5 And after sailing across the deep part along Cilicia and Pamphylia, we went down to Myra of Lycia.
6 And when the lieutenant found an Alexandrian boat there sailing to Italy, he boarded us into it.
7 In an adequate amount of days sailing slowly and after becoming along Cnidus with a lot of effort, the wind not permitting us *to go* further, we sailed under Crete along Salmone.
8 And since we were passing by it with a lot of effort, we went to a certain place called Nice Harbors that was near Lasea City.
9 After an adequate amount of time had elapsed and the voyage already being hazardous because of the *fact* for even the time of going without food *for the Day of Atonement* to have already passed by, Paul was suggesting,
10 saying to them, "Men, I see that the voyage *in the future* is going to be with injury and much loss, not only of the freight and the boat, but also of our souls."
11 But the lieutenant was being persuaded by the helmsman and the shipowner rather than by the *things* being said by Paul.
12 Since the harbor was not suitable for spending the storm season in, the majority were set in an intention to also take off from there, if somehow they might be able, after making it to Phoenix, to spend the storm season in a harbor of Crete looking aligned with Lips (*the southwest wind*) and aligned with Choros (*the northwest wind*).
13 When a south *wind* was blowing softly, when *their* purpose seemed to have merit, after taking off, they were passing closer by Crete.

14 After not much *time*, a hurricane-like wind, the *one* called Euros (*the east wind*) Aquilo (*the northeast wind*), thrust down from it.
15 When the boat was seized and not being able to be facing into the wind, after giving up, we were being driven off.
16 After running under a certain small island called Clauda, with a lot of effort we had *the* strength to become captors of the dinghy,
17 that, after they took up, they were using helps, tying up the underside of the boat. And fearing that they might fall out into the Syrtis, after lowering the gear, they were being driven along like this.
18 Since we were in a terrible storm, on the *day* afterward, they were doing a throwing out *of things*.
19 And on the third *day*, we tossed the furniture of the boat out with our own hands.
20 Neither sun, nor constellations shining over several days and not *just* a little storm lying on *us, the* rest *of the time* every anticipation of the "for us to be rescued" *kind* was being taken away all around.
21 Since *the* time without grain was long, at that time, when Paul was stood up in *the* middle of them, he said, "Certainly it was necessary *for you*, O men, after being loyal to me, not to be taking off from Crete and to gain this injury and loss.
22 And the *things* now, I suggest for you to be cheering up. You see, there will be not even one casualty of a soul from among you, other than the boat;
23 for there stood by me this night an angel of the God whose I am, whom I also minister to,
24 saying, 'Don't be afraid, Paul. It is necessary for you to stand up next to Caesar and, look, God as an act of generosity has given you all the *people* sailing with you.'
25 For this reason, cheer up, men. You see, I trust God that it will be like this: according to *the* way that has been spoken to me.
26 But it is necessary for us to fall out into a certain island."
27 As *the* fourteenth night happened of us being carried along *by the wind* in the Adriatic *Sea*, throughout *the* middle of the night the crewmen were suspecting *their course* to be leading a certain rural area toward them.
28 And when they measured the depth, they found *it to be* twenty fathoms *(120 feet)*. After standing a bit further and measuring the depth again, they found *it to be* fifteen fathoms *(90 feet)*.
29 And being afraid that somehow we might fall out into rugged places, after tossing four anchors from the back of the boat, they were wishing *for it* to become day.
30 As the crewmen were looking to escape from the boat and after lowering the dinghy into the sea for a sham (as *if they were* going to be putting anchors out from the front of the boat),
31 Paul said to the lieutenant and the soldiers, "If these *people* do not stay in the boat, you *all* are not able to be rescued."
32 Then the soldiers chopped off the ropes of the dinghy and allowed it to fall off.

33 Till *a time* that day was going to be happening, Paul was encouraging absolutely everyone to take a meal with *everyone else*, saying, "Today, *the* fourteenth day, you are thoroughly finishing without grain, expecting *this to end*, after taking in nothing.
34 For this reason, I encourage you to take in a meal. You see, this is toward your rescue; for a hair won't fall from the head of even one of you."
35 After he said these *things* and took bread, he thanked God in the sight of everyone, and after splitting *it*, he began to be eating.
36 After everyone became cheerful, they also took in a meal.
37 We were all the souls in the boat, two hundred seventy-six.
38 After they were stuffed from *the* meal, they were lightening the boat, throwing the grain out into the sea.
39 When it became day, they were not recognizing the land, but they were taking a closer look at a certain bay that had a beach, into which they advised, if they were able, to push out the boat.
40 And after taking the anchors away all around, they were allowing *them to remain* in the sea. At the same time, after they eased up on the bindings of the rudders and raised the foresail up to the blowing *breeze*, they were holding *it* steady into the beach.
41 When they fell surrounded into a place where two seas meet *causing a shallow sandbank*, they ran the ship aground. And when the front of the boat certainly got stuck, it stayed undisturbed, but the back of the boat was being broken by the force of the swells.
42 An intention of the soldiers became that they should kill the inmates *so that* no one would completely escape after swimming away.
43 But the lieutenant, intending to keep Paul safe, hindered them from *their* intention. And he gave the order for the *people* who were able to be swimming, after jumping off, to be out on the land first,
44 and for the rest *to go, some* that *are* on boards, *others* that *are* on some of the *things* off the boat. And this is how it happened for all to be safe on the land.

28

1 And after they were safe, then they correctly understood that the island is called Melita.
2 The foreigners were providing to us the benevolence not *usually* obtained. You see, after starting a bonfire, they took us all in because of the shower (the *shower* that had stood over *us*) and because of the cold.
3 After Paul bunched a large number of dry sticks together and placed *them* on the bonfire, when a poisonous snake came from the heat, it clamped down on his hand.
4 As the foreigners saw the wild animal hanging from his hand, they were saying to each other, "By all means, this person is a murderer whom, after being safe from the sea, *Lady* Justice did not allow to be living."
5 So after knocking the wild animal off into the fire, he certainly suffered nothing bad.
6 The *foreigners* were expecting for him to be going to be swollen or to suddenly be falling down dead. But over a long *time* as they expected and saw

nothing out of place happening to him, switching, they were saying for him to be a god.

7 In the *areas* around that place, there were parcels of land *belonging* to the most important *person* of the island with *the* name Publius, who, after welcoming us in, courteously provided a place *for us* to stay for three days.

8 It happened for the father of Publius, being constrained by a fever and severe diarrhea, to be lying down, to whom, when Paul went in and prayed, after placing *his* hands on him, he cured him.

9 So after this happened, also the rest (the *people* who had weaknesses in the island) were coming forward and being healed.

10 The *foreigners* also paid us with many valuables. And as we took off, they placed the *things* on *the boat* for *our* need.

11 We took off after three months in a boat that had spent the storm season in the island (an Alexandrian *boat* side-marked with *the* twin sons of Zeus).

12 And after landing at Syracuse, we stayed over for three days.

13 From there, after we went around, we made it to Rhegium. And after one day of a south *wind* coming again, we second-day *people* went to Puteoli.

14 When we found brothers there, we were encouraged based on them to stay over for seven days, and this is how we went to Rome.

15 And from there, after the brothers heard the *news* about us, they came out for a face-to-face meeting with us till Appii Forum and Three Shacks, whom, when Paul saw, after thanking God, he received courage.

16 When we went to Rome, the lieutenant handed over the prisoners to the head of the army camp, but permission was given to Paul to be staying by himself together with the soldier guarding him.

17 It happened after three days for Paul to call together the *people* who were most important of the Jewish *people*. When they came together, he was saying to them, "Men, brothers, although I did nothing opposing the ethnic group or the customs, the paternal *customs*, I was turned over *as* a prisoner from Greater Jerusalem to the hands of the Romans,

18 some who, after investigating me, were intending to dismiss *me* because of the *fact for there* to be not even one accusation of death in me.

19 But since the Jewish *people* were expressing opposition, I was urged to call on Caesar, not as a *person* who has any complaint to level against my nation.

20 So because of this accusation, I called you here to see and speak to *you*. You see, on account of the anticipation of Israel I am lying around this chain."

21 The *people* said to him, "We neither accepted documents out of Judea about you, nor did any of the brothers who showed up report or speak anything evil about you.

22 But we think that *things* from the side of you (*things* that you focus on) deserve to be heard. You see, concerning this sect it is certainly known to us that opposition is expressed everywhere."

23 After arranging a day with him, more *people* were arriving to him into the guesthouse, to whom he was laying *it* out, being a strong witness of the monarchy of God and persuading them in the *things* about Jesus out of both the law of Moses and the Preachers from in *the* morning until late afternoon.

24 And the *people* certainly were being persuaded by the *things* being said, but the *others* were not trusting.
25 They, being disagreeing toward each other, were dismissing themselves after Paul said one statement, "The Spirit, the Sacred *Spirit*, spoke nicely through Isaiah, the preacher, to our fathers,
26 saying *in Isaiah 6:9–10,* 'Travel to this ethnic group and say, "With *your* sense of hearing, you will hear and not in any way understand, and as you look, you will look and not in any way see.
27 You see, the heart of this ethnic group became fat, with *their* ears they hardly heard, and their eyes they shut so that they might never see with the eyes, with the ears hear, with the heart understand, and return back, and I would cure them."'
28 So it must be known to you that to the non-Jews is the rescue *process* of God sent out, and they will hear."
29 And when he said these *things*, the Jewish *people* went away having much back and forth questioning among themselves.
30 Paul stayed a whole two year period in *his* own rented house and was gladly accepting all the *people* traveling in to him,
31 speaking publicly about the monarchy of God and teaching the *things* about the Master Jesus, the Anointed King, unhindered with every clear public statement.

Romans

1 *From:* Paul, a slave of Jesus, *the* Anointed King, an invited missionary who has been isolated for God's good news,
2 that He previously promised through His preachers in *the* sacred *Old Testament* writings,
3 about His Son (the *One* who became from a seed of David according to *the* physical body,
4 the *One* who was designated *the* Son of God in ability according to *the* Spirit of sacredness from a return back to life of *the* dead), Jesus, *the* Anointed King, our Master,
5 through whom we received generosity and a mission for obedience of trust among all the nations on behalf of His name,
6 among whom you are also invited of Jesus, *the* Anointed King.
7 To: All the *people* who are in Rome: loved of God, invited, sacred *people*. Generosity to you and peace out from God, our Father, and Master Jesus, *the* Anointed King.
8 First *of all*, I certainly thank my God through Jesus, *the* Anointed King, on behalf of you all because your trust is proclaimed in the whole world.
9 You see, God (to whom I minister in my spirit in the good news of His Son) is my witness how I constantly make a mention of you,
10 always pleading over my prayers, if somehow, finally, I will be successful in what God wants, to come to you.
11 You see, I yearn to see you so that I might give out some spiritual gift to you for the "for you to be established" *part*,
12 that is, to be encouraged together in you through the trust in each other (of both you and me).
13 I don't want you to be unaware, brothers, that many times I put *my intention out there* beforehand to come to you (and was hindered till the *place* here) so that I might also have some fruit among you, just as *I* also *have* among the rest *of the* non-Jews.
14 I am a person who owes both Greeks and foreigners, both insightful and unobservant *people*.
15 This is why *there is* the eager *passion* regarding me to also share good news with you, the *people* in Rome.
16 You see, I am not ashamed of the good news of the Anointed King; for it is God's ability for a rescue to everyone who trusts, both Jewish first and Greek.
17 You see, God's right way in it is uncovered from trust for trust, just as it has been written *in Habakkuk 2:4*, "The *person* who does what is right will live from trust."
18 You see, God's punishment out of heaven is uncovered on all godlessness and wrong of people, the *ones* holding down the truth in wrong
19 because what *is* known of God is shown in them; for God showed *it* to them.

20 You see, as the invisible *things* of Him are perceived, from *the* creation of a world to the *things* done, both His eternal ability and divinity are clearly seen for the "for them to be defenseless" *part*
21 because when they knew God, they did not elevate Him as God to a place of magnificence, nor were they thankful. But they were futile in their ponderings, and their clueless heart was made dark.
22 Claiming to be insightful *people*, they became foolish
23 and changed the magnificence of the undeteriorating God in a likeness of an image of a deteriorating person, of winged birds, of four-legged animals, and of reptiles.
24 For this reason, God also turned them over (in the desires of their hearts) to what is not clean, of the "to be belittling their bodies among themselves" *kind*,
25 some who exchanged the truth of God in the Lie, and worshiped and ministered to the creation, contrary to the *One* who created *it*, who is conferred with blessings for the spans of time. Amen.
26 Because of this, God turned them over to lusts of no value. You see, even their females exchanged the natural use *of the body* for what *is* contrary to nature.
27 And likewise, when the males also left the natural use of the female, they burned out in their craving for each other, males among males, working on and completing what is improper and fully receiving among themselves the payback that is necessary for their misleading lie.
28 And just as they did not approve to be having God in a correct understanding, God turned them over to an unapproved way of thinking, to be doing the *things* not meeting even the lowest standard,
29 who have been filled with all wrong, sexual sin, evilness, desire for more, badness (full of envy, murder, fighting, deception, bad character), whisperers,
30 critical, God-detesting, injurers, proud, egoistic, inventors of bad *things*, unbelieving to parents,
31 clueless, not keeping agreements, hardhearted toward family, refusing to enter into agreements, unforgiving,
32 some who, after correctly understanding the right path of God (that the *people* who repeatedly do these types of *things* are deserving of death), not only do these *things*, but also agree that the *people* who repeatedly do *them* are good.

2

1 For this reason, you are defenseless, O person (everyone who judges). You see, what you judge the different *person* in *is what* you yourself are guilty *of*; for you (the *person* who judges) repeatedly do the same *things*.

2 We realize that the judgment of God is aligned with truth over the *people* who repeatedly do these types of *things*.
3 Do you consider this, O person (the *one* who judges the *people* repeatedly doing these types of *things* and who does them), that you will escape from the judgment of God?

4 Or do you ignore the wealth of His kindness, tolerance, and patience, unaware that the kindness of God leads you into a change of ways?
5 Aligned with your hardness and stubborn heart, you stockpile punishment for yourself during a day of punishment and an uncovering of *the* right judgment of God,
6 who will give back to each *person* aligned with his actions:
7 to the *people* who, aligned with persistence of *the* good action, look for magnificence, value, and non-deterioration — certainly life that spans *all* time;
8 but to the *people* who from contention certainly do not even believe the truth, but believe the wrong way — anger and punishment.
9 Hard times and difficulty *are* on every soul of a person, the *person* working on and completing what is bad (both of Jewish first and of Greek).
10 But magnificence, value, and peace *are* to everyone who works *on* the good thing (both to Jewish first and to Greek).
11 You see, there is no being swayed by appearances beside God;
12 for as many as sinned without *the* law will also be ruined without *the* law, and as many as sinned in *the* law will be judged through *the* law.
13 You see, the hearers of the law *are* not right beside God, but the doers of the law will be made right;
14 for when the non-Jews (who by nature don't have a law) do the *things* of the law, these who don't have a law are a law to themselves,
15 some who display the action of the law written in their hearts, their conscience concurring and *their* reasonings leveling complaints against or even defending between each other
16 in a day when God judges the hidden *things* of the people aligned with my good news through Jesus, *the* Anointed King.
17 Look, you identify yourself as Jewish, you relax based on the law, you brag about God,
18 you know what *He* wants, and you approve the *things* that carry through, being echoed down from the law.
19 And you have been confident for yourself to be a guide of blind *people*, a light of the *people* in darkness,
20 a discipliner of distracted *people*, a teacher of infants, having the framework of the information and the truth in the law.
21 So, the *person* who teaches a different *person*, don't you teach yourself? The *person* who speaks publicly *saying* not to be stealing, do you steal?
22 The *person* who says not to be cheating on a spouse, do you cheat on *your* spouse? The *person* who is disgusted with the idols, do you pilfer *idol* temples?
23 Do you who brag about the law belittle God through *your* violation of the law?
24 You see, the name of God is insulted among the non-Jews because of you, just as it has been written *in Isaiah 52:5 and Ezekiel 36:22-23.*
25 You see, circumcision certainly is a benefit if you are constantly doing *the* law, but if you are a violator of *the* law, your circumcision has become uncircumcision.

26 So if the uncircumcision observes the right paths of the law, won't his uncircumcision be considered for circumcision?
27 And the uncircumcision from nature that finishes the law will judge you, the violator of *the* law through a document and circumcision.
28 You see, it isn't the Jewish *person* in the shown *realm*, nor the circumcision in the shown *realm*, in the physical body,
29 but the Jewish *person* in the hidden *realm* and circumcision of a heart, in spirit, not a document; whose high praise *is* not from people, but from God.

3

1 So what *is* the much better *quality* of the Jewish *person*? Or what *is* the benefit of the circumcision?
2 *There is* much in every way. You see, first *is* certainly that they were trusted with the utterances of God.
3 You see, what if some did not trust? Their lack of trust won't make the trust of God useless, will it?
4 It could not happen. God must become valid, but every person a liar, just as it has been written *in Psalm 51:4*, "in order that You (*God*) might be made right in Your messages and will conquer in the *thing* to be decided by You."
5 If our wrong way stands together with God's right way, what will we state? God, the *One* bringing up the punishment, *is* not wrong, is He? (I am talking aligned with a person.)
6 It could not happen. Or else how will God judge the world?
7 You see, if the truth of God overflowed in my fabrication to His magnificence, why am I still even judged as a sinful *person*?
8 And *it is* not — just as we were insulted and just as some declare us to be saying — "we should do the bad *things* so that the good *things* might come," is it? Whose judgment *(that it is not good to do bad)* is reasonable.
9 So what? Are we held in a better position? Not by any means. You see, we already accused both Jewish *people* and Greeks, everyone to be under sin,
10 just as it has been written *in Psalm 14:1–3; 53:1–3*, "There is not a *person* who does what is right, not even one."
11 "He is not the *person* who understands. He is not the *person* intensively searching for God."
12 "All slid away. At the same time, they went bad. There is not a *person* showing kindness. There isn't so much as one."
13 "Their throat *is* a gravesite that has been opened. They were deceiving with their tongues" *(Psalm 5:9)*. "Venom of cobras *is* under their lips," *(Psalm 140:3)*
14 "whose mouth is packed full of cursing and bitterness" *(Psalm 10:7)*.
15 "Their feet *are* sharp to spill out blood.
16 Disaster and misery *are* in their roads,
17 and they didn't know a road of peace" *(Psalm 59:7–8)*.
18 "*The* fear of God isn't up in front of their eyes" *(Psalm 36:1)*.
19 We realize that as much as the law says, it speaks to the *people* in the law so that every mouth might be shut and the entire world might become legally liable to God
20 because from actions of *the* law, every physical body will not be made right in His sight. You see, a correct understanding of sin *is* through *the* law.

21 But right now, separate from *the* law, God's right way has been shown, being witnessed by the Law and the Preachers.
22 God's right way *is* through a trust of Jesus, *the* Anointed King, for all and on all the *people* trusting. You see, there is no difference *between Jew and non-Jew*;
23 for all *who trust* sinned and are lacking of the magnificence of God,
24 being made right for free by His generosity through the paid release, the *paid release* in *the* Anointed King Jesus,
25 whom God put beforehand *as* a source of remedy through the trust in His blood for a display of His right way because of the passing by of the sins that have already happened
26 in the tolerance of God, toward a display of His right way in the present time, for the "for Him to be right and *to be* the *One* who makes the *person* right from a trust of Jesus" *part*.
27 So where *is* the bragging? It was excluded. Through what kind of law? *A law* of the actions? No, but through a law of trust.
28 So we consider a person with trust to be made right separate from actions of *the* law.
29 Or *is He* only the God of Jewish *people*? *Is He* not also *the God* of non-Jews? Yes, also of non-Jews
30 since it is true that God is one *God* who will make circumcision right from trust and uncircumcision *right* through the *same* trust.
31 So do we make *the* law useless through *this* trust? It could not happen. No, we establish *the* law.

1 So what will we state for Abraham, our father, to have found regarding *the* physical body?
2 You see, if Abraham was made right from actions *of work*, he has something to brag about, but not to God.
3 You see, what does the *Old Testament* writing say *in Genesis 15:6*? "But Abraham trusted God, and it was considered to him for *the* right way."
4 To the *person* working, the pay is not considered aligned with generosity, but aligned with what is owed.
5 To the *person* not working, but trusting based on the *One* who makes the *person who is* not godly right, his trust is considered for *the* right way,
6 exactly as David also tells the blessedness of the person to whom God considers *the* right way *to be* separate from actions *of work in Psalm 32:1, 2*.
7 "*People* whose crimes are forgiven and whose sins are covered up *are* blessed.
8 A man to whom a master won't in any way consider sin *is* blessed."
9 So *is* this blessedness on the circumcision *only*? Or *is it* also on the uncircumcision? You see, we say that the trust was considered to Abraham for *the* right way.
10 So how was it considered *for the right way*? Being in circumcision or in uncircumcision? Not in circumcision, but in uncircumcision.
11 And he received an indicator of circumcision *as* a seal of the right way of the trust, the *trust* during the uncircumcision, for the "for him to be a father of all

the *people* who trust through uncircumcision (for the 'for *the* right way to also be considered for them' *part*)

12 and a father of circumcision" *part* (not to the *people* only from circumcision, but to the *people* who also march in step with the footsteps of the trust during the uncircumcision of our father Abraham).

13 You see, the promise to Abraham or to his seed (the "for him to be an inheritor of the world" *thing*) *is* not through *the* law, but through *the* right way of trust;

14 for if the inheritors *are* from *the* law, the trust has been meaningless, and the promise has been rendered useless.

15 You see, the law works on and completes punishment. You see, where there is no law, neither *is there* a violation.

16 Because of this, *it is* from trust so that *it is* aligned with generosity, for the "for the promise to be firm to every seed" *part*, not to the *seed that is* only from the law, but to the *seed that* also *is* from *the* trust of Abraham (who is a father of us all,

17 just as it has been written *in Genesis 17:5*, "I have placed you as a father of many nations," directly facing whom he trusted, God, the *One* who gives life to the dead and calls the *things* not existing as if existing),

18 who trusted beyond anticipation based on anticipation for the "for him to become a father of many nations" *part* aligned with what had been stated, "This is how your seed will be."

19 Even when he wasn't weak with the trust, didn't he take a closer look at his *own* body, already having been *as good as* dead (being somewhere around a hundred-year-old) and the deadness of the womb of Sarah?

20 For the promise of God, he didn't consider *it* to be wrong with the lack of trust, but he became competent with the trust when he gave magnificence to God

21 and was well-established *in the conviction* that *God* is also able to do what He has promised.

22 For this reason, it also was considered to him for *the* right way.

23 It was not written only because of him (that it was considered *for the right way* for him),

24 but also because of us, for whom it is going to be considered, the *people* trusting based on the *One* who got Jesus, our Master, up from *the* dead,

25 who was turned in because of our infractions and was gotten up because of our verdict declaring that *we* do what is right.

5

1 So after we are made right from trust, we have peace toward God through our Master Jesus, *the* Anointed King

2 (through whom we also have had the access to the trust into this generosity in which we have stood, and we are optimistic based on anticipation of the magnificence of God.

3 Not only *that*, but we also are optimistic about the hard times realizing that the hard times work on and complete a persistence *to do what is right*,

4 the persistence *works on and completes* a proven track record, the proven track record *works on and completes* anticipation.

5 The anticipation doesn't shame *us* because the love of God has been spilled out in our hearts through *the* Sacred Spirit, the *Spirit* that was given to us.
6 You see, we still being weak, *the* Anointed King died according to an appointed time on behalf of *people who are* not godly;
7 for with a lot of effort on behalf of a *person* who does what is right, some will die. You see, on behalf of the good *person*, some possibly even dare to die.
8 But God stands together with His *own* love for us, because we still being sinful *people, the* Anointed King died on our behalf.)
9 So, much more now, after being made right in His blood, we will be rescued through Him out of the punishment.
10 You see, if we, being enemies, were restored to God through the death of His Son, much more, after being restored, we will be rescued in His life.
11 Not only *that*, but *we are* also being optimistic about God through our Master Jesus, *the* Anointed King, through whom we now received the restored relationship.
12 Because of this, even as through one person the sin came into the world, and through the sin, the death, so also the death went through to all people based on *the fact* that all sinned.
13 (You see, till *the* law, sin was in *the* world, but sin is not put on *anyone's* account since there is no law.
14 But the death was king from Adam up to Moses, even over the *people* who didn't sin on the likeness of the violation of Adam, who is a type of the *One* that is going *to come*,
15 but not as the infraction, so also the gift. You see, if with the infraction of the one *person*, the many died, much more the generosity of God and the free handout in the generosity of the one Person (Jesus, *the* Anointed King) overflowed for the many.
16 And the free gift *is* not as through one *person* who sinned. You see, the judgment certainly *is* from one *person* to a guilty verdict, but the gift is from many infractions to *the* right path;
17 for if with the infraction of the one *person*, the death was king through the one *person*, much more the *people* receiving the overflow of the generosity and the free handout of the right way will be kings in life through the one *Person*, Jesus, *the* Anointed King.)
18 So clearly, as through one *person's* infraction, *it is* for all people for a guilty verdict, so also through one *Person's* right path, *it is* for all people for a verdict of life declaring that *they* do what is right.
19 You see, even as through the noncompliance of the one person were the many *people* placed as sinful *people*, so also through the obedience of the one *Person* will the many *people* be placed as *people* who do what is right.
20 *The* law quietly came in so that the infraction might increase. But where the sin increased, the generosity overflowed even more
21 so that even as the sin was king in the death, so also might the generosity be king through *the* right way for life that spans *all* time through Jesus, *the* Anointed King, our Master.

6

1 So what will we state? Will we stay over in the sin so that the generosity might increase?
2 It could not happen. How will we, some who died to the sin, still live in it?
3 Or are you unaware that as many of us as were submerged into *the* Anointed King Jesus, were submerged into His death?
4 So we were buried together with Him through the submersion into the death so that even as *the* Anointed King was gotten up from *the* dead through the magnificence of the Father, so also we might walk around in newness of life.
5 You see, if we have become integrated into the likeness of His death, still we will also be *a part* of the return back to life,
6 knowing this, that our former person was nailed to a cross together with *Him* so that the body of the sin might be rendered useless, of the "for us to no longer be a slave to the sin" *kind*;
7 for the *one* who died has been made right out of the sin.
8 If we died together with *the* Anointed King, we trust that we also will live together with Him
9 realizing that *the* Anointed King who was gotten up from *the* dead no longer dies. Death is no longer a master of Him.
10 You see, *the death* that He died to the sin, He died all at once, but *the life* that He lives, He is living for God.
11 This is how you also must consider yourselves to certainly be dead *people* with the sin, but *people* living with God in *the* Anointed King Jesus, our Master.
12 So the sin must not be a king in your dying body for the "to be obeying it in its desires" *part*.
13 Neither offer your body parts *to be* weapons of *the* wrong way, to the sin, but offer yourselves to God (as being alive from *the* dead) and your body parts *to be* weapons of *the* right way, to God.
14 You see, sin won't be a master of you *all*; for you aren't under *the* law, but under generosity.
15 So what? Will we sin because we aren't under *the* law, but under generosity? It could not happen.
16 Have you not seen that you are slaves to what you obey, to what you offer yourselves as slaves for obedience? Either then of sin for death, or of obedience for *the* right way.
17 Generosity *be* to God because you were slaves of the sin but you obeyed from *the* heart that type of teaching you were given over to.
18 After being set free out of the sin, you were enslaved to the right way.
19 I am telling *this* human *analogy* because of the weakness of your physical body. You see, even as you offered your body parts *to be* slaves to what is not clean and to the crime for the crime, so now offer your body parts *to be* slaves to the right way for sacredness;
20 for when you were slaves of the sin, you were free from the right way.
21 So what fruit were you having at that time over what you are now ashamed of? You see, the conclusion of those *fruits* is death.

22 Right now, after being set free out of the sin (but enslaved to God), you have your fruit for sacredness. The conclusion *of it is* life that spans *all* time.
23 You see, the wages of the sin *is* death, but the gift of God *is* life that spans *all* time in *the* Anointed King Jesus, our Master.

7

1 Or are you unaware, brothers, (you see, I am speaking to *people* who know *the* law) that the law is a master of the person over as much time as he lives?
2 You see, the 'under-a-husband' woman has been tied to the living husband by *the* law. But if the husband dies, she has been rendered exempt from the law of the husband.
3 So clearly, as the husband is living, it will notify *people that she is* a cheating wife if she becomes with a different man. But if the husband died, she is free from the law, of the "for her not to be a cheating wife when she becomes with a different man" *kind*.
4 In such a way, my brothers, you also were made dead to the law through the body of the Anointed King for the "for you to become with a different *man*" *thing*, the *Man* who was gotten up from the dead, so that we might produce fruit for God.
5 You see, when we were in the physical body, the hardships of the sins (the *hardships* through the law) were active in our body parts for the "to produce fruit for the death" *thing*.
6 But right now, we were rendered exempt from the law after dying in what we were being held down *by* in such a way for us to be slaves in newness of spirit and not *the* outdated nature of a document.
7 So what will we state? The law *is* sin? It could not happen. No, I didn't know the sin except through *the* law. You see, I hadn't even seen the desire, except the law was saying *in Exodus 20:17*, "You will not desire..."
8 But when the sin took an opportunity through the demand, it worked on and completed all kinds of desire in me. You see, separate from *the* law sin *is* dead.
9 I was living separate from *the* law in the past, but when the demand came, the sin came back to life. I died.
10 And this demand, the *demand* for life, was found by me *to be* for death.
11 You see, when the sin took an opportunity through the demand, it completely fooled me, and through this killed *me*.
12 In such a way, the law certainly *is* sacred, and the demand *is* sacred, right, and good.
13 So has the good *thing* for me become death? It could not happen. But the sin *came back to life* so that through the good *thing* for me sin might be shown working on and completing death, so that the sin might become even more sinful through the demand.
14 You see, we have seen that the law is spiritual, but I am physical, having been put up for sale by the sin.
15 You see, what I work on and complete, I don't know; for what I want, this I don't constantly do, but what I hate, this I do.
16 If I do this, what I don't want, I declare together with the law that *it is* nice.

17 Right now, I no longer work on and complete it, but the sin that has a house in me *does*.
18 You see, I have seen that good doesn't have a house in me, that is in my physical body; for the "to be wanting" *part* lies beside me, but not the "to be working on and completing the nice *thing*" *part*.
19 You see, I don't do *the* good that I want, but *the* bad that I don't want, this I repeatedly do.
20 If I do this, what I don't want, I no longer work on and complete it, but the sin that has a house in me *does*.
21 I clearly find the law for me (the *person* wanting to be doing the nice *thing*) *is* that the bad lies beside me.
22 You see, I admire the law of God according to the inner person,
23 but I see a different law in my body parts that is a soldier fighting against the law of my way of thinking and forcibly incarcerating me to the law of the sin, the *law* that is in my body parts.
24 I *am* a troubled person. What will save me from the body of this death?
25 I thank God through Jesus, *the* Anointed King, our Master. So clearly I myself am not only a slave to *the* law of God with *my* way of thinking, but to *the* law of sin with *my* physical body.

8

1 Clearly *there is* no guilty verdict now for the *people* in *the* Anointed King Jesus who do not walk around "aligned with *the* physical body," but "aligned with *the* Spirit."
2 You see, the law of the Spirit of the life in *the* Anointed King Jesus set me free out of the law of the sin and the death;
3 for the impossible *thing* of the law, in which it was weak through the physical body, God, when He sent His *own* Son in *the* likeness of a physical body of sin and concerning sin, found the sin in the physical body to be guilty
4 so that the right path of the law might be accomplished in us, the *people* not walking around aligned with *the* physical body, but aligned with *the* Spirit.
5 You see, the *people* who are aligned with *the* physical body focus on the *things* of the physical body, but the *people who are* aligned with *the* Spirit *focus on* the *things* of the Spirit;
6 for the focus of the physical body *is* death, but the focus of the Spirit *is* life and peace
7 because the focus of the physical body is a hostile relationship with God. You see, it doesn't place itself under the law of God; for neither is it able to.
8 The *people* who are in a physical body aren't able to do anything that God would like.
9 You aren't in a physical body, but in *the* Spirit, if it is true that God's Spirit has a house in you. If anyone doesn't have *the* Spirit of *the* Anointed King, this *person* is not His.
10 If *the* Anointed King *is* in you, the body certainly *is* dead because of sin, but *the* Spirit *is* alive because of *the* right way.
11 If the Spirit of the *One* who got Jesus up from *the* dead has a house in you, the *One* who got the Anointed King up from *the* dead will also give your dying bodies life through His Spirit that has a house in you.

12 So, brothers, we are clearly not people who owe the physical body, of the "to be living aligned with *the* physical body" *kind*.
13 You see, if you live aligned with *the* physical body, you are going to be dying, but if you make dead to *the* Spirit the things the body repeatedly does, you will live;
14 for as many *people* as are led by God's Spirit, these are God's sons.
15 You see, you didn't receive a spirit of slavery again for fear, but you received a spirit of adoption in which we yell, "Daddy, the Father!"
16 The Spirit itself concurs with our spirit that we are children of God,
17 but if children, also inheritors, not only inheritors of God, but inheritors together with *the* Anointed King if it so happens that we suffer together, so that we also might be elevated to a place of magnificence together.
18 You see, I consider that the hardships of the present time *are* not deserving of the magnificence that is going to be uncovered in us.
19 You see, the eager expectation of the creation patiently waits for the uncovering of the sons of God;
20 for the creation was placed under the futileness, not voluntarily, but because of the *One* who placed *it* under *it* based on anticipation
21 because even the creation itself will be set free out of the slavery of the deterioration into the freedom of the magnificence of the children of God.
22 You see, we realize that the entire creation groans together and together is in labor till the present.
23 Not only *the creation*, but we ourselves also, having the first-part-offering of the Spirit, even we ourselves groan within ourselves patiently waiting for an adoption, the paid release of our body.
24 You see, we were rescued with the anticipation *of good*, but anticipation that is seen is not anticipation; for what someone sees, why does he also anticipate *it*?
25 But if we anticipate what we don't see, we patiently wait through persistence.
26 Similarly, the Spirit also assists together with our weaknesses. You see, we don't realize what we should pray aligned with what is necessary, but the Spirit itself intervenes on behalf of us with unspeakable groans.
27 The *One* examining the hearts realizes what the focus of the Spirit *is* because He intervenes aligned with God on behalf of sacred *people*.
28 We realize that all *things* work together for good to the *people* who love God, to the *people* who are invited aligned with a purpose
29 because whom He knew beforehand, He also designated beforehand *to be people* formed together, of the image of His Son, for the "for Him to be *the* firstborn among many brothers" *part*.
30 Whom He designated beforehand, these He also invited, and whom He invited, these He also made right. Whom He made right, these He also elevated to a place of magnificence.
31 So what will we state toward these *things*? If God *does it* on behalf of us, who *is* against us?

32 He, who definitely didn't go easy on *His* own Son, but gave Him up on behalf of us all, how will He not also together with Him give us everything as an act of generosity?
33 Who will bring a charge against God's *people* who choose *Him*? God *is* the *One* making *them* right.
34 Who *is* the *one* finding *anyone* guilty? *The* Anointed King *is* the *One* who died, but more *than that*, who also was gotten up, who also is in *the* right *side* of God, who also intervenes on our behalf.
35 Who will separate us away from the love of the Anointed King? *Will* hard times, or difficulty, or persecution, or famine, or nakedness, or danger, or a dagger?
36 *It is* just as it has been written *in Psalm 44:23*, "On account of You, we are being put to death the whole day. We are considered as sheep of a slaughter."
37 But in all these *things*, we are more than conquerors through the *One* who loved us.
38 You see, I have been confident that neither death, nor life, nor angels, nor head rulers, nor abilities, nor *things* that have stood here, nor *things* that are going *to be,*
39 nor a high thing, nor depth, nor some different created being will be able to separate us away from the love of God in *the* Anointed King Jesus, our Master.

9

1 I am telling *the* truth in *the* Anointed King (I am not lying), my conscience concurring with me in *the* Sacred Spirit,
2 that great sadness and a constant agony is with me with my heart.
3 You see, I myself was wishing to be doomed away from the Anointed King on behalf of my brothers, my relatives regarding *the* physical body,
4 some who are Israelis, whose *are* the adoption, the magnificence, the deals, the making of the law, the sacrifice ritual, and the promises,
5 whose *are* the fathers and from whom *is* the Anointed King (the "according to *the* physical body" thing), *whose is* the God who is over all *things* conferred with blessings for the spans of time. Amen.
6 But *it is* not such *a thing* that the message of God has failed. You see, not all these *people* from Israel *are* Israel.
7 Neither *is it* that all *Abraham's people* (*his*) children) are Abraham's seed, but, "*The* seed with you will be called 'in Isaac.'"
8 That is, these children of the physical body *are* not children of God, but the children of the promise are considered for a seed.
9 You see, this message *in Genesis 18:14 is a message* of promise: "aligned with this time, I will come, and with Sarah there will be a son."
10 Not only *that*, but also Rebecca *received it* having a bed from one *man*, Isaac, our father.
11 (You see, *this happened* when *the children* were not yet born, nor repeatedly did anything good or bad, so that God's purpose regarding selection may remain, not from actions, but from the *One* calling.)

12 It was stated to her, "The bigger *group* will be a slave to the lesser *group*" (*Genesis 25:23*).
13 *It is* just as it has been written *in Malachi 1:2, 3*, "Jacob I loved, but Esau I hated."
14 So what will we state? *There is* not wrong beside God, is there? It could not happen.
15 You see, He says to Moses, "I will show forgiving kindness on whomever I show forgiving kindness, and I will have compassion on whomever I have compassion."
16 So clearly *it is* not of the *one* who wants *it*, nor of the *one* who runs, but of the *One* showing forgiving kindness, God.
17 You see, the *Old Testament* writing says to Pharaoh *in Exodus 9:16*, "For this very *thing* I got you up out *of there*, in order that I might display in you My ability and in order that My name might be announced everywhere in all the earth."
18 So clearly He shows forgiving kindness to whom He wants. He hardens whom He wants.
19 So you will state to me, "Why does He still find fault? You see, has anyone stood in opposition to His intention?"
20 No, of course not, O person, but who are you? The *person* responding in opposition to God? Will the sculpture state to the *One* who sculpted *it*, "Why did you make me like this?"
21 Or doesn't the clay worker have authority *over* the mud from the same batch to make *one* container that *is* for value, but *another* that *is* for no value?
22 *What* if God, wanting to display the punishment and to make known what *is* possible of Him, in much patience, put up with containers of punishment that have been developed for ruin,
23 even so that He might make known the wealth of His magnificence on containers of forgiving kindness that He had ready beforehand for magnificence,
24 whom He also invited, us, not only from Jewish *people*, but also from non-Jews?
25 As He also says in Hosea *2:23*, "I will invite the 'Not My Ethnic Group' *to be* My ethnic group, and the '*Woman* Who Hasn't Been Loved' *to be a woman* who has been loved."
26 And *in Hosea 1:10*, "It will be in the place where it was stated to them, 'You *are* "Not My Ethnic Group";' there they will be invited *to be* sons of *the* living God."
27 Isaiah *in Isaiah 10:22* yells over Israel, "Though the number of the sons of Israel is as the sand of the sea, *only* the part left behind will be rescued."
28 You see, an answer, as He is completely finishing and completely cutting *it* off in *the* right way ("an answer that has been completely cut off"), *the* Master will make on the earth.
29 And *it is* just as Isaiah had stated before *in Isaiah 1:9*, "If *the* Master of Sabaoth (*Hebrew for army, the name of God's army*) didn't leave a seed down in us, as Sodom we would have become, and as Gomorrah we would be like."

30 So what will we state? That the non-Jews not pursuing *the* right way have completely taken *the* right way, but the right way from trust,
31 but Israel pursuing *the* law of *the* right way didn't already come into *the* law of *the* right way.
32 Why? Because *they did* not *pursue it* from trust, but as *if* from actions of *the* law. You see, they tripped on the stone of the trip hazard.
33 *It is* just as it has been written *in Isaiah 28:16 and 8:14*, "Look, I place in Zion a stone of a trip hazard and a rock of an obstacle. And everyone trusting based on it will not be shamed."

10

1 Brothers, certainly the good notion of my heart and the plea, the *one* to God, over Israel is for rescue.
2 You see, I am a witness for them that they have a passion for God, but not aligned with a correct understanding;
3 for being unaware of the right way of God and looking to establish *their* own right way, they haven't placed themselves under the right way of God.
4 You see, *the* Anointed King *is the* conclusion of *the* law for *the* right way to everyone who trusts;
5 for Moses writes about the right way, the *one* from the law, *in Leviticus 18:5*, "The person doing these *things* will live in them."
6 But the right way from trust talks like this, "Don't say in your heart, 'Who will climb up into heaven?' (that is, to lead *the* Anointed King down)
7 or, 'Who will climb down into the bottomless area?' (that is, to lead *the* Anointed King up from *the* dead)."
8 But what does it say? "The statement is near you, in your mouth and in your heart," that is, the statement of the trust that we speak publicly about,
9 that if you acknowledge in your mouth Master Jesus and trust in your heart that God got Him up from *the* dead, you will be rescued.
10 You see, with *the* heart, He is trusted for *the* right way, but with *the* mouth, He is acknowledged for rescue;
11 for the *Old Testament* writing says *in Isaiah 28:16*, Everyone "who trusts based on Him won't be shamed."
12 You see, there is no difference between Jewish and Greek; for the same Master *is Master* of everyone, being wealthy to everyone who calls on Him.
13 You see, "Everyone, whoever calls on the name of *the* Master will be rescued" (*Joel 2:32*).
14 So how will they call on *a person* in whom they didn't trust? How will they trust *a person* of whom they didn't hear? How will they hear separate from *a person* speaking publicly?
15 How will they speak publicly, except they be sent out? Just as it has been written *in Isaiah 52:7*, "How beautiful *are* the feet of the *people* sharing the good news of peace, the *people* sharing the good news of the good *things*."
16 But not everyone obeyed the good news. You see, Isaiah says *in Isaiah 53:1*, "Master, who trusted what was heard from us?"
17 Clearly the trust *is* from what is heard. What is heard *is* through a statement of God.

18 But I say, "Didn't they in any way hear?" Yes, of course. "Their sound went out into all the earth and their statements to the ends of the civilized world" *(Psalm 19:4)*.
19 But I say, "Did Israel not in any way know?" First, Moses says *in Deuteronomy 32:21*, "I will make you jealous over *a nation that is* not a nation. Over a clueless nation I will incite rage in you."
20 Isaiah dares to come out and say *in Isaiah 65:1*, "I was found by the *people* not looking for me. I became explicitly shown to the *people* not asking about me."
21 To Israel he says *in Isaiah 65:2*, "The whole day I extended my hands to an ethnic group that doesn't believe and that expresses opposition."

11

1 So I say, "God didn't push His ethnic group away, did He?" It could not happen. You see, I am also an Israeli from a seed of Abraham, of Benjamin's family line.
2 God didn't push His ethnic group away whom He knew beforehand. Or don't you realize in Elijah what the *Old Testament* writing says (*1 Kings 19:10, 14*) as he intervenes to God against Israel? Saying,
3 "Master, they killed your preachers, they dug up and removed your altars, I was left after *that* alone, and they are looking for *me to take* my soul."
4 But what does the *divine* notice say to him? "I left seven thousand men down *there* for Myself, some who didn't bend a knee to Baal."
5 So this is also how in the present time a remaining few have become aligned with a selection of generosity.
6 If *it* is with generosity, *it is* no longer from actions *of work*, or else the generosity no longer becomes generosity. But if *it* is from actions *of work*, it no longer is generosity, or else the work no longer is work.
7 So what *is it*? Israel didn't obtain *any* of this *thing* that it is searching for, but the selection obtained *it*. The rest became hard as stone.
8 *It is* just as it has been written *in Isaiah 29:10*, "God gave them a spirit of numbness, eyes of the 'to not be seeing' *kind*," and ears of the "to not be hearing" *kind* until the day today.
9 And David says, "Their table must become for a trap, for a hunt, for an obstacle, and for a repayment to them.
10 Their eyes must be made dark, of the 'to not be seeing' *kind*. And their back, through everything, bend *it* completely over with *heavy loads*."
11 So I say, "They didn't slip so that they might fall, did they?" It could not happen. But with their infraction, the rescue *went* to the non-Jews for the "to make them *(the Jewish people)* jealous" *thing*.
12 If their infraction *is the* wealth of *the* world and their defeat *the* wealth of *the* non-Jews, how much more their fullness?
13 You see, I am talking to you, the non-Jews, based on as much as I certainly am a missionary to non-Jews. I elevate my *job of* serving to a place of magnificence
14 if somehow I might make my physical kin jealous and might rescue some from among them.

15 You see, if their casualty *is the* world's restored relationship, what *is their* readmission, if not life from *the* dead?
16 If the first-part-offering *is* sacred, *the rest of* the batch also *is*. And if the root *is* sacred, the branches also *are*.
17 If some of the branches were split off, but you, being a wild olive tree, were grafted in among them and became a sharer together of the root and the fatness of the olive tree,
18 don't brag about how much better you are than the branches. *Even* if you brag about how much better you are, you don't haul the root, but the root *hauls* you.
19 So you will state, "The branches were split off so that I might be grafted in."
20 Nicely, with the lack of trust, they were split off, but with the trust, you have stood. Don't be focused on high things, but be afraid.
21 You see, if God didn't go easy on the branches *that are* according to nature, neither will He somehow go easy on you.
22 So look at God's kindness and fierceness — certainly on the *people* who fell: fierceness; but on you: kindness if you stay over in *His* kindness. Or else you also will be chopped out.
23 If those *Jewish people* don't stay over in the lack of trust, they also will be grafted in. You see, God is able to graft them in again;
24 for if you were chopped out of the wild olive tree *that* according to nature *you were branches of* and contrary to nature you were grafted into a cultivated olive tree, how much more will these, the *branches* according to nature, be grafted into *their* own olive tree?
25 You see, I don't want you to be unaware, brothers, of this secret (so that you may not be focused with yourselves), that stone hardness out of a part *of it* has happened to Israel till *a* time that the fullness of the non-Jews might come in.
26 And this is how all of Israel will be rescued, just as it has been written *in Isaiah 59:20*, "The *One* who saves will arrive from Zion and will turn godlessness away from Jacob,"
27 and *in Isaiah 59:21 and Jeremiah 31:33, 34*, "This *is* to them, the deal from My side, when I will take away their sins."
28 Regarding the good news, *they* certainly *are* enemies because of you. But regarding the selection, *they are* loved because of the Father.
29 You see, the gifts and the invitation of God *are* not *things that are* regretted.
30 You see, even as you also in the past didn't believe in God but now you received forgiving kindness with the unbelief of these *people,*
31 so also these *people* now didn't believe so that with your forgiving kindness they also might receive forgiving kindness;
32 for God closed all the *people* up into unbelief so that He might show forgiving kindness to all the *people*.
33 O *the* depth of God's wealth, insight, and knowledge! How unexplorable *are* His judgments, and *how* impossible-to-track *are* His ways!
34 You see, "Who knew *the* Master's way of thinking?" or "Who became His counselor" *(Isaiah 40:13)*?
35 or "Who gave to Him before and will be repaid by Him" *(Job 41:11)*?

36 Because all *things are* from Him, through Him, and for Him. To Him *belongs* the magnificence for the spans of time. Amen.

12

1 So I encourage you, brothers, through the compassion of God to offer your bodies *as* a sacrifice, living, sacred, well-liked by God, your logical sacrifice ritual.
2 And don't be conformed to this span of time, but be transformed with the renewal of your way of thinking for the "for you to be proving what *is* the *thing* that God wants" *part*, the good, well-liked, and complete *thing*.
3 You see, through the generosity given to me, I say to everyone who is among you not to be focusing above *and* beyond what it is necessary to be focusing on, but to be focusing for the "to be properly focused on each *person*" *part* as God divided out an amount of trust;
4 for exactly as in one body we have many body parts, but all the body parts don't have the same repetitive action,
5 so we, the many, are one body in *the* Anointed King, but the *Anointed King* throughout each other *is* body parts,
6 *people* who have specialized gifts according to the generosity, the *generosity* given to us. If *the gift is* preaching, *it is* aligned with the portion of the trust *given to that person.*
7 If *the gift is* serving, *it is* in the serving *given to that person.* If *it is* the *person* teaching, *it is* in the instruction *given to him.*
8 If *it is* the *person* encouraging, *it is* in the encouragement *given to him.* The *person* giving *things* out *should do so* in dedication. The *person* presiding *should do so* in concern. The *person* showing forgiving kindness *should do so* in *the* providing of a remedy.
9 Love should not be faked. *You should be people* detested away from the evil *thing*, being stuck like glue to the good;
10 to the brotherly kindness, family-friendly to each other; to the value, lead the way in front of each other;
11 to the concern, not lazy; to the Spirit, being passionate; to the Master, being a slave;
12 to the anticipation *of good*, being happy; to the hard times, persisting *to do what is right*; to the prayer, staying close by;
13 to the needs of the sacred *people* — sharing, pursuing being nice to strangers.
14 Confer a blessing on the *people* pursuing you. Confer a blessing, and do not put a curse *on them*.
15 To be happy with *people* who are happy and to be crying with *people* who are crying
16 (focusing on the same *thing* for each other, not focusing on the high *things*, but being led away together with the lowly *things*), don't become *people* focused by the side of yourselves,
17 giving back bad for bad to no one, planning for nice *things* in the sight of all people,
18 if possible (what *is* from among you), being peaceful with all people,

19 not retaliating for yourselves, loved *ones*. But give a place for the punishment. You see, it has been written *in Deuteronomy 32:35*, "'Retaliation *is* for Me. I will repay,' says *the* Master."
20 So if your enemy is hungry, give him food. If he is thirsty, give him a drink. You see, doing this, you will pile coals of fire on his head.
21 Don't be conquered by the bad, but conquer the bad in the good.

13

1 Every soul must arrange itself under authorities that have a higher position. You see, there is no authority except from God. The existing authorities exist having been placed under God.
2 In such a way, the *person* placing himself in opposition to the authority has stood in opposition to the arrangement of God. The *people* who have stood in opposition to *it* will receive a judgment to themselves.
3 You see, the head people are not a fear of the good actions, but of the bad. Do you want to not be fearing the authority? Do the good *thing*, and you will have high praise from him;
4 for he is a servant of God to you for the good *thing*. But if you do the bad *thing*, be afraid. You see, he does not wear the dagger for no reason; for he is a servant of God, a retaliator for punishment to the *person* who repeatedly does the bad *thing*.
5 For this reason, *there is* an obligation to be placing yourself under *him*, not only because of the punishment, but also because of the conscience.
6 You see, because of this, you also pay protection fees; for they are public servants of God for this very *thing*, staying close by.
7 So give back to all *people* the amounts owed: to the *one owed* the protection fee, the protection fee; to the *one owed* the tax, the tax; to the *one owed* the fear, the fear; to the *one owed* the value, the value.
8 Don't owe anyone anything except the "to be loving each other" *thing*. You see, the one who loves the different *person* has accomplished *what the* law *says to do*;
9 for the "You will not cheat on *your* spouse, you will not murder, you will not steal, you will not lie when you are a witness, you will not be envious," *thing* (and if *there is* some different demand) is summed up in this saying, in the "You will love the *person* near you as yourself" *saying*.
10 The love does not work *anything* bad to the *person* nearby. So *the* fullness of *the* law *is* the love.
11 And this *is important*, realizing the time, because *it is* already *the* hour for us to get up from slumber. You see, now our rescue *is* nearer than when we trusted.
12 The night progressed. The day has come near. So we should put away the actions of the darkness, and we should put on the weapons of the light.
13 As during *the* day, we should walk around reputably: not in wild parties and bouts of drunkenness, not in beds and indulgent activities, not in fighting and hostile passion.
14 But put on the Master Jesus, *the* Anointed King, and of the physical body, don't make a plan for desires.

Romans 14

1 Take in the *person* who is weak in the trust, not into discernments of questions.
2 *There* certainly *is a person* who trusts to eat all *food*, but the *person* who is weak eats vegetables.
3 The *person* who eats must not treat the *person* who doesn't eat as a nobody, and the *person* who doesn't eat must not judge the *person* who eats. You see, God has taken him in.
4 Who are you, the *one* judging a domestic servant belonging to others? To *his* own master he stands or falls. He will be established. You see, God is able to establish him.
5 *There is one person* who judges a day beyond *another* day, *another* who judges every day. Each *person* must be well-established in *his* own way of thinking.
6 The *person* who focuses on the day, focuses on *it* with *the* Master; and the *person* who is not focusing on the day, *is* with *the* Master *as* he is not focusing. The *person* who eats, eats with *the* Master (you see, he thanks God); and the *person* who isn't eating, *is* with *the* Master *as* he isn't eating (he also thanks God).
7 You see, not one of us lives by himself, and not one dies by himself;
8 for both if we live, we live with the Master, and if we die, we die with the Master. So both if we live and if we die, we are the Master's.
9 You see, for this *the* Anointed King died, stood up, and came back to life, so that He might be the Master of both dead *people* and *people* living.
10 Why do you judge your brother? Or also, why do you treat your brother as a nobody? You see, we will all stand up next to the judicial bench of the Anointed King;
11 for it has been written *in Isaiah 45:23*, "*As* I live," says *the* Master, "every knee will bend down to Me, and every tongue will acknowledge God out loud."
12 So clearly each of us will give an answer concerning himself to God.
13 So we shouldn't judge each other anymore. But judge this instead, the "not to be putting a trip hazard or obstacle for the brother" *thing*.
14 I have seen and have been confident in Master Jesus that nothing by itself *is* shared except to the *person* who considers something to be shared. To that *person it is* shared.
15 If because of food your brother is sad, you no longer walk around aligned with love. Don't ruin that *brother* with your food on behalf of whom *the* Anointed King died.
16 So your good must not be insulted.
17 You see, the monarchy of God isn't dinner and drink, but *it is the* right way, peace, and happiness in *the* Sacred Spirit;
18 for the *person* who is a slave in these *things* to the Anointed King *is* well-liked by God and approved by the people.
19 So clearly we should pursue the *things* of the peace and the *things* of the construction, the *construction* for each other.
20 On account of food don't tear down the work of God. All *things* certainly *are* clean, but *it is* a bad *thing* for the person, the *one* who eats through a trip hazard.

21 The "not to eat meat" *thing is* nice (nor to drink wine, nor *to do anything* in which your brother trips, or stumbles, or is weak).
22 Do you have trust? Have *it* by yourself in the sight of God. The *person is* blessed who doesn't judge himself in what he approves.
23 The *person* considering *it* to be wrong has been guilty if he eats, because *it is* not from trust. Everything that is not from trust is sin.

15

1 We (the able *people*) are obligated to be hauling the frailties of the unable *people* and not to be doing what we ourselves would like.
2 You see, each of us must do what the *person* nearby would like for the good *thing* toward construction.
3 You see, even the Anointed King didn't do what He Himself would have liked, but just as it has been written *in Psalms 69:9*, "The criticisms of the *people* criticizing You (*God*) fell on Me."
4 You see, as much as was written about previously was written for our instruction so that through the persistence and the encouragement of the *Old Testament* writings we may have the anticipation.
5 May the God of the persistence and the encouragement give to you to be focusing on the same *thing* among each other aligned with *the* Anointed King Jesus,
6 so that unanimously with one mouth you *all* may elevate the God and Father of our Master Jesus (*the* Anointed King) to a place of magnificence.
7 For this reason, take each other in, just as the Anointed King also took us in for God's magnificence.
8 I am saying for Jesus, *the* Anointed King, to have become a servant of circumcision on behalf of God's truth for the "to authenticate the promises of the fathers" *part*,
9 but on behalf of forgiving kindness, for the non-Jews to elevate God to a place of magnificence, just as it has been written *in Psalm 18:49*, "Because of this, I will acknowledge You out loud among non-Jews and recite psalms to Your name."
10 And again he says *in Deuteronomy 32:43*, "Non-Jews, celebrate with His ethnic group."
11 And again *in Psalm 117:1*, "Praise the Master, all the non-Jews, and applaud Him, all the ethnic groups."
12 And again Isaiah (*11:10*) says, "He will be the root of Jesse and the *One* standing up to be heading non-Jews. Based on Him, non-Jews will anticipate good."
13 May the God of the anticipation fill you with all happiness and peace during the *time* to be trusting for the "for you to be overflowing in the anticipation" *part* in *the* ability of *the* Sacred Spirit.
14 I have been confident, my brothers, even I myself, concerning you that you yourselves also are full of goodness, who have been filled with all *the* information, being able also to be cautioning each other.
15 I wrote more daringly to you out of a part *of it*, brothers, as *a way of* prompting you because of the generosity, the *generosity* given to me by God

16 for the "for me to be a public servant of Jesus, *the* Anointed King for the non-Jews" *part*, being a temple worker for the good news of God so that the offering *that is comprised* of the non-Jews might become well-received, having been made sacred in *the* Sacred Spirit.
17 So I have something to brag about in *the* Anointed King Jesus of the *things* toward God.
18 You see, I won't dare to be speaking any of *the things* that *the* Anointed King didn't work on and complete through me (for obedience of *the* non-Jews in message and work)
19 in *the* ability of indicators and incredible things, in *the* ability of God's Spirit, in such a way for me out of Jerusalem and circling up to Illyricum to have filled up the good news of *the* Anointed King,
20 but like this, thinking it is important to be sharing good news where the name of *the* Anointed King hasn't been mentioned so that I may not build on a foundation belonging to others.
21 But *it is* just as it has been written *in Isaiah 52:15*, "People to whom it wasn't announced about Him will see, and the *people* who haven't heard will understand."
22 For this reason, I was also being interrupted by many *things* from the "to come to you" *part*.
23 But right now, having no more place in these slopes, but having an intense yearning for the "to come to you" *part* from many years,
24 whenever I may travel to Spain, I will come to you. You see, I am anticipating, as I travel through, to see you and by you to be brought on my way through there, if first out of a part *of it* I might be filled up from you.
25 But right now I am traveling to Jerusalem serving the sacred *people*.
26 You see, it seemed like a good idea to Macedonia and Achaia to do some sharing to the poor of the sacred *people* in Jerusalem.
27 You see, it seemed like a good idea to them, and they are people who owe them; for if they *(the sacred people in Jerusalem)* shared their spiritual *things*, the non-Jews also are obligated to serve the public for them in the physical *things*.
28 So after finishing this up and putting a seal on this fruit to them, I will go off through you into Spain.
29 I realize that as I come to you, I will come in fullness of a conferring of blessing on the good news of *the* Anointed King.
30 I encourage you, brothers, through our Master Jesus, *the* Anointed King, and through the love of the Spirit, to struggle together with me in the prayers on my behalf to God
31 that I might be saved from the *people* who don't believe in Judea and so that my serving, the *serving* in Jerusalem, might become well-received by the sacred *people*,
32 so that I might come to you in happiness through what God wants, and I might be relaxed together with you.
33 *May* the God of the peace *be* with you all. Amen.

1 I endorse Phoebe to you (our sister, who is a servant of the assembly, the *one* in Cenchrea)

16

2 so that you might accept her in in *the* Master in a manner deserving of the sacred *people* and stand by her in whatever item she may need of you. You see, she also became a sponsor of many and of myself.
3 Say hello to Priscilla and Aquila, my co-workers in *the* Anointed King Jesus,
4 some who on behalf of my soul have put their *own* neck under *the ax*, whom I not only thank, but also all the assemblies of the non-Jews.
5 And say hello to the assembly throughout their house, to Epenetus, my loved *one*, who is *the* first-part-offering of Achaia for *the* Anointed King.
6 Say hello to Mary, someone who labored with many *things* for us.
7 Say hello to Andronicus and Junias, my relatives and people incarcerated together with me, some who are well-known among the missionaries, who also have become in *the* Anointed King before me.
8 Say hello to Amplias, my loved *one* in *the* Master.
9 Say hello to Urbanus, our co-worker in *the* Anointed King, and Stachys, my loved *one*.
10 Say hello to Apelles, the approved *one* in *the* Anointed King. Say hello to the *people* from Aristobulus.
11 Say hello to Herodion, my relative. Say hello to the *people* from Narcissus, the *ones* who are in *the* Master.
12 Say hello to Tryphena and Tryphosa, the *women* laboring in *the* Master. Say hello to Persis, the loved *one*, someone who labored with many *things* in *the* Master.
13 Say hello to Rufus, the select *one* in *the* Master, and his mother and mine.
14 Say hello to Asyncritus, Phlegon, Hermas, Patrobas, Hermes, also the brothers together with them.
15 Say hello to Philologus and Julia, Nereus and his sister, Olympas, and all the sacred *people* together with them.
16 Say hello to each other with a sacred friendly gesture. The assemblies of the Anointed King say hello to you.
17 I encourage you, brothers, to be keeping an eye out for the *people* who cause the factions and the obstacles contrary to the teaching that you learned, and slide away from them.
18 You see, these types of *people* are not slaves to our Master Jesus, *the* Anointed King, but to their *own* belly, and through the kind message and conferring of blessings, they completely fool the hearts of the *people* who are not bad.
19 You see, your obedience was spread to everyone, so I am happy based on you. I want you to certainly be insightful *people* in the good *thing*, but unpolluted in the bad *thing*.
20 The God of the peace will crush the Opponent under your feet quickly. The generosity of our Master Jesus, *the* Anointed King, *is* with you. Amen.
21 Timothy (my co-worker) says hello to you, also Lucius, Jason, and Sosipater (my relatives).
22 I, Tertius (the *one* who wrote *out this* letter in *the* Master), say hello to you.
23 Gaius (the host of me and the whole assembly) says hello to you. Erastus (the manager of the city) says hello to you, also Quartus (the brother).
24 The generosity of our Master Jesus, *the* Anointed King, *is* with you all. Amen.

25 To the *One* who is able to establish you aligned with my good news and the public speaking of Jesus, the Anointed King, (aligned with *the* uncovering of a secret that has been kept quiet in times that span *all* time

26 — but that now is also shown through preached writings aligned with a directive of the God who spans *all* time for "obedience of trust" — that is made known to all the non-Jews),

27 to *the* only insightful God through Jesus, *the* Anointed King, *belongs* the magnificence for the spans of time. Amen. [Written to *the* Romans from Corinth, *and sent* through Phoebe, the servant of the assembly at Cenchrea.]

First Corinthians

1

1 *From*: Paul (an invited missionary of Jesus, *the* Anointed King, through what God wants) and Sosthenese (the brother).
2 To: the assembly of God (the *one* that is in Corinth), invited sacred *people* who have been made sacred in *the* Anointed King Jesus together with all the *people* who call on the name of our Master Jesus, *the* Anointed King, in every place (both theirs and ours).
3 Generosity to you and peace out from God, our Father, and Master Jesus, *the* Anointed King.
4 I always thank my God concerning you based on the generosity of God, the *generosity* given to you in *the* Anointed King Jesus
5 because in everything you became wealthy in Him, in every message and all *the* information,
6 just as the witness of the Anointed King was authenticated among you,
7 in such a way for you not to be lacking in any gift, patiently waiting for the uncovering of our Master Jesus, *the* Anointed King,
8 who will also authenticate you until *the* conclusion *as people* with no charges against them in the day of our Master Jesus, *the* Anointed King.
9 God can be trusted, through whom you were invited into a sharing of His Son Jesus, *the* Anointed King, our Master.
10 I encourage you, brothers, through the name of our Master Jesus, *the* Anointed King, that you should all say the same *thing* and there shouldn't be rifts among you, but you should be *people* who have been developed in the same way of thinking and in the same opinion.
11 You see, it was made obvious to me about you, my brothers, by the *people* of Chloe, that there are fights among you.
12 I say this, that each of you says: some, "I am of Paul;" others, "I *am* of Apollos;" others, "I *am* of Cephas *(Aramaic for Peter)*;" still others, "I *am* of *the* Anointed King."
13 Has the Anointed King been divided? Paul wasn't nailed to a cross on your behalf, was he? Or were you submerged in the name of Paul?
14 I thank God that I submerged none of you except Crispus and Gaius
15 so that no one might say that I submerged in my name.
16 I also submerged *the people living in* Stephanas' house. *Of the* rest, I don't know if I submerged anyone else.
17 You see, *the* Anointed King didn't send me out *on a mission* to be submerging, but to be sharing good news, not in insight of a message, so that the cross of the Anointed King might not be meaningless;
18 for the message, the *message* of the cross, certainly is foolishness to the *people* who are ruined, but to the *people* who are rescued, us, it is *the* ability of God.

19 You see, it has been written *in Isaiah 29:14*, "I will ruin the insight of the insightful *people* and invalidate the understanding of the understanding *people*."

20 Where *is* an insightful *person*? Where *is* an *Old Testament* transcriber? Where *is* a philosopher of this span of time? Didn't God make the insight of this world foolish?

21 You see, in the insight of God, since, for sure, the world didn't know God through *its* insight, it seemed like a good idea to God through the foolishness of the public speaking to rescue the *people* who trust.

22 Since, for sure, Jewish *people* also ask for an indicator and Greeks look for insight,

23 we speak publicly about *the* Anointed King who has been nailed to a cross — not only an obstacle to Jewish *people*, but foolishness to Greeks.

24 But to the invited *people* themselves, both Jewish and Greeks, *the* Anointed King *is* God's ability and God's insight

25 because the foolishness of God is more insightful than the people and the weakness of God is stronger than the people.

26 You see, look at your invitation, brothers, because *there are* not many insightful *people* regarding *the* physical body, not many competent, not many from a high-ranking family line.

27 But the foolish *things* of the world God selected so that He may shame the insightful *people*. And the weak *things* of the world God selected so that He may shame the strong *things*.

28 And the *things* of the world that don't have a family and the *things* that have been treated as if they are nothing God selected (even the *things* that don't exist) so that He might make the *things* that exist useless

29 in order that every physical body might not brag in the sight of Him.

30 From Him, you are in *the* Anointed King Jesus, who became insight to us out from God, also *the* right way, sacredness, and a paid release

31 so that just as it has been written *in Jeremiah 9:24–25*, "The *person* who brags must brag about *the* Master."

2

1 And when I came to you, brothers, I didn't come aligned with *the* higher position of *the* message or insight as I proclaimed to you the witness of God.

2 You see, I judged of the "to have seen nothing among you except Jesus, the Anointed King, and this *Anointed King* who had been nailed to a cross" kind.

3 And toward you I became in weakness, in fear, and in much trembling.

4 And my message and my public speaking *were* not in persuasive messages of human insight, but in a show of *the* Spirit and ability

5 so that your trust wouldn't be in people's insight, but in God's ability.

6 We speak insight among the complete *people*, but insight not of this span of time, nor of the head people of this span of time, the *ones* who are rendered useless.

7 But we speak God's insight in a secret, the *insight* that has been hidden away, that God designated beforehand (before the spans of time) for our magnificence,
8 that none of the head people of this span of time have known. You see, if they knew, they wouldn't have nailed the Master of the magnificence to a cross.
9 But just as it has been written *in Isaiah 64:4*, "*Things* that an eye didn't see, an ear didn't hear," and didn't step up to a person's heart, "*are things* that God got ready for the *people* who love Him,"
10 God uncovered *them* to us through His Spirit. You see, the Spirit examines everything, even the depths of God;
11 for who among people realizes the *things* of the person except the spirit of the person, the *one* in him? In this same way also, no one realizes the *things* of God except the Spirit of God.
12 We didn't receive the spirit of the world, but the Spirit, the *One* from God, so that we may realize the *things* that in an act of generosity were given to us by God,
13 *things* that we also speak, not in taught messages of human insight, but in taught *messages* of *the* Sacred Spirit, comparing spiritual *things* with spiritual *things*.
14 A psychological person doesn't accept the *things* of the Spirit of God. You see, it is foolishness to him, and he isn't able to know it because it is investigated spiritually.
15 The spiritual *person* certainly investigates everything, but he himself is investigated by no one.
16 You see, who knew *the* Master's way of thinking that he will pull Him together? But we have *the* Anointed King's way of thinking.

3

1 And I, brothers, wasn't able to speak to you as to spiritual *people*, but as to physical, as to infants in *the* Anointed King.
2 I gave you milk to drink and not food. You see, you weren't yet able, but neither are you still able now;
3 for you are still physical. You see, where *there is* hostile passion, fighting, and factions among you, are you not physical and walk around aligned with a person?
4 You see, when someone says, "I certainly am of Paul," but a different *person*, "I am of Apollos," are you not physical *beings*?
5 So who is Paul? Who is Apollos? But the servants through whom you trusted and to each as the Master gave.
6 I planted. Apollos watered. But God was growing *it*.
7 In such a way, neither is the *one* planting anything, nor the *one* watering, but *the one who is something is* the *One* growing *it*, God.
8 The *person* planting and the *person* watering are one. Each will receive *his* own pay aligned with *his* own labor.
9 You see, we are God's co-workers. You are God's farmland, God's building.
10 Aligned with the generosity of God, the *generosity* given to me, as an insightful general contractor, I have laid a foundation, but another *person* builds on *it*. Each *person* must watch how he builds on *it*.

11 You see, another foundation no one is able to lay contrary to the *one* lying *there*, that is Jesus, the Anointed King.
12 If someone builds on this foundation gold, silver, valuable stones, wood, grass, straw,
13 the work of each *person* will become shown. You see, the *Judgment* Day will make *it* obvious because it is uncovered in fire, and the work of each *person* (what kind it is) the fire will prove.
14 If the work of someone remains, what he built on *it*, he will receive pay.
15 If the work of someone will be burned up, he will sustain loss. He himself will be rescued, but like this: as through fire.
16 Don't you realize that you are a temple of God and the Spirit of God has a house in you?
17 If anyone worsens the temple of God, God will worsen this *person*. You see, the temple of God is sacred, something that you are.
18 No one must completely fool himself. If anyone among you seems to be insightful in this span of time, he must become foolish so that he might become insightful.
19 You see, the insight of this world is foolishness beside God; for it has been written *in Job 5:13*, "The *One* catching the insightful *people* in their slyness,"
20 and again *in Psalm 94:11*, "*The* Master knows the ponderings of the insightful *people*, that they are futile."
21 In such a way, no one must brag about people. You see, everything is yours.
22 Whether Paul, or Apollos, or Cephas *(Aramaic for Peter)*, or *the* world, or life, or death, or *things* that have stood here, or *things* that are going *to be*, all are yours.
23 You *are the* Anointed King's. *The* Anointed King *is* God's.

4

1 This is how a person must consider us: as underlings of *the* Anointed King and managers of God's secrets,
2 but *a thing* that for *the* rest *of the time* is looked for among the managers *is* that someone would be found who can be trusted.
3 With me, is it for a smallest *thing* that I might be investigated by you or by a human *judgment* day? But I don't even investigate myself
4 (you see, I have been aware of nothing by myself, but in this I haven't been made right). The *One* who investigates me is *the* Master.
5 In such a way, don't judge anything before *the* appointed time until the Master comes, who also will light up the hidden *things* of the darkness and show the intentions of the hearts. And at that time, the high praise will happen to each *person* out from God.
6 But these *things*, brothers, I refashion into myself and Apollos because of you, so that in us you might learn the "not to focus above what has been written" *thing*, so that not one *of* you may be conceited on behalf of the one *person*, against the different *person*.
7 You see, who is considering you to be wrong? What do you have that you didn't receive? If you also received *it*, why do you brag as *someone* who didn't receive *it*?

8 Are you *people* who have already been stuffed? Were you already wealthy? Were you kings without us? And If only you definitely were kings so that we also might be kings together with you.
9 You see, it seems to me that God showed us off last, the missionaries, as *people* doomed to death because we became a spectacle to the world, both to angels and to people.
10 We *are* foolish because of *the* Anointed King, but you *all are* focused in *the* Anointed King. We *are* weak, but you *all are* strong. You *all are* magnificent, but we *are* worthless.
11 Till the hour now, we even are hungry, thirsty, naked, slugged, and homeless.
12 And we labor, working with *our* own hands. As we are put down, we confer blessings. As we are persecuted, we tolerate *it*.
13 As we are insulted, we encourage. As the world's grime, we became what is scrapped off of everything until now.
14 I am writing these *things*, not embarrassing you, but as my loved children, I am cautioning *you*.
15 You see, if you may have ten thousand babysitters in *the* Anointed King, still *you do* not *have* many fathers; for in *the* Anointed King Jesus through the good news, I gave birth to you.
16 So I encourage you, become imitators of me.
17 Because of this, I sent you Timothy, who is my loved and reliable child in *the* Master, who will remind you again of my ways, the *ones* in *the* Anointed King, just as I teach everywhere in every assembly.
18 As *if* I *am a person* not coming to you, some were conceited.
19 But I will come to you soon, if the Master wants *me to*, and I will know, not the message of the *people* who have been conceited, but the ability.
20 You see, the monarchy of God *is* not in a message, but in ability.
21 What do you want? Should I come to you with a staff or with love and a spirit of humility?

5

1 Entirely heard among you is sexual sin, and this type of sexual sin, something that *is* not even named among the non-Jews, *sexual sin* in such a way to be having a certain wife of the father.
2 And you are *people* who have been conceited and didn't instead grieve so that the *man* who did this action might be taken from *the* middle of you.
3 You see, I certainly (as *if* being away from *you* in the body, but being beside *you* in the spirit) have already judged (as *if* being beside the *man* who worked on and completed this like this)
4 in the name of our Master Jesus, *the* Anointed King, (when you and my spirit are gathered together with the ability of our Master Jesus, *the* Anointed King)
5 to turn over this type of *man* to the Opponent for destruction of the physical body so that the spirit might be rescued in the day of the Master Jesus.
6 Your bragging *is* not nice. Don't you realize that a little yeast causes the whole batch *of dough* to rise?

7 So clean out the former yeast so that you may be a young batch *of dough*, just as you are yeast-free. You see, even our Passover was sacrificed on our behalf, the Anointed King.
8 In such a way, we may observe the festival, not with former yeast, nor with yeast of badness and evilness, but with yeast-free *loaves* of genuineness and truth.
9 I wrote you in the letter not to be interacting with people who commit sexual sin,
10 and not all the *people* of this world who commit sexual sin, or the *people* who desire more, or vicious *people*, or idol worshipers, or else you clearly are obligated to go out of the world.
11 I wrote you right now not to be interacting — if anyone who is named a brother is a *person* who commits sexual sin, or a *person* who desires more, or an idol worshiper, or a *person* who puts *others* down, or an alcoholic, or a vicious *person* — nor to be eating together with this type of *person*.
12 You see, how *is it* my *responsibility* to also be judging the *people* outside? Don't you judge the *people* inside?
13 But the *people* outside, God will judge, and you will take the evil *person* out from among yourselves.

6 1 Do any of you who have an item facing the different *brother* dare to be judged before the *people* who do what is wrong and not before the sacred *people*?
2 Don't you realize that the sacred *people* will judge the world? And if the world is judged among you, are you undeserving of *the* smallest courts?
3 Don't you realize that we will judge angels? *We can* definitely *judge* this life's things, *can we* not?
4 So if you certainly have courts for this life's things, seat these *people as judges*: the *people* who have been treated as nobodies in the assembly.
5 Toward embarrassment to you, I say *it* like this: Isn't there an insightful *person* among you, or even one *person* who will be able to consider what is wrong up in *the* middle of his brother?
6 But a brother with a brother is judged, even this, before untrusting *people*.
7 So it certainly already is a defeat among you entirely, because you have judgments with yourselves. Why not instead be wronged? Why not instead be robbed?
8 But you wrong and rob even these: brothers.
9 Or don't you realize that *people* who do what is wrong won't inherit God's monarchy? Don't be misled. Neither people who commit sexual sin, nor idol worshippers, nor cheating spouses, nor elegant *people*, nor homosexuals,
10 nor thieves, nor *people* who desire more, nor alcoholics, no *people* who put *others* down, no vicious *people* will inherit God's monarchy.
11 And some *of* you were these *things*, but you doused yourselves off, but you were made sacred, but you were made right in the name of the Master Jesus and in the Spirit of our God.

12 Everything is allowed to me, but not everything is advantageous. Everything is allowed to me, but I won't be controlled by anything.
13 The foods *are* for the belly, and the belly *is* for the foods, but God will make both this *belly* and these *foods* useless. The body *is* not for sexual sin, but for the Master and the Master for the body.
14 God both got the Master up and will get us up out *of here* through His ability.
15 Don't you realize that your bodies are body parts of *the* Anointed King? So after taking the body parts of the Anointed King, will I make *them* body parts of a prostitute? It could not happen.
16 Or don't you realize that the *person* being stuck like glue to the prostitute is one body? You see, "The two," He declares, "will be in one physical body."
17 The *person* being stuck like glue to the Master is one spirit.
18 Escape the sexual sin. Every sin that a person might ever do is outside of the body, but the *person* who commits sexual sin sins into *his* own body.
19 Or don't you realize that your body is a temple of the Sacred Spirit in you, that you have out from God and you are not your own?
20 You see, you were bought *with something* of value. Elevate God to a place of magnificence, for sure, in your body and in your spirit, some that are God's.

7

1 Concerning *things* that you wrote me, *it is* nice for a person not to be touching a woman.
2 Because of the sexual sins, each *man* must have his *own* wife and each *woman* must have *her* own husband.
3 The husband must give back the good attitude that is owed to the wife, but likewise also, the wife to the husband.
4 The wife doesn't have authority over *her* own body, but the husband *does*. Likewise, the husband also doesn't have authority over *his* own body, but the wife *does*.
5 Don't rob each of the other unless *it is* from a harmonious *decision* toward a certain time, so that you may hang out for the time of going without food and the prayer and you may come together again based on the same *harmonious decision*, so that the Opponent may not trouble you because of your lack of restraint.
6 This I say aligned with a suggestion, not aligned with a directive.
7 You see, I want all people to be even as I myself *am*. But each *person* has *his* own gift from God: *one* that certainly *is* like this, but *another* that *is* like this.
8 I say to the unmarried and to the widows, "*It is* nice for them if they stay even as I *am*.
9 But if they are not restraining themselves, they must marry." You see, it is better to marry than to be inflamed *with lust*.
10 I pass the order on (not I, but the Master) to the *people* who have married: for a wife not to be separated away from a husband
11 (if she actually is separated, she must stay unmarried or be restored to *her* husband), and for a husband not to be leaving a wife.

12 To the rest, I say (I, not the Master), "If any brother has an untrusting wife and she agrees that it is good to be having a house with him, he must not be leaving her.
13 And a wife, someone who has an untrusting husband and he agrees it is good to be having a house with her, she must not be leaving him."
14 You see, the husband, the untrusting *one*, has been made sacred in the wife, and the wife, the untrusting *one*, has been made sacred in the husband, or else clearly your children are not clean. But now they are sacred.
15 If the untrusting *person* separates, he must be separated. The brother or the sister hasn't been enslaved in these types of *situations*. God has invited us in peace.
16 You see, how do you know, wife, if you will rescue *your* husband? Or how do you know, husband, if you will rescue *your* wife?
17 If not, as God divided out to each *person*, as the Master has invited each *person*, this is how he must walk around. And this is how I specifically arrange *it* in all the assemblies.
18 Was anyone invited having been circumcised? He must not put *a foreskin back* on. Was anyone invited in uncircumcision? He must not be circumcised.
19 The circumcision is nothing, and the uncircumcision is nothing, but *what is something is the* keeping of God's demands.
20 Each *person* in the invitation with which he was invited, in this he must stay.
21 Were you invited *as* a slave? It must not be a concern to you. But if you also are able to become free instead, use *it*.
22 You see, the slave who was invited in *the* Master is a freed slave of *the* Master. Likewise also, the free *person* who was invited is a slave of *the* Anointed King.
23 You were bought *with something* of value. Don't become people's slaves.
24 Each *person* in what he was invited, brothers, in this he must stay, beside God.
25 Concerning the virgin women, I don't have a directive of *the* Master. I am giving an opinion as a *person* who has been shown forgiving kindness who can be trusted by *the* Master.
26 So I assume this to be nice because of the obligation that has stood here, because with a person, the "to be like this" *thing is* nice.
27 Have you been tied to a wife? Don't look for a release. Have you been released from a wife? Don't look for a wife.
28 But even if you married, you didn't sin, and if the virgin married, she didn't sin. These types of *people* will have hard times in the physical body. I am making it easy for you.
29 I declare this, brothers, because the appointed time is a *thing* that has been wrapping up, so that for the rest *of the time*, even the *people* who have wives should be as the *people* who don't have wives.
30 And the *people* crying *should be* as *people* not crying. And the *people* being happy *should be* as *people* not being happy. And the *people* buying *should be* as *people* not steadily having *anything*.

31 And the *people* using this world *should be* as *people* not overusing *it*. You see, the entity of this world is passing on by.
32 I want you to be without worries. The unmarried *man* worries about the *things* of the Master: how he will do what the Master would like.
33 But the *man* who is married worries about the *things* of the world: how he will do what the wife would like.
34 The woman has been divided. And the virgin, the unmarried *woman*, worries about the *things* of the Master so that she may be sacred both in the body and in the spirit. But the *woman* who is married worries about the *things* of the world: how she will do what the husband would like.
35 I say this toward what is advantageous for yourselves, not so that I might throw a lasso on you, but toward the reputable and good attending to the Master *thing* without distraction.
36 If anyone assumes *it* to be improper on his virgin daughter, if she is past the prime of her youth and so he is obligated *for it* to be happening, he must do what she wants. He isn't sinning. They must marry.
37 *A person* who has stood in *his* heart, stable, not having an obligation, but has authority concerning *his* own thing that he wants, and has decided this in *his* own heart, to be keeping his *own* virgin daughter, does nicely.
38 In such a way, even the *person* who gives *her* out in marriage does nicely, but the *person* who doesn't give *her* out in marriage does better.
39 A wife has been tied up by *the* law over as much time as her husband lives, but if her husband fell asleep, she is free to be married to whom she wants, only in *the* Master.
40 But she is more blessed if she stays like this, aligned with my opinion. I also seem to be having God's Spirit.

8

1 Concerning the idol sacrifices, we realize that we all have *the* information. The information brings conceit, but the love is constructive.
2 If anyone seems to realize something, he does not yet know even just what it is necessary to know.
3 But if anyone loves God, this *person* has been known by Him.
4 So concerning the dinner of the idol sacrifices, we realize that an idol *is* nothing in *the* world and that *there is* not even one different god except One.
5 You see, even if it is true that there are *beings* called gods, whether in heaven or on the earth, even as there are many gods and many masters,
6 but to us *there is* one God, the Father, from whom *are* all *things* (and we *are* in Him), and *there is* one Master, Jesus, *the* Anointed King, through whom *are* all *things* (and we *are* through Him).
7 But the information *is* not in all *people*. Some *people* eat with the conscience of the idol until now, as *if* they are eating an idol sacrifice. And their conscience that is weak is dirtied.
8 Food doesn't stand us up next to God. You see, neither if we ate, are we overflowing, nor if we didn't eat, are we lacking.
9 See to it that somehow this authority of yours doesn't become a trip hazard to the *people* who are weak.

10 You see, if anyone sees you, the *one* who has *the* information, lounging in an idol temple, won't the conscience of him who is weak be built for the "to be eating the idol sacrifices" *part*?
11 And the brother who is weak (because of whom *the* Anointed King died) will be ruined based on your information.
12 This is how, as you do sinful things to the brothers and hit their conscience that is weak, you do sinful things to *the* Anointed King.
13 For this very reason, if food causes my brother to stumble, I won't in any way eat meat for the span of time so that I won't cause my brother to stumble.

9

1 Am I not a missionary? Am I not free? Have I not seen Jesus, *the* Anointed King, our Master? Are you not my work in *the* Master?
2 If I am not a missionary to others, still I definitely am to you. You see, you (in *the* Master) are the seal of my mission.
3 My defense to the *people* investigating me is this.
4 Do we not in any way have authority to eat and drink?
5 Don't we in any way have authority to be leading around a sister, a wife, even as the rest *of the* missionaries, the brothers of the Master, and Cephas (*Aramaic for Peter*)?
6 Or do only I and Barnabas not have authority of the "to not be working" kind?
7 Who serves in the military at any time *paying his* own wages? Who plants a vineyard and doesn't eat from its fruit? Or who shepherds a flock and doesn't eat from the milk of the flock?
8 I am not speaking these *things* aligned with a person, am I? Or doesn't the law also say these *things*?
9 You see, it has been written in Moses' law *in Deuteronomy 25:4*, "You won't muzzle a cow processing grain." God doesn't care for the cows, does He?
10 Or does He say *it* by all means because of us? You see, because of us, it was written, because the *person* plowing is obligated to be plowing based on anticipation and the *person* processing grain to be taking part in his anticipation based on anticipation.
11 If we seeded the spiritual *things* in you, *is it* a great *thing* if we will harvest your physical *things*?
12 If others take part in your authority, *shouldn't* we more? But we don't use this authority. No, we put up with all *things* so that we might not give any interruption to the good news of the Anointed King.
13 Don't you realize that the *people* working with the temple *things* eat from the temple grounds? The *people* attending to the altar receive an allotment to the altar.
14 This is also how the Master specifically arranged *it* for the *people* proclaiming the good news: *for them* to be living from the good news.
15 But I have used none of these *things*. I didn't write these *things* so that it might become like this in me. You see, *it is* nice for me instead to die, than that someone would make my bragging meaningless.

16 You see, if I share good news, to me it isn't something to brag about; for an obligation is lying on me. What a tragedy it is to me if I don't share good news;

17 for if I constantly do this *thing* voluntarily, I get pay, but if involuntarily, I have been trusted with management.

18 So what is the pay to me? That as I share good news, I might place the good news of the Anointed King with no cost *to anyone* (for the "for my authority in the good news not to be overused" *part*).

19 You see, being free from all *people*, to all *people* I enslaved myself so that I might gain the majority *of people*.

20 And to the Jewish *people*, I became as a Jewish *person* so that I might gain Jewish *people*. To the *people* under *the* law, *I became* as *a person* under *the* law so that I might gain the *people* under *the* law.

21 To the criminals, *I became* as a criminal (not being a criminal to God, but a lawful *obeyer* to *the* Anointed King) so that I might gain criminals.

22 To the weak, I became as a weak *person* so that I might gain the weak. To all *people*, I have become all *things* so that by all means I might rescue some.

23 I do this because of the good news, so that I might become a sharer of it together with *you*.

24 Don't you *all* realize that all the *people* running in a lap *(200 yards)* race certainly run, but one takes the prize? This is how you *all* must run, so that you might completely take *it*.

25 Everyone struggling *for a race* restrains himself in everything. So those *people* certainly *restrain themselves* so that they might receive a deteriorating award wreath, but we, an undeteriorating *award wreath*.

26 Now then, this is how I run, not obscurely. This is how I box, not as *if I am* beating *the* air.

27 But I give my body a black eye and lead *it* as a slave, that somehow, after speaking publicly to others, I might not become unapproved myself.

10

1 I don't want you to be unaware, brothers, that all our fathers were under the cloud, they all went through the sea,

2 they all submerged themselves into Moses in the cloud and in the sea,

3 they all ate the same spiritual food,

4 and they all drank the same spiritual drink. You see, they were drinking from a spiritual rock following *them*. The rock was the Anointed King.

5 But God wasn't delighted with the majority of them. You see, *their dead bodies* were spread out down in the backcountry.

6 These *things* became examples for us for the "for us not to be desirers of bad *things*" *part*, just as those *people* also desired.

7 Neither become idol worshipers, just as some of them; as it has been written *in Exodus 32:6*, "The group was seated to eat and to drink and got up to be acting like children."

8 Neither should we commit sexual sin, just as some of them committed sexual sin and twenty-three thousand fell in one day.

9 Neither should we try to harass the Anointed King, just as some of them also tried to cause trouble and were ruined by the snakes.
10 Neither grumble, just as some of them grumbled and were ruined by the Destroyer.
11 All these *things* were transpiring with those *people as* examples. It was written toward our correction, to whom the conclusions of the spans of time have made it.
12 In such a way, the *person* who seems to have stood must see to it that he not fall.
13 Trouble has not taken *hold of* you, except human *trouble*. God can be trusted who won't allow you to experience trouble above what you are able, but together with the trouble He will also make the way out of the "for you to be able to endure *it*" *kind*.
14 For this very reason, my loved *ones*, escape away from the idol worship.
15 I am talking as to focused *people*. You *all* must judge what I declare.
16 The cup of the conferring of blessing that we confer a blessing on, is it not *the* sharing of the blood of the Anointed King? The bread that we split, is it not *the* sharing of the body of the Anointed King?
17 Because we, the many, are one bread, one body. You see, we all take part in *it* from the one bread.
18 Look at Israel regarding *the* physical body. Aren't the *people* eating the sacrifices sharers of the altar?
19 So what am I declaring? That an idol is anything? Or that an idol sacrifice is anything?
20 No, *I am declaring* that what the non-Jews sacrifice, they sacrifice to lesser deities, and not to God. I do not want you to become sharers with the lesser deities.
21 You are not able to be drinking *the* Master's cup and *the* lesser deities' cup. You are not able to be taking part in *the* Master's table and *the* lesser deities' table.
22 Or do we make the Master jealous? We are not stronger than Him, are we?
23 Everything is allowed to me, but not everything is advantageous. Everything is allowed to me, but not everything is constructive.
24 No one must look for what *is* his *own*, but each for what *is* the different *person's*.
25 Eat everything sold in a meat market, investigating nothing, because of the conscience.
26 You see, the earth and its fullness *are* the Master's.
27 If any of the untrusting *people* invite you and you want to be traveling *there*, eat everything placed beside you, investigating nothing, because of the conscience.
28 But if someone says to you, "This is an idol sacrifice," do not eat *it* because of that *person* (the *one* who disclosed *it*) and the conscience. You see, the earth and its fullness *are* the Master's.
29 I say conscience, definitely not the *conscience* of yourself, but the *conscience* of the different *person*. You see, why *is it* that my freedom is being judged by another's conscience?

30 If I am taking part in *it* with generosity, why am I insulted over what I am thankful *for*?
31 So whether you eat, or drink, or anything you do, do everything for God's magnificence.
32 Become *people* not offensive to both Jewish *people* and Greeks, and the assembly of God,
33 just as I also do all *things* that all *things* would like, not looking for what is advantageous for myself, but what *is advantageous* for the many, so that they might be rescued.

11

1 Become imitators of me, just as I also *am* of *the* Anointed King.
2 I applaud you, brothers, because you have always remembered me. And just as I gave the traditions over to you, you hold steady *to them*.
3 I want you to realize that the head of every man is the Anointed King. *The* head of a wife *is* the husband. *The* head of *the* Anointed King *is* God.
4 Every man praying or preaching having *something* down over *his* head shames his head.
5 Every wife praying or preaching with the head completely uncovered shames her *own* head. You see, it is one and the same with the *wife* having been shaved;
6 for if a wife is not completely covered, she also must cut *her hair*, but if *it is* shameful to a wife (the "to cut *her hair* or to be shaved" *thing*), she must be completely covered.
7 You see, a man certainly is not obligated for *his* head to be completely covered, being an image and *the* magnificence of God, but a woman is *the* magnificence of a man;
8 for a man is not from a woman, but a woman *is* from a man.
9 You see, also a man was not created because of the woman, but a woman because of the man.
10 Because of this, the woman is obligated to be having authority based on the head because of the angels.
11 More importantly, neither *is* a man separate from a woman, nor a woman separate from a man in *the* Master.
12 You see, even as the woman *is* from the man, so also *is* the man through the woman. All *things are* from God.
13 Judge among yourselves. Is it *a thing* that is appropriate for a woman to be praying to God completely uncovered?
14 Or doesn't even nature itself teach you that certainly if a man grows *his* hair out, it is no value to him?
15 But if a woman grows *her* hair out, it is magnificence for her because the long hair has been given to her for a cloak.
16 If anyone seems to be fond of quarreling, we don't have this type of policy, neither *do* the assemblies of God.
17 As I pass this order on, I don't applaud *you*, because you come together, not for the better, but for the worse.

18 You see, first *of all*, certainly as you come together in the assembly, I hear rifts to be among you, and I trust some part *of it*;
19 for it is necessary for even splinter groups to be among you so that the approved *people* will become shown among you.
20 So as you come together at the same *place*, it is not to eat a master feast.
21 You see, each *person* takes *his* own feast before *others arrive* during the *time* to eat. And *there is one* who is hungry, *another* who is drunk.
22 You see, do you not in any way have houses for the "to be eating and to be drinking" *part*? Or do you ignore the assembly of God and shame the *people* who don't have *food*? What should I say to you? Should I applaud you in this? I do not applaud *you*.
23 You see, I took in from the Master what I also turned in to you, that the Master Jesus took bread in the night that He was being turned in.
24 And after He was thankful, He split *it* and said, "Take. Eat. This is My body, the *body* that is torn on your behalf. Do this for the reminder again of Me."
25 Similarly, also the cup after the *time for them* to eat dinner, saying, "This cup is the new deal in My blood. Do this as often as you drink for the reminder again of Me."
26 You see, as often as you eat this bread and drink this cup, you proclaim the death of the Master till whenever He comes.
27 In such a way, whoever eats this bread or drinks the cup of the Master in an undeserving manner will be eligible to be sentenced for the body and blood of the Master.
28 A person must check himself, and this is how he must eat from the bread and drink from the cup.
29 You see, the *person* who eats and drinks in an undeserving manner, eats and drinks judgment on himself, not considering the body of the Master to be different.
30 Because of this, many *people* among you *are* weak and sick, and an adequate amount are asleep.
31 You see, if we were considering ourselves to be wrong, we would not be judged.
32 Being judged by *the* Master, we are disciplined so that we might not be found guilty together with the world.
33 In such a way, my brothers, as you come together for the "to eat" *part*, wait for each other.
34 If anyone is hungry, he must eat in a house so that you don't come together into judgment. I will specifically arrange the rest *of the things* whenever I come.

12

1 Concerning the spiritual *things*, brothers, I don't want you to be unaware.
2 You realize that you were non-Jews being led away to the idols, the voiceless *ones*, whenever you were being led.
3 For this reason, I am making known to you that no one speaking in God's Spirit says, "Jesus *is* doomed," and no one is able to say, "Jesus is *the* Master," except in *the* Sacred Spirit.

4 There are varieties of gifts, but the same Spirit.
5 And there are varieties of serving tasks and the same Master.
6 And there are varieties of actions, but the same God is the *One* being active all in all.
7 The showing of the Spirit is given to each *person* toward what is advantageous.
8 You see, *there is a person* to whom a message of insight certainly is given through the Spirit; but to another, a message of information aligned with the same Spirit;
9 to a different *person*, trust in the same Spirit; but to another, gifts of cures in the same Spirit;
10 but to another, actions of abilities; but to another, preaching; but to another, discernments of spirits; but to a different *person*, families of languages; but to another, interpretation of languages.
11 With all these, the one and the same Spirit is active, divvying out to each individually just as He intends.
12 You see, exactly as the body is one and has many body parts, but all the body parts of the body, the one *body*, being many, are one body, so also *is* the Anointed King;
13 for also in one Spirit, we all were submerged into one body, whether Jewish *people*, or Greeks, or slaves, or free. And we all were given a drink into one Spirit.
14 You see, also the body is not one body part, but many.
15 If the foot said, "Because I am not a hand, I am not from the body," it is not, beside this, not from the body.
16 And if the ear said, "Because I am not an eye, I am not from the body," it is not, beside this, not from the body.
17 If the whole body *is* an eye, where *is* the sense of hearing? If *the* whole *is the* sense of hearing, where *is* the sense of smell?
18 But right now God placed the body parts, each one of them, in the body just as He wanted.
19 If it was all one body part, where *is* the body?
20 Now *it is* certainly many body parts, but one body.
21 An eye is not able to say to the hand, "I have no need of you," or again the head to the feet, "I have no need of you."
22 But much more, the body parts of the body seeming to be weaker are essential.
23 And *parts* that seem to us to be more worthless, we place much more value around these *parts* of the body, and our improper *parts* have a much better reputation.
24 Our reputable *parts* have no need, but God mixed the body together, after giving much more value to the *person* that lacks
25 so that there may not be a rift in the body, but the body parts may have the same concern over each other.
26 And if one body part suffers, all the body parts suffer together with *it*. If a body part is elevated to a place of magnificence, all the body parts are happy together with *it*.

27 You *all* are a body of *the* Anointed King, body parts from a part *of it*,
28 and whom God certainly placed in the assembly: first, missionaries; second, preachers; third, teachers; following that, abilities; after that, gifts of cures, assists, counselings, families of languages.
29 Not all *are* missionaries, are they? Not all *are* preachers, are they? Not all *are* teachers, are they? Not all *are* abilities, are they?
30 Not all have gifts of cures, do they? Not all speak with languages, do they? Not all thoroughly interpret, do they?
31 But be passionate about the gifts, the better *gifts*, and yet I am showing you an even better way.

13

1 If I speak with the languages of the people and of the angels, but do not have love, I have become an echoing *piece of* copper or a clanging cymbal.
2 And if I have *the skill of* preaching and have seen all the secrets and all the information, and if I have all the trust in such a way to be dislodging mountains, but I don't have love, I am nothing.
3 And if I use all the *things* that are mine to give out food, and if I turn in my body so that I might be burned, but I don't have love, I am benefited with nothing.
4 The love is patient. It is kind. The love does not get mad. The love does not brag. It is not conceited.
5 It is not improper. It does not look for its *own things*. It is not annoyed. It does not consider the bad *thing*.
6 It is not happy based on the wrong way, but is happy together with the truth.
7 All *things* it puts up with. All *things* it trusts. All *things* it anticipates good from. All *things* it persists *to do what is right* in.
8 The love never ever fails, but if *there is* preachings, it will be rendered useless; if languages, they will stop; if information, it will be rendered useless.
9 You see, *what* we know *is* from a part, and *what* we preach *is* from a part.
10 But when the complete *thing* comes, at that time the *thing* from a part *of it* will be rendered useless.
11 When I was an infant, I was speaking as an infant, I was focusing on *things* as an infant *does*, I was considering *things* as an infant *does*. But when I have become a man, I have made the *things* of the infant useless.
12 You see, now we see through a mirror, in a puzzle, but at that time, face to face. *What* I know now *is* from a part, but at that time, I will correctly understand just as I also was correctly understood.
13 Right now trust, anticipation, love remain, these three. But *the* greatest of these *is* the love.

14

1 Pursue the love. Be passionate about the spiritual *things*, but rather that you may preach.
2 You see, the *person* who speaks with a language doesn't speak to people, but to God; for no one hears. He speaks secrets to a spirit.

3 The *person* who preaches speaks construction, encouragement, and comfort to people.
4 The *person* speaking with a language builds himself, but the *person* preaching builds an assembly.
5 I want you all to be speaking with languages, but rather that you may preach. You see, the *person* preaching is greater than the *person* speaking with languages, outside of except he thoroughly interprets, so that the assembly might receive construction.
6 Brothers, if I come to you right now speaking with languages, how will I benefit you if I don't speak to you either in *the thing* uncovered *to me*, or in information, or in preaching, or in a teaching?
7 In the same manner, the soulless *things* that give *off* a sound, whether a flute or a harp, if it didn't give a difference to the notes, how will it be known what is played on the flute or what is played on the harp?
8 You see, if a trumpet also gave an obscure sound, who will prepare for war?
9 In this way, you also through the language, if you don't give a clear message, how will it be known what is spoken? You see, you will be *people* speaking into *the* air.
10 There are (if it may be obtained) so many kinds of voices in *the* world, and none *are* voiceless.
11 So if I don't realize the ability of the voice, I will be a foreigner to the *person* speaking, and the *person* speaking *will be* a foreigner in me.
12 In this way you also, since you are people with passion for spirits, look for *them* toward the construction of the assembly so that you may overflow.
13 For this very reason, the *person* speaking with a language must pray that he may thoroughly interpret.
14 You see, if I pray with a language, my spirit prays, but my way of thinking is fruitless.
15 So how is it? I will pray to the Spirit, but I also will pray to the way of thinking. I will recite psalms to the Spirit, but I also will recite psalms to the way of thinking.
16 Or else if you confer a blessing on *someone* in spirit, how will the *person* who fills up the place of the uneducated, state the Amen over your thankfulness since, for sure, he doesn't realize what you are saying?
17 You see, you certainly are nicely thankful, but the different *person* is not built.
18 I thank my God, speaking with languages more than all of you.
19 But in an assembly I want to speak five words through my way of thinking so that I also might echo other *words* down, than ten thousand words in a language.
20 Brothers, don't become young children with the *things you* focus *on*. But with the badness, act like infants. With the *things you* focus *on*, become complete *people*.
21 It has been written in the law *in Isaiah 28:11–12*, "'In *people* of different languages and in different lips, I will speak to this ethnic group, and in this way, they won't listen to Me either,' says *the* Master."

22 In such a way, the languages are for an indicator, not to the *people* who trust, but to the untrusting *people*. The preaching *is* not to the untrusting *people*, but to the *people* who trust.

23 So if the whole assembly came together at the same *place* and everyone is speaking with languages, but uneducated people or untrusting *people* came in, will they not state that you are crazy?

24 If everyone is preaching, but a certain untrusting or uneducated person came in, he is reprimanded by everyone, he is investigated by everyone.

25 And in this way, the hidden *things* of his heart become shown, and in this way, after getting down on *his* face, he will bow to God, reporting that God is really in you.

26 So how is it, brothers? When you come together, each of you has a psalm, has a teaching, has a language, has *the thing* uncovered *to him*, has an interpretation. Everything must happen toward construction.

27 If someone speaks with a language, *it must be* by two, or *at* the most three, and *one* part apiece. And one must thoroughly interpret.

28 But if there is no interpreter, he must keep quiet in an assembly. He must speak to himself and to God.

29 Two or three preachers must speak and the others must consider what is wrong.

30 If it is uncovered to another who is sitting, the first must keep quiet.

31 You see, you are all able to be preaching *one* by one so that all may learn and all may be encouraged.

32 And spirits of preachers are placed under *the* preachers' control.

33 You see, God is not *a God* of conflict, but of peace, as *He is* in all the assemblies of the sacred *people*.

34 Your wives must keep quiet in the assemblies. You see, permission is not given to them to be speaking, but they *are* to be placed under *their husbands*, just as the law also says.

35 If they want to learn anything, they must ask *their* own husbands in a house. You see, it is shameful for a wife to be speaking in an assembly.

36 Or did the message of God come out from you? Or did it only make it to you?

37 If anyone seems to be a preacher or spiritual, he must correctly understand *things* that I write to you, that they are the Master's demands.

38 If anyone is unaware, he must be unaware.

39 In such a way, brothers, be passionate about the "to be preaching" *thing*, and don't hinder the "to be speaking with languages" *thing*.

40 Everything must happen reputably and according to an arrangement.

15

1 I am making the good news known to you, brothers, that I shared with you, that you also received in, in which you also have stood,

2 through which you also are rescued with a certain message (I myself shared good news with you), if you hold steady, outside of except you trusted for no reason.

3 You see, I turned over to you (among *the* first) what I also took in, that *the* Anointed King died on behalf of our sins aligned with the *Old Testament* writings,
4 that He was buried, that He has been gotten up on the third day aligned with the *Old Testament* writings,
5 and that He was seen by Cephas *(Aramaic for Peter)*, after that by the Twelve.
6 Following that, He was seen by over five hundred brothers all at once, from whom the majority remains until now, but some also fell asleep.
7 Following that He was seen by James, after that by all the missionaries.
8 But last of all, even as if by the aborted fetus, he was seen also by me.
9 You see, I am the smallest of the missionaries, who is not adequate to be called a missionary because I persecuted the assembly of God.
10 But with God's generosity, I am what I am. And His generosity, the *generosity* for me, didn't become meaningless, but I labored much more than they all, not I, but the generosity of God, the *generosity* together with me.
11 So whether I or those *missionaries*, this is how we speak publicly, and this is how you trusted.
12 If *the* Anointed King is publicly spoken about, that He has been gotten up from *the* dead, how do some among you say that there is no return back to life of dead *people*?
13 If there is no return back to life of dead *people*, neither has *the* Anointed King been gotten up.
14 If *the* Anointed King hasn't been gotten up, clearly our public speaking *is* meaningless. Your trust *is* also meaningless.
15 We also are found *to be* lying witnesses of God because we told what we witnessed down from God, that He got the Anointed King up, whom He didn't get up if it is clearly true that dead *people* aren't gotten up.
16 You see, if dead *people* aren't gotten up, neither has *the* Anointed King been gotten up.
17 If *the* Anointed King hasn't been gotten up, your trust *is* futile. You are still in your sins.
18 Clearly also the *people* who fell asleep in *the* Anointed King are lost.
19 If we who have anticipated good in *the* Anointed King are only in this life, we are more miserable than all people.
20 But right now *the* Anointed King has been gotten up from *the* dead. He became a first-part-offering of the *people* who have fallen asleep.
21 You see, since, for sure, the death *is* through a person, *the* return back to life of dead *people is* also through a person;
22 for even as in Adam all die, so also in the Anointed King all will be given life.
23 But each *is* in *its* own order: a first-part-offering (*the* Anointed King); following that, the *people* of *the* Anointed King during His arrival;
24 after that the conclusion, when He will turn the monarchy over to the God and Father, when He will make every head ruler and every authority and ability useless.

25 You see, it is necessary for Him to be king till whenever He *(God)* will put all the enemies under His feet *(Jesus')*.
26 *The* last enemy is rendered useless: the death.
27 You see, He placed all *things* under His feet. But when He said, "All *things* have been placed under *Him*," *it is* obvious that *it is* outside of the *One* who placed all *things* under Him.
28 When all *things* are placed under Him, at that time the Son Himself will also be placed under the *One* who placed all *things* under *Him* so that God may be all in all.
29 Or else what will the *people* do who are submerged over with the dead? If dead *people* aren't gotten up at all, why are they even submerged over with the dead?
30 Also why are we in danger every hour?
31 I die daily (as sure as the bragging about you that I have in *the* Anointed King Jesus, our Master).
32 If aligned with a person I fought against wild animals in Ephesus, what *is* the benefit to me? If dead *people* aren't gotten up, "we should eat and drink; for tomorrow we die."
33 Don't be misled; bad associations worsen useful morals.
34 Wake up from *your* drunkenness rightly, and don't sin. You see, some *people* have an ignorance of God. I say *this* toward embarrassment to you.
35 But some will state, "How are the dead gotten up? What kind of body do they come *back* with?"
36 Distracted *person*, what you seed is not given life, except it die.
37 And what you seed, you don't seed the body, the *one* that it will become, but a naked kernel of wheat (if it may be obtained) or some of the rest *of the seeds*.
38 God gives it a body, just as He wanted, and to each of the seeds, *its* own body.
39 Not every physical body *is* the same physical body, but certainly another physical body of people, another physical body of animals, another of fish, another of winged birds.
40 *And there are* heavenly bodies and earthly bodies, but certainly the magnificence of the heavenly *is* different, the *magnificence* of the earthly *is* different.
41 *There is* another magnificence of a sun, another magnificence of a moon, and another magnificence of stars. You see, a star is more substantial than a *different* star in magnificence.
42 This is also how the return back to life of the dead is seeded in deterioration; it is gotten up in non-deterioration.
43 It is seeded in no value; it is gotten up in magnificence. It is seeded in weakness; it is gotten up in ability.
44 It is seeded a soul body; it gets up a spiritual body. There is a soul body, and there is a spiritual body.
45 This is also what has been written *in* Genesis 2:7, "The first person, Adam, became into a living soul," the last Adam, into a life-giving spirit.

46 But *it is* not the spiritual *body* first, but the soul *body*; following that, the spiritual.
47 The first person *is* from *the* earth, a dirt *person*. The second person *is* the Master from heaven.
48 Such as the dirt *person was*, the dirt *people are* also these types *of people*; and such as the heavenly *person was*, the heavenly *people are* also these types *of people*.
49 And just as we wore the image of the dirt *person*, we will also wear the image of the heavenly *person*.
50 I declare this, brothers, that a physical body and blood are not able to inherit God's monarchy. Neither does the deterioration inherit the non-deterioration.
51 Look, I am telling you a secret: certainly not all of us will sleep, but all of us will be changed
52 in a moment, in *the* twitch of an eye, in the last trumpet. You see, it will blow, the dead will be gotten up undeteriorating, and we will be changed;
53 for it is necessary for this deteriorating *body* to put on non-deterioration and for this dying *body* to put on deathlessness.
54 When this deteriorating *body* will put on non-deterioration, and this dying *body* will put on deathlessness, at that time the message, the *one* that has been written *in Isaiah 25:8 and Hosea 13:14*, will happen, "The death was swallowed up into victory.
55 Death, where *is* your sting? Hades *(the underworld of the dead)*, where *is* your victory?"
56 The sting of the death *is* the sin. The ability of the sin *is* the law.
57 Generosity *be* to God, the *One* who gives us the victory through our Master Jesus, *the* Anointed King.
58 In such a way, my loved brothers, become stable *people*, unmovable, overflowing in the work of the Master, always realizing that your labor is not meaningless in *the* Master.

16

1 Concerning the collection *of money*, the *collection* for the sacred *people*, even as I specifically arranged with the assemblies of Galatia, so must you also do.
2 On each *Day* 1 after a Sabbath, each of you must put beside himself (as he stockpiles *stuff*) whatever he is successful in, so that no collections *of money* happen at the time when I come.
3 When I show up, whomever you approve, I will send these *people* through letters to carry off your generosity into Jerusalem.
4 If it is deserving of the "for me to also be traveling" *kind*, they will travel together with me.
5 I will come to you whenever I might go through Macedonia. You see, I am going through Macedonia,
6 but to you after *that* is obtained. I will stay with *you*, or even spend the storm season, so that you might bring me on my way to wherever I travel.
7 You see, I don't want to see you now while passing by; for I anticipate to stay over for some time with you if the Master gives permission.

8 But I will stay over in Ephesus until the Fiftieth *Day Festival*.
9 You see, a door has opened to me, large and active, and many *are* lying in opposition.
10 If Timothy comes, see *to it* that he might become fearlessly toward you. You see, he works *on* the work of *the* Master, as I also *do*.
11 So no one should treat him as a nobody, but bring him on his way in peace so that he might come to me. You see, I am waiting for him with the brothers.
12 Concerning Apollos, the brother, many *times* I encouraged him that he should come to you with the brothers, and by all means it was not what *he* wanted, that he would go now, but he will come when he has a good time *to come*.
13 Stay awake, stand in the trust, be a man, gain power.
14 Everything from you must happen in love.
15 I encourage you, brothers, (you realize the house of Stephanas, that it is a first-part-offering of Achaia, and they assigned themselves to *a task of* serving the sacred *people*)
16 that you also may be placed under these types of *people* and *under* everyone working together and laboring.
17 I am happy based on the arrival of Stephanas, Fortunatus, and Achaicus because these *people* filled up your deficiency.
18 You see, they relaxed my spirit and yours. So you must recognize these types of *people*.
19 The assemblies of Western Turkey say hello to you. Aquila and Priscilla together with the assembly throughout their house say hello many *times* to you in *the* Master.
20 All the brothers say hello to you. Say hello to each other with a sacred friendly gesture.
21 The greeting (with my hand) of Paul.
22 If anyone is not fond of the Master Jesus, *the* Anointed King, he must be doomed. Maranatha *(Aramaic for "the Master is coming")*.
23 *May* the generosity of the Master Jesus, *the* Anointed King, *be* with you.
24 My love *is* with all of you in *the* Anointed King Jesus. Amen. [*This* first *letter* was written to Corinth from Philippi *and sent* through Stephanas, Fortunatus, Achaicus, and Timothy.]

Second Corinthians

1 *From*: Paul (a missionary of Jesus, *the* Anointed King, through what God wants) and Timothy (the brother). To: the assembly of God, the *assembly* that is in Corinth, together with all the sacred *people*, the *ones* who are in all of Achaia.

1

2 Generosity to you and peace out from God, our Father, and *the* Master Jesus, *the* Anointed King.

3 The God and Father of our Master Jesus, *the* Anointed King, *is* conferred with blessings, the Father of the compassion, and God of every encouragement,

4 the *One* encouraging us over all our hard times for the "for us to be able to be encouraging the *people* in all *kinds of* hard times" *part* through the encouragement that we ourselves are encouraged with by God,

5 because just as the hardships of the Anointed King overflow to us, so our encouragement also overflows through *the* Anointed King.

6 Whether we go through hard times, *it is* on behalf of your encouragement and rescue, the *encouragement* that is active in persistence *to do what is right* in the same hardships that we also suffer; or whether we are encouraged, *it is* on behalf of your encouragement and rescue. And our anticipation on your behalf is firm

7 realizing that even as you are sharers of the hardships, so also *you are sharers* of the encouragement.

8 You see, we don't want you to be unaware, brothers, over our hard times, the *ones* that happened to us in Western Turkey, that even more than above *our* ability we were weighted down in such a way for us to be unable to find a way out even for the "to be living" *part*.

9 But we ourselves have had the sentence of the death in ourselves so that we may be *people* who haven't been confident based on ourselves, but based on God, the *One* who gets the dead up,

10 who saved us from such a great death as this and saves, in whom we have anticipated that He also will still save,

11 as you also work quietly together on our behalf in *your* plea so that the gift to us from many faces through many *methods* might be thankfulness for us.

12 You see, this is what we brag about, the witness of our conscience, that in dedication and genuineness of God, not in physical insight, but in God's generosity, we were busy in the world (but much more to you);

13 for we are not writing other *things* to you other than what you read or also correctly understand. I am anticipating that you will correctly understand *them* even until *the* conclusion,

14 just as you also correctly understood us out of a part *of it*, because we are what you brag about, exactly as you *are* also *what* we *brag about* in the day of the Master Jesus.

15 And with this confidence, I was intending previously to come to you so that you may have generosity a second *time*,

16 to go across past you into Macedonia, to come again out of Macedonia to you, and to be brought by you on my way to Judea.
17 So as I was advising this, I clearly didn't behave with a flippant attitude, did I? Or do I advise what I advise according to the physical body so that beside me the "yes, yes" may also be the "no, no"?
18 God can be trusted because our message, the *message* to you, did not become "yes and no."
19 You see, when the Son of God, Jesus, *the* Anointed King, the *One* among you, was spoken publicly through us (through me, Silas, and Timothy), it didn't become "yes and no," but in Him, it became "yes;"
20 for as many promises of God as *there are*, in Him *they are* the "yes," and in Him the "amen" *is* to God toward magnificence through us.
21 The God who authenticates us together with you for *the* Anointed King and who anointed us
22 *is* also the *One* who put a seal on us and gave the down payment of the Spirit in our hearts.
23 I call on God on my soul *as* a witness that *as a way of* making *it* easy on you I did not come into Corinth yet,
24 not because we are masters over your trust, but we are co-workers of your happiness. You see, you have stood with the trust.

2

1 I decided this myself, the "not to come to you again in sadness" *thing*;
2 for if I make you sad, who is the *one* who also celebrates with me except the *one* who is sad from me?
3 And I wrote this same *thing* to you so that when coming, I wouldn't have sadness from *people* whom it was necessary for me to be happy with, having been confident based on you all, because my happiness is of you all.
4 You see, from much hard times and distress of heart, I wrote you through many tears, not so that you might be sad, but so that you might know the love that I have much more of for you.
5 If anyone has caused sadness, he has not caused sadness for me (but out of a part *of it*) so that I may not be a burden on you all.
6 This pressure on this type of *man* by the majority *of you is* adequate.
7 In such a way, just the opposite, *it is* more *important* for you, as an act of generosity, to forgive and to encourage, that somehow this type of *person* might not be swallowed up with much more sadness.
8 For this reason, I encourage you to make *your* love for him official.
9 You see, for this I also wrote, so that I might know the proven track record of you, if you are obedient in all *things*.
10 To whom you forgive anything as an act of generosity, I also *forgive*. You see, as an act of generosity, I have even forgiven *it* (if *it is* anything) to whom I have forgiven, because of you, in *the* face of *the* Anointed King
11 so that we might not be taken advantage of by the Opponent; for we are not unaware of his patterns of thinking.

12 After going to Troas for the good news of the Anointed King and a door having been opened to me in *the* Master,
13 I have not had relief to my spirit (the *spirit* — for me not to find Titus, my brother). But after saying good-bye to them, I went out to Macedonia.
14 Generosity *be* to God, the *One* always bringing us out in a victory parade in the Anointed King and showing the aroma of His information through us in every place,
15 because we are a sweet fragrance of *the* Anointed King to God among the *people* being rescued and among the *people* being ruined,
16 *one*, to whom *we are* an aroma of death for death, *another*, to whom *we are* an aroma of life for life. Who *is* even adequate toward these *things*?
17 You see, we are not as the many *people* who are dishonest with the message of God, but as *people* from genuineness, but as *people* from God, we are speaking directly in the sight of God in *the* Anointed King.

3

1 Do we begin again to be endorsing ourselves? Or do we, not as some, need endorsement letters to you or endorsement *letters* from among you?
2 You are our letter that has been written in our hearts, known and read by all people,
3 as you are shown that you are a letter of *the* Anointed King, served by us, having been written not with ink, but with *the* Spirit of *the* living God, not in stone slabs, but in physical slabs of a heart.
4 We have this type of confidence through the Anointed King toward God
5 (not that we are adequate out from ourselves to consider anything, as *if it were* from ourselves, but our adequacy *is* from God),
6 who also made us adequate *to be* servants of a new deal, not of a document, but of a spirit. You see, the document kills, but the Spirit gives life.
7 If the serving of the death (that has been imprinted in alphabetic characters in stones) happened in magnificence in such a way for the sons of Israel to not be able to stare into the face of Moses because of the magnificence of his face (the *magnificence* that is rendered useless),
8 how will the serving of the Spirit not be more in magnificence?
9 You see, if the serving of the guilty sentence *is* magnificence, much more the serving of the right way overflows in magnificence;
10 for even the *thing* that has been elevated to a place of magnificence has not even been elevated to a place of magnificence in this part, on account of the superior magnificence.
11 You see, if the *thing* that is rendered useless *is* through magnificence, much more the *thing* that remains *is* in magnificence.
12 So having this type of anticipation, we use *it* with a very clear public statement
13 and not anything like Moses. He was putting a veil on his *own* face with the *intent* for the sons of Israel not to stare at the conclusion of the *thing* that is rendered useless.

14 But their patterns of thinking became hard as stone. You see, till the *day* today the same veil stays on the reading of the former deal, *it* not being unveiled that something is rendered useless in *the* Anointed King.
15 But until today, whenever Moses is read, a veil lies on their hearts.
16 Whenever it returns back toward *the* Master, the veil is taken away all around.
17 The Master is the Spirit. Where the Spirit of *the* Master *is*, freedom *is* there.
18 We all who see the reflection of the magnificence of *the* Master in a face that has been unveiled are transformed into the same image out of magnificence for magnificence, exactly as *it is* out of *the* Spirit of *the* Master.

4

1 Because of this, having this *task of* serving, just as we were shown forgiving kindness, we don't get discouraged.
2 But we denounced the hidden *things* of the shame, not walking around in slyness, nor using the message of God deceptively, but in the showing of the truth, endorsing ourselves to every conscience of people in the sight of God.
3 If our good news also is *a thing* that has been covered up, it is *a thing* that has been covered up among the *people* being ruined,
4 among whom, the god of this span of time blinded the patterns of thinking of the untrusting *people* for the "for the lighting of the good news of the magnificence of the Anointed King (who is *the* image of God) not to radiate out to them" *part*.
5 You see, we don't speak publicly about ourselves, but about *the* Anointed King Jesus, *the* Master (ourselves, your slaves because of Jesus),
6 because God, the *One* who told light *to shine* from darkness, who shined in our hearts, will shine toward a lighting of the information of the magnificence of God in *the* face of Jesus, *the* Anointed King.
7 We have this stockpile of treasure in ceramic containers so that the superiority of the ability may be God's and not from us:
8 in every *situation* going through hard times, but not restricted; unable to find our way, but not unable to find a way out;
9 persecuted, but not left down in *there*; thrown down, but not ruined;
10 always carrying the dying of the Master Jesus around in the body so that the life of Jesus also might be shown in our body.
11 You see, we, the *people* living, are always given over to death because of Jesus so that the life of Jesus might also be shown in our dying physical body.
12 In such a way, the death certainly is active in us, but the life *is active* in you.
13 Having the same spirit of the trust aligned with what has been written *in Psalm 116:10*, "I trusted, for this reason I spoke," we also trust, for this reason we also speak,
14 realizing that the *One* who got the Master Jesus up will also get us up through Jesus and will stand by together with you.
15 You see, all *things are* because of you, so that when the generosity increases through the majority *of things*, it might overflow the thankfulness for the magnificence of God.

16 For this reason, we don't get discouraged, but even if our outside person is devoured, still the inside is renewed day *in* and day *out*.
17 You see, the light *weight* of our hard times at this very instant works on and completes an even greater and greater weight of magnificence for us that spans *all* time,
18 not keeping an eye out for our *things* that are seen, but for the *things* that are not seen; for the *things* that are seen *are* for the time being, but the *things* that are not seen *are things* that span *all* time.

1 You see, we realize that if our earthly house of the tent is torn down, we have a building from God, a house made without hands, that spans *all* time in the heavens.
2 You see, we also groan in this *tent*, yearning to put our habitation, the *one* from heaven, on over *it*
3 if also after definitely putting *it* on, we won't be found naked.
4 You see, we, the *people* who are in the tent, also groan, being weighted down, based on which, we don't want to strip *it* off, but to put *this* on over *it* so that the dying *thing* might be swallowed up by the life.
5 The *One* who worked on and completed us for this same *thing is* God, the *One* who also gave us the down payment of the Spirit,
6 so *we are* always being courageous and realizing that as we are at home in the body we are absent away from the Master.
7 You see, we walk around through trust, not through a visual image.
8 We are courageous, and it seems like a good idea to us instead to be absent from the body and to be at home facing the Master.
9 For this reason, we also think it is important, whether being at home or being absent, to be well-liked by Him.
10 You see, it is necessary for all the *people*, us, to be shown in front of the judicial bench of the Anointed King so that each *person* might retrieve the *things* toward what he repeatedly did through the body, whether good or bad.
11 So realizing the fear of the Master, we persuade people. We have been shown to God, but I anticipate to have also been shown in your consciences.
12 You see, we are not endorsing ourselves again to you, but giving you an opportunity of bragging on our behalf so that you may have *it* for the *people* who brag about appearance and not *the* heart.
13 You see, if we are deranged, *it is* for God; if we are properly focused, *it is* for you;
14 for the love of the Anointed King constrains us who judge this, that if One died on behalf of all *people*, clearly all died,
15 and on behalf of all, He died so that the *people* living may no longer live for themselves, but for the *One* who died on their behalf and was gotten up.
16 In such a way, we, from the present *on*, have seen no one according to a physical body. Even if we have known *the* Anointed King according to a physical body, still, now we no longer know *Him according to a physical body*.
17 In such a way, if anyone *is* in *the* Anointed King, *he is* a new creation, the beginning *things* passed. Look, all *things* have become new.

18 All *things* are from God, the *One* who restored us to Himself through Jesus, *the* Anointed King, and gave us the *job of* serving the restored relationship;
19 how that God was in *the* Anointed King restoring *the* world to Himself (not considering to them their infractions), who also placed the message of the restored relationship in us.
20 So on behalf of *the* Anointed King we are representatives. As God, who is encouraging through us, we plead on behalf of *the* Anointed King, be restored to God.
21 You see, the *One* who didn't know sin He made *to be* sin on our behalf so that we might become God's right way in Him.

6

1 Working together, we also encourage you not to accept the generosity of God in a meaningless *way*.
2 You see, He says *in Isaiah 49:8,* "At an accepted time, I listened closely to you, and during a day of rescue, I helped you." Look! Now *is* a good accepted time. Look! Now *is* a day of rescue.
3 *We are people* not giving any type of trip risk in any way so that *our* serving might not be blamed,
4 but in everything endorsing ourselves as God's servants in much persistence *to do what is right*, in hard times, in shortages, in difficulties,
5 in wounds, in jails, in conflicts, in *times of* labor, in sleepless *nights*, in times of going without food,
6 in consecration, in *the* information, in patience, in kindness, in *the* Sacred Spirit, in love *that is* not faked,
7 in a true message, in God's ability through the weapons of the right way, the right *weapons (offensive)* and left *weapons (defensive)*,
8 through magnificence and no value, through harsh talk and good talk, as misleading and valid,
9 as being unaware and correctly understanding, as dying and, look, we live, as disciplined and not put to death,
10 as being sad but always being happy, as poor but making many wealthy, as having nothing and steadily having all *things*.
11 Our mouth has opened for you, Corinthians. Our heart has been widened.
12 You are not restricted in us. You are restricted in your sympathy.
13 For the same payback (I talk as to children), you also must be widened.
14 Don't become *people* who are strapped to a crossbeam with different *people*, with untrusting *people*. You see, what common element *does the* right way and crime *have*? What *kind of* sharing *does* light *have* facing darkness?
15 What harmonious agreement *does the* Anointed King *have* toward Belial *(a name for Satan)*? Or what part *does* a trusting *person have* with an untrusting *person*?
16 What consensus vote *does* God's temple *have* with idols? You see, you are a temple of *the* living God, just as God said *in Leviticus 26:12,* "I will have a house in and walk around among them," and *in Ezekiel 37:27,* "I will be their God, and they will be My ethnic group."

17 For this reason, "Come out from *the* middle of them, and be isolated," says *the* Master *in Isaiah 52:11*. "And don't touch what is not clean, and I will accept you in."
18 And *in 2 Samuel 7:8, 14*, "'I will be for a Father to you, and you will be for sons and daughters to Me,' says *the* Master, *the* All-Powerful One."

7

1 So having these promises, loved *ones*, we should clean ourselves off from every dirty spot of *the* physical body and spirit as we finish up sacredness in *the* fear of God.
2 Make room for us. We wronged no one. We worsened no one. We took advantage of no one.
3 I am not talking toward a guilty sentence. You see, I have stated before, "You are in our hearts for the 'to die together and to be living together' *part*."
4 I *have* a very clear public statement toward you. I *have* much bragging on your behalf. I have been filled with the encouragement. I overflow even more with the happiness over all our hard times.
5 You see, even when we came into Macedonia, our physical body has had not even one *bit of* relief, but in every *way* going through hard times: on *the* outside, arguments; on *the* inside, fears.
6 But God, the *One* encouraging the lowly *people*, encouraged us in Titus' arrival,
7 not only in his arrival, but also in the encouragement that *he received when* he was encouraged based on you, as he announced to us your yearning, your mourning, your passion over me in such a way for me instead to be happy
8 because even if I made you sad in the letter, I don't regret *it* (even if I was regretting *it*). You see, I see that that letter made you sad (if *it was* even toward an hour).
9 Now I am happy, not because you were saddened, but because you were saddened into a change of ways. You see, you were saddened aligned with God so that in nothing would you sustain loss from us;
10 for the sadness aligned with God works on and completes a change of ways for a rescue that no one regrets, but the sadness of the world works on and completes death.
11 You see, look, this same *thing* (the "for you to be sad aligned with God" *thing*), how much concern it worked on and completed with you, but *also* defense, but *also* outrage, but *also* fear, but *also* yearning, but *also* passion, but *also* retaliation. In everything, you endorsed yourselves to be consecrated *people* in *this* item.
12 Clearly, even if I wrote you, *it was* not on account of the *person* who did wrong, nor on account of the *person* who was wronged, but on account of the *need* for our concern, the *concern* on your behalf, to be shown to you in the sight of God.
13 Because of this, we have been encouraged based on your encouragement, but we were much happier instead based on Titus' happiness, because his spirit had been relaxed from you all,

14 because if I have bragged anything to him on your behalf, I was not ashamed. But as we spoke everything to you in truth, so our bragging, the *bragging* before Titus, also became true.

15 And his sympathy for you is much more as he reminds himself again of the obedience of you all, how with fear and trembling you accepted him.

16 So I am happy that in everything I am courageous in you.

8

1 We are making the generosity of God known to you, brothers, the *generosity* that has been given among the assemblies of Macedonia

2 because in a great proven track record of hard times the overflow of their happiness and their deep down poverty overflowed into the wealth of their dedication.

3 I am a witness that according to ability and above ability, on their own,

4 with much encouragement pleading of us for us to accept the generosity and the sharing of the serving, the *serving* for the sacred *people*,

5 and unlike what we anticipated, but they first gave themselves to the Master and to us through what God wanted

6 for the "for us to encourage Titus" *part*, so that just as he already began in on *it*, so also might he finish up for you even this generosity.

7 But even as in everything you overflow (with trust, *the* message, *the* information, every concern, and the love from you in us), *it is* so that you may also overflow in this generosity.

8 I am not saying *this* aligned with a directive, but through the concern of different *people* and proving the real *existence* of your love.

9 You see, you know the generosity of our Master Jesus, *the* Anointed King, that because of you He (being wealthy) became poor so that with the poverty of that *Person* you might become wealthy.

10 And I am giving an opinion in this. You see, this is advantageous to you, some who already began in on *it* since last year, not just the "to do" *part*, but also the "to be wanting" *part*.

11 But right now, also finish up the "to do" *part*, in order that, exactly as *there is* the eagerness of the "to be wanting" *part*, so also *is* the "to finish up" *part* from the "to be having" *part*.

12 You see, if the eagerness already lies *there*, "aligned with whatever someone has" *is* well-received, not "aligned with what he doesn't have;"

13 for *it is* not that relief *is* for others, hard times *are* for you, but out of equality in the present time, your excess *is* for the deficiency of those *people*

14 so that also the excess of those *people* might become for your deficiency, in order that equality might happen.

15 *This is* just as it has been written *in Exodus 16:18*, "The *person who gathered* the big *amount* didn't get more *than two liters*, and the *person who gathered* the little *amount* didn't get less."

16 Generosity *be* to God, the *One* who gives the same concern on your behalf in Titus' heart

17 because he certainly accepted the encouragement, but being more concerned *than I expected*, he went out to you on his own.

18 We sent the brother together with him whose high praise *is* in the good news through all of the assemblies,
19 not only *that*, but who was also handpicked by the assemblies *to be* our traveling companion together with this generosity, the *generosity* that is served by us toward the magnificence of his Master and our eagerness.
20 As we are setting this up, no one should blame us in this abundance, the *abundance* served by us.
21 We plan for nice things, not only in the sight of the Master, but also in the sight of people.
22 Together with them we sent our brother whom we proved that he is concerned in many ways many times, but right now *he is* much more concerned with much confidence for you.
23 Whether *it is* my partner and co-worker for you on behalf of Titus or *it is* our brothers (missionaries of assemblies), *it is the* Anointed King's magnificence.
24 So display to them the display of your love and of our bragging on your behalf even to *the* face of the assemblies.

9

1 You see, certainly concerning the serving, the *one* for the sacred *people*, to me it is much more *than I need to do*, the "to be writing to you" *thing*;
2 for I have seen your eagerness that I bragged about on your behalf to Macedonians, "Achaia has been prepared since last year." And the passion from you provoked the majority *of them*.
3 But I sent the brothers so that our bragging, the *bragging* on your behalf, might not be emptied in this detail, so that just as I was saying, you might be *people* that have been prepared.
4 What if somehow, when Macedonians came together with me, they actually found you unprepared? We (so that I may not say you) would be ashamed in this undertaking of *our* bragging.
5 So I regarded *it* essential to encourage the brothers so that they might go on ahead to you and develop beforehand your previously proclaimed conferring of blessing for this to be ready in this way, as a conferring of blessing *from you* and not even as a desire for more.
6 *Remember* this: the *one* who seeds lightly, lightly will he also harvest, and the *one* who seeds based on a conferring of blessing, based on a conferring of blessing will he also harvest.
7 Each *person must give* just as he chooses in *his* heart beforehand, not from sadness or from an obligation. You see, God loves a giver who wants to provide a remedy.
8 God *is* able to overflow every *bit of* generosity to you so that in everything always having every *bit of* contentment, you may overflow in every good action.
9 *This is* just as it has been written *in Psalm 112:9*, "He scattered *it*. He gave to the underprivileged. His right way stays for the span of time."

10 The *One* who further supplies seed to the *one* who seeds and bread for dinner will supply and increase your batch of seeds. And He will grow the produce of your right way
11 in everything as you become wealthy for every *bit of* dedication, something that works on and completes thankfulness to God through us
12 because the serving of this public service is not only furnishing the deficiencies of the sacred *people*, but also overflowing through many thanks to God
13 through the proven track record of this serving, elevating God to a place of magnificence based on the compliance of your acknowledgment to the good news of the Anointed King, *based on* dedication of the sharing relationship for them and for all,
14 and *based on* their plea over you, yearning for you, because of the superior generosity of God on you.
15 Generosity *be* to God based on His indescribable free handout.

10

1 I myself, Paul, encourage you through the humility and politeness of the Anointed King (*I* who right in front of *your* face certainly *am* lowly among you, but being away from *you* I am courageous to you).
2 I plead the "being beside *you* not to be courageous" *thing* to the confidence that I am considering to dare on some of the *people* who consider us as walking around aligned with a physical body.
3 You see, walking around in a physical body, not aligned with a physical body, we serve in *God's* military;
4 for the weapons of our military service *are* not physical, but *they are* able with God for a takedown of forts:
5 taking down reasonings and every high thing raising itself up against the information of God, forcibly incarcerating every pattern of thinking into the obedience of the Anointed King,
6 and holding in readiness to retaliate for every noncompliance when your obedience is accomplished.
7 Do you look at the *things* right in front of *your* face? If anyone has been confident of himself to be *the* Anointed King's, he again must consider this out from himself, that just as he *is the* Anointed King's, so also *are* we *the* Anointed King's.
8 You see, even if I also bragged somewhat much more concerning our authority that the Master gave us for construction and not for your takedown, I won't be ashamed
9 so that it might not seem to you as *if* to be frightening you through the letters
10 because, "The letters," he declares, "certainly *are* heavy and strong, but the presence of the body *is* weak and the message *is a message* that has been treated as if it is nothing."
11 This type of *person* must consider this, that such as we are with the message through letters being away from *you*, this is how *we will* also *be* with *our* action as we are beside *you*.

12 You see, we don't dare to judge *ourselves* in or compare ourselves with some of the *people* who endorse themselves. But they, who measure themselves in themselves and compare themselves to themselves, don't understand.
13 We definitely won't brag of the *things* that have no measurement, but aligned with the measurement of the standard that the God of measurement divided out to us to reach even till you.
14 You see, *it is* not as *if*, not reaching to you, we overextend ourselves; for we already came even till you in the good news of the Anointed King,
15 not bragging of the *things* that have no measurement, in labors belonging to others, but having an anticipation of your growing trust to become great in you (according to our standard) to an overflow,
16 to share good news to the *places* beyond you, not to brag about the *things that are* ready in a standard belonging to others.
17 The person who brags must brag in *the* Master.
18 You see, that *person* endorsing himself is not approved, but whom the Master endorses *is*.

11

1 If only you were tolerating me a little in *this* distraction, but you actually do tolerate me.
2 You see, I am passionate about you with God's passion; for I arranged your marriage to one man: for a consecrated virgin to stand up next to the Anointed King.
3 But I am afraid that somehow as the snake completely fooled Eve with his slyness, so your patterns of thinking might be worsened away from the dedication, the *dedication* for the Anointed King.
4 You see, certainly if the *person* coming speaks publicly about another Jesus whom we did not speak publicly about, or you receive a different spirit that you did not receive or different good news that you did not accept, you were tolerating *it* nicely.
5 You see, I consider *myself* to have lacked nothing from the super missionaries.
6 Even if *I am* an unskilled person with the message, still *I am* not *unskilled* with the information, still in every *way we are people* who were shown to you in all *things*.
7 Or did I commit a sin putting myself down low so that you might be put up high (because I shared the good news of God with you for free)?
8 I pilfered other assemblies when I took wages toward the *task of* serving you.
9 And as I was beside *you* facing you and when I was lacking, I didn't freeload off anyone. You see, my deficiency the brothers who came out of Macedonia furnished. And in everything, I kept and will keep myself weightless to you.
10 A truth of *the* Anointed King in me is that this bragging won't be shut up in me in the slopes of Achaia.
11 Why? Because I don't love you? God knows.
12 But what I do, I will also do so that I might chop out the opportunity of the *people* wanting an opportunity, so that they might be found in what they brag about *to be* also just like us.

13 You see, these types of *people are* counterfeit missionaries, deceptive workers, refashioning themselves into missionaries of *the* Anointed King.
14 And *this is* not amazing. You see, the Opponent refashions himself into an angel of light.
15 So *it is* not a great *thing*, if his servants are also refashioned as servants of *the* right way, whose conclusion will be aligned with their actions.
16 Again I say, "It should not seem to anyone for me to be distracted." But even if *it* definitely *does*, accept me as a distracted *person* so that I might also brag about a little something.
17 What I speak, I don't speak regarding *the* Master, but as in a distraction in this undertaking of the bragging.
18 Since many *people* brag regarding the physical body, I will also brag.
19 You see, you gladly tolerate the distracted *people, you* who are focused;
20 for you tolerate if someone makes you a complete slave, if someone eats up *your food*, if someone takes *your things*, if someone raises up, if someone beats you in *the* face.
21 Aligned with no value, I talk as *if it were* that we were weak. But in whatever some dare *to be* (I say in distraction), I also dare *to be*.
22 Are they Hebrew-speaking *Jews*? I also *am*. Are they Israelis? I also *am*. Are they Abraham's seed? I also *am*.
23 Are they servants of *the* Anointed King? (I who have *the* wrong focus am speaking) I *am* above *that*: much more in *times of* labor, too often in wounds, much more in jails, many times in life-threatening situations.
24 Under Jewish *people*, five times I received forty *stripes* minus one.
25 Three times I was beaten with a stick. Once I was attacked with stones. Three times I was shipwrecked. A night and day, I have done in the deep *sea*,
26 many times in road travels, in dangers of rivers, in dangers of bandits, in dangers from family, in dangers from non-Jews, in dangers in *the* city, in dangers in *the* uninhabited place, in dangers in *the* sea, in dangers among counterfeit brothers,
27 in labor and hard work, many times in sleepless *nights*, in famine and thirst, in many times of going without food, in cold and nakedness.
28 Separate from the *things*, besides *and* outside of *these*, my tension, the *tension* daily, *is* the concern for all the assemblies.
29 Who is weak, and I am not weak? Who stumbles, and I am not inflamed?
30 If it is necessary to be bragging, I will brag about the *things* of my weakness.
31 (The God and Father of our Master Jesus, *the* Anointed King, knows, the *One* who is conferred with blessings for the spans of time, that I am not lying.)
32 In Damascus, the governor under Aretas the king was watching over the city of Damascenes wanting to arrest me,
33 and through a window I was lowered in a rope basket through the wall and escaped from his hands.

12

1 It is not advantageous to me, for sure, to be bragging. You see, I will come to sightings and uncoverings of *the* Master.

2 I know a person in *the* Anointed King fourteen years ago (whether in a body, I don't know, or outside of the body, I don't know, God knows) after this type of *person* was snatched up to *the* third heaven.
3 And I know this type of person (whether in a body or outside of the body, I don't know, God knows)
4 that he was snatched up into the paradise and heard inexpressible statements that a person *is* not allowed to speak.
5 On behalf of this type of *person* I will brag, but on my *own* behalf I won't brag except in my weaknesses.
6 You see, though I might want to brag, I won't be distracted; for I will state *the* truth. I am going easy on *you* that no one might consider *anything* to me above what he sees me *to be* or something he hears from me.
7 And with the superiority of the uncoverings (so that I may not be raised too far up), a spike to the physical body, an announcer of an opponent, was given to me so that it may slug me, so that I may not be raised too far up.
8 On behalf of this, three times I encouraged the Master so that it might stand off away from me,
9 and He has stated to me, "My generosity is enough for you. You see, My ability is finished in weakness." So I will most gladly rather brag in my weaknesses so that the ability of the Anointed King might be set up over me.
10 For this reason, I am delighted in weaknesses, in injuries, in obligations, in persecutions, in difficulties on behalf of *the* Anointed King. You see, when I am weak, at that time I am able.
11 I have become distracted bragging. You urged me. You see, I ought to be endorsed by you; for I lack nothing from the super missionaries, even though I am nothing.
12 Certainly the indicators of the missionary were worked on and completed in you in every *bit of* persistence *to do what is right*, in indicators, incredible things, and abilities.
13 You see, how is it that you were inferior above the rest *of the* assemblies, except that I myself did not freeload off you? As an act of generosity, forgive me this wrong.
14 Look, I have *myself* ready a third *time* to come to you, and I will not freeload off you. You see, I don't look for your *things*, but for you; for the children aren't obligated to be stockpiling *stuff* for the parents, but the parents for the children.
15 I will most gladly spend and be completely spent on behalf of your souls. Though even loving you much more, I am loved less.
16 It must be. I didn't press a heavy load down on you. But did I, being sly, take you with deception?
17 Any of *the people* that I have sent out to you, I didn't take advantage of you through them, did I?
18 I encouraged Titus, and I sent the brother out *on a mission* together with *him*. Titus didn't take any advantage of you, did he? Didn't we walk around in the same spirit, in the same footsteps?

19 All this time, does it seem to you that we are defending ourselves to you? We are speaking directly in the sight of God in *the* Anointed King. All *things*, loved *ones*, are on behalf of your construction.
20 You see, I am afraid that somehow when I come I might not find you such as I want *you to be* and I might be found by you such as you do not want *me to be*, that somehow *there will be* fighting, hostile passion, bursts of anger, contentions, bad comments, whispers, conceited attitudes, conflicts;
21 that when I come again, my God will put *me* down low before you and I will grieve for many of the *people* who have previously sinned and did not change their ways over what is not clean, sexual sin, and indulgent activity that they repeatedly did.

13

1 This *is the* third *time* I am coming to you. Based on *the* mouth of two and three witnesses, every statement will be established.
2 I have stated before and I am telling beforehand (as *I did* being beside *you* the second *time* and now being away from *you*). I am writing to the *people* who have previously sinned and to all the rest, "If I come into the *situation* again, I won't go easy on *you*"
3 since you look for proven track record of the Anointed King speaking in me, who is not weak to you, but has *His* ability in you.
4 You see, even if He was nailed to a cross from weakness, still He lives from God's ability; for even we also are weak in Him, but we will live together with Him from God's ability for you.
5 Trouble yourselves whether *or not* you are in the trust. Prove yourselves. Or do you yourselves not correctly understand that Jesus, *the* Anointed King, is in you, unless you are unapproved?
6 I anticipate that you will know that we are not unapproved.
7 I wish to God for you not to do anything bad, not so that we might shine as approved *people*, but so that you may do the nice *thing* but we may be as unapproved *people*.
8 You see, we are not capable of anything against the truth, but over with the truth.
9 You see, we are happy when we may be weak, but you may be competent. We also wish for this: your development.
10 Because of this, I am writing these *things* as I am away from *you*, so that as I am beside *you* I might not behave severely aligned with the authority that the Master gave to me for construction, and not for a takedown.
11 For *the* rest *of the time*, brothers, be happy. Be trained. Be encouraged. Focus on the same *thing*. Be peaceful, and the God of the love and peace will be with you.
12 Say hello to each other with a sacred friendly gesture.
13 All the sacred *people* say hello to you.
14 *May* the generosity of the Master Jesus, *the* Anointed King, the love of God, and the sharing of the Sacred Spirit *be* with all of you. Amen. [*This* second *letter* was written to Corinth from Philippi, Macedonia *and sent* through Titus and Luke.]

Galatians

1 *From:* Paul (a missionary not out from people, nor through a person, but through Jesus, *the* Anointed King, and *through* Father God, the *One* who got Him up from *the* dead)

2 and all the brothers together with me. To: the assemblies of Galatia.

3 Generosity to you and peace out from Father God and our Master Jesus, *the* Anointed King,

4 the *One* who gave Himself on behalf of our sins in order that He might take us out of the evil span of time that has stood here, aligned with what our God and Father wants,

5 to whom the magnificence *belongs* for the spans of time of the spans of time. Amen.

6 I am amazed that this is how quickly you are transferred away from the *One* who invited you in generosity (*the* Anointed King) to different good news,

7 that is not other *good news* except there are some *people* agitating you and wanting to alter the good news of the Anointed King.

8 But even if we or an angel from heaven should share good news with you contrary to what we shared with you, he must be doomed.

9 As we have stated before, even now I say again, "If anyone shares good news with you contrary to what you received in, he must be doomed."

10 You see, do I now persuade people or God? Or do I look to be doing what people would like? You see, if I were still doing what people would like, I would not be a slave of *the* Anointed King.

11 I am making the good news known to you, brothers, the *good news* that was shared by me, that it is not according to a person;

12 for I neither received it in from the side of a person, nor was taught *it*, but *I* got it through *the thing* uncovered *to me*, Jesus, *the* Anointed King.

13 You see, you heard of my behavior in the past in Judaism, that even more *than others* I was pursuing the assembly of God and damaging it,

14 and I was progressing in Judaism above many my own age in my family being a person with much more passion for my patrimonial traditions.

15 But when it seemed like a good idea to God (the *One* who isolated me from my mother's belly and invited *me* through His generosity)

16 to uncover His Son in me so that I may share the good news of Him among the non-Jews, I didn't consult right away with a physical body and blood.

17 Neither did I go up into Jerusalem to the missionaries before me. But I went off into Arabia and returned again into Damascus.

18 Following that, after three years, I went up into Jerusalem to visit Peter. And I stayed over for fifteen days with him.

19 But a different *one* of the missionaries I didn't see except James, the brother of the Master

20 (*the things* that I am writing to you, look in the sight of God that I am not lying).
21 Following that, I went to the slopes of Syria and Cilicia.
22 I was *a person* that no one was aware of by the face in the assemblies of Judea, the *assemblies* in *the* Anointed King.
23 There were *people* only hearing, "The *one* pursuing us in the past, now shares the good news of the trust that in the past he was damaging,"
24 and in me they were praising God's magnificence.

2

1 Following that through fourteen years, I walked up to Jerusalem again with Barnabas when we also took Titus along together with *us*.
2 I walked up regarding *the thing* uncovered *to me*. And I laid out to them the good news that I speak about publicly among the non-Jews, but privately to the *people* who seem *to be something*, that somehow I may not run or ran for a meaningless *cause*
3 (but neither was Titus, the Greek who was together with me, urged to be circumcised)
4 because of the undetected counterfeit brothers, some who quietly came in to spy out *and plot against* our freedom that we have in *the* Anointed King Jesus so that they might make us complete slaves,
5 to whom we didn't even for an hour give in with the compliance, so that the truth of the good news might stay through *it all* to you.
6 To be something from the *people* seeming *to be something*, whatever kind of *people* they were in the past, is not more substantial to me. God does not receive *the* appearance of a person. You see, the *people* seeming *to be something* imposed nothing on me.
7 But just the opposite, when they saw that I had been trusted with the good news of the uncircumcision, just as Peter *had been trusted with the good news* of the circumcision
8 (you see, the *One* who was active with Peter for *his* mission to the circumcision, was also active with me for the non-Jews),
9 and after knowing the generosity, the *generosity* that was given to me, James, Cephas *(Aramaic for Peter)*, and John (the *ones* seeming to be pillars) gave right *hands* of a sharing relationship to me and Barnabas so that we *are* for the non-Jews, but they for the circumcision;
10 only of the poor: that we should remember *them*; this same *thing* that I also made every effort to do.
11 But when Peter came to Antioch, I stood in opposition to him right in front of *his* face because it was *something* that had been known against *him*.
12 You see, before the *time* for certain *people* to come out from James, he was eating together with the non-Jews. But when they came, he was backing off and isolating himself, fearing the *people* from *the* circumcision.
13 And the rest *of the* Jewish *people* also faked *it* together with him in such a way that Barnabas also was led away together with their faked behavior.
14 But when I saw that they are not straight-footed toward the truth of the good news, I said to Peter in front of everyone, "If you, being Jewish, are living

non-Jewishly and not Jewishly, why do you urge the non-Jews to become Jews?"

15 We *are* Jewish by nature and not sinful *people* from *the* non-Jews,

16 who realize that a person is not made right from actions of *the* law, except through trust of Jesus, *the* Anointed King. And we trusted in *the* Anointed King Jesus so that we might be made right from trust of *the* Anointed King and not from actions of *the* law because from actions of *the* law every physical body will not be made right.

17 But if, as we were looking to be made right in *the* Anointed King, we ourselves were actually found *to be* sinful *people*, so what *would the* Anointed King *be*, a servant of sin? It could not happen.

18 You see, if I again build these *things* that I tore down, I myself stand together with a violator.

19 You see, I through *the* law died to *the* law so that I might live for God.

20 Together with *the* Anointed King I have been nailed to a cross. I no longer live, but *the* Anointed King lives in me. What I now live in a physical body, I live in trust, the *trust* of the Son of God, the *One* who loved me and turned Himself in on my behalf.

21 I don't invalidate the generosity of God. You see, if *the* right way *is* through *the* law, clearly *the* Anointed King died for nothing.

3

1 O unobservant Galatians, who tricked you to not believe the truth (to whom, right in front of *your* eyes, Jesus, *the* Anointed King, was openly written about among you, that He had been nailed to a cross)?

2 I only want to learn this out of you, did you receive the Spirit from actions of *the* law or from what was heard of trust?

3 This is how you are unobservant. After beginning in on *it* with *the* Spirit, are you now finishing up with *the* physical body?

4 Did you suffer so many *things* for no reason, if *it* definitely even *is* for no reason?

5 So the *One* further supplying the Spirit to you and active with abilities among you, *is He* from actions of *the* law or from what is heard of trust?

6 Just as, "Abraham trusted God, and it was considered to him for *the* right way" *(Genesis 15:6)*,

7 you clearly know that the *people* from trust, these are sons of Abraham.

8 When the *Old Testament* writing saw beforehand that God makes the non-Jews right from trust, it shared good news with Abraham beforehand, "All the non-Jews will be conferred with blessings in you" *(Genesis 22:18)*.

9 In such a way, the *people* from trust are conferred with blessings together with trusting Abraham.

10 You see, as many as are from actions of *the* law are under a curse; for it has been written *in Deuteronomy 27:26*, "Everyone *is* cursed who does not stay in all the *things* that have been written in the scroll of the law, of the 'to do them' kind."

11 That no one is made right in *the* law beside God, *it is* obvious, because, "The *person* who does what is right will live from trust" *(Habakkuk 2:4)*.

12 The law is not from trust, but "the person who does these *things* will live in them."

13 *The* Anointed King purchased us from the curse of the law after becoming a curse on our behalf. You see, it has been written *in Deuteronomy 21:23,* "Everyone who hangs on a wooden cross is cursed,"

14 so that Abraham's conferring of blessing might become for the non-Jews in *the* Anointed King Jesus, so that we might receive the promise of the Spirit through the trust.

15 Brothers, in the same manner, a person's deal (I am talking regarding a person) that has been made official, no one invalidates *it* or adds to *it.*

16 To Abraham the promises were stated and to his seed. He does not say, "and to the seeds," as *if* based on many, but as *if* based on one, "and to your seed," who is *the* Anointed King.

17 I am saying this: a deal (that has been made official beforehand by God for *the* Anointed King), the law (that has happened after four hundred and thirty years) does not nullify for the "to make the promise useless" *part.*

18 You see, if the inheritance is from *the* law, *it is* no longer from a promise. But to Abraham through a promise, God, in an act of generosity, has given *the inheritance.*

19 So why *does* the law *exist*? Thanks to the violations. It was added till *a time* that the seed would come, to whom *(Abraham),* it has been promised after being specifically arranged through angels in *the* hand of a middleman.

20 The middleman is not *a middleman* of one. But God is one.

21 So *is* the law against the promises of God? It could not happen. You see, if the law was given that is able to give life, the right way really would have been from *the* law.

22 But the *Old Testament* writing closed everything up under sin, so that the promise from trust of Jesus, *the* Anointed King, might be given to the *people* trusting.

23 Before the *time* for the trust to come, we were being watched over by *the* law, having been closed up into the trust that is going to be uncovered.

24 In such a way, the law has become our babysitter for *the* Anointed King so that from trust we might be made right.

25 But when the trust comes, we are no longer under a babysitter.

26 You see, you are all sons of God through the trust in *the* Anointed King Jesus;

27 for as many of you as were submerged into *the* Anointed King put on *the* Anointed King.

28 There is not Jewish, nor Greek. There is not slave, nor free. There is not male and female. You see, you all are one in *the* Anointed King Jesus.

29 If you *are the* Anointed King's, clearly you are Abraham's seed and inheritors aligned with a promise.

4

1 I say, over as much time as the inheritor is an infant, he is nothing more substantial than a slave though he is master of *them* all.

2 But he is under administrators and managers till the predetermined time of the father.

3 This is how we also, when we were infants, were *people* who had been enslaved under the conventional practices of the world.
4 But when the fullness of the time came, God sent off His Son, who became from a woman, who became under *the* law,
5 so that He might purchase the *people* under *the* law from *the conventional practices* so that we might fully receive the adoption.
6 Because you are sons, God sent off the Spirit of His Son into your hearts, yelling, "Daddy, the Father!"
7 In such a way, you are no longer a slave, but a son. If *you are* a son, *you are* also an inheritor of God through *the* Anointed King.
8 But at that time, when you certainly didn't know God, you were slaves to the *things* that by nature are not gods.
9 Now, after knowing God, rather, being known by God, how are you turning back again to the weak and poor conventional practices that you want to be slaves to all over again?
10 You closely watch days, months, certain times, and years.
11 I am afraid *when it comes to* you that somehow I have labored for you for no reason.
12 Become as me because I also *am* as you, brothers. I plead with you. You didn't harm me in any way.
13 You realize that because of a weakness of *my* physical body, I shared good news with you the prior *time*,
14 and you didn't treat my trouble in my physical body as a bad thing, nor despise *it*, but as an angel of God, you accepted me as *the* Anointed King Jesus.
15 So what was your blessedness? You see, I am a witness to you that, if possible, after plucking out your eyes, you would have given *them* to me.
16 In such a way, have I become your enemy, being true to you?
17 They are passionate about you, not nicely. But they want to exclude you *from everything else* so that you may be passionate about them.
18 *It is* nice to always be passionate in a nice *way* and not only during the *time* for me to be beside *you* facing you.
19 My little children (with whom I am in labor again till *the time* that *the* Anointed King will be formed in you),
20 I was wanting to be beside *you* facing you now and to change my voice because I am not sure what to think about you.
21 Tell me, the *people* wanting to be under the law, don't you hear the law?
22 You see, it has been written *in Genesis 16:3 and 21:2* that Abraham had two sons: one from the servant girl and one from the free *woman*.
23 But the *one* from the servant girl certainly has been born aligned with a physical body, but the *one* from the free *woman*, through the promise —
24 some *things* that are having another meaning. You see, these are the two deals. One *is* certainly out of Mount Sinai giving birth to slavery, someone who is Hagar.
25 Hagar is Mount Sinai in Arabia. She is marching together now in step with Jerusalem, but she is a slave with her children.

26 The *one* from above is free Jerusalem, someone who is a mother of us all.
27 You see, it has been written *in Isaiah 54:1*, "Celebrate, infertile woman, the *one* not delivering *a baby*! Burst out and shout, the *woman* not in labor, because *there are* many children of the uninhabited *place*, more than *the children* of the *woman* who has the husband."
28 We, brothers, aligned with Isaac, are children of promise.
29 But even as *it was* at that time (the *one* who was born aligned with a physical body was persecuting the *one* aligned with *the* Spirit), so also *is it* now.
30 But what does the *Old Testament* writing say *in Genesis 21:10*? "Throw out the servant girl and her son. You see, the son of the servant girl won't in any way inherit with the son of the free *woman*."
31 Clearly, brothers, we are not children of a servant girl, but of the free *woman*.

5

1 So stand for the freedom that *the* Anointed King freed us for, and don't be held in again by a crossbeam of slavery.
2 Look, I, Paul, tell you that if you should be circumcised, *the* Anointed King will in no way benefit you.
3 Again, I am a witness to every person being circumcised that he is a person who owes to do the whole law.
4 You were rendered exempt away from the Anointed King, any who are made right in *the* law. You fell from the generosity.
5 You see, we (with a spirit from trust) patiently wait for *the* good anticipation of *the* right way;
6 for in *the* Anointed King Jesus, neither circumcision has strength for anything, nor uncircumcision, but *what has strength is* trust that is active through love.
7 You were running nicely. Who chopped you up *for you* to not be persuaded of the truth?
8 The persuasion *is* not from the *One* who invited you.
9 A little yeast causes the whole batch to rise.
10 I have been persuaded for you in *the* Master, that you will focus on nothing else. The *one* agitating you will haul the judgment, whoever he may be.
11 I, brothers, if I still speak publicly *for* circumcision, why am I still pursued? Clearly the obstacle of the cross has been rendered useless.
12 If only the *people* upsetting you will also chop themselves off *from you*.
13 You see, you were invited based on freedom, brothers, only not the freedom for an opportunity to the physical body, but through the love be slaves to each other;
14 for the entire law is accomplished in one message, in the "you will love the *person* near you as yourself" *message*.
15 If you bite and eat up each other, look out *that* you aren't consumed by each other.
16 I say, "Walk around in *the* Spirit, and you will not in any way finish *the* desire of *the* physical body."

17 You see, the physical body desires *what is* against the Spirit, but the Spirit *what is* against the physical body. These lie in opposition to each other so that whatever you may want, these you don't do.
18 If you are led by *the* Spirit, you are not under *the* law.
19 The actions of the physical body are shown, some that are cheating on a spouse, sexual sin, *desire* that is not clean, indulgent activity,
20 idol worship, drug abuse, hostile relationships, fightings, hostile passions, bursts of anger, contentions, factions, splinter groups,
21 envies, murders, bouts of drunkenness, wild parties, and the *things* like these that I am telling you beforehand, just as I also already said, that the *people* constantly doing these types of *things* will not inherit God's monarchy.
22 But the fruit of the Spirit is love, happiness, peace, patience, kindness, goodness, trust,
23 humility, restraint. Against these types of *things*, there is no law.
24 The *people* of the Anointed King nailed the physical body to a cross with the hardships and the desires.
25 If we live with *the* Spirit, with *the* Spirit also we should march in step.
26 We should not become *people* with delusions of grandeur, hassling each other, envying each other.

1 Brothers, if a person is also taken beforehand in a certain infraction, you, the spiritual *ones*, develop this type of *person* in a spirit of humility keeping an eye out for yourself (and you won't experience trouble).
2 Haul the heavy weights of each other, and in this way fully accomplish the law of the Anointed King.
3 You see, if someone seems to be something who is nothing, he is seducing himself.
4 Each *person* must check *and correct* his *own* work, and then for himself alone he will have the bragging and not for the different *person*.
5 You see, each *person* will haul *his* own load.
6 The *person* whom the message is echoed down to must share in all *kinds of* good *things* with the *person* echoing *it* down.
7 Don't be misled. God is not made into a fool. You see, whatever a person seeds, this he will also harvest,
8 because the *person* seeding into his *own* physical body, from the physical body he will harvest deterioration, but the *person* seeding into the Spirit, from the Spirit he will harvest life that spans *all* time.
9 We should not get discouraged doing the nice *thing*. You see, in *its* own time, we will harvest, not giving up.
10 So clearly, as we have time, we should work *on* the good *thing* toward everyone, but especially toward the *people* living in the house of the trust.
11 Look at how big *the* alphabetic characters *are that* I wrote to you with my hand.
12 These *people*, as many as want to look good in *the* physical body, urge you to be circumcised just so that they might not be persecuted for the cross of the Anointed King.

13 You see, neither do the circumcised *people* observe *the* law themselves, but they want you to be circumcised so that they might brag about your physical body.

14 It could not happen to me, *for me* to be bragging except about the cross of our Master Jesus, *the* Anointed King, through whom to me *the* world has been nailed to a cross, and I to the world.

15 You see, in *the* Anointed King Jesus, neither circumcision has strength for anything, nor uncircumcision, but *what has strength is* a new creation.

16 And as many as will march in step with this standard, peace *is* on them, and forgiving kindness *is* also on God's Israel.

17 For the rest *of the time*, no one must bother me. You see, I haul the branding scars of the Master Jesus in my body.

18 *May* the generosity of our Master Jesus, *the* Anointed King, *be* with your spirit, brothers. Amen. [Written to Galatia from Rome]

Ephesians

1

1 *From:* Paul, a missionary of Jesus, *the* Anointed King, through what God wants. To: The sacred *people* (the *ones* who are in Ephesus) and trusting *people* in *the* Anointed King Jesus.
2 Generosity to you and peace out from God, our Father, and Master Jesus, *the* Anointed King.
3 The God and Father of our Master Jesus, *the* Anointed King, *is* conferred with blessings, the *One* who conferred blessings on us in every spiritual conferring of blessings in the heavenly *regions* in *the* Anointed King,
4 just as He selected us in Him before *the* founding of *the* world for us to be sacred and unblemished directly in His sight, in love
5 after designating us beforehand for an adoption to Him through Jesus, the Anointed King, aligned with the good notion of what He wanted
6 for high praise of magnificence of His generosity in which He showed us generosity in the *One* who had been loved,
7 in whom we have the paid release through His blood, the forgiveness of the infractions, according to the wealth of His generosity
8 that overflowed into us in every insight and focus,
9 after making the secret known to us of what He wants aligned with His good notion that He put beforehand in Him,
10 for *the* management of the fullness of the appointed times to sum all the *things* up in the Anointed King: both the *things* in the heavens and the *things* on the earth.
11 In Him, in whom we also were assigned an inheritance after being designated beforehand aligned with *the* purpose of the *One* who is active with all *things*, aligned with the intention of what He wants,
12 for the "for us to be for high praise of His magnificence" *part*, the *people* who have anticipated good in the Anointed King beforehand,
13 in whom you also after hearing the message of the truth, the good news of your rescue, in whom after also trusting, you *all* were sealed by the Spirit of the promise, the Sacred *Spirit*,
14 who is a down payment of our inheritance for a paid release of the acquisition, for high praise of His magnificence.
15 Because of this, when I also heard of the trust of each of you in the Master Jesus and of the love, the *love* for all of the sacred *people*,
16 I didn't stop being thankful for you, making a mention of you over my prayers
17 that the God of our Master Jesus, *the* Anointed King, the Father of the magnificence, might give you a spirit of insight and of an uncovering in a correct understanding of Him,
18 the eyes of your mind having been lit up, for the "for you to have seen" *part*, what is the anticipation of His invitation, what *is* the wealth of the magnificence of His inheritance in the sacred *people*,

19 and what *is* the superior magnitude of His ability for us, the *people* who trust aligned with the influence of the power of His strength,
20 with which He was active in the Anointed King when He got Him up from the dead. And He seated *Him* in His right *side* in the heavenly *regions*
21 over *and* above every head ruler, authority, ability, government, and every name that is named, not only in this span of time, but also in the *span of time* that is going *to come*.
22 And He placed all *things* under His feet. And He gave Him (*the* head over everything) to the assembly
23 (something that is His body, the fullness of the *One* who fills all in all);

2

1 even you, being dead with the infractions and the sins,
2 in which in the past, you walked around aligned with the span of time of this world, aligned with the head of the authority of the air (the spirit, the *one* that is now active in the sons of the unbelief),
3 among whom we all also were messed up in the past, in the desires of our physical body, doing the *things* that the physical body and the mind wanted. And we were children of punishment by nature, even as the rest.
4 But God (being wealthy in forgiving kindness because of His great love that He loved us with)
5 brought even us (being dead with the infractions) to life together with the Anointed King. You are *people* who have been rescued by generosity.
6 And He got *us* up together and seated *us* together in the heavenly *regions* in *the* Anointed King Jesus
7 so that He might display in the spans of time, the upcoming *ones*, the superior wealth of His generosity in kindness on us in *the* Anointed King Jesus.
8 You see, with the generosity you are *people* who have been rescued through trust. And this *is* not from among you. *It is* the contribution of God,
9 not from actions, so that no one would brag.
10 You see, we are what He made, who were created in *the* Anointed King Jesus based on good actions that God had ready beforehand so that we might walk around in them.
11 For this reason, remember that you in the past *were* non-Jews in *the* physical body, the *people* who are called Uncircumcision by what is called Circumcision (handmade in *the* physical body),
12 because in that time you were without *the* Anointed King, having been alienated from the citizenship of Israel and strangers to the deals of the promise having no anticipation *of good*, and godless in the world.
13 But right now, in *the* Anointed King Jesus, you, the *people* who were a long way away in the past, became near in the blood of the Anointed King.
14 You see, He is our peace, the *One* who made the both of *them* one and broke down the partition of the barrier wall,
15 the hostile relationship, in His physical body after making the law of the demands in rules useless so that He might create the two in Himself into one new person, making peace,

16 and He might completely restore the both of *them* in one body to God through the cross after killing the hostile relationship in it.
17 And after coming, He shared the good news of peace to you, the *people* a long way away and the *people* near,
18 because through Him we have the access (the both in one Spirit) to the Father.
19 So clearly you are no longer strangers and foreign residents, but co-citizens of the sacred *people* and *people* living in God's house
20 after being built on the foundation of the missionaries and preachers, *the* primary corner of it being Jesus, *the* Anointed King,
21 in whom the entire building linked together grows into a sacred temple in *the* Master,
22 in whom you also are built together into a residence of God in *the* Spirit.

1 Thanks to this, I, Paul, *am* the prisoner of the Anointed King Jesus on behalf of you, the non-Jews,
2 if you definitely heard *about* the management of the generosity of God, the *generosity* that was given to me for you,
3 that according to *the thing* uncovered *to me* He made the secret known to me, just as I wrote about previously in a little *message*,
4 to which you are able by reading to be aware of my understanding in the secret of the Anointed King,
5 that in different generations was not made known to the sons of the people, as it is now uncovered to His sacred missionaries and preachers in *the* Spirit,
6 for the non-Jews to be inheritors together, a body together, and teammates together of the promise in *the* Anointed King Jesus through the good news,
7 of which I became a servant aligned with the free handout of the generosity of God, the *free handout* that was given to me aligned with the influence of His ability.
8 To me (the smaller smallest *one* of all sacred *people*) this generosity was given to share with the non-Jews the good news of the impossible-to-track wealth of the Anointed King
9 and to light up for everyone what is the sharing relationship of the secret, the *one* that has been hid away from the spans of time in God, the *One* who created everything
10 so that it might be made known now to the head rulers and the authorities in the heavenly *regions* through the assembly, the multifaceted insight of God,
11 aligned with a purpose of the spans of time that He made in *the* Anointed King Jesus, our Master,
12 in whom we have the clear public statement and the access in confidence through the trust of Him.
13 For this reason, I am asking *you* not to be getting discouraged in my hard times on your behalf, something that is your magnificence.
14 Thanks to this, I bend my knees down to the Father of our Master Jesus, *the* Anointed King
15 (from whom every family tree in heaven and on earth is named),

16 so that He might give to you aligned with the wealth of His magnificence in ability to gain power through His Spirit for the inner person,
17 for the Anointed King to live in your hearts through the trust, having been rooted and having a foundation laid in love,
18 so that you might be strong enough to take down together with all the sacred *people* what *is* the width, length, depth, and height,
19 and to know the love of the Anointed King that is superior to the knowledge, so that you might be filled to all the fullness of God.
20 To the *One* who is able above everything to do even much more of *things* that we ask for or are aware of aligned with the ability, the *ability* that is active in us,
21 to Him *belongs* the magnificence in the assembly in *the* Anointed King Jesus for all the generations of the span of time of the spans of time. Amen.

4

1 So I, the prisoner in *the* Master, encourage you to walk around in a manner deserving of the invitation that you were invited with,
2 with every *bit of* lowly focus and humility, with patience, tolerating each other in love,
3 making every effort to be keeping the oneness of the Spirit in the bond of the peace:
4 one body and one spirit, just as also you were invited in one anticipation of your invitation,
5 one Master, one trust, one submersion,
6 one God and Father of everyone, the *One* over everyone, through everyone, and in you all.
7 To each one of us was given the generosity aligned with the amount of the free handout of the Anointed King.
8 For this reason, it says *in Psalm 68:18*, "When He stepped up into a high position, He incarcerated incarceration and gave presents to the people."
9 The "He stepped up" *part*, what is *it* if *it is* not that He also stepped down first into the lower parts of the earth?
10 The *One* who Himself stepped down is also the *One* who stepped up, over *and* above all of the heavens so that He might accomplish all *things*.
11 And He Himself gave not only the missionaries, but the preachers, but the sharers of good news, but the shepherds and teachers
12 toward the developing of the sacred *people*, for a work of serving, for construction of the body of the Anointed King,
13 up to *the point when* we all will make it to the oneness of the trust and the correct understanding of the Son of God, to a complete man, to a measurement of size of the fullness of the Anointed King,
14 so that we may no longer be infants pushed back and forth and carried around by every wind of the instruction, in the rigged game of the people, in slyness toward the scheme of the misleading lie,
15 but, being true, in love we might grow everything into Him, who is the head, the Anointed King,
16 from whom, as the entire body is linked together and pulled together through every connection of the supply aligned with influence in an amount

of each one, a part, it makes the growth of the body for construction of itself in love.

17 So I say this (and I am a witness in *the* Master) for you not to be walking around anymore just as the rest *of the* non-Jews also walk around, in *the* futileness of their way of thinking,

18 being *people* who have been made dark in the mind, who have been alienated from God's life because of *their* lack of awareness, the *lack of awareness* that is in them because of the stone hardness of their heart,

19 some who, having stopped feeling pain, gave themselves over to the indulgent activity for work of all of what is not clean in a desire for more.

20 But this is not how you learned the Anointed King.

21 If you definitely heard Him and were taught in Him, just as truth is in Jesus,

22 *it is important* for you to put away, regarding the prior behavior, the former person, the *one* who is worsened aligned with the desires of the fraud,

23 but to be rejuvenated with the spirit of your way of thinking

24 and to put on the new person, the *one* who was created aligned with God in *the* right way and holiness of the truth.

25 For this reason, after putting away the lie, each of you must speak truth with the *person* near him because we are body parts of each other.

26 Be enraged, and don't sin. The sun must not go down on your fit of rage.

27 Neither give a place to the Accuser.

28 The *person* stealing must not steal anymore. Instead he must labor, working what is good with *his* hands so that he may have *something* to be giving out to the *person* who has a need.

29 Every defective message must not travel out from your mouth. But if something *is* good toward construction of the need, *say it* so that it might give generosity to the *people* hearing *it*.

30 And don't make the Spirit sad, the Sacred *Spirit* of God, in whom you were sealed to *the* day of *the* paid release.

31 Every *bit of* bitterness, anger, rage, yelling, and an insult must be taken away from you together with all badness.

32 Become kind to each other, goodhearted, forgiving each other as an act of generosity, just as God also in *the* Anointed King forgave you as an act of generosity.

5

1 So become imitators of God as loved children

2 and walk around in love, just as the Anointed King also loved us and turned Himself in on our behalf *to be* an offering and sacrifice to God for an aroma of a sweet fragrance.

3 Sexual sin and all of what is not clean or a desire for more must not be named among you either, just as it is *what is* appropriate for sacred *people*,

4 and shameful behavior and foolish talk or a snide remark, the *things* that don't meet the high standards, but instead thankfulness.

5 You see, you are *people* knowing this, that every person who commits sexual sin, or person who is not clean, or person who desires more (who an idol

worshiper is) does not have an inheritance in the monarchy of the Anointed King and God.
6 No one must fool you with empty words. You see, because of these *things*, the punishment of God comes on the sons of the unbelief.
7 So don't become teammates together with them.
8 You see, you once were darkness, but now *you are* light in *the* Master. Walk around as children of light
9 (for the fruit of the Spirit *is* in all goodness, *the* right way, and truth),
10 as you prove what is well-liked by the Master.
11 And don't share together in the fruitless actions of the darkness. But instead also reprimand *them*.
12 You see, the *things* becoming hidden by them are shameful to even be saying.
13 All things that are reprimanded are shown under the light. You see, everything that is shown is light.
14 For this reason, it says, "Get up, the *one* who sleeps, and come back to life from the dead; and the Anointed King will be a light over you."
15 So look how you specifically walk around, not as *people* who don't have insight, but as insightful *people*,
16 as you buy up the time because the days are evil.
17 Because of this, don't become distracted, but *become people* who understand what the Master wants.
18 And don't be drunk with wine (in which it is recklessness). But be filled in *the* Spirit,
19 speaking to yourselves in psalms, praise songs, and spiritual songs, singing and reciting psalms in your heart to the Master,
20 always being thankful for everything in *the* name of our Master Jesus, *the* Anointed King, to the God and Father,
21 being placed under each other in fear of God.
22 The Wives — Place yourselves under *your* own husbands as *under* the Master
23 because the husband is head of the wife as the Anointed King *is* also head of the assembly and He *is* a rescuer of the body.
24 But even as the assembly is placed under the Anointed King, so also the wives *under their* own husbands in everything.
25 The Husbands — Love your *own* wives, just as the Anointed King also loved the assembly and turned Himself in on its behalf
26 so that He might make it sacred after cleaning *it* with the bath of the water in a statement,
27 so that He might offer to Himself a magnificent *bride*, the assembly, not having a stain, or a wrinkle, or any of these types of *things*, but that it may be sacred and unblemished.
28 This is how the husbands are obligated to be loving their *own* wives as their *own* bodies. The *husband* loving his *own* wife loves himself.
29 You see, no one ever hates his *own* physical body, but he fully nurtures and keeps it warm, just as the Master also *does with* the assembly

30 because we are body parts of His body from His physical body and from His bones.
31 For this, a person will leave his father and mother down *there*, be stuck like glue to his wife, and the two will be in one physical body.
32 This secret is great, but I am talking in reference to *the* Anointed King and in reference to the assembly.
33 More importantly, you also, the *husbands*, *one* by one, must each love your *own* wife like this, as yourself, but the wife, that she should fear the husband.

6

1 The Children — Obey your parents in *the* Master. You see, this is right.
2 Value your father and mother, a certain *demand* that is *the* first demand with a promise:
3 that it might become well with you and you will be on the earth for a long time.
4 And the Fathers — Don't incite rage in your children, but fully nurture them in *the* Master's discipline and correction.
5 The Slaves — Obey *your* masters regarding *the* physical body with fear and trembling in dedication of your heart as to the Anointed King,
6 not aligned with eye-slavery, as people pleasers, but as slaves of the Anointed King, doing what God wants from a soul,
7 being a slave with a good attitude, as to the Master and not to people,
8 realizing that whatever good each person did, he will retrieve this from the side of the Master, whether *he is a* slave or free.
9 And the Masters — Do the same *things* toward them, easing up on the threat, realizing that your *own* Master also is in heavens and there is no being swayed by appearances beside Him.
10 For the rest *of the time*, my brothers, become competent in *the* Master and in the power of His strength.
11 Put on the full body armor of God with the *intent* for you to be able to stand facing the Accuser's schemes
12 because the wrestling match for us is not facing blood and a physical body, but facing the head rulers, facing the authorities, facing the global powers of the darkness of this span of time, facing the spiritual *elements* of the evilness in the heavenly *regions*.
13 Because of this, take up the full body armor of God so that you might be able to stand in opposition to *them* in the day, the evil *day*, even after working on and completing absolutely everything to stand.
14 So stand after putting a sash around your waist in truth, putting on the armored vest of the right way,
15 and tying *sole pads* on under the feet in readiness of the good news of the peace,
16 on everything, after taking up the shield of the trust, with which you will be able to extinguish all the arrows of the evil *one* that have been flaming.
17 And accept the head protection of the rescue *process* and the dagger of the Spirit that is God's statement,

18 through every prayer and plea praying in every right time in *the* spirit, and for this same *reason* not going to sleep in every *bit of* close involvement and plea concerning all the sacred *people*
19 and on my behalf that a message might be given to me in *the* opening of my mouth in a clear public statement to make known the secret of the good news
20 (on behalf of which I am an older man in chains) so that in it I might make clear public statements as it is necessary for me to speak.
21 So that you also may realize the *things* regarding me, what I constantly do, Tychicus (the loved brother and reliable servant in *the* Master) will make everything known to you,
22 whom I sent to you for this same *reason*, so that you might know the *things* about us and he might encourage your hearts.
23 Peace to the brothers and love with trust out from Father God and *the* Master Jesus, *the* Anointed King.
24 *May* the generosity *be* with all of the *people* who love our Master Jesus, *the* Anointed King, in non-deterioration. [Written to Ephesian *people* from Rome *and sent* through Tychicus]

Philippians

1

1 *From*: Paul and Timothy, slaves of Jesus, *the* Anointed King. To: All of the sacred *people* in *the* Anointed King Jesus, the *ones* who are in Philippi together with supervisors and servants.
2 Generosity to you and peace out from God, our Father, and Master Jesus, *the* Anointed King.
3 I am thankful to my God on every mention of you
4 always in every plea of mine over you all, making the plea with happiness
5 based on your sharing in the good news from *the* first day till the present,
6 having been confident of this very *thing*, that the *One* who began in on a good work in you will finish *it* up till *the* day of Jesus, *the* Anointed King.
7 Just as it is right for me to be focusing on this over you all because of the *fact* for me to be having you in *my* heart, both in my restraints and *in* the defense and authentication of the good news, since you all are sharers together of my generosity.
8 You see, God is my witness how I yearn for you all in *the* sympathy of Jesus, *the* Anointed King.
9 And I pray this, that your love may overflow yet more and more in correct understanding and all comprehension,
10 for the "for you to be approving the *things* that are more substantial" *part*, so that you may be genuine and not offensive for *the* day of *the* Anointed King,
11 having been filled with fruits of *the* right way, the *fruits* through Jesus, *the* Anointed King, for God's magnificence and high praise.
12 I intend for you to be knowing, brothers, that the *things* regarding me have instead come for *the* progress of the good news,
13 in such a way for my restraints to become shown *as being* in *the* Anointed King in the whole Roman palace and to all the rest.
14 And the majority of the brothers in *the* Master have been confident with my restraints to be much more daring to be speaking the message fearlessly.
15 Some also certainly speak publicly about the Anointed King because of envy and fighting, but some actually because of a good notion.
16 The *people* from contention certainly proclaim the Anointed King in a disingenuous way, supposing to be bringing up hard times to my restraints,
17 but the *people* from love *do it* realizing that I am lying *here* for *the* defense of the good news.
18 You see, more importantly, what *is important*? In every way, whether for a sham or for truth, *the* Anointed King is proclaimed and I am happy in this, yes, and will be happy;
19 for I realize that this will step out to me for a rescue through your plea and *the* supply of the Spirit of Jesus, *the* Anointed King,
20 aligned with my eager expectation and anticipation that in nothing I will be ashamed, but in every clear public statement, as always and now, *the* Anointed King will be made great in my body, whether through life or through death.

21 You see, to me, the "to be living" *thing is the* Anointed King and the "to die" *thing is* gain.
22 But if *it is* the "to be living" *thing* (in *the* physical body), this to me *is* fruit of work. And what will I choose? I am not making *that* known.
23 You see, I am constrained from the two, having the desire for the "to be released and to be together with *the* Anointed King" *part* (*it is* even much better),
24 but the "to be staying over in the physical body" *part is* more essential because of you.
25 And having been confident of this, I realize that I will stay and continue together with you all for your progress and happiness in the trust
26 so that your bragging may overflow in *the* Anointed King Jesus in me through my presence again to you.
27 Be law-abiding citizens only in a manner deserving of the good news of the Anointed King so that whether coming and seeing you or being away from *you*, I might hear the *things* about you: that you stand in one spirit, one soul, competing together as a team for the trust of the good news
28 and not spooked in anything by the *people* lying in opposition: something that certainly is a display of ruin to them, but of a rescue to you, and this out from God
29 because the *good news* was given as an act of generosity to you on behalf of *the* Anointed King, not only the "to be trusting in Him" *part*, but also the "to be suffering on His behalf" *part*,
30 having the same struggle such as you saw in me and now hear *to be* in me.

2

1 So if *there is* any encouragement in *the* Anointed King, if any comfort of love, if any sharing of *the* Spirit, if any sympathy and compassion,
2 fill up my happiness that you may focus on the same *thing*, united souls having the same love, focusing on the one *thing*,
3 nothing aligned with contention or a delusion of grandeur, but with the lowly focus as you regard each other as having a higher position than yourselves.
4 Each *of you* must not keep an eye out for the *things* of your *own*, but each also for the *things* of different *people*.
5 You see, this must be focused on in you: what *is* also in *the* Anointed King Jesus,
6 who being in *the* form of God, did not regard the "to be equal with God" *thing* as something that must be tightly held on to.
7 But He emptied Himself, after taking *on the* form of a slave when He became in *the* likeness of people.
8 And after being found in an entity as a person, He put Himself down low when He became obedient up to death, a cross' death.
9 For this reason, God also put Him up high and in an act of generosity gave Him the name over every name,
10 so that in the name of Jesus every knee would bend down (of heavenly *beings*, of earthly *beings*, and of underground *beings*)

11 and every tongue would acknowledge out loud that *the* Master *is* Jesus, *the* Anointed King, for *the* magnificence of Father God.
12 In such a way, my loved *ones*, just as you always obeyed, not only as in my presence, but now much more in my absence, with fear and trembling work on and complete your *own* rescue.
13 You see, God is the *One* who is active among you, both the "to be wanting" part and the "to be active" *part* on behalf of the good notion.
14 Do everything without grumblings and questions
15 so that you might become faultless and unpolluted, children of God unblamed in *the* middle of a generation, crooked and that has been twisted, among whom you appear as light sources in *the* world,
16 fixing *your* attention on *the* message of life (for bragging to me in *the* day of *the* Anointed King that I didn't run for a meaningless *cause*, nor labor for a meaningless *cause*).
17 But if my blood is also poured out as an offering on the sacrifice and public service of your trust, I am happy. And I am happy together with you all.
18 You also must be happy for the same *thing*. And be happy together with me.
19 I anticipate in Master Jesus to send Timothy to you soon so that I also may have a good soul when I know the *things* about you.
20 You see, I have no one with an equal soul, someone who will really worry about the *things* concerning you;
21 for the *people* all look for their *own things*, not the *things* of the Anointed King Jesus.
22 You know the proven track record of him, that, as a child to a father, together with me, he was a slave for the good news.
23 So I certainly anticipate to send this *person* immediately, as *soon as* I might look away from the *things* concerning me.
24 I have been confident in *the* Master that I myself also will come soon.
25 I regard *it* essential to send to you Epaphroditus (my brother, co-worker, and fellow soldier, but your missionary and public servant of my need)
26 since, for sure, he was yearning for you all and heavyhearted because you heard that he was weak
27 (you see, he actually was weak, near to *and* beside death, but God showed forgiving kindness to him, not only to him, but also to me, so that I would not have sadness on sadness).
28 So I more aggressively sent him so that when you see him again you might be happy, and I may not be as sad.
29 So accept him in with every *bit of* happiness in *the* Master and hold these types of *people* as valued
30 because he was near up to *the point of* death because of the work of the Anointed King when he shrugged off *his* soul so that he might fill up your deficiency, the public service to me.

1 For the rest *of the time*, my brothers, be happy in *the* Master. To be writing the same *things* to you *is* certainly not lazy of me, but certain for you.

2 Look out for the dogs. Look out for the bad workers. Look out for the mutilators.
3 You see, we are the circumcision, the *people* ministering in *the* Spirit to God, bragging about *the* Anointed King Jesus, and not having been confident in *the* physical body,
4 even though I *am a person* also having confidence in the physical body. If anyone else seems to have been confident in *the* physical body, I *have* more.
5 *I was* an eight-day-old at circumcision, from a family of Israel, *the* family line of Benjamin, a Hebrew-speaking *Jew* from Hebrew-speaking *Jews*, regarding *the* law: a Separatist;
6 regarding passion: persecuting the assembly; regarding *the* right way (the *one* in *the* law): *a person* who became faultless.
7 But certain *things* that were gains to me, these I have regarded *as* a loss because of the Anointed King.
8 But yes, so of course I also regard all *things* to be a loss because of the *thing* that has a higher position of the knowledge of *the* Anointed King Jesus, my Master, because of whom I sustained the loss of all *things* and I regard *them* to be garbage so that I might gain *the* Anointed King
9 and be found in Him, not having my right way, the *one* from *the* law, but the *one* through trust of *the* Anointed King, the right way from God based on the trust,
10 of the "to know Him, the ability of His return back to life, and the sharing of His hardships" *kind*, being formed together into His death,
11 if somehow I might make it to the *point of* standing up from the dead.
12 Not that I already took *it* or have already been completed, but I pursue *it* if I might also completely take *it* based on what I was also completely taken for by the Anointed King Jesus.
13 Brothers, I don't consider myself to have completely taken *it*, but one *thing I do*, certainly forgetting the *things* behind, but reaching forward to the *things* in front,
14 aligned with a goal I pursue *it* based on the prize of God's invitation above in *the* Anointed King Jesus.
15 So we, as many of us as are complete, should focus on this. And if you are focusing differently on something, God will also uncover this to you.
16 More importantly, *we are* to be marching in step to the same standard that we already came into, to be focusing on the same *thing*.
17 Become imitators together of me, brothers, and keep an eye out for the *people* walking around like this, just as you have us *for* an example.
18 You see, many walk around (*about* whom, many times I was talking to you, but now I am even talking crying) the enemies of the cross of the Anointed King,
19 whose conclusion *is* ruin, whose God *is* the belly and the magnificence in their shame, the *people* focusing on the earthly *things*.
20 You see, our community is in heavens, from which we also patiently wait for a Rescuer, Master Jesus, *the* Anointed King,

21 who will refashion the body of our lowliness for the "for it to become formed together to the body of His magnificence" *part* aligned with the influence of the "for Him to be capable and to place all *things* under Himself" *kind*.

4

1 In such a way, my loved and yearned for brothers, my happiness and award wreath, stand like this in *the* Master, loved *ones*.
2 I encourage Euodia and I encourage Syntyche to be focusing on the same *thing* in *the* Master.
3 And I also ask you, *my* real strapped together *with me brother*, take them in together, some who competed together as a team in the good news for me with both Clement and the rest of my co-workers, whose names *are* in *the* scroll of life.
4 Always be happy in *the* Master. Again I will state, "Be happy."
5 Your polite *nature* must be known to all people. The Master *is* near.
6 Worry about nothing, but in everything by the prayer and the plea with thankfulness, your requests must be made known to God.
7 And the peace of God, the *peace* that has a higher position of every way of thinking, will watch over your hearts and your patterns of thinking in *the* Anointed King Jesus.
8 For the rest *of the time*, brothers, as many *things* as are valid, as many as *are* respectful, as many as *are* right, as many as *are* consecrated, as many as *are* toward friendship, as many as *are* good sounding, if *there is* any achievement and if *there is* any high praise, consider these *things*.
9 What you also learned, took in, heard, and realized in me, these *things* you must constantly do, and the God of the peace will be with you.
10 But I was immensely happy in *the* Master because finally you again flourished the "to be focusing on my behalf" *thing*, on which you actually were focusing, but you were not at the right time.
11 Not that I am talking regarding a deficit, you see, I learned to be content in *situations* that I am *in*.
12 I realize both *what it is like* to be put down low and I realize *what it is like* to be overflowing. In every and in all *situations*, I have learned the secret to be both full and hungry, to be both overflowing and lacking.
13 I have strength for all *things* in the Anointed King who gives ability to me.
14 More importantly, you did nicely when you shared together in my hard times.
15 You also realize, Philippians, that in *the* beginning of the good news when I went out from Macedonia, not even one assembly shared with me for an account of giving and receiving except you alone,
16 that even in Thessalonica, both once and twice, you sent *money* to me for the need.
17 Not that I am searching for the present, but I am searching for the fruit, the *fruit* increasing in your account.
18 I have all of everything, and I overflow. I have been filled up after accepting from the side of Epaphroditus the *things* from the side of you, an aroma of a sweet fragrance, an accepted sacrifice well-liked by God.

19 My God will fill up every need of yours aligned with His wealth in magnificence in *the* Anointed King Jesus.
20 To our God and Father *belongs* the magnificence for the spans of time of the spans of time. Amen.
21 Say hello to every sacred *person* in *the* Anointed King Jesus. The brothers together with me say hello to you.
22 All the sacred *people* say hello to you, but especially the *people* from the house of Caesar.
23 *May* the generosity of our Master Jesus, *the* Anointed King, *be* with you all. Amen. [Written to Philippians from Rome *and sent* through Epaphroditus]

Colossians

1

1 *From:* Paul (a missionary of Jesus, *the* Anointed King, through what God wants) and Timothy (the brother).
2 To: The sacred and trusting brothers in *the* Anointed King in Colosse. Generosity to you and peace out from God, our Father, and Master Jesus, *the* Anointed King.
3 We are thankful to the God and Father of our Master Jesus, *the* Anointed King, always praying concerning you,
4 after hearing *of* your trust in *the* Anointed King Jesus and *your* love, the *love* for all the sacred *people*,
5 because of the anticipation, the *anticipation* that is set aside for you in the heavens, that you heard about before in the message of the truth of the good news,
6 the *good news* that is beside *you and* for you, just as it is also in all the world, even producing fruit, just as *it* also *does* in you from *the* day that you heard and correctly understood the generosity of God in truth,
7 just as you also learned from Epaphras, our loved fellow slave, who is a reliable servant of the Anointed King on your behalf,
8 the *one* who also made obvious to us your love in *the* Spirit.
9 Because of this, we also, since *the* day that we heard, don't stop praying over you and requesting that you might be filled up with the correct understanding of what He wants in every insight and spiritual understanding,
10 for you to walk around in a manner deserving of the Master, to every bit of what is liked in every good action, producing fruit and growing in the correct understanding of God,
11 gaining ability in every ability aligned with the power of His magnificence for every persistence *to do what is right* and *for* patience with happiness,
12 thanking the Father, the *One* who made us adequate for the part of the portion of the sacred *people* in the light,
13 who saved us from the authority of the darkness and dislodged *us* into the monarchy of the Son of His love,
14 in whom we have the paid release through His blood, the forgiveness of the sins,
15 who is an image of God, the invisible *God*, firstborn of every created being,
16 because in Him all *things* were created, the *things* in the heavens and the *things* on the earth, the visible and the invisible, whether thrones, or governments, or head rulers, or authorities. All *things* have been created through Him and for Him.
17 And He is before all *things*, and all *things* have stood together in Him.
18 And He is the head of the body of the assembly, who is *the* beginning, *the* firstborn from the dead, so that in everything, He might become *the One* who is first,
19 because it seemed like a good idea for all the fullness to live in Him

20 and through Him to completely restore all the *things* to Him (after He made peace through the blood of His cross through Him), whether the *things* on the earth or the *things* in the heavens,
21 and you, who in the past were *people* who had been alienated and enemies to the mind in the actions, the evil *ones*, but right now He completely restored
22 in the body of His physical body through *His* death to offer you up, sacred, unblemished, and with no charges against you directly in His sight,
23 if you definitely stay over in the trust: a foundation having been laid, stable, and not moved away from the anticipation of the good news that you listened to, the *good news* that was spoken publicly among every created being under the sky, of which I, Paul, became a servant,
24 I, who now is happy in the hardships on your behalf. And it is my turn to fill up the deficiencies of the hard times of the Anointed King in my physical body on behalf of His body, that is the assembly,
25 of which I became a servant aligned with the management of God, the *management* that was given to me for you to accomplish the message of God,
26 the secret, the *one* that has been hidden away from the spans of time and away from the generations, but right now it has been shown to His sacred *people*,
27 to whom God wanted to make known what *is* the wealth of the magnificence of this secret among the non-Jews, that is *the* Anointed King in you, the anticipation of the magnificence,
28 whom we proclaim cautioning every person and teaching every person in all insight so that we might offer up every person complete in *the* Anointed King Jesus,
29 for which I also labor struggling aligned with His influence, the *influence* that is active in me in ability.

2 1 You see, I want you to realize how great of a struggle I have concerning you and the *people* in Laodicea, and as many as have not seen my face in *the* physical body,
2 that their hearts might be encouraged after being pulled together in love and into all *the* wealth of the full accomplishment of the understanding, into a correct understanding of the secret of the God and Father and of the Anointed King,
3 in whom all the stockpiles of the insight and information are hidden away.
4 I say this so that no one may misguide you in a persuasive message.
5 You see, even if I am away from *you* in the physical body, still I am together with you in the Spirit being happy and seeing your arrangement and the solidness of your trust in *the* Anointed King.
6 So as you received the Anointed King Jesus in, the Master, walk around in Him
7 having been rooted, being built on in Him, and being authenticated in the trust, just as you were taught, overflowing in it in thankfulness.
8 See that no one will be the *one* carrying you off as stolen property through the philosophy and meaningless fraud aligned with the tradition of the

people, aligned with the conventional practices of the world, and not aligned with *the* Anointed King,

9 because in Him lives all the fullness of the Godhead bodily.

10 And you are in Him, having been filled up, who is the head of every head ruler and authority,

11 in whom you also were circumcised with circumcision made without hands, in the stripping away of the body of the sins of the physical body in the Anointed King's circumcision

12 when you were buried together with Him in the submersion, in which you also were gotten up together with *Him* through the trust of the influence of God, the *One* who got Him up from the dead.

13 And you being dead in the infractions and the uncircumcision of your physical body He brought to life together with Him when, in an act of generosity, He forgave you of all the infractions

14 after erasing the handwritten document against us in the rules, that was a covert opponent to us. And He has taken it from the middle by nailing it to the cross.

15 After stripping away the head rulers and the authorities, He made an exhibit *of them* in a clear public statement when He brought them out in a victory parade in it.

16 So no one must judge you in dinner, or in drink, or in a detail of a festival, or a new moon, or Sabbaths,

17 (that are a shadow of the *things* that are going *to come*, but the body *is* the Anointed King's).

18 No one must disqualify you from receiving your prize, wanting *to be* in a lowly focus and with a religion of the angels, intruding into *things* that he has not looked at, being conceited for no reason by the way of thinking of his physical body,

19 and not holding on to the head, from which the entire body through *its* connections and bonds, being further supplied and pulled together, grows the growth of God.

20 So if you died together with the Anointed King out of the conventional practices of the world, why do you consider rules as *if you are people* living in *the* world?

21 "You should not touch, nor should you taste, nor should you come into contact with *it*,"

22 that are all for deterioration with the consumption aligned with the regulations and instructions of the people,

23 some *things* that are a message that certainly has insight in invented religion, lowly focus, and not going easy on *the* body, not with any value toward a filling up of the physical body.

1 So if you were gotten up together with the Anointed King, look for the *things* above where the Anointed King is sitting in *the* right *side* of God.

2 Focus on the *things* above, not the *things* on the earth.

3 You see, you died and your life has been hidden together with the Anointed King in God.
4 When the Anointed King (our life) is shown, at that time you also will be shown with Him in magnificence.
5 So deaden your body parts (the *ones* on the earth): sexual sin, *desire* that is not clean, lust, bad desire and the desire for more (something that idol worship is),
6 because of which, the punishment of God comes on the sons of the unbelief,
7 among whom you also walked around in the past when you were living among them.
8 But right now you also must put away all *these things*: punishment, anger, badness, an insult, a shameful word from your mouth.
9 Don't lie to each other after stripping away the former person together with the things it repeatedly does
10 and after putting on the young *person*, the *one* who is renewed to a correct understanding aligned with *the* image of the *One* who created him,
11 where there is not Greek and Jewish, circumcision and uncircumcision, foreigner, savage, slave, free, but *the* Anointed King *is* all and in all.
12 So put on (as God's select *people*, sacred and having been loved) sympathy of compassions, kindness, lowly focus, humility, patience
13 (as you tolerate each other and forgive each other as an act of generosity; if anyone has a complaint toward anyone, just as the Anointed King also forgave you as an act of generosity, so you also *must forgive*),
14 but over all these *things*, the love, something that is a bond of the maturity.
15 And the peace of God must referee in your hearts, into which you were also invited in one body. And become thankful.
16 The message of the Anointed King must have a house in you richly in every insight, teaching and cautioning yourselves with psalms, praise songs, and spiritual songs as you sing in generosity in your hearts to the Master.
17 And everything, whatever you do in word or in action, *do* all *things* in *the* name of *the* Master Jesus, being thankful to the God and Father through Him.
18 The Women — Place yourselves under *your* own husbands, as it was meeting the high standards in *the* Master.
19 The Men — Love the wives, and do not be bitter toward them.
20 The Children — Obey the parents regarding all *things*. You see, this is well-liked to the Master.
21 The Fathers — Don't provoke your children so that they may not feel dejected.
22 The Slaves — Regarding all *things*, obey the masters regarding *the* physical body, not in eye-slavery, as people pleasers, but in dedication of heart, fearing God.
23 And everything, whatever you do, work from *the* soul as *if it is* for the Master and not for people,
24 realizing that you will fully receive the repayment of the inheritance out from *the* Master. You see, you are slaves to the Master, *the* Anointed King.

25 The *person* who does wrong will retrieve what he did wrong *in*, and there is no being swayed by appearances.

1 The Masters — Provide the right *thing* and the equality to the slaves, realizing that you also have a master in heavens.
2 Stay close to the prayer, staying awake in *the* same in thankfulness,
3 praying at the same time also about us that God might open to us a door of the message, to speak the secret of the Anointed King (because of which we also have been locked up)
4 so that I might show it as it is necessary for me to speak.
5 Walk around toward the *people* outside in insight, buying up the time,
6 your message always having been seasoned with generosity salt to realize how it is necessary for you to be answering each one.
7 All the *things* regarding me, Tychicus (the loved brother, reliable servant, and fellow slave in *the* Master) will make known to you,
8 whom I sent to you for this same *purpose* (so that he might know the *things* about you and encourage your hearts)
9 together with Onesimus (the reliable and loved brother who is from among you). They will make everything here known to you.
10 Aristarchus (the person incarcerated together with me) says hello to you, and Mark (the cousin of Barnabas, about whom you received demands; if he comes to you, accept him)
11 and Joshua (the *one* who is called Justus). The *people* who are from *the* circumcision, these *are my* only co-workers for the monarchy of God, some who became a boost to me.
12 Epaphras (the slave of *the* Anointed King from among you) says hello to you, who is always struggling over you in the prayers so that you, complete and having been filled, might be established in everything God wants.
13 You see, I am a witness for him that he has much passion over you, the *people* in Laodicea, and the *people* in Hierapolis.
14 Luke (the doctor, the loved *one*) and Demas say hello to you.
15 Say hello to the brothers in Laodicea and to Nymphas and the assembly throughout his house.
16 And when *this* letter is read beside you, make *sure* that it is also read in the assembly of Laodiceans and that you also read the *one* from Laodicea.
17 And say to Archippus, "See to the *task of* serving that you received in *the* Master, so that you may accomplish it."
18 The greeting of Paul with my hand. Remember my restraints. *May* the generosity *be* with you. Amen. [Written to Colossians from Rome *and sent* through Tychicus and Onesimus]

First Thessalonians

1

1 *From:* Paul, Silas, and Timothy. To: The assembly of Thessalonians in Father God and Master Jesus, *the* Anointed King. Generosity to you and peace out from our Father God and Master Jesus, *the* Anointed King.

2 We are always thankful to God concerning you all, making mention of you over our prayers,

3 constantly remembering your work of the trust, *your* labor of the love, and *your* persistence of the anticipation of our Master Jesus, *the* Anointed King, in front of our God and Father,

4 realizing your selection, brothers, having been loved by God,

5 because our good news didn't happen to you in message only, but also in ability, in *the* Sacred Spirit, and in a very full accomplishment; just as you realize, we became such among you because of you.

6 And you became imitators of us and the Master when you accepted the message in very hard times with *the* Sacred Spirit's happiness,

7 in such a way for you to become examples to everyone trusting in Macedonia and Achaia.

8 You see, the message of the Master has been reverberated out from you (not only in Macedonia and Achaia, but also in every place your trust, the *trust* toward God, has gone out to) in such a way for us to be having no need to be speaking anything;

9 for they themselves report concerning us what kind of inroad we had to you and how you returned back to God from the idols to be slaves to *the* living and true God

10 and to stay and wait for His Son from the heavens, whom He got up from *the* dead, Jesus, the *One* saving us from the punishment, the coming *punishment*.

2

1 You see, you yourselves, brothers, realize our inroad, the *inroad* to you, that it has not become meaningless.

2 But even after we previously suffered and were injured in Philippi (just as you know), we made clear public statements in our God to speak the good news of God to you in a great struggle.

3 You see, our encouragement *is* not from a misleading lie, nor from what is not clean, nor in deception.

4 But just as we have been approved by God to be trusted with the good news, so we speak, not as doing what people would like, but *as doing what* God *would like*, the *One* who approves our hearts.

5 You see, neither in the past did we become in a message of flattery, just as you know, nor in a sham of a desire for more (God *is* a witness),

6 nor looking for magnificence from people (not from you, not from others), being able to be in a heavy weight as missionaries of *the* Anointed King,
7 but we became gentle in *the* middle of you, as when a nursing mother keeps her *own* children warm.
8 Being affectionately desirous of you like this, it seemed like a good idea to us to not only give out the good news of God to you, but also our *own* souls, because you have become loved to us.
9 You see, brothers, you remember our labor and hard work; for night and day working with the *intent* to not be a burden on any of you, we spoke publicly to you about the good news of God.
10 You and God *are* witnesses how holily, rightly, and faultlessly we became to you, the *people* trusting,
11 exactly as you realize how *we were with* each one of you, as a father *with* his *own* children, encouraging you, comforting *you*, and telling what we witnessed
12 for the "for you to walk around in a manner deserving of God" *part*, the *One* who invited you into His *own* monarchy and magnificence.
13 Because of this, we also are constantly thankful to God because when you took in a message of what was heard from the side of us, of God, you accepted *it*, not *as* a message of people, but, just as it truly is, a message of God, who also is active in you, the *people* trusting.
14 You see, you became imitators, brothers, of the assemblies of God, the *ones* that are in Judea in *the* Anointed King Jesus, because you also suffered these *things* under *your* own countrymen, just as they also *suffered* under the Jewish *people*,
15 the *people* who also killed the Master Jesus and *their* own preachers, who chased us out, who do not do what God would like, and oppose all people,
16 hindering us (for the "to always fill up their sins" *part*) to speak to the non-Jews so that they might be rescued. The punishment for *the* conclusion already came on them.
17 But when we were made orphans by being away from you, brothers, toward an hour's time to *the* face, not to *the* heart, we made much more of an effort with much desire to see your face.
18 For this reason, we wanted to come to you, certainly I, Paul, both once and twice, and the Opponent interrupted us.
19 You see, what *is* our anticipation *of good*, or happiness, or award wreath of bragging? Or *is it* not even you in front of our Master Jesus, *the* Anointed King, during His arrival?
20 You see, you are our magnificence and happiness.

3

1 For this reason, no longer being able to stand *it*, it seemed like a good idea to us to be left down in Athens alone.
2 And I sent Timothy (our brother, God's servant, and our co-worker in the good news of the Anointed King) for the "to establish you and to encourage you concerning your trust" *part*,
3 the "for no one to be swayed in these hard times" *thing*. You see, you yourselves realize that we are lying *here* for this;

4 for even when we were facing you, we were telling you beforehand that we are going to be going through hard times, just as it also happened, and you have seen *it*.
5 And because of this, no longer being able to stand *it*, I sent *Timothy to you* for the "to know your trust" *part*, in case somehow the *one* who tries to cause trouble was trying to cause trouble with you and our labor should become for a meaningless *thing*.
6 Just now, after Timothy came to us from you and shared with us the good news of *your* trust, your love, and that you always have a good mention of us, yearning to see us, exactly as we also you:
7 because of this, brothers, we were encouraged based on you over all our hard times and shortages through your trust
8 because now we live if you stand in *the* Master.
9 You see, what thanks are we able to repay to God concerning you over all the happiness that we are happy with because of you in front of our God,
10 night and day pleading even much more for the "to see your face and to develop the deficiencies of your trust" *part*?
11 May our God and Father Himself and our Master Jesus, *the* Anointed King, direct our way to you.
12 May the Master increase and overflow you with the love for each other and for everyone, exactly as we also *have* for you,
13 for the "to establish your hearts faultless in sacredness" *part* in front of our God and Father in the arrival of our Master Jesus, *the* Anointed King, with all His sacred *people*.

4

1 So for the rest *of the time*, brothers, we ask and encourage you in Master Jesus (just as you received in from us the "how it is necessary for you to be walking around and to be doing what God would like" *part*) that you may overflow more.
2 You see, you realize what orders we gave to you through the Master Jesus;
3 for this is what God wants: your sacredness, for you to be keeping yourselves away from the sexual sin,
4 for each of you to realize the "to be getting his *own* container in sacredness and value" *part*
5 (not in lust of desire exactly as the non-Jews, the *ones* who don't even know God),
6 the "not to be stepping beyond and to be taking advantage of his brother in the item" *part*, because the Master *is* a retaliator concerning all of these, just as we also already told you and were a strong witness to.
7 You see, God didn't invite us based on what is not clean, but in sacredness.
8 So you see then, the *person* invalidating *these things* doesn't invalidate a person but God, the *One* who also gave His Spirit to us, the Sacred *Spirit*.
9 But concerning the brotherly kindness, you have no need *for me* to be writing to you. You see, you yourselves are God-taught for the "to be loving each other" *part*;

10 for you actually do it to all the brothers, the *ones* in all of Macedonia, but we encourage you, brothers, to be overflowing more,

11 to be thinking it is important to remain calm, to constantly be doing *your* own *things*, and to be working with your own hands just as we passed the order on to you

12 so that you may walk around reputably toward the *people* outside and may have need of nothing.

13 I don't want you to be unaware, brothers, about the *people* who are asleep so that you are not sad just as the rest, the *ones* who actually have no anticipation *of good*.

14 You see, if we trust that Jesus died and came back to life, this is how God will also lead together with Him the *people* who fell asleep through Jesus;

15 for we are saying this to you in *the* Master's message, that we, the *people* living, the *ones* who are left here for the arrival of the Master, will not in any way precede the *people* who fell asleep,

16 because the Master Himself in *the* giving of an order (in *the* head angel's voice and in God's trumpet) will step down out of heaven, and the dead in *the* Anointed King will come back to life first.

17 Following that, we, the *people* living, the *ones* who are left here, at the same time together with them will be snatched up in clouds for a face-to-face meeting of the Master in *the* air. And this is how we will always be together with *the* Master.

18 In such a way, encourage each other in these messages.

5

1 Concerning the amounts of time and the appointed times, brothers, you have no need *for anything* to be written to you.

2 You see, you yourselves accurately realize that the day of *the* Master comes like this, as a thief in *the* night.

3 You see, when they say peace and certainty, then unexpected destruction stands over them, even as the *labor* pain *stands over* the *woman* having *a baby* in *her* womb. And they will not in any way escape from *it*.

4 But you, brothers, are not in darkness that the day might take you down as a thief.

5 You all are sons of light and sons of day. We are not of night, nor of darkness.

6 So clearly we should not sleep, even as the rest *do*, but we should stay awake and be sober.

7 You see, the *people* who sleep, sleep at night, and the people who get drunk are drunk at night.

8 But we who are of *the* day should be sober, after putting on an armored vest of trust and love; and head protection, anticipation of rescue;

9 because God didn't place us into punishment, but into an acquisition of rescue through our Master Jesus, *the* Anointed King,

10 the *One* who died on our behalf so that whether we may stay awake or whether we may be sleeping, we might live at the same time together with Him.

11 For this reason, encourage and build each other, one *for* the one, just as you also are doing.
12 We ask you, brothers, to know the *people* laboring among you, presiding over you in *the* Master, and cautioning you;
13 and to be regarding them even much more in love because of their work. Be peaceful among yourselves.
14 We are encouraging you, brothers. Caution the defiant. Comfort the downhearted. Have the weak in front of *you*. Be patient toward everyone.
15 Look. No one should give back bad for bad to anyone, but always pursue the good *thing*, both for each other and for all.
16 Always be happy.
17 Constantly pray.
18 In everything, be thankful. You see, this is what God wants in *the* Anointed King Jesus for you.
19 Don't extinguish the Spirit.
20 Don't treat preachings as if they are nothing.
21 Check all *things*. Hold the nice *thing* steady.
22 Keep yourselves away from every visual image of evil.
23 May the God of the peace Himself make you sacred, entirely complete *people*. And may your entirely whole spirit, soul, and body be kept faultlessly in the arrival of our Master Jesus, *the* Anointed King.
24 The *One* inviting you can be trusted, who will also do *it*.
25 Brothers, pray about us.
26 Say hello to all the brothers with a sacred friendly gesture.
27 I place you under an oath to the Master for *this* letter to be read to all the sacred brothers.
28 *May* the generosity of our Master Jesus, *the* Anointed King, *be* with you. Amen. [*This* first *letter* was written to Thessalonians from Athens]

Second Thessalonians

1

1 *From:* Paul, Silas, and Timothy. To: The assembly of Thessalonians in our Father God and Master Jesus, *the* Anointed King.
2 Generosity to you and peace out from our Father God and Master Jesus, *the* Anointed King.
3 We are obligated to always be thankful to God concerning you, brothers, just as it is deserving because your trust grows over and the love of each one of you all is increasing for each other,
4 in such a way for us ourselves to be bragging about you in the assemblies of God over your persistence *to do what is right* and trust in all your persecutions and the hard times that you tolerate.
5 *It is* a display of the right judgment of God for the "for you to be considered deserving of the monarchy of God" *thing* over what you also suffer,
6 if it so happens that *it is* right beside God to repay hard times to the *people* causing you hard times
7 and to you (the *people* going through hard times) relief with us in the uncovering of the Master Jesus out of heaven with angels of His ability
8 in a fire of a blaze, making a retaliation against the *people* not knowing God and the *people* not obeying the good news of our Master Jesus, *the* Anointed King,
9 some who will pay a penalty of justice (destruction that spans *all* time away from *the* face of the Master and away from the magnificence of His strength)
10 when He comes to be elevated to a place of magnificence among His sacred *people* and to amaze *people* among all the trusting *people* (because what we witnessed over you was trusted) in that day;
11 for which we also always pray concerning you that our God might think that you deserve the invitation and might fill *you* with every good notion of goodness and action of trust in ability,
12 in order that the name of our Master Jesus, *the* Anointed King, might be elevated to a place of magnificence in you and you in Him aligned with the generosity of our God and Master Jesus, *the* Anointed King.

2

1 We ask you, brothers, on behalf of the arrival of our Master Jesus, *the* Anointed King, and our coming together in one place to Him,
2 for the "for you not to be quickly disturbed away from the way of thinking, not to be alarmed" *thing*, not through a spirit, not through a message, not through a letter (as *if* through us), as that the day of the Anointed King has stood here.
3 No one should completely fool you aligned with any way because *it will not happen* unless the divorce comes first and the person of the sin, the son of the ruin, is uncovered,

4 the *one* lying in opposition and being raised up over everything that is called a god or a worshipped object in such a way for him to be seated as God in the temple of God showing himself off that he is God.
5 Don't you remember that as I was still facing you, I was telling you these *things*?
6 And now you realize the *thing* that holds *it* down for the "for him to be uncovered in his *own* time" *part*.
7 You see, the secret of crime is already active. The *one* who holds down now *is* only until it will become out of *the* middle.
8 And then the criminal will be uncovered whom the Master will consume with the Spirit of His mouth and will make useless at the manifestation of His arrival,
9 whose arrival (*the criminal's*) is aligned with the Opponent's influence in every ability, indicators, and incredible things of a lie,
10 and in every fraud of the wrong way in the *people* being ruined for *the times* that they did not accept the love of the truth for the "for them to be rescued" *part*.
11 And because of this, God sends them *the* influence of a misleading lie for the "for them to trust in the lie" *part*,
12 so that they might be judged, all the people who didn't trust the truth but who were delighted in the wrong way.
13 But we are obligated to always be thankful to God concerning you, brothers, who have been loved by *the* Master because God chose you from *the* beginning for rescue in sacredness of spirit and trust of truth,
14 into which He invited you through our good news into an acquisition of *the* magnificence of our Master Jesus, *the* Anointed King.
15 So clearly, brothers, stand and hold on to the traditions that you were taught, whether through a message or through our letter.
16 May our Master Jesus Himself, *the* Anointed King, and our God and Father, the *One* who loved us and gave encouragement that spans *all* time and good anticipation in generosity,
17 encourage your hearts and establish you in every good message and action.

3

1 For the rest *of the time*, brothers, pray about us that the message of the Master may run and be elevated to a place of magnificence, just as *it* also *is* toward you,
2 and that we might be saved from the out of place and evil *people*. You see, the trust *is* not everyone's.
3 But the Master can be trusted who will establish and guard you from the evil *one*.
4 We have been confident in *the* Master over you, that the orders that we pass on to you, you are both doing and will do.
5 May the Master direct your hearts into the love of God and into the persistence of the Anointed King *to do what is right*.
6 We are passing the order on to you, brothers, in the name of our Master Jesus, *the* Anointed King, for you to be setting yourself up away from every brother

walking around defiantly and not aligned with the tradition that he took in from the side of us.

7 You see, you yourselves realize how it is necessary to be imitating us because we were not defiant among you.

8 Neither did we eat bread for free from the side of anyone, but with labor and hard work night and day working with the *intent* to not be a burden on any of you,

9 not because we don't have authority, but so that we might give ourselves *as* an example to you, for the "to be imitating us" *part*.

10 You see, even when we were facing you, we were passing this order on to you, "If anyone does not want to be working, he must not eat either;"

11 for we hear *about* some *people* who are walking around defiantly among you, working nothing but working *their way* around *work*.

12 We pass the order on to these types of *people* and encourage *them* through our Master Jesus, *the* Anointed King, that working with calmness, they should eat their *own* bread.

13 You, brothers, should not get discouraged doing nice things.

14 If anyone does not obey our message through *this* letter, make an indication of this *person*, and don't interact with him so that he might be embarrassed.

15 And don't regard *him* as an enemy, but caution *him* as a brother.

16 May the Master of the peace Himself give you the peace through everything in every way. The Master *is* with you all.

17 *This is* the greeting of Paul with my hand that is an indicator in every letter. This is how I write.

18 *May* the generosity of our Master Jesus, *the* Anointed King, *be* with you all. Amen. [*This* second *letter* was written to Thessalonians from Athens]

First Timothy

1 *From:* Paul, a missionary of Jesus, *the* Anointed King, aligned with a directive of God, our Rescuer and Master, Jesus, *the* Anointed King, our anticipation *of good*.
2 To: Timothy, a real child in trust. Generosity, forgiving kindness, peace out from our Father God and Jesus, *the* Anointed King, our Master.
3 Just as I encouraged you to still stay in Ephesus as I was traveling to Macedonia so that you might pass the order on to some not to be teaching a different *doctrine*,
4 nor to be paying attention to myths and endless genealogies, some that provide questionings rather than the construction of God in trust;
5 the conclusion of the order is love from a clean heart, a good conscience, and trust *that is* not faked,
6 of which, after some missed the target, they were turned from *it* to empty chatter,
7 wanting to be law teachers, not being aware of both what they say and about what they thoroughly authenticate.
8 We realize that the law *is* nice if someone uses it according to the rules,
9 realizing this, that *the* law is not lying *here* for a *person* who does what is right, but for criminals and unruly *people*, for godless and sinful *people*, for unholy and profane *people*, for father-beaters and mother-beaters, for murderers,
10 for people who commit sexual sin, for homosexuals, for human traffickers, for liars, for oath breakers, and if something different lies in opposition to the instruction that is healthy
11 aligned with the good news of the magnificence of the blessed God that I was trusted with.
12 And I have generosity for the *One* who gave ability to me, *the* Anointed King Jesus, our Master, because He regarded me *to be someone* who can be trusted when He put *me* into *the job of* serving,
13 though the prior *time* I was a insulting *person*, a persecutor, and an injurer. But I was shown forgiving kindness because, being unaware, I did *it* in a lack of trust.
14 The generosity of our Master greatly increased with the trust and love in *the* Anointed King Jesus.
15 The message can be trusted and *is* deserving of every *bit of* acceptance, that *the* Anointed King Jesus came into the world to rescue sinful *people* of whom I am first.
16 But because of this, I was shown forgiving kindness so that in me first Jesus, *the* Anointed King, might display every *bit of* the patience to a prototype of the *people* who are going to be trusting based on Him for life that spans *all* time.

17 To the King of the spans of time (*the* undeteriorating, invisible, only insightful God) *belongs* value and magnificence for the spans of time of the spans of time. Amen.

18 I am placing this order beside you, child Timothy, aligned with the preachings going ahead over you so that you may serve in the military of these, the nice military service,

19 having trust and a good conscience that some, after pushing away, were shipwrecked concerning the trust,

20 of whom are Hymenaeus and Alexander, whom I turned over to the Opponent so that they might be disciplined to not be insulting *God*.

2

1 So I encourage, first of all, for pleas, prayers, interventions, thanks to be made on behalf of all people,

2 on behalf of kings and all the *people* who are in a higher position so that we may lead through a quiet and calm life in every *bit of* godliness and respect.

3 You see, this *is* nice and acceptable in the sight of our Rescuer, God,

4 who wants all people to be rescued and to come into a correct understanding of truth.

5 You see, *there is* one God, also one middleman between God and people, a person, *the* Anointed King Jesus,

6 the *One* who gave Himself *to be* a release payment on everyone's behalf, the witness at *its* own right times,

7 into which I was put *as* a public speaker and missionary (I am telling *the* truth in *the* Anointed King; I am not lying), a teacher of non-Jews in trust and truth.

8 So I intend for the men to be praying in every place raising up holy hands without rage and questioning,

9 similarly also, for the women to be decorating themselves in an orderly demeanor with modesty and proper focus, not in hair weaves, gold, pearls, or very expensive clothing,

10 but what is appropriate for women promising God-worship through good actions.

11 A woman must learn in calmness in total compliance.

12 I don't give a woman permission to be teaching, nor to be domineering over a man, but to be in calmness.

13 You see, Adam was sculpted first, after that Eve.

14 And Adam was not fooled, but the woman, after being fooled, has become in violation.

15 But she will be rescued through the raising of children if they stay in trust, love, and sacredness with proper focus.

3

1 The message can be trusted: "If anyone reaches out for *a position of* supervision, he desires nice work."

2 So it is necessary for the supervisor to be unattackable, one woman's husband, sober, properly focused, orderly, friendly to strangers, able to teach,

3 not beside wine, not a hitter, not pursuing shameful gain, but polite, a non-arguer, without greed,
4 presiding over *his* own house nicely, having children in compliance with all respect
5 (if someone does not realize *how* to preside over *his* own house, how will he take care of God's assembly?),
6 not a young convert so that when he gets blinded by smoke, he might not fall into the accuser's judgment.
7 It is also necessary for him to be having a nice witness account from the outside so that he might not fall into a criticism and trap of the accuser.
8 Similarly, *it is necessary* for servants *to be* respectful, not double-talkers, not paying attention to a lot of wine, not pursuing shameful gain,
9 having the secret of the trust in a clean conscience.
10 These also must first *be* checked. After that they must serve being *people* with no charges against them.
11 Similarly, *it is necessary* for wives *to be* respectful, not accusers, sober, reliable in all *things*.
12 Servants must be husbands of one wife, presiding over children and over *their* own houses nicely.
13 You see, the *ones* who serve nicely acquire a nice foothold for themselves and a very clear public statement in trust, the *trust* in *the* Anointed King Jesus.
14 I am writing these *things* to you anticipating to come to you faster.
15 But if I am slow, *I am writing these things* so that you may realize how it is necessary to be busying yourself in God's house, something that is an assembly of *the* living God, a pillar and stabilizer of the truth.
16 And the secret of the godliness is admittedly great. God was shown in a physical body, was made right in *the* Spirit, was seen by announcers, was publicly spoken about among nations, was trusted in *the* world, was taken up in magnificence.

1 The Spirit distinctly says that in later times some *people* will stand off away from the trust, paying attention to misleading spirits and instructions of lesser deities,
2 in faked behavior of lying *people*, who have been scarred in *their* own conscience,
3 who hinder *people* to be marrying, *for them* to be keeping themselves away from foods that God created for receiving with thankfulness by the trusting *people* and *people* who have correctly understood the truth,
4 because every created *thing* of God *is* nice and nothing being received with thankfulness *is* trash.
5 You see, it is made sacred through God's message and intervention.
6 Putting these *things* under the brothers, you will be a nice servant of Jesus, *the* Anointed King, nurtured in the messages of the trust and the nice instruction that you have followed alongside.
7 Refuse the profane and old wives' myths. Strenuously exercise yourself toward godliness.

8 You see, the strenuous bodily exercise is beneficial toward a few *things*, but the godliness is beneficial toward everything, having a promise of the life now and the *life* that is going *to be*.
9 The message can be trusted and *is* deserving of every *bit of* acceptance.
10 You see, for this we also labor and are criticized, because we have anticipated good based on *the* living God who is a rescuer of all *kinds of* people, especially trusting *people*.
11 Pass these orders on and teach *them*.
12 No one must ignore *you because* of your youth. But become an example of the trusting *people* in message, in behavior, in love, in spirit, in trust, in consecration.
13 Until I come, pay attention to the reading, the encouragement, the instruction.
14 Don't stop caring for the gift in you that was given to you through preaching with *the* laying on of the hands of the board of older men.
15 Be concerned about these *things*. Be in these *things* so that your progress may be shown in everyone.
16 Fix *your* attention on yourself and the instruction. Stay over in them. You see, doing this, you will rescue both yourself and the *people* listening to you.

5

1 You shouldn't pound on an older *man*, but encourage *him* as a father. *Encourage* younger *men* as brothers,
2 older *women* as mothers, younger *women* as sisters in all consecration.
3 Value widows, the real widows.
4 If any widow has children or grandchildren, they must first learn to be reverencing *their* own house and to be giving reimbursements back to the predecessors. You see, this is nice and acceptable in the sight of God.
5 The real widow who has also been alone has anticipated good based on God and still stays in the pleas and the prayers night and day.
6 The *widow* living in luxury has died as she lives.
7 And pass these orders on so that they may be unattackable.
8 If anyone does not plan for *his* own, and especially for the *people* living in *his* house, he has denied the trust and is worse than an untrusting *person*.
9 A widow must be inducted not less than sixty years *old* who has become one man's wife,
10 who is witnessed *by you* among nice actions: if she nurtured children, if she accepted strangers, if she washed sacred *people*'s feet, if she supported *people* going through hard times, if she followed closely behind every good action.
11 Refuse younger widows. You see, when they might be dominant against the Anointed King, they want to be marrying,
12 having judgment *against them* because they invalidated the first trust.
13 At the same time idle *women* also learn to go around to the houses, not only idle, but also gossips and *people* who work *their way* around *work*, speaking the *things* that are not necessary.

14 So I intend for younger *women* to be marrying, to be raising children, to be running the house, to be giving the *one* who lies in opposition *to them* not even one opportunity, thanks to a put-down.
15 You see, some were already turned from *it* behind the Opponent.
16 If any trusting *man* or trusting *woman* has widows, they must support them and the assembly must not be weighted down, so that it might support the real widows.
17 The older *men* who have presided nicely must be thought of as deserving double value, especially the *ones* laboring in message and instruction.
18 You see, the *Old Testament* writing says *in Deuteronomy 25:4*, "You will not muzzle a cow processing grain." And, "The worker *is* deserving of his pay."
19 Don't accept with a warm welcome a criminal complaint against an older *man*, outside of except *it is* based on two or three witnesses.
20 Reprimand the *people* who sin in the sight of everyone so that the rest may also have fear.
21 I am a strong witness in the sight of God, Master Jesus (*the* Anointed King), and the select angels, *to the fact* that you should observe these *things* without prejudice, doing nothing aligned with bias.
22 Place hands on no one quickly. Don't share sins belonging to others. Keep yourself consecrated.
23 Don't be a water drinker anymore, but use a little wine because of your stomach and your frequent weaknesses.
24 The sins of some people are evident, going ahead *of them* into judgment, but with some *people* they actually follow closely behind.
25 Similarly, the nice actions also are evident, and the *things* having *it* otherwise are not able to be hidden.

6

1 As many as are under a crossbeam (slaves) must regard *their* own owners as deserving of all value so that the name and the instruction of God may not be insulted.
2 The *slaves* who have trusting owners must not ignore *them* because they are brothers. But instead they must be *their* slaves because they are trusting and loved *owners*, the *owners* assisting in the humane thing. Teach and encourage these *things*.
3 If anyone teaches a different *doctrine* and does not come forward to messages that are healthy (the *messages* of our Master Jesus, *the* Anointed King) and to the instruction that is aligned with godliness,
4 he has been blinded by smoke, being aware of nothing, but ill concerning questionings and arguments over words, from which happen envy, fighting, insults, evil suspicions,
5 societies of people who have been devoured in *their* way of thinking and who have been robbed of the truth, assuming the godliness to be a way to get gain. Stand off away from these types of *people*.
6 The godliness with contentment is a way to get great gain.
7 You see, we carried nothing into the world. *It is* obvious that neither are we able to carry anything out.
8 Having nourishments and covers, with these we will be content.

9 But the *people* intending to be wealthy fall into trouble, a trap, and desires (many unobservant and hurtful), some that sink the people into destruction and ruin.
10 You see, a root of all *kinds of* the bad *things* is the fondness for money, of which, as some reached out for *it*, they were misled away from the trust and stabbed themselves through with many agonies.
11 But you, O person of God, escape these *things*. Pursue *the* right way, godliness, trust, love, persistence *to do what is right*, humility.
12 Struggle in the nice struggle of the trust. Latch on to the life that spans *all* time, into which you also were invited and acknowledged the nice acknowledgment in the sight of many witnesses.
13 I pass the order on to you in the sight of God (the *One* who gives life to all *things*) and the Anointed King Jesus (who told what He witnessed before Pontius Pilate in the nice acknowledgment)
14 for you to keep the demand unspotted, unattackable up to the manifestation of our Master Jesus, *the* Anointed King,
15 that He will show at *their* own right times, the blessed and only competent ruler, the King of the *ones* who are kings and *the* Master of the *ones* who are masters,
16 the only *One* having deathlessness, having a house in unapproachable light, whom no one (of people) saw, neither is able to see, to whom *belongs* value and power that spans *all* time. Amen.
17 To the wealthy *people* in the present span of time, pass on the order not to be focusing on high things, neither to have anticipated good based on *the* obscurity of wealth but in God, the living *God*, the *One* who richly provides everything to us for enjoyment,
18 to be working on good *things*, to be wealthy in nice actions, to be benevolent, sharing,
19 stockpiling for themselves in a safe place a nice foundation for the *time* that is going *to come*, so that they might latch on to the life that spans *all* time.
20 O Timothy, guard the thing placed down alongside *of you*, turning from the profane meaningless voices and opposing positions of the falsely named knowledge,
21 that as some promise *to have it*, they miss the target concerning the trust. *May* the generosity *be* with you. Amen. [*This* first *letter* was written to Timothy from Laodicia, a certain *city* that is a mother city of Phrygia Pacatiana]

Second Timothy

1

1 *From:* Paul, a missionary of Jesus, *the* Anointed King, through what God wants aligned with a promise of the life in *the* Anointed King Jesus.

2 To: Timothy, a loved child. Generosity, forgiving kindness, peace out from Father God and *the* Anointed King Jesus, our Master.

3 I have generosity for God (to whom I minister out from predecessors in a clean conscience) as I have the constant mention concerning you in my pleas night and day,

4 yearning to see you (having remembered your tears) so that I might be full of happiness

5 receiving a quiet reminder of the trust in you *that is* not faked, something that first had a house in your grandmother Lois and in your mother Eunice. I have been confident that *it is* also in you,

6 which *is the* reason why I am reminding you again to be rekindling the gift of God that is in you through the laying on of my hands.

7 You see, God did not give us a spirit of cowardice, but of ability, of love, and of proper focus.

8 So you shouldn't be ashamed of what our Master witnessed, nor of me, His prisoner, but suffer tough hardships together with *me* for the good news aligned with God's ability,

9 the *One* who rescued and invited us with a sacred invitation, not aligned with our actions, but aligned with *His* own purpose and the generosity that was given to us in *the* Anointed King Jesus before *the* times that span *all* time,

10 but now was shown through the manifestation of our Rescuer, Jesus, *the* Anointed King (who not only made the death useless, but lit up life and non-deterioration through the good news),

11 into which I was placed *as* a public speaker, a missionary, and a teacher of non-Jews,

12 which *is the* reason why I also suffer these *things*. But I am not ashamed. You see, I know whom I have trusted, and I have been confident that He is able to guard the thing placed alongside of me for that day.

13 Have a prototype of messages that are healthy (that you heard from the side of me) in the trust and love in *the* Anointed King Jesus.

14 Guard the nice thing placed down alongside *of you* through the Sacred Spirit that has a house in us.

15 You realize this, that all the *people* in Western Turkey turned away from me, of whom are Phygellus and Hermogenes.

16 May the Master give forgiving kindness to the house of Onesiphorus because many times he refreshed me and was not ashamed of my chain.

17 But when he became in Rome, he looked with more concerned for me and found *me*.

18 May the Master give to him to find forgiving kindness from the side of a master in that day. And as much as he served in Ephesus, you know better *than I*.

2

1 So, you, my child, become competent in the generosity, the *generosity* in *the* Anointed King Jesus.
2 And what you heard from the side of me through many witnesses, place these *things* beside people who can be trusted, some who will be adequate to also teach different *people*.
3 So you must suffer tough hardships as a nice soldier of Jesus, *the* Anointed King.
4 No one serving in the military is entangled with the transactions of *his* life so that he might do what the *one* who enlisted the soldiers would like.
5 Also if someone competes, he is not crowned with an award wreath unless he competes according to the rules.
6 It is necessary for the laboring farmer to first be receiving of the fruits with *others*.
7 Be aware of what I say. You see, the Master will give you understanding in all *kinds of things*.
8 Remember Jesus, *the* Anointed King, who has been gotten up from *the* dead, from David's seed, aligned with my good news,
9 in which I suffer tough hardships up to restraints, as *if I am* an outlaw, but the message of God has not been locked up.
10 Because of this, I persist *to do what is right* in all *things* because of the select *people*, so that they also might obtain the rescue in *the* Anointed King Jesus with magnificence that spans *all* time.
11 The message can be trusted. You see, if we died together, we will also live together.
12 If we persist *to do what is right*, we will also be kings together. If we deny *Him*, that *One* will also deny us.
13 If we don't trust, that *One* stays *as the One* who can be trusted. He is not able to deny Himself.
14 Quietly remember these *things*, being a strong witness in the sight of the Master not to be arguing about words based on nothing useful, based on a disaster of the *people* listening.
15 Make every effort to offer yourself up, approved to God, an unashamed worker, being straight with the message of the truth.
16 Stand clear of the profane meaningless voices. You see, they will progress on to more of godlessness,
17 and their message will have a pasture as gangrene, of whom is Hymenaeus and Philetus,
18 some who missed the target concerning the truth (saying the return back to life to have already happened) and overturn the trust of some.
19 However, the solid foundation of God has stood having this seal: "*The* Master knew the *people* who are His." And, "Everyone who names the name of the Master must stand off away from *the* wrong way."

20 In a large house, there is not only gold and silver containers, but also wooden and ceramic, and *some* that *are* for value, *others* that *are* for no value.
21 So if anyone cleans himself off from these *things*, he will be a container for value that has been made sacred and very useful to the owner, that has been readied for every good action.
22 Escape the more youthful desires. Pursue *the* right way, trust, love, peace with the *people* who call on the Master from a clean heart.
23 Refuse the foolish and undisciplined questionings, realizing that they give birth to arguments.
24 It is not necessary for a slave of *the* Master to be arguing, but to be gentle to everyone, able to teach, tolerant of bad things,
25 in humility disciplining the *people* who oppose *God's* deal, so that perhaps God might give them a change of ways to a correct understanding of truth,
26 and they might be sober again out of the trap of the Accuser, who have been caught alive by him for what that *Accuser* wants.

3

1 Know this, that in *the* last days, fierce times will stand here.
2 You see, the people will be fond of themselves, fond of money, egoistic, proud, insulting, unbelieving to parents, ungenerous, unholy,
3 hardhearted toward family, refusing to enter into agreements, accusers, lacking restraint, mean, not fond of good,
4 traitors, obnoxious, having been blinded by smoke, fond of pleasure rather than fond of God,
5 having a form of godliness, but having denied its ability. And from these *people*, turn away.
6 You see, out of these *people* are the *people* who sneak into the houses and incarcerate the wacky women who have been piled with sins, being led by various desires,
7 always learning and never able to come to a correct understanding of truth.
8 *In the* way that Jannes and Jambres stood in opposition to Moses, so these *people* also stand in opposition to the truth, people who have been entirely worsened by *their* way of thinking, unapproved concerning the trust.
9 But they will not progress on to more. You see, their insanity will be quite obvious to everyone, as the *insanity* of those *people* also became.
10 You have followed alongside my instruction, *my* leading, *my* purpose, *my* trust, *my* patience, *my* love, *my* persistence *to do what is right*,
11 *my* persecutions, *my* hardships (such as happened to me in Antioch, in Iconium, in Lystra). Such persecutions I endured, and from all *of them* the Master saved me.
12 All the *people* who also want to be living godly in *the* Anointed King Jesus will be persecuted.
13 Evil people and impostors will progress on to the worse *thing*, misleading and being misled.
14 You must stay in what you learned and come to trust, realizing from whose side you learned

15 and that from a baby you have seen the temple documents, the *ones* that are able to provide you with insight into rescue through trust, the *trust* in *the* Anointed King Jesus.
16 Every God-breathed writing *is* also beneficial toward instruction, toward a reprimand, toward rehabilitation, toward the discipline in *the* right way,
17 so that the person of God may be developed having been fully developed toward every good action.

4

1 So I am a strong witness in the sight of God and the Master Jesus, *the* Anointed King (the *One* who is going to be judging living *people* and dead *people*) regarding His manifestation and His monarchy.
2 Speak publicly about the message. Take a stand at easy times, at inconvenient times. Reprimand. Shush. Encourage in every *bit of* patience and teaching.
3 You see, there will be a time when they will not tolerate the instruction that is healthy, but aligned with the desires (*their* own), they will pile up teachers for themselves who tickle the sense of hearing.
4 And away from the truth they certainly will turn the hearing; over the myths they will be turned out.
5 You must be sober in all *things*. Suffer tough hardships. Do *the* work of a sharer of good news. Be well-established in your *job of* serving.
6 You see, my blood is already being poured out as an offering, and the time of my release has stood over *me*.
7 I have struggled in the struggle, the nice *one*. I have finished the race. I have kept the trust.
8 For *the* rest *of the time*, the award wreath of the right way is set aside for me that the Master (the judge who does what is right) will give back to me in that day, not only to me, but also to all the *people* who have loved His manifestation.
9 Make every effort to come to me soon.
10 You see, Demas left me down in *here* (who loved the present span of time) and traveled to Thessalonica, Crescens to Galatia, Titus to Dalmatia.
11 Only Luke is with me. After taking up Mark, lead *him here* with yourself. You see, he is very useful to me in serving.
12 I sent Tychicus out *on a mission* to Ephesus.
13 Bring the coat that I left behind in Troas beside Carpus as you come, and the scrolls, especially the sheep skins.
14 Alexander, the coppersmith, displayed many bad *things* to me. The Master will give back to him aligned with his actions,
15 whom you also must beware of. You see, he has stood very *much* in opposition to our messages.
16 In my first defense, no one came out together for me. But everyone left me down in *here*. May it not be considered to them.
17 The Master stood by me and gave ability to me so that through me the public speaking might be well-established and all the non-Jews might hear. And I was saved from *the* lion's mouth.

18 And the Master will save me from every evil action and will rescue *me* into His monarchy, the heavenly *one*, to whom *belongs* the magnificence for the spans of time of the spans of time. Amen.
19 Say hello to Prisca (*the formal name of Priscilla*), Aquila, and *the people in* Onesiphorus' house.
20 Erastus stayed in Corinth, but I left Trophimus behind in Miletus (who is weak).
21 Make every effort to come before *the* storm season. Eubulus, Pudens, Linus, Claudia, and all the brothers say hello to you.
22 *May* the Master Jesus, *the* Anointed King, *be* with your spirit, the generosity with you all. Amen. [*This* second *letter* was written to Timothy (first elected supervisor of the assembly of the Ephesian *people*) from Rome when Paul stood before Caesar Nero at *the* second *time*]

Titus

1

1 *From:* Paul, God's slave, but a missionary of Jesus, *the* Anointed King, aligned with *the* trust of God's select *people* and a correct understanding of the truth aligned with godliness
2 based on an anticipation of life that spans *all* time, that the God who does not lie promised before *the* times that span *all* time.
3 At *His* own right times, He showed His message in public speaking with which I was trusted aligned with a directive of our Rescuer God.
4 To: Titus, a real child according to a shared trust. Generosity, forgiving kindness, peace out from Father God and Master Jesus, *the* Anointed King Jesus, our Rescuer.
5 Thanks to this, I left you down *there* in Crete so that you might set the *things* straight that are missing and put older *men* in charge in each city as I specifically assigned you:
6 if someone is a *person* with no charges against him, one woman's husband, having trusting children not in a criminal complaint of recklessness or unruly.
7 You see, it is necessary for the supervisor to be a *person* with no charges against him as God's manager, not self-pleasuring, not easily mad, not beside wine, not a hitter, not pursuing shameful gain,
8 but friendly to strangers, fond of good, properly focused, right, holy, restrained,
9 having in front of *him* the message that can be trusted *that is* aligned with the teaching so that he may be able both to be encouraging with the instruction (the *instruction* that is healthy) and to be reprimanding the *people* expressing opposition.
10 You see, many are also unruly meaningless talkers and seducers, especially the *people* from *the* circumcision,
11 with whom it is necessary to be putting something over their mouths, some who overturn whole houses teaching what is not necessary (thanks to shameful gain).
12 Someone from among them, their own preacher, said, "Cretans always *are* liars, bad, wild animals, idle stomachs."
13 This witness account is valid, which *is the* reason why you must reprimand them severely so that they may be healthy in the trust,
14 not paying attention to Judean myths and demands of people who turn away from the truth.
15 All *things are* certainly clean to the clean *people*, but to the *people* who have been desecrated and *who are* untrusting, nothing *is* clean, but both their way of thinking and conscience have been desecrated.
16 They acknowledge to know God, but with *their* actions they deny *Him*, being disgusting, unbelieving, and unapproved toward every good action.

2

1 *As for* you, speak what is appropriate for the instruction that is healthy:
2 for old men to be sober, respectful, properly focused, being healthy in the trust, the love, the persistence;
3 for old women, similarly, *to be* temple-appropriate in conduct, not accusers, not having been enslaved to much wine, teachers of nice things
4 (so that they may properly focus the young *women* to be fond of *their* husbands, fond of children),
5 properly focused, consecrated, housekeepers, good, being under *their* own husbands so that the message of God may not be insulted;
6 for the younger *men*, similarly, encourage to be properly focused
7 about everything, providing yourself *as* an example of nice actions in the instruction: durability, respect, non-deterioration,
8 a healthy message with no known problems (so that the *person* from an opposing *view* might be embarrassed, having nothing useless to be saying about you);
9 for slaves to be placing themselves under *their* own owners in all *things*, to be well-liked, not expressing opposition,
10 not secretly keeping anything for themselves, but displaying every *bit of* good trust so that they may decorate the instruction of our Rescuer God in all *things*.
11 You see, the generosity of God, the rescuing *generosity*, was shined on all people
12 disciplining us so that after denying the godlessness and the global desires, we might live properly focused, rightly, and godly in the present span of time
13 awaiting the blessed anticipation and manifestation of the magnificence of the great God and our Rescuer Jesus, *the* Anointed King,
14 who gave Himself on our behalf so that He might pay the price to release us out of every crime and clean for Himself a special ethnic group with passion for nice actions.
15 Speak, encourage, and reprimand these *things* with every directive. No one must circumvent you.

3

1 Quietly remind them to be placing themselves under head rulers and authorities, to be loyal, to be ready toward every good action,
2 to be insulting no one, to be non-arguers, polite, displaying all humility to all people.
3 You see, we ourselves in the past were also unobservant, unbelieving, being misled, being slaves to desires and various pleasures, leading through *it* in badness and envy, detestable, hating each other.
4 When the kindness and the benevolence of our Rescuer God was shined on us
5 (not from actions, the *ones* in *the* right way that we did, but aligned with His forgiving kindness), He rescued us through a bath: a rebirth and renewal of *the* Sacred Spirit,

6 that He spilled out richly on us through Jesus, *the* Anointed King, our Rescuer,

7 so that when we were made right by that *One's* generosity, we might become inheritors aligned with anticipation of life that spans *all* time.

8 The message can be trusted. And concerning these *things*, I intend for you to be thoroughly authenticating *them* so that the *people* who have trusted in God may be made to focus to be presiding over nice actions. These are the nice and beneficial *things* for the people.

9 But stand clear of foolish questionings, genealogies, fightings, and law arguments. You see, they are nonbeneficial and futile.

10 Refuse a person of a sect after one and a second correction,

11 realizing that this type of *person* has been turned inside out and sins, being found guilty by himself.

12 When I will send Artemas to you or Tychicus, make every effort to come to me to Nicopolis. You see, I have decided to spend the storm season there.

13 Bring Zenas (the law *expert*) and Apollos aggressively on their way so that nothing may be missing to them.

14 Our *people* must also learn to be presiding over nice actions for the essential needs so that they may not be fruitless.

15 All the *people* with me say hello to you. Say hello to the *people* that we are fond of in trust. *May* the generosity *be* with you all. Amen. [Written to Titus (first elected supervisor of the assembly of Cretans) from Nicopolis, Macedonia]

Philemon

1

1 *From:* Paul (a prisoner for *the* Anointed King Jesus) and Timothy (the brother). To: Philemon (the loved *one* and our co-worker),
2 Apphia (the loved *woman*), Archippus (our fellow soldier), and the assembly throughout your house.
3 Generosity to you and peace out from God, our Father, and Master Jesus, *the* Anointed King.
4 I am always thankful to my God, making mention of you over my prayers,
5 as I hear your love and trust that you have toward the Master Jesus and for all the sacred *people*
6 in order that the sharing of your trust might become active in a correct understanding of every good *thing* in you for *the* Anointed King Jesus.
7 You see, I have much happiness and encouragement based on your love because the sympathy of the sacred *people* has been relaxed through you, brother.
8 For this reason, having a very clear public statement in *the* Anointed King to be giving the directive to you for what meets the high standards,
9 because of the love instead I am encouraging *you*, being this type of *person* as Paul, an old man, but right now also a prisoner for *the* Anointed King Jesus.
10 I am encouraging you concerning my child whom I gave birth to in my restraints, Onesimus *(his name means Profitable)*,
11 the *one* not useful to you in the past, but right now he *is* very useful to you and to me,
12 whom I am sending up *to you* (you yourself must take *him* in — this is my sympathy),
13 whom I was intending to steadily be having facing myself so that he may serve me on your behalf in the restraints of the good news.
14 But without your opinion, I didn't want to do anything, so that your good may not be, as *it were*, aligned with an obligation, but aligned with volunteering.
15 You see, possibly because of this he was separated *from you* toward an hour, so that you may have all of him that spans *all* time,
16 no longer as a slave, but above a slave, a loved brother, especially to me, but how much more to you, both in *the* physical body and in *the* Master.
17 So if you have me *as* a partner, take him in as me.
18 But if he wronged you or owes anything, put this to me on account.
19 I, Paul, wrote it with my hand (I will pay the penalty in full) so that I may not tell you that you also additionally owe yourself to me.
20 Yes, brother, may I profit from you in *the* Master. Relax my sympathy in *the* Master.
21 Having been confident of your obedience, I wrote you realizing that you will do even above what I say.

22 Also at the same time get a guesthouse ready for me. You see, I anticipate that through your prayers I will be given to you as an act of generosity.
23 Epaphras, the person incarcerated together with me in *the* Anointed King Jesus, says hello to you,
24 *as do* Mark, Aristarchus, Demas, Luke, my co-workers.
25 *May* the generosity of our Master Jesus, *the* Anointed King, *be* with your spirit. Amen. [Written to Philemon from Rome *and sent* through Onesimus, a domestic servant]

Hebrews

1

1 God, who in many parts and in many ways a long time ago spoke to the fathers in the preachers,
2 over these last days spoke to us in *the* Son, whom He placed *as* an inheritor of all *things*, through whom He also made the spans of time,
3 who being radiance of the magnificence and an exact expression of His undertaking, also carrying all *things* with the statement of His ability, after doing a cleansing of our sins by Himself, He was seated in *the* right *side* of the Majesty in high *places*,
4 after becoming so much better than the angels, as much as He has inherited a more substantial name than they.
5 You see, to which of the angels did He ever say *(as He said in Psalms 2:7)*, "You are My Son, I today have given birth to You?" And again *in 2 Samuel 7:14*, "I will be for a father to Him, and He will be for a son to Me?"
6 Again, when He led the Firstborn into the civilized world, He says *in Deuteronomy 32:43*, "And all God's angels must bow down to Him."
7 And toward the angels, He certainly says *in Psalm 104:4*, "The *One* who makes His angels spirits and His public servants a blaze of fire,"
8 but toward the Son *in Psalm 45:6–7*, "Your throne, God, *is* for the span of time of the span of time. A staff of straightness *is* the staff of Your monarchy.
9 You loved *the* right way and hated crime. Because of this, God, Your God, anointed You with olive oil of excitement rather than Your teammates."
10 And *in Psalm 102:25-27*, "You, throughout *the* beginning, Master, laid the earth's foundation, and the skies are works of Your hands.
11 They will be ruined. But You stay through *it all*, and they all will be worn out as a robe.
12 And as if *they were* a cloak, You will fold them up, and they will be changed. But You are the same, and your years will not cease."
13 Toward which of the angels has He ever stated, "Sit down at *places to the* right of Me until I place Your enemies *as* a footrest for Your feet?"
14 Aren't they all spirits that serve the public being sent out *on a mission* for serving because of the *people* who are going to be inheriting a rescue?

2

1 Because of this, it is necessary for us to be paying much more attention to the *things* that were heard so that we might not flow past *them*.
2 You see, if the message spoken through angels became firm and every violation and noncompliance received a reasonable earned payment,

3 how will we escape from *it* after not caring for such a great rescue as this, something that after it received a beginning to be spoken through the Master, it was authenticated for us by the *people* who heard *it*,
4 God corroborating *it* together with indicators, incredible things, various abilities, and distributions of *the* Sacred Spirit aligned with what He wanted.
5 You see, He didn't place under angels the civilized world, the *one* that is going *to come*, about which we are speaking.
6 But someone somewhere was a strong witness *to the fact*, saying *in Psalm 8:4–6*, "What is a person that You remind Yourself of him or a person's son that You keep an eye on him?
7 You made him some bit less than angels. You also crowned him with an award wreath of magnificence and value. You also put him in charge over the works of Your hands.
8 You placed all *things* beneath his feet." You see, during the *time* to place all the *things* under Him, He left nothing unruly to Him. But now we see that all *things* are not yet placed under Him.
9 We see Jesus *as* the *One* who has been made some bit less than angels, who because of the hardship of the death has been crowned with an award wreath of magnificence and value, in order that by God's generosity He might taste death on behalf of everyone.
10 You see, it was appropriate for Him (because of whom all the *things exist*, and through whom all the *things exist*), after leading many sons into magnificence, to complete the Head Leader of their rescue through hardships;
11 for both the *One* making *people* sacred and the *people* being made sacred *are* all from one, which *is the* reason why He is not ashamed to be calling them brothers,
12 saying *in Psalm 22:22*, "I will report Your name to My brothers. In *the* middle of an assembly I will sing praise songs to You."
13 And again *in Isaiah 8:17*, "I will be *someone* who has been confident based on Him." And again *in Isaiah 8:18*, "Look, I and the young children that God gave to Me."
14 So since the young children have shared a physical body and blood, He Himself also, in a way *that was* near *and* beside *them*, took part in the same *things*, so that through the death He might make useless the *one* who has the power of the death (that is, the Accuser)
15 and He might relieve these *people*, as many as with fear of death through every *bit of* the "to be living" *part* were eligible to be sentenced to slavery.
16 You see, maybe He does not latch on to angels, but He does latch on to a seed of Abraham.
17 From this, He ought to be like the brothers regarding all *things* so that He might become a kind forgiving and reliable head priest *in* the *things* toward God for the "to be providing a remedy for the sins of the ethnic group" *part*.
18 You see, in what He has suffered when He Himself experienced trouble, He is able to help the *people* experiencing trouble.

3

1 From this, sacred brothers (teammates of a heavenly invitation), take a closer look at the Missionary and Head Priest of our acknowledgment, *the* Anointed King Jesus,
2 who is reliable to the *One* who made Him *the Head Priest*, as Moses also *was* in his whole house.
3 You see, this *Head Priest* has deserved more magnificence than Moses, inasmuch as the *One* who constructed it *(the house)* has more value than the house;
4 for every house is constructed by someone, but the *One* who constructed all the *things is* God.
5 And Moses certainly *is* reliable in His whole house (as an attending servant) for a witness of the *things* that will be spoken.
6 But *the* Anointed King (as a son) *is* over His house, whose house we are if it is true that we steadily have the clear public statement and the bragging of the anticipation firm up to *the* conclusion.
7 For this reason, *it is* just as the Spirit, the Sacred *Spirit*, says *in Psalm 95:7–11*, "Today, if you will listen to His voice,
8 you should not harden your hearts as in the rebellion throughout the day of the trouble in the backcountry
9 where your fathers tried to cause trouble with Me. They checked Me and saw My actions forty years.
10 For this reason, I was aggravated with that generation, and I said, 'They are always misled with the heart. They didn't know My ways.'
11 *It is* as I guaranteed in My punishment, 'If they will come into My resting place, *may I be punished*.'"
12 Brothers, see that there will never be in any of you an evil heart of a lack of trust during the *time for you* to stand off away from *the* living God.
13 But encourage yourselves throughout each day till *a time* that is called the "Today," so that no one from among you might be hardened by the sin's fraud.
14 You see, we have become teammates of the Anointed King if it is true that we steadily have the beginning of the undertaking firm up to *the* conclusion,
15 during the *time for it* to be said, "Today, if you will listen to His voice, you should not harden your hearts as in the rebellion."
16 You see, who rebelled after they heard? But *who*? Not all the *people* who came out of Egypt through Moses.
17 Who was He aggravated with for forty years? Was it not with the *people* who sinned, whose carcasses fell in the backcountry?
18 To whom did He guarantee *for them* not to go into His resting place, except to the *people* who did not believe?
19 And we see that they were not able to go in because of a lack of trust.

4

1 So we should be afraid that as a promise is left down *here* to go into His resting place, some from among you may not ever seem to have lacked *it*.
2 You see, we are also *people* with whom the good news has been shared, exactly as those *people* also *were*, but the message of what

was heard didn't benefit those *people*, not having been mixed together with the trust with the *people* who heard.

3 You see, we (the *people* who trusted) come into the resting place, just as it has been stated *in Psalm 95:11* ("As I guaranteed in My punishment, 'If they will come into My resting place...'") even yet from the actions *of work* that happened from *the* world's founding;

4 for He has stated somewhere *(Genesis 2:2)* about the seventh *day* like this, "And God rested in the day, the seventh, from all His actions *of work*."

5 And in this *place* again, "If they will come into My resting place...."

6 So since it is left behind for some to go into it, and the *people* with whom the good news was previously shared did not go in because of unbelief,

7 again He designated a certain day, "Today," saying in David after so much time, just as it has been stated, "Today, if you will listen to His voice, you should not harden your hearts."

8 You see, if Joshua gave them rest, *David* would not be speaking about another *day* after these days.

9 Clearly a Sabbath-rest is left behind for God's ethnic group.

10 You see, the *person* who went into His resting place also himself rested from his actions *of work*, even as God *rested* from *His* own *actions of work*.

11 So we should make every effort to go into that resting place so that someone might not fall in the same demonstration of the unbelief.

12 You see, the living message of God *is* also active, sharper above every double-edged dagger, penetrating till dividing both soul and spirit, joints and marrows, and judgeable of a heart's contemplations and internal ways of thinking.

13 And creation is not *something* unapparent in His sight. All *are* naked and *things* that have been exposed to His eyes (facing whom the message *is* for us).

14 So having a great head priest who has gone through the heavens, Jesus, the Son of God, we should hold on to the acknowledgment.

15 You see, we don't have a head priest who is not able to empathize with our weaknesses, but *a head priest* who has experienced trouble in each *and* everything, in each likeness, without sin.

16 So we may come with a clear public statement to the throne of the generosity so that we might receive forgiving kindness and find generosity for well-timed help.

5

1 You see, every head priest taken from people is put in charge of the *things* toward God on behalf of people, so that he may offer up both contributions and sacrifices on behalf of sins,

2 being able to be sympathizing to a certain extent with the *people* who are unaware and who are misled since weakness is also lying around him.

3 And because of this, he is obligated (just as concerning the ethnic group, so also concerning himself) to be offering up *sacrifices* concerning sins.

4 And someone does not take the importance for himself, but *he is* the *one* who is invited by God, exactly as Aaron also *was*.

5 In this way also, the Anointed King did not elevate Himself to a place of magnificence to become *the* head priest, but the *One* who spoke to Him ("You are My Son. I today have given birth to You.") *elevated Him to a place of magnificence.*
6 Just as He also says in a different *place in Psalm 110:4,* "You *are* a priest for the span of time aligned with the arrangement of Melchizedek,"
7 who, in the days of His physical body, after bringing both pleas and petitions to the *One* who is able to be rescuing Him from death with a strong yell and tears and was listened to out of the devotedness,
8 even though being a son, learned the obedience out of what He suffered.
9 And when He was completed, He became (for all the *people* obeying Him) *the* cause of *the* rescue that spans *all* time
10 when He was publicly addressed by God *as* Head Priest aligned with the arrangement of Melchizedek,
11 about whom, the message to us *is* a lot and of a hard interpretation to be telling, since you have become sluggish with the hearing.
12 You see, even though you ought to be teachers because of the time, again you have a need of the "for us to be teaching you some primary elements of the beginning of the utterances of God" *kind*. And you have become *people* having a need of milk and not a solid meal.
13 You see, everyone who takes part in milk *is* inexperienced with *the* right way's message; for he is an infant.
14 But the solid meal is for complete *people*, the *people* who because of the habit have the senses that have been strenuously exercised toward discernment of both nice and bad.

6

1 For this reason, after leaving the message of the beginning of the Anointed King, we should be carried up to the maturity, not throwing down a foundation again of a change of ways out of dead actions and of trust based on God,
2 of *the* teaching of submersions, of laying on of hands, of *the* return back to life of dead *people*, and of judgment that spans *all* time.
3 And this we will do if it is true that God gives permission.
4 You see, *it is* impossible for the *people* who were once lit up and who tasted of the free handout (the heavenly *one*), who became teammates of *the* Sacred Spirit,
5 who tasted God's nice statement and *the* abilities of *the* span of time that is going *to come,*
6 and who fell away, to again make *themselves* renewed in a change of ways, again nailing the Son of God to a cross for themselves and making a public exhibit *of it.*
7 You see, after the ground drinks the shower coming on it many times, as it also delivers feed that is suitable for those who, because of *them*, it is even farmed, with *others* it receives *some* of *the* conferring of blessings out from God.
8 But as it brings out thorns and thistles, *it is* unapproved and near a curse of which the conclusion *is* for a burn.

9 But we have been confident concerning you, loved *ones*, of the better *things* and of *things* that include rescue, even though we speak like this.
10 You see, God doesn't do what is wrong: to be forgetful of your work and the labor of love that you displayed in His name after you served and as you serve the sacred *people*.
11 We desire each of you to be displaying the same concern toward the full accomplishment of the anticipation *of good* till *the* conclusion
12 so that you might not become sluggish, but imitators of the *people* who inherit the promises through trust and patience.
13 You see, when God promised to Abraham, since He had no one greater to guarantee *it* under, He guaranteed *it* under Himself,
14 saying *in Genesis 22:17*, "Most certainly, as I confer blessings, I will confer blessings on you, and as I increase, I will increase you."
15 And this is how after he was patient, he obtained the promise.
16 You see, people certainly guarantee under the bigger *one* and the oath for authentication is the end of every dispute for them,
17 in which, since God intends much more to show the inheritors of the promise the unchangeable *attribute* of His intention, He ratified *it* with an oath
18 so that through two unchangeable items (in which *it is* impossible for God to lie), we may have strong encouragement, the *people* who escaped down to take hold of the anticipation *of good* that is lying up ahead,
19 that we have as an anchor of the soul, certain, firm, and going into the inner *side* of the *temple's* curtain,
20 where a scout went in on our behalf, Jesus, who became a head priest (aligned with the arrangement of Melchizedek) for the span of time.

7

1 You see, this Melchizedek, king of Salem, priest of God (the highest *God*), *is* the *one* who met together with Abraham as he was returning out of the slaying of the kings and who conferred a blessing on him,
2 to whom, Abraham also divided ten percent out of everything. First, *his name* certainly *is* interpreted "king of *the* right way," but following that *he is* also king of Salem, that is king of peace,
3 fatherless, motherless, genealogyless, having neither beginning of days, nor conclusion of life, but having been made very much like the Son of God, he stays a priest forever.
4 See how great this *man was* to whom even Abraham, the head father, gave ten percent from the tops of the piles.
5 And certainly the *people* from the sons of Levi who receive the office of the priesthood have a demand to be taking ten percent out from the ethnic group according to the law (that is, *from* their brothers, even though *they are people* who have come out of the groin of Abraham).
6 But the *one* who is not genealogically traced from them has received ten percent from Abraham and conferred a blessing on the *one* who has the promises.

7 Separate from every dispute, the lesser *person* is conferred with a blessing by the better *person*.
8 And here, people who certainly die receive ten percent, but there, *a person* who is witnessed *by the Old Testament* that he lives.
9 And as *a part of this, there is* a saying to say: through Abraham even Levi (the *one* who receives ten percent) has paid ten percent *to him*.
10 You see, he was still in the groin of *his* father when Melchizedek met together with him.
11 So certainly if there was a completion through the Levitical priesthood (you see, laws have been made for the ethnic group based on it), what further need *would there be* for a different priest to be standing up, to be called aligned with the arrangement of Melchizedek and not aligned with the arrangement of Aaron?
12 You see, as the priesthood is transferred, from an obligation, a transfer of law also happens.
13 You see, He (on whom these *things* are said) has taken part in a different family line out of which no one has paid attention to the altar;
14 for *it is* evident that our Master has come up from Judah, a family line to which Moses spoke nothing about a priesthood.
15 And it is still much more than very obvious: if *He is* aligned with the likeness of Melchizedek, a different priest is standing up,
16 who hasn't become aligned with *the* law of a physical demand, but aligned with *the* ability of an indestructible life.
17 You see, He tells what He witnessed *in Psalm 110:4*, "You *are* a priest for the span of time aligned with the arrangement of Melchizedek."
18 You see, a demand leading the way certainly becomes an invalidation because of the weak and nonbeneficial *nature* of it;
19 for the law completed nothing, but what was brought in over it *has* a better anticipation *of good* through which we come near to God.
20 And inasmuch as *it is* not without an oath of guarantee
21 (you see, certainly, the *people* are without an oath of guarantee who have become priests, but the *Anointed King is* with an oath of guarantee through the *One* saying to Him, "*The* Master guaranteed *it* and will not regret *it*, You *are* a priest for the span of time aligned with the arrangement of Melchizedek")
22 aligned with so much, Jesus has become a security deposit of a better deal.
23 And certainly, the *people* who have become priests are more *in number* because of the *fact for them* to be hindered by death to be continuing on.
24 But *Jesus* (because of the *fact* for Him to be staying for the span of time) has the nontransferable priesthood.
25 From this, He is also able to be rescuing to the maximum the *people* who come to God through Him since He is always living for the "to be intervening on their behalf" *part*.
26 You see, this type of head priest was appropriate for us, holy, not bad, not desecrated, separate away from the sinful *people*, who even became higher than the heavens,
27 who does not have a daily obligation, even as the head priests *do*, to be carrying up sacrifices, previously on behalf of *their* own sins, following that *on*

behalf of the *sins* of the ethnic group. You see, He did this when He carried Himself up all at once;
28 for the law puts people in charge *as* head priests who have weakness, but the message of the oath of guarantee (the *one* after the law) *puts the* Son (who has been completed) *in charge* for the span of time.

8

1 The main point on the *things* being said *is*, we have this type of head priest, *one* who is seated in *the* right *side* of the throne of the Majesty in the heavens,
2 a public servant of the Sacred *Things* and the tent (the true *one*), that the Master and not a person set up.
3 You see, every head priest is put in charge for the "to be offering both contributions and sacrifices" *part*. From this, *it is* essential for this *person* to also be having something that he might offer.
4 So certainly, if He were on earth, He would not even be a priest since the priests exist, the *ones* who offer up the contributions aligned with the law,
5 some who minister for a demonstration and shadow of the heavenly *things*, just as Moses had been *divinely* notified as he was going to be finishing up the tent. "You see, look," He declared, "you should make everything according to the example, the *one* shown to you in the mountain."
6 But right now, He has obtained a more substantial public service, as much as He is also a middleman of a better deal, something that law has been made with based on better promises.
7 You see, if that first *deal* were faultless, *the* place of *the* second *deal* would not be looked for;
8 for finding fault with them, He says *in Jeremiah 31:31–34*, "'Look, days are coming,' says *the* Master, 'and I will completely finish a new deal over the house of Israel and over the house of Judah,
9 not aligned with the deal that I made with their fathers in a day when I latched on to their hand to lead them out of *the* land of Egypt. Because they didn't stay in My deal, I also didn't care for them,' says *the* Master.
10 'Because this is the deal that I will make with the house of Israel after those days,' says *the* Master, 'giving my laws, I will inscribe them into their mind and on their hearts. And I will be to them for a God, and they will be to Me for an ethnic group.
11 And they will not in any way teach (each *one* the *person* near him and each *one* his brother), saying, 'Know the Master,' because everyone will know Me, from a little *one* up to their great *one*,
12 because I will be remedied for their wrong ways, and their sins and their crimes I will not in any way remember anymore.'"
13 During the *time* to be saying, "New," He has outdated the first. What is outdated and aging *is* near disappearance.

9

1 So the first *deal* certainly also was having right paths of a sacrifice ritual and the global Sacred *Thing*.

2 You see, a tent was constructed: the first *room* in which *were* both the lampstand and the table and the display of the *loaves of* bread, a certain *room* that is called *the* Sacred *Room*,

3 but after the second curtain, the tent being called Sacred *Room* of Sacred *Things*

4 having *the* gold incense altar and the box of the deal that has been covered around on all sides with gold, in which *is* a gold jar (having the manna and the staff of Aaron, the *one* that budded) and the slabs of the deal,

5 over *and* above this, cherubim of magnificence throwing a shadow on the source of remedy; about which *things* there is not *time* now to be talking of each part.

6 These having been constructed like this, into the first *room of the* tent through everything the priests certainly enter finishing up the sacrifice rituals,

7 but into the second *room* once a year, the head priest *enters* alone, not without blood, that he offers up on behalf of himself and the undiscovered things of the ethnic group.

8 This *is* what the Spirit, the Sacred *Spirit*, makes obvious: for the way of the Sacred *Things* to not yet have been shown as the first *room of the* tent still has a standing,

9 something that *is* an illustration for the time, the *time* that has stood here, aligned with which, both contributions and sacrifices are offered up that are not able, regarding *the* conscience, to complete the *person* ministering,

10 only lying on food, drink, specialized submersions, and right paths of a physical body up to *the* right time of reformation.

11 But when *the* Anointed King showed up *as* a head priest of the good *things* that are going *to come* through the greater and more complete tent, not handmade, that is, not of this creation,

12 nor through *the* blood of male goats and calves, but through *His* own blood, He went all at once into the Sacred *Things* after He found a release payment that spans *all* time.

13 You see, if the blood of bulls and male goats and ash of a young cow sprinkling the *people* who have been shared makes *them* sacred toward the cleaning of the physical body,

14 how much more the blood of the Anointed King (who through *the* Spirit that spans *all* time offered Himself up unblemished to God) will clean your conscience off from dead actions for the "to be ministering to the living God" *part*.

15 And because of this, He is *the* middleman of *the* new deal in order that, after a death happened for *the* paid release from the violations on the first deal, the *people* who have been invited might receive the promise of the inheritance that spans *all* time.

16 You see, where *there is* a deal, *there is* an obligation for *the* death of the *person* making the deal to be carried;

17 for a deal *is* firm over *the* dead, or else it never has strength when the *person* who made *it* is alive.

18 From this, neither has the first *deal* been initiated without blood.

19 You see, after every demand according to *the* law was spoken by Moses to all the ethnic group, when he took the blood of the calves and the male goats with water, red wool, and hyssop, he sprinkled both the very scroll and all the ethnic group,
20 saying, "This *is* the blood of the deal that God demanded to you."
21 Both the tent and all the containers for public service he likewise sprinkled with the blood.
22 And nearly everything is cleaned in blood according to the law, and without a spilling out of blood, forgiveness does not happen.
23 So *there is* certainly an obligation for the demonstrations of the *things* in the heavens to be cleaned with these, but the heavenly *things* themselves with better sacrifices than these.
24 You see, the Anointed King didn't go into *the* handmade Sacred *Things* (a corresponding type of the true *Sacred Things*), but into heaven itself to be made apparent now to the face of God on our behalf,
25 nor so that he may offer Himself up many times (even as the head priest goes into the Sacred *Things* yearly with blood belonging to others),
26 or else it was necessary for Him to suffer many times since *the* founding of *the* world, but now, once, over *the* very conclusion of the spans of time, He has been shown for *the* invalidation of sin through His sacrifice.
27 And inasmuch as it is set aside for the *people* to die once, but after this, judgment,
28 in this way, the Anointed King, after being offered up once for the "to carry up *the* sins of many" *part*, will appear from a second *time* without sin to the *people* who patiently wait for Him for rescue.

10

1 You see, the law (having a shadow of the good *things* that are going *to come*, not the very image of the items) is never ever able to complete the *people* coming to *it* yearly with the same sacrifices that they offer up forever.
2 Or else wouldn't they stop being offered up? Because of the *fact for them* to be having no conscience of sins anymore (the *people* serving the public who have been pruned once).
3 But in these *sacrifices there is* a reminder again of sins yearly.
4 You see, *it is* impossible for *the* blood of bulls and male goats to be taking away sins.
5 For this reason, as He is coming into the world, He says *in Psalm 40:6–8*, "A sacrifice and an offering You didn't want, but a body You developed for Me.
6 You were not delighted *by* entirely burned offerings and *offerings* concerning sin.
7 At that time, I said, 'Look, I have arrived (in a roll of a scroll it has been written about me) for the *purpose* to do what You want, God.'"
8 Further up as it says that You didn't want a sacrifice, an offering, entirely burned offerings, and *offerings* concerning sin, neither were You delighted *by them*, some *offerings* that are offered up according to the law,

9 then He has stated, "Look, I have arrived for the *purpose* to do what You want, God;" He takes away the first so that the second might stand.

10 In a *thing* that He wants, we are *people* who have been made sacred through the offering of the body of Jesus, *the* Anointed King, all at once.

11 And every priest certainly has stood daily ministering and offering up the same sacrifices many times, some that are never ever able to take sins away all around.

12 But when He offered up one sacrifice on behalf of sins forever, He was seated in *the* right *side* of God,

13 the rest *of the time* waiting until His enemies are placed *as* a footrest of His feet.

14 You see, with one offering He has completed forever the *people* who are made sacred.

15 The Spirit, the Sacred *Spirit*, also is a witness to us *of this fact*, you see, after the *time for Him* to have stated beforehand *in Jeremiah 31:33*,

16 "'This *is* the deal that I will make toward them after those days,' says *the* Master. 'Giving My laws, I will inscribe them on their hearts and on their minds,'"

17 and *in Jeremiah 31:34*, "I will not in any way remember their sins and their crimes anymore."

18 Where *there is* forgiveness of these, *there* no longer *is* an offering concerning sin.

19 So, brothers, having a clear public statement for the entrance of the Sacred *Things* in the blood of Jesus

20 (that for us He initiated a way, recent and living, through the curtain, that is, *through* His physical body)

21 and a great priest over the house of God,

22 we should come forward with a true heart in full accomplishment of trust, having been sprinkled away from an evil conscience (the hearts) and having been given a bath in clean water (the body).

23 We should hold steady the acknowledgment of the anticipation *of good* without tilting. You see, the *One* who promised can be trusted.

24 And we should take a closer look at each other in reference to a stimulation of love and nice actions,

25 not leaving down in *there* the coming together of ourselves in one place, just as *it is* a custom to some, but encouraging, and so much more as much as you see the day coming near.

26 You see, if we are voluntarily sinning after the *time for us* to receive the correct understanding of the truth, a sacrifice is no longer left behind concerning sins,

27 but a certain fearful wait for judgment and a passion of fire that is going to be eating up the covert opponents.

28 Anyone who invalidates Moses' law dies without compassion based on two or three witnesses.

29 How much worse of an honor punishment does it seem to you the *person* will deserve who trampled on the Son of God, who regarded the blood of the

deal as shared (*the blood* in which he was made sacred), and who maimed the Spirit of the generosity?

30 You see, we know the *One* who said *in Deuteronomy 32:35*, "'Retaliation *is* for Me. I will repay,' says *the* Master," and again *in Deuteronomy 32:36*, "*The* Master will judge His ethnic group."

31 The fearful *thing is* to fall into hands of a living God.

32 But remind yourselves again of the days previously, in which, after you were lit up, you persisted *to do what is right* during much competition of hardships,

33 not only this: being made a public spectacle in both criticisms and hard times; but this: becoming partners of the *people* who were busy like this.

34 You see, you also empathized with my restraints and accepted the looting of the *things* that are yours with happiness, knowing in yourselves to be having a better and remaining possession in heaven.

35 So you shouldn't throw away your clear public statement, something that has a large earned payment.

36 You see, you have a need of persistence so that after doing what God wants, you might retrieve the promise;

37 for yet as much as, as much as a little while, the *One* who is coming will arrive, and it will not take a long time.

38 "The *person* who does what is right will live from trust" *(Habakkuk 2:4)* and if he backs off, My soul is not delighted with him.

39 We are not of a backing off into ruin, but of trust into an acquisition of *the* soul.

11

1 Trust is an undertaking of *things* that are anticipated, a validation of items that are not seen.

2 You see, in this the older *men* were witnessed *by others*.

3 With trust, we are aware for the spans of time to have been developed by God's statement for the "for the *things* that are seen to not have come into existence from *things* that appear" *part*.

4 With trust, Abel offered up to God more of a sacrifice than Cain, through which he was witnessed *by others* to be right, God telling what He witnessed based on his contributions. And through it, after dying, he still speaks.

5 With trust, Enoch was transferred, of the "to not see death" *kind*, and he was not being found because God transferred him. You see, before his transfer, he had been witnessed *by others* to have been well-liked by God.

6 Without trust *it is* impossible to be well-liked *by Him*. You see, it is necessary for the *person* who comes to God to trust that He is and He becomes a payer of earnings to the *people* intensively searching for Him.

7 With trust, when Noah was *divinely* notified about the *things* not yet seen, after taking *it* seriously, he constructed a box for *the* rescue *of the people* of his house, through which he found the world guilty and became an inheritor of *the* right way *that is* aligned with trust.

8 With trust, *a man* called Abraham obeyed to go out to the place that he was going to be receiving for an inheritance. And he went out, not even aware of where he is going.

9 With trust, he was a foreign resident in the land of the promise, as *land* belonging to others, who lived in tents with Isaac and Jacob, the inheritors together of the promise, the same *promise*.
10 You see, he was waiting for the city that had the foundations, whose skilled worker and craftsman *is* God.
11 With trust, also Sarah herself received *the* ability for *the* founding of a seed and delivered beyond *the* right time in age since she regarded the *One* who promised *to be someone* who can be trusted.
12 For this reason, also out of one who had been dead, even these *descendents* were born to the large number, just as the constellations of the sky and as if *they were* the sand along the shore of the sea, the countless *sand*.
13 Aligned with trust, these all died after not receiving the promises, but after seeing them from far away, greeting *them*, and acknowledging that they are strangers and refugees on the earth.
14 You see, the *people* saying these types of *things* make *it* apparent that they are searching for a hometown.
15 And certainly if they were remembering that *hometown* that they came out away from, they would have had a time to double back.
16 But right now they are reaching out for a better *hometown* (that is, a heavenly *hometown*). For this reason, God is not ashamed of them, to also be called their God. You see, He got a city ready for them.
17 With trust, Abraham had offered Isaac up, being troubled. And he was offering up the only biological *son, he,* the *one* who welcomed the promises in,
18 to whom it was spoken, "In Isaac, a seed will be called to you."
19 After he considered that God *is* able to be getting *him* up, even from *the* dead, from this he retrieved him, also in an illustration.
20 With trust, concerning *things* that were going *to come,* Isaac conferred a blessing on Jacob and Esau.
21 With trust, Jacob, as he was dying, conferred a blessing on each of the sons of Joseph, and bowed down over the edge of his staff.
22 With trust, Joseph, as he was passing away, remembered about the exit of the sons of Israel and demanded *them* about his bones.
23 With trust, Moses, after being born, was hidden for a three-month *period* by his parents because they saw the young child *to be* well behaved and they didn't fear the ruling of the king.
24 With trust, Moses, after he became great, denied to be called a son of Pharaoh's daughter,
25 after choosing rather to be mistreated together with the ethnic group of God than to be having enjoyment of sin for the time being,
26 who regarded the criticism of the Anointed King *as* greater wealth than the stockpiles of Egypt. You see, he was looking off to the earned payment.
27 With trust, he left Egypt down *there,* not fearing the anger of the king. You see, he was empowered by the invisible *One,* as *if* seeing *Him*.
28 With trust, he has done the Passover and the public spilling of the blood so that the *one* destroying the firstborn *children* would not come into contact with them.

29 With trust, they walked across the Red Sea as across dry *land*, that after the Egyptians received trouble, they were swallowed up by *it*.
30 With trust, the walls of Jericho fell after being surrounded over seven days.
31 With trust, Rahab, the prostitute, was not ruined together with the *people* who didn't believe after she accepted the spies with peace.
32 And what else may I say? You see, the time will leave on me describing about Gideon, Barak, Samson, and Jephthah; David, Samuel, and the preachers,
33 who through trust struggled against monarchies, worked for *the* right way, obtained promises, shut lions' mouths,
34 extinguished fire's ability, escaped *the* mouths of a dagger, became competent out of weakness, became strong in war, toppled barracks of *soldiers* belonging to others.
35 Women received their dead from a return back to life. Others were clubbed *to death* after not accepting the paid release so that they might obtain a better return back to life.
36 Different *people* received trouble from *incidents of* mockery and whips, but still *others* from restraints and jail.
37 They were attacked with stones. They were sawed *in half*. They experienced trouble. They died in a murder with a dagger. They went around in sheepskins, in goat skins, lacking, going through hard times, being mistreated
38 (of whom the world was not deserving), wandering around in uninhabited places, mountains, caves, and the openings of the earth.
39 And these all (who were witnessed *by others* through the trust) did not retrieve the promise
40 of God who beforehand looked at something better concerning us, that they would not be completed without us.

12

1 So you see then, since we also *are people* who have so much cloud cover of witnesses lying around us, after putting away all extra weight and the sin that easily stands around *us*, through persistence, we should run in the struggle that is lying up ahead of us,
2 looking away to the head leader and completer of the trust, Jesus, who for the happiness lying up ahead of Him, persisted *to do what is right* after ignoring a cross of shame and was seated in *the* right *side* of the throne of God.
3 You see, think about the *One* who has persisted *to do what is right* in this type of a dispute (in reference to Him) by the sinful *people* so that you might not be exhausted in your souls, giving up.
4 You didn't yet resist up to the point of blood, struggling in opposition to the sin, did you?
5 And you have been completely forgetful of the encouragement *in Proverbs 3:11*, something that has a discussion with you as sons, "My son, don't consider *the* Master's discipline to be a small thing, neither give up as you are being reprimanded by Him."

6 You see, whom *the* Master loves, He disciplines. He whips every son that He accepts with a warm welcome.
7 If you persist *to do what is right* with discipline, God brings Himself to you as to sons. You see, what son is it that a father does not discipline?
8 If you are without discipline, that everyone has become teammates of, clearly you are illegitimate and not sons.
9 Add to that, we certainly had discipliners (the fathers of our physical body) and were embarrassed. Will we not much more place ourselves under the Father of the spirits and live?
10 You see, the *fathers* certainly toward a few days were disciplining aligned with what seemed *good* to them, but the *Father*, based on what is advantageous for the "to receive with *others* of His sacredness" *part*.
11 All discipline toward the *thing* beside *you* certainly doesn't seem to be happiness, but sadness. Later it gives back peaceful fruit of *the* right way to the *people* who have been strenuously exercised through it.
12 For this reason, straighten up the hands that have been neglected and the knees that have been disabled.
13 And make straight tracks for your feet so that the crippled *foot* might not be turned outward, but instead it might be cured.
14 Pursue peace with everyone and the sacredness without which no one will see the Master,
15 supervising *that* no one *is* lacking from the generosity of God, *that* some root of bitterness sprouting up may not crowd in and through this many would be desecrated,
16 *that there is* not someone who commits sexual sin or a profane *person* (as Esau, who for one dinner gave away his firstborn rights;
17 you see, you must realize that even later afterward, wanting to inherit the conferring of blessing, he was rejected; for he did not find a place of a change of ways even though he intensively searched for it with tears).
18 You see, you have not come to a mountain that is felt, that has been burning with fire, to overcast skies, to darkness, to a blowing storm,
19 to an echo of a trumpet, and to a voice of statements, of which *voice*, after the *people* heard, they refused *another* word to be added to them;
20 for they were not putting up with what was warned. Even if a wild animal might come into contact with the mountain, stones will be thrown at it or it will be shot down with a dart.
21 And this is how fearful the *thing* being revealed was: Moses said, "I am frightened and trembling inside."
22 But you have come to Mount Zion, to *the* city of *the* living God, heavenly Jerusalem, to tens of thousands of angels,
23 a mass rally, to an assembly of firstborn who have been registered in heavens, to *the* Judge of all *people* (God), to spirits of *people* who are right, who have been completed,
24 to *the* Middleman of a young deal (Jesus), and to blood of sprinkling speaking better *things* than Abel.

25 See that you won't refuse the *One* speaking. You see, if those *people* didn't escape who refused *the man* on the earth *divinely* notifying *people*, much more we (the *people* who turn away the *One* out of heavens
26 whose voice disturbed the earth at that time) *also will not escape*. But now He has promised, saying *in Haggai 2:6*, "Yet, once *more* I am causing not only the earth to shake, but also the sky."
27 The *phrase* "yet once *more*" makes the transfer obvious of the *things* that are disturbed (as what has been made), so that the *things* that are not disturbed might stay.
28 For this reason, as we receive an undisturbed monarchy in, we may have generosity through which we may minister in a way that is well-liked by God with modesty and devotedness.
29 You see, our God also *is* a completely consuming fire.

13

1 The brotherly kindness must stay.
2 Don't be forgetful of being nice to strangers. You see, through this, some were unnoticed who provided angels a place to stay.
3 Remind yourselves of the prisoners (as *if* having been locked up together with *them*), the *people* who are mistreated (as *if* even being yourselves in *their* body).
4 Marriage *is* valuable in all *situations*, and the bed *is* not desecrated. But people who commit sexual sin and cheating spouses God will judge.
5 The way *to live is* without greed, being content with what is beside *you*. You see, He has stated, "I will not in any way ease up from you, neither will I in any way leave you down in *there*"
6 in such a way for us (as we are courageous) to be saying, "*The* Master *is* a helper to me, and I will not fear what a person will do to me."
7 Remember the *people* being leaders of you, some who spoke the message of God to you, whose trust you must imitate, observing the way out of the behavior.
8 Jesus *is the* Anointed King, the same yesterday, today, and in the spans of time.
9 Don't be carried around by various and strange teachings. You see, *it is* nice for the heart to be authenticated with generosity, not with foods (that the *people* who walked around in were not benefited by).
10 We have an altar from which the *people* ministering with the tent don't have authority to eat,
11 you see, of animals, of which the blood concerning sin is carried into the Sacred *Things* through the head priest, the bodies of these are burned up outside of the camp.
12 For this reason, Jesus also (so that He might make the ethnic group sacred through *His* own blood) suffered outside of the gate.
13 Now then, we should go out to Him outside of the camp, carrying the criticism of Him.
14 You see, we don't have a city remaining here, but we are searching for the *city* that is going *to come*.

15 So through Him, we should carry up a sacrifice of praise through everything to God, that is, fruit of lips acknowledging to His Name.
16 Don't be forgetful of the doing of good and sharing. You see, these types of sacrifices are well-liked by God.
17 Believe the *people* being leaders of you, and surrender *to them* (you see, they don't go to sleep on behalf of your souls as *people* who will give an answer back) so that they may do this with happiness and not groaning (you see, this *has* no fitting compensation for you).
18 Pray about us. You see, we have been confident that we have a nice conscience in all *things*, wanting to be nicely busy.
19 But much more, I encourage *you* to do this so that I might be reestablished to you faster.
20 May the God of the peace, the *One* who led the Shepherd of the sheep (the Great *Shepherd*) up from *the* dead in *the* blood of a deal that spans *all* time, our Master Jesus,
21 develop you in every good action for the "to do what He wants" *part* as He does in you what *is* well-liked in His sight through Jesus, *the* Anointed King, to whom *belongs* the magnificence for the spans of time of the spans of time. Amen.
22 I am encouraging you, brothers. Tolerate the message of the encouragement. You see, even through bits, I wrote you a letter.
23 You know that *our* brother Timothy has been dismissed, with whom, if he comes faster, I will see you.
24 Say hello to all the *people* being leaders of you and to all the sacred *people*. The *people* out of Italy say hello to you.
25 *May* the generosity *be* with you all. Amen. [*This letter* was written to Hebrew *people* out of Italy *and sent* through Timothy]

James

1

1 *From:* James, a slave of God and of *the* Master Jesus, *the* Anointed King. To: The twelve family lines, the *ones* in the scattering. Happy to meet you.
2 Regard *it* total happiness, my brothers, when you fall into being surrounded by various troubles,
3 knowing that the proving of your trust works on and completes persistence *to do what is right*.
4 The persistence must have a complete work so that you *all* may be complete and entirely whole, lacking in nothing.
5 If any of you lack insight, he must ask from the side of the God who gives to everyone in a dedicated way and who does not criticize, and it will be given to him.
6 He must ask in trust, considering nothing to be wrong. You see, the *person* considering *it* to be wrong has depicted a wave of *the* sea blown by the wind and tossed;
7 for that person must not suppose that he will receive anything from the side of the Master.
8 A double-souled man *is* inconsistent in all his ways.
9 The brother, the lowly *one*, must be optimistic about his high position,
10 but the wealthy *person*, about his lowliness because he will pass as a flower of grass.
11 You see, the sun came up together with the hot wind, it shriveled up the grass, its flower fell off, and the beauty of its appearance was ruined. This is also how the wealthy *person* in his journeys will be snuffed out.
12 A man who persists *to do what is right* during trouble *is* blessed because when he becomes approved, he will receive the life's award wreath that the Master promised to the *people* loving Him.
13 No one who is experiencing trouble must say, "I am experiencing trouble out from God." You see, God is untroubled from bad *things*. He Himself does not try to cause trouble with anyone.
14 Each *person* experiences trouble as he, under *his* own desire, is drawn out and enticed.
15 After that, when the desire conceives, it delivers *a baby*, sin; but the sin, when it is finished out, brings death out of the womb.
16 Don't be misled, my loved brothers.
17 All good giving and every completely free gift is from above, stepping down out of the Father of the lights, beside whom there is no change or shade of turning.
18 He who intended *it* brought us out of the womb with a message of truth for the "for us to be a certain first-part-offering of His created *things*" part.
19 In such a way, my loved brothers, every person must be quick for the "to hear" *part*, slow for the "to speak" *part*, slow for rage.

20 You see, a man's rage does not work on and complete God's right way.
21 For this reason, after you put away all filthiness and overflow of badness, in submissiveness accept the implanted message, the *one* that is able to rescue your souls.
22 Become doers of *the* message and not just hearers, misguiding yourselves,
23 because if anyone is a hearer of *the* message and not a doer, this *person* has depicted a man taking a closer look in a mirror at the face of his birth.
24 You see, he took a closer look at himself, he has gone away, and right away he forgot whatever kind of *thing* he was.
25 But the *one* who stooped and peered into the complete law of the freedom and stayed with *it*, this *one*, who did not become a hearer of forgetfulness, but a doer of work, this *one* will be blessed in the doing of it.
26 If anyone among you seems to be religious as he is not bridling his tongue but fooling his heart, the religion of this *person is* futile.
27 Religion that is clean and not desecrated beside the God and Father is this, to be keeping an eye on orphans and widows in their hard times, to be keeping oneself unspotted away from the world.

2

1 My brothers, don't have the trust of our Master Jesus, *the* Anointed King, the Magnificence, in being swayed by appearances.
2 You see, if a man with a gold ring on *his* finger comes into your synagogue in a dazzling outfit, but also a poor *man* comes in in a filthy outfit,
3 and *if* you *all* take a look at the *person* wearing the outfit, the dazzling *one*, and say to him, "You sit here nicely," and you say to the poor *man*, "You stand over there or sit down here under my footrest,"
4 you didn't even consider what is wrong among yourselves and become judges of evil ponderings.
5 Listen, my loved brothers, didn't God select the poor *people* of this world *to be* wealthy in trust and inheritors of the monarchy that was promised to the people who love Him?
6 But you belittled the poor *man*. Don't the wealthy *people* suppress you and themselves drag you into courts?
7 Don't they themselves insult the nice name, the *one* that was called over you?
8 However, if you finish the royal law aligned with the *Old Testament* writing, "You will love the *person* near you as yourself," you do nicely.
9 But if you are swayed by appearances, you are working sin, being reprimanded by the law as violators.
10 You see, anyone who will keep the whole law, but slip in one *point* has become eligible to be sentenced for *breaking it* all;
11 for the *One* who said, "You will not cheat on *your* spouse," also said, "You will not commit murder." If you won't cheat on *your* spouse, but you will commit murder, you have become a violator of *the* law.
12 Speak like this and do *things* like this, as *people* who are going to be judged through *the* law of freedom.

13 You see, the judgment *is* without a remedy to the *person* who didn't show forgiving kindness, and forgiving kindness brags about how much better it is than judgment.
14 What *is* the benefit, my brothers, if someone says to be having trust, but doesn't have *its* actions? The trust is not able to rescue him, is it?
15 If a brother or sister is naked and is lacking the day's meal,
16 but some from among you might say to them, "Make *your* way back in peace. Be warm and be full," but you won't give them the needful *things* of the body, what *is* the benefit *of that*?
17 This is also how the trust, if it doesn't have actions, is dead according to itself.
18 But someone will state *that* you have trust and I have actions. Show me your trust separate from your actions, and I will show you my trust from my actions.
19 You trust that there is one God. You do nicely. Even the lesser deities trust and shudder.
20 Do you want to know, O empty person, that the trust separate from the actions is dead?
21 Wasn't Abraham, our father, made right from actions when he carried Isaac, his son, up onto the altar?
22 Do you see that the trust was working together with his actions, and from the actions the trust was completed?
23 And the *Old Testament* writing, the *one* saying, "Abraham trusted God, and it was considered to him for *the* right way," *(Genesis 15:6)* was accomplished, and he was called a friend of God *in Isaiah 41:8 and 2 Chronicles 20:7*.
24 You see now then that from actions a person is made right and not from trust only.
25 Likewise also, was not Rahab, the prostitute, made right from actions when she accepted the announcers under *her roof* and took *them* out a different way?
26 You see, even as the body separate from a spirit is dead, so also the trust separate from the actions is dead.

1 Don't become many teachers, my brothers, realizing that we will receive greater judgment.
2 You see, absolutely all of us slip often. If anyone does not slip in word, this *person is* a complete man, able to also bridle the whole body.
3 Look, we put the bridles into the mouths of the horses with the *intent* for them to be persuaded by us, and we lead their whole body about.
4 Look also at the boats being such big *boats* as these and being driven by harsh winds. It is led about by *the* smallest rudder to wherever the sudden impulse of the *person* steering intends.
5 This is also how the tongue is a little body part and brags about great things. Look, a little fire starts such a *large* forest on fire.

6 And the tongue *is* a fire, the world of the wrong way. This is how the tongue is placed among our body parts: the *tongue* staining the whole body, igniting the running wheel of the birth, and being ignited by the Hinnom Valley.
7 You see, every nature of both wild animals and winged birds, of both reptiles and marine *animals*, is being tamed and has been tamed by the nature, the human *nature*,
8 but the tongue of people no one is able to tame. *It is* restless, bad, full of lethal poison.
9 With it, we confer a blessing on the God and Father, and with it we put curses on the people, the *ones* who have become aligned with God's likeness.
10 From the same mouth comes a conferring of a blessing and a curse. My brothers, these *things* do not need to be happening like this.
11 The spring doesn't emit from the same opening the sweet and the bitter, does it?
12 My brothers, a fig tree is not able to produce olives (or a vine, figs), is it? This is how not even one spring *is able* to produce salt and sweet water.
13 Who *is* insightful and intelligent among you? He must show his actions from the nice behavior in submissiveness of insight.
14 But if you have bitter hostile passion and contention in your heart, do not brag and lie against the truth.
15 This insight is not coming down from above, but *is* earthly, psychological, like lesser deities.
16 You see, where hostile passion and contention *are*, there *is* conflict and every useless item.
17 But the insight from above certainly is first consecrated, following that, peaceful, polite, easily persuaded, full of forgiving kindness and good fruits, not considering the wrong things, not faked.
18 The right way's fruit is seeded in peace for the *people* who make peace.

4
1 Where *are* wars and arguments from among you? Aren't *they* from here, from your pleasures, the *ones* that serve in the military of your body parts?
2 You desire and do not have. You murder, get mad, and are not able to obtain. You argue and wage war. But you do not have because of the *fact* for you to not be asking.
3 You ask and do not receive because you ask in a bad way, so that you might spend *it* in your pleasures.
4 Cheating husbands and cheating wives, don't you realize that the friendship of the world is a hostile relationship of God? So whoever intends to be a friend of the world is placed as an enemy of God.
5 Or does it seem to you that the *Old Testament* writing meaninglessly says, "The spirit that lives in you yearns toward envy."
6 But He gives more generosity. For this reason, He says, "God places Himself in opposition to proud *people*, but gives generosity to lowly *people*."
7 So place yourselves under God. Stand in opposition to the Accuser, and he will escape away from you.

8 Come near to God, and He will come near to you. Clean *your* hands, sinful *people*, and consecrate *your* hearts, double-souled *people*.
9 Be troubled, grieve, and cry. Your laughter must be turned into grief and the happiness into dismay.
10 Put yourselves down low in the sight of the Master, and He will put you up high.
11 Don't speak badly about each other, brothers. The *person* speaking badly about a brother and judging his brother speaks badly about *the* law and judges *the* law. If you judge *the* law, you are not a doer of *the* law, but a judge.
12 There is one Lawmaker, the *One* who is able to rescue and to ruin. Who are you, the *one* who judges the different *person*?
13 Bring *your attention here* now, the *people* who say, "Today or tomorrow we will travel to the city here, do *things* there one year, travel among *them*, and make money,"
14 some who are not even aware of the *content* of the *day* tomorrow. You see, what kind of *life is* your life? You see, it is a fog, the *kind* that appears toward a little *while*, but following that disappears.
15 In place of *that, there should be* the "for you to be saying, 'If the Master wants, we will also live and do this or that'" *thing*.
16 But now you brag about your egos. All of this type of bragging is evil.
17 So to a *person* who knows to be doing a nice *thing* and does not do *it*, to him it is sin.

5

1 Bring *your attention here* now. The wealthy *people* — cry, howling over your miseries, the *ones* coming on *you*.
2 Your wealth has rotted, and your clothes have become moth-eaten.
3 Your gold and silver have become covered with tarnish, and their tarnish will be for a witness to you and will eat your physical body as fire. You stockpiled *wealth* in *these* last days.
4 Look! The pay of the workers, the *ones* who brought in the crops of your rural areas, the *pay* that has been robbed by you, yells. And the shouts of the *people* who harvested have come into the ears of *the* Master of Sabaoth (*Hebrew for army, the name of God's army*).
5 You had lavish things on the earth and lived in luxury. You nurtured your hearts as in a day of slaughter.
6 You found guilty, you murdered the *person* who did what is right. He did not place himself in opposition to you.
7 So be patient, brothers, until the arrival of the Master. Look! The farmer waits for the valuable fruit of the earth, being patient over it until it receives early and late shower.
8 You also must be patient. Establish your hearts because the arrival of the Master has come near.
9 Don't groan against each other, brothers, so that you might not be guilty. Look! The judge has been standing in front of the doors.

10 Take a demonstration of the hard suffering, my brothers, and the patience of the preachers who spoke with the name of *the* Master.

11 Look! We consider the *people* to be blessed who persist *to do what is right*. You heard of the persistence of Job and saw the conclusion of *the* Master, that the Master is very sympathetic and compassionate.

12 Before all *things*, my brothers, don't guarantee, not with the sky, nor with the earth, nor with any other oath, but your "yes" must be yes and *your* "no," no, so that you might not fall under judgment.

13 Is anyone among you suffering tough hardships? He must pray. Is anyone cheered up? He must recite psalms.

14 Is anyone weak among you? He must call for the older *men* of the assembly, and they must pray over him after dabbing olive oil on him in the name of the Master.

15 And the vow of the trust will rescue the *person* who is exhausted, and the Master will get him up. And if he is *a person* who has committed sins, it will be forgiven him.

16 Acknowledge the infractions out loud to each other, and wish *for good* over each other in order that you *all* might be cured. A plea that is active from a *person* who does what is right has much strength.

17 Elijah was a person suffering like us. And he prayed a prayer of the "not to rain" *kind*, and it did not rain on the earth for three years and six months.

18 And again he prayed, and the sky gave a shower, and the earth budded its fruit.

19 Brothers, if anyone among you wanders off from the truth and someone returns him back,

20 he must know that the *person* who returned a sinful *person* back from his wandering way will rescue a soul from death and cover up a large number of sins.

First Peter

1 *From:* Peter, a missionary of Jesus, *the* Anointed King. To: Select refugees of a scattering throughout Pontus, Galatia, Cappadocia, Western Turkey, and Bithynia
2 aligned with what Father God knew beforehand in *the* sacredness of *the* Spirit for obedience and *the* sprinkling of *the* blood of Jesus, *the* Anointed King. May generosity to you and peace increase.
3 The God and Father of our Master Jesus, *the* Anointed King, is conferred with blessings, the *One* who aligned with His great forgiving kindness gave us a rebirth for good anticipation that lives through Jesus, *the* Anointed King's, return back to life from *the* dead,
4 for an inheritance that isn't deteriorating, isn't desecrated, and isn't snuffed out that has been kept in heavens for you,
5 the *people* in God's ability being watched over through trust, for rescue, ready to be uncovered in *the* last time,
6 in which you are a little excited now, though it is *a thing* that is necessary after being sad in various troubles
7 so that the proving of your trust (much more valuable than the gold that is ruined, but proved, through fire) might be found for high praise, value, and magnificence during *the* uncovering of Jesus, *the* Anointed King,
8 whom, though you did not see, you love, for whom, not seeing now, but trusting, you are excited with happiness, inexpressible and that has been elevated to a place of magnificence,
9 retrieving the conclusion of your trust, a rescue of souls,
10 about which rescue, the preachers who preached about the generosity for you, intensively searched for and intensively examined,
11 examining for whom or which time the Spirit in them of *the* Anointed King was making obvious, as He witnessed beforehand about the hardships for *the* Anointed King and the magnificent *things* after these,
12 to whom it was uncovered that they were serving these *things*, not to themselves, but to us, *things* that now were announced to you through the *people* who shared good news with you in *the* Sacred Spirit that was sent out from heaven, *things* that announcers desire to stoop and peer into.
13 For this reason, after tying up the waists of your mind, being completely sober, anticipate good based on the generosity brought to you during *the* uncovering of Jesus, *the* Anointed King.
14 As children of obedience, not conforming to the prior desires in your lack of awareness,
15 but, aligned with the Sacred *One* who invited you, you yourselves also must become sacred in every behavior
16 because it has been written *in Leviticus 11:44*, "Become sacred because I am sacred."

17 And if you call on the Father who is not swayed by appearances *and* judges according to the work of each *person*, turn over the time of your foreign residency in fear,
18 realizing that not with deteriorating *things* (silver or gold) a price was paid to release you from your futile behavior (*the* traditional *behavior* of the forefathers),
19 but with valuable blood (as of a lamb unblemished and unspotted) of *the* Anointed King,
20 who certainly had been known beforehand, before *the* founding of *the* world, but who was shown over the last times because of you,
21 the *ones* who through Him trust in God, the *One* who got Him up from *the* dead and gave Him magnificence in such a way for your trust and anticipation to be in God.
22 Having consecrated your souls in the obedience of the truth through *the* Spirit to brotherly kindness *that is* not faked, from a clean heart, love each other intensively
23 being reborn, not from a deteriorating reproduction process, but from an undeteriorating *reproduction process* through God's living and remaining message for the span of time,
24 because every physical body *is* as grass and all *the* magnificence of a person, as a flower of grass. The grass shriveled up, and its flower fell off,
25 but the statement of *the* Master remains for the span of time. This is the statement, the *statement* of good news that was shared to you.

2

1 So when you put away all badness, every deception, faked behaviors, envies, and all bad comments,
2 as newborn babies, yearn for the message's deception-free milk so that in it you might grow
3 if it is true that you tasted that the Master *is* kind,
4 to whom (a living stone, that certainly has been rejected by people, but beside God, select, valued), as you come,
5 you (yourselves also as living stones) are built, a spiritual house, a sacred order of priests, to carry up well-received spiritual sacrifices to God through Jesus, *the* Anointed King.
6 For this reason, it also has itself around *this* in the *Old Testament* writing *in Isaiah 28:16*, "Look, I put in Zion a primary corner stone, select, valued. And the *person* trusting based on it will not in any way be shamed."
7 So the value *is* to you, the *people* trusting, but to *people* not believing, a stone that the *people* who are building rejected, this became for a corner's head,
8 a stone of a trip hazard, and a rock of an obstacle (*people* who trip on the message, not believing what they actually were put into).
9 But you *are* a select family, a kingly order of priests, a sacred race, an ethnic group for an acquisition (in order that you might promote the achievements of the *One* who invited you *to come* from darkness into His amazing light);
10 the *people* not an ethnic group in the past, but now God's ethnic group; the *people* who had not received forgiving kindness, but who now received forgiving kindness.

11 Loved *ones*, I encourage *you* as foreign residents and refugees to be keeping yourselves away from the physical desires, some that serve in the military against the soul,

12 keeping your behavior nice among the non-Jews, so that in what they speak badly about you (as *if you are people* who do bad things), from the nice actions, as they watch, they might praise God's magnificence in a day of supervision.

13 So place yourself under every human creation because of the Master, whether under a king as *one* that has a higher position,

14 or under leaders as being sent through him certainly for retaliation against *people* who do bad things but *for* high praise of *people* who do good things,

15 because what God wants is like this: for *people* doing good to be muzzling the ignorance of the distracted people.

16 As free *people* (and not as *people* who have the freedom as a cover for the badness, but as slaves of God)

17 value all *people*, love the brotherhood, fear God, value the king

18 (the domestic servants being placed under the owners in all fear, not only under the good and polite, but also under the crooked).

19 You see, this *is* generosity, if, because of a conscience of God, someone endures sadnesses as he suffers wrongfully;

20 for what kind of recognition *is there* if you who sin and are slugged will persist *to do what is right*? But if you who do good and suffer will persist *to do what is right*, this is generosity beside God.

21 You see, into this you were invited, because even *the* Anointed King suffered on our behalf, leaving a master copy behind to us so that you might follow closely behind in His footsteps,

22 who did not commit sin, neither was deception found in His mouth,

23 who as He was being put down, was not responding with put-downs, as He was suffering, was not threatening, but giving in to the *One* who judges rightly,

24 who Himself carried up our sins in His body on the wooden cross, so that after getting away from the sins, we might live in the right way, by whose *own* bruising you were cured.

25 You see, you were as sheep wandering off, but now you were turned back to the Shepherd and Supervisor of your souls.

3

1 Likewise, the wives *should be* placing themselves under *their* own husbands so that even if any do not believe the message, they will be won through the wives' behavior unaccompanied by *the* message

2 when they watch your consecrated behavior in fear;

3 whose makeup must not be on the outside, of elaborate braiding of hair and decoration of gold or of a dressing up in clothes,

4 but the hidden person of the heart in the undeteriorating *clothes* of the submissive and calm spirit that is very expensive in the sight of God.

5 You see, this is also how in the past the sacred wives, the *ones* anticipating good based on God, were decorating themselves, placing themselves under *their* own husbands,

6 as Sarah obeyed Abraham calling him master, whose children you became, doing good and not fearing any *bit of* panic.
7 The husbands likewise *should be* living in a house together with *them* aligned with knowledge, as to a weaker container, the woman *container*, doling out value as also inheritors together of life's generosity, for the "for your prayers to not be chopped out" *part*.
8 The conclusion *is that* everyone *is* agreeable, empathetic, brotherly, goodhearted, courteous,
9 not giving back bad for bad, or put-down for put-down, but just the opposite, conferring blessings (realizing that for this you were invited, so that you might inherit a conferring of blessing).
10 You see, the *person* wanting to be loving life and to see good days must stop his tongue away from bad and his lips from the "to not speak deception" *part*.
11 He must slide away from bad and do good. He must look for peace and pursue it
12 because the eyes of *the* Master *are* on *people* who do what is right and His ears *are* into their plea. *The* Master's face *is* on *people* who do bad *things*,
13 and who *is* the *person* who will do bad to you if you become imitators of the good *thing*?
14 But if you also suffer because of *the* right way, *you are* blessed. Don't fear the fear of them, neither should you be uneasy.
15 Make *the* Master (God) sacred in your hearts, always ready toward a defense to everyone asking you for an answer concerning the anticipation in you with submissiveness and fear,
16 having a good conscience so that in what they may speak badly about you (as *if you are people* who do bad things), they might be ashamed, the *people* being spiteful of your good behavior in *the* Anointed King.
17 You see, *it is* better to be suffering for doing good (if what God wants wants *it*) than for doing bad,
18 because *the* Anointed King also suffered once concerning sins, a *Man* who does what is right on behalf of *people* who do what is wrong, so that He might bring us to God, who certainly has been put to death in *the* physical body, but was given life in the Spirit,
19 in which, after traveling, He also spoke publicly to the spirits in jail,
20 to *people* who did not believe in the past when once the patience of God was waiting in *the* days of Noah, as a box was being constructed, in which a few (that is, eight) souls were completely rescued through water
21 to which a corresponding type also now rescues us, submersion, (not a physical body's putting away of filth, but an asking for God from a good conscience) through *the* return back to life of Jesus, *the* Anointed King,
22 who is in *the* right *side* of God, after traveling into heaven, when angels, authorities, and abilities were placed under Him.

4 1 So since *the* Anointed King suffered on our behalf in a physical body, you also must arm yourselves with the same internal way of thinking because the *person* who suffered in a physical body has stopped sin

2 for the "for the remaining time in a physical body to no longer be lived for desires of people but for what God wants" *part*.
3 You see, the time of the life that has passed by *is* enough for us to work on and complete what the non-Jews want, having traveled in indulgent activities, desires, times with too much wine, wild parties, drinking binges and forbidden idol worship;
4 in which they think it is strange that you don't run together with *them* in the same obsession of the recklessness as they insult *you*,
5 who will give back an answer to the *One* who has *Himself* ready to judge living *people* and dead *people*.
6 You see, for this, good news was also shared with dead *people*, so that they might certainly be judged aligned with people in *the* physical body, but they may live aligned with God in *the* spirit.
7 The conclusion of everything has come near. So you *all* must be properly focused and sober for the prayers,
8 but having intensive love among yourselves before everyone (because the love covers up a large number of sins),
9 friendly to strangers among each other, unaccompanied by grumblings.
10 Just as each *person* received a gift, *they should be* serving *the* same *thing* among themselves as nice managers of *the* varied generosity of God.
11 If someone speaks, *he should speak* as God's utterances. If someone serves, *he should serve* as from strength that God supplies so that in all *things* God may be elevated to a place of magnificence through Jesus, *the* Anointed King, with whom is the magnificence and the power for the spans of time of the spans of time. Amen.
12 Loved *ones*, don't think the burning among you is strange, that is becoming pointed toward trouble for you, as a strange *thing* transpiring with you.
13 But aligned with what you share in the hardships of the Anointed King, be happy so that also during the uncovering of His magnificence you would be happy, being excited.
14 If you are criticized for *the* Anointed King's name, *you are* blessed because the spirit of the magnificence and the *Spirit* of God relaxes on you. Throughout them, He certainly is insulted, but throughout you *all*, He is elevated to a place of magnificence.
15 You see, none of you must suffer as a murderer, or a thief, or a *person* who does bad things, or as a meddler.
16 But if *someone suffers* as a Christian, he must not be ashamed. He must elevate God to a place of magnificence in this part
17 because *it is* the time of the "for the judgment to begin out from the house of God" *part*. If *it is* first out from us, what *will* the conclusion *be* of the *people* who do not believe the good news of God?
18 And if the *person* who does what is right is rescued with a lot of effort, the godless and sinful *person*, where will he appear?
19 In such a way, the *people* who suffer aligned with what God wants must also place their *own* souls as *if* beside a Creator who can be trusted in doing good.

5

1 I am encouraging the older *people* among you, I, the older colleague and witness of the hardships of the Anointed King, also the sharer of the magnificence that is going to be uncovered.
2 Shepherd the flock of God among you, supervising, not *because you are* urged to (but voluntarily), neither for shameful gain (but eagerly),
3 neither as *people* who act like masters over *their* portions (but becoming examples to the flock).
4 And when the Head Shepherd is shown, you will retrieve the unfading award wreath of the magnificence.
5 Likewise, you younger *people* must place yourselves under older *people*. As you all place yourselves under each other, you must put on the lowly focus of a servant because God places Himself in opposition to proud *people*, but gives generosity to lowly *people*.
6 So put yourselves down low under the powerful hand of God so that He might put you up high at *the* right time
7 after tossing your every worry on Him because there is concern with Him about you.
8 Stay sober; stay awake; because your opponent in the court case, *the* Accuser, as a growling lion, is walking around looking for someone to swallow up,
9 to whom you solid *people* must stand in opposition with the trust having seen the same *aspects* of the hardships to be finished up by your brotherhood in *the* world.
10 But the God of all generosity (the *One* who invited us into His magnificence that spans *all* time in *the* Anointed King Jesus) will Himself (after you suffer a little) develop you, establish, strengthen, lay a foundation.
11 To Him *belongs* the magnificence and the power for the spans of time of the spans of time. Amen.
12 I wrote to you through Silas, the reliable brother (as I consider *him to be*), through a few *words* encouraging and corroborating this to be God's valid generosity in which you have stood.
13 The *woman* selected together with *you* in Babylon says hello to you, and Mark, my son.
14 Say hello to each other with a friendly gesture of love. Peace to you, all the *people* in *the* Anointed King Jesus. Amen.

Second Peter

1 *From:* Simon Peter, a slave and missionary of Jesus, *the* Anointed King. To: The *people* who took their turn with us in equally valuable trust in *the* right way of our God and our Rescuer Jesus, *the* Anointed King.

2 May generosity to you and peace increase in a correct understanding of God and Jesus, our Master:

3 as all *things* to us of His divine ability that has been given for free, the *things* toward life and godliness through the correct understanding of the *One* who invited us through magnificence and achievement

4 through which the biggest and valuable promises have been given to us for free so that through these *things* you might become sharers of *the* divine nature after escaping away from the deterioration in *the* world in desire;

5 even this very *thing*: after summoning every effort, further supply in your trust, the achievement; in the achievement, the information;

6 in the information, the restraint; in the restraint, the persistence *to do what is right*; in the persistence *to do what is right*, the godliness;

7 in the godliness, the brotherly kindness; in the brotherly kindness, the love.

8 You see, these *things* existing and increasing in you, place you as not idle nor fruitless in the correct understanding of our Master Jesus, *the* Anointed King;

9 for *a person* who doesn't have these *things* beside him is blind, not being able to see very well, who took no notice of the cleansing of his sins a long time ago.

10 For this reason, brothers, make more of an effort to be making your invitation and selection firm. You see, as you do these, you will not ever in any way slip;

11 for this is how the entrance into the monarchy that spans *all* time of our Master and Rescuer Jesus, *the* Anointed King, will be richly further supplied to you.

12 For this reason, I will not stop caring about always to be quietly reminding you about these *things*, even though *you are people* who realize *them* and have been established in the truth that is beside *you*.

13 I regard *it to be* right, over as long as I am in this shelter, to be waking you up with a quiet reminder,

14 realizing that the putting away of my shelter is soon, just as our Master Jesus, *the* Anointed King, also made obvious to me.

15 I will also make every effort at each juncture to be having you, after my exit, to be making the remembrance of these *things*.

16 You see, we made the ability and arrival known to you of our Master Jesus, *the* Anointed King, not after closely following insight-making myths, but after becoming eyewitnesses of the greatness of that *Man*;

17 for when He received value and magnificence from the side of Father God, when such a great voice was carried to Him by the appropriately great magnificence, "This is My Son, the loved *Son*, in whom I am delighted,"
18 we actually heard this voice that was carried from heaven as we were together with Him on the sacred mountain.
19 We also have the firmer preached message, that you are doing nicely paying attention to, as to a lamp shining in a dingy place until *the time* that day will radiate through and a light-carrier will come up in your hearts,
20 knowing this first, that all preaching of an *Old Testament* writing does not happen of *its* own explanation.
21 You see, preaching in the past was not carried to what a person wanted, but sacred people of God spoke being carried by *the* Sacred Spirit.

2

1 But there also became counterfeit preachers among the ethnic group, as counterfeit teachers will also be among you, some who will quietly introduce sects of ruin, even denying the Owner who bought them, bringing quick ruin onto themselves.
2 And many will closely follow their ruining behaviors, because of whom, the way of the truth will be insulted.
3 And in a desire for more, they will travel among you with manipulating messages, to whom the judgment from a long time ago isn't idle, and their ruin isn't nodding off.
4 You see, if God did not go easy on angels that sinned, but turned *them* over to cords of gloom when He put *them* in *the lowest part of hell* (Tartarus), being kept for judgment,
5 and *if* He did not go easy on *the* original world, but guarded an eighth *person*, Noah, a public speaker for *the* right way, when He brought a flood onto a world of godless *people*,
6 and *if* when cremating *the* cities of Sodom and Gomorrah, He found *them* guilty with a disaster, having put a demonstration *out there* for *people* who are going to be godless,
7 and *if* He saved Lot who did what is right, who was oppressed by the behavior of the noncompliant *people* in indulgent activity
8 (you see, by what was seen and what was heard, as the *person* who did what is right lived among them from day to day, with criminal actions he was torturing a soul that was right),
9 *the* Master knows to be saving godly *people* from troubles, but to be keeping *people* who do what is wrong curtailed for a day of judgment,
10 especially the *people* traveling behind a physical body in a desire of desecration and ignoring government. Self-pleasuring, daring people, they do not tremble as they insult magnificent *things*.
11 Where angels, who are greater in strength and ability, don't bring a insulting judgment against them beside *the* Master,
12 these *people* (as natural irrational animals having been born for capture and decomposition), insulting in *ways* that they are unaware of, will be entirely worsened in their deterioration,

13 who will retrieve *the* wrong way's pay, regarding the lavish things in a day *as* pleasure, *they are* stains and blemishes, being lavish in their frauds, partying together with you,
14 having eyes full of cheating on spouses and addicted to sin, enticing unestablished souls, having a heart that has been strenuously exercised with a desire for more, children of a curse.
15 Leaving the straight way down *here*, they were misled after closely following the way of Balaam (the *son* of Beor), who loved *the* wrong way's pay.
16 But he had a reprimand of *his* own lawlessness. A voiceless workhorse that verbalized in a person's voice hindered the wrong focus of the preacher.
17 These *people* are springs without water, clouds driven by a blast, for whom the gloom of the darkness has been kept for *the* span of time.
18 You see, verbalizing exaggerated *statements* of futileness, they entice the *people* in indulgent activities in desires of *the* physical body who really are escaping away from the *people* who are messed up in a misleading lie,
19 promising them freedom, they themselves being slaves of the deterioration. You see, what someone has been defeated by, to this he has also been enslaved.
20 You see, if after escaping away from the desecrations of the world in a correct understanding of the Master and Rescuer Jesus, *the* Anointed King, but being entangled again to these *things*, they are defeated, the last *things* have become worse for them than the first *things*;
21 for it was better for them not to have correctly understood the road of the right way, than, after correctly understanding *it*, to turn back from the sacred demand given over to them.
22 The *picture* of the valid analogy has transpired with them: "A dog that turned back to *its* own vomit and a pig that bathed itself into a rolling around of muck."

3

1 Loved *ones*, I am already writing this second letter to you in which I am waking up your genuine mind in a quiet reminder
2 to remember the statements stated before by the sacred preachers and the demand from our missionaries of the Master and Rescuer.
3 Knowing this first, that over the last days, mockers will come traveling aligned with their own desires
4 and saying, "Where is the promise of His arrival? You see, since *the day* that the fathers fell asleep, all *things* through *it all* stay like this from *the* beginning of creation;"
5 for this is unnoticed by them (since they want *it to be unnoticed*): that there were skies from a long time ago and land that had stood together from water and through water with the message of God,
6 through which, the world at that time was ruined when it was flooded with water.
7 The skies now and the land that have been stockpiled with the same message are kept for fire in a day of judgment and ruin of the godless people.

8 This one *thing* must not be unnoticed by you, loved *ones*: that one day beside *the* Master *is* as a thousand years, and a thousand years as one day.
9 The Master of the promise is not slow as some regard slowness, but He is patient to us, not intending for anyone to be ruined, but for all *people* to make room for a change of ways.
10 *The* Master's day will arrive as a thief in *the* night, in which the skies will pass with a loud crash. Primary elements being on fire will be undone, and land and the actions in it will be burned up.
11 So since all these *things* are being undone, what kind of *people* is it necessary for you to be in sacred behaviors and *expressions of* godliness,
12 expecting and hurrying the arrival of the day of God, because of which, flaming skies will be undone, and primary elements being on fire are melted?
13 But we expect new skies and new land (according to His promise) in which *the* right way lives.
14 For this reason, loved *ones*, as you expect these *things*, make every effort to be found by Him in peace, unspotted and unblamed *people*.
15 And regard the patience of our Master *as* a rescue, just as our loved brother Paul aligned with the insight given to him also wrote to you,
16 as also in all the letters, speaking in them about these *things*, in which there are some hard to understand *things* that the unlearned and unestablished *people* pervert (as also the rest *of the* writings) to their own ruin.
17 So you, loved *ones*, since you know *these things* beforehand, beware that, after being led away together with the misleading lie of the noncompliant, you don't fall from *your* own established position.
18 But grow in generosity and information about our Master and Rescuer Jesus, *the* Anointed King. To Him *belongs* the magnificence both now and for a day of a span of time. Amen.

First John

1

1 What was from *the* beginning, what we have heard, what we have seen with our eyes, what we viewed and our hands felt concerning the message of the life
2 (actually, the life was shown, we have seen *it*, we are telling what we witnessed, and we are reporting to you about the life, the *life* that spans *all* time, something that was pointing toward the Father and was shown to us),
3 what we have seen and heard, we are reporting to you so that you also may have a sharing relationship with us, even the sharing relationship (our *sharing relationship*) with the Father and with His Son Jesus, *the* Anointed King.
4 And we are writing these *things* to you so that your happiness may be *happiness* that has been filled up.
5 And this is the announcement that we have heard out from Him and are announcing to you: "God is light, and darkness is not in Him, not even one *bit*."
6 If we say that we have a sharing relationship with Him and we walk around in the darkness, we lie and do not do the truth.
7 But if we walk around in the light as He is in the light, we have a sharing relationship with each other, and the blood of Jesus, *the* Anointed King, His Son, cleans us off from every sin.
8 If we say that we don't have sin, we mislead ourselves and the truth is not in us.
9 If we acknowledge our sins, He can be trusted and does what is right so that He might forgive us of the sins and clean us off from every wrong.
10 If we say that we haven't sinned, we make Him a liar and His message is not in us.

2

1 My little children, I am writing these *things* to you so that you might not sin. And if anyone sins, we have an Encourager pointing toward the Father, Jesus, *the* Anointed King, who does what is right.
2 And He is a remedy concerning our sins, not concerning ours only, but also concerning the whole world's.
3 And in this we know that we have known Him, if we keep His demands.
4 The *person* saying, "I have known Him," and not keeping His demands is a liar, and the truth is not in this.
5 But whoever keeps His message, truly in this, the love of God has been completed. In this, we know that we are in Him.
6 The *person* saying to be staying in Him is obligated, just as that *One* Himself also walked around, so to be walking around.
7 Brothers, I am not writing a new demand to you, but a former demand that you were having from *the* beginning. The demand, the former *one*, is the message that you heard from *the* beginning.

8 Again I am writing a new demand to you, that is valid in Him and in you, because the darkness is passing on by and the light, the true *light*, is already shining.
9 The *person* saying to be in the light and hating his brother is in the dark until now.
10 The *person* loving his brother stays in the light, and there is no obstacle in him.
11 But the *person* hating his brother is in the dark, walks around in the dark, and does not realize where he is making *his* way back to because the dark blinded his eyes.
12 I am writing to you, little children, because the sins have been forgiven you because of His name.
13 I am writing to you, fathers, because you have known the *One who is* from *the* beginning. I am writing to you, young lads, because you have conquered the evil *one*. I am writing to you, young children, because you have known the Father.
14 I wrote to you, fathers, because you have known the *One who is* from *the* beginning. I wrote to you, young lads, because you are strong, the message of God stays in you, and you have conquered the evil *one*.
15 Don't love the world, neither the *things* in the world. If anyone loves the world, the love of the Father is not in him
16 because everything in the world (the desire of the physical body, the desire of the eyes, and the ego of the life) is not from the Father, but is from the world.
17 And the world passes on by and its desire. But the *person* doing what God wants stays for the span of time.
18 Young children, it is a last hour. And just as you heard that *the* Opponent to the Anointed King is coming, and now many have become opponents to the Anointed King, from this we know that it is a last hour.
19 From us they went out, but they were not from us. You see, if they were from us, they would have stayed with us. But *this happened* so that they might be shown, because not all are from us.
20 And you have an anointing out from the Sacred *One*, and you realize all *things*.
21 I didn't write to you because you don't realize the truth, but because you realize it and that every lie is not from the truth.
22 Who is the liar if *it is* not the *one* denying that Jesus is the Anointed King? This *one* is the opponent to the Anointed King, the *one* who denies the Father and the Son.
23 Everyone denying the Son does not have the Father either. The *person* acknowledging the Son also has the Father.
24 So *as for* you, what you heard from *the* beginning must stay in you. If it stays in you (what you heard from the beginning), you also will stay in the Son and in the Father.
25 And this is the promise that He promised us, the life, the *life* that spans *all* time.
26 I wrote these *things* to you about the *people* misleading you.

27 And *as for* you, the anointing that you received out from Him stays in you, and you have no need that someone should teach you, but as the same anointing teaches you about all *things*, is valid, and is not a lie, and just as He taught you, you will stay in Him.
28 And now, little children, stay in Him so that when He is shown, we may have a clear public statement and not be shamed away from Him during His arrival.
29 If you realize that He is right, you know that everyone doing *things* the right way has been born from Him.

3

1 Look at what kind of love the Father has given to us, that we would be called God's children. Because of this, the world does not know us, because it did not know Him.
2 Loved *ones*, now we are God's children, and it was not yet shown what we will be. But we realize that if it might be shown, we will be like Him because we will see Him just as He is.
3 And everyone who has this anticipation based on Him consecrates himself, just as that *One* is consecrated.
4 Everyone committing the sin is also committing the crime. Actually the sin is the crime.
5 And you realize that that *One* was shown so that He might take away our sins, and sin is not in Him.
6 Everyone staying in Him is not sinning. Everyone sinning has not seen Him, nor known Him.
7 Little children, no one must mislead you. The *person* doing *things* the right way is right, just as that *One* is right.
8 The *person* committing the sin is from the Accuser because the Accuser is sinning from *the* beginning. For this, the Son of God was shown, so that He might undo the actions of the Accuser.
9 Everyone who has been born from God is not committing sin because His seed stays in him and is not able to be sinning because it has been born from God.
10 In this, the children of God and the children of the Accuser are shown: everyone not doing *things the* right way is not from God, also the *person* not loving his brother,
11 because this is the announcement that you heard from *the* beginning, that we should love each other.
12 Just not like Cain, he was from the evil *one* and slaughtered his brother. And thanks to what did he slaughter him? Because his actions were evil, but the *actions* of his brother *were* right.
13 Don't be amazed, my brothers, if the world hates you.
14 We realize that we have stepped from the death into the life because we love the brothers. The *person* not loving the brother stays in the death.
15 Everyone hating his brother is a people-killer, and you realize that every people-killer does not have life that spans *all* time staying in him.

16 In this we have known the love of God: because that *Person* put His soul *out there* on our behalf. We are also obligated to put *our* souls *out there* on behalf of the brothers.
17 Whoever has the livelihood of the world, watches his brother having a need, and closes his sympathy off from him, how *is* the love of God staying in him?
18 My little children, we should not love with words, nor with the tongue, but with action and truth.
19 And in this, we know that we are from the truth, and in front of Him we will persuade our hearts
20 that *it is alright* if our heart knows something against *us* because God is bigger than our heart and knows all *things*.
21 Loved *ones*, if our heart knows nothing against us, we have a clear public statement facing God.
22 And whatever we request, we receive from the side of Him because we keep His demands and do the *things* that are liked in His sight.
23 And this is His demand, that we should trust in the name of His Son Jesus, *the* Anointed King, and love each other, just as He gave us a demand.
24 And the *person* keeping His demands stays in Him and He in him. And in this we know that He stays in us, from the Spirit that He gave us.

4

1 Loved *ones*, don't trust every spirit, but check the spirits (if *every spirit* is from God) because many counterfeit preachers have gone out into the world.
2 In this you know the spirit of God: every spirit that acknowledges Jesus *as the* Anointed King who has come in a physical body is from God.
3 And every spirit that doesn't acknowledge that Jesus, *the* Anointed King, has come in a physical body is not from God. And this is the *spirit* of the opponent to the Anointed King that you have heard that it is coming and now is already in the world.
4 You are from God, little children, and have conquered them because the *One* in you is greater than the *one* in the world.
5 They are from the world. Because of this, they speak from the world, and the world listens to them.
6 We are from God. The *person* who knows God listens to us. *A person* who isn't from God doesn't listen to us. From this we know the Spirit of the Truth and the spirit of the misleading lie.
7 Loved *ones*, we should love each other because the love is from God and everyone who loves has been born from God and knows God.
8 The *person* not loving did not know God because God is love.
9 In this, the love of God was shown among us, because God has sent His Son, the only biological *Son*, out *on a mission* into the world so that we might live through Him.
10 In this is the love, not because we have loved God, but because He loved us and sent His Son out *as* a remedy concerning our sins.
11 Loved *ones*, if this is how God loved us, we also are obligated to be loving each other.

12 No one has viewed God at any time. If we love each other, God stays in us, and it is His love that has been completed in us.
13 In this we know that we stay in Him and He in us, because He has given to us from His Spirit.
14 And we have viewed and are telling what we witnessed, that the Father has sent the Son out *on a mission as* a rescuer of the world.
15 Whoever acknowledges that Jesus is the Son of God, God stays in him and he in God.
16 And we have known and have trusted the love that God has in us. God is love, and the *person* staying in the love stays in God and God in him.
17 In this the love has been completed with us: so that we may have a clear public statement during the day of the judgment, because just as that *One* is, we also are in this world.
18 Fear is not in the love. But the complete love throws the fear out because the fear has confinement. The *person* fearing has not been completed in the love.
19 We love Him because He first loved us.
20 If anyone says, "I love God," and hates his brother, he is a liar. You see, the *person* not loving his brother (whom he has seen), how is he able to be loving God (whom he has not seen)?
21 And we have this demand out from Him, that the *person* loving God should also love his brother.

5

1 Everyone who trusts that Jesus is the Anointed King has been born from God, and everyone loving the *One* who gave birth should also love the *one* who has been born from Him.
2 In this we know that we love the children of God: when we love God, and keep His demands.
3 You see, this is the love of God, that we should keep His demands. And His demands are not heavy
4 because everything that has been born from God conquers the world and this is the conquering element, the *thing* that conquered the world, our trust.
5 Who is the *person* conquering the world, if *it is* not the *person* trusting that Jesus is the Son of God?
6 This is the *One* who went through water and blood, Jesus, the Anointed King, not in the water only, but in the water and the blood. And the Spirit is the *One* telling what He witnessed because the Spirit is the truth,
7 because there are the three telling what they witness in the heaven: the Father, the Message, and the Sacred Spirit. And these three are One.
8 And there are the three that tell what they witness in the earth: the Spirit, the water, and the blood. And the three are for the one *thing*.
9 If we receive the witness account of the people, the witness account of God is greater because this is the witness account of God that He has witnessed about His Son.
10 The *person* trusting in the Son of God has the witness account in himself. The *person* not trusting God, has made Him a liar because he has not trusted in the witness account that God has witnessed about His Son.

11 And this is the witness account: that God gave us life that spans *all* time and this life is in His Son.
12 The *person* having the Son has the life. The *person* not having the Son of God does not have the life.
13 I wrote these *things* to you (the *people* trusting in the name of the Son of God) so that you may realize that you have life that spans *all* time and so that you may trust in the name of the Son of God.
14 And this is the clear public statement that we have toward Him that if we request anything aligned with what He wants, He listens to us.
15 And if we realize that He listens to us, whatever we request, we realize that we have the requests that we requested from the side of Him.
16 If anyone saw his brother sinning a sin not toward death, he will request, and He will give life to him, to the *people* sinning not toward death. There is sin toward death. I don't say that he should ask about that.
17 Everything that is wrong is sin, and there is sin not toward death.
18 We realize that everyone who has been born from God is not sinning, but the *person* who was born from God keeps himself, and the evil *one* does not touch him.
19 We realize that we are from God, and the whole world lies in the evil.
20 We realize that the Son of God has arrived, He has given us a mind so that we may know the True *One*, and we are in the True *One*, in His Son Jesus, *the* Anointed King. This is the true God and life that spans *all* time.
21 Little children, guard yourselves away from the idols. Amen.

Second John

1 *From:* The older *man*. To: *The* select Kuria and her children, whom I love in truth and not only I, but also all the *people* who have known the truth
2 because of the truth, the *truth* staying in us, and it will be with us for the span of time.
3 With you will be generosity, forgiving kindness, peace from the side of Father God and from the side of Master Jesus, *the* Anointed King, the Son of the Father in truth and love.
4 I was very happy that I have found *some* from among your children walking around in truth, just like *the* demand we received from the side of the Father.
5 And now I am asking you, Kuria (not as though I am writing a new demand to you, but *a demand* that we had from *the* beginning) that we should love each other.
6 And this is the love: that we should walk around aligned with His demands. This is the demand, just as you heard from *the* beginning, that you should walk around in it
7 because many misleading *people* came into the world, the *people* not acknowledging *that* Jesus *is the* Anointed King coming in a physical body. This is the misleading *person* and the opponent to the Anointed King.
8 Watch yourselves so that we might not ruin what we worked for, but we might fully receive full pay.
9 Everyone walking in violation of and not staying in the teaching of the Anointed King doesn't have God. The *person* staying in the teaching of the Anointed King, this *person* has both the Father and the Son.
10 If someone comes to you and doesn't bring this teaching, do not receive him into *the* house and don't say, "Happy to meet you," to him.
11 You see, the *person* saying "Happy to meet you" to him, shares in his actions, the evil *actions*.
12 Having many *things* for you, I did not intend to be writing through paper and ink, but I am anticipating to come to you and to speak mouth to mouth so that our happiness may be *happiness* that has been filled up.
13 The children of your sister, the select *one*, say hello to you. Amen.

Third John

1 *From:* The older *man*. To: The loved Gaius, whom I love in truth.
2 Loved *one*, concerning all *things*, I wish you to be successful and to be healthy, just as your soul is successful.
3 You see, I was very happy as brothers came and told what they witnessed about your truth, just as you walk around in truth.
4 I have no greater happiness than these, that I may hear my children walking around in truth.
5 Loved *one*, you are doing a *thing* that can be trusted, whatever you work *on* for the brothers and for the strangers.
6 The *brothers* told what they witnessed of your love in the sight of *the* assembly, for whom you will do nicely when you bring them on their way in a manner deserving of God.
7 You see, on behalf of His name, they went out taking nothing away from the non-Jews.
8 So we are obligated to be fully receiving these types of *people* so that we may become co-workers to the truth.
9 I wrote to the assembly, but the *one* who is fond of being first among them, Diotrephes, does not accept us.
10 Because of this, if I come, I will quietly remember his actions that he does, gossiping with evil words about us. And not content over these, neither does he accept the brothers, he hinders the *ones* intending *to accept them*, and he throws *them* out of the assembly.
11 Loved *one*, do not imitate the bad, but *imitate* the good. The *person* doing good is from God, but the *person* doing bad has not seen God.
12 It has been told to Demetrius what was witnessed by everyone and by the truth itself. We also are telling what we witnessed, and you realize that our witness account is valid.
13 I had many *things* to be writing, but I do not want to write to you through ink and a stick.
14 I am anticipating to see you right away, and we will speak mouth to mouth. Peace to you. *Your* friends say hello to you. Say hello to *our* friends by name.

Jude

1

1 *From:* Jude (a slave of Jesus, *the* Anointed King, but a brother of James). To: The invited *people* who have been considered sacred in Father God and have been kept by Jesus, *the* Anointed King.
2 May forgiving kindness to you, peace, and love increase.
3 Loved *ones*, making every effort to be writing you about the shared rescue, I had an obligation to write you, encouraging *you* to be strenuously struggling for the trust that was once turned over to the sacred *people*.
4 You see, some people sneaked in undetected (the *ones* who previously had been written about a long time ago into this judgment: *they are* godless) transferring the generosity of our God into indulgent activity and denying the only Owner (God) and our Master, Jesus, *the* Anointed King.
5 But I intend to quietly remind you (though you realized this once) that the Master who rescued *the* ethnic group from *the* land of Egypt, the second *time*, ruined the *people* who did not trust.
6 And the angels that did not keep the beginning of themselves, but left *their* own habitation behind, He has kept for *the* judgment of a great day in eternal restraints under gloom;
7 as Sodom, Gomorrah, and the cities around them (that were sexually promiscuous the same way as these *people* and went off behind a different physical body) are already laid *as* an exhibit, holding *them* under *the* justice of fire that spans *all* time.
8 However, likewise also, these *people*, being inspired while they sleep, not only desecrate *the* physical body, but they invalidate government, but they insult magnificent *things*.
9 But when Michael, the head angel, considering the Accuser to be wrong, was having a discussion about the body of Moses, he didn't dare to bring up a judgment of an insult, but said, "May *the* Master stop you."
10 These *people* insult, not only as many *of the things* as they have not seen, but as many *of the things* as they are naturally (as the irrational animals) well acquainted with. They are worsened in these.
11 What a tragedy *it is* to them because they traveled the road of Cain, they were spilled out in the misleading lie of the pay of Balaam, and they ruined themselves in the dispute of Korah.
12 These *people* are in your love *events*, submerged boulders, partying together with you, fearlessly shepherding themselves; clouds without water being carried around by winds; leafless, fruitless trees that died twice, that were uprooted;
13 wild swells of *the* sea foaming out their *own* shames; stars, wanderers, to whom the gloom of the darkness has been kept for the span of time.
14 Enoch, *the* seventh from Adam, also preached to these *people*, saying, "Look, *the* Master came in His sacred tens of thousands

15 to do judgment against all and to fully reprimand all of their godless *people* concerning all the actions of their godlessness that were godless and concerning all of the harsh *things* that godless sinful *people* spoke against Him."

16 These *people* are complaining grumblers traveling aligned with their desires, and their mouths speak exaggerated *statements* as they are amazed at appearances (thanks to *it being* a benefit *to them*).

17 You, loved *ones*, remember the statements, the *ones* that have been stated before by the missionaries of our Master Jesus, *the* Anointed King,

18 because they were telling you that in *the* last time there will be mockers traveling aligned with their *own* desires of the godlessness.

19 These are the *people* drawing lines dividing themselves, psychological *people* not having a spirit.

20 You, loved *ones*, building yourselves on your most sacred trust, praying in *the* Sacred Spirit,

21 keep yourselves in God's love, accepting the forgiving kindness of our Master Jesus, *the* Anointed King, for life that spans *all* time.

22 And *there are some* to whom, as they consider *it* to be wrong, you must show forgiving kindness,

23 but *others* whom, as you snatch from fire, you must rescue in fear, hating even the long undershirt that has been stained from the physical body.

24 To the *One* who is able to guard you *to be* non-slipping, and to stand *you* directly in the sight of His magnificence *as* unblemished *people* in excitement,

25 to *the* only insightful God, our Rescuer, *belongs* magnificence and majesty, power and authority, both now and for all the spans of time. Amen.

Revelation

1

1 *The* Uncovering of Jesus, *the* Anointed King, that God gave to Him to show His slaves what is necessary to happen quickly and *what* He indicated when He sent *it* out through His angel to His slave John
2 (who told what he witnessed of the message of God and the witness account of Jesus, *the* Anointed King, even as many *things* as he saw).
3 The *person* reading and the *people* hearing the messages of the preaching and keeping the *things* that have been written in it *are* blessed. You see, the appointed time *is* near.
4 *From*: John. To: The seven assemblies (the *ones* in Western Turkey). Generosity to you and peace out from the *One* (the *One* who is, the *One who* was, and the *One* who is coming), out from the seven spirits that are in the sight of His throne,
5 and out from Jesus, *the* Anointed King (the Witness, the *One* who can be trusted, the Firstborn from the dead and the Head of the kings of the earth). To the *One* who loved us and gave us a bath *to wash* off our sins in His blood
6 and made us kings and priests to God and His Father, to Him *belongs* the magnificence and the power for the spans of time of the spans of time. Amen.
7 Look, He is coming with the clouds, and every eye will look at Him, even certain *people* who impaled Him. And all the family lines of the earth will beat their chests in grief over Him. Yes. Amen.
8 "I am the A and the O *(the last letter in the Greek alphabet)*, Beginning and Conclusion," says the Master, "the *One* who is, the *One who* was, and the *One* who is coming, the All-Powerful One."
9 I, John (also your brother and a sharer together with *you* in the hard times, in the monarchy and persistence of Jesus, *the* Anointed King), became on the island (the *one* called Patmos) because of the message of God and because of the witness account of Jesus, *the* Anointed King.
10 I became in a spirit in the master day and heard a loud voice behind me as if *it were* from a trumpet,
11 saying, "I am the A and the O *(the last letter in the Greek alphabet)*, the First and the Last. And what you look at, write into a scroll and send to the seven assemblies (the *ones* in Western Turkey): to Ephesus, to Smyrna, to Pergamos, to Thyatira, to Sardis, to Philadelphia, and to Laodicea."
12 And I turned around to be looking at the voice, something that spoke with me, and when I turned around, I saw seven gold lampstands.
13 And in *the* middle of the seven lampstands *was someone* like a son of a person having put on a robe that went down to the ankles and around whom a gold sash had been put toward the breasts.
14 His head and hairs *were* white as if *they were* wool (white as snow), His eyes as a blaze of fire,

15 His feet like fine copper (as *feet* that had been refined in a furnace), His voice as *the* voice of many waters,

16 having seven stars in His right hand, a sharp double-edged sword traveling out from His mouth, and His eyes as the sun shines in its ability.

17 And when I saw Him, I fell toward His feet as a dead *man*. And He placed His right hand on me, saying to me, "Don't be afraid. I am the First, the Last,

18 and the Living *One*. And I became dead, and, look, I am living for the spans of time of the spans of time, Amen. And I have the keys of Hades *(the underworld of the dead)* and Death.

19 Write *things* that you saw, that are, and that are going to be happening after these.

20 The secret of the seven stars that you saw on My right *hand* and the seven lampstands, the gold *ones, is that* the seven stars are announcers of the seven assemblies and the seven lampstands that you saw are *the* seven assemblies."

2

1 To the announcer of the Ephesianite assembly, write, "The *One* holding on to the seven stars in His right *hand*, the *One* walking around in *the* middle of the seven lampstands (the gold *ones*), says the *things* here,

2 'I have seen your actions, your labor, your persistence *to do what is right*, that you are not able to put up with bad *people*, and you tried to cause trouble with the *people* claiming to be missionaries (and they are not) and found them *to be* lying.

3 And you put up with *things*, have persistence, and because of My name, have labored and have not gotten exhausted.

4 But I have *something* against you because you left your love, the first *love*.

5 So remember where you have fallen from, change your ways, and do the first actions. But if not, I am coming to you quickly, and I will move your lampstand from its place if you don't change your ways.

6 But this you have, that you hate the actions of the Nicolaitans that I also hate.'

7 The *person* who has an ear must hear what the Spirit says to the assemblies, 'To the *person* who conquers, I will give him *the right* to eat from the wooden tree of the life that is in *the* middle of the paradise of God.'"

8 And to the announcer of the assembly of Smyrnaeans, write, "The First and the Last who became dead and lived, says the *things* here,

9 'I have seen your actions, the hard times, the poverty (but you are wealthy), and the insult from the *people* saying for themselves to be Jewish (and they are not, but *they are* a synagogue of the Opponent).

10 Fear nothing, *not even things* that you are going to be suffering. Look, the Accuser is going to be throwing *some* from among you into jail so that you might experience trouble, and you will have hard times for ten days. Become trusting till death, and I will give you the award wreath of the life.'

11 The *person* who has an ear must hear what the Spirit says to the assemblies, 'The *person* who conquers will not in any way be harmed from the death, the second *one*.'"

12 And to the announcer of the assembly in Pergamos, write, "The *One* who has the sword, the double-edged *one*, the sharp *one*, says the *things* here,
13 'I have seen your actions and where you live (where the throne of the Opponent *is*), and you hold on to My name and did not deny the trust of Me, even in the days in which Antipas *was* My witness, the reliable *witness*, who was killed beside you where the Opponent lives.
14 But I have a few *things* against you, because you have *people* there who hold on to the teaching of Balaam, who was teaching Balak to throw an obstacle in the sight of the sons of Israel, to eat idol sacrifices and to commit sexual sin.
15 In this way, you, even you, have *people* who hold on to the teaching of the Nicolaitans that I hate.
16 Change your ways. But if not, I am coming to you quickly, and I will wage war with them with the sword of My mouth.'
17 The *person* who has an ear must hear what the Spirit says to the assemblies, 'To the *person* who conquers, I will give him *the right* to eat of the manna, the *manna* that has been hidden, and I will give him a white pebble and on the pebble a new name that has been written that no one knew except the *one* receiving *it*.'"
18 And to the announcer of the assembly in Thyatira, write, "The Son of God, the *One* who has His eyes as a blaze of fire and His feet like fine copper, says the *things* here,
19 'I have seen your actions, the love, the serving, the trust, your persistence *to do what is right*, and your actions, the last *actions* more than the first.
20 But I have a few *things* against you because you allow the woman Jezebel, the *one* calling herself a preacher, to teach and for My slaves to be misled to commit sexual sin and to eat idol sacrifices.
21 And I gave her time so that she might change her ways from her sexual sin, and she didn't change her ways.
22 Look, I am throwing her onto a cot and the *people* cheating on *their* spouses with her into great hard times, unless they will change their ways from their actions.
23 And I will kill her children with death and all the assemblies will know that I am the *One* who examines kidneys *(inner thoughts)* and hearts *(intentions)*. And I will give to you each aligned with your actions.
24 But I say to you and to the rest in Thyatira, as many as don't have this teaching and any who didn't know "the depths of the Opponent" (as they say), I will not throw another weight on you.
25 More importantly, hold on to what you have till whenever I might arrive.
26 And the *person* who conquers and the *person* who keeps My actions till *the* conclusion, I will give him authority over the nations,
27 and he will shepherd them with an iron staff (as the containers, the clay *ones*, are crushed), even as I have received from the side of My Father.
28 And I will give him the star, the morning *star*.
29 The *person* who has an ear must hear what the Spirit says to the assemblies.'"

3

1 And to the announcer of the assembly in Sardis, write, "The *One* who has the seven spirits of God and the seven stars says the *things* here, 'I have seen your actions, that you have the name that you live, and you are dead.

2 Become *a person* who stays awake and establish the rest of the *things* that are going to die. You see, I haven't found your actions that have been accomplished in the sight of God.

3 So remember how you have received and heard; keep guard; and change your ways. So if you don't stay awake, I will arrive upon you as a thief, and you won't in any way know which hour I will arrive upon you.

4 You have a few names even in Sardis that didn't dirty their clothes. And they will walk around with Me in white because they are deserving.

5 The *person* who conquers, this *person* will put *clothes* around himself in white robes. And I won't in any way erase his name from the scroll of the life, and I will acknowledge his name out loud in the sight of My Father and in the sight of His angels.

6 The *person* who has an ear must hear what the Spirit says to the assemblies.'"

7 And to the announcer of the assembly in Philadelphia, write, "The sacred *One*, the true *One*, the *One* who has the key of David, the *One* who opens and no one closes and who closes and no one opens, says the *things* here,

8 'I have seen your actions. Look, in your sight I have given a door having been opened and no one is able to close it because you have little ability, you kept My message, and you did not deny My name.

9 Look, I am giving *you some* from the synagogue of the Opponent (the *people* saying for themselves to be Jewish, and they are not, but they are lying). Look, I will make them so that they will arrive and bow down in the sight of your feet. And they will know that I loved you.

10 Because you kept the message of My persistence *to do what is right*, I also will keep you from the hour of the trouble, the *hour* that is going to be coming on the whole civilized world to trouble the *people* living on the earth.

11 Look, I am coming quickly. Hold on to what you have so that no one might take your award wreath.

12 The *person* who conquers, I will make him a pillar in the temple of My God, and he will not in any way go outside anymore. And I will write on him the name of My God, the name of the city of My God, the New Jerusalem (the *one* stepping down from the sky out of My God), and My name, the new *name*.

13 The *person* who has an ear must hear what the Spirit says to the assemblies.'"

14 And to the announcer of the assembly of Laodiceans, write, "The Amen, the Witness, the reliable and true *Witness*, the Beginning of the creation of God, says the *things* here,

15 'I have seen your actions, that you are neither cold, nor hot. If only you were cold or hot.

16 This is why (because you are lukewarm and neither cold, nor hot) I am going to vomit you from my mouth

17 because you say, 'I am wealthy, I have been wealthy, and I have need of nothing,' and you have not seen that you are the troubled, miserable, poor, blind, and naked *person*.
18 I strongly advise you to buy from the side of Me gold that has been refined from fire (so that you might be wealthy), white robes (so that you might put *them* around yourself and the shame of your nakedness might not be shown), and collyrium *(medicated eye wash)* to anoint in your eyes (so that you might see).
19 However many that I am fond of, I reprimand and discipline. So be passionate and change your ways.
20 Look, I have been standing at the door, and I am knocking. If anyone listens to My voice and opens the door, I will come in to him, eat dinner with him, and he with Me.
21 The *person* who conquers, I will give him *the right* to be seated with Me in My throne, as I also conquered and was seated with My Father in His throne.
22 The *person* who has an ear must hear what the Spirit says to the assemblies.'"

1 After these *things* I looked, and look, a door having been opened in the sky and the voice (the first *one* that I heard as a trumpet speaking with me) saying, "Step up here, and I will show you what is necessary to happen after these."
2 And right away I became in a spirit, and look, a throne was situated in the sky and *One* sitting on the throne.
3 And the *One* sitting was like *the* sight of a jasper stone and a sardine *stone*. And a halo surrounding the throne *was* like the sight of an emerald *stone*.
4 And surrounding the throne *were* twenty and four thrones, and on the thrones, I saw the twenty and four older *men* sitting, around whom *clothes* had been put in white robes. And they had gold award wreaths on their heads.
5 And from the throne travel out lightnings, thunders, sounds, and seven torches of fire burning in the sight of the throne (that are the seven spirits of God).
6 And in the sight of the throne *was* a glassy sea like crystal. And in the middle of the throne and circling the throne *were* four animals packed full of eyes, in front and behind:
7 and the animal (the first *one*), like a lion; the second animal, like a calf; the third animal, having the face as a person; and the fourth animal, like a flying raptor.
8 And *the* four animals each one itself were having six wings apiece packed full of eyes surrounding *it* and on *the* inside. And they don't have relief, day and night, saying, "Sacred, sacred, sacred Master God, the All-Powerful One, the *One who* was, the *One* who is, and the *One* who is coming."
9 And when the animals will give magnificence, value, and thanks to the *One* sitting on the throne (the *One* living for the spans of time of the spans of time),

10 the twenty and four older *men* will get down in the sight of the *One* sitting on the throne, bow to the *One* living for the spans of time of the spans of time, and throw their award wreaths in the sight of the throne, saying,
11 "You, Master, are deserving to receive the magnificence, the value, and the ability because You created all *things*. And because of what You wanted, they exist and were created."

5

1 And I saw on the right *side* of the *One* sitting on the throne, a scroll that had been written on *the* inside and on *the* back, having been sealed with seven seals.
2 And I saw a strong angel speaking publicly in a loud voice, "Who is deserving to open the scroll and to break its seals?"
3 And no one in the heaven, nor on the earth, nor beneath the earth was able to open the scroll, nor to be looking at it.
4 And I was crying a lot because not even one deserving *person* was found to open and to read the scroll, nor to be looking at it.
5 And one from the older *men* says to me, "Don't cry. Look, the Lion (the *One* who is from the family line of Judah, the Root of David) conquered to open the scroll and to break its seven seals."
6 And I looked, and look, in *the* middle of the throne and the four animals and in *the* middle of the older *men*, a lamb that had stood as having been slaughtered, having seven horns and seven eyes that are the seven spirits of God that have been sent out *on a mission* into all the earth.
7 And He went and has taken the scroll from the right *side* of the *One* sitting on the throne.
8 And when He took the scroll, the four animals and the twenty-four older *men* got down in the sight of the Lamb, each having a harp and gold bowls (packed full of incense) that are the prayers of the sacred *people*.
9 And they sing a new song, saying, "You are deserving to take the scroll and to open its seals because You were slaughtered and You purchased us for God in Your blood from every family line, language, ethnic group, and nation.
10 And You made us a monarchy and priests to our God, and we will be kings on the earth."
11 And I looked and heard *the* voice of many angels surrounding the throne, the animals, and the older *men* (and their number was tens of thousands of tens of thousands and thousands of thousands),
12 saying with a loud voice, "The Lamb, the *One* that has been slaughtered, is deserving to receive the ability, wealth, insight, strength, value, magnificence, and conferring of blessings."
13 And every created thing that is in the heaven, in the earth, beneath the earth, on the sea that exist, and all the *things* in them, I heard saying, "To the *One* sitting on the throne and to the Lamb *belong* the conferring of blessings, the value, the magnificence, and the power for the spans of time of the spans of time."
14 And the four animals were saying, "Amen." And the twenty-four older *men* got down and bowed to *Him* who lives for the spans of time of the spans of time.

1 And I looked when the Lamb opened one from the seals and listened to one from the four animals saying as a voice of thunder, "Come and see."
2 And I looked, and, look, a white horse and the *one* sitting on it having a bow. And an award wreath was given to him, and he went out conquering and so that he might conquer.
3 And when He opened the second seal, I listened to the second animal saying, "Come and see."
4 And another horse went out, a fiery *one*, and to the *one* sitting on it, it was given to him to take the peace away from the earth, even so that they will slaughter each other. And a large dagger was given to him.
5 And when He opened the third seal, I listened to the third animal saying, "Come and see." And I looked, and, look, a black horse and the *one* sitting on it having a beam balance in his hand.
6 And I heard a voice in *the* middle of the four animals saying, "A quart of wheat *is* a denarius ($50), three quarts of barley *are* a denarius ($50), and you should not harm the olive oil and the wine."
7 And when He opened the seal, the fourth *one*, I heard *the* voice of the fourth animal saying, "Come and see."
8 And I looked, and, look, a green horse and the *one* sitting up on top of it. A name for him *is* Death, and Hades *(the underworld of the dead)* follows with him. And authority was given to them over the fourth *part* of the earth to kill with a sword, with famine, with death *(a plague)*, and by the wild animals of the earth.
9 And when He opened the fifth seal, I saw beneath the altar the souls of the *people* who had been slaughtered because of the message of God and because of the witness account that they were having.
10 And they yelled with a loud voice, saying, "Until when, the Owner, the sacred and the true *One*, are you not judging and retaliating for our blood out of the *people* living on the earth?"
11 And long white robes were given to each *of them*, and it was stated to them that they should relax for a short time yet, until *the time* that both their fellow slaves and their brothers, the *ones* that are going to be killed as they also *had been*, will be accomplished.
12 And I looked when He opened the seal, the sixth *one*. And, look, a great earthquake happened, the sun became black as cloth made of goat hair, the moon became as blood,
13 the stars of the sky fell to the earth as a fig tree throws its unripe figs as it is shook by a strong wind,
14 *the* sky was separated apart as a scroll being folded up, and every mountain and island were moved from their places.
15 And the kings of the earth, the greatest people, the wealthy, the commanding officers, the competent *ones*, every slave, and every free *person* hid themselves in the caves and in the rocks of the mountains.
16 And they say to the mountains and the rocks, "Fall on us, and hide us away from *the* face of the *One* sitting on the throne and away from the punishment of the Lamb

17 because the day, the great *day*, of His punishment came, and who is able to be stood up?"

7

1 And after these *things*, I saw four angels that had stood on the four corners of the earth holding on to the four *directional* winds of the earth so that wind may not blow on the earth, nor on the sea, nor on any tree.

2 And I saw another angel stepping up out of *the* rising of *the* sun having *the* seal of *the* living God. And he yelled with a loud voice to the four angels to whom it was given to them to harm the earth and the sea,

3 saying, "You should not harm the earth, nor the sea, nor the trees till *a time* that we might put a seal on the slaves of our God, on their foreheads."

4 And I heard the number of the *people* that had been sealed, 144 thousand that had been sealed from every family line of Israel's sons:

5 from Judah's family line, 12 thousand *people* that had been sealed; from Reuben's family line, 12 thousand *people* that had been sealed; from Gad's family line, 12 thousand *people* that had been sealed;

6 from Asher's family line, 12 thousand *people* that had been sealed; from Naphtali's family line, 12 thousand *people* that had been sealed; from Manasseh's family line, 12 thousand *people* that had been sealed;

7 from Simeon's family line, 12 thousand *people* that had been sealed; from Levi's family line, 12 thousand *people* that had been sealed; from Issachar's family line, 12 thousand *people* that had been sealed;

8 from Zebulon's family line, 12 thousand *people* that had been sealed; from Joseph's family line, 12 thousand *people* that had been sealed; from Benjamin's family line, 12 thousand *people* that had been sealed.

9 After these *things*, I looked, and, look, a big crowd (that no one was being able to number it) from every nation, *from* family lines, ethnic groups, and languages that had stood in the sight of the throne and in the sight of the Lamb, around whom long white robes had been put, and palm branches in their hands,

10 and yelling with a loud voice, saying, "The rescue *belongs* to our God (to the *One* sitting on the throne) and to the Lamb."

11 And all the angels had stood circling the throne, the older *men*, and the four animals. And they got down in the sight of the throne on their faces and bowed to God,

12 saying, "Amen. The conferring of blessings, the magnificence, the insight, the thanks, the value, the ability, and the strength *belong* to our God for the spans of time of the spans of time. Amen."

13 And one from the older *men* responded, saying to me, "These around whom the long robes, the white *ones*, have been put, who are they? And where did they come from?"

14 And I have stated to him, "Master, you know." And he said to me, "These are the *people* coming from the hard times, the great *hard times*. And they rinsed their long robes and whitened them in the blood of the Lamb.

15 Because of this, they are in the sight of the throne of God and they minister to Him day and night in His temple. And the *One* sitting on the throne will camp over them.
16 They won't be hungry anymore, nor thirsty anymore, nor will the sun fall on them, nor any burning heat,
17 because the Lamb, the *Lamb* up in *the* middle of the throne will shepherd them and guide them over living springs of waters. And God will dab off every tear from their eyes."

1 And when He opened the seal, the seventh *one*, there became a hush in the heaven as *if it were* half an hour.
2 And I saw the seven angels that had stood in the sight of God. And seven trumpets were given to them.
3 And another angel went and was stood on the altar having a gold incense burner. And much incense was given to him so that he might give *it* with the prayers of all the sacred *people* on the altar, the gold *altar*, the *altar* in the sight of the throne.
4 And the smoke of the incense tumbled up with the prayers of the sacred *people* from the angel's hand in the sight of God.
5 And the angel has taken the incense burner, filled it full *of coals* from the fire of the altar, and threw *it* to the earth. And there became sounds, thunders, lightnings, and an earthquake.
6 And the seven angels, the *ones* having the seven trumpets, got themselves ready so that they might blow the trumpets.
7 And the first angel blew a trumpet, and there became hail and fire that had been mixed with blood. And it was thrown to the earth, the third *part* of the trees were burned up, and all green grass was burned up.
8 And the second angel blew a trumpet, and *what was* as a large mountain being burned with fire was thrown into the sea. And the third *part* of the sea became blood,
9 the third *part* of the created things (the *ones* in the sea, the *ones* having souls) died, and the third *part* of the boats were devoured.
10 And the third angel blew a trumpet, and a large star fell from the sky being burned as a torch. And it fell on the third *part* of the rivers and on the springs of *the* waters.
11 And the name of the star is called Absinthium. And the third *part* of the waters became into absinthium, and many of *the* people died from the waters because they were bitter.
12 And the fourth angel blew a trumpet, and the third *part* of the sun, the third *part* of the moon, and the third *part* of the stars was affected so that the third *part* of them would be made dark. And the day may not shine, the third *part* of it, and the night likewise.
13 And I looked and heard one angel flying in *the* middle of the sky, saying with a loud voice, "What a tragedy! What a tragedy! What a tragedy to the *people* living on the earth from the rest of *the* sounds of the trumpet of the three angels, the *angels* that are going to be blowing."

9 1 And the fifth angel blew a trumpet, and I saw a star that had fallen from the sky to the earth. And the key of the shaft of the bottomless area was given to it.

2 And it opened the shaft of the bottomless area, and smoke tumbled up from the shaft as *the* smoke of a large furnace. And the sun and the air were made dark from the smoke of the shaft.

3 And out of the smoke came grasshoppers to the earth, and authority was given to them as the scorpions of the earth have authority.

4 And it was stated to them that they shouldn't harm the grass of the earth, nor any green *thing*, nor any tree, just the people only, any who don't have the seal of God on their foreheads.

5 And it was given to them that they may not kill them, but that they would be tortured five months. And the torture from them *was* as torture from a scorpion when it strikes a person.

6 And in those days, the people will look for death and won't find it. And they will desire to die, and the death will escape away from them.

7 And the likenesses of the grasshoppers *were* like horses having been readied for war, on their heads *were* as *if they were* award wreaths, like gold, their faces *were* as faces of people,

8 they had hair as women's hair, their teeth were as lions',

9 they had vests as iron vests, the sound of their wings *was* as *the* sound of chariots of many horses running to war,

10 and they have tails like scorpions and stingers, in their tails also was their authority to harm the people five months.

11 And they have a king over them, the angel of the bottomless area. A name for him in Hebrew *is* Abaddon, and in the Greek *language* he has a name, Apollyon (*Ruiner*).

12 The tragedy, the one, went away. Look, two tragedies are still coming after these.

13 And the sixth angel blew a trumpet, and I heard one voice from the four horns of the altar, the gold *altar*, the *altar* in the sight of God,

14 saying to the sixth angel that had the trumpet, "Release the four angels, the *ones* that have been locked up over the river, the great Euphrates."

15 And the four angels were released, the *ones* that have been readied for the hour, day, month, and year so that they may kill the third *part* of the people.

16 And the number of military forces of the horse *unit was two hundred million* (two ten thousands of ten thousands). And I heard the number of them.

17 And this is how I saw the horses in the sighting and the *ones* sitting on them: having flaming (*red*), hyacinth (*dark blue*), and sulfurous (*yellow*) vests, the heads of the horses as lions' heads, and from their mouths travel out fire, smoke, and sulfur.

18 By these three, the third *part* of the people were killed: from the fire, from the smoke, and from the sulfur, the *thing* traveling out from their mouths.

19 You see, the authority of them is in their mouth and in their tails; for their tails having heads *are* like snakes, and they cause harm with them.

20 And the rest of the people, the *ones* who were not killed in these devastations did not change their ways from the works of their hands, so that

they would not bow down to the lesser deities and idols (the gold *ones*, the silver *ones*, the brass *ones*, the stone *ones*, and the wooden *ones*) that are able neither to be seeing, nor to be hearing, nor to be walking around.

21 And they did not change their ways from their murders, nor from their drug abuses, nor from their sexual sin, nor from their thefts.

10

1 And I saw another strong angel stepping down from the sky around whom a cloud has been put, a halo *was* on *his* head, his face *was* as the sun, his feet *were* as pillars of fire,
2 and he had in his hand a little scroll that had been opened. And he put his foot (the right *foot*) on the sea, but the left *foot* on the land.
3 And he yelled with a loud voice even as a lion roars. And when he yelled, the seven thunders spoke their *own* voices.
4 And when the seven thunders spoke their *own* voices, I was going to be writing, and I heard a voice from the sky saying to me, "Put a seal on what the seven thunders spoke, and you will not write these."
5 And the angel that I saw that had stood on the sea and on the land raised up his hand to the sky,
6 and guaranteed with the *One* who lives for the spans of time of the spans of time (who created the sky and the *things* in it, the land and the *things* in it, and the sea and the *things* in it) that there will be no more time left.
7 But in the days of the sounding of the seventh angel, whenever he is going to be blowing the trumpet, the secret of God will also be finished as He shared good news with His *own* slaves, the preachers.
8 And the voice that I heard from the sky *is* speaking with me again and saying, "Make *your* way back, take the little scroll, the *one* that has been opened in the hand of the angel that has stood on the sea and on the land."
9 And I went off to the angel, saying to him, "Give me the little scroll." And he says to me, "Take and eat it up. And it will make your belly bitter, but in your mouth, it will be sweet as honey."
10 And I took the little scroll from the hand of the angel and ate it up. And it was sweet as honey in my mouth. And when I ate it, my belly became bitter.
11 And he says to me, "It is necessary for you to preach again over many ethnic groups, nations, languages, and kings."

11

1 And a stick like a staff was given to me, and the angel had stood, saying, "Get up, and measure the temple of God, the altar, and the *people* bowing down in it.
2 And the courtyard, the *one* outside of the temple, throw *it* outside, and you should not measure it because it was given to the non-Jews. And they will trample the city (the sacred *one*) forty-two months.
3 And I will give to My two witnesses, and they will preach a thousand two hundred sixty days having put cloth made of hair around themselves.
4 These are the two olive trees and the two lampstands, the *ones* having stood in the sight of the God of the earth.

5 And if anyone wants to harm them, fire travels out from their mouth and eats up their enemies. And if anyone should want to harm them, this is how it is necessary for him to be killed.

6 These have authority to close the sky so that a shower may not dampen in *the* days of their preaching. And they have authority over the waters to be turning them into blood and to strike the earth with every devastation as often as they might want.

7 And when they finished their witness account, the wild animal, the *one* stepping up from the bottomless area, will make war with them, conquer them, and kill them.

8 And their corpses *will be* on the plaza of the great city, a certain *city* that spiritually is called Sodom and Egypt, where our Master was also nailed to a cross.

9 And *people* from the ethnic groups, family lines, languages, and nations will look at their corpses three and a half days. And they are not leaving their corpses to be put into a grave.

10 And the *people* living on the earth will be happy over them. And they will celebrate and send contributions to each other because these two preachers tortured the *people* living on the earth.

11 And after the three and a half days, a spirit of life from God came into them, and they stood on their feet. And great fear fell on the *people* watching them.

12 And they heard a loud voice from the sky saying to them, "Step up here," and they stepped up into the sky in the cloud. And their enemies watched them.

13 And in that hour, a large earthquake happened, and the tenth *part* of the city fell. And seven thousand names of people were killed in the earthquake, and the rest became afraid and gave magnificence to the God of the heaven.

14 The tragedy, the second *one*, went away. And look, the tragedy, the third *one*, is coming quickly.

15 And the seventh angel blew a trumpet, and loud voices happened in the heaven, saying, "The monarchies of the world became our Master's and His Anointed King's. And He will be king for the spans of time of the spans of time."

16 And the twenty and four older *men*, the *ones* in the sight of God sitting on their thrones, got down on their faces and bowed to God,

17 saying, "We are thankful to You, Master, God, the All-Powerful One, the *One* who is, the *One who* was, and the *One* coming, because You have taken Your ability, the great *ability*, and became king.

18 And the nations were enraged. And Your rage came and the time of the dead to be judged, to give the pay to Your slaves (the preachers, the sacred *people*, and the *people* who fear Your name, the little and the great), and to devour the *people* who devour the earth."

19 And the temple of God in the heaven was opened; the box of His deal was seen in His temple; and lightnings, sounds, thunders, an earthquake, and large hail happened.

12

1 And a great indicator was seen in the heaven: a woman that has put the sun around herself, the moon beneath her feet, on her head an award wreath of twelve stars,
2 and having *a baby* in *her* womb; she yells being in labor and being tortured to deliver.
3 And another indicator was seen in the heaven. And look, a great fiery dragon having seven heads and ten horns, on his heads seven crowns,
4 and his tail drags the third *part* of the stars of the heaven and threw them to the earth. And the dragon has stood in the sight of the woman, the *one* who is going to deliver, so that whenever she delivers, he might eat up her child.
5 And she delivered a male son who is going to be shepherding all the nations with an iron staff. And her child was snatched up to God and His throne.
6 And the woman escaped into the backcountry where she has a place that has been readied out from God so that they may nurture her there a thousand two hundred sixty days.
7 And there became a war in the heaven: Michael and his angels waged war against the dragon. And the dragon waged war and his angels.
8 And they did not have strength, neither was a place found for them anymore in the heaven.
9 And the dragon (the great *dragon*), the snake (the original *snake*), the *one* called Accuser and the Opponent, the *one* misleading the whole civilized world, was thrown *out*. He was thrown to the earth, and his angels were thrown with him.
10 And I heard a loud voice in the heaven, saying, "Just now there became the rescue, the ability, the monarchy of our God, and the authority of His Anointed King because the complainant against our brothers was thrown down, the *one* leveling complaints against them in the sight of our God day and night.
11 And they conquered him because of the blood of the Lamb and because of the message of their witness account. And they did not love their soul till death.
12 Because of this, celebrate, the heavens and the *ones* camping in them. What a tragedy *it is* to the *people* living on the earth and in the sea because the Accuser stepped down to you having great anger, realizing that he has little time."
13 And when the dragon saw that he was thrown to the earth, he pursued the woman, someone who delivered the male.
14 And two wings of the raptor (the great *one*) were given to the woman so that she may fly into the backcountry, into her place where she is nurtured there for a time, times, and half a time away from *the* face of the snake.
15 And the snake threw water from his mouth behind the woman as a river so that he might make this *woman to be* washed away by the river.
16 And the earth helped the woman. And the earth opened its mouth and swallowed up the river that the dragon threw from his mouth.
17 And the dragon was enraged over the woman and went off to make war with the rest of her seed, the *people* keeping the demands of God and having the witness account of Jesus, *the* Anointed King.

13 1 And I was placed on the sand of the sea. And I saw a wild animal stepping up from the sea having seven heads, ten horns, on his horns ten crowns, and on his heads a name of an insult.

2 And the wild animal that I saw was like a leopard, his feet as a bear's, and his mouth as a lion's mouth. And the dragon gave him his ability, his throne, and great authority.

3 And I saw one from his heads as *a head* that had been slaughtered to death, and the wound of his death was healed. And the whole earth was amazed behind the wild animal.

4 And they bowed down to the dragon that gave authority to the wild animal, and they bowed down to the wild animal, saying, "Who *is* like the wild animal? Who is able to wage war with him?"

5 And a mouth was given to him speaking great *things* and insults. And authority was given to him to do forty two months.

6 And he opened his mouth in insults toward God to insult His name, His tent, and the *ones* camping in heaven.

7 And it was given to him to make war with the sacred *people* and to conquer them. And authority was given to him over every family line, language, and nation.

8 And they will bow down to him, everyone living on the earth whose names have not been written in the scroll of the life of the Lamb who has been slaughtered out from *the* founding of *the* world.

9 If anyone has an ear, he must hear.

10 If anyone gathers *innocent people* for incarceration, he makes *his* way back into incarceration. If anyone kills with a dagger, it is necessary for him to be killed with a dagger. Here is the persistence *to do what is right* and the trust of the sacred *people*.

11 And I saw another wild animal stepping up from the earth. And he was having two horns like a lamb and was speaking as a dragon.

12 And every authority of the first wild animal, he did in his sight. And he made the earth and the *people* living in it so that they will bow down to the wild animal, the first *one* whose wound of his death was healed.

13 And he did great indicators so that he may even make fire to be tumbling down from the sky to the earth in the sight of the people.

14 And he misleads the *people* living on the earth because of the indicators that were given to him to do in the sight of the wild animal, saying to the *people* living on the earth to make an image to the wild animal that has the wound of the dagger and lived.

15 And it was given to him to give a spirit to the image of the wild animal so that the image of the wild animal would both speak and make however many did not bow down to the image of the wild animal, that they would be killed.

16 And he made all the little *people*, the great *people*, the wealthy *people*, the poor *people*, the free *people*, and the slaves so that they would give them a mark on their hand (the right *one*) or on their foreheads,

17 and that no one may be able to buy or to sell except the *person* having the mark, or the name of the wild animal, or the number of his name.

18 Here is the insight. The *person* having the way of thinking must count the number of the wild animal. You see, it is *the* number of a person, and his number *is* 666.

14

1 And I looked and, look, a Lamb that has stood on Mount Zion and with Him a hundred forty-four thousand having the name of His Father that has been written on their foreheads.
2 And I heard a sound from the heaven as a sound of many waters and as a sound of loud thunder. And I heard a sound of harpists playing on their harps.
3 And they sing as *if it were* a new song in the sight of the throne and in the sight of the four animals and the older *men*. And no one was able to learn the song except the hundred forty-four thousand, the *people* who have been bought out of the earth.
4 These are the *people* who were not dirtied with women. You see, they are virgins. These are the *people* who follow the Lamb wherever He may make *His* way back to. These were bought out of the people, a first-part-offering to God and the Lamb.
5 And deception was not found in their mouth. You see, they are unblemished in the sight of the throne of God.
6 And I saw another angel flying in the middle of the sky having good news that spans *all* time to share good news with the *people* living on the earth, with every nation, family line, language, and ethnic group,
7 saying in a loud voice, "Fear God, give magnificence to Him because the hour of His judgment came, and bow down to the *One* who made the sky, the earth, the sea, and springs of waters."
8 And another angel followed, saying, "It fell. It fell, Babylon, the city, the great *one*, because she has given all nations a drink from the wine of the anger of her sexual sin."
9 And a third angel followed them, saying in a loud voice, "If anyone bows down to the wild animal and his image and receives a mark on his forehead or on his hand,
10 he also will drink from the wine of the anger of God, the *anger* that has been poured undiluted in the cup of His punishment. And he will be tortured in fire and sulfur in the sight of the sacred angels and in the sight of the Lamb.
11 And the smoke of their torture tumbles up for spans of time of spans of time. And they don't have relief day and night (the *people* bowing down to the wild animal and his image and if anyone receives the mark of his name).
12 Here is *the* persistence *to do what is right* of the sacred *people*. Here *are* the *people* keeping the demands of God and the trust of Jesus."
13 And I heard a voice from the sky, saying to me, "Write, 'The dead *are* blessed, the *ones* in *the* Master dying after right now.'" "Yes," says the Spirit, "so that they might relax from their labors. Their actions follow with them."
14 And I looked and, look, a white cloud and sitting on the cloud *someone* like a son of a person having on His head a gold award wreath and in His hand a sharp sickle.

15 And another angel came out of the temple yelling in a loud voice to the *One* sitting on the cloud, "Send Your sickle and harvest because the hour to harvest came to You, because the harvest of the earth is shriveled up."
16 And the *One* sitting on the cloud threw His sickle over the earth, and the earth was harvested.
17 And another angel came out of the temple, the *one* in the heaven, he also having a sharp sickle.
18 And another angel came out of the altar having authority over the fire. And he hollered with a loud yell to the *one* who has the sickle, the sharp *one*, saying, "Send your sickle, the sharp *one*, and pick the grape bunches of the vine of the earth," because her grape clusters were ripe.
19 And the angel threw his sickle into the earth, picked the vine of the earth, and threw *it* into the grape smashing pit of the anger of God, the great *pit*.
20 And the grape smashing pit was trampled outside of the city, and blood came out of the pit till the bridles of the horses from a thousand six hundred track laps *(200 miles)*.

15

1 And I saw another indicator in the heaven, great and amazing, seven angels having seven devastations, the last *ones*, because in them the anger of God was finished.
2 And I saw as *if it were* a glassy sea (that had been mixed with fire) and the *people* conquering from the wild animal, from his image, and from his mark from the number of his name, having stood on the sea, the glassy *one*, having the harps of God.
3 And they sing the song of Moses (the slave of God) and the song of the Lamb, saying, "Great and amazing *are* Your actions, Master, the God, the All-Powerful One. Right and true *are* Your ways, the King of the sacred *people*.
4 Who would not in any way fear You, Master, and praise Your name's magnificence? Because only *You are* holy. Because all the nations will arrive and will bow in Your sight. Because Your right paths were shown."
5 And after these *things*, I looked, and look, the temple of the tent of the witness in the heaven was opened.
6 And the seven angels who have the seven devastations came out of the temple having put on clean and dazzling linen and around whom gold sashes have been put around the chests.
7 And one from the four animals gave the seven angels seven gold bowls packed full of the anger of God, the *One* who lives for the spans of time of the spans of time.
8 And the temple was full of smoke from the magnificence of God and from His ability. And no one was able to go into the temple till the seven devastations of the seven angels were finished.

16

1 And I listened to a loud voice from the temple saying to the seven angels, "Make *your* way back and spill the bowls of the anger of God out into the earth."

2 And the first *angel* went off and spilled his bowl out on the earth. And there became a bad and evil sore into the people, the *ones* having the mark of the wild animal and the *ones* bowing to his image.
3 And the second angel spilled his bowl out into the sea, and it became blood, as a dead *person's blood*. And every living soul died in the sea.
4 And the third angel spilled his bowl out into the rivers and into the springs of the waters, and it became blood.
5 And I listened to the angel of the waters saying, "You are right, Master, the *One* who is, the *One who* was, and the *One* who will be holy, because You decided these *things*,
6 because they spilled out *the* blood of sacred *people* and preachers, and You gave them blood to drink. You see, they are deserving *of it*."
7 And I listened to another from the altar saying, "Yes, Master, the God, the All-Powerful One, true and right *are* Your judgments."
8 And the fourth angel spilled his bowl out on the sun, and it was given to it to scorch the people in fire.
9 And the people were scorched with a great burning heat, and they insult the name of God, the *One* having authority over these devastations. And they did not change their ways to give magnificence to Him.
10 And the fifth angel spilled his bowl out on the throne of the wild animal, and his monarchy became *one* that had been darkened. And they were gnawing their tongues from the anguish
11 and insulted the God of the heaven from their anguishes and from their sores. And they did not change their ways from their actions.
12 And the sixth angel spilled his bowl out on the river, the great *river*, the Euphrates, and its water dried up so that the way of the kings (the *ones* out from *the* rising of *the* sun) might be readied.
13 And I saw from the mouth of the dragon, from the mouth of the wild animal, and from the mouth of the counterfeit preacher three spirits that were not clean, like frogs.
14 You see, they are spirits of lesser deities doing indicators that travel out on the kings of the earth and of the whole civilized world to gather them together for the war of that day, the great *day* of God, the All-Powerful One.
15 Look! I come as a thief. The *person is* blessed who stays awake and keeps his clothes so that he may not walk around naked and they may see what is improper of him.
16 And he gathered them together into the place, the *one* called in Hebrew, Armageddon (*Hill of Rendezvous*).
17 And the seventh angel spilled his bowl out into the air, and a loud voice came out from the temple of the heaven out from the throne, saying, "It has happened."
18 And sounds, thunders, and lightnings happened. And a large earthquake happened, such as did not happen from *the time* that the people happened on the earth, such a great earthquake, this is how great.
19 And the city, the great *city*, became into three parts, the cities of the nations fell, and Babylon the Great was remembered in the sight of God to give her the cup of the wine of the anger of His punishment.

20 And every island escaped, and mountains were not found.
21 And large hail (as *in* one hundred pounds) tumbled down from the sky on the people. And the people insulted God from the devastation of the hail, because its devastation is terribly great.

17

1 And one from the seven angels, the *ones* having the seven bowls, came and spoke with me, saying, "Come here. I will show you the judgment of the prostitute, the great *one*, the *one* sitting on the waters, the many *waters*,
2 with whom the kings of the earth committed sexual sin, and the *people* living on the earth got drunk from the wine of her sexual sin."
3 And he carried me off into *the* backcountry in *the* spirit, and I saw a woman sitting on a red wild animal packed full of names of an insult having seven heads and ten horns.
4 And it was the woman that has put purple and red around herself and has embellished herself with gold, valuable stones, and pearls, having a gold cup in her hand packed full of disgusting things and *the* uncleanness of her sexual sin.
5 And on her forehead *is* a name that has been written, "A Secret — Babylon the Great, the Mother of the Prostitutes and of the Disgusting Things of the Earth."
6 And I saw the woman getting drunk from the blood of the sacred *people* and from the blood of the witnesses of Jesus. And I was amazed, after seeing her, with great amazement.
7 And the angel said to me, "Why were you amazed? I will state to you the secret of the woman and of the wild animal, the *one* hauling her, the *one* having the seven heads and the ten horns.
8 The wild animal that you saw, was, is not, and is going to be stepping up from the bottomless area and to be making *his* way back into ruin. And they will be amazed, the *people* living on the earth (whose names have not been written on the scroll of the life since *the* founding of *the* world) as they see the wild animal, someone that was, and is not, even though he is.
9 Here *is* the way of thinking, the *one* having insight. The seven heads are seven mountains where the woman sits on them.
10 And they are seven kings: the five fell, and the one is, the other did not come yet. And when he comes, it is necessary for him to stay a little *while*.
11 And the wild animal that was and is not, even he is eighth. And he is from the seven and makes *his* way back into ruin.
12 And the ten horns that you saw are ten kings, some that did not receive a monarchy yet. But they receive authority as kings one hour with the wild animal.
13 These have one opinion. And their *own* ability and authority they pass out to the wild animal.
14 These will wage war with the Lamb, and the Lamb will conquer them because He is Master of masters and King of kings. And the *people* with Him *are* invited, select, and trusting."

15 And he says to me, "The waters that you saw where the prostitute sits are ethnic groups, crowds, nations, and languages.
16 And the ten horns that you saw on the wild animal, these will hate the prostitute and will make her *a woman* that has become uninhabited and naked. And they will eat her physical body and burn her up in fire.
17 You see, God gave into their hearts to do His opinion, to do one opinion, and to give their monarchy to the wild animal till the statements of God will be finished.
18 And the woman that you saw is the city, the great *one*, the *one* having a monarchy over the kings of the earth."

18

1 And after these *things*, I saw another angel stepping down from the sky having great authority. And the earth was lit up from his magnificence.
2 And he yelled in strength with a loud voice, saying, "It fell. It fell, Babylon the Great. And it became a residence of lesser deities, a guard station of every spirit that is not clean, and a guard station of every bird that is not clean and that has been hated
3 because all the nations have drunk from the wine of the anger of her sexual sin, the kings of the earth committed sexual sin with her, and the wholesalers of the earth were wealthy from the ability of her dominance.
4 And I heard another voice from the sky, saying, "Come out from her, My ethnic group, so that you might not share together in her sins and so that you might not receive from her devastations
5 because her sins were pasted as high as the sky and God remembered the wrong things she did.
6 Give back to her even as she gave back to you, and double to her *the* double *punishments from her* according to her actions. In the cup that she poured, pour double to her.
7 As much as she elevated herself to a place of magnificence and was dominant, give her so much torture and grief, because in her heart she says, "I sit *as* a queen, I am not a widow, and I will not in any way see grief."
8 Because of this, in one day, her devastations will arrive: death, grief, and famine. And in fire, she will be burned up because the Master God (the *One* who judged her) *is* strong.
9 And they will cry for her and beat their chests in grief over her (the kings of the earth, the *ones* who committed sexual sin with her and were dominant) when they see the smoke of her burning,
10 having stood off at a distance because of the fear of her torture, saying, "What a tragedy! What a tragedy, the city, the great Babylon, the city, the strong *city*, because in one hour your judgment came!"
11 And the wholesalers of the earth cry and grieve over her because no one buys their cargo anymore:
12 cargo of gold, silver, valuable stone, pearls, elegant linen, purple color, silk, and red *color*, all citrus wood, every ivory container, every container from *the* most valuable wood, copper, iron, and marble,

13 cinnamon, scents, perfume, high quality incense, wine, olive oil, fine flour, grain, animals, sheep, *things* for horses, *things* for four-wheeled vehicles, *things* for bodies, and souls of people.
14 "And the harvest season of the desire of your soul went away from you, and all the extravagant and the dazzling *things* went away from you. And you will not in any way find them anymore."
15 The wholesalers of these *things* (the *ones* who were wealthy from her) will stand off at a distance because of the fear of her torture, crying, grieving,
16 and saying, "What a tragedy! What a tragedy, the city, the great *city*, the *one* that has put elegant linen *fabric*, both purple and red, around itself and has embellished itself in gold, valuable stone, and pearls
17 because in one hour so much wealth became uninhabited!" And every helmsman, every passenger on the boats, crewmen, and as many as work the sea stood off at a distance.
18 And they were yelling, seeing the smoke of her burning, saying, "What *city* is like the city, the great *city*?"
19 And they threw dirt on their heads and were yelling, crying and grieving, saying, "What a tragedy! What a tragedy, the city, the great *city* in which all the *people* having boats in the sea were wealthy from her valuableness, because in one hour it became uninhabited!"
20 Celebrate over her, heaven (both the sacred missionaries and the preachers), because God judged your judgment from her.
21 And one strong angel picked up a stone as a large millstone and threw *it* into the sea, saying, "Like this, with violence, Babylon, the great city, will be thrown and will not in any way be found anymore.
22 And *the* sound of harpists, musicians, flute players, and trumpeters will not in any way be heard in you anymore. And every skilled worker of every trade will not in any way be found in you anymore. And *the* sound of a millstone will not in any way be heard in you anymore.
23 And *the* light of a lamp will not in any way shine in you anymore. And *the* sound of a bride and groom will not in any way be heard in you anymore because your wholesalers were the greatest people of the earth because in your drug abuse all the nations were misled.
24 And in her was found *the* blood of preachers, sacred *people*, and all the *people* who have been slaughtered on the earth."

19

1 And after these *things*, I heard *the* loud sound of a big crowd in the heaven saying, "Hallelujah (*Hebrew for "praise Yahweh"*)! The rescue, the magnificence, the value, and the ability *belong* to *the* Master, our God,
2 because true and right *are* His judgments because He judged the prostitute, the great *one*, someone who was worsening the earth in her sexual sin, and He retaliated for the blood of His slaves from her hand."
3 And a second time they have stated, "Hallelujah!" And her smoke tumbles up for the spans of time of the spans of time.
4 And the older *men* (the twenty-four) and the four animals got down, bowed to God (the *One* sitting on the throne) saying, "Amen! Hallelujah!"

5 And a voice came out of the throne saying, "Praise our God, all His slaves, the *ones* fearing Him, the little, and the great."
6 And I heard as *if it were the* sound of a big crowd, as *the* sound of many waters, and as *the* sound of strong thunders, saying, "Hallelujah, because He was king, *the* Master, God, the All-Powerful One.
7 We may be happy and excited. And we will give the magnificence to Him because the wedding of the Lamb came and His wife got herself ready.
8 And it was given to her that she might put clean and dazzling elegant linen *fabric* around herself." You see, the elegant linen is the right paths of the sacred *people*.
9 And he says to me, "Write, 'The *people are* blessed who have been invited to the feast of the wedding of the Lamb.'" And he says to me, "These messages of God are true."
10 And I got down in front of his feet to bow to him, and he says to me, "Look! No! I am a fellow slave of you and of your brothers, the *ones* who have what Jesus witnessed. Bow to God. You see, what Jesus witnessed is the spirit of the preaching."
11 And I saw the sky that had been opened and, look, a white horse and the *One* sitting on it who is called "Reliable and True." And in *the* right way He judges and wages war.
12 His eyes *are* as a blaze of fire and on His head many crowns, who has a name that has been written that no one knows except He Himself,
13 and around whom a robe has been put that has been dipped in blood. And His name is called the Message of God.
14 And the military forces, the *ones* in the heaven, were following Him on white horses having put on elegant linen *fabric*, white and clean.
15 And out of His mouth travels a sharp sword so that with it He might strike the nations, He Himself will shepherd them with an iron staff, and He Himself tramples the grape smashing pit of the wine of the anger and the punishment of God, the All-Powerful One.
16 And He has on *His* robe and on His thigh a name that has been written, "King of kings and Master of masters."
17 And I saw one angel that had stood in the sun, and he yelled with a loud voice, saying to all the birds, the *ones* flying in *the* middle of the sky, "Come on, and be gathered together for the feast of the great God,
18 so that you might eat physical bodies of kings, physical bodies of commanding officers, physical bodies of strong *people*, physical bodies of horses and of the *people* sitting on them, and physical bodies of all *kinds of people*, both free and slave, both little and great."
19 And I saw the wild animal, the kings of the earth, and their military forces that had been gathered together to make war with the *One* sitting on the horse and with His military unit.
20 And the wild animal was captured and with this, the counterfeit preacher, the *one* who did the indicators in his sight with which he misled the *people* who received the mark of the wild animal and the *people* bowing down to his image. *Still* living, the two were thrown into the lake of the fire, the *one* burning with the sulfur.

21 And the rest were killed with the sword of the *One* sitting on the horse, the *sword* traveling out of His mouth. And all the birds were full from their physical bodies.

20

1 And I saw an angel stepping down from the sky who had the key of the bottomless area and a large chain over his hand.
2 And he took hold of the dragon (the snake, the original *one*, who is an accuser and opponent) and locked him up a thousand years.
3 And he threw him into the bottomless area, closed it, and put a seal up on top of it so that he would not mislead the nations anymore till the thousand years were finished. And after these, it is necessary for him to be released for a short time.
4 And I saw thrones (and they were seated on them, and judgment was given to them) and the souls of the *people* that had been executed with a double-headed axe because of what Jesus witnessed and because of the message of God (and anyone who did not bow down to the wild animal, nor his image, and did not receive the mark on their forehead and on their hand also lived). And they were kings with the Anointed King a thousand years.
5 The rest of the dead did not come back to life until the thousand years were finished. This *is* the return back to life, the first *one*.
6 Blessed and sacred *is* the *person* who has a part in the return back to life, the first *one*. Over these *people*, the death (the second *death*) doesn't have authority, but they will be priests of God and of the Anointed King and will be kings with Him for a thousand years.
7 And when the thousand years are finished, the Opponent will be released from his jail.
8 And he will go out to mislead the nations, the *ones* in the four corners of the earth, Gog and Magog, to gather them together to a war, whose number *is* as the sand of the sea.
9 And they walked up over the width of the earth and surrounded the camp of the sacred *people* and the city, the *one* that had been loved. And fire tumbled down out from God from the sky and ate them up.
10 And the Accuser, the *one* misleading them, was thrown into the lake of the fire and sulfur, where the wild animal and the counterfeit preacher *are*. And they will be tortured day and night for the spans of time of the spans of time.
11 And I saw a great white throne and the *One* sitting on it, away from whose face the earth and the sky escaped, and a place was not found for them.
12 And I saw the dead, little and great, that had stood in the sight of God. And scrolls were opened, and another scroll was opened that is of the life. And the dead were judged from the *things* that had been written in the scrolls regarding their actions.
13 And the sea gave *up* the dead in it. And Death and Hades (*the underworld of the dead*) gave *up* the dead in them. And they were judged, each regarding their actions.
14 And Death and Hades (*the underworld of the dead*) were thrown into the lake of the fire. This is the second death.

15 And if anyone was found that had not been written in the scroll of the life, he was thrown into the lake of the fire.

21

1 And I saw a new sky and a new earth. You see, the first sky and the first earth passed, and the sea does not exist anymore.
2 And I, John, saw the city, the sacred new Jerusalem, stepping down out from God from the sky that had been readied as a bride that has been decorated for her husband.
3 And I listened to a loud voice from the sky saying, "Look, the tent of God *is* with the people, and He will camp with them. And they will be His ethnic groups, and God Himself will be with them, their God.
4 And God will dab off every tear out of their eyes. And the death will not exist anymore. Neither grief, nor yelling, nor anguish will exist anymore because the first *things* went away."
5 And the *One* sitting on the throne said, "Look, I am making all *things* new." And He says to me, "Write that these messages are true and reliable."
6 And He said to me, "It has happened. I am the A and the O *(the last letter in the Greek alphabet)*, the Beginning and the Conclusion. To the *person* who is thirsty, I will give *water* from the spring of the water of the life for free.
7 The *person* conquering will inherit these *things*, and I will be a God to him, and he will be the son to Me.
8 But to cowardly, to untrusting, to *people* who have been disgusting, to murderers, to people who commit sexual sin, to drug abusers, to idol worshipers, and to all the liars, their part *is* in the lake, the *one* burning with fire and sulfur, that is the death, the second *one*."
9 And one of the seven angels (the *angels* having the seven bowls, the *bowls* packed full of the seven devastations, the last *ones*) came to me and spoke with me, saying, "Come here. I will show you the bride of the Lamb, the wife."
10 And he carried me off in *the* spirit on to a large and high mountain and showed me the city, the great *one*, the sacred Jerusalem, stepping down from the sky out from God
11 having the magnificence of God (and its light source like a valuable stone, as a jasper stone that is crystal-clear),
12 also having a large and high wall, having twelve gateways and at the gateways twelve angels and names having been inscribed that are of the twelve family lines of Israel's sons
13 (out from *the* east three gateways, out from *the* north three gateways, out from *the* south three gateways, and out from *the* western regions three gateways),
14 the wall of the city having twelve foundations, and in them names of the twelve missionaries of the Lamb.
15 And the *one* speaking with me had a gold stick so that he might measure the city, its gateways, and its wall.
16 And the city lies four-cornered. And its length is so much, as much as also the width. And he measured the city with the stick at twelve thousand track laps *(1500 miles)*. The length, the width, and the height of it are equal.

17 And he measured its wall, a hundred forty-four cubits (*approximately 216 feet*), *elbow to fingertip lengths*, a measurement of a person, that is, of an angel.
18 And the composition of its wall was jasper; and the city, clean gold, like clean glass.
19 And the foundations of the wall of the city that have been assembled with every valuable stone *are*: the foundation, the first *one*, jasper; the second, sapphire; the third, chalcedony; the fourth, emerald;
20 the fifth, sardonyx; the sixth, sardius; the seventh, chrysolite; the eighth, beryl; the ninth, topaz; the tenth, chrysoprasus; the eleventh, jacinth; the twelfth, amethyst.
21 And the twelve gateways *are* twelve pearls (each one of the gateways was from one pearl apiece). And the plaza of the city *is* clean gold as transparent glass.
22 And I didn't see a temple in it. You see, the Master, God, the All-Powerful One is its temple (and the Lamb).
23 And the city has no need of the sun, nor the moon, so that they may shine in it. You see, the magnificence of God lit it up, and its lamp *is* the Lamb.
24 And the nations of the rescued *people* will walk around in its light. And the kings of the earth bring their magnificence and value into it.
25 And its gateways won't in any way be closed after a day. You see, night won't be there.
26 And they will bring the magnificence and the value of the nations into it.
27 And everything that is shared and that does a disgusting *thing* and a lie won't in any way go into it, just the *people* who have been written in the scroll of the life of the Lamb.

22

1 And he showed me a clean river of water of life, dazzling as crystal, traveling out of the throne of God and of the Lamb
2 in *the* middle of its plaza. And on this side and on this side of the river *is* a wooden tree of life producing twelve fruits aligned with one each month, giving away its fruit and the leaves of the wooden tree for healing of the nations.
3 And all adverse doom will no longer exist. And the throne of God and of the Lamb will be in it, and His slaves will minister to Him.
4 And they will see His face, and His name *will be* on their foreheads.
5 And night will not exist there, and they have no need of a lamp and *the* light of *the* sun because *the* Master God will light *things* up for them. And they will be kings for the spans of time of the spans of time.
6 And he said to me, "These messages are reliable and true. And *the* Master, the God of the sacred preachers, sent out His angel *on a mission* to show His slaves *things* that are necessary to happen quickly."
7 "Look, I am coming quickly. The *person is* blessed who keeps the messages of the preaching of this scroll."
8 And I, John, *am* the *one* seeing and hearing these *things*. And when I heard and saw, I got down to bow in front of the feet of the angel, the *one* showing me these *things*.

9 And he says to me, "Look! No! You see, I am a fellow slave of you, of your brothers (the preachers), and of the *ones* keeping the messages of this scroll. Bow down to God."

10 And he says to me, "You should not put a seal on the messages of the preaching of this scroll because the appointed time is near.

11 The *person* doing wrong must still do wrong. And the *person* who is filthy must still be filthy. And the *person* who does what is right must still be made right. And the sacred *person* must still be made sacred."

12 "And look, I am coming quickly and My pay *is* with Me to give back to each *person* as his work will be.

13 I am the A and the O *(the last letter in the Greek alphabet)*, Beginning and Conclusion, the First and the Last."

14 The *people are* blessed who do His demands so that their authority will be over the wooden tree of the life and they might go into the city by the gateways.

15 But outside *are* the dogs, the drug users, the people who commit sexual sin, the murderers, the idol worshipers, and everyone who is fond of and makes a lie.

16 "I, Jesus, sent My angel to tell you these *things* that he witnessed before the assemblies. I am the Root and the Family of David, the Star, the Dazzling and Daybreaking *Star*."

17 And the Spirit and the bride say, "Come." And the *person* who hears must say, "Come." And the *person* who is thirsty must come. And the *person* wanting water of life must take *it* for free.

18 You see, I am a witness together with everyone hearing the messages of the preaching of this scroll, "If anyone should add to these *things*, God will add on to him the devastations, the *ones* that have been written in this scroll.

19 And if anyone should take away from the messages of the scroll of this preaching, God will take his part away from the scroll of the life and from the city, the sacred *one*, even the *things* that have been written in this scroll.

20 The *One* who is a witness to these *things* says, "Yes, I am coming quickly." Amen. Yes, come, Master Jesus.

21 *May* the generosity of our Master Jesus, *the* Anointed King, *be* with all of you. Amen.